new york
CITY

FODOR'S TRAVEL PUBLICATIONS
NEW YORK • TORONTO • LONDON • SYDNEY • AUCKLAND

WWW.FODORS.COM

Contents

KEY TO SYMBOLS

- ✚ Map reference
- ✉ Address
- ☎ Telephone number
- 🕐 Opening times
- Admission prices
- Subway station
- Bus number
- Train station
- Ferry/boat
- Tours
- Guidebook
- 🍴 Restaurant
- Café
- Shop
- Toilets
- Number of rooms
- P Parking
- No smoking
- Swimming pool
- Gym

How to Use this Book

Understanding New York is an introduction to the city, its geography, economy and people. **Living New York** gives an insight into the city today, while **The Story of New York** takes you through its past.

For detailed advice on getting to New York—and getting around once you are there—turn to **On the Move**. For useful practical information, from weather forecasts to emergency services, turn to **Planning**.

New York's key attractions are listed alphabetically in **The Sights** and are located on the maps on pages 58–61. The key sightseeing areas are described on pages 62–66 and are circled in blue on the map on the inside front cover.

Turn to **What to Do** for information on shops, entertainment, nightlife, sport, health and beauty, children's activities, and festivals and events. Entries are listed by these themes, then alphabetically. Shops are located on the maps on pages 160–163 and theatres on the maps on pages 186–189. The top shopping areas are described on pages 164–168 and circled in green on the map on the inside front cover.

Out and About offers ten walks around New York and two excursions that encourage you to explore further afield.

Eating and Staying gives you selected restaurants and hotels, listed alphabetically. Restaurants are located on the maps on pages 266–269 and hotels on the maps on pages 294–297.

Map references refer to the locator maps within the book or the street atlas at the end. For example, Empire State Building has the grid reference 60 E19, indicating the page on which the map is found (60) and the grid square in which the building sits (E19). Grid squares remain the same whatever page the map is on.

UNDERSTANDING NEW YORK

New York City is an international center for entertainment, fashion, creative arts and finance. It has great shopping, dynamic theater, superb concert halls and clubs, world-class museums, gorgeous parks and gardens, and sports events all year long. The variety and quality of restaurants is incomparable.
As a world financial center, it soars and plummets with the fluctuations on Wall Street. New Yorkers move fast, talk fast and are passionate about politics and style. They come in all shapes, sizes, colors and ethnicities; the city's multiculturalism is part of its charm. Although known for being brusque, New Yorkers are often surprisingly warm. Sometimes infuriating, the city is never dull. And chances are, with its vibrant whirl of activity, it's nothing like home.

NEW YORK

THE MANHATTAN LAYOUT
Manhattan is just one of five boroughs that comprise New York City. The others, sometimes known as the Outer Boroughs, are the Bronx, Brooklyn, Queens and Staten Island.

Manhattan is the long, narrow island jutting southwest off the mainland and is the smallest borough at 13.5 miles (22km) long and 2.25 miles (3.5km) wide. On the east side of the island is the East River. On the west is the Hudson River. To the north is the Harlem River. Upper New York Bay—the city's fine harbor—is to the south.

In Manhattan, most streets are numbered and laid out in a grid. The exception to this is Lower Manhattan, south of 14th Street, which grew up before the grid system was established. On the grid, "avenues" run from north to south, and "streets" run east and west. Broadway, a chief exception to this rule, cuts across town diagonally from northwest to southeast. First Avenue is on the eastern side of town, while Twelfth Avenue is on the western side. Fifth Avenue divides the city into the East Side and the West Side (except south of Washington Square, where Broadway becomes the east–west divide).

No matter where you are in Manhattan, if you are heading north you're going "uptown" and if you're heading south you're going "downtown."

If you want to travel east to west or west to east, you want to go "crosstown."

CLIMATE
From January to March, New York can be very cold, and occasional blizzards can obliterate your view of skyscrapers. But cheaper air fares and hotel rooms can make it worth your while to visit then—and sometimes the weather can be temperate. The best times to visit are in late April and May, when temperatures are generally no lower than 61°F (16°C), and attractions are crowded only at peak times, and in September to early November, when temperatures range from 50°F (10°C) to 77°F (25°C). The city is hot and humid in July and August, with extremes of 95°F (35°C) or higher, but the pleasures of Central Park, open-air concerts and ferry rides are compensations, and almost everything is air-conditioned.

STREET LIFE
Walking is the best way to fully appreciate the city, with its architectural splendors, intriguing sculptures, pretty fountains, beautiful parks and iconic landmarks. The street life is entertaining and colorful. New Yorkers speak Spanish, Chinese, Russian, Yiddish, Korean, Greek and English, to name just a few of the languages you will hear on the streets.

Financial District Oldest part of the city and nexus of the securities industry anchored by the New York Stock Exchange and Wall Street.

TriBeCa It means *Triangle Below Canal* and is defined by Canal and Barclay streets and Broadway and the Hudson River. A mixed-use neighborhood of gritty warehouse lofts, loft-style restaurants and low-end retail.

Chinatown Stretching over about 30 blocks, from Kenmare and Delancey streets to East Broadway and Worth Street, and from Broadway to Allen Street. Throngs of people shop for fish, meat, vegetables and herbal remedies or dine in the many affordable restaurants.

Little Italy Consists largely of Mulberry Street, lined with tourist-oriented restaurants, plus one or two genuine delis and pastry stores.

SoHo An ultra-expensive, chic shopping mall that is crowded with non-residents on weekends.

Lower East Side From 14th Street to Fulton and Franklin and from the East River to Broadway,

Take the Staten Island Ferry for one of the best views of the Manhattan skyline

the area takes in Chinatown, Little Italy and the East Village neighborhoods. Haunt of young professionals and artists.

Greenwich Village/West Village Stretches from 14th Street to Houston and from the Hudson River to Bowery and Fourth Avenue. Boutiques line the west end of Bleecker Street.

Noho Between SoHo and Greenwich Village (from Houston to Eighth streets and Mercer to Bowery/Third Avenue), this youth-oriented neighborhood has plenty of fashionable shopping, bars and restaurants.

East Village Filled with restaurants, bars and a youth-oriented street scene.

Union Square/Flatiron District Hot new neighborhood south of the Flatiron Building on 22nd Street and around Madison Square with plenty of bars, restaurants and clubs. From 14th to 23rd streets and Park Avenue to Sixth Avenue.

Chelsea Center of the gay community. Numerous warehouse/garage galleries along 24th Street, and a lively club and restaurant scene. Stretches from 14th to 30th streets and from Sixth Avenue to the Hudson River.

Hell's Kitchen The latest neighborhood undergoing gentrification (from Eighth Avenue to the Hudson River between 30th and 59th streets).

Midtown Commercial heart of the city between 34th and 59th streets on the West Side and from 40th to 59th streets on the East Side.

Times Square/Theater District The area around 42nd Street and Broadway is now occupied by major corporations and national chain stores, as well as new hotels, clubs and theaters.

Upper East Side From 59th to 96th streets and from Fifth Avenue to the East River. Madison Avenue is the ultra-chic shopping street.

East/Spanish Harlem From 96th to 142nd streets between Park Avenue and the East River. A mixed neighborhood of Italians, African-Americans and Hispanics.

Upper West Side Broadway cuts right through this section that extends from 59th to 125th streets between the Hudson River and Central Park West.

Harlem Stretching from 110th Street to the Harlem River and from Fifth to St. Nicholas avenues, Harlem is the city's most famous black community.

The Bronx North of and linked to Manhattan by bridges and subway. Home of the New York Botanical Garden, the Bronx Zoo and Yankee Stadium.

Brooklyn Southeast of Manhattan and connected by bridges, a tunnel and subway, it is New York's most populous borough. Take in great views of Manhattan from Brooklyn Heights.

Queens A 20-minute subway trip east from Manhattan takes you to Queens, one of New York's fastest-growing and most ethnically diverse areas.

Staten Island The most southerly and least populous borough, with attractions such as Historic Richmond Town. Good views of Manhattan and the Statue of Liberty from the ferry.

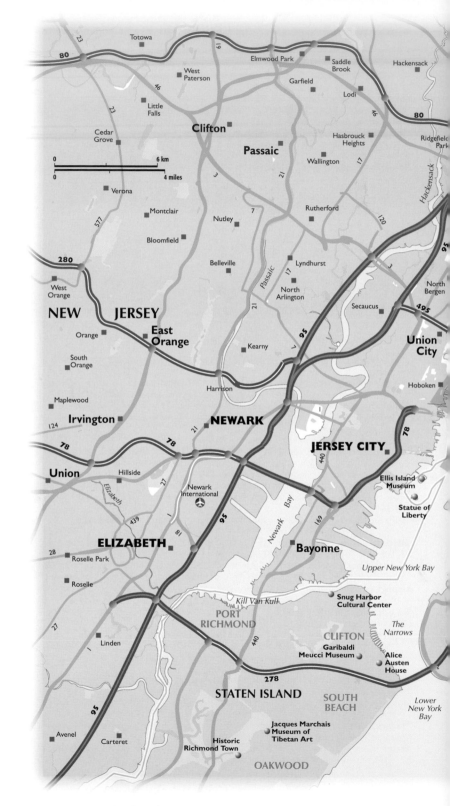

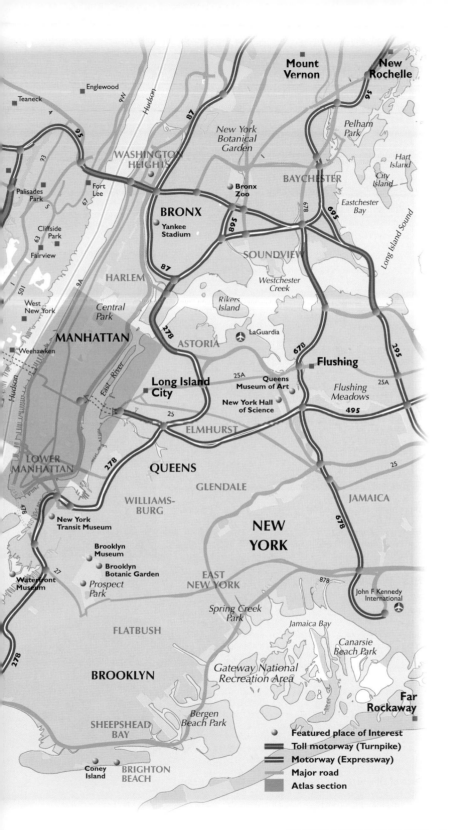

Teaneck

Englewood

Mount
Vernon

New
Rochelle

Hudson

New York
Botanical
Garden

Pelham
Park

Palisades
Park

Fort
Lee

WASHINGTON
HEIGHTS

Bronx
Zoo

BAYCHESTER

Hart
Island

City
Island

Cliffside
Park

BRONX

Yankee
Stadium

678

695

Eastchester
Bay

Fairview

SOUNDVIEW

Long Island Sound

West
New York

HARLEM

87

Westchester
Creek

Central
Park

Rikers
Island

Weehawken

MANHATTAN

278

ASTORIA

LaGuardia

678

295

East River

Long Island
City

25A

Queens
Museum of Art

Flushing

Flushing
Meadows

25A

Hudson

New York Hall
of Science

495

25

ELMHURST

LOWER
MANHATTAN

278

QUEENS

GLENDALE

JAMAICA

New York
Transit Museum

WILLIAMS-
BURG

NEW
YORK

678

Brooklyn
Museum

Brooklyn
Botanic Garden

EAST
NEW YORK

878

Waterfront
Museum

27

Prospect
Park

Spring Creek
Park

John F Kennedy
International

278

FLATBUSH

Jamaica Bay

Canarsie
Beach Park

25

BROOKLYN

Gateway National
Recreation Area

Bergen
Beach Park

Far
Rockaway

SHEEPSHEAD
BAY

278

Coney
Island

BRIGHTON
BEACH

Featured place of Interest
Toll motorway (Turnpike)
Motorway (Expressway)
Major road
Atlas section

THE BEST OF NEW YORK

BEST PLACES TO SHOP

B & H Photo (▷ 184) The professional place for cameras, video equipment and film, all at great prices.

Barneys (▷ 176) For cutting-edge fashion. Don't miss the handbag department.

Bloomingdale's (▷ 176) A department store that's so very New York.

Century 21 (▷ 177) For seriously discounted designer wear and a crowd scene worthy of the annals of shopping.

Dean & DeLuca (▷ 177) Everything in this fancy food emporium is absolutely the best of its kind. A sensuous browsing and tasting experience.

Tiffany's window displays on Fifth Avenue are worth a peek

FAO Schwarz (▷ 184) The ultimate toy store, as seen in the film *Big* with Tom Hanks.

J & R (▷ 179) Audiophiles and technophiles can satisfy every craving for audio components and CDs, computers and peripherals, cameras and other gadgets at good prices.

Jeffrey (▷ 171) The shoe department at this expensive clothing store is stellar, and the best place to see high-designer selections in a single location.

Sherry-Lehmann (▷ 178) An education; the inventory of international wine selections is worth $10 million.

Tiffany (▷ 183) Superb silver, crystal and other luxury gifts are the attraction at this famous American name, in business since 1837.

Big names on the bags: Barney's (top left) and FAO Schwarz (above)

BEST MUSEUMS AND GALLERIES

American Museum of Natural History (▷ 68–72) Not only for dinosaur fossils and moon rocks, but also a planetarium complex that is out of this world.

Frick Collection (▷ 100) A large collection of masterpieces by Rembrandt, Vermeer, El Greco and Goya housed in Henry Clay Frick's splendid mansion.

International Center of Photography (▷ 101) More than 60,000 photographs by top names.

Metropolitan Museum of Art (▷ 114–119) 5,000 years' worth of art from around the world.

Museum of Modern Art (▷ 125) Now doubled in size after architect Yoshio Taniguchi's expansion, MOMA displays masterworks of modern sculpture and painting.

BEST OUTDOOR SCULPTURES

Barosaurus at the American Museum of Natural History

Alice in Wonderland (▷ 82) by José de Creeft (1959). In Central Park Alice perches on a giant mushroom while the March Hare holds out a watch and the Mad Hatter looks on.

Bronze Bull by Arturo Di Modica (1989). Reminds many stock-market traders who pass by daily that better times are ahead. At Bowling Green (▷ 73).

The Immigrants (▷ 73) by Luis Sanguino (1973). A heart-rending sculpture evoking the hardships of early immigrants. In Battery Park.

Prometheus by Paul Manship (1934). Rockefeller Center's (▷ 128) famous gold-leaf and bronze statue overlooks the ice-skating rink.

The Sphere (▷ 73) Fritz Koenig's 22-ton symbol of global peace, rescued from the plaza between the twin towers after 9/11, is now a memorial to the victims. In Battery Park.

Statue of Liberty (▷ 136–137) America's symbol of freedom, by Frédéric-Auguste Bartholdi (1885). Take the ferry to Liberty Island for a close-up look.

The gilded figure of Prometheus at the Rockefeller Center

BEST PLACES TO EAT

Restrained elegance, in decor and cuisine, at Jean-Georges

Babbo (▷ 271) Mario Batali's flagship is the place to sample his lusty cuisine.

Le Bernardin (▷ 280) Everything about this seafood specialist is perfect—the service, the flowers and the exquisitely refined, thoughtful cuisine.

DB Bistro Moderne (▷ 275) Eating at one of Daniel Boulud's restaurants is a must for every food-loving visitor. This is the most relaxed and joyous of them all.

Four Seasons (▷ 277) Even though it has been around since 1959, it remains supremely modern and the darling of the city's movers and shakers. Christian Albin's cuisine is another bonus.

Jean-Georges (▷ 279) All of Jean-Georges Vongerichten's restaurants (Jo Jo, Vong, 66, Mercer Kitchen and Spice Market) showcase his brilliance, but this is his flagship.

Nobu (▷ 283) Nobu Matsuhisa's sushi is inspirational.

Per Se (▷ 284) Thrilling cuisine by Thomas Keller, of French Laundry, Napa Valley fame. Currently the city's most coveted reservation.

Tabla (▷ 200) Seductive neo Indian cuisine by master spice blender Floyd Cardoz.

BEST BARS

The bar scene lasts till dawn in the city that never sleeps

Flute (▷ 214) A luxury subterranean retreat serving 20 champagnes by the glass. Perfect for pre- or post-theater.

King Cole Bar (▷ 214 215) Where the Bloody Mary was invented. Maxfield Parrish's mural adds vibrant color. In the St. Regis Hotel.

MO Bar (▷ 303) Romantic hot spot in the Mandarin Oriental Hotel.

P. J. Clarke's (▷ 218) A beloved New York saloon, home to a rakish crowd.

Pen Top Bar (▷ 216) Who can resist a rooftop bar in Midtown?

Pravda (▷ 216) Sixty-five vodkas, plus caviar and Russian snacks at this trendsetter.

Rainbow Grill Bar (▷ 216) The bartenders mix a great cocktail at this romantic only-in-New York locale.

Top of the Tower (▷ 217) A nostalgic 26th-floor piano-bar overlooking the East River.

BEST PLACES TO STAY

Carlyle (▷ 299) The city's most discreet retreat.

Four Seasons (▷ 301) Legendary for its service and its immense bathtubs.

Library (▷ 303) A book-lovers' haunt notable for its hip minimalist design and good service.

Marcel (▷ 303) and the **Metro** (▷ 304) Chic on the cheap (by New York standards).

Le Parker Meridien (▷ 302) Very French uptown hotel with hip downtown style. Pool with a view and a rooftop jogging track.

Ritz Carlton (▷ 306) The opulent Central Park star offers superb service, the latest techno amenities and the only La Prairie spa in the United States.

St. Regis (▷ 307) A gilded Beaux-Arts beauty just off Fifth Avenue.

Soho Grand (▷ 307) First of the hip downtown hostelries. Pets get the red-carpet welcome.

Wyndham (▷ 309) Stay across from the Plaza Hotel for half the price.

The art deco Carlyle Hotel (above); welcome to the St. Regis (right)

BEST BUILDINGS AND SKYSCRAPERS

Ansonia Hotel (2101 Broadway) The Upper West Side's largest Beaux-Arts apartment-hotel. Soundproof partitions between floors attracted musicians and singers, many of them now famous.

Cathedral Church of St. John the Divine (▷ 67) It dates from 1892 and still isn't finished, but the mix of architectural styles inside is amazing.

Chrysler Building (▷ 85) An art deco masterpiece, a shrine to the Chrysler automobile.

Flatiron Building (▷ 87) New York's first skyscraper got its nickname from its triangular shape.

Guggenheim Museum (▷ 110–111) Frank Lloyd Wright's only New York building, a whirling wonder both inside and out.

42nd Street/Times Square (▷ 236–237 and 138–140) Architecture as performing art, with luminous façades of pulsating color. Best at night.

New York Public Library (▷ 127) Archetypal Beaux-Arts magnificence.

City icons: the Guggenheim (left) and the Chrysler Building

BEST FREE SIGHTS

Central Park (▷ 78–83) New York's green lung and Frederick Law Olmsted's masterpiece of landscape architecture.

The Hispanic Society of America (▷ 101) An extraordinary collection of paintings, sculpture and decorative arts. See El Grecos, Goyas and an exceptional collection of works by Joaquin Sorolla y Bastida. The 100-year-old buildings are architectural treasures too.

Parades (▷ 324) A festival of color and the city's best people-watching. There are many every year.

Staten Island Ferry (▷ 54) A wonderful trip across the harbor. Just hop on.

Whitney Museum of American Art at Philip Morris (▷ 148–151) A branch of the Whitney with wonderful exhibitions by living artists and a charming sculpture court. Worth a stop if you're in the Grand Central neighborhood.

Rockefeller Center and Grand Central Terminal (▷ 128–130 and 102–104) Two architectural gems worth a self-guided tour.

Outdoor New York: Staten Island Ferry (left) and Central Park

BEST EXPERIENCES

Empire State Building (▷ 94–96) The Observation Deck offers a panoramic view of all Manhattan, very romantic at sunset.

A Broadway show Seeing one is quintessential New York and various discount pricing schemes make it more affordable for all.

M4 bus to the Cloisters (▷ 48) A great trip past Columbia University (▷ 77) and through colorful neighborhoods.

Bronx Zoo (▷ 157) Always entertaining—the people are sometimes as interesting as the animals.

Waldorf-Astoria Hotel (▷ 308) A study in opulence. Ogle the amazing floral displays in the lobby.

A walk across the Brooklyn Bridge (▷ 74–75) A terrific view of the skyscrapers in Lower Manhattan and the East River.

Allow a day to visit the Bronx Zoo (left), and an hour or two for the Empire State Building

Living
New York

The stylish Chelsea District has an artsy edge (above), while Mott Street is home to one of the oldest Chinese communities in New York (right)

From the Empire State Building, skyscrapers can look tiny—even the Chrysler Building (above)

Make yourself dizzy looking down on Grand Army Plaza and Fifth Avenue from the General Motors Building (left)

The Urban
Landscape

Manhattan is only 13.5 miles (22km) long and 2.25 miles (3.5km) wide. Geologically it consists of bedrock made of gneiss, marble or mica schist. These two factors, plus population density, have played major roles in shaping the city's land- and streetscape, making it more vertical than most. Tall buildings line the streets, and people think nothing of riding elevators to their 50th-floor offices. Daily the population swells as commuters pour into Manhattan from the suburbs, creating a crowded environment that throbs with energy. Commuters access the city via ferry, tunnels and bridges, the most graceful of which are the Brooklyn (1883) and George Washington (1931) bridges. North of 14th Street the streets are laid out in a grid. There are few open spaces or green parks to provide relief—only one or two squares, such as Union, Washington and Madison, or small pockets of asphalt with benches, statues and fountains. Instead, there is one vast park, Central Park, separating East and West Sides uptown. It functions as the city's playground.

Commuting on the subway is part of daily life (above), as is taking a break in the park (below)

The grid and the warren

Most visitors to New York City quickly grasp the logic of the streetscape north of 14th Street. A series of broad north–south avenues is crossed by east–west streets, numbered logically. Below 14th Street things get more complicated. Here the narrow streets twist and turn, reminiscent of a medieval city, and have names rather than numbers. This came about because the city grew haphazardly and there were only a few long arteries connecting farms and villages. So in 1811 an orderly grid of 12 broad avenues and 155 streets was established, subdivided into lots measuring 25 by 100ft (7.5 by 30m). It was thought that traffic would be heaviest on the east–west routes, so more streets than avenues were planned. This pattern remains.

Central Park (right) is great for recreation: You can walk, jog, cycle, roller-blade, sail model boats or just take a picnic and chill

With only one major park in the city, every possible space is turned into an outdoor haven (right); street vending (left); locally made produce (bottom)

Underground city

First-time visitors to Manhattan often notice the rooftop water towers, fire hydrants, potholes and, weirdest of all, steam-belching funnels. The last give an inkling of what lies below—a multi-level network of electric and telephone cables, plus steam, water, gas and sewage pipes, all laid above the subway. A large water tunnel under the subway supplies the city's drinking water. The subway alone has 660 miles (1,062km) of track and 490 stations. There's 100 million miles of telephone cable. City water comes from upstate New York reservoirs, and the 1,500 million gallons a day is delivered by more than 6,000 miles of tunnel and water mains. Installed before 1930 and made of cast iron, they can rupture, which causes chaos. When the piped gases build up, they cause manhole explosions. The steam-belching funnels help to relieve the pressure and stop the 60,000 manholes from erupting.

Robert Moses—New York's Baron Haussmann

Robert Moses (1888–1981), who served on the Parks and Planning commissions, had a huge impact on the city's overall design. Between 1924 and 1968, he transformed the city, building 17 parkways, 14 expressways (including the Brooklyn–Queens Expressway), the FDR and Harlem River drives, the Triborough and Verrazano bridges, Lincoln Center and Stuyvesant Town. In the process he destroyed whole neighborhoods, tearing down slums and relocating residents in dehumanizing public housing in Harlem, the Lower East Side, the Bronx and Brooklyn. The citizens got angry. And when he moved to route cars through Washington Square and put parking lots in Central Park they mobilized to preserve the small scale of their neighborhoods. Still, Moses left a gigantic imprint on the city.

Waking up to the waterfront

For years New York City's 580 miles (920km) of waterfront lay blighted, the site of rusting piers, crumbling warehouses and refuse-strewn lots. Suddenly it's as if the city has woken up to its potential pleasures, as citizens go kayaking, fishing and sailing. A 28-mile (45km) bike path now encircles Manhattan, and the waterfront has been converted into a park with promenade and gardens from the Battery to 58th Street. It's hard to pinpoint when it began. In the 1980s, South Street Seaport, Battery Park City and Chelsea piers were important beginnings, followed by Riverbank State Park (1993). The rest has followed, culminating in Stuyvesant Cove Park (2002) and Hudson River Park (2003).

Urban gardens

New York City has one large park and only two major botanical gardens, so resident horticulturists create their own gardens in unlikely corners. If you look up at the residential buildings you might see green fronds peeking out from the roofline. Some of these roof gardens are luxurious indeed, planted with trees and flowers and decorated with urns and statues. In contrast are the hundreds of community gardens, usually created on vacant city-owned lots, which serve as neighborhood social centers. The impetus for such gardens can be traced to 1972 and a garden at Bowery and Houston tended by the Green Guerrillas. Mayor Giuliani sought to destroy such gardens and battled with neighborhood activists, but Mayor Michael Bloomberg has moved quickly to make peace.

Berkshire Berries
Rooftop Magic®

New York City
Rooftop Honey
1/2 Lb

You can play a game of softball on the Great Lawn in Central Park anytime

Shoe-shining outside Grand Central

Formal suit, fun transportation— New Yorkers like to be different

A New York cop

Peruvian celebrations in Bryant Park, Midtown (above)

The
People

International express—the number 7 train

In the census of 2000, Queens had the fastest-growing population, having risen by 11 per-cent in the preceding decade. Much of that rise can be attributed to the arrival of new immigrants from all over the globe— Indians, Colombians, Ecuadorians and Peruvians in Jackson Heights; Dominicans, Colombians and Mexicans in Corona; Chinese, Koreans and Vietnamese in Flushing. Queens is the city's new melting pot—the new gateway to America. A ride on the number 7 train will confirm this. The first few stations (40th to 61st streets and Queens Boulevard) are in Sunnyside and Woodside, where the most recent influx of Irish immigrants has settled. It then proceeds along Roosevelt Avenue, stopping in Jackson Heights (74th Street), Corona (111th Street) and, finally, Flushing.

Playing chess in Chinatown (above); many waiters earn most of their money from tips (below)

New York City is a city of immigrants. Between 1892 and 1924, 16 million immigrants poured through Ellis Island, many heading to the Lower East Side. Today, the gateways are Kennedy and Newark airports, and the immigrants' destinations are often the ethnic mosaics of Brooklyn and Queens, where such high schools as New Town have students who speak 30 different languages, and where the Central Library caters to a population that speaks nearly 40 languages. The Dutch, of course, were the first immigrants. They were interested in talent and enterprise and opened the city to immigrants of all sorts—Huguenots, Jews, Germans, Africans (slave and free) and the English, Scottish, French and Irish. At the turn of the 20th century, large numbers of Jews, Italians and Russians arrived, and after 1965, people from the Caribbean, Central America and Asia. The percentage of foreign-born has always fluctuated. At 40 percent, it is today at its highest. The lowest was in 1970 (18 percent). The population is 8 million, of which 35 percent are white, 27 percent Latino, 25 percent black and 10 percent Asian.

The Polish Day parade (left) takes place every October

A bright mural covers a wall in Chinatown (above); many early settlers were Jews, and there is still a large Jewish community in New York

Cool clothing for a steamy New York summer's day (left)

Hispanics—second in strength

The 1961 movie *West Side Story* depicted the struggle of Puerto Ricans, the city's first Hispanic community. Today, joined by nationals from Cuba, Ecuador, Colombia, El Salvador, the Dominican Republic and Mexico, Hispanics are the city's largest minority, representing 27 percent of the population. The Hispanic influence can be seen everywhere, from media and music to politics and cuisine. Turn on the TV and you'll find Telemundo and Univision offering Spanish talk shows and steamy soap operas. Scan a stand for newspapers *El Diario/La Prensa, Hoy, El Nacional* and *El Tiempo*. Baseball teams are peppered with Latin names; the Latino music craze continues, as more artists cross over in the footsteps of Ricky Martin; and chefs deliver the latest Spanish and Latino cuisine at such hot spots as Bolo and Casa Mono.

Bollywood on the Hudson

Before 1965 only a few South Asian students lived in the city, but after 1965, the Indian, Pakistani, Bangladeshi, Sri Lankan and Nepalese presence increased noticeably. Asians ran the news-stands, and suddenly it seemed everyone who worked in a Duane Reade drugstore was Asian. Gradually Asian cuisine, music and culture registered on the consciousness of New Yorkers. Now even fusion is occurring. Witness Panjaba MC and Jay-Z's hit *Beware of the Boys*, in which hip-hop meets British *bhangra*. In the 1970s more Asian professionals settled in Queens. Jackson Heights became the commercial center, with Sam and Raj opening in 1976 on 74th Street, a must-stop for all visiting Indians. Here are stores selling saris, South Asian videos, music and cooking staples. There are also several Hindu temples. And Madison Square Garden headlines Bollywood entertainers.

Tracing African-American heritage

A scholar interested in the black experience would begin at the Schomburg Center on 125th Street. Documents here chart the growth of the community from 14,000 in 1830 to 1.96 million today, along with the lives of such famous black New Yorkers as abolitionists Henry Highland Garnet and Alexander Crummell, and civil rights leaders Adam Clayton Powell and Malcolm X. A casual visitor might start at the African Burial Ground at Broadway and Duane. Here, from 1712 to 1794, 10,000–20,000 black people were buried as they were excluded from the Trinity Church graveyard. Few traces remain of Manhattan's 19th-century black communities, but much is found in Harlem: the church where Adam Clayton Powell, Sr. and Jr. preached, at 138th Street; the mosque associated with Malcolm X; and many Harlem Renaissance sites.

Understanding Yiddish

Every New Yorker knows what *chutzpah, mensch* and *kvetch* mean, and what the difference is between *shlep*, *shlemiel* and *schmozzle*. New York has the largest Jewish community outside Israel, but it's not its size so much as its spirit that counts. The greatest number of Jews came in the late 19th century, fleeing pogroms in Russia and Eastern Europe and settling on the Lower East Side. Their story is told in Irving Howe's history, *World of Our Fathers*. A tale of struggle rewarded by success and assimilation, it's a journey seen in the contrast between Woody Allen's Jewish outsider and Jerry Seinfeld's totally assimilated incidental Jew. Successful Jews moved from the Lower East Side and Brooklyn to the Upper West Side and the suburbs. They became financiers, doctors, lawyers, stand-up comedians and schoolteachers, and passed along Yiddish.

The 1959 Guggenheim Museum (right) was designed as a flowing building to please the eye

Brooklyn Bridge was the world's first steel suspension bridge (below)

The 1902 Flatiron Building (above) is barely a skyscraper, measuring only 285ft (87m)

The New York skyline, now without the World Trade Center (above); Lee Lawrie's *Wisdom* at the G. E. Building (right)

WISDOM AND KNOWLEDGE SHALL BE THE STABILITY OF THY TIMES

New York
Architecture

Beyond signature skyscrapers

Yes, the Empire State and the Chrysler buildings are two stunning skyscrapers, but they're not alone. The Bayard Condict Building (1898) on Bleecker Street is the only example of Louis Sullivan's work in the city. Later skyscrapers often incorporated elements from earlier eras, as did Daniel Burnham's Renaissance Revival Flatiron Building (1902). Raymond Hood's Radiator Building is a beauty—black brick and blue-green tiles with gold ornamentation. The Seagram Building on Park Avenue, by Mies van der Rohe and Philip Johnson, is a good example of 1950s modernism. Architects are still building the skyscrapers of tomorrow—Daniel Libeskind's design was chosen for the new complex to be built at the site of the former World Trade Center.

There are so many great buildings in New York that it can be overwhelming. Many great buildings have also been lost to redevelopment, and that too is overwhelming, but not surprising, given the city's commercial nature. Skyscrapers dominate the island of Manhattan, a building style made possible by the confluence of several factors—the geological bedrock, the availability of steel, and the techniques of engineering. City governments had always emphasized growth and innovation, which helped create such real-estate moguls as John Jacob Astor, William Zeckendorf, Harry Helmsley and Donald Trump. Zoning laws arrived only in 1916 and conservation came even later. Robert Moses razed whole neighborhoods, and between 1900 and 1965 many architectural gems were replaced with inferior substitutes. New Yorkers finally woke up in 1965, after Penn Station was demolished and replaced with the sorry station there today. A Landmarks Preservation Commission was founded, but it still had to be re-affirmed by the Supreme Court in 1978 when Grand Central Station was threatened.

The Chrysler Building, with its gleaming stainless-steel spire, is a 1930s art deco masterpiece

Brownstones in TriBeCa (left inset); the Empire State Building (right)

Tenements with their fire escapes clearly visible (below left); vast columns decorate the former U.S. Custom House (right); a quirky statue in SoHo (below)

Brownstones and tenements

Besides skyscrapers there are plenty of other building types to appreciate. Brownstones —named after the sandstone from the banks of the Connecticut and Hackensack rivers—line the streets of Greenwich Village, Chelsea and other districts. Today they make elegant residences. In the mid-19th century, cast iron was used for the façades of factories, shops and warehouses, many in SoHo. They seem to be carved in stone, but are in fact some of the first pre-fabs ever made. The most spectacular examples are at Nos. 260–561 Broadway and Mercer Street in SoHo.

Humble tenements with fire escapes are also city trademarks. Built to house the 19th-century immigrants, they were narrow, cramped and unsanitary, but cheap— $2–$3 per month. Examples still line the streets of the Lower East Side and East Village. Today the rent is 500 times more.

Mews, and other nooks and crannies

Visitors soon discover Midtown's pocket parks and plazas, but if you wander farther you'll find more charming oddities. Pomander Walk (West 94th and 95th streets), for example, is 16 two-story Tudor-style cottages. Sniffen Court, 150–158 East 36th Street, is a beguiling collection of brick carriage houses now used as residences. The Village has several oddities. The enclaves of Patchin Place (1848), West 10th Street, and Milligan Place, on Sixth Avenue between West 10th and 11th streets (1852), were originally built to house Basque waiters, who worked at the Brevoort House on Fifth Avenue. Later residents were more famous—among them e e cummings. Along Bedford Street, between Morton and Commerce, stands the narrowest house in the city—it's only 9ft (3m) wide and was home to Edna St. Vincent Millay in 1924.

Sculptors and painters help to gild the lily

Visitors often focus on the number and size of Manhattan skyscrapers, failing to notice the many embellishments created by famous and not so famous stonemasons, sculptors and painters. Daniel Chester French adorned the U.S. Custom House with monumental portraits of Asia, America, Europe and Africa. Reginald Marsh painted the interiors, celebrating the maritime wealth of the city. The lower façades of the art deco Rockefeller Center are encrusted with sculptures and bas-reliefs. Lee Lawrie's *Wisdom* hovers above the entrance to the G. E. Building, while inside José Maria Sert's mural, *Man's Conquests*, covers the walls. Portraits of Mary Pickford and Ethel Barrymore by Alexander Stirling Calder grace the Miller Building at West 46th Street and Seventh Avenue. French artist Marc Chagall adorned the Metropolitan Opera House.

Cass Gilbert

Cass Gilbert stands out as the designer of some of the city's most beautiful and luxuriant buildings. Go into the Woolworth Building (1910–1913) at 233 Broadway, for example. Woolworth, who paid the $15.5 million price tag in cash, certainly got his money's worth. The exterior soars 792ft (240m) without a setback. The interior is stunning. The vaulted lobby is swathed in veined marble, gold leaf and mosaic, and decorated with humorous sculptures, including one of Cass Gilbert himself holding the building and another of Woolworth counting his dimes. Gilbert's other great building is the U.S. Custom House (1907), a suitably grand repository for the wealth of the early city. He also contributed the New York Life Insurance Building (1907) at 51 Madison Avenue, between 26th and 27th streets, and the Federal Courthouse on Foley Square (1936).

You can visit some famous graves in Trinity Church (above); a choir sings out loud and proud in Harlem (left)

Katz's Deli (above) serves Jewish deli food; hot dogs and bagels are part of the NYC experience

New York Way of Life

Thousands of commuters pass through Grand Central Station every day

Most New Yorkers are not born in the city. They come to it. They come for many reasons, most of which involve dreams of success and the money, power and fame that follow. So the city is full of competitive people trying to make it on stage, in music, in real estate, on Wall Street, Madison Avenue or in any other arena. Even though many citizens are in "success overdrive," there are other factors that affect the rhythms of city life. New York is not monolithic. It's a cluster of neighborhoods, each with a different ambience and energy. The West Village wakes up late and operates at a slow pace; the East Village wakes up very late and parties very late; Washington Heights is loud and moves to a Dominican rhythm; Beekman Place is always subdued. The city may stay open 24 hours, but each neighborhood plays its own rhythmic variation.

A hot dog with mustard and ketchup—lunch on the run

Worship at your choice of altar

Many visitors are surprised to learn how religious Americans are and how many people attend religious services. New York City is no exception. From its founding it has offered an array of religious options, when Anglicans, Presbyterians, Quakers, Anabaptists, Jews, Catholics and Lutherans co-existed. Today, Christians, Buddhists, Hindus, Sikhs, Jews and Muslims all have a place to worship in the city. If you want to understand a culture, attend a religious service. In New York, head to Harlem and hear the gospel choirs raising the roofs of the Baptist churches, or go to East 96th Street to the Islamic Cultural Center. Take the train to the Hindu temples or Sikh gurdwaras in Queens, or drop in to one of the Buddhist temples in Chinatown. Or visit St. John the Divine or St. Patrick's.

The first yellow cabs hit the streets in 1907 (above)

Sex and the City's four sirens of singledom: Kim Cattrall, Kristin Davis, Sarah Jessica Parker and Cynthia Nixon (below)

Doing weights at the gym is much more interesting with the Manhattan skyline to look at (above)

Roller-blading is a speedy and healthy option (right)

Convenience greases the daily wheels

To the average New Yorker, speed and convenience take precedence over everything else. Time is, after all, money. So meals on the run are habitual. Workers en route to their offices, the women sporting Adidas, stop for an Egg McMuffin at McDonald's or coffee and a danish at Starbucks. At lunch, New Yorkers "order in" a sandwich or salad and soft drink, instead of going out for a leisurely meal. Or if they have a corporate cafeteria they go there. Some of these are extraordinary, the most famous being the Philippe Starck version at Condé Nast. If workers do go out, it will often be to "brown bag it," taking a sandwich to a pocket park.

At night, they may go home and order take-out from one of the many neighborhood menus that they keep by their phone—Thai, Chinese, Mexican, Indian, Italian or Japanese.

Exercise, exercise!

Although a recent study reported that 35 percent of New Yorkers are over-weight or obese, you would not know it from the frequent sightings of earnest New Yorkers pumping iron or running on treadmills. Keeping fit is a serious business. Most executives receive a standard gym membership and many have personal trainers, who show them how to work the machines and set their fitness goals. Of course, the Old Guard have always had their clubs, where they go to swim, exercise or get a massage—The Knicker-bocker, the Union, the Colony or the Harmonie are just some examples. After these come luxury gyms like the Sports Club/L.A. Average New Yorkers are more likely to join Bally Fitness or Crunch and take some aerobics classes. It's all part of the endless New York regimen of health and beauty.

Yellow cabs—love or hate?

The average New Yorker rides the bus or the subway, but many prefer to hail a cab, one of the 12,760 licensed to roam the city streets. You can't miss the yellow chariots. They have been in business since 1907. Early operators were so corrupt that in 1923 a Taxi and Limousine Commission began issuing licenses. LaGuardia sold the first medallion for $10 in 1937. Today they cost as much as $360,000. Every immigrant group has driven cabs—initially Jewish settlers, Italians and Irish and more recently people from Russia, Africa, Haiti and South Asia. They receive only 24 hours of instruction and earn about $5 an hour. Some cabs perform some wild maneuvers to grab passengers. The bullet-proof partitions separating passenger from driver were installed in 1967. A handful of televisions arrived in 2002 but were discontinued in 2003.

New York solutions to singledom

There are 100 million "singles" in the United States. Several million of them live in New York, and many are looking for the perfect mate, supporting a veritable marriage market industry. Even in the 1860s, matrimonial brokers' ads ran in the press. For example, John Johnson and Co. offered services to "ladies wishing agreeable and wealthy husbands," and to men desiring "beautiful, rich and accomplished wives." If you scan the ads in the local media, you'll find little has changed. Now, though, individuals advertise themselves, posting photographs in such publications as *New York Magazine*, revealing their most intimate data online at itsjustlunch.com, or signing up for TV shows such as "Perfect Partner" and "Boy Meets Boy." There are singles groups of all kinds, from speed-dating specialists to one for tall people only.

The
Metro-
politan
Opera
House
stages
excellent
performances
(right); one
of a series
of Jackson
Pollock's
modern, some
say aggressive,
pieces (below)

Everything from ancient Egypt to Van Gogh is in the Metropolitan Museum of Art (above); the all-singing, all-dancing 1980s musical *42nd Street* has been revived (right)

The Arts

New York City leads the nation in arts and entertainment. It's the world's center of contemporary art, and also has a phenomenal collection of performing arts companies in dance, music and theater. The city's cultural groups have also led the way in finding innovative ways to fund their endeavors. For years, although they have received some funding from government, city cultural institutions and groups have developed their own funding resources—private donors, memberships, bookstores and other ancillary profit centers. The arts scene is constantly evolving. There is an uptown mainstream scene and a downtown more experimental scene, and within each shifts are always occurring—SoHo galleries migrating to Chelsea, for example. Don't worry, whatever excites you in the arts can be found in New York.

Thoroughly Modern Millie is a big, bright, upbeat story of a young girl from Kansas arriving in New York in 1922 (above); modern art in SoHo (below)

Culture and money

Wealthy dynasties have always served as patrons of the arts, and New York's are no different. Mayor Bloomberg donates a large part of his fortune to cultural institutions, as do many in the Social Register. Today, the money is likely to be dispensed by the 525 city-based foundations, which control $82 billion. These cultural donors are copying earlier magnates whose names still resonate throughout the city—Astor, Carnegie, Morgan, Rockefeller, Vanderbilt and Whitney. John D. Rockefeller gave away $1.5 million annually and launched the Rockefeller Foundation in 1913 with $100 million. His son, John, Jr., founded Rockefeller University and donated the Cloisters, Fort Tryon Park and the site for the United Nations building. John Jacob Astor left $400,000 for a library, which Brooke Astor, the wife of his great-great grandson, still supports.

New York and jazz are synonymous (above); this huge red cube (right) by Isamu Noguchi is on Church Street; unmissable house number outside 9 West 57th Street (below)

Martin Scorsese's movie is about Irish immigrants in 1863 (above)

New York, New York, it's a helluva town

The film industry may have moved from New York to Hollywood after World War I, but it is still a film town, thanks to the renovation of old studios and the encouragement of the Mayor's Office of Film. Film-makers have long conducted a love affair with the city, sometimes using fake studio backdrops, as they did in *King Kong*, and other times filming the reality on location. The directors most associated with New York are Martin Scorsese, Paul Mazursky, Sidney Lumet, John Cassavetes, Spike Lee and Wes Anderson (*The Royal Tenenbaums*). But the love affair goes back a long way to such films as *Miracle on 34th Street* (1947), *The Naked City* (1948) and *On the Waterfront* (1954).

If you want an architectural tour of New York plus an insight into its collective unconscious, treat yourself to any Woody Allen film.

They still make Steinways in New York

The name Steinway signifies the best pianos in the world, and it has done so since 1853, when Henry Steinweg started the company. The company was so successful that by 1873 the family was able to build a company town in Astoria, Queens, complete with factory, housing, a school and other amenities. At one time, the company made 6,000 grand pianos a year, but the industry collapsed in 1927 with the introduction of radio and the phonograph. The company survived, although the family sold it in 1972. Today it continues to operate with 450 workers, who handcraft about 2,000 grand pianos (and 500 uprights) a year, which cost from $25,000 to $147,000. Even though the eight-month process is the same, each one has a different musical personality, depending on the wood and other subjective factors.

Chelsea—new center of contemporary art

In 1987 the Dia Center for the Arts opened on 22nd Street in Chelsea, making it the new vortex for contemporary art, surpassing SoHo and 57th Street. In 1991 it opened its innovative rooftop urban park. Since then, the area between 19th and 29th streets and 10th and 11th avenues has grown into a large gallery district with more than 200 spaces. All the former big names in SoHo and Uptown are now represented here—Matthew Marks, Larry Gagosian, Mary Boone, Pace Wildenstein, Paula Cooper, Robert Miller, Barbara Gladstone, Holly Solomon and Sonnabend. Some galleries have hangar-like spaces large enough to accommodate massive works by such artists as Richard Serra. In some cases entire buildings (529 West 20th Street and 526 West 26th Street, for example) now house multiple galleries.

The challenge of Broadway

Every year Broadway is reported teetering on the edge of economic disaster and accused of abandoning serious theater for warmed-over revivals. It's tough to make money on Broadway. Back in 1866, *Black Crook*, a musical melodrama, ran for only 475 performances and took in $1.1 million, easily recouping the $24,000 investment. Today a musical costs on average $8 million to put on, and the show has to run for at least 520 performances just to break even. When producers have to rely on tourists to fill the seats, it gets really tough. Success then depends on low costs, good press, a Tony Award and lots of luck. Few shows meet the test. In fact, about 80 percent of Broadway shows fail to recoup their investments. So producers of serious theater turn to Off- and Off-Off Broadway, where costs are lower and they can afford to nurture new playwrights.

QUIET ZONE

Library sign (above); film crews shoot in the streets (left)

Media and politics inescapably entwined: The Grand Old Party (Republican) elephant slugs it out with the Democrat donkey (left), and Mayor Bloomberg gets a hug from media queen Jennifer Lopez

GOP

DEMO

Politics and Media

Summarizing New York City politics is difficult. It's a complex city divided into five boroughs—Manhattan, Brooklyn, the Bronx, Queens and Staten Island—populated by 8 million people of different races and religions and diverse socio-economic interests. As a consequence, city politics are often contentious, with ethnic rivalries playing a large part in the political process. The municipal employee unions— police, fire, teachers, sanitation and transit—also play a major role in city politics and can make the city a more, or less, pleasant place to live and work. As far as national politics goes, New York City is firmly Democratic, even though it has voted for two Republicans in the last three mayoral elections. Only Staten Island votes pretty solidly Republican. The print media cut across party lines. The *New York Times*, the *Daily News* and *Newsday* lean toward the Democratic Party while the *Wall Street Journal*, the fledgling *New York Sun* and Rupert Murdoch's *New York Post* take a more Republican tack.

For some, the alternating political processes are nothing but a failure

WILL WORK FOR FOOD MAY GOD BLESS YOU PEOPLE!

Who's in charge?

It's hard for outsiders to determine who is in charge. Under the federal system, the responsibilities are divided among the federal, state and municipal governments. Although there have been many powerful mayors— LaGuardia, Koch, and Giuliani in particular— their power is limited by the state governor, the state assembly and senate, the borough presidents and the city council, to name the major challengers. Currently, for example, even though Mayor Bloomberg presides over a city containing 38 percent of the state's population, he is battling Governor Pataki over the redevelopment of Lower Manhattan and the building of a water filtration plant. The city lives under a tough set of fiscal rules imposed by the state 30 years ago, with four agencies monitoring city finances. If the city fails to balance the budget or pay its debt, the state will assume financial control.

The presidential seal (left); a New York cycling cop (right)

Mayor Michael Bloomberg's 2003 ban on smoking in all public places did not go down well with New Yorkers (below and left)

Radio City Hall is lit up for Christmas (above)

Education is the topic of the day

From the 1960s to the early 1990s crime and race dominated the headlines, but under Mayor Guiliani crime dropped dramatically and although race continued to play a divisive role, it diminished as a headline issue. Today, education is such a compelling issue that among the wealthy even getting into the "right" nursery matters. Although there are top-notch schools (Stuyvesant, Bronx Science), the public (state) school system is in crisis. It educates 1.1 million students in 1,200 schools, many of which are in disrepair, require students to pass through metal detectors, and have truancy problems. Bloomberg has staked his reputation on reforming it by streamlining the bureaucracy and imposing a standard curriculum.

The smoking edict

Mayor Giuliani disciplined New Yorkers for such "bad behavior" as jay-walking, panhandling, staging scatological art shows, squeegeeing and sleeping on, or occupying, two seats on the subway. New Yorkers grumbled, but came to appreciate the improvement in the quality of life that followed. When Bloomberg tried the same, he ran into resistance, particularly when he banned smoking from all public spaces, including bars. Bar and nightclub owners, libertarians and dedicated smokers were irate. A few years on, everyone has calmed down. In fact smokers even admit to enjoying smoke-free interiors and the camaraderie of smoking outside with others. Business has not been adversely affected.

Gossip

Gossip has a high profile in New York City because power, money, sex and celebrity drive society and gossip helps keep score on who's in and who's out. Gossip may have begun with Mrs. William Astor and her 400 and continued on the zebra-striped banquettes at El Morocco and at Walter Winchell's table at the Stork Club, but now it's everywhere. It's not confined to the tabloids, either. It may not be called a gossip column, but that's what it is. The New York Times has "boldface names;" New York Magazine has "The Intelligencer;" The New Yorker calls it the "Talk of the Town" and Town & Country insists that it's "Parties." Tina Brown leavened Vanity Fair with it. Everyone has to read the New York Post's Liz Smith, Cindy Adams and Page Six. And it's becoming even more center stage, as the Star moves into Manhattan and gossip drives the content of glossies U.S. and People.

Madison Avenue

Madison Avenue may be the Golden Mile of designer retailing, but it is also synonymous with one of the largest and most important city industries. In 2002, a massive $117 billion was spent on advertising, plus $6.8 billion on focus groups alone. With consumer spending accounting for 60 percent of the national economy and 22,000 new packaged products being launched annually, advertising plays a huge marketing role. New York City remains the advertising capital, because all the TV networks and publishing companies have their headquarters or offices here. Although the advertising companies are not necessarily on or near Madison Avenue anymore—Saatchi & Saatchi is at 375 Hudson in the West Village—they do need to be near the media buyers and sellers, so that they can easily participate in the seasonal media buying frenzy.

Alan Greenspan (above) became Chairman of the Federal Reserve Board in 1987, a post he held for more than 18 years

Nasdaq and Wall Street are familiar names in the world of money

The New York Stock Exchange is the heart of financial America

Commerce and Finance

New York City has always been a money-making city. John Jacob Astor made his fortune in real estate, J. P. Morgan in banking, Cornelius Vanderbilt in transportation and John D. Rockefeller in oil. Today wealth is still made in finance, real estate and commodities, but the new money is in technology and communications and less in manufacturing and trade. Manufacturing has moved South or to Mexico and Asia, while the once mighty port business has shifted to New Jersey. New York is still the financial capital of the world, the global center of banking and insurance (more than 70 banks had their headquarters here in the mid-1990s), even though some have moved, like Goldman Sachs, to New Jersey. The securities industry is vital to the city's economy. When it is booming, the city flourishes and when it declines, the city does too. When the dot-com bubble burst in March 2000 and was followed a year and half later by the tragedy of 9/11, the city suffered and by fall 2002 the city had a projected deficit of $5 billion. Under Mayor Bloomberg the city has staged a remarkable economic recovery.

Seventh Avenue hangs on

From the 1930s to the 1950s, the garment industry was the biggest in the city. Cutters, pattern-makers and sewing-machine operators and button and zipper makers jammed the blocks between 36th and 38th streets between Madison and Eighth Avenues. (Seventh Avenue is also called Fashion Avenue between 23rd and 42nd streets.) Today the only evidences of the trade are the racks being pushed along the sidewalks and the "seconds" bins. Most manufacturing has gone to low-cost countries like China. What remains is on the Lower East Side, and in Chinatown and Queens, where Chinese, Thai and Dominican staff sweatshops. The Garment Industry Development Corporation is working to reinvigorate the industry.

The NYSE, Amex and Nasdaq—the three pillars

The New York Stock Exchange, whose 1,366 seats are for sale by auction, is the most prestigious of the three. The first seats sold in 1868 for $4,000; in October 2002 a seat sold for $2.3 million. Only the most carefully scrutinized companies—2,800 of them—are listed on the NYSE, which has a global market capitalization of $20 trillion and trades on average 1.46 billion shares a day.

Those who could not afford to join the NYSE started the Amex, on Trinity Place. It lists only 696 companies. It was originally called the Curb Market because the brokers did their business at the curbside.

In 1971 the National Association of Securities Dealers Automated Quotation (Nasdaq) was launched as the world's first electronic stock market. It lists 3,300 mostly high-growth companies and is the world's largest market in trading volume.

The Story of New York

Early Colonial Days

In the 16th century the area now known as Manhattan was a land of natural beauty, populated by wild animals and Native American tribes. Early explorers' engravings and vellum maps depict the hilly terrain and early settlements, including the Indian longhouses near Coney Island. In the early 16th century, Giovanni da Verrazano, a Florentine navigator and merchant working for the French, attempted to find the supposed Northwest Passage, a more direct route between Europe and Asia. Instead, he found himself sailing into the wonderful natural harbor that is now New York Harbor on April 17, 1524, and was greeted by the astonished native Algonquians.

However, not much exploring went on until the arrival in 1609 of Henry Hudson, an English navigator working for the Dutch East India Company. He sailed up the river that now bears his name and reported back on the abundance of otter, beaver, mink and wildcat and on the possibilities of the fur trade. The Dutch, recognizing the potential, went into business and brought traders to settle the area. One farm belonged to Jonas Bronck, whose name has stuck firmly to the area known today as The Bronx.

Native Algonquian (left); Giovanni da Verrazano (right) gave his name to the Verrazano Narrow Bridge

Native Americans

During the early colonial days, the Algonquians were often at war with each other and with the Iroquois. To protect themselves, the tribes lived in tight-knit groups under strong chiefs.

In the beginning, the Algonquians were a friendly people and showed the Dutch colonists where to hunt, farm and fish. The Native Americans enjoyed trading just as much as the Dutch, but then, as the colonists tried to take land away, fighting broke out. The Dutch attacked two encampments, killing 80 Native Americans, and started a very bloody war. Reports of this fighting got back to Holland, discouraging emigration to the New World.

1500

Manhattan (right) was named New Amsterdam after the Dutch took control; the trial of John Peter Zenger (below) ended in victory for the press

Dutch colony

Peter Minuit bought Manhattan Island in 1626 for a cool $24 worth of kettles, axes and cloth. However, the Native Americans he paid did not share his concept of land ownership and didn't understand the sale; furthermore, the transaction was made with the Canarsie tribe, who were merely passing by on that day. Dutch garrisons built a windmill, a fort, a barracks, a jail, a church, a tavern and a governor's house. There were about 120 houses by 1656, and about 300 four years later. Merchants and traders ran the municipal government and everyone was happy until the Dutch governor tried civilizing the rowdy populace.

Peter Minuit purchased Manhattan illegally for next to nothing (below)

Peter Stuyvesant

The early colonists were a fairly lawless lot, and drunkenness and violence were common. Then, in 1647, the one-legged Peter Stuyvesant stepped in as governor. Under his strict control, law and order were established, along with a school, hospital, prison and post office. But Stuyvesant was not popular, and he eventually surrendered to English attackers, then returned to Holland in 1665 to defend himself against charges of misconduct. In 1667, he came back to his New York farm, the *bouwerij* that has given its name to New York's Bowery. Stuyvesant died in 1672 and was buried on his farm, now the site of St. Mark's Church-in-the-Bowery (▷ 131).

Peter Stuyvesant's lack of a limb never held him back (below)

The English

In 1664, with 8,000 unhappy Dutch colonists living on the island, now known as New Amsterdam, Colonel Richard Nicolls easily seized the territory from the Dutch on the orders of King Charles II of England. The king's brother, the Duke of York, took control and changed the colony's name to New York. The terms of the surrender were generous, and not a single Dutch resident took Nicolls up on his offer to repatriate them. Nicolls became governor and was both efficient and popular. In 1673, when a war between Holland and England broke out, New York returned to Dutch control, but it bounced back to the English in 1674 under the Treaty of Westminster.

King of New York: Charles II of England (below)

Freedom of the press

German immigrant John Peter Zenger became the editor of the *New York Weekly Journal* in 1733 and quickly grew unpopular with Governor William Cosby. His opposition to the governor's arbitrary acts gained support from lawyers, merchants and others of independent spirit. In 1734 he was arrested for seditious libel. His lawyer, Andrew Hamilton, refuted the libel charge on the basis that the offensive article was not actually false. The court disagreed, stating that whether or not the publication was true was irrelevant and that merely publishing such wicked words about the government was enough to convict.

However, Hamilton's eloquent appeal to the judge and jury resulted in Zenger's acquittal and a victory for freedom of the press, setting a precedent against judicial tyranny in libel suits and leading eventually to the First Amendment to the Constitution.

1750

A view of the early settlement of New York (above)

Revolutionary Period

King's College, now Columbia University (▷ 77), was established in 1754 by royal charter of King George II with the twin aims of preventing the growth of republican principles and promoting the teachings of the Anglican Church. As the American colonies grew more independently minded, students such as Alexander Hamilton emerged to become America's patriot leaders.

In 1765 a Stamp Act passed by Parliament in London taxed marriage licenses, playing cards, newspapers and 40 other necessities of life, and infuriated the colonists. Leading opposition to the Stamp Act, New York sent a formal protest to the king; 28 delegates from nine colonies attended the Stamp Act Congress in New York. After protests that included the virtual suspension of all port activity for nearly two weeks, Parliament repealed the Act in March 1766. New York joined the fight against taxation that eventually led to the American Revolution. Although New York did not see a great deal of action, it was Britain's military headquarters and was the only city occupied by the British throughout the conflict. When the war ended, many loyalists left America for the West Indies or Canada and the population dwindled to 12,000. But within six years of the British departure, New York had become America's most vibrant city.

You'll find Alexander Hamilton (left) on a $10 bill; the Stamp Act imposed by London (right)

British occupation

The city's Tories, who supported the British Crown, were jubilant when British troops entered New York in June 1776. Patriots surrounded the city, denying the British easy communications with other colonies. Under military occupation, the city suffered terrible fires and loss of life and property. A fire on September 21, 1776 destroyed a quarter of the city, including Trinity Church (▷ 142–143). On August 3, 1778, 100 houses burned. The guerrilla war between the two opposing sides involved cattle-rustling, abductions and deliberate burning of crops. American prisoners of war were either incarcerated in a crowded, appalling dungeon on Liberty Street or in ships anchored in the harbor. Almost 11,000 soldiers perished in the horrendous conditions.

1750

The impressive entrance to the library at prestigious Columbia University (above)

Raging fires in New York in 1776 claimed many lives and destoyed parts of the city (right)

Defeat on Long Island

After forcing the British General William Howe to evacuate Boston in March 1776, General George Washington arrived in Manhattan on April 13. Knowing that he would meet General Howe's army again, forts were built in Brooklyn Heights and Lower Manhattan. On July 2, Howe's force landed on Staten Island. On July 9, the Declaration of Independence was read to Washington's soldiers on Bowling Green. The delighted soldiers and civilians tore down the statue of King George III and melted it down to make bullets—42,088 of them. Meanwhile, Howe's army moved to the south of Brooklyn, where his 20,000 British regulars surprised Washington's 7,000 militiamen. The Battle of Long Island, a terrible defeat for Washington, left 2,000 Americans dead.

Benedict Arnold

In today's United States, the name Benedict Arnold is synonymous with traitor. After Arnold had fought for General Washington against the British at Lake Champlain and in Connecticut, he was placed in command of Philadelphia in 1778. But he became disillusioned with Congress after he was overlooked for promotion. He knew British General Clinton was bribing Americans to desert and he began a treasonable correspondence with Clinton. He was in the process of making plans to surrender West Point, the military academy then under his command, to the British when the plot was revealed. Arnold managed to escape and became a leader of British troops in New York. After the British surrendered, he and his wife moved to England, where they were deeply unpopular.

From general to president

On November 25, 1783, General Washington made his ceremonial entry into New York and gave a farewell address to his troops in front of Fraunces Tavern at 54 Pearl Street, then returned to his home at Mount Vernon in Virginia. On February 4, 1789, he was unanimously chosen as president of the new United States at a convention in Philadelphia.

On April 30, 1789, Washington took the oath of office on the balcony of L'Enfant's Federal Hall, on the site of today's Federal Hall National Monument (▷ 97). Thousands lined Murray's Wharf at the end of Wall Street as he arrived by ceremonial barge. The cheering crowds, waving their hats, then followed him on his route through the downtown streets.

The Tea Party

The British Parliament approved the Tea Act in 1773, giving the British East India Company a monopoly on all the tea sold in the colonies. The angry Manhattan Sons of Liberty encouraged the public to repel the tea ships; New Yorkers boycotted all establishments offering East India tea. On December 16, 1773, the Boston Tea Party, a protest in which a group of men masquerading as Mohawks dumped 342 cases of East India tea into Boston Harbor, further fueled radicalism in New York. Britain passed the Intolerable Acts which closed Boston's port, alarming New Yorkers. On April 22, 1774, New York had its own Tea Party and dumped 18 boxes of tea into the bay. This led to the establishment of the revolutionary government in New York State.

The hero of the piece—George Washington (left)

Benedict Arnold (left) played a large part in the shaping of New York

_1800_

The inauguration of the United States' first president, George Washington, on the balcony of Federal Hall (above)

Troops were employed to escort the stamped paper for the 1765 Stamp Act to City Hall (below)

Commercial Growth

The first half of the 19th century brought New York conflict, epidemics and disaster, as well as an explosion of commerce and riches. During the War of 1812 between the United States and Britain, New York's port was blockaded. Ten years later, a yellow fever epidemic broke out in Front Street, and in 1832 a cholera epidemic killed 4,000. The Great Fire of 1835 gutted 700 buildings in a 17-block area below Wall Street; in 1845, another fire destroyed 300 buildings in Lower Manhattan.

The achievement that brought growth, prosperity and international commerce to the city was the building of the Erie Canal in 1825, a project of Governor DeWitt Clinton. In following years, powerful men went from rags to riches practically overnight. Cornelius Vanderbilt (1794–1877), an uneducated Staten Island farm boy, became one of the wealthiest men in America when he took control of much of the shipping business in the harbor and along the Hudson River to Albany.

The swelling city needed news. William Cullen Bryant, whose name is now associated with Bryant Park, became editor of the New York *Evening Post* in 1829. In 1834 Horace Greeley founded the *New Yorker*, a weekly literary and news journal unrelated to the modern magazine. In 1841, he became the founding editor of the *New York Tribune*, while other newspapers also flourished.

1800

Knickerbocker

The word knickerbocker was a literary invention of author Washington Irving (1783–1859) in his *Diedrich Knickerbocker's History of New York* (1809). A satire on pedantry, manners, politics and history told by an imaginary Dutch colonist, Knickerbocker, it won Irving much acclaim in the United States and Europe. New Yorkers of Dutch descent, and by extension the entire city, became known as Knickerbockers. The group of writers including Irving, novelist James Fenimore Cooper and poet William Cullen Bryant was known as the Knickerbocker Group.

Writer Washington Irving (left) and editor William Cullen Bryant (above) left their mark

This was how New York appeared in 1849, looking south from Union Square

Parts of the city were left in ruins after the Great Fire on December 16 and 17, 1835 (above)

John Jacob Astor

By 1808, John Jacob Astor—who emigrated to America from Germany in 1783—had amassed a fortune in the fur trade and was the sole owner of the American Fur Company. When he grew fat and his health deteriorated, he sold the company and took up real estate. After he invested in farmland north of New York City, in what is now the heart of Manhattan, the city's rapid expansion turned his farmland into a goldmine. Astor House, the biggest hotel in the world at the time, stood on what is now City Hall Park (▷ 77) and was the first building to bear the family's name. The Astor Library, which he bequeathed to the city, is now part of the New York Public Library (▷ 127).

John Jacob Astor was the richest man in the world when he died

Grid system

New York City's grid system of streets was devised in 1811, at a time when the population was increasing rapidly. In need of new streets for the undeveloped land north of Washington Square, city officials accepted the plans put forward by engineer John Randel, Jr. The commissioners dismissed the idea of ovals, circles or stars and opted for the economy of straight lines and right angles. The Commissioner's Plan called for 2,000 long, narrow blocks, disregarded the contours of the land, and provided for neither parks nor open spaces.

Erie Canal

The Erie Canal, connecting the Hudson River and the Great Lakes, made New York the only eastern port with a waterway route to the farmlands of the Midwest, and instantly turned the city into America's center of commerce. It was New York governor DeWitt Clinton who oversaw the $7 million project, which skeptics at the time called "Clinton's Folly." The 10-day canal trip from New York to Buffalo meant that goods from around the world could be transported via New York to the interior of the New World. There was an explosion of new office space and warehouses along the harbor, and New York began its career as a major world trading center.

Artist and inventor

By 1825, many of the most respected American painters were living in New York—that is the ones who stayed in the country and did not flee to Paris. A significant artist of the Romantic School and a successful portrait painter, Samuel F. B. Morse is best remembered as the inventor of the Morse Code. He moved permanently to New York in 1824 and became a founder of the National Academy of Design in 1826. *The House of Representatives* (1822–23), one of Morse's most notable paintings, includes more than 80 portraits of politicians. By the early 1830s, he was more interested in electrical experiments than in painting, and in 1844 he tapped out in code the famous message, "What hath God wrought?"

DeWitt Clinton (above) was a governor with invaluable foresight

1850

The first barges arrived from Buffalo along the Erie Canal (above)

City Hall, finished in 1812, gave the city a venue for meetings and events

Social Unrest and Reform

By 1875 more than a million people lived in New York. The poor, many of them recent immigrants, lived in tenements that bred hatred, violence and disease, especially tuberculosis. Jacob Riis published a book of photographs, *How the Other Half Lives* (1890), which called the public's attention to the atrocious living conditions. As a result, reformers like Theodore Roosevelt and Frances Perkins joined a crusade to rid the city of these inhumane dwellings.

The enormous task of transportation in the growing city was a major problem. In 1858, about 35 million passengers used horse-drawn trams to move around. In the 1860s, trains were a welcome improvement. Washington Bridge, opened in 1889, made it easier to go from Manhattan to the Bronx. Commissioner George Waring reorganized the sanitation system, and in 1893, New York began chlorinating its drinking water. Progressive reformers brought education to immigrant children and they were offered free medical examinations in 1895. The changes came too late for many immigrants, but at last something was being done to improve their lives.

Immigrants poured into the city in the second half of the 19th century (right); Dr Elizabeth Blackwell was the first woman on the British Medical Register (far right)

Elizabeth Blackwell

Elizabeth Blackwell came from Bristol, England, to New York in 1832 to train as a doctor. She applied to eight medical schools before being accepted at Geneva Medical School. Graduating in 1847, she was ostracized by the profession because she was a woman. With great determination, she opened a dispensary for the poor in the slums of the Lower East Side. In 1857 she founded the New York Infirmary for Indigent Women and Children (the New York Infirmary). In 1868, after creating a training school for nurses, she founded the Women's Medical College of the New York Infirmary. In 1910, she died in Hastings, England.

ELIZABETH BLACKWELL M D 1849

1850

A pictorial railway ticket (above); the elevated railway on Third Avenue (right)

Slavery

By the middle of the 18th century, New York had the highest concentration of slaves north of Virginia. They were sold at the slave market at the foot of Wall Street until slavery was abolished in New York State in 1827. But slavery was to continue, especially in the South, for another 38 years. New York provided a pivotal stage for its demise. On February 27, 1860, Abraham Lincoln arrived in New York City to give his celebrated antislavery address in the Great Hall of the Cooper Union Foundation Building on East 7th Street, now a designated historic landmark. His eloquent defense of the Constitution and the call for the freedom of slaves helped him secure the Republican presidential nomination.

The famous features of President Abraham Lincoln

Tammany Hall

In 1850 William Marcy Tweed organized a volunteer fire department, a move which made him popular enough to get elected to city and state posts. In the 1860s and 1870s, under Tweed's direction, corrupt politicians at the Democratic Party headquarters, Tammany Hall, ran the party by bribery, coercion and vote rigging. Having swindled the city at every opportunity, Tweed was finally caught after the Tweed Ring reneged on a deal with the sheriff, who went to the press. *The New York Times* revealed the facts, and on November 19, 1873, Tweed was sentenced to 12 years in prison.

Draft riots 1863

A dearth of volunteers for the Civil War led to conscription in 1862. In New York, as in other places, the draft met with great opposition and bounty hunters found substitutes for men who could pay. Others with $300 in their pocket could pay to be exempt. The cost of living in New York had doubled and the mostly Irish dock workers had gone on strike for higher wages; they were furious when 'scabs' were brought in to work. Under the circumstances the Irish could see no reason to fight for black freedom and bitterly resented conscription. Four days of rioting in scorching heat ended on July 17, 1863, but not before 120 men had died, mostly African-Americans killed by Irish immigrants.

Jewish immigrants

The first Jewish people, 27 of them, arrived in New York in 1633. But the pogroms in Russia and Eastern Europe resulted in the great influx of Jewish immigrants at the turn of the 19th century. In 1892, around 81,000 Jewish people arrived at Ellis Island (▷ 90–93) and 258,000 more between 1905 and 1906. They crowded into the tenements on the Lower East Side (▷ 109), alongside the Irish, who had come earlier and who resented the newcomers. Given that many of the police officers of the day were Irish, it is not surprising that Mayor McClellan's police commissioner claimed that 50 percent of the city's crimes were committed by Jewish people. The outraged Jewish community forced him to make a public retraction.

A cartoon satirizing William Marcy "Boss" Tweed (1823–78), the corrupt politician who defrauded New York City of $30 million

1900

The building on Ellis Island that was the first sight of New York for most immigrants (above)

Ulysses S. Grant, the Union and Republican President, tans the hides of Confederate generals and his electoral opponents (left)

World's Second-Largest City

By 1900 Greater New York had a population of 3.5 million and was the world's second-largest city after London. In Manhattan, 42,700 tenements housed the 1.5 million poor in dire conditions. By the 1920s a campaign to restrict immigration resulted in legislation that brought a decline in the number of newcomers from Poland, Russia and Italy. The great metropolis experienced terrible disasters and celebrated remarkable triumphs. In 1901, a heatwave killed nearly 100 New Yorkers in just 24 hours. The first skyscrapers went up, starting with the Flatiron Building in 1902, symbolizing the city's wealth and hopes for the future. Meanwhile, Prohibition drove New Yorkers to illegal speakeasies. Many went uptown to Harlem for nights of pleasure. Then, on October 24, 1929, the New York stock market collapsed, bringing the Roaring Twenties to a sudden halt. A loudspeaker attached to a dirigible above the skyscrapers cried out to the employed, "Give until it hurts." Books like Theodore Dreiser's *Sister Carrie* (1900), and F. Scott Fitzgerald's *This Side of Paradise* (1920) and *The Great Gatsby* (1925) depicted a New York that had lost much of its sparkle.

The Empire State Building is a powerful symbol (left); at the Cotton Club (right) whites were entertained by blacks, who were banned from watching

Harlem

Jazz flourished in Harlem in the 1920s and 1930s as white New Yorkers discovered establishments such as the Cotton Club, famous for its "Colored Revues" and as the home of Duke Ellington, the Great Orchestrator of Jazz. Ellington's band, the Washingtonians, and his arrangements dominated big-band jazz for three decades. In 1932, he wrote a song whose title served as a slogan for the next 10 years: *It Don't Mean a Thing If It Ain't Got That Swing.* Cotton Club owner Owney Madden, a gangster and bootlegger, strictly enforced segregation. The Depression took the swing out of these Harlem night-spots, and the Cotton Club moved down-town to West 48th Street, eventually closing in 1940.

1900

Speakeasies flourished during Prohibition

The subway in 1909 was only five years old

Edwardian New York is apparent in the 20-floor Flatiron Building

Triangle Shirtwaist Fire

Sweatshops in the Lower East Side at the beginning of the 20th century employed immigrant families in dreadful conditions at very low wages. Wages were increased after a series of strikes, but the tragedy of the Triangle Shirtwaist Fire in 1911 was to bring improvements in safety standards. The factory, on the top three floors of a 10-story building at the corner of Washington Place and Greene Street, employed 600 workers, mainly young women. They were ready to go home when the fire broke out. Many doors to the fire escapes were locked, as was common during working hours, and 146 workers perished, some leaping to their deaths. Public outrage brought new legislation for safety in the workplace.

Tin Pan Alley

By 1900 New York was the place to be for the young, ambitious songwriter. Theaters were flourishing and music publishers needed as many songs as they could get their hands on. Hundreds of composers and small publishing firms crowded into the abandoned brownstones on 28th Street, between Fifth Avenue and Broadway, and the area became known as Tin Pan Alley because of the cacophony coming from the open windows. Two of the great songwriters of this era were George and Ira Gershwin, sons of Russian immigrants. At 15 years old, George was the youngest song demonstrator. The brothers' many hits included the classics *I Got Rhythm, Embraceable You* and *Somebody Loves Me.* George died of a brain tumor in 1937 at the age of 38.

The subway

The elevated railways, financed by Jay Gould, Russell Sage and J. P. Morgan in the 1860s, improved public transportation, but were already inadequate by 1900. It was time to go underground. The Interborough Rapid Transit Company was born. The first line, 22 miles (35km) long, opened in 1904, carrying 600,000 passengers each day. It was a huge success and the profits enabled the city to expand the system. In 1921, New York and New Jersey joined forces to create the Port of New York Authority to develop and operate transportation. Delightful Coney Island, with its family entertainment, vaudeville and exhibitions, became accessible to everyone, thanks to New York's subways, which now total 660 miles (1,062km) in length, across 25 lines.

Organized crime

Just before Mayor William O'Dwyer, first elected as New York's mayor in 1946, began a re-election campaign, the *Brooklyn Eagle* published some very damning news about the mayor's connection to organized crime in the city. The newspaper charged that policemen and judges were being paid off in return for protection for 4,000 bookies. The mayor fled to Florida "for health reasons." In the hope of avoiding prosecution, more than 110 policemen resigned. In August 1950, the mayor also resigned. Subpoenaed and left with little choice, O'Dwyer admitted he knew about the corruption and that he too had associations with mobsters. Yet for a lack of hard evidence of willful wrongdoing, he went unpunished.

George Gershwin (far left) wrote the classical *Rhapsody in Blue* (1924), while Irving Berlin (left; 1888–1989) gave the world *White Christmas*, among other classics, before living as a recluse in Manhattan

New Yorkers got their kicks on Coney Island's Boardwalk (below)

Boardwalk   Looking East from Steeplechase Pier, Coney Island, N.Y.

1950

Although America entered World War II in 1941 (below), New York City was physically unaffected

The Stock Exchange (above) is still a powerful financial institution

35

The Late 20th Century

The years between 1950 and 2000 swung back and forth between economic booms (1950s, 1980s, 1990s) and financial crisis (1970s), and Wall Street struggled and soared with the times. New York's Abstract Expressionist painters inspired the art world in the late 1940s and 1950s; the Pop Artists shocked and thrilled the public from the late 1950s to the 1970s. Music and theater got a big boost when the Lincoln Center was built in the 1960s. The number of Asian and Hispanic immigrants swelled, with Hispanics overtaking the African-American population as the city's largest minority group. In 1989 the city elected its first black mayor, David Dinkins, who beat Rudolph Giuliani. Crime soared in the 1970s and 1980s, and vandals defaced landmarks with graffiti. After Rudolph Giuliani was elected mayor in 1994, the number of recorded crimes dropped from 430,460 per year in 1993 to 161,956 in 2001, and the city had bright hopes for the future.

The Vietnam Veterans' Memorial is a moving display of letters written home by the troops

Mayor David Dinkins

Greenwich Village

By the 1950s, New York was America's cultural marketplace and Greenwich Village, with its cheap rents and bohemian flair, attracted America's finest artists and writers. Cedar Street Tavern at 24 University Place was the favorite Village hang-out for Abstract Expressionist painters Jackson Pollock, Willem de Kooning and Franz Kline. Regulars at the San Remo bar on the corner of Bleeker and MacDougal streets included writers James Agee, James Baldwin, Allen Ginsberg, Jack Kerouac and William Burroughs. It was here that the word Beatnik entered the language. Writers Dylan Thomas and Norman Mailer preferred the White Horse at Hudson and West 11th Street. Mailer's disregard for the Beats produced the Hip Generation.

1950

Nonconformist Greenwich Village (above); counting the national debt (right)

Sweet success

In 1962, astronaut John Glenn, the first American to orbit the earth, arrived in New York and jubilant throngs lined Broadway for a tickertape parade, an honor bestowed only on visiting heads of state, generals, victorious baseball teams, athletes and great politicians. New Yorkers flung 3,474 tons of tickertape, more than anyone had ever seen before, from office buildings and skyscrapers along the route.

In 1969 the New York Mets rose from ninth place in the National League, defeating the Baltimore Orioles in the World Series and ending up with their first victory pennant. But they only received a tickertape flurry compared to the blizzard that welcomed John Glenn (below).

Andy Warhol

Pop Art changed the art scene when Andy Warhol (below) opened his Factory in 1963. His Coca-Cola bottle, Campbell's Soup cans and multicolor silk-screen images of icons Marilyn Monroe, Elvis Presley and Jackie Kennedy were as astonishing at the time as the openly gay lifestyle he confidently espoused in an era when "homophobic" wasn't even a word. As a movie director he filmed *Kiss* and *Blow Job* in friends' apartments on the Lower East Side and in Greenwich Village. He lived as a recluse for the last 13 years of his life at 57 East 66th Street and died in 1987 rather bizarrely after routine gallbladder surgery.

Woody Allen

Allan Konigsberg changed his name when he started out as a comedian in Greenwich Village comedy clubs. He went on to make about a movie a year after 1965, most of them about New Yorkers. In 1977, *Annie Hall* took the brainy, scrawny actor and director to heights when he won Oscars for Best Director and Best Screenplay. But he did not attend the Academy Awards ceremony; he plays clarinet most Monday nights at Michael's Pub (211 East 55th Street). His 1992 affair with and later marriage to the adopted daughter of his partner Mia Farrow shook his fans and damaged his career.

Ed Koch

The Big Apple was in such dire financial straits in the 1970s that it seemed only a miracle could prevent a collapse. In October 1975, for instance, the city was only 53 minutes from defaulting on its almost $477 million debt. After the Federal government proved unwilling to extend a hand, money from teacher pension funds inched the city back from the brink of disaster. When Ed Koch ran for mayor, he vowed to restore prosperity. He kept his promise after winning the 1977 election, and was re-elected by a landslide victory in 1981. His tax cuts, along with changes to investment banking, restored corporate America's confidence in New York.

Ed Koch, Ronald Reagan and a large U.S. Treasury check

Andy Warhol

2000

Public safety officers are on hand in Times Square, although it's a lot tamer than it used to be

The New Millennium

New York City's financial situation was not rosy at the start of the millennium. Mayor Rudolph Giuliani had cut taxes by $3 billion, and the city was heavily in debt. Then came the terrorist attack on September 11, 2001, that killed nearly 3,000 people, destroyed 25 million square feet (2.25 million square meters) of office space and closed the Stock Exchange for four days. Mayor Giuliani's courage and compassion immediately after the attack was admired by all. For plain-speaking Michael Bloomberg, elected mayor in 2002, Giuliani has proved a hard act to follow. The Republican billionaire businessman spent $70 million on his first election campaign. The city has largely recovered from the economic impact of 9/11 and slowly New Yorkers have come to appreciate Bloomberg.

strategy of implementing noise abatement laws and health statutes helped to close down brothels, gambling joints and massage parlors. A new zoning law banned "adult entertainment" from within 500ft of a residential district. In the 1990s Mayor Giuliani's tough policies made the area more desirable. Subsequent investment in the New Amsterdam Theater encouraged revitalization.

Grand Central Terminal (below); Mayor Giuliani (below left)

Crime

In 2003, New York happily boasted that it was America's safest large city, and given its history of disturbing crime statistics, this is good news. New York was ranked 160th in total crime among 205 American cities. The 15-year trend of crime reduction, with homicides at a 40-year low, is continuing. It was the controversial, aggressive policing during the Giuliani years that helped to cut crime by 62 percent. The mayor beefed up the police force with 4,000 new officers and sent them out to tackle jaywalking, sleeping on subways, defacing property, and other petty crime and quality of life issues. Mayor Bloomberg has continued to fight crime.

Cleaning up

Between the 1960s and 1980s, the district from 40th Street to 53rd Street between 6th and 8th avenues was a sleazy area overrun by hookers, pimps and gamblers. In the 1970s and 1980s a

2000–today

Messages and prayers were everywhere after 9/11 (right)

Neon and color are de rigueur in Times Square (below)

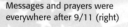

38

On the Move

ARRIVING

Arriving by Air

ON THE MOVE

You can fly direct to New York from most major European cities and from many other destinations around the world. International carriers fly into John F. Kennedy International Airport, 15 miles (24km) from Manhattan, on Jamaica Bay, and Newark Liberty International Airport, 16 miles (26km) west of town. LaGuardia Airport handles mainly domestic flights and is 8 miles (13km) from Manhattan in the borough of Queens.

John F. Kennedy International Airport (JFK)

JFK has nine passenger terminals. Terminals 2 and 3 are dedicated to Delta Airlines, Terminal 7 handles all British Airways flights, jetBlue uses Terminal 6, and Virgin Atlantic Terminal 4. All other terminals service international carriers. There are information desks, restaurants and concession stands in all terminals. An AirTrain links the

TRANSPORTATION FROM MAJOR AIRPORTS		
	JOHN F. KENNEDY INTERNATIONAL AIRPORT (JFK)	**LA GUARDIA AIRPORT (LGA)**
Distance from Manhattan:	15 miles (24km).	8 miles (13km).
Journey time to Manhattan:	Taxi 45–60 minutes, Subway 60–100 minutes.	Taxi 20–35 minutes, Bus 40–50 minutes.
Ground transportation information:	Baggage claim level of all terminals.	Baggage claim level of all terminals.
Transport	**Shuttle/subway** • A free yellow, white and blue Long-Term Parking Lot shuttle bus runs to the Howard Beach Station, where you get the A subway train to Manhattan. • The free shuttle runs every 10 to 15 minutes during rush hour, every 20 minutes at all other times. • The subway costs $2 but you will need to buy a MetroCard (▷ 43). **AirTrain** • Buy your ticket ($5 each way) at the station, or from a vending machine in the airport. • These connect to the LIRR at Jamaica station, subways at Howard Beach/JFK Airport station and Sutphin Blvd.-Archer Ave./Jamaica station, and local bus lines.	**Bus** • Follow the "Ground Transportation" signs out of the terminal. You will see the M60 bus stop sign at the curb. • The fare is $2, but you save on the transfer if you use a MetroCard (▷ 43). • Take the M60 to 106th Street at Broadway. • Get off at Lexington Avenue to catch the 4, 5 and 6 subway trains; at Malcolm X Boulevard for the 2 and 3 trains; at St. Nicholas Avenue for the A, B, C and D trains; at 116th Street-Columbia University for the 1 train. • The bus runs daily between 4am and 1am, leaving every 30 minutes. • For more information, visit www.mta.nyc.ny.us/nyct.

airport and the New York subway, local bus lines and the LIRR.

LaGuardia Airport (LGA)

Most domestic flights go through LaGuardia Airport, with United Airlines and Continental Airlines operating the lion's share. If you need assistance, look out for the Customer Service Agents in their red jackets or go to the information desk between concourse C and D on the departure level. There's a selection of restaurants in the USAir and Delta terminals, which are accessible via a free shuttle service.

TIP
● Avoid airport hustlers offering taxi services. City cabs and car services are a better option and equally convenient—they wait outside terminals in designated areas.

Newark Liberty International Airport (EWR)

Major carriers that fly into this airport include Virgin Atlantic, British Airways, Lufthansa and Continental Airlines. All passenger terminals—A, B, C and D—have restaurants on the concourse level, and the Information desk is in Terminal B, lower level. The AirTrain system links the airport with the subway, NJ Transit, Amtrak and LIRR, and makes for a quick and cheap way of getting into the city.

LEAVING THE AIRPORT

After collecting your bags and going through Customs, you can get into the city in several different ways.

TAXI

You will easily find taxi stands outside airport terminals. Dispatchers work during peak hours at JFK and LaGuardia, and 24 hours a day at Newark. For more information about

USEFUL TELEPHONE NUMBERS AND WEBSITES

John F. Kennedy International Airport (JFK)
718/244-4444
www.panynj.gov

LaGuardia Airport
718/533-3400
www.panynj.gov

Newark Liberty International Airport
973/961-6000
www.panynj.gov

taxis, ▷ 51. Tip your drivers 15 percent to 20 percent.
● At JFK, you are charged a flat rate of $45, plus tolls.
● At LaGuardia, you pay by the meter ($24–28), plus tolls.
● At Newark, dispatchers ask you where you are going. Give an address and you will be quoted the fare ($69–$75, plus tolls and a $15 surcharge).

NEWARK LIBERTY INTERNATIONAL AIRPORT (EWR)

16 miles (26km).

Taxi 35–50 minutes,
Airtrain 30 minutes.

On the baggage claim level.

AirTrain
• This modern speedy monorail/rail link operated by NJ Transit and Amtrak is comfortable and fast, and also easy, provided you do not have a lot of baggage.
• Follow signs to the AirTrain from any Newark arrivals terminal.
• Buy your ticket at the station (NJ Transit trains $11.55/children under 5 free; Amtrak trains $27) or from a vending machine in the airport or at the train station.
• These take you to Penn Station at Eighth Avenue and 31st Street in Manhattan.
• Do not get off at Newark's Penn Station if you want to go to Manhattan—stay on board until the next stop to reach New York's Penn Station. From there, you can easily catch a cab, the subway or a bus to your hotel.
• NJ Transit trains run two to three times an hour during peak travel times, once an hour off-peak.
• It is easy to make connections to destinations beyond Manhattan from the Newark International Airport Station. For details, phone NJ Transit 800/626-RIDE or visit www.njtransit.com or phone Amtrak 800/USA-RAIL or visit www.amtrak.com.

ADDITIONAL INFORMATION

Telephone contact
The Air-Ride number, 800/247-7433, describing transportation to and from all three airports, is answered by an operator Monday to Friday between 8am and 6pm; at all other times you get recorded information.

NYC and Co.
810 Seventh Ave., New York, NY 10019
212/484-1200
www.nycvisit.com
Contact NYC and Co. to order the *Official NYC Guide* listing hotels, restaurants, theaters, attractions and events. The visitor's kit also includes a map, brochures, a newsletter and information on services.

ON THE MOVE

PRIVATE TRANSPORTATION FROM MAJOR AIRPORTS
New York Airport Service express bus
Tel 718/875-8200
www.nyairportservice.com
Follow the "Ground Transportation" signs to the pick-up point outside the terminal.

From JFK
This service runs between 6.15am and 11.10pm, and travel time is 45 to 65 minutes, longer during rush hour. The trip to the Port Authority Bus Terminal, at 42nd Street and Eighth Avenue, costs $15 ($27 round-trip). The journey to Grand Central Terminal at Vanderbilt Avenue and 42nd Street or to Bryant Park costs $15 ($27 round-trip), or $31 round-trip to hotels between 31st and 60th streets. The service to New York's Penn Station costs $15 ($27 round-trip).

From LaGuardia
This service runs between 7.20am and 11pm, and travel time is 30 to 45 minutes, longer during rush hour. The journey costs $12 ($21 round-trip) to Port Authority Bus Terminal at 42nd Street and Eighth Avenue or Grand Central Terminal at Vanderbilt Avenue and 42nd Street or Bryant Park, and $26 round-trip to hotels between 31st and 60th streets. The service to New York's Penn Station runs every 60 minutes from 8am to 8pm, takes 40 minutes and costs $12.

SuperShuttle
Tel 800/451 0455 or 212/315-3006
www.supershuttle.com
Go to the Ground Transportation desk and dial SuperShuttle on the courtesy phone in the baggage claim area of JFK, LaGuardia or Newark airports. Vans run 24 hours a day, throughout all five boroughs of New York City. Reservations are not required. The fares range from $15 to $19.

Coach USA
Tel 877/8-NEWARK (639275)
www.coachusa.com
Operating only out of Newark Airport, Coach USA takes passengers to Penn Station, at 34th Street and Eighth Avenue; to Grand Central Terminal, at Vanderbilt Avenue and 42nd Street; to the Port Authority Bus Terminal, at Eighth Avenue and 42nd Street; and to Chinatown and Lower Manhattan. The bus leaves every 15 minutes to Midtown and every 30 minutes to Lower Manhattan and costs $12 ($20 round-trip); children under 12 ride free.

SECURITY AT CUSTOMS
Since 9/11, security has been stepped up at airports, tunnels, bridges and train stations. To facilitate departure, do cooperate. Do not carry sharp items on your person or in your carry-on bags.

Empty your pockets before walking through the security detection scanner. Be prepared to open bags or remove your shoes for inspection or to allow a security officer to scan your body with a hand-held scanner.

Arriving by Road
Driving into Manhattan is not for the faint-hearted and once you've got into the city, you then have the problem of finding somewhere to park. Expect lengthy delays on the bridges and tunnels that cross to the island of Manhattan, especially on the bridges that cross the East River (repairs are ongoing). It is best to avoid the morning, lunchtime and evening rush-hour traffic.

Arriving by Rail
Most commuter trains from Connecticut and the suburbs north of the city serve Grand Central Station (on 42nd Street at Park Avenue). Amtrak's long-distance trains from across the United States pull into Penn Station at 31st Street and Seventh Avenue and for journeys to and from Long Island and New Jersey, the Long Island Railroad and New Jersey Transit are the trains to catch, also operating out of Penn Station.

A New York Airport Service express bus

GETTING AROUND

The best way to see Manhattan is on foot. Streets in most Manhattan neighborhoods are safe both by day and after dark. However, walking takes time, and if you want to visit several museums or neighborhoods, or if the weather is bad, the subways are a better option. They are easy to use, inexpensive, and relatively clean and safe. Buses are more pleasant than subways because you get a chance to see street life as you travel, although you need to pay with correct change, and during rush hour traffic slows your progress—sometimes it's faster to walk.

ON THE MOVE

OPTIONS

If you will be in New York for seven days or more, buy a MetroCard to save money on transit fares. You swipe the card at the subway turnstile or as you get on the bus, and you do not have to worry about having the correct change. Taxis are the quickest way for many to travel but the most expensive. When you take a cab, don't forget to tip the driver 15 percent or more.

Driving your own car in New York is not usually the best option. Besides the traffic, you will need to park on the street, and garages are expensive. If you do arrive in New York by car, the best course is to leave your car in a garage until you are ready to leave town (head for the eastern or western fringes of Manhattan if saving money matters more to you than convenience).

WALKING IN NEW YORK

- Always use crosswalks; jaywalking is against the law.
- Stay to the right as you would when driving.
- When the light changes and you are about to cross, check the intersection to make sure that no drivers or bicyclists have decided to make a dash through the light. This is not uncommon.

METROCARD

What is it?
A magnetically encoded card that debits the fare when you swipe it through the turnstile in the subway or the fare box on a bus.

What about transfers?
When you use a MetroCard for a trip, transfers between subways and buses within a 2-hour period are free.

Where can I buy one?
From staffed subway booths (cash only), special vending machines in most subway stations (cash, credit cards, debit cards), drugstores like Rite Aid, Hudson News at Penn Station and Grand Central Terminal, or at the Times Square Visitors Center at 1560 Broadway between 46th and 47th streets (cash, credit cards, debit cards). Many hotels sell them, too.

What's the cost?
Pay-Per-Ride MetroCard: $10 buys 6 rides, $20 buys 12 rides. These can be swiped four times

in succession, so are good for up to four people traveling together. Just swipe, walk through, and hand the card to the person behind you, who swipes, walks through, and hands it to the person behind. You can refill these cards—that is, put more rides on them—in the vending machines located in most subway stations. Just put the card in, indicate how much money you want to spend, and insert your credit card or cash.
Unlimited Ride MetroCard: $7 buys a 1-Day Fun Pass, $24 buys a 7-Day Card, $76 buys a 30-Day Card. These can't be used by

more than one person—an 18-minute interval must elapse between journeys. These cards go into effect the first time you use them, not the day you buy them.

Can I get a discount?
Seniors and visitors with disabilities can get reductions; phone 718/243-4999.

How do you use a MetroCard?
When you swipe your card, the turnstile indicator shows how much money is left on the card. If you swipe the card too fast or too slowly, the indicator asks you to swipe it again. If this happens, swipe it again. Do not go to a different turnstile, as you may end up paying twice.

Where can I get more information?
Phone 800/METROCARD or 212/638-7622, from Monday through Friday between 9 and 5 or visit www.mta.nyc.ny.us/metrocard.

Subways

The Metropolitan Transit Authority (MTA) runs the subway system. It runs 24 hours a day, seven days a week. Rush hour is roughly between 7.30 and 9.30am and again from 4.30 to 6.30pm Monday through Friday except holidays. The subway is quick, inexpensive, efficient, generally safe, and fairly easy to figure out.

TIP

• New Yorkers refer to subway lines as trains. "Take the A train" means "Take subway line A."

Fares are $2 ($1 for seniors and people with disabilities); children under 44 inches (1.13m) ride free. The best way to pay is by MetroCard (▷ 43).

A campaign promotes polite behavior, and posters ask passengers to give their seats to the elderly and infirm, to move to the center of the train so as not to block the doors, and to walk rather than run.

Stations are clearly marked

UNDERSTANDING THE SUBWAY MAP

MTA maps are free and easy to understand. You can get them in any subway station, at information centers and in hotel lobbies.

The map (▷ 45) shows each line as a different color, but it is the number or letter that you need to know. No one refers to trains by color.

Solid black circles on the colored lines indicate stops for local trains, which make more stops than express trains.

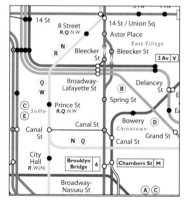

Black and white lines connecting white and black circles indicate free subway transfers.

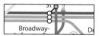

White circles on the colored lines indicate express train stops. Express trains skip about three stops for every one they make.

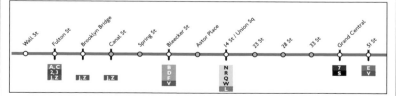

Below the name of every stop, the letters or numbers of the lines that stop there are indicated. Boldface type, for example **B**, indicates that the line offers a full-time service. Lightface type, for example B, indicates a part-time service. At 72nd Street, you see B, **C**, indicating part-time service on line B and full-time on line C.

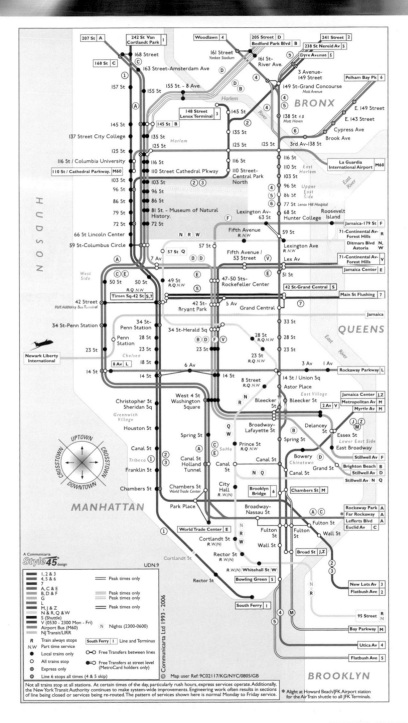

● The Lower East Side and the East Village are not well served by subways. If you are traveling to or from these areas at night, it is best to take a taxi.

SUBWAY HELP

● Station clerks are very helpful, and many subway stations are manned.

● For help in English, call 718/330-1234, 24 hours a day.

● For help in other languages, call 718/330-4847, between 7am and 7pm.

FINDING A SUBWAY

● In the station look for the signs with colored circles showing the subway line letter (A, B, C, etc.) or the subway line numbers of the trains that stop there.

● If you need help finding a subway station, ask a policeman or step into a hotel lobby, museum or store to ask. Most people working in such places are used to helping tourists but even regular New Yorkers on the street do so quite happily.

FINDING THE RIGHT SUBWAY LINE

● After you have paid and walked through the turnstile, look for the colored circles. Find the line you want, and follow the signs. Above the platform edge, signs indicate the trains that stop there, their destinations and hours of operation. Changes to the line's service are usually posted, but signs are not very large, so you need to look carefully.

● Uptown or downtown? If you want to go north of where you are, no matter where in the city you happen to be, you want an uptown train. If you want to go south of where you are, you want a downtown train. Some stations are Uptown Only or Downtown Only—clearly marked at street level. If you find the color circle

A MetroCard ticket machine

HOW TO USE THE SUBWAY

● Although the New York subway once had a bad reputation for safety, trains are now safer and cleaner. However, pickpockets and beggars are perennial, so keep a close eye on your bags. Keep your money well hidden and do not wear expensive jewelry or even jewelry that looks expensive.

● Do not wait for trains near the edge of the platform; stand back a bit.

● If there are few people on the platform or if you are alone, stand under the yellow sign "During Off Hours Trains Stop Here." When the train stops, the conductor sticks his or her head out the window from a middle car, which is where he or she rides, and you should, too.

● Let passengers off first before getting on.

● Stay out of empty cars.

● After 11pm or midnight, take a taxi until you know your way around in the subway.

● If you find yourself on an express train speeding past your destination, get off at the next stop and either take the same line back to where you got on or ask the station clerk for directions. Be prepared to pay an extra fare to re-enter the platform; at some stations, you may need to exit the station, cross the street, and re-enter the station on the other side to catch the train that's going in the right direction for you.

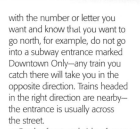

with the number or letter you want and know that you want to go north, for example, do not go into a subway entrance marked Downtown Only—any train you catch there will take you in the opposite direction. Trains headed in the right direction are nearby—the entrance is usually across the street.

● On the front and side of every train, the route number or letter is displayed. Make sure you look for this before getting on the train to be sure it is the one you want.

● If you really want to be sure, stand in the middle of the platform, halfway between the two ends of the train, and when the train rolls into the station, look for the conductor leaning out of a window in the center car—he or she can tell you definitively where the train is headed.

KNOWING WHEN TO GET OFF

● Conductors make announcements before each stop. On new trains, these are recorded.

● Every subway car has a map posted on the wall by a door, so you can check to make sure you are traveling in the right direction and can see how many stops you need to go.

● Look for signs on the station walls as you pull into the station.

LEAVING THE SUBWAY

After you get off the train, go upstairs (usually via stairway, but sometimes via escalator). You have to go back through the turnstiles to exit the station, but you do not need to use your MetroCard again. Make sure you choose the right exit for your destination.

DISRUPTIONS

● Coney Island services on lines N, R and W were being rerouted at the time of research due to construction work. Service may be restored by the time you use this guide, so check with the MTA for an update.

● Weekend service is sometimes altered on some lines to allow for maintenance work. Announcements are posted in the affected stations.

IN CASE OF EMERGENCY

● Look for a police officer. The

Passengers travel way above a Harlem street on an elevated section of the subway

Transit Bureau Police patrol the subways.

● Look for a telephone and call 911. This is a free call.

● Go to the station clerk in the booth.

● On the subway train, make your way to the middle of the train to find the conductor or to the front of the first car to find the operator.

TRAVELERS WITH DISABILITIES

Not all subways are wheelchair accessible. You can find information on the 30 or more stations that are by visiting www.mta.nyc.ny.us.

TRAINS MOST USEFUL FOR VISITORS	
4, 5 and 6	The trains run up and down the east side of Manhattan, to the Bronx and to Brooklyn.
1, 2, 3, 9, A, B, C, D, E and F	The trains run up and down the west side of Manhattan, to the Bronx and to Brooklyn.
N, R, Q and W	The trains run from Brooklyn and Queens in and out of Manhattan.
S	The train runs between Times Square and Grand Central Terminal, operating as a shuttle.
L	The train runs across 14th Street to Brooklyn.

Lexington Avenue subway

Buses

ON THE MOVE

The Metropolitan Transit Authority (MTA) runs the city's buses, and fares are the same as for subways (▷ 44–47). You can use your MetroCard or exact change to pay for your ride. Bus drivers do not give change, so travel with plenty of quarters if you do not buy the more practical and economical MetroCard. Buses are slower than subways. Buses run 24 hours a day on most routes but less often at night, and on weekends. Drivers are helpful, so if you need advice, don't be afraid to ask.

FINDING A BUS

● Go to a designated bus stop, recognized by the yellow-painted curb and blue-and-white sign.
● Look at the posted Guide-A-Ride boxes, showing the route map and service schedule.
● Most major avenues have their own bus routes, running north or south.
● Crosstown buses, running east and west, are strategically located on major streets across Manhattan.

GETTING ON AND OFF

Board buses at the front. Swipe your MetroCard or pay in exact change. Leave seats in front for the elderly, the infirm and adults with small children. You will notice a tape strip above and beside the windows. To indicate to the driver where you wish to get off, push on this about one block before your stop. Front doors open automatically; to exit by the back, wait for the green light to go on above the doors, then press the yellow tape on the doors to open them.

WHICH BUS TO TAKE

The routes given here are the ones most used by visitors for the main attractions. If you need further guidance, see the Bus Buster Chart opposite, or pick up an MTA bus map from any visitor center (▷ 324), subway station or hotel lobby.

ADDRESS LOCATOR

To locate the cross street of an address on an avenue:
● Drop the last digit of the street number.
● Divide by 2.
● Add or subtract the number given below.
● The answer is approximately the nearest number cross street (for example 54th Street).

AVENUES

A, B, C, D, First, Second	add 3
Third, Eighth	add 10
Fourth	add 8
Sixth	subtract 12
Seventh	add 12
Ninth	add 13
Tenth	add 14
Amsterdam	add 60
Broadway (23rd to 192nd St)	subtract 30
Fifth	up to 200	add 13
	up to 400	add 16
	up to 600	add 18
	up to 775	add 20
	up to 1286	drop last digit and subtract 18
	up to 1500	add 45
	above 2000	add 24
Central Park West	divide by 10 and add 60
Columbus	add 60
Lexington	add 22
Madison	add 26
Park	add 35

Bus routes criss-cross the city

North–South buses

● **M1, M2, M3** and **M4** basically run north up Madison and south down Fifth. These buses take you to the museums along Fifth Avenue, also called Museum Mile; M4 travels as far north as The Cloisters in Fort Tryon Park (▷ 252).
● **M5** runs from Houston Street north along Sixth Avenue, then up Riverside Drive and Broadway to Washington Heights.
● **M6** runs from Central Park South down Broadway to South Ferry, through Times Square, Union Square, Greenwich Village, SoHo and the Financial District, then back up Sixth Avenue.
● **M7** runs between Union Square and West 147th Street/ Adam Clayton Powell Boulevard.

The Coach USA sign

It runs up Sixth Avenue, over Broadway, up Amsterdam Avenue, and across Central Park North, then up to 147th Street. On the return, it travels south on Columbus, Seventh Avenue and Broadway back to Union Square.

● **M9** runs from Union Square to Battery Park along Manhattan's Lower East Side.
● **M10** runs from West 31st Street/Seventh Avenue (Penn Station) to West 159th Street/Frederick Douglass Boulevard. It travels up Central Park West, stopping at the American Museum of Natural History, and is a good bus for getting to Central Park.
● **M11** runs along the west side of Manhattan, north on Tenth Avenue/Amsterdam Avenue right up into Harlem.
● **M15** runs from South Ferry, north along the East Side to Second Avenue/East 126th Street.

● **M60** runs from West 106th Street/Broadway to LaGuardia Airport.
● **M100** runs from West 220th Street/Broadway to East 125th Street/Second Avenue.

Crosstown buses
● **M8** runs from Avenue D to West Street through the East Village and Greenwich Village.
● **M14A** and **M14D** run from the Chelsea Piers to the Lower East Side.
● **M27** runs between West 41st Street/Eighth Avenue (Port Authority Bus Terminal) and East 42nd Street/First Avenue.
● **M34** runs from Jacob Javits Convention Center at Eleventh

BUS BUSTER CHART

CHANGE AT OR WALK TO/FROM:

☐ Union Square ☐ Times Square ☐ Broadway and East 8th/9th Streets
☐ Central Park South ☐ South Street
w = walk   F = South Ferry from South Street

Use this chart to find out which buses will take you to your chosen destination. Follow the rows of squares horizontally and vertically from the name of the destinations until they meet. This square contains the number(s) of the bus(es) you'll need to catch. Bus numbers on white squares are direct. Numbers in shaded squares show that you have to change buses or take a bus some of the way and walk the rest. Start out on the first bus listed, then change to the second bus. Look at the key to find out where you must change buses or walk to/from. Note that the bus stop may be a few minutes' walk away from the destination.

Routes change regularly, and often differ on Sundays, so check an up-to-date timetable or bus map before setting out.

(Triangular bus-change reference chart with destinations along the diagonal: American Museum of Natural History, Brooklyn Bridge, Central Park, East Village and NoHo, Ellis Island Museum of Immigration and History Center, Empire State Building, Grand Central Terminal, Greenwich Village, Guggenheim Museum, Lincoln Center, Metropolitan Museum of Art, Rockefeller Center, SoHo, South Street Seaport, Statue of Liberty, Times Square/Broadway, Trinity Church, Whitney Museum of Art.)

MAIN TOURIST BUS ROUTES

Certain bus routes link key attractions. All routes shown are circular (north to south section of M15 shown only). Start and end stops are given as well as stops near to main attractions.

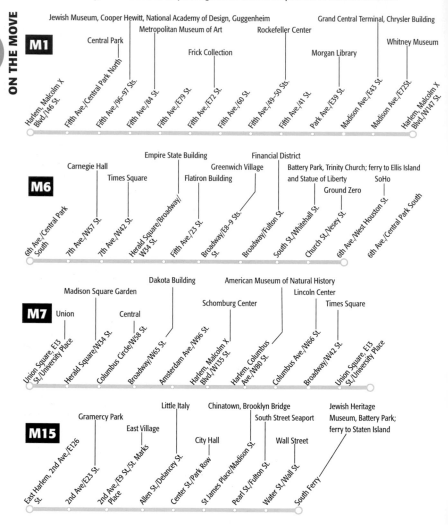

M1

Attractions: Jewish Museum, Cooper Hewitt, National Academy of Design, Guggenheim; Central Park; Metropolitan Museum of Art; Frick Collection; Rockefeller Center; Grand Central Terminal, Chrysler Building; Morgan Library; Whitney Museum

Stops: Harlem, Malcolm X Blvd./146 St.; Fifth Ave./Central Park North; Fifth Ave./96-97 Sts.; Fifth Ave./84 St.; Fifth Ave./E79 St.; Fifth Ave./E72 St.; Fifth Ave./60 St.; Fifth Ave./49-50 Sts.; Fifth Ave./41 St.; Park Ave./E39 St.; Madison Ave./E43 St.; Madison Ave./E72St.; Harlem, Malcolm X Blvd./W147 St.

M6

Attractions: Carnegie Hall; Times Square; Empire State Building; Flatiron Building; Greenwich Village; Financial District; Battery Park, Trinity Church; ferry to Ellis Island and Statue of Liberty; Ground Zero; SoHo

Stops: 6th Ave./Central Park South; 7th Ave./N57 St.; 7th Ave./W42 St.; Herald Square/Broadway/W34 St.; Fifth Ave./23 St.; Broadway/E8-9 Sts.; Broadway/Fulton St.; South St./Whitehall St.; Church St./Vesey St.; 6th Ave./West Houston St.; 6th Ave./Central Park South

M7

Attractions: Madison Square Garden; Union; Central; Dakota Building; American Museum of Natural History; Schomburg Center; Lincoln Center; Times Square

Stops: Union Square, E13 St./University Place; Herald Square/W34 St.; Columbus Circle/W58 St.; Broadway/W65 St.; Amsterdam Ave./W96 St.; Harlem, Malcolm X Blvd./W135 St.; Harlem, Columbus Ave./W80 St.; Columbus Ave./W66 St.; Broadway/W42 St.; Union Square, E13 St./University Place

M15

Attractions: Gramercy Park; East Village; Little Italy; City Hall; Chinatown, Brooklyn Bridge; South Street Seaport; Wall Street; Jewish Heritage Museum, Battery Park; ferry to Staten Island

Stops: East Harlem, 2nd Ave./E126 St.; 2nd Ave./E23 St.; 2nd Ave./E9 St./St. Marks Place; Allen St./Delancey St.; Center St./Park Row; St James Place/Madison St.; Pearl St./Fulton St.; Water St./Wall St.; South Ferry

Avenue/West 34th Street to East 34th Street/FDR Drive.

• **M42** runs along 42nd Street from Circle Line Pier to the United Nations Headquarters.

• **M72** runs from the Upper West Side to the Upper East Side from West 68th Street/Freedom Place to East 72nd Street/York Avenue.

• **M79** runs from West 79th Street/Riverside Drive to East 79th Street/East End Avenue.

SAFETY

Buses are safe throughout the day and the early hours of the night, but after 10pm it is best to take a taxi rather than wait for a bus on a deserted street. If a beggar asks you for money, just shake your head and do not get embroiled in conversation.

TRAVELERS WITH DISABILITIES

Buses are equipped with wheelchair lifts, and drivers can make the buses "kneel" by lowering the front step of the vehicle for people who have difficulty getting on.

Taxis and Car Services

New York's official taxicabs are licensed by the Taxi and Limousine Commission (TLC). They are easily recognizable; they are always yellow, always display the rates on the door, and always have a light on the roof and a flat bronze medallion on the hood. Do not get into any other taxi; only yellow cabs with the distinctive markings are legally licensed. Car services operated by private companies are available at an hourly rate and must be arranged in advance; they are not allowed to pick up passengers who hail them. Limousines are also available to rent.

A distinctive yellow New York taxi

HOW TO GET A TAXI

You can hail a taxi on any street by holding out your arm at the curb. When the light on the roof is turned on, the taxi is available. If the light is turned off, it is occupied. Usually you don't have to wait long before getting one, but it sometimes takes a while—after the theater, in the theater district and just about anywhere with the approach of rush hour time (4pm). Try to hail a taxi in the direction you would like to travel, which saves travel time and money. The best way to direct the driver is by giving the cross street and the avenue—for example, 42nd Street and Fifth Avenue. As you get closer to your destination, you can let the driver know the exact address. Many taxi drivers do not have a great command of the English language, so speak clearly and not too quickly when giving addresses or asking questions.

HOW MUCH IS THE FARE?

● As soon as you get into the cab, the meter is turned on; this flag-drop fare is $2.50.
● After that, it's 40 cents for every one-fifth mile (0.3km) or 20 cents per minute in stopped or very slow traffic.

● Tolls at tunnels and bridges cost extra. The driver may ask you for the toll money as you approach or may pay it himself then charge you at the end of the journey. Tolls range from $2 to $6. For more information on toll charges, visit www.panynj.gov.
● Between 8pm and 6am, you pay a night surcharge of 50 cents; during weekday peak hours from 4 to 8pm the surcharge is $1.
● Tip your driver between 15 percent and 20 percent on the fare excluding tolls.
● Note down the taxi driver's four-digit medallion identity number, which is posted on the divider behind the driver's head and ask for a receipt. These will be useful if you accidentally leave one of your possessions in the taxi or if you want to make a complaint.
● There is no extra charge per passenger, but taxis cannot take more than four people. There is also no extra charge for luggage.

KNOW YOUR RIGHTS

Drivers are required by law to:
● Be polite.
● Take passengers anywhere in the five boroughs, to Westchester and Nassau counties, and to Newark Airport.
● Provide air conditioning.
● Turn off the radio if asked.
● Refrain from smoking while a passenger is in the taxi.

For full information on the Taxi Rider's Bill of Rights, call the 24-hour Consumer Hotline 212/NYC-TAXI or visit www.ci.nyc.ny.us/taxi.

Some visitors choose to arrive at their hotel by taxi

TRAVELERS WITH DISABILITIES

Taxis are required to carry passengers with folding wheelchairs, as well as those with guide dogs and therapy dogs.

CAR SERVICES

Most car services have a two-hour minimum rental period and rates start at $35 per hour. Try Allstate Car and Limousine Service (tel 212/741-7440), Carmel (tel 212/666-6666) or Tel Aviv (tel 212/777-7777). The Yellow Pages has a complete listing. Alternatively, you can contract with a car service, through a concierge. It might be possible to agree a pre-set rate for a specific trip.

Driving

Driving in New York City is not for everyone. Garage parking runs to $25 a day or more, and finding on-street parking is nearly impossible; restrictions are designed to discourage drivers from using their cars. Plus tow trucks are out in force, and to get your car back if it's towed, you have to pay a hefty fine—in cash, often in a neighborhood you would rather not visit. Traffic is taxing during rush hours, between 7.30 and 9.30am and again from 4.30 to 6.30pm. Drivers are aggressive, unpredictable, or both.

DRIVING CUSTOMS AND LAWS
● Most streets in New York are

SPEED LIMITS	
Major streets	30mph (48kph)
Residential areas	25mph (40kph)
Major expressways	65mph (104kph)
Highways in rural areas out of town	55mph (88kph)

one-way. Newcomers from Britain and Australia need to remember to drive on the right.
● No right turn is permitted on red lights in New York City.
● Drivers must wear seatbelts. By law, front-seat passengers and children aged 4 to 10 in the back seat must also wear them. Children under 4 ride in child safety-seats.
● Passing (overtaking) is permitted on the inside and outside lanes of Interstate Highways.

PARKING
● Check street parking signs carefully. For street cleaning, parking is prohibited on alternate sides of the street on different days.
● For on-street parking you may need to feed the parking meter with change, sometimes on an hourly basis. In Midtown, look for Mini Meters, kiosks that dispense timed parking chits to leave locked inside your car, visible to parking inspectors.
● Do not park within 15ft (4.6m) of a fire hydrant.
● Never leave anything inside a

Nose to tail on Madison Avenue

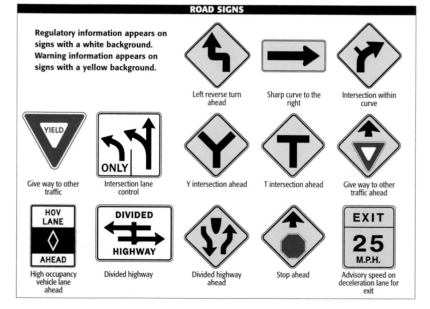

ROAD SIGNS

Regulatory information appears on signs with a white background. Warning information appears on signs with a yellow background.

Left reverse turn ahead

Sharp curve to the right

Intersection within curve

Give way to other traffic

Intersection lane control

Y intersection ahead

T intersection ahead

Give way to other traffic ahead

High occupancy vehicle lane ahead

Divided highway

Divided highway ahead

Stop ahead

Advisory speed on deceleration lane for exit

Exits are clearly signed (above). Traffic policeman (below).

parked vehicle, not even in the trunk (boot). Even an empty shopping bag can provoke a thief's curiosity—and yield a broken window or locks.
• Parking garages are easy to find but expensive, in the range of $15 for the first hour to $40 a day, with special rates if you arrive before 10 or 11am. Midtown is the priciest area; to save money, park closer to the rivers.

CAR RENTAL COMPANIES

NAME	TELEPHONE	WEBSITE
Alamo	800/462-5266	www.alamo.com
Avis	800/331-1212	www.avis.com
Budget	800/527-0700	www.budget.com
Dollar	800/800-3665	www.dollar
Hertz	800/654-3131	www.hertz.com
National	212/875-8204	www.nationalcar.com

CAR RENTALS

Car rental companies are at all three major airports and at various locations around the city. Prices vary considerably, but as a general rule, a one-day weekday rental costs between $75 and $100, weekly rates run between $277 and $300, and weekend rates run around $65 for one day to $175 for two days.

If you require a specific type of car then make sure the rental company is aware of your needs because in a lot of cases you will be reserving the rental rate and not an actual car model when you make your booking. When working out costs, remember to consider the 13.63 percent tax in addition to the quoted price and remember that rates are calculated using the 24-hour clock. Most rental companies will offer various insurance packages which may include Collision Damage Waiver (CDW), Loss Damage Waiver (LDW), Physical Damage Waiver (PDW) or Additional Liability Insurance (ALI) in their cover. Another

charge to look out for is the "dropping off" charge levied when you want to leave the car in a different place to where you collected it. This charge is usually minimal but can be quite high if you decide to journey interstate. Most car rental companies have a stock of childrens' car safety seats but these need to be requested when you make your initial booking.

TIPS

To rent a car you must:
• Be 25 years old to rent a car from most companies (and be aware that some companies may have an upper age limit, too).
• Have a valid driver's license bearing your photo.
• Produce a major credit card and, if you're not an American citizen, your passport.
• Have your own insurance or purchase maximum insurance from the rental company.
• Return the car with a full tank of fuel or the company will fill it up and add the cost to your bill.

Alternatives

Depending on where you want to go, your trip can be a travel experience.

FERRIES

Ferries offer a comfortable ride with spectacular views. The free Staten Island Ferry has been running since 1905; it gives you a great view of the Statue of Liberty and New York Harbor. Boats depart from Whitehall Terminal 1 (Whitehall Street, tel 718/727-2508, www.nyc.gov) and operate from Staten Island to Manhattan from 6am to 10pm and from Manhattan to Staten Island from 6.30am to 11pm. Taking your car costs $3. The trip, 5.2 miles (8.4km), takes 20 minutes. Listed below are only some of the ferry commuter services available. For sightseeing cruises, ▷ 260.

NY Waterway (tel 800/53-FERRY, www.nywaterway.com) operates commuter ferries from New Jersey to points in Manhattan and from Manhattan to Yankee Stadium and Shea Stadium using several piers: Pier 78 at West 38th Street, Pier 11 at Wall Street, and the World Financial Center. Ferries run between 6am and 9.30pm, depending on location. Harbor sightseeing cruises are also available.

New York Water Taxi (tel 212/742-1969, www.nywatertaxi.com) runs a shuttle between several piers around Manhattan, including Chelsea Piers on West 23rd Street and at the Circle Line at West 42nd Street. Packages are available.

Circle Line operates sightseeing cruises (▷ 260).

NYC Department of Transportation (tel 311) can give you information on all New York City ferries.

PEDICABS

On weekends and evenings in Greenwich Village, SoHo, Times Square, Midtown and the East Village, consider a pedicab for a unique view of town. Some drivers are licensed NYC tour guides. Most fares from Manhattan Rickshaw (tel 212/604-4729, www.manhattan-rickshaw.com) are approximately $50 an hour. Consult a driver or contact the company by telephone. Pedicabs may be hailed in the street; there are no stands.

CARRIAGES

A good old-fashioned carriage ride around Central Park can be an idyllic experience. Carriages stand at Fifth Avenue and Central Park South. Most charge $40 for 20 minutes. For specific information call Central Park Carriages (547 West 37th Street, tel 212/736-0680, www.centralparkcarriages.com).

Pedicab and driver

New York Water Taxi

LEAVING NEW YORK

If you want to sample life away from the metropolis for a day then head out to the boroughs. If you have more time then travel north into the beautiful Hudson Valley, with its pretty towns and historical buildings, or go south to Philadelphia or Washington, D.C. Trains and buses serve all major routes out of town if you decide not to take to the road yourself.

BY RAIL

New York has two train stations: Grand Central Terminal on the east side and Pennsylvania Station on the west.
● Local Metro-North commuter trains run in and out of Grand Central Terminal to New York and Connecticut suburbs. Information: 212/532-4900 or 800/METRO-INFO; www.mta.info/mnr.
● Long Island Railroad (LIRR) runs commuter trains to and from Long Island. Information: 718/217-5477; www.mta.nyc.ny.us/lirr.
● PATH connects Manhattan to many New Jersey cities. Information: 201/216-6000 or 800/234-7284; www.panynj.gov/path.
● Amtrak's high-speed Acela trains serve Penn Station as well

as Boston, Philadelphia and Washington, D.C. Amtrak also has a daily service to cities throughout the US. Information: 800/872-7245 or 212/630-6400; www.amtrak.com.

BY ROAD

Long-distance and commuter buses, as well as airport buses, operate from the Port Authority

Travel by Greyhound bus is quick and comfortable

Bus Terminal (42nd Street and Eighth Avenue, tel 212/564-8484), which is New York's main bus station.
Greyhound buses travel to cities and towns across the US. Information: 800/231-2222; www.greyhound.com.

BUS VERSUS TRAIN

All prices are based on one-way tickets. To ensure availability, bookings should be made at least 24 hours in advance. Some train journeys involve transfers; contact Amtrak for further information.

ALBANY–HUDSON RIVER VALLEY
Train 2 hours 30 min. $50
Coach 2 hours 49 min. $33.50

HARTFORD
Train 2 hours 45 min. $45
Bus 2 hours 45 min. $24

BOSTON
Train Acela Express 3 hours 30 min. $99
Bus 5 hours. $49

PHILADELPHIA
Train 1 hour 30 min. $50
Bus 2–3 hours. $18

WASHINGTON, D.C.
Train 3 hours 15 min. $76
Bus 4 hours 20 min. $35

CHICAGO
Train 19 hours, reservations only. $85
Bus 17 hours 15 min, reservations only. $85

ATLANTA
Train 18 hours, reservations only. $162
Bus 18–22 hours. $95

The mileages given on the chart below represent recommended driving routes and are not the shortest distances between cities.

ALBANY - HUDSON RIVER VALLEY 141 MILES (226KM)

BOSTON 194 MILES (310KM)

HARTFORD 120 MILES (192KM)

CHICAGO 807 MILES (1291KM)

NEW YORK

PHILADELPHIA 104 MILES (166KM)

WASHINGTON, DC 235 MILES (376KM)

ATLANTA 888 MILES (1421KM)

VISITORS WITH A DISABILITY

Thanks to the Americans with Disabilities Act, New York City is a fairly accessible place for wheelchair users. Most streets are level with curbs, cut at corners. Buses have lifts for wheelchairs, and taxis are required to pick up those with folding wheelchairs or guide dogs.

ON THE MOVE

GETTING ABOUT

All three airports serving New York are wheelchair accessible and have restrooms for travelers with disabilities as well as TDD telephones in all terminals.

Most subway stations provide elevators and ramps, and there are tactile and audio features on ticket vending machines. If you use a wheelchair, alert the station clerk, who will collect your fare and buzz you through the entry gate near the turnstile; customers can enter the subway with a special Autogate MetroCard (▷ 43).

The MTA buses are equipped with wheelchair lifts that are at the rear of most vehicles and are operated by the bus driver. Once on board, the driver makes sure that the wheelchair is secure. The buses are also fitted with a device that lowers the front of the vehicle so that people with impaired mobility are able to board and alight safely.

The car rental companies Avis and Hertz have some hand-operated cars for rent (▷ 53). There are car rental desks at each airport.

Many theaters offer discounts to people with disabilities, and most cultural events are sign-language interpreted. Museums are accessible, but some old buildings have not yet been converted.

USEFUL CONTACTS

If you have accessibility concerns and require information on visiting sights, contact individual venues or any of the following:

Mayor's Office for People with Disabilities (tel 212/788-2830) will send the free book *Access New York* to people who phone in a request. This large-type book provides resources and reviews.

Metropolitan Transit Authority (tel 718/596-8585, TTY 718/596-8273; 718/330-3322 for subway maps in Braille; 646/252-5252 for Access-a-Ride) provides information on New York's public transportation system.

Gray Line Air Shuttle (tel 212/315-3006) provides transportation between the three major airports and area hotels with 24-hour notice.

Travel Information Center for Hearing Impaired Visitors (tel TTY 718/596-8273) can help.

Society for Accessible Travel and Hospitality (SATH; tel 212/447-7284; www.sath.org) gives information on travel worldwide.

Big Apple Greeter (tel 212/669-8159, 212/669-3602, TTY 212/669-8273; www.bigapplegreeter.org) provides free tours of New York's neighborhoods with native New Yorkers. If you wish, you may ask for a volunteer guide with a disability. Reserve at least a week in advance.

Scoot Around (tel 888/441-7575; www.scootaround.com) provides wheelchairs and scooters for rental.

Hospital Audiences (tel 212/575-7676, 888/424-4685, TTY 212/575-7673; www.hospitalaudiences.org) arranges seats at theaters, concert halls and other venues.

Hands On Sign Interpreted Performances (tel 212/740-3087; www.handson.org) can tell you where you will find sign language interpreters at exhibitions, performances and film screenings citywide.

New York City Sports Commission (tel 877/NYC-SPORTS; www.nyc.gov/sports) gives information on accessible sports leagues and venues.

AT&T Relay Operator (tel voice 800/421-1220, TTY 800/662-1220; www.consumer.att.com/relay). Operators act as interpreter between a TTY user and a voice telephone user. The operator reads the TTY user's typed message back to the other party.

This section is divided into three parts: Sightseeing Areas, consisting of five areas (circled in blue on the map inside the front cover) highlighting what to see; A–Z of Sights, an alphabetical listing of places to visit in New York City, all located on the maps on pages 58–61; and Farther Afield, which describes attractions outside New York City (see map on pages 6–7).

The Sights

For quick reference, the top sights are listed below with the key ones highlighted in bold type.

East 95th Street
East 95th Street

East 94th Street
East 94th Street

East 93rd Street
East Harlem,
El Museo del Barrio,
Museum of the City of New York,
Studio Museum in Harlem,
Schomburg Center for
Research in Black Culture

East 92nd Street
Jewish Museum

East 91st Street
Cooper-Hewitt National
Design Museum
National Academy
of Design

East 90th Street

Guggenheim
Museum
East 88th Street
Gracie
Mansion

East 87th Street
86th Street

Neue
Galerie
East 86th Street

East 85th Street

East 84th Street

The Metropolitan
Museum of Art
East 83rd Street

East 82nd Street

East 81st Street

East 80th Street

East 79th Street
Park

East 78th Street
John Jay Park

East 77th Street
77th Street

East 76th Street

Whitney Museum
of American Art
East 75th Street

East 74th Street

East 73rd Street

East 72nd Street

Frick
Collection
East 71st Street
Asia Society
and Museum
ROOSEVELT
ISLAND

East 70th Street

East69th Street
68th Street
Hunter College

East68th Street
East 68th Street

East 67th Street

East 66th Street

East 65th Street

FIFTH AVENUE
East 64th Street

East 63rd Street
Lexington Avenue

East 62nd Street
Roosevelt
Island
Main
Street

East 61st St
Mount Vernon Hotel
Museum and Garden

East 60th Street
HIGHWAY 25
QUEENSBORO
BRIDGE
Main Street

5th Avenue
East 59th Street
59th Street

West 58th Street
East 58th Street
East 58th Street

57th Avenue of the Americas (6th Avenue)
WEST 57TH STREET   EAST 57TH STREET
Trump Tower
Dahesh Museum of Art
East Road
West Road

West 56th Street
West 56th Street

West 55th Street
East 55th Avenue

Museum of
Modern Art
West 54th Street

Museum of
Arts and
Design
West 53rd Street
Seagram
Building

West 52nd Street
Museum of
Television and Radio

St Patrick's
Cathedral
Municipal
Art Society
51st Street

West 51st Street
Radio City
Music Hall
Rockefeller
Center

West 50th Street
Mitchell Pl

G E Building
West 49th Street
East 49th Street

Rockefeller
Center
West 48th Street
East 48th Street

DIAMOND
DISTRICT
West 47th Street
MIDTOWN
MANHATTAN
East 47th Street

West 46th Street
East 46th Street

West 45th Street
East 45th Street

Park Avenue
Lexington Avenue
3rd Avenue
2nd Avenue
1st Avenue
York Avenue
Franklin Delano Roosevelt Drive
Sutton Place

Mill Rock Park
Carl Schurz Park

SIGHT LOCATOR

West 52nd Street

Museum of Arts and Design
Museum of Television and Radio

West 52nd street

Seagram Building

West 51st Street
St Patrick's Cathedral
Municipal Art Society
51st Street

Radio City Music Hall
East 50th Street

47th - 50th Streets Rockefeller Center
GE Building

50th Street
58th Street
49th Street

West 49th Street

West 48th Street
Rockefeller Center
West 48th Street

West 47th Street
DIAMOND DISTRICT
West 47th Street
East 47th Street

MIDTOWN MANHATTAN

BROADWAY

West 46th Street
West 46th Street

West 45th Street
West 45th Street
East 45th Street

18

West 43rd Street
Int'l Center of Photography
East 44th Street
Grand Central Terminal
Chrysler Building

West 44th Street

Times Square

West 43rd Street
West 43rd Street

Holy Cross Church
42nd Street
5th Avenue
Grand Central 42nd St
Daily News Building

WEST 42ND STREET
WEST 42ND STREET
EAST 42ND STREET

Reuters Building

42nd Street Port Authority Bus Terminal
New Amsterdam Theater
Times Square
42nd Street
New York Public Library
Chanin Building

West 41st Street
West 41st Street
East 41st Street

Bryant Park

West 40th Street
West 40th Street
East 40th Street

West 39th Street
West 39th Street
East 39th Street

FASHION AVENUE

AVENUE OF THE AMERICAS (6th Avenue)

West 38th Street
West 38th Street
East 38th Street

West 37th Street
West 37th Street
East 37th Street

Morgan Library

West 36th Street
West 36th Street
East 36th Street

PARK AVENUE

West 35th Street
West 35th Street
East 35th Street

Macy's

West 34th Street
WEST 34TH STREET
EAST 34TH STREET

34th Street Penn Station
34th Street Penn Station
34th Street Herald Square
Empire State Building
33rd Street

19

West 33rd Street
East 33rd Street

Madison Square Garden
Pennsylvania Station

West 32nd Street
East 32nd Street

West 31st Street
West 31st Street
East 31st Street

West 30th Street
Little Church Around the Corner
East 30th Street

West 29th Street
West 29th Street
East 29th Street

28th Street
28th Street

Chelsea Park

West 28th Street
West 28th Street
East 28th Street

West 27th Street
West 27th Street

West 26th Street
West 26th Street

Madison Square Park

West 25th Street
East 25th St

20

West 24th Street
Metropolitan Life Insurance Tower
East 24th St
23rd Street

23rd Street

West 23rd Street
Flatiron Building
23rd Street

West 22nd Street
East 22nd Street
Gramercy Park North
Gramercy Park
Gramercy Park South

CHELSEA

West 21st Street
East 21st Street

West 20th Street
East 20th Street

18th Street

West 19th Street
Theodore Roosevelt Birthplace
East 19th Street

GRAMERCY PARK HISTORIC DISTRICT

West 18th Street
East 18th Street
Irving Place

West 17th Street
West 17th Street
East 17th Street

West 16th Street
West 16th Street
East 16th St

Union Square Park

West 15th Street
West 15th Street
East 15th Street
14th Street Union Square
3rd Avenue

21

WEST 14TH STREET
14th Street
8th Avenue
14th Street
UNION SQUARE
WEST 14TH STREET
EAST 14TH STREET

West 13th
13th
Street
East 13th Street

6th Avenue

Little West 12th Street
Forbes Magazine Galleries
East 13th Street

West 12th Street
Grace Church

Jefferson Market Library
West 11th Street
East 11th Street

Wanamaker Place

West 10th Street
East 10th Street
5TH AVENUE

West 9th Street
East 9th Street

8th Street NYU

Astor Place
8th Street

Christopher Street
Sheridan Square
Macdougal Alley
Washington Mews
University Place

Ukrainian Museum

GREENWICH VILLAGE

Christopher Park
Washington Square
WASHINGTON SQ NORTH
Washington Square Park
WASHINGTON SQUARE EAST
Waverly Place
Washington Place

NOHO

McNulty's Rare Teas and Choice Coffee Shop
West 4th St - Washington Square
WASHINGTON SQ SOUTH
West 3rd Street
Merchant's House Museum

Church of St Luke-in-the-Fields
Minetta Lane
La Guardia Place

Bond

House of Oldies
Bleecker Street
Jones Aly

C   D   E   F

Around Museum Mile

🚌 M1, M2, M3, M4
🚇 4, 5, 6

Several of New York's finest museums are on the stretch of Fifth Avenue going north from 79th Street—an area known as Museum Mile.

This chic part of town, once known as Millionaires' Row, is also called the Carnegie Hill Historic District. Running from 86th to 98th streets between Fifth and Lexington avenues, Carnegie Hill is home to a concentration of imposing mansions by some of New York's most prestigious architects. Today's museums are housed in what were the great mansions of wealthy industrialists, who turned their attentions to this part of town in the 1890s. Central Park runs along the western edge, and provided stunning views for the former residents.

The Guggenheim Museum is a Frank Lloyd Wright masterpiece

MAIN SIGHTS

From 79th Street going north the main museums are the Metropolitan Museum of Art, the Guggenheim Museum and the Jewish Museum, but there are several others that are also worth a visit.

Metropolitan Museum of Art

The Great Hall of this enormous museum, the third-largest in the world, is one of the city's great public spaces. It costs nothing to walk in and spend a few minutes admiring it; the splendid collections could keep you awestruck for weeks (▷ 114–119).

Guggenheim Museum

To fully appreciate Frank Lloyd Wright's unsurpassable 1940s swirl, step inside, go to your right and look up. The fine collection and special exhibitions are ranged along a spiral walkway and are more than worthy of the setting (▷ 110–111).

Jewish Museum

This Loire Valley-style chateau, designed by Charles P. H. Gilbert, was completed in 1908 and was the home of financier Felix Warburg. Now it houses a museum of Jewish art and culture and offers an in-depth look into the lives of 19th- and 20th-century European and American Jewish communities (▷ 109).

OTHER PLACES OF INTEREST

Cooper-Hewitt National Design Museum

Completed in 1902 to a design by the architectural firm of Babb, Cook & Willard, this 64-room Georgian mansion was originally the home of industrialist Andrew Carnegie and his wife Louise until his death in 1919. Now owned by the Washington, D.C.-based Smithsonian Institution, the industrialist's splendid home displays a superb design collection assembled by the Cooper and Hewitt families (▷ 77).

National Academy of Design

This museum, also a school of fine art founded in 1826, owns a large collection of 19th- and 20th-century American art painted by its members (▷ 124).

Neue Galerie

Built in 1914 in the style of a place des Vosges mansion, and once the home of Mrs Cornelius Vanderbilt III, the top society hostess of her time, the

Go to the Great Hall of the Metropolitan Museum of Art to pick up information for your visit

residence was designed by Carrère & Hastings. Today it displays 20th-century German and Austrian works of art and design (▷ 124).

Sarabeth's
Delicious breakfasts and filling lunches (▷ 286).

● The Whitney Museum of American Art (▷ 148–151) and the Frick Collection (▷ 100) are not far south along Fifth Avenue.

THE SIGHTS

Map labels:
E13
Jewish Museum — East 92nd Street
Cooper-Hewitt National Design Museum — East 91st Street
East 90th Street
National Academy of Design
Guggenheim Museum — East 88th Street
Central Park Reservoir — East 87th Street
F13
East 86th Street — 86th Street
86th Street Transverse Road — East 86th Street — Neue Galerie
Central Park — East 85th Street
East 84th Street
F14
East 83rd Street
The Metropolitan Museum of Art — East 82nd Street
East 81st Street
E14
5th Avenue · PARK AVENUE · MADISON AVENUE · PARK AVENUE · Lexington Avenue
0 100 m / 0 100 yds

Around St. Patrick's Cathedral

HOW TO GET THERE

🚌 M1, M2, M3, M4, M5, M6, M7

🚇 B, D, E, F, V

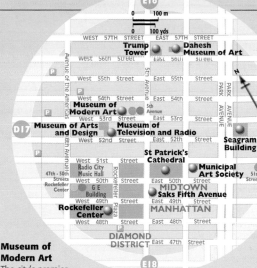

When St. Patrick's Cathedral was built in 1878, architect James Renwick, Jr. must have had a premonition of the skyscrapers to come. Everything in this tightly packed area of Midtown Manhattan reaches to the heavens.

Unlike Lower Manhattan, where the streets tend to have names, Midtown is all numbered streets and avenues, which makes navigating easier for the visitor. Get caught up in the fast pace of life and you can easily spend an entire day here as there is so much to see and do. Aside from the sights, this is one of New York's main shopping districts, with the flagship store of the venerated national chain Saks Fifth Avenue.

The double-spired, Roman Catholic St. Patrick's Cathedral

MAIN SIGHTS

St. Patrick's Cathedral is right in the middle of this area, encircled by entertainments at Rockefeller Center, the museums of Modern Art, of Arts and Design and Television and Radio, and the stunning Seagram Building.

St. Patrick's Cathedral

The twin towers and ornate white spires, reaching to 330ft (100m), remain impressive and are still often photographed, though dwarfed now by taller neighbors. The windows and stonework are beautiful and the space impressive (▷ 131).

Museum of Modern Art

The city's premier collection of contemporary art recently doubled its size. Go to see the great Impressionist and Post-Impressionist art and to relax in the serene sculpture garden (▷ 125).

Seagram Building

The plaza of this bronze and glass giant, built in 1958, offers Midtown workers a place to soak up the sun over lunch (▷ 141).

Trump Tower

The ultimate in shopping malls and decadence, with its many pricey shops, waterfalls and acres of marble and brass (▷ 144).

Museum of Television and Radio

Access 75 years of programs and commercials through theaters, screening rooms and individual consoles. A good shop is the icing on the cake (▷ 124).

Rockefeller Center

This city within a city is home to entertainment, shopping, dining, an ice-skating rink in winter and NBC's "Today" show. Some of New York's finest public sculptures, murals and friezes are here (▷ 128–130).

OTHER PLACES OF INTEREST
Dahesh Museum of Art

Dedicated to 19th- and 20th-century European academic art (▷ 77).

Museum of Arts and Design

Huge exhibition of 20th-century crafts (▷ 123).

Saks Fifth Avenue

Flagship store (▷ 176).

Trump Tower is about as ostentatious as it gets

WHERE TO EAT

Oceana
French-Asian cuisine and lots of wines by the glass (▷ 283).

'21' Club
A former speakeasy frequented by such figures as Humphrey Bogart and F. Scott Fitzgerald (▷ 289).

TIPS

● Shopping at Saks Fifth Avenue, Thomas Pink or Cartier could liven up a visit.
● Try and catch a show at the Radio City Music Hall or at the TV studios.

The Flatiron District, Union Square and Gramercy Park

HOW TO GET THERE

🚌 M1, M2, M3, M5, M6, M7
🚇 4, 5, 6 or N, Q, R, W

These three overlapping neighborhoods stretch east of Sixth Avenue (Avenue of the Americas) between 15th and 28th streets, south of Midtown Manhattan.

Each has managed to retain something of its historic charm. The Flatiron District has its early 20th-century classic skyscrapers around Madison Square Park, while Gramercy Park Historic District has leafy squares and fine old brownstones, and Union Square some of the first theaters. The area also provides some of New York's hottest restaurants (there's loads of choice) and hip, trendy shops like Emporio Armani and Diesel.

The Flatiron was built for the Fuller Construction Company

MAIN SIGHTS

The Flatiron District, Gramercy Park, Theodore Roosevelt Birthplace and Union Square form a cluster of sights centered on the Flatiron Building.

Flatiron Building and District

When Daniel Burnham's triangular, steel-framed skyscraper went up in the city's most prominent site on Madison Square in 1902, it was dubbed "the Flatiron" because it was shaped like an iron (then called a flat iron). Painters and photographers have made it into one of the city's enduring symbols (▷ 87).

Gramercy Park Historic District

Only residents around this lovely little park, or guests of the few hotels that front it, are allowed to enter the park; the gates are kept well locked. But you can see it well enough from the other side of the fence. Fine 1840s row houses line the west and south sides (▷ 101).

Theodore Roosevelt Birthplace

The house is not the actual birthplace of Teddy Roosevelt, the 26th president, but a 1923 reconstruction. It was built for the Women's Roosevelt Memorial Association. Roosevelt is the only native New Yorker to have become president (▷ 141).

Union Square

If you arrive at the Lincoln Statue in Union Square Park at 2pm on a Saturday, you can join a free walking tour of this neighborhood—a thriving theater, shopping, dining and entertainment area. If you go on Monday, Wednesday, Friday or Saturday you will find one of the best of the city's green markets—farmers' markets that inspire New York's ambitious chefs and delight New York food lovers (▷ 145).

OTHER PLACES OF INTEREST
Little Church Around the Corner

In 1870, when a minister of a nearby church refused to conduct an actor's funeral service, he suggested that mourners try "the little church around the corner" (▷ 109).

Metropolitan Life Insurance Tower

Designed in 1907 by Pierre Le Brun to be the world's tallest building, the Met Life skyscraper, at 700ft (214m), was soon

The National Arts Club in Gramercy Park Historic District

overshadowed by the Woolworth Building. A four-faced clock is its most prominent feature (▷ 120).

WHERE TO EAT

Eleven Madison Park
International menu and stylish interior (▷ 276).

Veritas
Plenty of wines to choose from, and a tasty menu (▷ 290).

TIP

● The Empire State Building (▷ 94–96) is only a few blocks north, at East 33rd Street and Fifth Avenue.

THE SIGHTS

SoHo and Little Italy

HOW TO GET THERE

M1, M5, M6

4, 5, 6 or N, Q, R, W

In these adjacent neighborhoods, some of the best galleries display works by innovative contemporary artists from around the world, and there are also many historic landmarks.

SoHo, between Broadway and Sixth Avenue and West Houston and Canal streets, became of particular interest when mid-19th-century Italianate and French Second Empire cast-iron-fronted buildings were discovered. Its former manufacturing buildings are now apartments, and its artists' studios are still thriving, although today they're for wealthy artists only. Chic boutiques and restaurants ensure that the area is mobbed on weekends.

Little Italy, next door to SoHo to the east and bordered by East

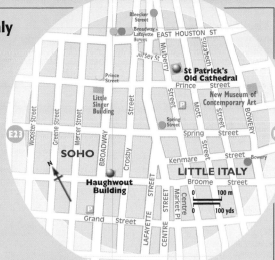

MAIN SIGHTS

Aside from the many galleries that dot the streets in SoHo, St. Patrick's Old Cathedral is an early 19th-century landmark.

St. Patrick's Old Cathedral

This Gothic-style landmark has a grand interior with cast-iron columns supporting a timber roof. Construction began in 1809 on what is now the oldest Roman Catholic church in the city. In 1866, after suffering severe fire damage, it was restored. In 1879, after a new cathedral was built on Fifth Avenue, this building was renamed St. Patrick's Old Cathedral and it was demoted to parish church status (▷ 131).

WHERE TO EAT

Bread
Soups and salads (▷ 273).

Honmura An
All kinds of noodles at this highly

Shopping for the unusual in SoHo's unique shops

Houston and Canal streets and Broadway to the Bowery, has at its heart Mulberry Street, once almost entirely inhabited by Italians, but now also home to a large Chinese community. Since the shrinking of Italian influence, trendy shops and restaurants have tended to move just north of Little Italy, to an area known as NoLita (*North of Little Italy*).

Even so, Little Italy still boasts a couple of *salumerias* (delicatessens) worth seeking out—Di Palo's, 206 Grand Street at Mott and the Italian Food Center at 186 Grand Street at Mulberry.

OTHER PLACES OF INTEREST
New York City Fire Museum

At 278 Spring Street in a Beaux Arts-style firehouse this collection shows how firefighting developed from the 18th to the 20th centuries (▷ 124).

Haughwout Building

This building, on the corner of Broadway and Broome Street, is a classic example of the restored cast-iron buildings in SoHo, completed in 1857 (▷ 242).

Little Italy still exists but is also home to a Chinese community

recommended establishment (▷ 278–279).

Nyonya
A favorite for Malaysian cuisine (▷ 283).

TIP

● Little Italy's Feast of San Gennaro in September is 10 days of colorful festivities. Vendors offer tempting foods.

The Financial District

HOW TO GET THERE

- M9, M15
- 2, 3, 4, 5, 6 or J, M, Z

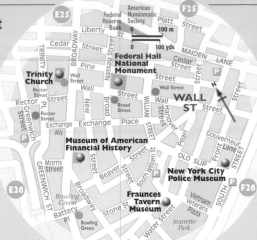

The oldest part of Manhattan, the Financial District grew from the 1800s into a global focus for trade and commerce.

It is packed with historic landmarks, grand neoclassical buildings and contemporary high-rise steel and glass skyscrapers, and it's one area no visitor should miss. Come on a weekday to appreciate its vitality and robust flavor.

THE SIGHTS

MAIN SIGHTS

Wall Street has been synonymous with high finance since the days of Dutch governor Peter Stuyvesant, and here too are the Federal Hall National Monument and Museum of American Financial History. Trinity Church provides a peaceful sanctuary from all that money.

George Washington surveys the New York Stock Exchange

Wall Street

The skyscrapers lining this old, narrow street cast a shadowy gloom even on sunny days. But the passion for creating wealth that suffuses the offices overlooking this 'canyon' makes this little superhighway the city's most famous street. With many American flags waving overhead, it's a sight to see. The New York Stock Exchange is also on Wall Street (▷ 146–147).

Federal Hall National Monument

As you stroll along Wall Street, you can't miss the imposing bronze statue of the country's first president, George Washington, on the steps of the Federal Hall National Monument across from the New York Stock Exchange. On this site, Washington took the oath of office. Inside is an exquisite rotunda, among the finest Greek Revival rooms in the city. There are free exhibits, including the Bible on which Washington placed his right hand during the swearing-in (▷ 97).

Trinity Church

At the west end of Wall Street is Trinity Church. Do pause for a look at this 1846 landmark's beautifully carved front doors, white marble altar and wooden vault. At 280ft (85m), Trinity Church was Manhattan's tallest building from 1846 to 1890 (▷ 142–143).

Museum of American Financial History

As you stroll down Broadway, you know you've reached the Museum of American Financial History when you see the bronze *Charging Bull* statue across from it. This Smithsonian affiliate displays some surprisingly interesting coins, documents and artifacts, and the interactive financial news terminals keep children amused (▷ 120).

OTHER PLACES OF INTEREST
Fraunces Tavern Museum

On this site in 1783 General George Washington bade farewell to his officers at the end of the American Revolution. Fires in the 19th century all but destroyed the original building; what was left of it was bought by the Sons of the Revolution in 1904, who renovated it in Colonial Revival style. The tavern is now a museum and restaurant (▷ 99).

Beautiful stained-glass windows adorn Trinity Church

New York City Police Museum

The New York Police Department is proud of its achievements. This museum offers a glimpse into the arrest records of famous criminals, a look at police weapons, and an introduction to forensic science (▷ 126).

WHERE TO EAT

Mark Joseph Steakhouse
A steakhouse for the power brokers (▷ 281).

TIP

- Century 21 is a designer discount heaven. (▷ 177).

Battery Park City Esplanade is popular with the city's joggers

Detailed carvings front the Cathedral of St. John the Divine

AMERICAN ACADEMY AND INSTITUTE OF ARTS AND LETTERS

✚ Off map 58 C12 • Broadway at 155th Street 10032 ☎ 212/368-5900 🕐 Thu–Sun 1–4 🚇 M4, M5 🚇 B, C, D

One of America's first planned cultural centers, the Renaissance Revival complex now known as the Audubon Terrace Historic District was the brainchild of Archer M. Huntington, the son of Collis P. Huntington, builder of the Central Pacific Railroad, who founded the Hispanic Society of America in 1904 (▷ 101). The American Academy of Arts and Letters gives grants and prizes to artists and each year holds two month-long special exhibitions of works by member artists, composers or authors (in April and mid-May to mid-June).

AMERICAN MUSEUM OF NATURAL HISTORY

See pages 68–72.

AMERICAN NUMISMATIC SOCIETY AT THE FEDERAL RESERVE BANK OF NEW YORK

✚ 61 F25 • 96 Fulton Street 10038 ☎ 212/571-4470 🕐 Mon–Fri 10–4 🚇 Free 🚇 M1, M6, M15 🚇 Wall Street (2, 3, 4, 5) www.amnumsoc.org

This society "advances the study and appreciation of coins, medals and related objects of all cultures." Housed in the magnificent Florentine palazzo-style bank building, the society has a huge collection of coins, estimated at approximately 800,000 items, as well as maps and photographs. The shows here document the heritage of American coins and medals and the history of money—a suitable subject for this commercial city.

ASIA SOCIETY AND MUSEUM

✚ 59 F15 • 725 Park Avenue at 70th Street 10021 ☎ 212/288-6400 🕐 Tue–Sun 11–6, Fri 11–9 🚇 Adult $10, under 16s and members free, Fri 6pm–9pm free for all 🚇 M1, M2, M3, M4, M66, M72 🚇 6 🚇 📷 🍴 www.asiasociety.org

Founded by John D. Rockefeller III in 1956 to promote relations between America and Asian countries, the society mounts exhibitions, lectures, conferences, concerts and workshops. A $30-million renovation of the 1981 building completed in 2001 doubled the exhibition space. The collection is based on Rockefeller's donation of acquisitions from all over Asia, and ranges from 11th-century BC Chinese ceramics to Japanese prints and Cambodian sculptures to 19th-century objects.

BATTERY PARK

See page 73.

A 14th-century Nepalese sculpture on display in the Asia Society and Museum

BATTERY PARK CITY

✚ 61 E25 • Southwest tip of Manhattan 🚇 M20, M22 🚇 1, 2, 3, 9, E, N, R www.batteryparkcity.org

From Pier A to Chambers Street, the $4-billion, 92-acre (37 ha) Battery Park City development was created using the earth excavated in the 1970s during construction of the World Trade Center. It's a great place for a stroll along the waterfront, or for watching the boats on the Hudson River. Cesar Pelli's World Financial Center (1987) sits amid residential towers, plazas and parks. The Gardens of Remembrance were planted here two months after 9/11.

BROOKLYN BRIDGE

See pages 74–75.

CARNEGIE HALL

See page 76.

CATHEDRAL CHURCH OF ST. JOHN THE DIVINE

✚ Off map 58 C12 • 1047 Amsterdam Avenue at 112th Street 10025 ☎ 212/316-7540 🕐 Services Mon–Sat 8, 8.30, 12.15, 5.30, Sun 8, 9, 11, 6 🚇 Fee for tour 🚇 M3, M4, M7, M11 🚇 B, C 🔎 Tue–Sat 11, Sun 1; $5 📷 www.stjohndivine.org

Seat of the Episcopal Diocese of New York, the cathedral is the largest Gothic church in the world. Building began in 1892 and has stopped and started many times, as funds dried up; the end is still not in sight. Besides the dizzying scale and contrasting architectural styles, admire the Mortlake Tapestries, woven from a design by Raphael in 1623, and the Barberini tapestries. Chapels around the cathedral are dedicated to other world faiths; memorials pay tribute to victims of genocide and racism, and to those who died on 9/11.

AMERICAN ACADEMY OF ARTS AND LETTERS–CATHEDRAL OF ST. JOHN THE DIVINE 67

American Museum of Natural History

36 million specimens, from dinosaur fossils to moon rock, and state-of-the-art exhibitions.

The main entrance to the museum on Central Park West

Biology and evolution of humans on Earth

Hanging around the Hall of Biodiversity

SEEING THE AMERICAN MUSEUM OF NATURAL HISTORY

There are three entrances to the museum: the main entrance on Central Park West, where you will see the impressive bronze statue of President Theodore Roosevelt on horseback; the Columbus Avenue entrance onto West 77th Street; and an entrance on West 81st Street into the Rose Center for Earth and Space, a planetarium with a narrated history of the universe. The museum has grown over the years and now has 40 grand exhibition halls, so you will have to decide what interests you most and save the rest for other visits. A good way to start a visit is to join one of the free Highlights Tours; you will hear about some of the museum's prized treasures and get orientation on the layout of the exhibits. Ask at the information desk inside the main entrance, where the tour begins. The tour guides are friendly, well informed, usually very entertaining and easy to spot: They hold up a yellow flag as they proceed through the museum. You can join in along the way.

HIGHLIGHTS

ROTUNDA

Inside the main entrance is the Rotunda, a city landmark, where colorful murals depict great accomplishments of Theodore Roosevelt, the first New Yorker to become president of the United States. The *Barosaurus* in the middle of the Rotunda is the tallest mounted dinosaur in the world at 50ft (15m). The real bones are stored elsewhere; the ones you see here are casts.

TIPS
- Go on a free Highlights Tour.
- On Friday evenings the museum is less crowded.
- On the first Friday of every month top jazz musicians entertain for free at 5.30 and 7.15. Tapas and drinks are available.
- Purchase a CityPass (▷ 317), good for nine days, to save money and avoid standing in line for tickets.
- The gift shop has a wide range of jewelry, pottery, metalwork and glasswork from all over the world.

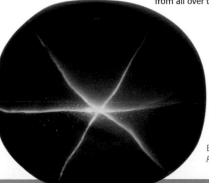

The 563-carat Star of India sapphire in the Hall of Gems (left); the Barosaurus *in the Rotunda (far left)*

The gorilla diorama (top); the Hall of Northwest Coast Indians

Totem poles dominate the Native American exhibition

The Hall of the Universe, on the lower level of the Rose Center

ROSE CENTER FOR EARTH AND SPACE
Hayden Sphere
Part of the four-story, $210-million Rose Center for Earth and Space, opened in 2000, which occupies a glass cube designed by James Polshek, the great Sphere contains the planetarium. Take a 30-minute virtual ride through the Milky Way and find out about distant planets and superclusters elucidated through the fascinating commentary and stellar special effects. The spiral Cosmic Pathway winds down around the course of the Sphere.

FIRST FLOOR
Dzanga-Sangha Rainforest (Hall of Biodiversity)
The full-size rainforest diorama, 90ft (27m) long, 26ft (8m) wide and 18ft (6m) high, re-creates a forest in the Central African Republic. Visitors can go behind the glass into a world where high-resolution imagery, video, sound and smell take you into a rainforest experience. On the forest floor, insects, reptiles and small mammals scuttle through the saplings, shrubs, herbs, ferns and leaf litter; a stream runs past, and in the distance you may get glimpses of elephants moving about, while birds and primates hang around in the tangle of overhead vines, branches and trunks.

Blue Whale (Hall of Ocean Life)
One of the museum's favorite exhibits, the 94ft (31m) model of a blue whale dominates the state-of-the-art Hall of Ocean Life. Video projection screens and interactive computer stations help you to understand marine environments across the world.

Discovery Room
Designed to interest children between the ages of 5 and 12, the Discovery Room has puzzles, games, scientific challenges and investigations to explore.

SECOND FLOOR
Elephant Diorama (Akeley Hall of African Mammals)
This venerable diorama, constructed in the 1930s, set the standard for natural history museum displays. The group of

A decorative mask

KEY TO MAIN ROOMS

FOURTH FLOOR
1: Research library
2: Vertebrate origins
4: Advanced mammals
5: Primitive mammals
7: Ornithischian dinosaurs (*Stegosaurus* and *Triceratops*)
9: Saurischian dinosaurs (*Tyrannosaurus* and *Apatosaurus*)

THIRD FLOOR
1: Pacific peoples
2, 3: Plains and Woodlands Indians
4: Primates
5: North American birds
6: New York State mammals
7: New York City birds
8: African mammals
9: Reptiles and amphibians (including the world's largest lizard, the 10ft/3m Komodo dragon)
10: Hayden Planetarium Space Theater

SECOND FLOOR
1: South American peoples
2: Mexico and Central America
3: Birds of the world
4: Asian peoples
5: Asian mammals
6: Main entrance and Rotunda
7: Oceanic birds
8: Scales of the universe
9: Cosmic pathway
10: Big Bang
11: African mammals
13: African peoples

FIRST FLOOR
1: Ross Hall of Meteorites
2: Human biology and evolution
3: Discovery Room
4: New York state environment
5: North American forests
6: Hall of Biodiversity
7: Theodore Roosevelt Memorial Hall
8: Hall of Planet Earth
9: Cosmic pathway
10: Rose Gallery (space show boarding)
11: North American mammals
12: Hall of Ocean Life
14: Northwest Coast Indians
15: IMAX theater
19, 20: Gems and minerals (Star of India sapphire)

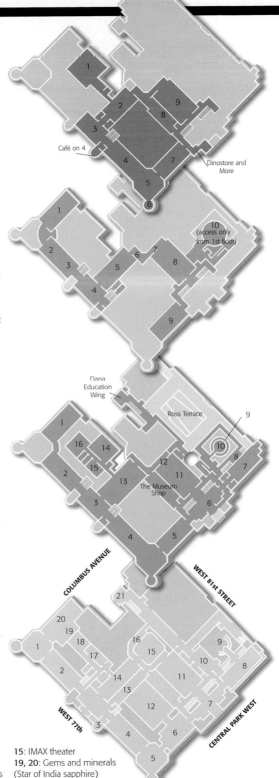

Café on 4

Dinostore and More

10 (access only from 1st floor)

Dana Education Wing

Ross Terrace

The Museum Shop

COLUMBUS AVENUE

WEST 81st STREET

WEST 77th

CENTRAL PARK WEST

THE SIGHTS

✚ 58 D14 • Central Park West at 79th Street 10024-5912

☎ 212/769-5100

🕐 Daily 10–5.45 (Fri until 8.45). Space shows Sun–Thu, Sat 10.30–4.30, Fri 10.30–7 (tickets can sell out, so buy in advance online or phone 212/769-5200)

💲 Museum and Rose Center suggested donation: adult $13, child $7.50. Admission and Space Show suggested donation: adult $22, child $13. Additional charge for IMAX and some special exhibitions

🚌 M7, M10, M11

🚇 B, C

🎧 Rose Center audiotours at desk near the Planetarium shop on the lower level, free. Hour-long guided Highlights Tour on the hour 10.15–3.15, free. Free thematic Spotlight Tours change each month

🍴 Museum Food Court on the lower level (daily 11–4.45); Café on 4 on the fourth floor (usually 10–5); Café 77 on the first floor (daily 11–4.45); Tapas Bar on the lower level (Fri 5.30–8)

🏛 🚻

www.amnh.org
Comprehensive information to help you plan your visit, including a map of the area and tips on parking. There's a floor plan, a guide to current exhibitions, and the facility to book advance tickets.

The Rose Center glass cube is made up of 736 panes of glass

elephants is set amid vegetation typical of their natural habitat. Other dioramas in the hall show more of Africa's stunning wildlife.

THIRD FLOOR
Passenger pigeon (Hall of New York City Birds)
Two centuries ago, the passenger pigeon was one of the most abundant birds in North America. Now extinct, the bird's life is traced through vivid displays.

FOURTH FLOOR
Stegosaurus and *Triceratops* (Hall of Ornithischian Dinosaurs)
These two huge dinosaurs were vegetarians, protected from rapacious attacks by massive bony jaw plates. Begin with a visit to the Wallach Orientation Center for an overview of the six fossil halls. Did you know that the word dinosaur means "terrible lizard"?

Tyrannosaurus and *Apatosaurus* (Hall of Saurischian Dinosaurs)
You may feel very small when you enter the Hall of Saurischian Dinosaurs and meet the giants displayed here. *Tyrannosaurus rex* is an awesome sight, with the horrendous teeth of a meat-eater.

BACKGROUND
Increasing interest in natural history and the discovery of fossils, particularly of dinosaurs, across the United States provided the inspiration for this great museum, founded in 1869 by Albert S. Bickmore. Originally the museum was in the Arsenal building in Central Park. Construction on this site began in 1874, to plans conceived by Calvert Vaux and J. Wrey Mould. President Ulysses S. Grant laid the cornerstone, and President Rutherford B. Hayes formally opened the museum in 1877. Additions in many architectural styles have expanded the museum since. The Theodore Roosevelt Memorial Hall, finished in 1936, was designed by John Russell Pope. Roosevelt, a keen hunter and collector, donated specimens from his many expeditions, including a bat and the skull of a red squirrel. The museum also includes a research center with numerous laboratories, teaching and other facilities, and a library that has the largest collection of natural history books in the Western hemisphere. The collection of dinosaurs and other fossils is the largest in the world, and many of those on view are real, not cast reproductions.

THE SIGHTS

Heading for the relative peace and quiet of Battery Park

BATTERY PARK

Spectacular views take in New York Bay to the south and the Financial District skyscrapers rising to the north.

These 21 acres (8.5ha), at the southern tip of Manhattan, are the site of Castle Clinton, a national monument, where you can buy tickets for the ferries to Liberty Island (▷ 136–137) and Ellis Island (▷ 90–93). The park's meandering paths are scattered with large, poignant memorials to more than 200 years of war dead. With its terrific view of the harbor, it is a pleasant place to get away from the busy, skyscraper-packed Financial District. Once a rocky ledge, Battery Park was created with landfill to protect the island from British attack in 1811, and it was named for the cannons that stood here.

CASTLE CLINTON

Castle Clinton was built between 1807 and 1809 for defense. In 1823 the U.S. government ceded it to the city, and it became a center for theatrical and musical entertainment, hosting such events as the triumphal 1850 appearance of the Swedish soprano Jenny Lind. From 1855 to 1890 almost 8 million newly landed immigrants passed through Castle Clinton, when it was the immigration processing center, recalled by the statue in front of the castle, *The Immigrants* by Luis Sanguino. In 1889 immigration processing moved to Ellis Island. From 1896 to 1911, Castle Clinton was home to New York's first aquarium, now at Coney Island. Dioramas in the small museum depict Castle Clinton's history.

THE HARBOR

At the south end of Battery Park is the terminal for the Staten Island Ferry. From here, looking out across the city's harbor, you have a magnificent view of the Statue of Liberty, Ellis Island, Governors Island, and the Verrazano Narrows Bridge with the Atlantic Ocean beyond. Just past Slip 6 is a sculpture by Marisol, the *American Merchant Mariners Memorial*, dedicated to all merchant mariners who have served the United States since the Revolutionary War. Throughout the park vendors sell everything from T-shirts to ice cream.

Artruro Di Modica's bronze bull–Financial District landmark since the 1980s

The relocated Sphere statue by Fritz Koenig

RATINGS	
Good for kids	●●●○
Historic interest	●●●●●
Photo stops	●●●○
Walkability	●●●●●

BASICS

✚ 344 E26 • Southwest tip of Manhattan on the Hudson River
🚌 M9, M15, M20, M22
🚇 1, 4, 5, 9, N, R

TIP

● If you enter the park from Bowling Green subway station, you will pass the damaged 22-ton bronze *Sphere,* which once stood between the twin towers of the World Trade Center. It was recovered and placed temporarily in the park as a memorial to the victims of the 9/11 attack.

Brooklyn Bridge

**A walk across Brooklyn Bridge yields a memorable view of
Lower Manhattan and New York Harbor.
A symbol of true pioneering spirit.**

*The bridge has been described as the crowning glory of an age
memorable for great industrial achievements*

*The walkway is a good place to
enjoy the cityscape*

RATINGS

Historic interest	● ● ● ○
Photo stops	● ● ● ● ●

BASICS

🔲 61 G25 • From southern Manhattan
over the East River to Brooklyn
🚩 Free
🚌 M9, M15, M103
🚇 2, 3, 4, 5, 6, N, R

TIP

● Walk across the bridge at
dusk on a summer evening as
the sun slowly sets behind
Liberty Island and the city
lights begin to twinkle.

This remarkable feat of 19th-century engineering, designed by John
Roebling and built between 1867 and 1883, was the world's first
steel suspension bridge. It spans a mile (1.6km) across the East
River, roughly between Cadman Plaza in Brooklyn and Park Row
in Manhattan.

CONSTRUCTION CASUALTIES

The construction of the bridge cost several lives, including that of the
chief engineer. While doing the final survey for the bridge, John
Roebling suffered a severe injury to his foot. He survived the
amputation of his toes, but died on July 22, 1869, of the resulting
tetanus infection. His son, Washington Roebling, an engineer with the
Union Army during the Civil War, took over as chief engineer. Working
underwater on the caissons one day in 1872, Washington surfaced
too quickly and was partially paralyzed by the resulting attack of the
bends, also known as decompression sickness. He carried on,
directing construction from his window in Brooklyn Heights with the
aid of a telescope, while his wife Emily marched back and forth
delivering his instructions to workers. Of the 600 laborers who
worked on this project, 20 lost their lives in construction accidents.

When the bridge opened in May 1883, the public marveled at the
Gothic-inspired span with its stone pylons and web of steel cables.
Roebling's understanding of aerodynamic stability was very advanced
for the time and he was the first to introduce radiating stays extending
from the tops of the towers to the lower end of the suspender cables.
It is estimated that 150,000 people walked across Brooklyn Bridge on
opening day—but not Roebling, who refused to come after a bitter
dispute with the company that financed the project. Disaster struck days
later. A woman stumbled and fell while walking across. As people tried
to see what was happening, there was much pushing and shoving.
It was Memorial Day, a national holiday commemorating American
servicemen killed in action, so there were great crowds on the bridge.
A rumor started that the bridge was about to collapse, and everyone
panicked and rushed toward land. Twelve people were trampled to
death and many were injured. On a cheerier note, in 1884 the great
circus entertainer P. T. Barnum led 21 elephants across the bridge,
which bore the weight without incident.

THE BRIDGE TODAY

As you walk along the wooden pedestrian walkway, you will come to a viewing spot where a bronze plaque gives information about the Roeblings. Take a look at the map etched in metal alloy, so that you know which skyscrapers loom ahead.

American poet Walt Whitman once described the bridge and the views as the best medicine his soul had ever experienced. He might balk at the number of skyscrapers, and probably at the number of bicycle-riders, roller skaters and joggers racing across it today, but they have their own lane so pedestrians can stroll at their own pace and in safety.

The twin Gothic arches tower 277ft (84m) above the East River. The bridge was repainted in 1973, in its original beige and light brown. The walkway was reconstructed in 1983.

Jogging across the one-mile span of the bridge is a popular way to keep in shape

Many famous conductors have appeared on this great stage, conducting music by names like Gershwin and Stravinsky

CARNEGIE HALL

The outstanding acoustics of this world-famous concert hall attract the world's most gifted musicians.

This superb Italian-Renaissance-inspired concert hall took seven years to build, opening in 1891. With 2,804 seats and excellent acoustics, it remains one of New York's most highly prized music centers. The Rose Museum on the second floor (daily 11–4.30 and available to concert patrons in the evenings; free) has archival treasures relating to the history of the building and famous figures who have performed here.

EARLY HISTORY

Late 19th-century New York was an important place but it did not have a concert hall. When the steel magnate Andrew Carnegie heard this, he put up the $2 million needed to construct the building, on the condition that the city provide the land on which to build it: At that time New York was a stretch of vacant lots, coal yards and row houses. Chief architect William B. Tuthill was a gifted amateur cellist, so was determined to get the acoustics right. Tchaikovsky opened the hall, making his American conducting debut in 1891. In the years since, the world's greatest musicians, including Rachmaninoff, Horowitz, Stravinsky, Ravel and George Gershwin, have all performed here. The New York Philharmonic orchestra made this its home until moving to the Lincoln Center (▷ 112–113) on the Upper West Side in 1962.

The second building, added in 1894, housed famous musicians, architects, dancing classes and agencies. In 1894 the green mansard roof of the main building was removed to build the studio floor. There is a small recital hall within the original building and an elegant auditorium, which was a movie theater until 1997.

THE HALL TODAY

In the 1960s, Carnegie Hall was saved from demolition largely by violinist Isaac Stern. So it is for good reason that the main auditorium is named after him. The Weill Recital Hall features singers and chamber groups; Zankel Hall offers contemporary innovative programming. Between 1981 and 1990, Carnegie Hall underwent a $50-million renovation. The modern 60-story office tower next door, sensitively designed by Cesar Pelli, was built in 1990.

The distinctive red-brick exterior of Carnegie Hall

RATINGS

Good for kids	● ●
Historic interest	● ● ● ●
Value for money	● ● ● ●

BASICS

✚ 58 D17 • 156 West 57th Street at Seventh Avenue 10019
☎ 212/247-7800
ⓘ For performance schedule, check website or phone 212/903-9765
🎫 Check website or phone 212/247-7800
🚶 One-hour tours Mon–Fri 11.30am, 2pm, 3pm when concert schedule permits
🚌 M7, M10, M20, M30
Ⓜ N, Q, R, W
🍴 ♿ 👥
www.carnegiehall.org

The Civic Center dates from the 19th century

The Alma Mater statue, Columbia University

Painting by François-Xavier Fabre, Dahesh Museum of Art

CENTRAL PARK

See pages 78–83.

CHELSEA

✛ 60 D20 • Seventh to Eleventh avenues between 14th and 28th streets 🚇 M20 🅰 C, E 🍴 🛍 🖼

Galleries, studios and dance and media centers add the artsy edge to this now-stylish district. Before World War I the US movie industry developed in disused warehouses and theaters here before moving to California. The Kitchen, at 512 West 19th Street, has film, music and dance. Among the many galleries worth visiting are the Gagosian (555 West 24th Street, tel 212/741-1111) and Cheim & Read (547 West 25th Street, tel 212/242-7727). The Dia Center for the Arts (548 West 22nd Street, tel 212/989-5566; www.diacenter.org) hides wonderful exhibits behind an unappealing facade. Currently being renovated, it is due to reopen in 2006.

West of the West Side Highway, a series of piers on the Hudson, known as Chelsea Piers, forms a sports and entertainment complex with ice skating, roller skating, swimming and restaurants.

CHINATOWN

See page 84.

CHRYSLER BUILDING

See page 85.

CITY HALL AND CIVIC CENTER

✛ 61 E25 • Broadway and Chambers Street 10007 ☎ 212/788-3000 🚇 M1, M6, M15 🅰 2, 3, 4, 6, N, R 🚌 Tours by appointment, tel 212/788-6865

Built between 1802 and 1812 in the Federal style with French influence, City Hall is one of New York's most elegant buildings. The heart of the city's administration, it is where the City Council meets and where the mayor has his office. Since 9/11 it has been closed to the public and can be seen only from outside (though this may change). The surrounding Civic Center area includes City Hall Park and Foley Square, several city, state and federal government offices and police headquarters, including the New York State Supreme Court, the U.S. Courthouse and the New York City Criminal Courts Building.

THE CLOISTERS

See page 86.

COLUMBIA UNIVERSITY

✛ Off map 58 C12 • West 114th to 120th streets 10027 ☎ 212/854-4900 🚇 M4, M11, M60, M104 🍴 🛍 🖼 🚹 🚌 Free guided tours weekdays www.columbia.edu

Founded as King's College in 1754 as a rival to the by then well-established Harvard and Yale, this was New York's first college and the fifth-oldest in the nation, and is among the Ivy League's wealthiest universities. Originally located in the schoolhouse of Trinity Church (▷ 142–143), the college has occupied several Manhattan locations. It moved to the current 36-acre (15ha) campus, originally the site of Bloomingdale's Insane Asylum, in 1897. The heart of the campus is the magnificent Low Library, inspired by the Pantheon in Rome; academic buildings are arranged around it. In 1934 the Low became the university's administrative center, and the library was moved.

COOPER-HEWITT NATIONAL DESIGN MUSEUM

✛ 59 E13 • 2 East 91st Street 10128-9990 ☎ 212/849-8400 🕐 Tue–Thu 10–5, Fri 10–9, Sat 10–6, Sun noon–6 🎟 Adult $10, under 12 free 🚇 M1, M2, M3, M4 🅰 4, 5, 6 🍴 🖼 🚹 www.si.edu/ndm

This elegant, 64-room, wood-paneled Georgian mansion, built from 1899 to 1902, was the home of the industrialist and philanthropist Andrew Carnegie. Designed by the architectural firm Babb, Cook & Willard, it was the first private residence in New York to have an Otis elevator, and also came with air-conditioning. Today it houses one of the largest design collections in the world, with more than 250,000 items. The collection, originally from the Cooper Union School for the Advancement of Science, was donated in 1967 to the Smithsonian, which moved it here. It includes a drawing by Michelangelo, furniture designs by Frank Lloyd Wright and industrial design drawings by Donald Deskey and Henry Dreyfuss.

DAHESH MUSEUM OF ART

✛ 59 E17 • 580 Madison Avenue 10017 ☎ 212/759-0606 🕐 Tue–Sat 11–6 🎟 Adult $9, under 12 free 🚇 M1, M2, M3, M4 🅰 F4, 5, 6 🍴 🛍 🖼 🚹 www.daheshmuseum.org

The museum occupies three floors of architect Edward Larrabee Barnes' black granite IBM Building. Established in 1995, the Dahesh is the only museum in America dedicated to 19th- and 20th-century European academic art.

Dr. Dahesh is in fact the Lebanese writer and philosopher Salim Achi; his collection of some 3,000 works of art was moved here from Beirut in 1975 to protect it from the civil war there. A subterranean concourse houses exhibitions, educational activities and public events; visitor services and the museum store are at street level. The mezzanine, overlooking Madison Avenue and the IBM Building's bamboo-forest atrium, is used as a venue for casual dining and public events.

Central Park

New York's "great green lung," designed by Frederick Law Olmsted and Calvert Vaux in 1851. Enjoy 843 acres (340ha) of green space with woods, gardens, playing fields and a zoo. Great for birdwatching, cycling, rowing, ice skating, rollerblading, strolling or jogging along 58 miles (95km) of paths.

Softball games often take place on the Great Lawn

The city's 843 green acres are perfect for dog walking

Cyclists enjoy the park's car-free roads on the weekends

RATINGS	
Good for kids	● ● ● ● ●
Historic interest	● ● ●
Photo stops	● ● ● ●
Walkability	● ● ● ● ●

TIPS

● Don't stroll alone in deserted areas, and stay out of the park at night unless you are going to a play or concert. The park is now generally safe by day and after dark when there are crowds on hand. Police and park rangers patrol in vehicles, on skates and on horseback.
● Count on spending a half day or more here, depending on what you want to see.
● On the roads, watch out for bicycle traffic, and always look carefully when crossing.
● The park has 21 children's playgrounds. Many are state of the art and no two are alike.

SEEING CENTRAL PARK

Several entrances lead into Central Park from Central Park South (59th Street) at the southern edge and 110th Street at the northern. The most popular entrance is at Grand Army Plaza, at 59th Street and Fifth Avenue. From Fifth Avenue on the east side, you can enter at 66th, 72nd, 79th, 85th, 97th and 102nd streets. On the west side, from Central Park West, you can enter at 66th, 72nd, 81st, 86th, 96th and 100th streets. North of 96th Street, the park is more rugged and less suitable for visitors with disabilities. Because there are so many different access points, study the map before entering, read about the highlights, then decide on a route through the park. Many roads that cut through the park are closed to vehicular traffic on weekends in summer, which makes it perfect for joggers, bikers, rollerbladers and baby-strollers. There are bronze statues throughout the park, including monuments to Beethoven, Christopher Columbus, William Shakespeare and Mother Goose in the south end. At the entrance to the Delacorte Theater are lovely statues of Romeo and Juliet, and from Shakespeare's *The Tempest,* Prospero with his daughter, Miranda. Bring binoculars; especially in the Ramble or on the lake.

HIGHLIGHTS

SOUTH QUADRANT

The Pond is a lovely first impression of Central Park for visitors who come in at Grand Army Plaza. The gilded bronze statue of Civil War Union General William Tecumseh Sherman by sculptor Augustus Saint-Gaudens is one of the most distinguished equestrian groupings in Western art. Along Central Park South, drivers of horse-drawn carriages wait for passengers. Nearby, the wooded Hallett Nature Sanctuary juts into the Pond, which has an island inhabited by turtles and birds and a lovely waterfall.

The Wildlife Center fills 5.5 acres (2ha) just north of Grand Army Plaza. This state-of-the-art zoo (tel 212/439-6500; Apr–end Oct Mon–Fri 10–5, Sat–Sun 10–5.30; rest of year daily 10–4.30; adult $6, child (3–12) $1) is home to more than 130 species from three

Mature trees surround the lake in the Ramble

climate zones: monkeys, crocodiles and snakes in the Rain Forest, Asian and North American animals in the Temperate Territory, and polar bears, penguins and polar foxes in the Polar Circle. The sea lion pool in the central courtyard is very popular, especially at feeding times (daily 11, 2 and 4). Young children can feed goats, sheep and a cow in the Children's Zoo. There are also daily animal shows in the Acorn Theater. North of the zoo, the George Delacorte Clock plays a nursery rhyme every hour on the hour as miniature animals glide around the base playing musical instruments. There is a café.

Wollman Memorial Rink (tel 212/439-6900, www.wollmanskating-rink.com; Mon–Tue 10–2.30, Wed–Thu 10–10, Fri–Sat 10am–11pm, Sun 10–9; Mon–Thu adult $8.50, child $4.25, Fri–Sun $11, $4.50, respectively, skate rental $4.75) is filled with ice skaters in winter. With its classic New York views of the Midtown skyline and its terrace overlooking the rink, this is one of the park's gems. Lessons are available and there's a snack shop.

   The Dairy (Apr–Oct daily 11–5; rest of year daily 11–4) a 19th-century building overlooking the Wollman Rink, has an exhibit about the history and design of the park. There's a 12ft (4m) model of the park.

Friedsam Memorial Carousel (tel 212/879-0244; Apr–end Nov daily 10–6; rest of year Sat–Sun 10–4.30, weather permitting), in the middle of the park at 64th Street, is one of the largest carousels in the U.S., with 58 handcarved, painted horses. Every year about 250,000 people mount a steed for a magical ride.

Dine at the Tavern on the Green, perhaps before the theater

Horse-drawn carriage rides are popular with visitors year round

BASICS

✚ 58 D16–off map • Central Manhattan from 59th to 110th streets between Fifth and Eighth avenues

☎ Administration 212/794-6564

🕐 30 min before sunrise to 1am

🚌 M1, M2, M3, M4 to Fifth Avenue (East Side) and M10 (West Side)

Ⓜ A, B, C, D, 1, 9 to Columbus Circle (southwest corner)

🚏 Look for park lamp posts to find out where you are in relation to city streets. The first two digits on the lamp post are those of the nearest street. There are direct-line emergency phones throughout the park and a 24-hour Park Line (tel 212/570-4820) you can call from mobile phones.

🍽 The lavish Tavern on the Green ▷ 288–289, reservations advised

🍴 The open-air Boathouse Café serves contemporary American cuisine from early spring to late October. Other cafés and food stalls throughout the park

🚲 Guided Central Park Conservancy Walking Tours (tel 212/360-2726) and Central Park Bicycle Tours (tel 212/541-8759); horse-drawn hansom cabs (tel 212/246-0520)

🚻

www.centralparknyc.org
Excellent online tours include details of the park's highlights, maps and information on events and things to do.

There are plenty of places to stop for a snack or a drink

The park is a favorite with joggers (top); Bow Bridge (above)

MID-PARK QUADRANT

The Sheep Meadow is 15 acres (6ha) of grass where you can have a picnic, fly kites and sunbathe. Some 300 sprinkler heads now keep the grass green and lush. A flock of sheep grazed here until 1934; their sheepfold is now a restaurant, the Tavern on the Green. On the east side of the meadow is a patch of pavement where you can watch talented roller skaters practice their moves.

Bethesda Terrace, in Olmsted and Vaux's original design, was "the heart of the park." By the 1980s it had fallen into disrepair and was rebuilt. Stand on the Upper Terrace for a splendid view of the lake and the wooded area known as the Ramble. The fountain, *Angel of the Waters* (1870), was the work of sculptor Emma Stebbins.

Strawberry Fields was created in 1981 with funds provided by Yoko Ono, widow of musician John Lennon, after his murder in 1980 outside the Dakota (▷ 87), and named after his song *Strawberry Fields Forever*. Italian craftsmen made the black-and-white mosaic embedded in the path near the entrance at West 72nd Street, directly across the street from the Dakota apartment building where he was killed. It is centered around the word "imagine," recalling another of Lennon's most popular songs. Yoko Ono provides $1 million annually to the Central Park Conservancy for the upkeep of these 2.5 acres (1ha). Fans often stop to pay their respects and leave flowers or candles, and a huge crowd gathers every year on the singer's birthday (October 9) to sing, pray and celebrate his life and work.

Loeb Boathouse rents out rowboats and bicycles (Apr–end Oct daily 10–5). Rowboats cost $10 for the first hour, $2.50 for each additional 15 minutes; each boat takes up to five people. A $30 cash deposit is required. Renting a bicycle costs between $9 and $15 per hour, and you must leave a credit card, driver's license or a passport as a deposit. In June and August (weather permitting) another option is a gondola ride—not cheap at $30 per half hour, but memorable. A fast-food restaurant in the Boathouse offers cold drinks and snacks. The Boathouse Restaurant is a lovely spot, serving brunch and lunch year round, and dinner from May to end October (reservations are a

THE SIGHTS

Charles A Dana
Discovery Center

El Museo
del Barrio

Museum of the
City of New York

Central Park

Gustave L
Levy Place

Jewish
Museum

Cooper-Hewitt
National Design
Museum

National
Academy
of Design

Guggenheim
Museum

Neue
Galerie

Central
Park
Reservoir

UPPER WEST
SIDE

CENTRAL PARK

The Metropolitan
Museum of Art

Central Park

Belvedere
Lake

American Museum
of Natural History

New-York
Historical Society

San Remo
Apartments

Ansonia
Building

The Dakota

The Lake

Whitney Museum
of American Art

Conservatory
Water

Frick
Collection

Asia Society
and Museum

68th Street
Hunter College

The
Sheep
Meadow

Juilliard School

Tavern on
the Green

FIFTH
AVENUE

Lincoln
Center

Museum of
Biblical Art

Central
Park

The Pond

COLUMBUS
CIRCLE

THE SIGHTS

CENTRAL PARK 81

Children love to climb on the bronze Alice in Wonderland *sculpture by Jose de Creeft, in Conservatory Water*

must, tel 212/517-2233). Birdwatchers record their observations in the Bird Register, inside the Boathouse, and other visitors' sightings also make for interesting reading.

Conservatory Water is the park's famous pond. On Saturdays at 10am from spring through fall, the Model Yacht Club races its radio-powered craft. You can rent miniature boats. North of the pond is the delightful *Alice in Wonderland* sculpture and to the west is the Hans Christian Andersen sculpture; children climb up on it to sit on his lap, and there are story hours on summer Saturdays at 11am.

Belvedere Castle (Wed–Mon 11–4) was Olmsted and Vaux's folly, an open-air flight of fancy that served as an elaborate scenic lookout across the lake. But during an extensive restoration in the early 1980s windows and doors were put in and it is now the Henry Luce Nature Observatory. Here you will find interesting displays—telescopes, microscopes, skeletons, feathers—intended to help children understand how naturalists observe the world. The US Weather Bureau has been operating from here since 1919, and you can get up-to-the-minute weather reports on the second floor. Also on this floor is a tree loft with a wonderful collection of papier-mâché models of bird species found in the park.

The Delacorte Theater, built in 1962, is where Shakespeare in the Park performances delight large audiences in summer. Waiting in line for a free ticket is part of the experience. New Yorkers bring picnic baskets and books when they line up (starting around 10am) and make a day of it. The box office begins distributing tickets at 1pm. Tickets are also handed out at the Public Theater at 425 Lafayette Street on the day of the performance from 1 to 3pm.

RESERVOIR QUADRANT

The Jacqueline Kennedy Onassis Reservoir, named for the widow of President John F. Kennedy because of her fondness for the place and her contributions to the city, is noted for the 1.58-mile (2.55km) track around it. Joggers and walkers come here by the thousands every day. This 106-acre (43ha) body of water no longer supplies

Manhattanites with fresh water, but it still feeds the other ponds in the park. In spring glorious ornamental cherry trees blossom on the slopes.

NORTH QUADRANT

The Conservatory Garden is 6 acres (2.5ha) of formal gardens with lovely fountains in an area that has been landscaped in a more rustic, naturalistic style than the southern part of the park. If you enter from Fifth Avenue at East 104th Street, you will pass through giant Parisian wrought-iron gates from the mansion of Cornelius Vanderbilt II.

Harlem Meer, Dutch for "little sea," is a pretty pond, well stocked with about 50,000 fish. Catch-and-release fishing (Apr–end Oct Tue–Sun 11–5) is great entertainment for kids, big and small. Fishing rods can be rented at the Charles A. Dana Discovery Center.

PARK GUIDE

SOUTH QUADRANT

The Arsenal (Mon–Fri 9–5), originally the New York State National Guard's munitions supply depot, was built between 1847 and 1851. Now a New York City Landmark, the Arsenal houses Olmsted and Vaux's original blueprint for Central Park, called the Greensward Plan. You can see it in a glass case on the third floor.

Looking across at the city from Bow Bridge in the Ramble

The park's waterways provide different ways to relax

The Chess and Checkers House is a magnet for children

Lasker Memorial Rink and Pool (tel 212/534-7639; Mon, Wed, Thu 10–3.45, Tue, Fri 10–10, Sat 12.30–10, Sun 12.30–4.30; adults $4.50, child (under 12) $2.25), built in the 1960s, is a wonderful ice-skating rink from November through March and a great roller-skating rink for the rest of the year. Skate rental is available. Very popular in summer, the swimming pool opens on July 1 and closes after Labor Day.

BACKGROUND

In the 1850s, many New Yorkers felt that their growing city needed a park. A large central site was chosen, and a competition in 1858 attracted 33 entries. A farmer and an architect, Frederick Law Olmsted and Calvert Vaux respectively, won the $2,000 commission. Olmsted was appointed superintendent of Central Park. Jacob Wrey Mould took on the ornamental side and designed the bridges, the Belvedere and the terrace. Construction took 16 years and cost more than $14 million. Three thousand workers, mostly unemployed Irish immigrants, and 400 horses moved stone and earth and planted 500,000 trees, shrubs and vines. The park got its own police force to discourage lawlessness. In 1925, the first of 19 playgrounds, the Heckscher Playground at 61st Street and 7th Avenue, was constructed. Between 1913 and 1919, decay took its toll on some of the fine designs. By 1934 Vaux's Marble Bridge was beyond repair and had to be demolished. In 1934, when parks commissioner Robert Moses moved the sheep from Sheep Meadow to Brooklyn's Prospect Park, the sheepfold, designed by Mould, was turned into the restaurant that's now the Tavern on the Green. The addition of the Wollman Skating Rink came in 1951 and the Delacorte Theater in 1963. Many statues were added along the way. The 1970s brought another period of neglect and lawlessness and the park was for a while not a safe place to visit. But that changed after the Central Park Conservancy, headed by Elizabeth Barlow Rogers, took the initiative in the 1970s and 80s to clean up the park and raise funds to establish a safer and cleaner space. The Sheep Meadow, the first area to be restored by the conservancy, was reopened in 1981 and remains one of the safest, most pleasant areas of the park.

MID-PARK QUADRANT

The Dairy, a Gothic Revival cottage, was once a place where children could go for a glass of fresh milk. It now houses a visitors center with video information terminals and a permanent exhibit on the history of the park. To the west of the Dairy is the octagonal Chess and Checkers (draughts) House, where you can test your skills at one of the 24 chess tables.

RESERVOIR QUADRANT

As you walk, or run, around the reservoir, note the three pedestrian wrought-iron bridges, called 24, 27 and 28. New Yorkers call Bridge 28 the Gothic Arch because of its lace-like quality.

NORTH QUADRANT

The Charles A. Dana Discovery Center, opened in 1993 on the northern shore of the Harlem Meer, is a visitor and community center with free educational exhibits relating to Central Park.

Signs are in Cantonese and English along the busy shopping streets

CHINATOWN

The largest Chinatown in the United States—colorful, noisy and exotic, with 300 restaurants.

Chinatown, northeast of City Hall and below Canal Street, has been home to generations of immigrants from China, Hong Kong, Taiwan, Korea, Vietnam and other Asian countries for more than 150 years. Now covering 3 square miles (8sq km), it has all but crowded out its neighbors, Little Italy and the Lower East Side. For cheap restaurants, bargain clothing, souvenirs, and exotic herbs and spices, no other Manhattan neighborhood compares.

The district occupied by today's densely populated Chinatown was dominated by the hog and cattle industry in the 17th and early 18th centuries; many streets were named for prominent local butchers (including Joshua Pell and John Mott). During the 1800s, the area was populated by Irish and German immigrants; some of New York's dirtiest and most crowded tenements were around the intersection of today's Mosco, Worth and Baxter streets, then known as the Five Points—the setting for Martin Scorsese's 2002 movie *Gangs of New York*. Chinese immigrants arrived in the late 1870s.

PLACES TO VISIT

Visit the Church of the Transfiguration, a Georgian church with Gothic windows at 25 Mott Street, built in 1801 by the English Lutheran Church and later the Zion Protestant Episcopal Church, and a Roman Catholic church in 1853. Columbus Park, created in 1897 at Mulberry Street and Baxter Street below Bayard Street, is popular among Chinese women, who bring their swords to practice tai chi in the morning, and senior citizens, who meet for Chinese chess or mah-jongg.

The Museum of Chinese in the Americas (▷ 123) is dedicated to the history and culture of the Chinese and their descendants in the Western world. The Kim Lau Chinese Memorial Arch, in Chatham Square, commemorates the Chinese-Americans who died in World War II. Facing the arch is a statue of imperial commissioner Lieutenant B. R. Kim Lau, who fought against the opium-smuggling that led to the Opium Wars. The 15ft (4.5m) statue of Confucius at Confucius Plaza on the Bowery has been a landmark since 1976. It was sculpted by Liu Shih, and a proverb inscribed on its base commends the virtues of a government that cares for the weak. The 1785 Edward Mooney House, at 18 Bowery, is the oldest townhouse in New York.

Street markets are an integral part of everyday life here

RATINGS

Historic interest	● ● ●
Photo stops	● ● ●
Specialist shopping	● ● ● ●
Walkability	● ● ● ●

BASICS

✚ 61 F24 • Between Little Italy and the Lower East Side, bounded by Canal and Worth streets between Broadway and Bowery

🚍 M1, M6, M103

🚇 J, M, N, Q, R, W, Z, 6

🍴 Hundreds of restaurants

☕ Saint's Alp Teahouse, 51 Mott Street 10013, tel 212/766-9889

ℹ Lower East Side Visitors' Center, 261 Broome Street between Orchard and Allen streets

🛍 Dozens of souvenir shops; a few concentrate in the mini-mall at 15 Elizabeth Street

With its shining stainless-steel spire, the Chrysler Building is an icon

CHRYSLER BUILDING

New York's most stunning art deco skyscraper has a magnificent lobby with walls of African marble and steel.

The Chrysler Building's diamond-honed Enduro KA-2 steel is as incandescent today as it was in 1929. From the street, look up at the spire with its pattern of 30 radiating triangular windows. Note the 9ft (3m) pineapples on the spire and the mighty, gargoyle-like eagle heads at the corners of the building. Around the 30th floor, a brick frieze depicts hubcaps. Go inside to view the lobby's sumptuous walls of African marble and steel and the Parisian-style elevators. The elaborate ceiling was painted by Edward Trumbull.

Walter Chrysler, the third-biggest car manufacturer in America, spent $2 million of his own money to buy the skyscraper's site. Chrysler had been an automobile mechanic for most of his life and had very little formal education, but when it came to machines he was a genius. After saving General Motors a fortune with his new techniques, he moved to New York from Chicago at the age of 45. Already earning a million dollars a year, he produced his first line of Chryslers in January 1924. They appealed to the rich and were a symbol of wealth and luxury—they were the right product for the booming 1920s. For Chrysler, building a skyscraper more fantastic than anything anyone had ever seen was a challenge he could not resist.

THE TALLEST BUILDING IN THE WORLD
In late 1929, architect William Van Alen watched anxiously as the spire was raised above the 77-story structure to make it, at 1,048ft (320m), the world's tallest building, beating the Bank of the Manhattan Company Building at 40 Wall Street. It held the title for only a short time. Opened on May 1, 1931, the 1,250ft (381m) Empire State Building surpassed it. Securing an object at such a height had never been done before, and the job had been kept so secret that no reporters were around when it actually happened—probably on October 24, 1929, the day before the Wall Street Crash. The spire was as daring as it was ingenious and took the city by surprise. Many thought the building a crass bit of architectural advertising; today it is a symbol of an age when anything was possible.

In 1978, the Chrysler Building was designated a New York City Landmark. In 1997, Tishman Speyer Properties took it over and restored the art deco lobby. The lancet crown was first switched on in 1981.

The view from Lexington Avenue (above); the lobby (below)

RATINGS				
Good for kids	●	●		
Historic interest	●	●	●	●
Photo stops	●	●	●	●	●

BASICS
✚ 60 F18 • 405 Lexington Avenue at 42nd Street
☎ 212/682-3070
🕐 Mon–Fri 8.30–5.30
🚌 M98, M101, M102, M103
Ⓜ 4, 5, 6, 7, S

The exterior of the Cloisters surrounded by the flowering plants and trees of Fort Tryon Park (above); Bonnefont Cloister (left)

RATINGS

Historic interest	●●●●●
Photo stops	●●●●●
Specialist shopping	●●●●○
Walkability	●●●●●

BASICS

✚ Off map 58 C12 • Fort Tryon 10040
☎ 212/923-3700
🕐 Mar–end Oct Tue–Sun 9.30–4.45, rest of year Tue–Sun 9.30–5.15
💵 Adult $15, under 12 free. Ticket includes same-day admission to the Metropolitan Museum of Art
🚇 M4
Ⓐ A
🍽 New Leaf Café, on the grounds of Fort Tryon, tel 212/568-5323; Tue–Sat noon–3, 6–10, Sun 11–3, 5.30–9.30
🎧 Free guided tours Tue–Sun 3pm; audioguide adult $6, under 12 $4
♿ 👫
www.metmuseum.org

TIPS

● Take the subway ride if you are in a hurry. Get off at 190th Street and take the elevator to street level. Enter Fort Tryon Park and walk up the Promenade to the Cloisters.
● In summer there is a direct bus from the Metropolitan Museum of Art—more expensive than public transportation but quicker.

THE CLOISTERS

An outstanding collection of medieval art and architecture from Europe in idyllic Fort Tryon.

Perched high above the Hudson River, the Cloisters is in delightful Fort Tryon Park in Washington Heights, at the northern tip of Manhattan, with spectacular views across the river to the steep rock-faced cliffs known as the Palisades. The Cloisters opened in 1938 as a branch of the Metropolitan Museum of Art (▷ 114–119) and is devoted to the art and architecture of medieval Europe. The building, in the style of a fortified monastery, includes large sections transported from five 12th- to 15th-century cloisters in southern France and Spain.

The collection is based on medieval sculptures and segments of architecture acquired by American sculptor George Grey Barnard during trips to Europe, and includes 5,000 sculptures, tapestries, illuminated manuscripts, paintings, stained glass and other priceless objects. He brought them to New York and exhibited them in a brick building on Fort Washington Avenue. In 1925, John D. Rockefeller donated a large sum of money to the Met to purchase the Barnard collection. Then in 1930, Rockefeller gave his beautiful Fort Tryon estate to the Met, stipulating that the Cloisters be built to house a medieval collection.

HIGHLIGHTS

On the main floor is the Fuentidueña Chapel, whose 1160 apse comes from the Church of San Martín in Castile, Spain. The capital on the right side depicts Daniel in the Lions' Den, while the one on the left shows the Adoration of the Magi. The Virgin and Child fresco in the semidome came from a small Catalan church in the Pyrenees. The Romanesque doorway in the nave of the chapel was carved in about 1175 in Tuscany. Also on this floor is the Saint-Guilhem Cloister, whose imposing covered walkway is from a Benedictine abbey near Montpellier, France. The columns have intricately carved capitals and date from the 12th to 13th centuries.

In the center of the main floor is the Cuxa Cloister, from a Benedictine monastery near Prades, France. The cloister was abandoned during the French Revolution and was later sold off in parts. Barnard managed to collect about half the original capitals, 25 bases and 12 columns. In the Nine Heroes Tapestries Room are some of the oldest surviving tapestries from a set dating from 1385.

Detail above the entrance of the Daily News Building

The Dakota Building was the city's first luxury apartment block

The distinctive triangular Flatiron Building was built in 1902

DAILY NEWS BUILDING

✚ 338 F18 • 220 East 42nd Street 10036 🕒 Daily 9–5, lobby only
🚇 M42, M104 🚊 4, 5, 6, 7

Founder of the *Daily News*, James Patterson commissioned this modernist steel-and-concrete song of praise to popular journalism in 1925. It was one of the first skyscrapers in New York not built in Gothic style. On the ground floor, outside and in, abstract art deco ornamentation contrasts with the modernist strips on the upper facade. Inside, the lobby is still mostly original. Note the revolving globe, 12ft (3.5m) in diameter; the frieze representing the early days of the paper; and the clock that gives the time in 17 different time zones. The floor is laid out like a giant compass.

In 1995, the *Daily News* moved out and the building was renamed the News Building.

THE DAKOTA

✚ 58 D15 • 1 West 72nd Street 10023 🚇 M7, M10, M11 🚊 B, C

A vaguely Germanic Upper West Side landmark, this marble-floored, mahogany-paneled structure was the first luxury apartment block on Central Park.

Far beyond the city's bright lights or even the power supply, it seemed as far away from the city as the Dakotas when it opened; the name was a joke on its remoteness. It wasn't long before the city moved uptown, however. Prices soared, and the rich and famous moved in—among them musician Leonard Bernstein and actress Lauren Bacall. John Lennon was tragically shot dead on the sidewalk outside the door as he returned home one night, and his widow, Yoko Ono, still lives here.

No one can move into this building without the agreement of all the other inhabitants.

EAST HARLEM

✚ Off map 59 E12 • Fifth to First avenues, East 97th to East 125th streets
🚇 M15, M101, M102, M103 🚊 4, 5, 6

Above the Upper East Side is East Harlem, once known as Spanish Harlem and now as El Barrio (the neighborhood). Unlike Central Harlem, this area developed in the 1870s and 1880s. Its poor-quality working-class dwellings were home to immigrants—first the Irish and then, from the 1890s, Italians. As the Puerto Ricans moved on up the social and employment ladder, they began to move in and soon made the area their own. The city's Puerto Rican population numbered 45,000 by the 1930s and 600,000 by the 1960s; today more than a million Puerto Ricans live in New York, and Spanish is an unofficial second language. El Barrio has a vibrant Hispanic flavor, with family-owned stores and restaurants lining the avenues and a busy street scene.

EAST VILLAGE AND NOHO

See pages 88–89.

ELLIS ISLAND IMMIGRATION MUSEUM

See pages 90–93.

EL MUSEO DEL BARRIO

✚ Off map 59 E12 • 1230 Fifth Avenue 10029 between 104th and 105th streets
☎ 212/831-7272 🕒 Wed–Sun 11–5 (Thu until 8) 💲 Suggested donation: adult $7 (free Thu 4–8), under 12 free. Special exhibition rates apply 🚇 M1, M2, M3, M4 🚊 6 ♿ 🚻 www.elmuseo.org

Growing out of a classroom display and opened in 1969, this is the only museum in the United States dedicated to Puerto Rican, Latin American and Caribbean culture and art.

There is a permanent display of hand-carved religious statuettes known as *santos de palo*, and another of artifacts from Caribbean cultures that welcomed Christopher Columbus to the New World.

Changing exhibits of Latin American and Caribbean art and crafts regularly eclipse the permanent displays. With its lectures and workshops, the museum is a cultural focal point.

EMPIRE STATE BUILDING

See pages 94–96.

FEDERAL HALL NATIONAL MONUMENT

See page 97.

FIFTH AVENUE

See page 98.

FLATIRON BUILDING AND DISTRICT

✚ 60 E20 • 175 Fifth Avenue at Broadway 10017 🚇 M2, M3, M5, M6 🚊 N, R

Squeezed into the angle where Broadway crosses Fifth Avenue, the Flatiron Building, at a mere 285ft (87m), never competed for New York's tallest-building status. Originally known as the Fuller Building, it was built to designs by architect Daniel Burnham in 1902. The unusual proportions and elaborate architecture have attracted the interest of photographers and the amazement of tourists for more than a century. Below 23rd Street, Fifth and Sixth avenues and Broadway were once the swankiest shopping district of New York, and this stretch of Sixth Avenue was called Ladies' Mile. Large department stores brought commercialism, a new style of architecture, and prestige to the area. Just northeast of the Flatiron Building is Madison Square Park.

THE SIGHTS

East Village and NoHo

A funky area of vintage-clothing shops, ethnic diners, innovative restaurants and trendy clubs, with numerous historic sites.

The Joseph Papp Theater   *Hippy chic on St. Mark's Place*   *Music is a part of Village life*

RATINGS	
Historic interest	●●●●●
Photo stops	●●●●○
Specialist shopping	●●●●○
Walkability	●●●●●

The East Village and NoHo (*North of Houston*) extend between 14th Street and Houston Street, between Broadway and Avenue B. Once farmland owned by Dutch governor Peter Stuyvesant, this area was home to Irish, German, Jewish, Ukrainian and Italian immigrants in the 1800s and 1900s. Today you can visit the Ukrainian Museum (▷ 144) to appreciate the culture of immigrants from the Ukraine.

New York's second-oldest church, St. Mark's-in-the-Bowery (▷ 131), on Second Avenue at 10th Street, is on land that was once part of the Stuyvesant farm; the old governor is buried in the churchyard. Poet W. H. Auden, who lived at 77 St. Mark's Place from 1953 to 1972, was a parishioner at the church.

In the 1830s the richest of the rich lived at 428–434 Lafayette Street, south of Astor Place, known as Colonnade Row. Among them were John Jacob Astor, some of the Vanderbilts, and the Delano family. Today only four of the original nine houses remain. Cooper Union, at 51 Astor Place, was founded by one of America's great engineering geniuses, Peter Cooper. Now a designated New York landmark, it was completed in 1859 and was where Abraham Lincoln made the antislavery speech that helped earn him the Republican Party's presidential nomination. In the 1870s, wealthy New York women attended services at Grace Church (▷ 99), by architect James Renwick, Jr., one of the finest examples of Gothic Revival architecture in the United States.

JEWS, RUSSIANS AND TURKS

At the beginning of the 20th century, Second Avenue between Houston Street and 14th Street became a center of Yiddish culture and came to be known as the Jewish Rialto. Edward G. Robinson and Walter Matthau got their start in the Yiddish theater here. At the Second Avenue Deli (156 Second Avenue), known for its wonderful renditions of classic Jewish dishes, plaques in the sidewalk honor Yiddish theater stars. The Christadora House, on the corner of 9th Street and Avenue B, was where George Gershwin gave his first public recital. On 10th Street, between First Avenue and Avenue A, the Russian and Turkish Baths (tel 212/674-9250) opened in 1892; unlike many similar establishments, it has survived to become a New York institution. Inside, the baths are not glamorous but poignantly evoke 19th-century New York.

Artists sell their wares along the sidewalk in the East Village

A BOHEMIAN DISTRICT

In the 1960s and 1970s, the East Village was a focal point of the American hippie culture. Anarchist Abbie Hoffman lived on St. Mark's Place and Allen Ginsberg, Timothy Leary, Andy Warhol and a motley collection of Hell's Angels, Hare Krishnas and political rebels frequented the area, often meeting for protest rallies and rock concerts in Tompkins Square Park. For years, until a 1990s restoration, the area attracted the homeless and drug-users. Today it is lovely by day, but still best avoided after dark.

The Joseph Papp Public Theater on Lafayette Street is one of the city's most famous off-Broadway theaters. Impresario Joseph Papp rescued the old Astor Library from demolition, and his theater opened in 1967 with the original production of the musical *Hair*.

The mix of ethnic restaurants in the East Village gives visitors a choice of great food at budget prices. For more stylish dining at higher prices, head for NoHo, the area around Lafayette and Broadway between Bleecker and 4th streets.

The farthest area east, known unofficially as Alphabet City because the streets are designated by letters not numbers, is less accessible by subway, so it's best to arrive and leave by taxi. The area has some chic shops and fashionable bistros.

BASICS

✚ 61 F22 • South of 14th Street, east of Bowery
🚌 M8, M15
🚇 4, 5, 6

TIPS

● Skip the area east of Avenue B—it's not really worth visiting and can be intimidating.
● Check local listings to find out what's on at other theaters.
● Visit in late afternoon or early evening for a stroll and an inexpensive dinner.

Ellis Island
Immigration Museum

A deeply moving memorial to the 12 million immigrants who arrived from distant lands between 1892 and 1924. Permanent exhibits include passports, clothing, baggage and family heirlooms donated by immigrants and their families.

THE SIGHTS

BASICS

✚ Page 6 • Ellis Island, New York 10004 ☎ Information 212/363-3200, ferry 212/269-5755; audiotours, café and gift shop 212/344-0996
◎ Daily 9–5, last outbound ferry departs 3.30
💵 Museum free, including film. Ferry ticket: adult $10, child (4–12) $4. Audiotours free
🎫 Buy tickets in Castle Clinton, Battery Park. Ferry runs approximately every 30 min daily 9–3.30, depending on season
🚌 M1, M6, M9, M15
🚇 1, 4, 5, 9 to Bowling Green
🚶 Park Rangers periodically conduct tours; check schedules on arrival
🍴 Ellis Island Café serves burgers, pizza, sandwiches, soft drinks and beer and wine. Outdoor seating
♿

www.ellisisland.com
The museum's website, complete with practical details, island map and a virtual tour. It's a little confusing to navigate but packed with useful information and links.

www.ellisisland.org
Website of the family history facility (in the museum on the first floor), which has passenger records for immigrants arriving between 1892 and 1924. You can search these online.

SEEING ELLIS ISLAND

To reach Ellis Island, buy a ferry ticket at Castle Clinton in Battery Park (▷ 73). Boarding is on a first-come, first-served basis, so in spring and summer, catch the ferry early to avoid long lines. From Battery Park, take the Circle Line-Statue of Liberty ferry; en route you can stop at Liberty Island (▷ 136–137). Upon arrival at Ellis Island, walk under the glass-and-metal canopy from the ferry slip to the museum, an ornate Beaux Arts building with fanciful copper-domed turrets. The magnificent arched portals must have been both imposing and intimidating to the arriving immigrants. There are three floors with permanent and changing exhibits about the immigration process, the living conditions of the detainees, memorabilia and displays on the building itself and its restoration. Upon entering, collect your free ticket for the 30-minute film *Island of Hope, Island of Tears*. The audiotour is also well worth getting.

HIGHLIGHTS

FIRST FLOOR
The Peopling of America Exhibit, in the old railroad ticket office, provides statistical information on the history of immigration to the US from as early as the 17th century. Trace migration patterns since the 18th century on the 6ft (180cm) globe.
The American Family Immigration History Center helps anyone to research their ancestors using high-tech facilities. Visit the website at www.ellisislandrecords.org.

SECOND FLOOR
The Registry Room is reached by climbing the stairs to the Great Hall, as every immigrant did, with doctors scrutinizing their walk for physical impairment. The voices of thousands of people speaking in many different languages filled this hall as inspectors and their interpreters questioned each adult and asked any child who looked old enough to give his or her name. The inspectors asked each immigrant up to 29 questions he or she had already answered on the ship's manifest. If the immigrants' answers did not match their previous answers, they were detained and questioned further. It was a harrowing experience for people who had traveled far, leaving family and possessions behind and enduring a long and difficult journey across the Atlantic. The railings that were here to keep the immigrants in orderly lines were removed in 1911 and replaced with benches. Today visitors pay tribute to the immigrants in this quiet space.

In 1916 the spectacular arched ceiling with Guastavino tiles and the red Ludowici tiled floor were added. During the 1980s restoration, only 17 of the 28,000 tiles needed replacing.

In the West Wing is an exhibit re-creating the step-by-step immigration process. In the East Wing, photographs and memorabilia explore the immigrants' hopes and expectations, fears and hardships. You can also listen to first-hand accounts of the process.

Study the moving portraits in Treasures from Home

THIRD FLOOR

Treasures from Home displays more than 1,000 objects, including clothing, jewelry, family heirlooms and photographs donated by immigrants and their descendants. There are touching reminders of the life each person left behind and of the bright future they were hoping to find. A wedding dress, a grandmother's bracelet, a child's teddy bear—all testify to the heartbreaking sacrifices made by people desperate to find freedom and hoping for prosperity.

IN THE GROUNDS

The American Immigrant Wall of Honor displays the names of over 500,000 immigrants whose descendants made donations to the Ellis Island Restoration Project. It serves as a memorial to all those who passed through here as they fled persecution and disease, poverty and hopelessness.

BACKGROUND

Dutch settlers named this 3-acre (1.2ha) island Oyster Island because of the abundance of oyster beds in the area. In the 1760s, after the execution of pirates on the island, it was known as Gibbet Island. It then came under the ownership of Samuel Ellis, and when the city of New York bought it after his death in 1807, it was renamed again. Expanded by landfill to 272 acres (110ha), it became home to Fort Gibson and housed munitions. The original wooden fort burned down in 1897.

IMMIGRATION

From 1892 Ellis Island replaced Castle Clinton as the inspection center for newly landed immigrants. The architectural firm Boring & Tilton designed its current Beaux Arts buildings. Until 1924, while the island was active, 70 percent of the immigrants to the US passed through the receiving facility; it served as a hospital, detention facility and transportation station. First- and second-class passengers were processed on board ship in more comfortable quarters, but steerage passengers were herded onto the island. Because it was assumed that these huddled masses came from countries with substandard hygiene, no one was allowed to

TIP

● Allow at least three hours; the museum alone usually takes two to three hours. Add extra time to visit the gift shop if you are interested in immigration or genealogy.

The Registry Room is where arriving immigrants would have their first taste of America

Immigrants arriving with all their worldly belongings

The Baggage Room is the first room you will see

The copper-domed turrets stand out from the water

MAKE A DAY OF IT
Your ferry ticket is also good for a visit to Liberty Island to see the Statue of Liberty (▷ 136–137). Since 9/11 the Statue of Liberty has been closed to the public, so call ahead. Even if you don't climb the 354 steps to the crown, you can walk around the island and see the statue up close.

sleep on a bed provided by Uncle Sam without first having a bath. Public Health Service doctors examined every person and if they detected signs of heart problems, mental problems or moral degradation, they would return the individual to their homeland. Eyes were examined for signs of trachoma, a highly contagious eye disease that led to blindness and even death; doctors, who came to be called "buttonhook men," used their fingers or a button-hook to turn eyelids inside out in search of redness caused by inflammation. Via translators, immigrants had to answer questions about their finances, their intended residence, and any waiting relatives. They had to prove they were strong, intelligent and able to find work. Fearful, many immigrants gave contradictory answers and corrupt immigration officers took advantage of many by accepting bribes when they gave a "wrong" answer. Inspectors questioned 400 to 500 individuals each day, spending only a few minutes with each. The bureaucracy was daunting, and Ellis Island became known as the Island of Tears, although most new arrivals received the landing card that allowed them to enter the US. Despite this, immigrants were often overcharged for their first train tickets in their new homeland so that many began their new lives in the poverty and squalor of New York City tenements.

AFTER WORLD WAR I
During World War I, the island came under US Army control and was used as a hospital. In 1924, after changes in legislation, prospective immigants were checked in US consulates abroad and Ellis Island became a deportation center for illegal aliens. A new immigration building, a ferry house and a recreation building were added between 1934 and 1936 under the Public Works Administration. During World War II, the US Army used the island to detain enemy aliens. Between 1945 and 1954, the buildings were abandoned and deteriorated. In 1952, despite a proposal to convert the main building into a museum, it remained unused and was closed in 1954. In 1965, President Lyndon Baines Johnson designated the island part of the Statue of Liberty National Monument. In the 1980s, architects Beyer Blinder Belle led a massive restoration project. The museum opened in 1990.

The Circle Line-Statue of Liberty ferry passes Ellis Island

KEY TO MAIN ROOMS

THIRD FLOOR

17: Restoring a Landmark: photographs of the restoration

16: Silent Voices: large photographs of the abandoned building before restoration

15: Treasures from Home: immigrants' memorabilia

14: Ellis Island Chronicles: detailed models depicting the island's history 1897–1940

13: Dormitory Room: early 20th-century furnished room showing cramped conditions

12: Changing exhibits

SECOND FLOOR

11: Peak Immigration Years: photographs, memorabilia and recorded commentaries on immigration 1880–1924

10: Theater 2: shows *Island of Hope, Island of Tears* film, where immigrants tell their stories

9: Registry Room: the now empty great hall where immigrants were processed

8: Through America's Gate: 14 rooms with exhibits on the inspection process and the "Stairs of Separation"

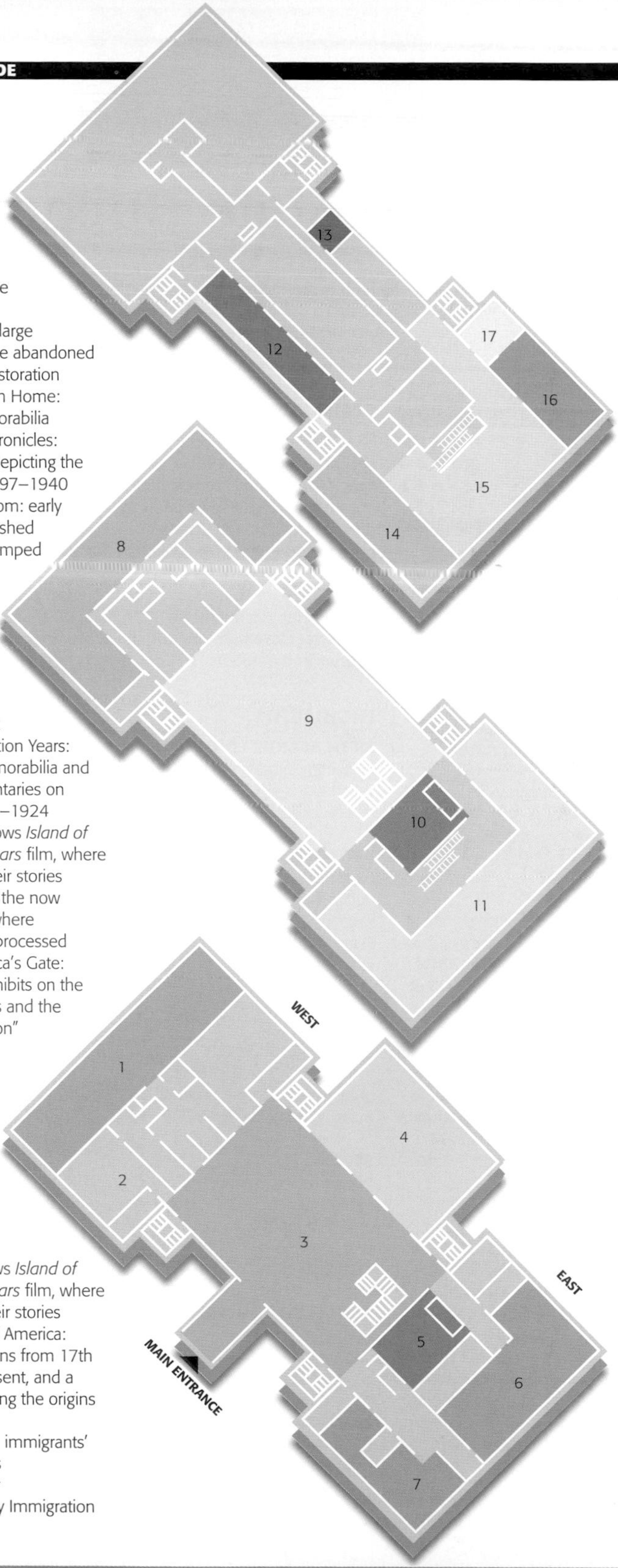

FIRST FLOOR

7: Shop

6: Ellis Island Café

5: Theater 1: shows *Island of Hope, Island of Tears* film, where immigrants tell their stories

4: The Peopling of America: immigration patterns from 17th century to the present, and a Word Tree explaining the origins of words

3: Baggage Room: immigrants' suitcases and bags

2: Learning Center

1: American Family Immigration History Center

THE SIGHTS

WEST

EAST

MAIN ENTRANCE

Empire State Building

**This New York City icon is the most famous skyscraper in the world.
Millions of visitors a year go up to the 86th-floor Observation Deck for spectacular
panoramas of the great metropolis.**

RATINGS	
Good for kids	●●●●●
Photo stops	●●●●●
Value for money	●●●●

BASICS
✚ 60 E19 • 350 Fifth Avenue 10118
☎ 212/736-3100
🕐 Daily 9.30am–midnight, last elevator ascends at 11.15pm
🎫 Adult $13, child (12–17) $10, child (6–12) $8, under 6s free, military in uniform free
🚌 M1, M2, M3, M4, M6, M7
🚇 6 to 33rd Street or B, D, F to 34th Street/Herald Square
📼 Observatory audiotour $6, corresponds to signs on the Observation Deck so you know exactly what buildings you are seeing
🍴 🏧 🚻

www.esbnyc.com
Listen to an audiotour sample, take an online tour, buy tickets and shop online, get the lighting schedule and a list of special events, and information about the ESB in the news and in the movies.

TIPS
● **To avoid waiting in line for tickets, buy them online, or in advance at the NYC & Company Visitor Center (tel 212/484-1200) at 810 Seventh Avenue between 52nd and 53rd streets.**
● **Come on a clear day and bring some quarters for the binoculars outside.**
● **The elevators carry only 16 people at a time, so be patient.**
● **Dusk is a popular time, so buy a ticket in advance if you can. Starry nights are magical and you can stay until closing time. There is no time limit on your visit.**

SEEING THE EMPIRE STATE BUILDING

The main entrance is on Fifth Avenue. You pass through a security checkpoint similar to those at airports. There is no coat check (cloakroom), so you must carry your belongings. If you have not purchased a ticket in advance, take the escalator or elevator down to the Concourse level and the Observatory ticket office. Signs indicate the waiting time and visibility. After buying your tickets, go back up the escalator to the main floor and follow the signs to the Observatory elevators on the second floor. Elevators let you out on the 80th floor, where staff direct you to the Tower elevator to the 86th floor. Viewing areas are both indoors and outdoors.

HIGHLIGHTS

FIFTH AVENUE LOBBY
Interesting exhibits show off memorabilia from New York's museums, galleries and artists. The marble walls are stupendous and the metal relief sculpture of the building dazzling.

34TH-STREET LOBBY
Eight huge color panels by artists Roy Sparkia and Renee Nemerov depict the Seven Wonders of the Ancient World and the eighth wonder from the modern world: the Great Pyramid of Cheops, the Hanging Gardens of Babylon, the Statue of Zeus, the Temple of Diana, the Lighthouse of Pharos, the Colossus of Rhodes, the Tomb of King Mausolus and the Empire State Building. The tallest Wonder of the Ancient World is the 600ft (183m) Lighthouse of Pharos.

CONCOURSE LEVEL
In addition to the Observatory ticket office, there is a collection of photographs of famous people who have visited the Empire State Building, including Queen Elizabeth II and Fidel Castro.

SECOND FLOOR
Special exhibits about New York City and its museums, cultural institutions and tourist attractions are on this floor. NY SKYRIDE (tel 212/279-9777, www.skyride.com, daily 10–10) gives a thrilling simulated tour of the city via the same simulator hardware that is used to train 747 commercial pilots.

86TH-FLOOR OBSERVATION DECK
On the outside deck you can get close-up views of the surrounding buildings and area using the high-powered binoculars. There is also an indoor, enclosed deck, which is useful if it's raining.

FLOODLIGHTS
Powerful floodlights illuminate the upper 30 floors between 9pm and midnight every night. Significant colors are used for special occasions —red, white and blue for Independence Day (July 4); green on St. Patrick's Day (Mar 17); red, black and green on Martin Luther King Day (third Mon in Jun); yellow and white for Easter; lavender and

white on Gay Pride Day (Jun). The stainless-steel window frames glimmer by day and night. In spring and fall during the bird migration season, the lights are turned off on foggy nights because the light shining through the fog confuses them.

THE TOWER
Broadcast cameras and microwave antennae on the east and west sides of the building monitor city traffic conditions for major TV and radio stations. The National Broadcasting Company (NBC) sent out the United States' first experimental transmission from the TV station here on December 22, 1931. Since 1965, FM radio has been transmitting from the tower. The New York Telephone Company also has transmission facilities on the tower. It's not open to visitors.

The Empire State Building looks most dramatic at dusk (above); jostling for a good view on the 86th floor outside deck (inset left); the Fifth Avenue entrance lobby is dominated by the shining relief of the skyscraper (inset right)

STATISTICS

- The Empire State Building weighs 365,000 tons; took 7 million man-hours to build; and is made up of 60,000 tons of steel, 2.5 million ft (790,000m) of electrical wire, 10 million bricks, 62 miles (100km) of water pipes, 6,500 windows, 72 elevators, 7 miles (11km) of elevator shafts, 1,860 steps, and a foundation that extends 55 ft (17m) below street level.

- The purchase price for the land, the site of the old Waldorf-Astoria Hotel, was $16 million; construction costs were $25 million. Construction time was an amazing 14 months. The building opened on May 1, 1931.

- With 102 stories, the Empire State Building stands 1,454ft (436m) tall. Eighty-six stories are usable office space. The Observation Tower is 16 stories.

- The TV antenna, installed in 1985, is 22 stories high.

- Three million visitors ascend annually. The stupendous 360-degree view extends for around 80 miles (130km) on a clear day.

- The Fleet Empire State Building Run-Up Race, a New York Road Runners Club event, was first run in 1978 and is now held annually in February. Competitors run up 1,567 steps. The current record is 9 minutes 33 seconds.

BACKGROUND

In 1827, William B. Astor bought the farm where the Empire State Building now stands for $16,000 and erected the first Waldorf-Astoria hotel. In 1928 the hotel was sold for $20 million and demolished to make way for the present structure. Excavation began in 1930. The developer was General Motors' vice-president, John Jacob Raskob, who wanted to create the world's tallest structure as quickly as possible. As a result, designs to decorate the limestone facade and the chromium-steel windows were machine-stamped. Completed in 1931, and $5 million under budget, the Empire State Building replaced the Chrysler Building as the world's tallest building and held this title until surpassed by the World Trade Center in 1971. Since 9/11 it has again become the tallest building in New York City, but not the world.

The Depression and then World War II put an end to the city's prosperity and much of its office space stood vacant. The tallest building in the world was dubbed the Empty State Building. However, the Observation Deck was so popular that the income from admission charges paid the taxes on the building. In 1933 the thriller *King Kong* was released and the Empire State Building became a movie star for the first time. Concerns about the stability of the building were put to rest on July 28, 1945, when a U.S. Army B-25 bomber crashed into the 78th and 79th floors, killing 13 people and causing extensive damage.

Looking east toward the borough of the Bronx from the top of the Empire State Building

The present Federal Hall building dates from 1842

FEDERAL HALL NATIONAL MONUMENT

The site of the nation's first capitol, where the first president of the newly created United States, George Washington, took the oath of office.

As you approach the Federal Hall National Monument there's no escaping the massive bronze John Quincy Adams Ward statue of George Washington on the front steps. This Doric-columned, Greek Revival building resembles a simplified Parthenon, and looks a bit out of place among Wall Street's massive structures. Inside, the rotunda has 16 marble Corinthian columns, a domed ceiling and ornate bronze railings. One exhibit explores the Constitution. Another showcases the Bible used to administer the solemn oath to Washington.

A HISTORIC SITE

New York's first City Hall was built on this site in 1699 and petty offenders were flogged in front of the building. In 1789 it was reconstructed by Pierre Enfant, who later designed Washington, D.C., and the First Continental Congress met here to draft the Bill of Rights, guaranteeing the rights to freedom of worship, speech, press, assembly, keeping and bearing arms, trial by jury, and the right against unreasonable searches and seizures. April 30, 1789, the day Washington took the oath of office, was an occasion for massive celebrations. The building remained the nation's first capitol until 1790, when the "famed deal" between Thomas Jefferson and Alexander Hamilton moved the seat of government along the Potomac River.

Many other important historic events took place on this site. Newspaper publisher John Peter Zenger was imprisoned here for seditious libel in 1734; a brilliant defense by lawyer Alexander Hamilton secured him victory in court and was an important step towards freedom of the press (▷ 27). In 1765, the Stamp Act Congress assembled here to protest taxation without representation. In 1787, after the colonies won their independence, the First Continental Congress met here to establish procedures for the creation of new states. The state, war and treasury departments were established here, as was the Supreme Court. Customs stayed for 20 years before moving to Wall Street. The building became a National Historic Site on May 26, 1939, and a National Memorial to George Washington on August 11, 1955.

Doric temple on the outside and graceful rotunda on the inside

RATINGS	
Good for kids	●●●
Historic interest	●●●●●
Photo stops	●●●●
Walkability	●●●●●

BASICS
✚ 61 E26 • 26 Wall Street 10005
☎ 212/825-6870
🕐 Mon–Fri 9–5
💲 Free
🚇 M9
🚌 4, 5

Fifth Avenue—one of the most famous streets in the world

FIFTH AVENUE

One of New York's most fashionable avenues, with shopping, museums and a few landmark skyscrapers.

The Empire State Building was completed in 1931, on Fifth Avenue at 34th Street. From its 86th-floor Observation Deck all of Fifth Avenue stretches out below you. The avenue begins downtown in Washington Square Park. Nearby, at No. 47, the Salmagundi Club, in an elegant Italianate brownstone, is America's oldest club for artists, founded in 1871. At No. 62 are the Forbes Magazine Galleries (▷ 99). At 23rd Street is Manhattan's first skyscraper, the triangular Flatiron Building (▷ 87).

St. Patrick's Cathedral (▷ 131) is between 50th and 51st streets. At No. 645 is the Olympic Tower, the headquarters of the late Aristotle Onassis's empire, with shops, offices, apartments and a restaurant. These two landmarks are at the heart of a section famous for its luxury shopping, between 49th and 59th streets. Tiffany & Co., founded in 1837, is now at 57th Street. Along with Saks Fifth Avenue, between 50th and 51st, and Bergdorf Goodman, also at 57th Street, are the Disney Store and many other retailers. Beyond the Trump Tower (▷ 144), Central Park (▷ 78–83) spreads out on the west side.

MANSIONS AND MUSEUMS

In the 19th century, Fifth Avenue was the fashionable address for the very wealthy, such as coke-and-steel tycoon Henry Clay Frick, tobacco magnate James Duke and railroad baron Jay Gould, who built increasingly large mansions. Some of them were demolished in the 1920s to make way for luxury apartments, but many remain. The first one, at No. 998, built in 1912, was such a success that it became the model that hundreds copied in form and detail. The starched doormen are an indication of the wealth of the residents, who enjoy spectacular views of Central Park. Henry Clay Frick's mansion at 70th Street is now open to the public, displaying his outstanding collection of European art in a residential setting. Andrew Carnegie's 64-room home at 91st Street is now the Cooper-Hewitt National Design Museum (▷ 77). The Jewish Museum, at 92nd Street, occupies another fine old home. The stretch between 79th and 104th streets is also punctuated by museums and has become known as Museum Mile, with the Metropolitan Museum of Art (▷ 114–119), the Guggenheim Museum (▷ 110–111) and the Museum of the City of New York (▷ 123).

RATINGS

Historic interest	●●●●●
Photo stops	●●●●●
Specialist shopping	●●●●●
Walkability	●●●●●

BASICS

✚ 59 E16 • From Washington Square north to the Harlem River

🚌 M1, M2, M3, M4

🚇 4, 5, 6

TIP

● Be sure to catch a parade on Fifth. The St. Patrick's Day Parade on March 17 is the biggest, but there are others. Check the NYC & Company events calendar for details. Crowds are so thick on the sidewalks during parades that you will not be able to shop or sightsee.

The elegant facade of the Fraunces Tavern Museum

Ulysses S. Grant's tomb was completed in 1897

Gracie Mansion has a prime location by the East River

FORBES MAGAZINE GALLERIES

✚ 60 E21 • 60–62 Fifth Avenue 10011
☎ 212/206-5548 🕐 Tue–Wed, Fri–Sat 10–4 💲 Free 🚌 M2, M3, M5, M7 🚇 F, L, V 🔦

www.forbes.com/forbescollection

Publishing magnate and adventurer Malcolm Forbes (1919–1990) had a passion for collecting, and the former home of the Macmillan publishing house, now the offices of *Forbes* magazine, includes a gallery that displays the result: old Monopoly games, model boats, whole battlefields with model soldiers, about 3,000 historical documents (including Abraham Lincoln's *Emancipation Proclamation*) and, among a display of objets d'art, a dozen of the fabled, bejewelled Easter eggs crafted for Russian czars by the house of Fabergé.

Children enjoy the antique toy collection and the model boats and other watercraft.

FRAUNCES TAVERN MUSEUM

✚ 61 F26 • 54 Pearl Street 10004
☎ 212/425-1778; restaurant 212/968-1776 🕐 Tue–Fri 10–4.45, Sat 10–5 💲 Adult $3, child (7–18) $2 🚌 M6, M15 🚇 4, 5 🍴 🏛 🔦

www.frauncestavernmuseum.org

The 18th-century Queen's Head Tavern on this site, run by one Samuel Fraunces, was visited in 1783 by George Washington himself. Here, in the Long Room, now reproduced in the style of a dining room of the period, he met with fellow officers and gave his famous farewell address at the end of the American Revolution. The current structure is a 1907 reconstruction sponsored by the Sons of the Revolution and now, together with adjacent 19th-century buildings, contains a museum of early American history and culture. Children can dress up in costume and try writing with quills. Separate from the museum is a restaurant busy all day serving all-American dishes to downtown workers.

FRICK COLLECTION

See page 100.

GENERAL GRANT NATIONAL MEMORIAL

✚ Off map 58 C12 • Riverside Drive at West 122nd Street 10077 ☎ 212/666-1640 🕐 Daily 9–5 🚌 M4, M5, M104 🚇 A

Generally called Grant's Tomb, this may be the nation's largest and most impressive sepulcher. Rising dramatically 150ft (46m) next to the Hudson River, the squat, dome-topped granite building fronted by six Doric columns proclaims the importance of wildly popular Civil War general, and later president, Ulysses S. Grant (1822–1885).

The design, chosen after a competition, was copied from the fourth-century BC tomb of Mausolus at Halicarnassus. Work began soon after Grant's death, with contributions from more than 90,000 people, many of them African-Americans, for whom Grant's achievements at the head of the Union army outweighed his less successful efforts as president.

Inside the massive bronze doors, below the domed rotunda and set off by the gleaming white marble, two 9-ton polished black sarcophagi hold the remains of Grant and his wife, Julia.

GRACE CHURCH

✚ 60 F21 • 800 Broadway at 10th Street 10004 ☎ 212/254-2000 🕐 Mon–Fri 10–4, Sun for services only 🚌 1, 2, 3 🚇 N, R, W, 6

www.gracenyc.org

By the time James Renwick, Jr. began building churches, the Gothic Revival was in full swing. Renwick, like Richard Upjohn, who designed Trinity Church (▷ 142–143) on Lower Broadway, took up the style with enthusiasm. Grace Church, completed in 1846, was one result, another was St. Patrick's Cathedral (▷ 131), on Fifth Avenue at 50th Street.

The church's original wood steeple was replaced by marble in 1888. It stands on the first bend of Broadway, so that it anchors the view up Broadway from downtown. The complex that surrounds the church includes Renwick's Grace House (1881) and the Rectory, and, on Fourth Avenue South, Renwick's Grace Memorial House.

GRACIE MANSION

✚ 59 G13 • East End Avenue 10128
☎ 212/570-4751 🕐 Guided tour only–late Mar to mid-Nov Wed 10, 11, 1 and 2. Reservations required 💲 $7 🚌 M15, M31, M86 🚇 4, 5, 6

Nothing remains for long without modification in the city of permanent change, and Archibald Gracie's stately home is no exception. A fine example of Federal architecture, it has survived against the odds. A quiet country retreat overlooking the East River when it was built in 1799, it was enlarged in 1804. It was sold in 1823, when Gracie's shipping business went under. It then spent an ignominious period as a refreshment stand, before being bought by the city's Department of Parks in 1896 and converted into the Museum of the City of New York in 1924. In 1942, after renovation, it became the official residence of the mayor of New York, although Mayor Bloomberg declined to use it. Major restoration renewed it in 1985.

The Frick mansion was designed in 18th-century European style (above); Sir Thomas More *(1527) by Hans Holbein (left)*

FRICK COLLECTION

A striking collection of masterpieces tastefully displayed in Henry Clay Frick's luxurious mansion.

RATINGS

Historic interest	⬤ ⬤ ⬤ ⬤ ⬤
Value for money	⬤ ⬤ ⬤ ⬤ ⬤
Walkability	⬤ ⬤ ⬤ ⬤ ⬤

BASICS

✚ 58 E15 • 1 East 70th Street at Fifth Avenue 10021

☎ 212/288-0700

🕐 Tue–Sun 10–6; closed Mon; limited hours, 1–6, on Presidents' Day, Election Day and Veterans' Day

💵 Adult $12, no children under 10

🚇 M1, M2, M3, M4

🚌 4, 5, 6

🎫 Books, cards, CDs, videos and museum-inspired gifts

👫

www.frick.org

TIP

• Try to come for a chamber music concert (year round on occasional Sundays at 5pm). Check website for details.

Henry Clay Frick (1849–1919) has gone down in history as a ruthless businessman, staunchly anti-union, obsessed with acquiring wealth—in other words, a master entrepreneur. Frick had his own successful business, the Frick Coke Company in Pittsburgh, when Andrew Carnegie made him his partner in the Carnegie Steel Company. Together they made the Carnegie steel empire one of the most important businesses in the country, and both men became multimillionaires. Frick's sole interest outside the world of steel and coke was art. He collected works painted by the world's masters from the 14th to the 19th centuries. At the age of 64 he had a palatial residence on Fifth Avenue built as his private home and gallery, to plans drawn up by Carrère & Hastings. Frick and his wife lived in the home until their deaths—his in 1919, hers in 1931. Frick, in an uncharacteristically generous move, bequeathed the house and paintings to the public.

After Frick's wife's death, the house was enlarged and became a museum in 1935. There is a reference library next door on East 71st Street, designed by John Russell Pope, the architect of the National Gallery in Washington, D.C. The house is set back from Fifth Avenue behind an elevated garden designed by Russell Page. As part of multimillion dollar improvements, the stone wall surrounding the site was replaced in 2002 and the wrought-iron fence was restored.

ARTISTIC HIGHLIGHTS

Through the 16 galleries, the paintings are not arranged by period or national origin, but in the way Frick would have had them displayed in his home. The Fragonard Room shows the large Fragonard paintings depicting *The Progress of Love* and contains 18th-century French furniture and porcelain. In the Living Room are paintings by Holbein, El Greco, Titian and Bellini. Through the Library, past Italian bronzes and Chinese vases, is the West Gallery, where there are landscapes by John Constable and portraits by Rembrandt and Velázquez. Especially delightful is the East Gallery, with works by Degas, Goya, Turner, Van Dyck and Whistler. After your visit, pause in the peaceful Garden Court (the enclosed Palm Court is the perfect oasis on a cold New York day), which occasionally hosts special exhibitions.

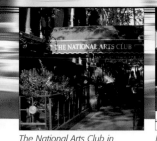

The National Arts Club in
Gramercy Park

Harlem's most famous club,
now on 125th Street

A veteran aircraft in the Intrepid
Sea, Air and Space Museum

GRAMERCY PARK HISTORIC DISTRICT

🔢 60 F20–F21 • Between Park Avenue South and Third Avenue from 18th to 21st streets 🚌 M1, M2, M3, M6, M7 🚇 N, Q, R, 6

Copied from elegant London squares by the developer Samuel Ruggles in 1831, Gramercy Park is the only private park in New York City and is still surrounded by the original high iron railings. The elegant area, full of attractive buildings, has long been favored by well-to-do citizens. At No. 16 Gramercy Park South the actor Edwin Booth, brother of Lincoln's assassin, lived in a superb brownstone. Booth's statue is inside the park. At No. 15, Samuel Tilden, Governor of New York from 1875 to 1877, installed steel doors and a tunnel to 19th Street in fear of the mob.

GRAND CENTRAL TERMINAL

See pages 102–104.

GREENWICH VILLAGE

See pages 105–107.

GROUND ZERO

See page 108.

GUGGENHEIM MUSEUM

See pages 110–111.

HARLEM

🔢 Page 7 • Fifth Avenue to Morningside Avenue north of 110th Street 🚌 M2, M3, M7, M10, M102 🚇 2, 3, A, B, C, D 🏢 Harlem Tourist Center and Gift Shop, 2224 Frederick Douglass Boulevard www.hatt.org

Harlem is forever linked with the speakeasies and jazz of the Prohibition era. Today the bleak landscape that saw the departure of middle-class families in the 1960s has given way to housing renovation and a growing, upbeat population. There is much of architectural interest, but many are attracted by the nightlife, jazz clubs and cultural attractions, including Manhattan's oldest residence, the Morris-Jumel Mansion Museum (65 Jumel Terrace, tel 212/923-8008, Wed–Sun 10–4, adult $3), and the Schomburg Center (▶ 131) After completing his second term as president, Bill Clinton opened an office in Harlem.

HISPANIC SOCIETY OF AMERICA

🔢 Off map 58 C12 • 613 West 155th Street at Broadway 10032 ☎ 212/926-2234 🕐 Tue Sat 10–4.30, Sun 1–4 💵 Free 🚌 M4, M5 🚇 1 🏢 www.hispanicsociety.org

This museum, described as one of the best-kept secrets of New York, is well worth the half-hour subway ride from Times Square. Audubon Terrace was the brainchild of philanthropist and Spanish scholar Archer Huntington. He founded the Hispanic Society in 1904 and commissioned his cousin to design the buildings. A little jewel devoted to the arts and culture of Iberia, the museum is a lavishly appointed showcase of all things Spanish, from Paleolithic tools to the masterpieces of Velázquez and Goya.

INTERNATIONAL CENTER OF PHOTOGRAPHY

🔢 60 E18 • 1133 Avenue of the Americas at 43rd Street 10036 ☎ 212/857-0000 🕐 Tue–Thu 10–6, Fri 10–8, Sat–Sun 10–6 💵 Adult $10 🚌 M5, M6, M7 🚇 B, D, F, V 🏢 www.icp.org

In the heart of Midtown Manhattan, the ICP is both a school and a museum. Temporary exhibitions are always on view, and the permanent collection has 60,000 photographs ranging from old daguerreotypes to iris prints, mainly from American and European reportage and documentation from the 1930s to the present. There are photographs by such well-known names as Henri Cartier-Bresson, Elliott Erwitt and Harold Edgerton, along with an impressive collection of 13,000 original prints by Weegee, who photographed crime scenes and New York nightlife in the 1930s and 1940s.

INTREPID SEA, AIR AND SPACE MUSEUM

🔢 58 B18 • Hudson River Pier 86, west end of 46th Street 10036 ☎ 212/245-0072 🕐 Apr–end Sep Mon–Fri 10–5, Sat–Sun 10–7; rest of year Tue–Sun 10–5 💵 Adult $16.50, child (6–17) $11.50, child (2–5) $4.50, under 2/those on active duty with ID free 🚌 M16, M42, M50 🚇 A, C, E 🎦 Free tours www.intrepidmuseum.org

The veteran aircraft carrier Intrepid, built in 1943 at a cost of $44 million, makes a fascinating museum. It is 898ft (275m) long, weighs 42,000 tons, and had a crew of 3,500. The Hangar Deck is divided into four exhibits: Pearl Harbor and World War II, Life Aboard an Aircraft Carrier, the Story of Intrepid, and Space Exploration, Satellite Communication and Weaponry. On the Flight Deck you can inspect aircraft apparently ready for take-off, including a Lockheed A-12 Blackbird, a Russian MIG and a Cobra helicopter. You can also tour the destroyer Edson and the submarine Growler; take a seven-minute SR-2 flight simulator ride; and rent a two-hour audiotour, during which veterans tell how they survived kamikaze attacks, and astronaut Scott Carpenter talks about the Intrepid scooping him up upon his return to Earth.

THE SIGHTS

Grand Central Terminal

•

**New York's most magnificent public space and one of the city's finest landmarks.
Full of sophisticated shops and interesting places for a quick bite.
Every day, trains running on 48 pairs of railroad tracks bring in half a million commuters
from the northern suburbs.**

Thousands of commuters use the station every day

The brass four-faced clock tells the time from all angles

Passengers make a beeline for the central information booth

SEEING GRAND CENTRAL TERMINAL

Enter Grand Central on 42nd Street at Park Avenue in order to experience the full impact and grandeur of the main concourse. As you enter, the feeling of space, sophistication and city bustle creates an awesome introduction to Manhattan. The careful $200-million renovation project that has restored its grandeur fills even cynical New Yorkers with civic pride. Notice the 75ft (29m) windows, the Tennessee marble floor, the brass clock over the central kiosk, and the gold-and-nickel chandeliers. Stroll around the arcades leading to Lexington Avenue and the lower level where you'll find restaurants and shops, including The Children's General Store, The Discovery Channel Store, Banana Republic and Godiva Chocolatier. Off the main concourse is the Grand Central Market, packed with fresh produce. The New York Transit Museum Annex & Store is worth visiting if you've got time. A maze of underground walkways links the terminal to surrounding streets; you can stay underground as far north as 48th and Park streets.

HIGHLIGHTS

THE MAIN CONCOURSE CEILING

With 59 electric stars replicating the zodiac constellations, in reverse, the design is based on an illustration from a medieval manuscript. It is not known whether the ceiling's French creator, Paul Helleu, was aware that depicting the heavens in reverse, or from God's point of view, was a common practice of medieval illustrators. The main concourse itself is 375ft long (114m) and 120ft wide (36m).

JULES ALEXIS COUTAN'S SCULPTURE

Mercury, the Roman god of travel and commerce, is the central figure of this 1935 sculpture over the south entrance. He is supported by Minerva and Hercules, representing mental and physical strength.

GRAND CENTRAL OYSTER BAR AND RESTAURANT

This restaurant, with its low-vaulted ceiling, is worth seeing. The tiles are by Guastavino. Order a bowl of clam chowder—either Manhattan (tomato-based) or New England (cream-based) style (▷ 278).

RATINGS	
Good for food	●●●●●
Historic interest	●●●●
Photo stops	●●●●
Specialist shopping	●●●●

BASICS

✚ 60 E18 • East 42nd Street at Park Avenue 10017

☎ 212/340-2210; for travel information 718/330-1234

🕐 Daily 5.30am–1.30am

🎟 Free

🚌 M1, M2, M3, M4

Ⓜ 4, 5, 6, 7, S

🎫 Excellent free tour by the Municipal Arts Society on Wed at 12.30. Meet at the information desk, under the clock, in the main concourse

🍴 Grand Central Oyster Bar & Restaurant on the lower level; Mon–Sat, tel 212/490-6650, www.oysterbarny.com. Michael Jordan's The Steak House N.Y.C. serves just that; tel 212/655-2300, www.theglaziergroup.com. Métrazur serves Charlie Palmer's progressive American cuisine along with seafood and pasta; tel 212/687-4600, www.métrazur.com.

🏬 50 specialist shops on the mezzanine and lower levels

www.grandcentralterminal.com
Phone numbers for stores and shops, menus and prices for all the restaurants, travel information and information on events.

Make time for a shoeshine (above); the famous Oyster Bar and Restaurant (above right)

TIPS

● Take one of the free area tours sponsored by Grand Central Partnership (GCP), one of the largest business improvement districts, every Friday at 12.30, rain or shine. Meet inside the Whitney Museum Annex at the Philip Morris Building at 42nd Street and Park Avenue.
● For lunch in New York, the food concourse on the lower level is fun, with its many interesting options from Cajun pizza to Vietnamese sandwiches. But go early—after 12.30 it's next to impossible to find a seat.
● Don't rush, take your time to enjoy the shopping, restaurants and most of all the architecture. This is not just a train station, it's a New York experience.
● When you leave the building, walk a couple of blocks south to 40th Street, then turn around and look back at Coutan's neoclassical sculpture over the south entrance.

THE SIGHTS

THE CAMPBELL APARTMENT

This elegant (if pricey) cocktail bar was built by John Campbell as an office and pied-à-terre in the 1920s in the style of a 13th-century Florentine palazzo, with its stained-glass windows by Louis Comfort Tiffany and elegant dark paneling. Follow signs to the small staircase across from Michael Jordan's The Steak House off the west balcony.

NEW YORK TRANSIT MUSEUM GALLERY & STORE

Here you'll find changing exhibits on the history, impact and future of public transportation (tel 212/878-0106, www.mta.nyc.us/museum).

SPECIAL EVENTS

Exhibitions, food tastings, treasure hunts and concerts take place regularly. The Christmas Market in Vanderbilt Halt showcases the work of dozens of innovative regional craftspeople and retailers.

BACKGROUND

New York Central Railroad magnate Cornelius Vanderbilt ordered the construction of Grand Central Terminal. Built between 1903 and 1913, it replaced the 42nd Street Terminal, an iron and glass train shed dating from 1871. At the turn of the 20th century, this area was the northern edge of the city, but as the new station flourished, stores, hotels, restaurants and offices grew up around it. By the 1920s it had become a fine boulevard graced with luxury apartment buildings.

Grand Central is an outstanding example of Beaux Arts design, with triumphal arches filled with glass and steel, a grand waiting room, sumptuous concourse, superb vaulted ceiling and imposing sculptures of Roman deities. The innovative design, by engineer William Wilgus and architects Reed & Stem, included extensive tunnels, a ramp system instead of stairs to keep people moving, and upper and lower level concourses. Architect Whitney Warren, a Vanderbilt cousin, was responsible for the outstanding facades and interior. The public was delighted with this marvel, but by the 1970s, the station had acquired layers of grime and was not a place to linger. The steel was rusty, the asbestos was falling out and the stairways stank: It had become a symbol of decay.

A NEW LEASE OF LIFE

In 1978, a New York City developer proposed building a 55-story office tower on top of the station, obliterating the facade. After a series of legal challenges, a US Supreme Court decision sided with the New York City Landmarks law and saved it from this fate. Jacqueline Kennedy Onassis was a prime force in the battle against the tower. Restoration was completed in 1998 under architects Beyer Blinder Belle, who examined 4,500 of Warren's original drawings and blueprints. Over a period of four years, 80-year-old wiring and plumbing were replaced, air conditioning was installed and new entrances were built. All of this was done while the station continued to operate, and not a single train was late or delayed owing to construction.

Greenwich Village

A fascinating, once bohemian, now celebrity-studded area bursting with funky shops, unique bookstores, sidewalk cafés and cool clubs. Where famous artists, writers and radical thinkers lived and hung out.

George Segal's sculpture Gay Liberation *was installed in 1992*

Lively Bleecker Street has great shops and cafés

Chumleys' walls are lined with photos of its literary patrons

SEEING GREENWICH VILLAGE

Broadway divides Greenwich Village into the East Village (▷ 88–89) and the West Village. Bleecker Street is the main thoroughfare of the West Village and is full of cafés, restaurants and shops. Coffeehouses, music and poetry still thrive, and this definitely is a lively place for a late night out, whether you take in the bars and clubs, or just go for a stroll.

HIGHLIGHTS

CHRISTOPHER PARK

Bordered by Christopher Street, West 4th Street and Seventh Avenue, Christopher Park is home to George Segal's life-size sculpture *Gay Liberation*, which depicts a gay couple standing in front of a bench where two lesbians sit. Behind them is the Stonewall Bar & Grill, where riots in 1969 sparked the nation's Gay Liberation movement. Christopher Street is a focal point of gay life in New York City.

CHUMLEY'S

At 86 Bedford Street, near Grove Street, this former speakeasy is not easy to find—it has no sign outside and the number does not appear on the front of the building. Over time many New York writers, including John Steinbeck (1902–68), have found solace in a drop or two here. Photos of famous patrons decorate the interior walls. The bar has appeared in several movies, including Woody Allen's *Sweet and Lowdown*.

JEFFERSON MARKET LIBRARY

In 1885, a survey of architects found this Gothic building at 425 Sixth Avenue, designed by Calvert Vaux and Frederick Clarke Withers between 1874 and 1877, to be the fifth most beautiful building in the United States. The richly ornamented facades include a pediment depicting the trial scene from Shakespeare's *The Merchant of Venice*. The tower has been used as a fire watch, and originally the building housed a police court and a district court. After years of neglect, it was about to be demolished when local activists saved it and it became a branch of the New York Public Library in 1967.

RATINGS	
Historic interest	●●●●○
Photo stops	●●●○○
Specialist shopping	●●●●○
Walkability	●●●●●

BASICS

➕ 60 D22 • From Broadway west to the Hudson River, between Houston Street to the south and 14th Street to the north

🚌 M1, M2, M3, M5–8, M20

🚇 A, C, E, F, N, R, V 1/9, 2, 3

🍴 A huge number of restaurants on Bleecker Street, Greenwich Avenue and streets in between provide a choice of international cuisines

🍽 Florent, 69 Gansevoort Street, tel 212/989-5779, open daily 24 hours, French-American cuisine and a full bar

🛍 Shops on Bleecker Street and Greenwich Avenue and many others

ℹ Information centers at Sixth Avenue and Christopher Street and at Astor Place Triangle, both Jul 1–Labor Day daily noon–6

TIPS

• Enjoy the outrageous costumes and partying up and down Sixth Avenue at the Village Halloween Parade.
• Stop at the Village Chess Shop at 230 Thompson Street, between Bleecker and West 3rd streets, for a friendly game of chess (www.chessshop.com).

ARTISTS

24 University Place: The site of the Cedar Street Tavern, where Jackson Pollock, Franz Kline and Willem de Kooning shared ideas, along with Beat writers Allen Ginsberg and Jack Kerouac.

8 West 8th Street: The first address of the Whitney Museum of American Art (▷ 148–151).

Garrick Theater, Bleecker Street: Crowds flocked here for

Skyscrapers north of Washington Square Park

seven months to see Andy Warhol's movie *Flesh*, which premiered in October 1968.

WRITERS

145 Bleecker Street: Home to James Fenimore Cooper, author of *The Last of the Mohicans*, in 1833.

172 Bleecker Street: Where James Agee wrote the screenplay for *The African Queen*.

130–132 MacDougal Street: Louisa May Alcott stayed in this house, and it is believed, wrote *Little Women* here.

137 MacDougal Street: Home to the Liberal Club. Writers such as Upton Sinclair, Jack London, Theodore Dreiser and Sinclair Lewis regularly met in the house that once stood here.

85 West 3rd Street: Edgar Allen Poe lived on the third floor in 1845 (his was the last window on the right).

11 Commerce Street: Washington Irving wrote *The Legend of Sleepy Hollow* while living here.

14 West 10th Street: Home of Mark Twain when he moved to New York at the age of 65.

(Continued on page 107)

SHERIDAN SQUARE

Sheridan Square is at the point where Seventh Avenue, West 4th Street and Barrow Street intersect. Named after the Civil War general Philip Henry Sheridan, it is the site of the first protests that culminated in the Draft Riots of 1863 when 120 were killed, mostly African-Americans, by Irish immigrants (▷ 33). You can see the statue of General Sheridan in Christopher Park.

WASHINGTON MEMORIAL ARCH IN WASHINGTON SQUARE

Built in 1889 as the entrance to the park at the base of Fifth Avenue, the original triumphal arch commemorated the centenary of George Washington's inauguration. Architect Stanford White designed the first arch, which was made of wood, plaster and papier mâché. It was so successful that a fund to erect a permanent stone arch of the same design soon raised $134,000. The arch you see today, 30ft (9m) across and 77ft (23m) high, became the gateway to fashionable Fifth Avenue in the 1950s, when cars passed directly underneath it and the avenue cut through the park, and remains a treasured city icon.

Many artists have painted or drawn the arch, including Childe Hassam in his 1894 *Washington Arch, Spring*. Many New Yorkers feel that New York University's 12-story Helen and Martin Kimmel Center on Fifth Avenue at Washington Square North detracts from the magnificence of the arch.

WASHINGTON MEWS

As you approach Memorial Arch from Fifth Avenue, on your left is a lovely little cobblestone street called Washington Mews. Originally the houses here were the stables and servants' quarters for the elite town houses on Washington Square North, known as "The Row," a street lined with fashionable homes built in 1833 by John Jacob Astor and Cornelius Vanderbilt.

The delightful old houses lining Washington Mews have long been sought as residences by artists and painters, including Gertrude Vanderbilt Whitney, founder of the Whitney Museum of American Art (▷ 148–151). Members of the faculty of New York University have more recently taken up residence here.

WASHINGTON SQUARE PARK

Washington Square is the heart of Greenwich Village. In warm weather the park is alive with street musicians, students, skateboarders, rollerbladers, the occasional film crew and chess players (bring your own set), so this lively little park is great for people-watching.

Originally the site was marshland and a hunting ground; until the 1820s, criminals were hanged from the large elm in the northwest corner, and from 1797 until 1926 it was a potters' field, where paupers were buried. The remains of about 10,000 people rest here in peace, if not quiet. Washington Square was eventually acquired by the city, cleared, and laid out as a military parade ground. The Common Council then purchased more land, and the 9 acres (3.5ha) became the city's largest park in the 1840s. In 1963 the city closed the park to traffic, making it even more attractive to the students in the area. By the 1970s, alcohol and drug abusers had taken over. A clean-up over the past decade has left it the mellow, genial place you see today.

BACKGROUND

By 1700 Greenwich Village, named after a town in England, had grown to become a small village of wood-framed houses and tree-lined, mud streets north of the city. A single grand estate, Richmond Hill, built by a British paymaster-general at what is today the intersection of Varick and Charlston streets, was George Washington's headquarters during the attempt to defend New York in 1776 and was later home to vice presidents John Adams (1767–1848) and Aaron Burr (1756–1836). Burr sold much of the land to John Jacob Astor, who divided it up into 456 lots, which he leased for a tidy little profit.

The streets grew up, sometimes along former cowpaths, before the grid street plan was introduced in 1811. When yellow fever struck in the 1820s, half the population fled the city, and prominent families looking for fresh air settled in Greenwich Village, tearing down most of the original frame houses and rebuilding in brick. The Village was a fashionable residential area by July 4, 1826, when Washington Military Parade Ground (Washington Square) was officially opened to celebrate the 50th anniversary of the signing of the Declaration of Independence. African-Americans moved in after the Draft Riots in 1863 and soon Italian immigrants from Little Italy were spilling over into the neighborhood. Tenements and factories were built, and wealthy New Yorkers moved north.

In the early 1900s, social changes and new zoning laws created cheap housing, attracting artists looking for studio space and low

RADICALS

12 Charles Street: Home of suffragette Crystal Eastman and a suffragist gathering place.

91 Greenwich Avenue. Where *The Masses* was published. This left-wing publication backed the Communist Party and was a precursor to the counter-culture of the 1960s.

147 West 4th Street: John Reed rented a room in this house while he wrote *Ten Days That Shook the World*.

Regular jamming sessions still liven up the park

Pretty brownstone townhouses characterize the streets

Bustling markets fill the streets on Sunday mornings

rents. Intellectuals, writers and rebels took up residence, creating a bohemian enclave. Social critics, including suffragists, anarchists and Communist sympathizers turned the Village into a hotbed of disaffection. Writers such as Henry James, O. Henry, Mark Twain, Edgar Allen Poe and Stephen Crane all lived here. The Village's artist-residents, including Edward Hopper, Jackson Pollock, Franz Kline and Willem de Kooning, created a new American style. Today, the Village is one of the liveliest parts of the city, and maintains its artsy overtones, despite being a very expensive place to live and therefore also popular with wealthy professionals.

Memorial Arch provides a sedate backdrop to performances in Washington Square Park

A poignant tribute to lost loved ones

A symbol of hope and strength, the iron cross at Ground Zero

GROUND ZERO

Ground Zero looks like nothing so much as a construction site. But seeing this corner of Lower Manhattan brings vividly home the horrors of 9/11.

The World Trade Center once filled seven buildings on the 16 acres (6.5ha) bordered by Church Street, Liberty Street, Park Place and West Street. The center's twin towers became the tallest buildings in the world in 1973, and for the next 28 years more than a million visitors visited every year, thrilling to the views from the open-air rooftop observation level. Then, on the morning of September 11, 2001, New Yorkers and the rest of the world watched with horror on their televisions as two hijacked commercial jets slammed into the towers. A total of 2,752 people were killed, 343 of them firefighters. When the towers collapsed, six buildings were destroyed and about 100,000 jobs were lost. Mayor Rudolph Giuliani was on the scene within minutes. Streets like Church and Vesey were completely enshrouded in thick white dust, people were in shock, and emergency crews and firemen rushed to the scene, hoping to find survivors, but there were very few. When the fires were eventually extinguished, Ground Zero was all that was left.

LOOKING TO THE FUTURE

Within a year, clean-up crews had completed their gruesome task and workers had started rebuilding affected subway stations. The Lower Manhattan Development Corporation (LMDC) staged a design competition, inviting top architects around the world to create plans for the site. Six were unveiled in July 2002; all were rejected. Calling for more plans, the LMDC got responses from 406 teams of architects, and in March 2003 the governor and the mayor announced the winner: Daniel Libeskind, a Polish immigrant who arrived in the U.S. in 1960, aged 13.

An avant-garde architect, known for his commemorations of tragic events, Libeskind designed the Imperial War Museum in Manchester, England, and the Jewish Museum in Berlin. The heart of his under-ground memorial is the enormous slurry wall that kept the Hudson River from eroding the World Trade Center foundation. It surrounds the footprints of the two towers. Rising above is a symbolic 1,176ft (359m) tower with landscaped gardens. An elevated promenade allows visitors to view the memorial, and at ground level, a named marker will be put in the pavement for each rescue company that responded on 9/11. Commercial and cultural buildings are also planned.

BASICS

➕ 61 E25 • Church to West streets, Liberty to Vesey streets

🚌 M6, M9, M20

🚇 1, 9, E, N, R

A Culture and Continuity gallery in the Jewish Museum

Go to Little Italy for the flavors and colors of the Mediterranean

An interior display from the Tenement Museum

JEWISH MUSEUM

✠ 59 E13 • 1109 Fifth Avenue at 92nd Street 10128 ☎ 212/423-3200 ◷ Mon–Wed 11–5.45, Thu 11–8, Fri 11–3, Sun 10–5.45 💲 Adult $10, under 12s free 🚇 M1, M2, M3, M4 🚇 6 🔲 ♿
www.thejewishmuseum.org

A faux Loire Valley chateau, the former family home of banker Felix Warburg, this greystone mansion dating from 1908 contains the Jewish Museum's collection of Jewish ceremonial objects and works of art.

A generous philanthropist, Warburg died in 1938 and his widow left the house to the museum in 1944. The permanent exhibit, entitled Culture and Continuity: The Jewish Journey, is based on Warburg's personal collection of artifacts, covering an impressive scale and time-span.

In a re-created 1900s café, oral histories reveal Jewish life in Europe at that time and explore the immigrant experience in the U.S. Family workshops and other events celebrate Jewish culture, holidays and traditions.

LINCOLN CENTER

See pages 112–113.

LITTLE CHURCH AROUND THE CORNER

✠ 60 E19 • East 29th Street between Fifth and Madison avenues ☎ 212/684-6770 ◷ Daily 9–5 🚇 M2, M3, M4 🚇 6
www.littlechurch.org

The Episcopal Church of the Transfiguration is affectionately called the Little Church Around the Corner. Nothing could better demonstrate changed attitudes to all things theatrical than the way in which this charming little church acquired its nickname. In 1870, a nearby church declined to conduct funeral rites for actors, and directed one such request to

"the little church around the corner." It has been favored by theater folk ever since.

An English-style lychgate leads to the church, set back from the street in a quiet garden. The interior maintains the intimate, modest atmosphere with carved wooden pillars and beams.

LITTLE ITALY

✠ 61 F23 • Between Canal, Lafayette, and Houston streets and the Bowery 🚇 6 🚇 M1, M103

Once the overcrowded destination of Italian immigrants coming from Ellis Island, Little Italy is shrinking under pressure from New York's burgeoning Chinatown (▷ 84). A few blocks recall the friendly, festive area chock-a-block with Italian restaurants and grocery stores, where lavish displays of cheese, olives and salami entice visitors. Descendants of the initial immigrants still gather for family occasions. In mid-September the Feast of San Gennaro, patron saint of Naples, fills Mulberry Street, the main artery, from Canal Street to Spring Street. With gaudy lights and carnival booths, it's definitely a scene to see if you don't mind crowds.

LOWER EAST SIDE

✠ 61 G23 • East of the Bowery, south of East Houston to the East River 🚇 M9, M14A 🚇 F, J, M, V, Z

A slum tenement here was the next stop for most 19th-century immigrants after the ordeal of Ellis Island. The squalor, stench and disease in these overcrowded apartments during the area's heyday—from the mid-19th century until the 1920s—can barely be imagined today. Few of the original town houses survived the frenzied 19th-century building of tenement blocks, but most of these survived later rebuilding.

Today, although there is little to admire in the architecture, the area is thick with history. It is also one of New York shoppers' best bargain-hunting destinations, particularly on Sundays. Almost every day except Saturday (when stores are closed), the discount garment stores in the streets off Delancey and Orchard streets are crowded. Ethnic food shops in the area are wonderful; Essex Street Market (Mon–Sat) shows the changes in the ethnic mix of residents.

LOWER EAST SIDE TENEMENT MUSEUM

✠ 61 G23 • 90 and 97 Orchard Street, between Broome and Delancey streets ☎ 212/431-0233 ◷ Guided tours only; available from the Visitor Center. Times vary but normally every 30 or 40 min Apr–end Nov Tue–Fri 1–4, Sat–Sun 11–4.30. Interactive program Sat–Sun noon, 1pm, 2pm, 3pm 💲 Adult $12, under 5 free. Interactive program: adult $11. Advance tickets (advisable), tel 800/965-4827 🚇 M9, M14A, M15 🚇 F, I, M, V, 7 🔲 ♿ 🛒 Guided tours
www.tenement.org

Four re-created apartments in a typical, five-story tenement dating from 1863 give a disturbing insight into how the other half lived, or at least managed to exist, in the overcrowded, unsanitary conditions common on the Lower East Side between the 1870s and 1920s.

Some 10,000 seekers of the American Dream and refugees from violent pogroms passed through this building over 70 years, as you learn on a guided tour. Fewer people go on each of these—never more than 15—than lived in a typical apartment. None of this is really for kids. For them, take in the interactive living history program, where they can try on period clothes and talk to "Victoria Confino," a Jewish teenager who lived here in 1916.

Guggenheim Museum

A masterpiece of modern architecture designed by Frank Lloyd Wright. Exhibiting one of the world's finest collections of modern and contemporary art.

The dramatic sweeping curves of the Guggenheim's exterior

Permanent exhibit Still Life: Flask, Glass and Jug *by Paul Cézanne*

Under the rotunda (above) the ramp spirals downward (right)

BASICS

✚ 59 E13 • 1071 Fifth Avenue at 89th Street 10028
☎ 212/423-3500
🕑 Sat–Wed 10–5.45, Fri 10–8
💲 Adult $18, under 12 free, Fri 5–8 pay-as-you-wish
🚌 M1, M2, M3, M4
🚇 4, 5, 6
📖 Free *Guggenheim Guide* containing listing of exhibits and programs, available at admission desk
🏪 Sat–Wed 9.30–5.45, Thu 9.30–3, Fri 9.30–8
🍽 Sat–Wed 9.30–6.15, Thu 11–6, Fri 9.30–8.30
🎧 Free tours daily. Reservations are taken at the information desk from 1.30

www.guggenheim.org
Links to the Guggenheim's museums in Venice, Berlin, Bilbao and Las Vegas; online listings of exhibitions with detailed information about each piece of art; museum store with innovative contemporary collectables.

SEEING THE GUGGENHEIM

As you enter, to your right is the admission desk, where you can pick up a free exhibitions program with a floor plan. As you look up at the five levels above the low white walls bordering the ramp you see a tall empty atrium-like space so dramatic that it is easy to forget that you came here to see modern art. Frank Lloyd Wright designed this building with the belief that the eye should not be confronted with angles and sudden changes of form when viewing works of art. From a logistical point of view, the best way to see the works hung here is to take the elevator to the skylit top and meander down the spiral ramp. However, the exhibits are often hung with the opposite path in mind.

HIGHLIGHTS

PAUL CÉZANNE, *STILL LIFE: FLASK, GLASS AND JUG*

In this 1877 still life, Cézanne (1839–1906) perceived objects in space as being interrelated. He created an illusion of objects resting and flowing simultaneously, calling attention to the two-dimensional canvas. This painting, and others, made Cézanne the foremost precursor of Cubism.

PABLO PICASSO, *WOMAN IRONING*

Painted in 1904 at the end of his Blue Period, *Woman Ironing* is Picasso's (1881–1973) quintessential work of labor and fatigue, reminiscent of the years he spent among the Paris working class. His expressionist style, with strong angular contours and attenuated proportions, expresses the woman's movement poetically, making her the metaphor for the pathos of the working poor.

MAX ERNST, *ATTIREMENT OF THE BRIDE*

This 1940s Surrealist painting by Max Ernst (1891–1976) evokes late 19th-century Symbolist painting, while the sleek, round-bellied figures recall motifs of 16th-century German art. The background architecture indicates the strong influence of the Italian painter Giorgio De Chirico. Ernst's invented alter-ego, the bird-man on the left, depicts the artist with a symbolic phallic spear. The picture-within-a-picture shows the same bride walking amid overgrown Classical ruins, indicating the role

of the bride throughout history. Garish colors and beastly figures suggest something violent about to happen.

BACKGROUND

The Solomon R. Guggenheim Museum, designed by Frank Lloyd Wright, opened on October 21, 1959. The inverted-ziggurat design, with its ramp encircling the walls, is as surprising today as it was when it was created. Solomon R. Guggenheim, a wealthy New Yorker whose father was a prominent 19th-century mining and smelting capitalist, used some of his wealth to buy works of art. He was content with Old Masters until 1927, when at the age of 66 he met baroness Hilla Rebay von Ehrenwiesen. The baroness favored European abstract art and introduced Guggenheim to such artists as Wassily Kadinsky, Fernand Léger and Robert Delaunay. It was she who suggested that Wright design a museum to house the great collection Guggenheim was amassing. Guggenheim died in 1949 and never saw the wondrous building, but Wright took on the job with enthusiasm and later pronounced it his "Pantheon."

Jeanne in a Yellow Jumper by Amedeo Modigliani (1919)

Lincoln Center

The Upper West Side's performing arts center offers the best in opera, classical music, chamber music, jazz, ballet and theater.

The Lincoln Center's fountains are dramatically lit at night

Take in a concert at Damrosch Park in summer

Colorful cafés line the Lincoln Center plaza

RATINGS

Good for kids	●●●
Photo stops	●●●●●
Specialist shopping	●●●●●
Value for money	●●●●●

BASICS

✚ 58 C16 • 70 Lincoln Center Plaza 10023-6583

☎ 212/546-2656 for main Lincoln Center

🚌 M5, M7, M10, M11, M66, M104

🚇 1, 9

🚶 One-hour tours daily from the concourse level of the Metropolitan Opera House 10.30–4.30, adult $12, child $5; backstage tours weekdays at 3.30 from Oct–end Jun only, Sat–Sun 10.30 (reservations tel 212/769-7020)

🍴 Avery Fisher Hall: Panevino Ristorante, tel 212/874-7000, Mon–Sat for dinner, lunch on matinée days

☕ Avery Fisher Hall: Café Vienna, 5pm–intermission nightly, opens at noon for matinées

🏬 The Performing Arts Shop, tel 212/441-1195; Metropolitan Opera Shop, tel 212/580-4090; Avery Fisher Hall Shop, tel 212/580-4356; New York Philharmonic Shop, tel 212/875-5437

♿

www.lincolncenter.org
Order tickets online, get visitor information about all events and performances.

With 14 venues offering everything from classical music to performances for children, the Lincoln Center is New York's premier center for performing arts. In the 1960s, a block of old tenements on the Upper West Side, where some of *West Side Story* was filmed, was demolished in a 12-block urban renewal project, and the Lincoln Center for the Performing Arts was built on the site. The initial investment for the Lincoln Center was more than $165 million. The state contributed the site and the rest of the money came from private contributions.

In 1962 the New York Philharmonic moved here from Carnegie Hall (▷ 76), which at the time was threatened with demolition. But the acoustics were never good, so in 1973 Avery Fisher donated $10 million to improve them. The hall closed for a time to undergo this work, but musicians and music-lovers were still not satisfied, so in 1992 the hall underwent further renovation.

OPERA, BALLET, THEATER, JAZZ

The New York State Theater is home to the New York City Opera and the New York City Ballet. The theater seats 2,700.

The Metropolitan Opera House, affectionately known as the Met, is home to both the opera company and the American Ballet Theater and seats 3,800. General manager Joe Volpe started as an apprentice carpenter and has worked his way up; he knows what attracts crowds and what doesn't.

The Guggenheim Bandshell in Damrosch Park, on 62nd Street near Amsterdam Avenue, hosts open-air concerts in summer.

The Lincoln Center Theater consists of the Vivian Beaumont Theater, with seating for 1,140, and the Mizi E. Newhouse Theater, an established Off Broadway venue.

Jazz, led by trumpeter and composer Wynton Marsalis, has moved from the Lincoln Center to the massive new Time Warner headquarters at nearby Columbus Circle, after receiving a $10 million gift from the Coca-Cola Company. The $128-million jazz venue is the focal point of the building, with three main performance spaces.

THE JUILLIARD SCHOOL OF MUSIC

The Juilliard School of Music is the top music school in the United

States. The campus includes Alice Tully Hall, a wonderful venue for chamber music and solo recitals, and the Walter Reade Film Theater, where the New York Film Festival sends up sparks every fall.

FUTURE PLANS

There is currently a plan to tear down Philharmonic Hall and start again; it is estimated that renovation of the existing building will cost half the amount of the projected $325 million reconstruction. When the New York Philharmonic is not in residence, leading orchestras give concerts in the house.

There are also plans to turn West 65th Street into a broad boulevard, much like a central artery of the Lincoln Center. This will be the first step in the $150-million redesign of the public areas and the center's buildings and grounds. The avant-garde design team of Diller and Scofidio, who are described as "artist architects," and specialize in experimental installations, have been selected for the project. Other features of the plan include technologically sophisticated signs with information about events, a sweeping staircase into the plaza, and a new look to a number of the buildings.

Marc Chagall's murals are visible through the windows of the Metropolitan Opera House

TIPS

● There is a vast underground parking area, if you dare drive in New York.
● Special events take place all year, from summer's Mostly Mozart concert series and swing dancing to live jazz under the stars and the annual run of the Big Apple Circus, which pitches its tent in Damrosch Park at the beginning of November.

Metropolitan Museum of Art

A spectacular collection spanning 5,000 years.

The entrance to the museum is imposing from any angle

Mary Cassatt's Lady at the Tea Table (1885)

The Petrie European Sculpture Court is an idyllic spot for a rest

SEEING THE METROPOLITAN MUSEUM OF ART

The grand main entrance, with its impressive neoclassical facade, is on Fifth Avenue at 82nd Street. Take a moment to look at the three-story banners announcing exhibits. As you enter the Great Hall inside the main entrance, go to the information desk to pick up a museum plan, which lists special exhibitions and new installations, and ask about the day's activities, including gallery talks. Allow plenty of time—there is much to see. The collections number more than 2 million items, with around 100,000 on display at any given time. It can be confusing if you simply wander around, so begin by deciding which galleries you want to see and go straight to them. You may wish to rent an audioguide; some focus on special exhibitions, others on selections from the permanent collection. Or join a free guided tour; sign up at an information desk in the Great Hall.

HIGHLIGHTS

GREEK AND ROMAN ART

Statue of a *Kouros*

With more than 35,000 works ranging from the Neolithic period to AD312, in beautifully renovated galleries, the Greek and Roman Art collection is one of the most comprehensive in North America.

In the center of the Steinhardt Gallery is the marble statue of a *kouros* (youth), one of the earliest of such statues of boys to survive complete. Carved in Naxian marble in Attica, the boy's rigid stance reflects the influence of Egyptian art. It is believed to have marked the grave of a young Athenian aristocrat.

Other Highlights

In the Belfer Court is a collection of terracotta pots, gemstones, figures and sculptures from the Neolithic period to the fifth century BC. There are interesting pieces from the Minoan Palace of Knossos in Crete and Roman copies of Hellenistic sculptures from classical Greece.

Upstairs are bronze mirrors from the sixth century BC, painted amphoras from the fifth century BC, Corinthian and Hellenistic pottery, and bronze reliefs from the Etrusco-Roman period.

Enter via the Great Hall, with its large ornamental flower planters

Take in the view from the Roof Garden, where a modern sculpture overlooks the museum's environs

BASICS

🚇 59 E14 • 1000 Fifth Avenue at East 82nd Street 10028-0198

☎ 212/879-5500

🕐 Tue–Thu, Sun 9.30–5.15, Fri–Sat 9.30–8.45

💰 Suggested donation (includes main building and same-day visit to The Cloisters) adult $15, under 12 with adult free

🚌 M1, M2, M3, M4 to 79th Street

🚇 4, 5, 6 to 86th Street

🎧 Audioguide to special exhibitions and selections from the permanent collection in English, Chinese, French, German, Italian, Korean, Portuguese, Russian, Spanish or Japanese: adult $6, under 12 $4. The Key to the Met Audio Guide provides commentary on selected works of art

🍴 Petrie Court Café plus cafeteria on first floor behind Medieval Hall

🏪 The Met Store prides itself on being the largest museum bookstore in America and offers reproductions of the collection's jewelry, china and other objets d'art

🚻

www.metmuseum.org
Informative introductions to collections. View highlights of 3,500 works of art online, get information on current exhibits, shop online from the Met Store.

THE SIGHTS

EUROPEAN SCULPTURE AND DECORATIVE ARTS
Bacchanal: A Faun Teased by Children
With 60,000 exhibits ranging from the Renaissance to the early 20th century, European sculpture is one of the largest departments in the museum. In the Northern Renaissance and Florence galleries is a sculpture by Rome's Gian Lorenzo Bernini (1598–1680), which he created when he was only 18. Distinctive of his revolutionary style, it breathes life into the marble with profound emotional and spiritual intensity. The satin-like texture, strong accented lines and bacchic subject are typical Bernini.

Small Desk *(Bureau Brisé)*
In the Louis XIV Gallery, this little oak, pine and walnut veneered desk, engraved with tortoiseshell, brass, ebony and rosewood, is one of a pair made in France for Louis XIV. It was made to fit into the king's small study in the north wing of the Palace of Versailles by a little-known cabinetmaker by the name of Alexandre-Jean Oppenordt (1639–1715). On the closed top is a barely distinguishable engraved mask of Apollo above the crown, and inlaid Apollo lyres on the top's sides.

Other Highlights
In the English galleries are a rococo-style dining room from Kirtlington Park, Oxfordshire, and a lavish dining room from Lansdowne House, London. The French galleries include a Paris shopfront from 1775, a daybed made for Marie Antoinette in the boudoir of the Hotel de Crillon, and in the Louis XVI Gallery, the king's desk from his study at Versailles .

Petrie European Sculpture Court
Not to be missed is the beautiful Petrie European Sculpture Court. Fountains and greenery and a splendid view of Central Park and Cleopatra's Needle provide a peaceful setting for fine Italian and French sculptures. Cleopatra's Needle was a gift from the Pasha of Egypt.

THE AMERICAN WING
One of the Met's most popular areas, the American Wing has three floors and centers on the splendid Charles Englehard Court. Focusing on the development of art and design in America, the collection fills 25 rooms with period furniture and furnishings, more than 1,000 paintings by American artists, 600 sculptures, 2,500 drawings and numerous examples of the decorative arts.

Louis Comfort Tiffany Vase
This vase, one of the first pieces of American glass in the collection, came from Louisine and Henry Havemeyer in 1896. Tiffany (1848–1933) showed his talents as a colorist, designer and naturalist in this beautiful example of his Favrile glass peacock vases—the fan shaped like a peacock's outspread plumage, the eyes of sliced glass millefiori canes, and the graceful lines depicting each individual feather.

Emmanuel Gottlieb Leutze, *Washington Crossing the Delaware*
Painted in 1851 by the German-born painter E. G. Leutze (1816–68), this American icon depicts General George Washington's surprise

KEY TO MAIN ROOMS

SECOND FLOOR
1: Modern art
2: 19th-century European paintings and sculpture
3: Islamic art
4: Cypriot art
5: Ancient Near Eastern art
6–7: Asian art
8: Musical instruments
9: American Wing: American paintings, sculpture, decorative arts and period rooms
10: European paintings
11: Special exhibitions

FIRST FLOOR
14: 20th-century paintings
15: Sculpture and artifacts from Africa, Oceania and the Americas
16: Greek and Roman art from prehistoric to classical
17: Egyptian art, Sackler Wing and Temple of Dendur
18: American Wing: American paintings, sculpture, decorative arts and period rooms
19: Arms and Armor: European, Islamic and Japanese armor, weaponry from Ottoman Turkish and Mughal Indian courts
20: European sculpture and decorative arts
21: Medieval art
22: Robert Lehman Collection: Old Masters, Impressionist, Post-Impressionist paintings
23: Library

GROUND FLOOR
25: Costume Institute: Late 16th-century to present clothing and costumes
26: Robert Lehman Collection

1
11
2
11
3
11
10
4
5
9
6
8
7
14
15
Museum Café
20
22
Central Park
21
16
23
20
18
The Great Hall
19
MAIN ENTRANCE
Grace Rainey Rogers Auditorium
17
Fifth Avenue
26
24
81st STREET ENTRANCE
25

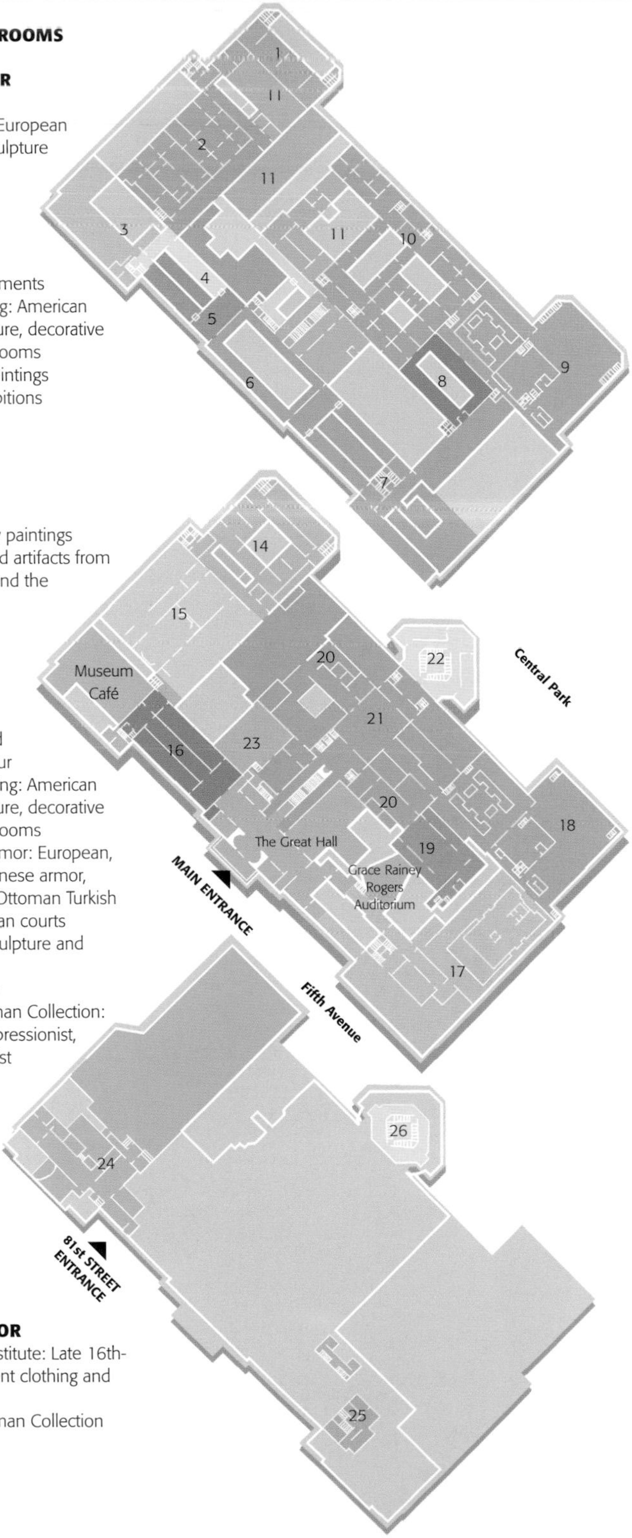

attack on the Hessians at Trenton, New Jersey, on Christmas night 1776. Washington's physical stamina and indomitable spirit as he leads 2,400 men to victory is central. In attempting to mythologize, Leutze takes liberties with history and focuses attention on inaccuracies such as the flag, not adopted until six months after the crossing. Leutze painted three versions of this work: The original went to the Kunsthalle in Bremen, the second was made for engraving.

Hart Room

The earliest interior in the American Wing, the Hart Room is from the home of Thomas Hart of Ipswich, Massachusetts. Built sometime between 1639 and 1674, this is a typical example of homes of the early New England settlers. The post-and-beam construction, much used in England, was both simple and sturdy. The bed is a reproduction ash and pine frame. The handwoven and sewn wool hangings around the bed helped to keep drafts away from the sleeper.

Other Highlights

In the airy Charles Englehard Court, linger to study Tiffany's *Garden Landscape and Fountain* and the beautiful stained-glass *Autumn Landscape*. The former was inspired by the Byzantine churches Tiffany saw while traveling in Europe. Turn to the right to see Tiffany's extravagant loggia from Laurelton Hall. The dahlias at the top of the columns are in three stages of growth: bud, full bloom and seed pod.

The sculptures in this glass-enclosed garden are by American artists Augustus Saint-Gaudens, Frederick MacMonnies and Daniel Chester French. In Gallery 127 is the work of the world-famous architect Frank Lloyd Wright. *Living Room from the Little House*, a very modern design in 1912, was designed for Francis Little.

Paintings and sculptures by American artists on this floor include John Singleton Copely's *Midshipman August Brine*, *The Falls of Niagara* by S. F. B. Morse, James McNeill *Whistler's Arrangement in Flesh, Color and Black*, John Singer Sargent's *Madame X* (1884), Mary Cassatt's *Lady at the Tea Table* (1885), and from the Hudson River School Frederic Church's *Heart of the Andes*.

EUROPEAN PAINTINGS

Albrecht Dürer, *Virgin and Child with St. Anne*

Germany's greatest Renaissance artist portrays St. Anne with her daughter, the Virgin Mary, holding the infant Jesus. It is believed that Dürer (1471–1528) painted this in 1519, at the time he was becoming an ardent follower of Martin Luther. By including St. Anne, who was a much-venerated saint in Germany, the artist was perhaps questioning the veracity of a virgin birth.

Vincent Van Gogh, *Cypresses*

Painted in 1889 when Van Gogh (1853–90) began his year-long confinement in the asylum at St-Rémy, *Cypresses* was one of several paintings the artist produced of familiar landscapes during this time. The illuminating shades of the background contrast sharply with the tree's splash of black. The use of swirls evokes the unpredictability of weather and the possible threat of the unknown.

Claude Monet, *Terrace at Sainte-Adresse*

Painted in 1867 at a time when Monet (1840–1926) was exploring new ways of representing modern life, this painting shocked his con-temporaries. The bold use of pure colors and strong contrasts combine to capture the blinding glare of the sun's reflection off the water, the paths and flowers. Giving balance and depth to the painting, the flags' movement gives the impression that the painter has caught a moment in time, like photographers would later be able to do with the camera.

Other Highlights

Among the many Italian masters' works are Raphael's *Madonna Enthroned with Child and Saints* (1505), Titian's *Venus and the Lute Player* (c1560), Tintoretto's *Finding of Moses* (c1550), Botticelli's *Last Communion of St. Jerome* (c1450) and Caravaggio's *Musicians* (1504). Early Dutch painters include a Rembrandt *Self-Portrait* (1660),

The marble statue of a youth, kouros, in the Steinhardt Gallery

Stroll among the statues in the Petrie European Sculpture Court

The Rocky Mountains, Lander's Peak, by Albert Bierstadt (1863)

Degas' The Dance Lesson (c1879)

Take an audiotour or a guided tour from the Great Hall

Vermeer's *Woman with a Water Jug* (1664) and works by de Hooch, van Goyen and others. French paintings include Poussin's *Rape of the Sabine Women* (c1635) and Jean Clouet's *Guillaume Budé*. Spanish works include El Greco's *View of Toledo* and *Grand Inquisitor Cardinal Don Fernando Niño de Guevara*. The English collection is represented by William Hogarth, Joshua Reynolds and Thomas Gainsborough.

European paintings of the 19th century include Millet's *Autumn Landscape with a Flock of Turkeys* (1872–73) and many Impressionist and Post-Impressionist paintings. Besides 100 works by Degas, there are paintings by Manet, Renoir, Seurat, Toulouse-Lautrec, Cézanne, Gauguin and Van Gogh. Worth seeing are one of Cézanne's best still lifes, *Still Life with Apples and a Pot of Primroses* (1895), and Monet's *Terrace at Sainte-Adresse* (c1867).

BACKGROUND

Members of New York's Union League Club—businessmen, artists and scholars—founded the Metropolitan Museum of Art in 1870. Originally at 681 Fifth Avenue, the museum moved to its present site in 1880. The original red-brick building, designed by Jacob Mould and Calvert Vaux, has been incorporated into the present museum and is visible in the Lehman Wing. The Richard Morris Hunt facade fronting Fifth Avenue was built in 1902. Beginning with a Roman sarcophagus, donations have continued over the years, but it was in 1904, when multimillionaire J. P. Morgan was elected president of the Board of Trustees, that world masterpieces became the main acquisitions. Morgan was not very interested in American art, nor in contemporary artists like Paul Gauguin and Henri de Toulouse-Lautrec, but preferred the Old Masters. A former Cypriot consul sold his collection of 6,000 objects to the museum, and Catherine L. Wolfe handed over 143 paintings of the Dutch and Flemish schools. Louis Comfort Tiffany's work was first presented in 1896 with 56 Favrile glass vases and in 1951 the Tiffany Foundation donated spectacular pieces from a private collection. In 2003, more than 100 works of art by Henri Matisse were given to the museum. The Met has also been running excavations for more than 30 years, and the finds are added to the collection.

TIPS

● To avoid long lines at the main entrance, enter at 81st Street, where there is a ticket and information desk.
● If you plan to visit the Cloisters (▷ 86) on the same day, it's best to visit the two sites on a Friday or Saturday, when the Met stays open later. Do the Cloisters in the morning and the Met in the afternoon.
● To avoid crowds, weekday mornings are optimal. Or plan a Friday or Saturday evening visit.
● Plan to take in the Roof Garden (May–end Oct). It's worth visiting not only for the splendid views of Central Park, the sandwiches and drinks, but also for the magnificent collection of sculptures.

The Metropolitan Life Insurance Tower stands proud

The elegant Ladies Parlour at the Mount Vernon Hotel

Stock-market ticker at the Museum of American Financial History

THE SIGHTS

MERCHANT'S HOUSE MUSEUM

✚ 60 F22 • 29 East 4th Street 10003
☎ 212/777-1089 ⏰ Thu–Mon 12–5
🚇 Adult $8, under 12 free 🚌 M1, M5, M6, M102 🚊 6, N, R 🚆 Tours every half hour Sat–Sun 🚻 ♿
www.merchantshouse.com

This museum is an 1832 time capsule, one of six Federal-style row houses with a charmingly gracious Greek Revival doorway. Bought by wealthy merchant Thomas Tredwell in 1835, the house was lived in by his daughter for 93 years. Renovated after her death in 1933, it was opened to the public as a museum in 1936 with the original furnishings intact, including personal family possessions. It is the only 19th-century house in Manhattan to be so completely preserved. Seven rooms on three floors and a secret garden are on view. Miss Tredwell is thought to have been the model for a character in Henry James' *Washington Square*.

METROPOLITAN LIFE INSURANCE TOWER

✚ 60 E20 • 1 Madison Avenue 🚌 M1, M3 🚊 4, 5, 6

Met Life's 1893 main building on 23rd Street stands on the site of the Madison Square Presbyterian Church, whose minister savagely attacked the corrupt politicians who ran the city in 1892. This 54-story tower, built in 1909, was their revenge. Planned as the tallest building in the world and a proud symbol of Met Life's promi-nence, it was soon overtaken by the Woolworth Building (▷ 144). The Met's campanile was 700ft (214m); in 1913, the Woolworth surpassed it by 92ft (28m).
   In 1962, the tower was stripped of its original ornamentation, leaving the gold dome and the huge clock faces.

METROPOLITAN MUSEUM OF ART

See pages 114–119.

MIDTOWN MANHATTAN

See page 121.

MORGAN LIBRARY

See page 122.

MOUNT VERNON HOTEL MUSEUM AND GARDEN

✚ 59 G16 • 421 East 61st Street at York Avenue ☎ 212/838-6878 ⏰ Tue–Sun 11–4; closed Aug 🚇 Adult $5, child free 🚌 M15, M31, M57 🚊 4, 6, N, R,
www.mountvernonhotelmuseum.org

In this splendid hotel, eight of the rooms were filled with Federal period furnishings by the Colonial Dames of America when they bought the structure in 1924. In the Gentlemen's Tavern Room, you're welcome to sit down and read a newspaper from 1828, and don't miss the museum's delightful 18th-century gardens. To get a feel for the place, visit the website and take a tour. The museum was a house that once belonged to Abigail Adams, the daughter of US president John Adams and the wife of George Washington's aide, William Stephens Smith. The Smiths had to sell the property in 1798 before all the buildings were complete and so never lived here. In 1826 the building underwent substantial internal alterations to convert it into a hotel. There are regularly scheduled events such as talks on American furniture of the early 19th century.

MUNICIPAL ART SOCIETY

✚ 59 E17 • 457 Madison Avenue 10022 ☎ 212/935-3960 reservations; 212/439-1049 for tours and meeting places ⏰ Mon–Wed, Fri–Sat 11–5 🚇 Guided walking tour weekdays $12; weekend walking and bus tour $15
www.mas.org

Founded in 1893, MAS is a non-profit, private, membership society aiming to promote a "more livable city." It advocates excellence in architecture, design and planning, public art and preservation of historic buildings, and believes sensible development is critical to the city's economic health and social well-being. It also organizes exhibitions and walking tours. The guides on these tours are highly qualified and give insights into the history and significance of the urban scene. Exhibitions are held at the headquarters, the Urban Center Galleries in one of the Villard Houses at the Helmsley Hotel, and are free and open to the public.

MUSEUM OF AMERICAN FINANCIAL HISTORY

✚ 61 E26 • 28 Broadway 10004 ☎ 212/908-4110 ⏰ Tue–Sat 10–4 🚊 4, 5 🚇 $2 contribution requested 🚻 ♿
www.financialhistory.org

On the site of Alexander Hamilton's law office, once the headquarters of multimillionaire John D. Rockefeller's Standard Oil Company, this four-room, Smithsonian Museum affiliate celebrates America's spirit of entrepreneurship with exhibits of coins, tickertape from the Wall Street Crash of 1929, curiously interesting photographs and murals of Wall Street and other documents and artifacts. Interactive financial news terminals help children understand the stock market. Special exhibitions have included informative displays about the history of the Dow Jones Industrial Average, banknote engraving and counterfeiting. The shop has interesting gifts for that person who has everything.

The view across town from the dizzying heights of the legendary Empire State Building

MIDTOWN MANHATTAN

Chic shopping, high-priced hotels, skyscrapers, landmarks and bright lights.

Midtown Manhattan stretches from 34th Street to 59th Street, with Fifth Avenue—where shopping is a big attraction—splitting it into east and west. Megastores have made it big in Times Square and the Theater District, while Fifth Avenue and 57th Street are lined with the most glamorous names like Gucci and Chanel. In the past few years, retailers Niketown, Banana Republic and Liz Claiborne have moved in, joining classic Saks Fifth Avenue, Tiffany & Co. and Bergdorf Goodman on the stretch of Fifth Avenue from 49th to 59th streets.

Midtown has New York's major train station, bus stations, the largest concentration of hotels, big stores and corporate headquarters. Midtown West includes the Garment District and the Theater District, with Times Square and New York's longest street, Broadway (▷ 138–140), at the heart of it.

Bryant Park is where tents are set up in September for New York's Fashion Week, no matter what the weather. Here there are museums like the International Center of Photography (▷ 101), Museum of Arts and Design (▷ 123), the Museum of Television and Radio (▷ 124) and the Museum of Modern Art (▷ 125). Rockefeller Center (▷ 128–130) and the home of the Rockettes, Radio City Music Hall (▷ 129), are in Midtown. Along the Hudson River, there's the Intrepid Sea, Air and Space Museum (▷ 101).

LANDMARK SIGHTS

Architectural landmarks in Midtown East include the Chrysler Building (▷ 85), the Chanin Building and the Daily News Building (▷ 87). Nearby is Grand Central Terminal (▷ 102–104). At 301 Park Avenue is the famous Waldorf-Astoria Hotel (▷ 308), where kings, queens and presidents have stayed. Along Madison Avenue are the stunning Villard Houses, notable for their turn-of-the-20th-century extravagance, now part of the Helmsley Palace Hotel. At the east end of 42nd Street is Tudor City, with 3,000 apartments and its own restaurants, parks, stores and post office. The United Nations Headquarters (▷ 144) stands on the East River, not actually on U.S. land, but on international territory belonging to the member nations. It has a serenity that sets it apart here.

Broadway is synonymous with theater and entertainment

RATINGS	
Historic interest	● ● ● ● ●
Photo stops	● ● ● ●
Specialist shopping	● ● ● ● ●
Walkability	● ● ● ●

BASICS

✚ 59 E18 • 34th to 59th streets
🚌 M1, M2, M3, M4, M6
Ⓜ 4, 5, N, R
🍴 Oyster Bar Grand Central Terminal lower level, tel 212/490-6650
☕ Café Soleil, 135 East 56th Street, tel 212/832-0199; Bryant Park Café, 25 West 40th Street (behind New York Public Library), tel 212/840-6500, in summer eating outdoors

The Adoration of the Magi, *from a choirbook executed in about 1540*

MORGAN LIBRARY

An astonishing collection of rare books, illuminated and literary manuscripts and drawings by the Western world's most creative geniuses.

The decorated facade of the Morgan Library

RATINGS	
Cultural interest	● ● ● ● ●
Historic interest	● ● ●
Specialist shopping	● ● ●
Value for money	● ● ● ●

BASICS
✚ 60 E19 • 29 East 36th Street 10016
☎ 212/685-0610
⏱ Tue–Thu 10.30–5, Fri 10.30–8, Sat 10.30–6, Sun noon–6
💷 Suggested admission: adult $7, under 16 with adult free
🚇 M2, M3, M4
Ⓜ 6
🍴 Morgan Court Café serves lunch and afternoon tea
📖 Bookshop closes 15 min before galleries
🚻
www.morganlibrary.org

The Morgan Library reopened in spring 2006 with twice the gallery space, an enlarged auditorium, a café, a bigger shop and more open public spaces, following three years of improvement work. The Reading Room is now better equipped and the storage areas are improved.

By the end of the 19th century, John Pierpont Morgan was one of New York's wealthiest financiers. To fulfill his desire to match Europe's greatest libraries, he began his opulent private library of European cultural treasures: manuscripts, paintings, prints and furniture. His travels abroad resulted in this priceless collection of nearly 10,000 draw- ings and prints, including some by Leonardo da Vinci and Albrecht Dürer. In 1902, he commissioned Charles McKim to design the magnificent Renaissance-style building. Later additions include those by Benjamin Morris in 1928, the annex, which was Morgan's private residence, at 231 Madison Avenue, and the garden courtyard in the 1990s.

MORGAN'S STUDY

The West Room of the library remains as Morgan left it when he died in 1913. He used it as a study and his huge wooden desk is still here, along with the Italian Renaissance paintings lining the walls. From the study you pass green-veined marble columns as you proceed toward the rotunda and the East Room. The beautiful three-tiered, walnut and bronze bookcases are almost as amazing as the ceiling covered with frescoes and the signs of the zodiac. Notice the 16th-century Flemish tapestry above the fireplace. But it is the collection of letters and manuscripts that most intrigues.

Morgan acquired nearly 600 medieval and Renaissance manuscripts, including the 9th-century Lindau Gospels, a rare vellum copy of the Gutenberg Bible, and the medieval Dutch masterpiece *The Hours of Catherine of Cleves*. He also purchased handwritten scores by such composers as Beethoven, Mozart and Puccini, which are protected under glass. The collection also includes manuscripts by authors of the calibre of Jane Austen, Charles Dickens, Henry David Thoreau and Mark Twain.

The Museum of Chinese in the Americas was founded in 1980

Modern and chic objects for daily use are on display in the Museum of Arts and Design

THE SIGHTS

MUSEUM OF ARTS AND DESIGN

➕ 59 E17 • 40 West 53rd Street 10019 ☎ 212/956-3535 🕐 Daily 10–6, Thu until 8 💰 Adult $9, under 12 free, pay-as-you-wish Thu 6–8 🚇 M1, M2, M3, M4 🚇 E, V 🏧 👬
www.americancraftmuseum.org

In this museum (formerly the American Craft Museum), the American Craft Council displays the nation's biggest exhibition of 20th-century American and international crafts. From jewelry to baskets, furniture to teapots, everything is carefully selected to represent the finest in form and function. Stimulating special exhibitions are chosen from the extensive, wide-ranging collections, augmented by loans from other collections, to illustrate contemporary trends in technique and design. It's all shown to great advantage in a spacious, three-story atrium. Past exhibitions have included a retrospective on U.S. design from 1975 to 2000 and another showcasing elaborate cake decorating.

MUSEUM OF BIBLICAL ART

➕ 58 D16 • 1865 Broadway at 61st Street 10023 ☎ 212/408-1500 🕐 Tue–Sun 10–6 (Thu until 8) 💰 Free 🚇 M5, M7, M10, M104 🚇 59th Street/Columbus Circle (A, B, C, D, 1, 9)
www.mobia.org

This museum aims to foster an understanding and appreciation of art inspired by the Bible. It opened its new building in 2005 with an inaugural exhibition of works by self-taught Southern folk artists. The museum evolved out of the American Bible Society (1816), which had amassed a huge collection of scripture, now on view behind a glass curtain wall in the main gallery. Exhibitions focus on the collection's highlights, such as the recent For Glory and for Beauty, which displayed 29 rare scriptures.

MUSEUM OF CHINESE IN THE AMERICAS

➕ G1 F24 • 70 Mulberry Street, 2nd Floor 10013 ☎ 212/619-4785 🕐 Tue–Sun noon–6 (Fri until 7) 💰 Adult $3 🚇 M103 🚇 N, Q, R 🏧 👬
www.moca-nyc.org

This museum exhibits photographs and other works of visual art, rare historical documents, musical instruments, clothing and artifacts that help to explain Chinese history and culture. MoCA's very moving core exhibit, Where is Home?, interprets themes such as migration, abandonment, customs, women and home. Temporary exhibits are equally interesting. Post 9/11, Recovering Chinatown displayed images, artwork and other materials documenting the experience of Chinatown residents during and after the attack on the World Trade Center. Gotta Sing Gotta Dance! offered insight into the world of Chinese-American performers from the 1930s and the 1940s.

MUSEUM OF THE CITY OF NEW YORK

➕ Off map 59 E12 • 1220 Fifth Avenue 10029 ☎ 212/534-1672 🕐 Tue–Sun 10–5. Preregistered groups only Tue 10.30–noon 💰 Suggested admission: adult $7, child $4, family $15 🚇 M1, M2, M3, M4, M106 🚇 6 📷 Highlights tour Sat noon 🏧 👬
www.mcny.org

A neo-Georgian, colonial-style villa built in 1929 houses this museum devoted to New York's history and life. The collections here hold more than 1.5 million objects relating to the social and economic life of the city— paintings, photographs, costumes, toys, decorative arts and other artifacts. Some are world-class, like the silver collection and the collection on American theater; the photography, marine and costume collections are also outstanding. The museum has sometimes been criticized for taking a dull approach to display, but lively exhibitions such as those devoted to Glamor New York Style and Puerto Rican New York have helped to change that reputation.

MUSEUM OF JEWISH HERITAGE

➕ 61 E26 • 36 Battery Place 10280 ☎ 646/437-4200 🕐 Sun–Tue, Thu 10–5.45, Wed 10–8, Fri and eve of Jewish holidays 10–5; closed Jewish holidays and Thanksgiving 💰 Adult $10, under 12 free 🚇 M1, M6, M9, M10, M15 🚇 4, 5 📷 🖥 🏧 👬
www.mjhnyc.org

This museum, opened in 1996 and designed by Kevin Roche and John Dinkeloo in a hexagonal shape to represent the Star of David, houses an exhibition of 20th-century Jewish history and culture. Presenting the story of Jewish tragedy and suffering, survival and renewal, the museum has three main sections: Jewish Life a Century Ago, The War Against the Jews, and Jewish Renewal.

Displays take you back to the now-vanished worlds of a century ago, through the horror of industrialized mass murder, to the resurgence of hope in a world not yet free of hatred and intolerance. Film clips, interspersed with displays of physical objects, include testimonies from Spielberg's Survivors of the Shoah project and footage from the museum's own archives.

Statue of Diana the Hunter in the National Academy of Design

Christian Schad's Maika (1929) *in the Neue Galerie*

Nineteenth-century fire carriages at the New York City Fire Museum

MUSEUM OF MODERN ART

See page 125.

MUSEUM OF TELEVISION AND RADIO

✚ 59 E17 • 25 West 52nd Street 10019
☎ 212/621-6800 ◷ Tue–Sun noon–6, Thu until 8, Fri theater programs until 9
🚻 Adult $10, under 14 $5 🚇 M1, M2, M3, M4 🚊 E, V ✇ 🍴 📷 🚻
www.mtr.org

William S. Paley, former chairman of CBS and now chairman of the museum, donated the land for this 17-story building, erected in 1989, to a design by architects Philip Johnson and John Burgee. Theaters, screening rooms, three public galleries and individual viewing and listening consoles are your access to the museum's collection of tapes of 100,000 programs and commercials celebrating more than 75 years. Thousands of new programs are added every year.

When you arrive, make a reservation to use the computer catalog on the fourth floor to locate what interests you, then reserve it and watch it in one of the museum's consoles. Or take in a show or two at one of the screening rooms or theaters. Seminars and classes, as well as exhibitions, are held throughout the year.

NATIONAL ACADEMY OF DESIGN

✚ 59 E13 • 1083 Fifth Avenue 10128
☎ 212/369-4880 ◷ Wed–Thu noon–5, Fri 10–6, Sat–Sun 11–6 🚻 Adult $10
🚇 M1, M2, M3, M4 🚊 4, 5, 6
✇ Gallery talks Wed 12.30; docent tours Wed–Thu after 11am, Fri–Sun after 10am
📷 Wed–Thu 10–5, Fri 10–6, Sat–Sun 11–6 🚻
www.nationalacademy.org

The National Academy of Design was founded in 1825 by a group of accomplished artists, architects,

sculptors and engravers, including artist/inventor Samuel Morse. It is both a museum and a school of fine art, and also owns the largest collection of 19th- and 20th-century American art in the country—an astonishing collection with more than 5,000 works ranging from portraiture of the Federalist period, landscapes of the Hudson River School, gritty realism of the Ashcan Movement, and paintings representing movements from Fauvism to photo-realism. The building was the home of Archer Milton Huntington and his wife, the sculptor Anna Hyatt Huntington. In 1913, they expanded and remodeled the house and lived here until 1939, when they gave it to the National Academy of Design, who moved in three years later. Tours covering the collection's highlights and Edith Wharton's New York are available.

NEUE GALERIE

✚ 59 E13 • 1048 Fifth Avenue 10028
☎ 212/628-6200 ◷ Fri 11–9, Sat–Mon 11–6 🚻 Adult $10, no children 🚇 M1, M2, M3, M4 🚊 4, 5, 6 🍴 📷 🚻
www.neuegalerie.org

This museum, dedicated to early 20th-century German and Austrian art and design, has a marvelous collection of fine paintings, decorative arts and other media, including works by Gustav Klimt, Paul Klee, Egon Schiele, Josef Hoffmann and Adolf Loos.

On Friday nights there are cabarets in Café Sabarsky, which serves Austrian fare, including delicious pastries. Some of the furniture is by Adolf Loos, and lighting fixtures are by Josef Hoffmann. The 1914 Carrère & Hastings mansion housing the museum was built for Mrs. Cornelius Vanderbilt III, and is every bit as remarkable as the collection.

NEW MUSEUM OF CONTEMPORARY ART

✚ 61 F23 • 556 West 22nd Street at Eleventh Avenue ☎ 212/219-1222
◷ Tue–Wed, Fri–Sun noon–6, Thu noon–8 🚻 Adult $6 (Thu 6–8 $3), under 18 free 🚇 M11 🚊 C, E 📷 🚻
www.newmuseum.org

The museum has been inviting international contemporary artists to mount shows of experimental work since 1977. It presents six major exhibits each year and five Media Lounge shows in a space dedicated to digital art, experimental video and sound works. This address is temporary while the museum builds a new home at 235 Bowery at Prince Street (61 E23), designed by Tokyo-based architects SANAA. It is scheduled to open in 2007.

NEW YORK CITY FIRE MUSEUM

✚ 61 E23 • 278 Spring Street at Hudson/Varick 10013 ☎ 212/691-1303
◷ Tue–Sat 10–5, Sun 10–4
🚻 Contribution requested (adult $5, child $1) 🚇 M10, M21 🚊 C, E
✇ Tours by appointment 📷 🚻
www.nycfiremuseum.org

A former firehouse of Rescue Company No.1, built in 1904, this museum packs three floors with firefighting paraphernalia, the most comprehensive collection in the United States. Equipment from the 1700s to the present includes buckets, pumps, horse-drawn fire engines, a fire hydrant, hosepipes, axes, uniforms and helmets old and new, and there's an exhibit on fire safety and burn prevention. Firefighters are usually around to explain and share stories.

This is one of the best places in the city to pay tribute to the 343 firefighters who lost their lives on September 11, 2001. You can also see exhibits relating to the disaster.

Among many fine works is Van Gogh's The Starry Night *(1889)*

MUSEUM OF MODERN ART

The world's greatest collection of painting and sculpture from the late 19th century to the present.

When MoMA opened in 1929 it occupied six rooms on 57th Street. Today, after a dramatic $425 million renovation by architect Yoshio Taniguchi, it offers an unparalleled collection of modern and contemporary art. The new MoMA opened in November 2004 to much acclaim. Taniguchi's redesign doubled the institution's space, allowing it to display much more of its superb collection. Visitors can now enter from 53rd or 54th streets to view the galleries, which are clustered around a 110ft tall (34m) atrium, which diffuses light throughout the building and gives great views of the sculpture garden, which features Aristide Maillol's *The River*, Henry Moore's *Family Group* and other works in an inviting outdoor setting.

COLLECTIONS AND EXHIBITIONS

The permanent collection, spanning art from the late 19th century to the late 1960s, is displayed on the fourth and fifth floors. The works are displayed in chronological sequence to create a comprehensive history of modern art. The 12 galleries on the fifth floor cover Post-impressionism, Cubism, Italian Futurism, Austrian and German Expressionism, Social Realism and Surrealism. Each boasts a string of masterpieces; Vincent Van Gogh's *The Starry Night* and Salvador Dalí's *The Persistence of Memory* are just two of the most celebrated examples. One gallery is devoted entirely to Matisse. Fourth-floor galleries present works from the late 1940s to the late 1960s and include works by such major artists as Willem de Kooning, Jasper Johns, Francis Bacon and Andy Warhol, as well as some splendid holdings of Jackson Pollock's work.

Contemporary works created since 1970 are shown in the second-floor galleries, which also include a dedicated media gallery. The collections of drawings, photography, architecture, and design are found on the third floor. The drawing collection contains 7,000 works from 1880 onward and the photography collection 25,000 works, which document the development of photography from the 1840s. The photograph collection ranges from Henri Cartier-Bresson to Diane Arbus, highlighted by William Fox Talbot's *Lace* and Paul Strand's *Fifth Avenue, New York*. With 19,000 films and four million film stills, the Film and Media Department is also impressive. The sixth floor is reserved for special exhibits.

Yoshio Taniguchi's new MoMA, from 53rd Street

RATINGS	
Good for kids	● ● ●
Historic interest	● ● ● ●
Specialist shopping	● ● ●
Value for money	● ● ● ●

BASICS

✚ 59 E17 • 11 West 53rd Street 10019

☎ 212/708-9400

🕐 Sat–Mon 10.30–5.30, Wed–Thu 10.30–5.30, Fri 10.30–8; closed Tue

💵 Adult $20, under 16 with adult free, free Fri 4–8; audioguide $5

Ⓔ Fifth Avenue/53rd Street (E, V), 47th–50th St/Rockefeller Center (B, D, F)

🚌 M1, M2, M3, M4, M5

🎧 Audioguide $5

🍴 2 restaurants, 3 cafés

🏬 MoMA Design and Book Store at museum, tel 212/708-9700; MoMA Design Store, 44 West 53rd Street, tel 212/767-1050; MoMA Design Store SoHo, 81 Spring Street, tel 646/613-1367

👥
www.moma.org

100 Old Slip in former days, now the New York City Police Museum

Indian, at the New-York Historical Society

The Gothic Revival interior of the Riverside Church

THE SIGHTS

NEW YORK CITY POLICE MUSEUM

✠ 61 F26 • 100 Old Slip 10005 ☎ 212/480-3100 ⏰ Tue–Sat 10–5, Sun 11–5 💰 Suggested donation adult $5, child (6–18) $2 🚌 M9, M15 🚇 2, 3, N, R 🏛 ♿
www.nycpolicemuseum.org

This small museum exhibits a collection of uniforms, ceremonial batons, New York Police Department (NYPD) shields, handguns, and even the machine gun used by Al Capone's gang to assassinate Frankie Yale, the first homicide in New York by such a weapon.

Visit a prison cell and see the display on vintage weapons and notorious criminals, which includes arrest records. Learn about fingerprinting and forensics, then view the NYPD Hall of Heroes, which now has a memorial to the 23 policemen and women who died in the attack on the World Trade Center.

NEW-YORK HISTORICAL SOCIETY

✠ 58 D14 • 170 Central Park West at 77th Street 10024 ☎ 212/873-3400 ⏰ Museum: Tue–Sun 10–6. Library: Tue–Sat 10–5 (mid-May to end Aug Tue–Fri 10–5). Print Room by appointment only 💰 Adult $10, child under 13 free 🚌 M10, M79 🚇 B, C 🎧 Audiotours, docent tours Tue–Sun at 1pm, 3pm 🏛 ♿
www.nyhistory.org

At Central Park West, this Upper West Side museum is a great place to spend a morning or afternoon. For nearly 200 years, the New-York Historical Society has been collecting, preserving and interpreting books, paintings, sculpture, photographs and newspapers. The fascinating Henry Luce III Center on the fourth floor displays lamps by Louis Comfort Tiffany, Hudson River School landscapes, a

complete set of original watercolors by John James Audubon for *The Birds of America*, George Washington's inaugural chair, and much more. The library is the oldest research library in the country.

NEW YORK PUBLIC LIBRARY

See page 127.

RECTORY OF THE SHRINE OF ELIZABETH ANN SETON

✠ 344 E26 • 7 State Street ☎ 212/269-6865 ⏰ Mon–Fri, ring bell for admission

From 1801 to 1803, this red-brick town house was the home of the New York socialite and mother of five, Elizabeth Ann Seton, the first American-born woman to be canonized by the Roman Catholic Church.

Born in 1774, she converted to Catholicism as an adult and became a spiritual leader and educator. She founded the first order of nuns in the US: the Sisters of Charity. Her legacy includes six religious communities with more than 5,000 members, hundreds of schools, and social service centers and hospitals in the US and all over the world. Pope Paul VI declared her a saint in 1975.

RIVERSIDE CHURCH

✠ Off map 58 C12 • 490 Riverside Drive 10027 ☎ 212/870-6700 ⏰ Gift shop: Tue–Thu, Sat 10.30–5, Wed 10.30–7, Sun 9.45–10.45, noon–4 🚌 M4, M5, M60, M104 🚇 1, 9 🏛 ♿
www.riversidechurch.net

Philanthropist John D. Rockefeller, Jr. funded the construction of this 21-story, steel-frame Gothic Revival church. Designed to resemble Chartres Cathedral in France, and completed in 1930,

it is an interdenominational, interracial and international church. Nelson Mandela, Martin Luther King, Jr., and the Children's Defense funder Marion Wright-Edelman have all spoken from the pulpit. The bell tower houses the world's largest carillon, with 74 bells, as well as a 20-ton brass bell. A viewing platform on top of the tower gives a glorious view over the Hudson River (call ahead to check when it's open). Inside are beautiful stained-glass windows and a cast of Jacob Epstein's *Christ in Majesty*. Another work by Epstein, *Madonna and Child,* is on the lawn.

ROCKEFELLER CENTER

See pages 128–130.

ROOSEVELT ISLAND

✠ 59 G15 • In the East River between Manhattan and Queens 🚡 Tram fare $2 🚌 Q102 🚇 F

You can take the subway to Roosevelt Island if you are afraid of heights, but the East 60th Street Heliport Aerial Tramway is a much more fun way to travel the 300 yards (274m) over the East River. Today there are 8,000 residents on the island, which is 2 miles (3.4km) long and only 800ft (250m) wide.

With its quiet streets, well-planned housing and great views of the Manhattan skyline, Roosevelt Island is a much sought-after area in which to live thanks to Roosevelt Island Operating Corporation, which was created in 1984 to run this "town-in-town." Up to the 19th century it was farmed by the Blackwell family, then it housed a prison, a mental health facility, the Octagon Building (1842), as well as the Smallpox Hospital (1854) and at the northern tip, a lighthouse (1872), both designed by James Renwick, Jr.

Looking down on the Main Reading Room, where the reading tables are often fully occupied

NEW YORK PUBLIC LIBRARY

Fascinating exhibits of New York culture inside a grand and beautifully restored Beaux Arts building.

Some things in New York are surprises, and this amazing research library is one of them. The massive white marble building, one of the first major commissions of the firm Carrère & Hastings in 1911, is absolutely gorgeous. Half of its $9-million cost was donated by steel magnate and philanthropist Andrew Carnegie (1835–1918). The two lions at the foot of the staircase fronting the museum are New York icons affectionately named Patience and Fortitude by New York's 1930s mayor, Fiorello LaGuardia; in the gift shop they adorn tote bags, spoons, charm bracelets, bookends, paperweights and more.

Up the imposing staircase and through the triple-arched portico is beautiful Astor Hall, named after John Jacob Astor (1763–1848), whose private library, along with that of James Lenox, was the foundation of this great collection. (Former New York governor Samuel J. Tilden bequeathed the $2.4 million to combine the libraries and erect the building.)

WHAT TO SEE, AND WHERE

Upon entering, pick up a floor plan at the information desk and ask about free tours. Gottesman Hall, straight ahead, displays temporary exhibits. The DeWitt Wallace Periodical Room, to the left, is embellished with Richard Haas murals of New York magazine and newspaper offices. At the top of the marble stairs is the McGraw Rotunda. The stupendous Main Reading Room, restored in 1998 so that the oak and brass gleam, is to your right. Across the hall is the Edna Barnes Salomon Room, where recent popular exhibitions have included New York Eats Out, Baseball at the Library, Prints of James McNeill Whistler (1834–1903) and The Charles Adams Mother Goose.

This is not a lending library, but there are more than 80 branches in Manhattan and the outer boroughs. Occasionally, you can see important items here from the vast collection, which include a Gutenberg Bible, a 1493 folio edition of a letter written by Christopher Columbus describing his discoveries in the New World, a first folio edition of Shakespeare's works from 1623, an early draft of Thomas Jefferson's Declaration of Independence, and much more.

One of two stone lions lounging on the front steps of the library

RATINGS	
Historic interest	● ● ●
Photo stops	● ● ●
Specialist shopping	● ● ● ● ●

BASICS
✚ 60 E18 • Fifth Avenue and 42nd Street 10018
☎ 212/661-7220 or 930-0830
🕐 Thu–Sat 10–6, Tue–Wed 11–7.30, Sun 1–6
👆 Free
🚌 M1, M2, M3, M4
Ⓜ B, D, F
🎫 Free tours Mon–Sat 11 and 2 from Astor Hall
📷 👬

www.nypl.org
The library catalog, Digital Library Collections, sections for teenagers, health information and an online exhibition.

Rockefeller Center

**A vital urban enclave in the heart of Manhattan.
More than 100 art deco works by 30 artists, including Paul Manship's iconic
gilded bronze *Prometheus* and Lee Lawrie's *Atlas*.
Home of Radio City Music Hall, a spectacular art deco landmark and home of the Rockettes.**

Gilded sculpture on the front of the center

New Yorkers frequently take time out at Rockefeller Center

Radio City Music Hall is used for live concerts and film premieres

BASICS

✚ 59 E17 • West 48th to West 51st streets, between Fifth and Sixth avenues

☎ 212/664-3700

🎟 Free

🚌 M1, M2, M27, M50

Ⓜ B, D, F, Q

📖 Free walking-tour brochure from the main information desk in the lobby of the G. E. Building

🍴 Many eateries and restaurants including Cucina & Co., Mendy's Kosher Deli, Hale and Hearty, Ben & Jerry's. The Rainbow Room, 65th floor of the G. E. Building, tel 212/632-5000, is famous for its art deco revolving dance floor

☕ Rockefeller Center Café, 20 West 50th Street, tel 212/332-7620

👬

www.RockefellerCenter.com
View artwork from Rockefeller Plaza online; links to restaurants and cafés, Radio City Music Hall, NBC Store, ice-skating rink.

SEEING ROCKEFELLER CENTER

To get a good sense of the place begin at Channel Gardens, on Fifth Avenue between 49th and 50th streets, which are six pools surrounded by pretty flower boxes running between the Maison Française and the British Empire Building (hence the name). Straight ahead as you face the Channel Gardens, with your back to Fifth Avenue, is Rockefeller Plaza, with its sunken garden, which is turned into an ice-skating rink in winter and a restaurant in summer. The gilded *Prometheus,* stealing the sacred fire from the Greek gods to give to man, rises ahead, while flags flutter around the plaza's perimeter. At the top of the steps down to the Lower Plaza a bronze plaque from multimillionaire and philanthropist John D. Rockefeller, whose fortune built Rockefeller Center, praises the virtues of hard work. On the southeast corner of the Lower Plaza is a branch of the Metropolitan Museum of Art Store, full of elegant souvenirs and gifts. As the complex is large, it is best to pick up a walking-tour guide from the information desk in the lobby of the G. E. Building to help you decide what to see and do.

HIGHLIGHTS

THE G. E. BUILDING

Over the east entrance of this prominent tower, the former RCA Building, is Lee Lawrie's limestone-and-glass frieze, *Wisdom*, inspired by William Blake's painting of the same name. The beautiful granite and marble east lobby is worth visiting; it houses José Maria Sert's sepia mural *Man's Conquests*, commissioned to replace one by Diego Rivera, which was rejected because it included an image of Joseph Stalin. The anticommunist Rockefellers had insisted that Rivera remove the offending portrait, but Rivera refused and his mural was destroyed. The signature clock on the 51st Street corner has projecting arms grasping electric bolts (RCA was a subsidiary of General Electric). The stylized figures at the building's crown have haloes of electric rays. The viewing platform is open to patrons of the elegant Rainbow Room restaurant on the 65th floor; for a drink and a view, stop in at the adjacent Rainbow Grill.

ICE-SKATING RINK

Ⓒ Mid-Oct to mid-Apr Mon–Thu 9am–10.30pm, Fri–Sat 8.30am–midnight, Sun 8.30am–10pm Ⓓ Adult $9 weekdays/$13 weekends, child $7 weekdays/$8 weekends, skate rental $6

When this ice rink in the Lower Plaza opened on Christmas Day 1933, it was a novelty made possible by new refrigeration technology. Today, a quarter of a million skaters test their blades here every year. The rink is small—only 122ft long (37m) and 59ft (18m) wide.

RADIO CITY MUSIC HALL

With about 6,000 seats, Radio City was the world's largest theater when it opened in 1932. Impresario Samuel (Roxy) Rothafel's original plans were for live entertainment, but movies soon became the main fare, with the high-kicking Roxyettes, later called the Rockettes, performing before each feature film. Donald Deskey was the interior design co-ordinator. The great arched proscenium in the form of a setting sun is an art deco masterpiece. The Grand Foyer's 24-carat gold-leaf ceiling, sweeping staircase and elegant chandeliers are breathtaking. Radio City was designated a New York City Landmark in 1979 and a National Historic Landmark in 1987. Intensive renovation in the late 1990s then won it a National Preservation Award in 2000.

"LATE NIGHT WITH CONAN O'BRIEN"

To get standby tickets to join the studio audience of this popular late-night show, line up at 9am on the day of taping outside 30 Rockefeller Plaza on 49th Street under the NBC Studios awning. Or reserve tickets in advance by calling 212/664-3056. You must be aged at least 16 to attend.

"TODAY SHOW"

Every weekday between 7 and 9am, hundreds of people crowd the blue police barricades at the corner of West 49th Street and Rockefeller Plaza, just outside the ground-level NBC studio of the long-running morning "Today Show." The lure is a glimpse of anchors Katie Couric and Matt Lauer, a brief chat with weatherman Al Roker, or national exposure for a greeting for the folks back home scrawled on

In winter skaters show off their flashier moves at the Lower Plaza ice-skating rink

RATINGS				
Good for kids	● ●			
Photo stops	● ● ● ●			
Specialist shopping	● ● ● ● ●			
Walkability	● ● ● ● ●			

TIPS

● If you're in town between early December and early January don't miss Rockefeller Center. An enormous Christmas tree is put up and decked with 20,000 tiny lights—a favorite New York tradition.

● Go early if you plan to ice-skate on the rink in the Lower Plaza. The rink can hold only 150 skaters at a time and it gets busy, especially at lunchtime. Skate rentals and rink fees are cash only—and not cheap.

● NBC Experience store, 49th Street and Rockefeller Plaza, offers one-hour tours of news and entertainment studios. See the "Saturday Night Live" set: Arrive before noon in the busy holiday and summer period to get tickets, which are on a first-come, first-served basis.

The gilded Prometheus *heralds the entrance to the center*

WISDOM AND KNOWLEDGE SHALL BE THE STABILITY OF THY TIMES

Lee Lawrie's relief over the entrance to the G. E. Building (above right); one of Jose Maria Sert's sepia murals (above)

a piece of cardboard. Spirits are high and the mood almost giddy. In good weather, a segment or two may be presented outdoors on the street. In winter, you can get a good view of the action from the Dean & Deluca coffee shop across the street.

BACKGROUND

The land on which Rockefeller Center stands belonged to Columbia University at the beginning of the 20th century. The university rented the land to farmers, but eventually developers came along and put up brownstones. By the late 1920s, the area was noisy and unpleasant, with elevated trains rumbling down Sixth Avenue and many residents too poor to spend money on the upkeep of the buildings. During Prohibition, the area was known as the "speakeasy belt," and along 52nd Street police raids were common. When liquor regained its legal status, the area became a popular setting for jazz clubs, where great musicians like Count Basie and Harry James entertained.

In 1928, John D. Rockefeller leased 12 acres (5ha) from Columbia University in order to build a colossal new opera house for the Metropolitan Opera. Rockefeller had a 24-year lease, but the project was dropped when the stock market crashed in 1929. But the rent still had to be paid, so Rockefeller decided to build a commercial center. In all, 228 buildings were demolished to make way for 12 new buildings to be designed by Associated Architects, a group directed by Raymond Hood. Between 1932 and 1940, this "city within a city," to use Rockefeller's words, was built. The central tower, the former RCA Building (now the G. E. Building) was planned with dense concentration of facilities for the creation and broadcasting of sound, with a vision of television's bright future. Today NBC occupies 11 floors.

Building Rockefeller Center was the largest privately sponsored real-estate venture in New York City's history. The complex was an instant success, and seven more buildings were added between 1947 and 1973. Today, 19 buildings cover 22 acres (9ha), about 65,000 people work in the offices here, and many more visit daily. In 1985, Columbia University sold the land underneath the buildings to Rockefeller Center, which had remained in the hands of the Rockefeller family; at the end of 1989, the family sold a half interest to Japan's Mitsubishi Estate Company.

Six pools surrounded by flower boxes lead to the entrance

St. Mark's in the Bowery's Greek Revival steeple dates from 1828

The St. Patrick's Cathedral spires were completed in 1888

The striking interior of St. Patrick's Old Cathedral

ST. MARK'S CHURCH-IN-THE-BOWERY

✚ 61 F21 • East 10th Street 10004
☎ 212/674-6377 ⏰ Events only
🚌 M8, M15 🚇 6, N, R
www.stmarkschurch-in-the-bowery.com

Peter Stuyvesant, New Amsterdam's last Dutch governor, had a *bouwerij* (farm) in the quiet countryside north of the bustling settlement. As the city expanded and land values soared, Stuyvesant's grandson sold off plots for development. In 1779, a year after the Stuyvesant mansion was destroyed by fire, his great-grandson sold the site of Stuyvesant's private chapel to the Episcopal Church for a nominal dollar. And so it was that St. Mark's Church-in-the-Bowery was built and named. The original church was Federal-style; in keeping with the area's increasing affluence it later acquired a cast-iron portico. Stuyvesant and six generations of his descendants are buried in the graveyard.

ST. PATRICK'S CATHEDRAL

✚ 59 E17 • Fifth Avenue (between 50th and 51st streets) 10022 ⏰ Daily
🚌 M1, M2, M3, M4 🚇 6, B, D, E, F, V
www.ny-archdiocese.org/pastoral/cathedral_about.html

Each year the largest Roman Catholic cathedral in the United States, seating about 2,200, welcomes more than three million visitors. Designed by James Renwick, Jr., this Gothic Revival cathedral was inspired by European originals, most notably Cologne Cathedral in Germany. The spire is 330ft (100m) above street level. The pietà inside is three times the size of the one in St. Peter's in Rome. Tiffany & Co. designed the beautiful St. Michael and St. Louis altar. Work began on the church in

1853 and it was consecrated in 1879. The cathedral's arrival encouraged the rich and powerful to move north and contributed to the development of Fifth Avenue's many sumptuous mansions.

ST. PATRICK'S OLD CATHEDRAL

✚ 61 F23 • 260–264 Mulberry Street 10013 🚌 M15, M103 🚇 N, Q, R 📷
www.oldsaintpatricks.com

French architect Joseph François Mangin had been busy with the building of City Hall until 1809, when he began work on this Gothic structure, the first Roman Catholic cathedral of New York. At 120ft long (36m) and 80ft (24m) wide, it opened in 1815, when the area was heavily populated by Irish immigrants. The work of enlarging the cathedral was well under way in 1866, when a fire destroyed it. Restored and completed by 1868, the cathedral remained the seat of the archdiocese until the dedication of the new St. Patrick's in 1879. At that time the old cathedral was demoted to the status of parish church. Now restored, the interior is grand and gloomy, the timber roof is supported on iron columns and the organ is one of only a handful of good organs in the city. The building was named a New York City Landmark in 1966, one of the first buildings to receive this designation.

ST. PAUL'S CHAPEL

✚ 61 E25 • Broadway between Fulton and Vesey Streets 10007 ☎ 212/602-0800 ⏰ Mon–Fri 9–3, Sun 7–3 🚌 M1, M22 🚇 4, 5 📷 Classical music Mon noon–1pm $2

This church was one of the outbuildings of the wealthy Episcopalian parish of Trinity Church (▷ 142–143). Modeled on London's St. Martin-in-the-

Fields, it was built of local stone between 1764 and 1768, with the graceful spire added in 1796. In 1789 the inaugural prayer service for George Washington, the new nation's first president, was held here. Pierre l'Enfant, the soldier-architect who laid out the plan for Washington, D.C. as the new capital city and designed the Federal Hall, is credited with the altar. After his inauguration, Washington worshiped here regularly and his pew, together with Governor Dewitt Clinton's, is preserved. On Mondays at noon, you can come for a marvelous hour of classical music—it costs just $2.

SCHOMBURG CENTER FOR RESEARCH IN BLACK CULTURE

✚ Off map 59 E12 • 515 Malcolm X Boulevard 10037-11801 ☎ 212/491-2200 ⏰ Tue–Wed noon–7.45, Thu–Fri noon–6, Sat 10–5.45 🎫 Free 🚌 M7, M102 🚇 2, 3 📷 Tue–Fri 10–3 🎭
www.schomburgcenter.org

A research library that serves a national and international constituency, the Schomburg Center was founded in 1925 as a special collection in a branch of the New York Public Library (▷ 127). Arthur A. Schomburg, a Puerto Rican black scholar and bibliophile, had collected 5,000 books, 2,000 etchings and 3,000 manuscripts, among other material on African-American culture, which was acquired by the library. The collection has now grown to more than 5 million items, including books, art, artifacts, photographs, prints, manuscripts, rare books, moving images and recorded sound.

The focus is on preserving and providing access to this important collection, documenting the lives of people of African descent throughout the world. Past exhibitions have included *The Art of African Women*.

SoHo

Stylish boutiques and stores, fashionable restaurants, fascinating architecture and plenty of art galleries.

Kors on Mercer Street keeps the designer fashions coming

The gilded Puck statue on the Puck Magazine Building

Shopping addicts should head for West Broadway

RATINGS	
Historic interest	●●●○
Photo stops	●●●○
Specialist shopping	●●●●●
Walkability	●●●●●

BASICS

✚ 61 E23 • Canal Street to Houston Street, between Sixth Avenue and Lafayette Street

ℹ️ Lower East Side Visitor Center, 261 Broome Street, between Orchard and Allen streets

🚌 M1, M6

Ⓜ️ C, E, N, R, 6

🍴 Rocky's, 45 Spring Street, tel 212/274-9756 ☕ Le Pain Quotidien, 100 Grand Street, tel 212/625-9009 📧

www.lowereastsideny.com
Easy-to-navigate website with listings of local shops and restaurants.

There are still many art galleries

BACKGROUND

This area *South of Houston* (pronounced *how-stun*)—which actually extends as far south as Canal Street, and runs from Sixth Avenue on the west to Lafayette Street on the east—started out in the 19th century as an industrial zone. Architects kept catalogues of cast-iron window frames, balustrades and columns then pieced together what they liked; an Italian Renaissance motif was very popular. Fashion moved uptown in the early 20th century, taking industry and business out of the area. Development stalled; nothing went up—but nothing came down, either. Rents plummeted, opening up opportunities for artists and sculptors in need of cheap accommodation and studio space. Preservationists caught wind of the phenomenon and soon all New York was singing the praises of SoHo.

Today, there are 50 cast-iron structures on Greene Street alone. The most admired include the Haughwout Building at the corner of Broome Street and Broadway, the Little Singer Building at 561 Broadway, and the St. Nicholas Hotel, where Mark Twain met his future wife, at 521–523 Broadway. Across the street at 504 Broadway, Harry Houdini worked as a tie-cutter before his career as an escape artist took off. It was in the Haughwout Building that Elisha Graves Otis installed his first passenger elevator; unfortunately it is no longer in the building. (▷ 242–243 for a walk around this neighborhood.)

SOUGHT-AFTER NEIGHBORHOOD

By the 1970s, SoHo was one of the most desired addresses in town, rents shot up and struggling artists left. But many dealers and galleries thrived, like The Leo Castelli Gallery, which exhibited Andy Warhol, Frank Stella and Roy Lichtenstein in the 1960s, at 420 Broadway.

By the end of the 20th century there were about 200 other art galleries, as well more photography galleries than anywhere else in New York. Today many of the galleries have moved to Chelsea (▷ 77) and, to a lesser extent, to Tribeca (▷ 141), but some survive. At 119 Wooster Street, the Tony Shafrazi Gallery (tel 212/274-9300) has exhibited artists such as Keith Haring and Julian Schnabel. Across

the street at No. 120 is the well-established Howard Greenberg Gallery (tel 212/334-0010), devoted to 20th-century photography. The innovative New York Earth Room (tel 212/473-8072; Wed–Sat), at 141 Wooster Street, displays 14 tons of soil, rather intriguingly.

Stores followed the galleries, pushing out both galleries and artists. But in the interim, many well-to-do New Yorkers moved into the loft spaces on the buildings' upper floors, attracting still other high-end retailers to SoHo, along with chic cafés and lots of bars and music venues. Rents for apartments here can rise to $15,000 per month.

No matter what the season, SoHo's streets offer the ultimate New York experience.

Fashionable places in which to eat and be seen eating are what SoHo is all about

South Street Seaport

A landmark district of historic buildings, a maritime museum, and more than 100 shops, cafés and restaurants on the waterfront.

Look out over the East River from South Street Seaport's Pier 17 sun decks

The inside areas at South Street have been attractively restored

SEEING SOUTH STREET SEAPORT

This "museum without walls" is a 12-square-block landmark district at the eastern edge of downtown Manhattan on the East River. Buildings include the Fulton Fish Market, Pier 17 Pavilion, the South Street Seaport Museum and retail outlets on the surrounding blocks. Begin your visit at Pier 17, where the eateries and shops are concentrated. Pick up a visitors' leaflet from one of the many display racks at the entrance to the pier. The clear, well-labeled map and listing of the stores and restaurants will enable you to decide the route that appeals to you most.

HIGHLIGHTS

PIER 17
From this impressive three-story glass-and-steel pier, transformed into a shopping center with dozens of restaurants and eateries, you can enjoy the magnificent views of the East River from the outdoor terrace.

SOUTH STREET SEAPORT MUSEUM
Historic Ships
Berthed between piers 15 and 17, the collection of ships includes the 1911 *Peking*, a four-masted cargo vessel built by Blohm and Voss in Hamburg, Germany, which made several trips around Cape Horn. After numerous voyages between Europe and South America, then serving as a stationary school ship for the British, it came to New York in 1975. The *Pioneer*, an 1885 schooner, takes visitors on a 2.5-hour harbor cruise, including close-up looks at the Statue of Liberty and Governor's Island (late May–late Sep; reservations tel 212/748-8786).

World Port New York
The museum's core exhibition, with 24 galleries on the upper floors of the renovated Schermerhorn Row and the A. A. Low Building, explores the history of the port from colonial times to the present.

THE TITANIC MEMORIAL LIGHTHOUSE
At the Water Street entrance to the seaport, this monument to the victims of the *Titanic*, which sank on April 15, 1912 on its maiden

Advertising the Titanic's *tragic maiden voyage to New York*

voyage from Southampton, England, to New York, was put up in 1913 overlooking the East River. It was moved to its present site in 1968. John Jacob Astor, owner of the Astoria Hotel, which stood on the site of the Empire State Building, was one of the 1,513 people who died.

BACKGROUND

The South Street Seaport Museum, at 207 Front Street, opened in 1967 and was the original draw to this then-neglected area, leading to a complete restoration project. Schermerhorn Row is the most significant historical landmark in the South Street Seaport complex. Nos. 191 and 193 Front Street were built in the 1790s by Peter Schermerhorn, a leading merchant from a prominent New York family. He built further groups of four-story Georgian and Federal-style warehouses and counting houses on Fulton Street in 1812. The stone warehouse at 167–171 John Street was built in 1849 for A. A. Low & Brothers. By the 1860s, the South Street area was no longer the hub of commercial port activity and only the Fulton Fish Market remained. In the 1980s the Rouse Company moved in to start restoring.

The collection of ships berthed between piers 15 and 17

BASICS

✚ 61 F25 • South of Brooklyn Bridge at Fulton Street

ℹ 12 Fulton Street, Apr–end Oct daily 10–6; rest of year daily 10–5; tel 212/732-7678 for event info, 212/732-8257 for administration

☎ Museum: 212/748-8600

🛍 Most shops Apr–end Oct Mon–Sat 10–9, Sun 11–8. Museum: Apr–end Oct daily 10–6; rest of year Fri–Sun 10–5

✋ Museum: adult $8, child (5–12) $4

🚌 M15

Ⓜ 2, 3, 4, 5

🚶 Guided walking tours: Ask at the ticket booth across from Pier 17

🍴 15 restaurants and food outlets

☕ Seaport Cafe on Pier 17, tel 212/964-1120; Pier 17 Pavilion, tel 212/267-8310

www.southstreetseaport.com
Events calendar, complete list of restaurants and shops.

www.southstseaport.org
Preview museum's permanent collection, information about exhibits and ships.

There is often some sort of street music or entertainment at South Street Seaport

Statue of Liberty

The city's most important landmark, in New York Harbor, recognized throughout the world as a symbol of freedom, a must-see for millions of visitors every year.

The statue is often affectionately referred to as Lady Liberty

Buy your very own statue headgear and wear it with pride

You can get up close on a ferry for a better look

RATINGS	
Good for kids	● ● ● ● ●
Historic interest	● ● ● ●
Photo stops	● ● ● ● ●

A symbol of freedom and democracy, the Statue of Liberty was the first sight for millions of immigrants as they approached their new homeland. As you sail toward her today, it's easy to imagine how they felt.

A JOINT PROJECT

When the Statue of Liberty was unveiled on October 28, 1886, thousands of spectators were filled with awe. Nearly three times the height of the Colossus of Rhodes, one of the Seven Wonders of the World, this gift from the people of France was in recognition of the friendship established between the two countries during the American Revolution. The French statesman Edouard de Laboulay proposed that the statue be made in France, but that the pedestal be made by the Americans. Alexandre-Gustave Eiffel, who designed the Eiffel Tower in Paris, came up with the revolutionary support system of interlocking angle irons for the enormous statue, which was designed by Frédéric-Auguste Bartholdi.

Paying for the project was a problem for both nations and great effort was put into fundraising events, such as theatrical performances, art exhibitions, auctions and prize-fights. But the public showed little interest. Joseph Pulitzer, who established the Pulitzer Prize, criticized the rich in his newspaper *The World* for failing to help finance the pedestal construction. He also criticized the middle classes for expecting the rich to provide all the money. Donations then came pouring in and the pedestal was completed in 1886. The French shipped the statue to New York in June 1885; it took four months to assemble.

VITAL STATISTICS

Lady Liberty, as she is often affectionately called, came to Bedloe's Island, renamed Liberty Island, in 1956. By presidential proclamation the Statue of Liberty became a National Monument in 1924; the United Nations designated her a World Heritage Site in 1984. After almost 100 years, the statue needed some attention; an $87-million restoration project ended with fireworks to celebrate the statue's centennial, coinciding with Independence Day, on July 4, 1986.

Her measurements are impressive. She weighs 225 tons and measures 151ft 1in (46.05m) from the top of the base to the torch.

The statue provides an inspiring welcome to the city

Her hands measure a whopping 16ft 5in (5m) and even her nose is 4ft 6in (1.37m). Richard Morris Hunt's magnificent pedestal measures 154ft (46.9m).

VISITING LADY LIBERTY

She can be fully appreciated only up close so it's unfortunate that the Statue of Liberty has been closed to the public for security reasons since September 11, 2001. Only the grounds are now open to visitors.

Still, it's worth taking the trip across the harbor to peer up at this monolith to liberty. For a panoramic view of the harbor, you can climb to an observation deck on the 16th floor at the top of the pedestal. There's also a museum. Note the tablet in her hand, inscribed with the date July 4, 1776 in Roman numerals. You can't help but ponder what excitement her crowned head and mighty torch must have generated in the hearts of millions of immigrants who first arrived here in the New World.

To visit Liberty Island, take the Statue of Liberty & Ellis Island Ferry from Battery Park. In advance, buy tickets online, by telephone or at the ticket office. In person, use the CityPass (▷ 317) or get your ticket from Castle Clinton ticket office (▷ 73). Lines are long during peak season so, as there are no reservations, arrive early.

The statue arrived in 350 pieces packed in 214 crates

BASICS

✚ Page 6 • Liberty Island in New York Harbor

☎ General information 212/363-3200, ferry tickets 212/269-5755

🕐 Daily 9.30–5, extended hours in peak season

🎫 Ferry tickets (good for a round-trip that includes a stop at Ellis Island) adult $11.50, child (4–12) $4.50. Free admission to Liberty Island and the Statue of Liberty

🚇 1, 4, 5, 9 🚌 M1, M6, M15

🍴 Refreshments on ferries; café on Liberty Island 🎫 On ferries 🚻

www.nps.gov/stli
History and statistics, museum exhibits and security updates.

Times Square and Broadway

New York at its flashiest.
Neon signs, huge billboards, live TV broadcasts, enormous stores and
gigantic family-friendly theme restaurants, not to mention theaters.

THE SIGHTS

RATINGS	
Good for kids	● ● ● ○
Photo stops	● ● ● ○
Specialist shopping	● ● ● ●
Walkability	● ● ● ●

BASICS
✚ 60 D18
ℹ️ Times Square Information Center, 1560 Broadway between 46th and 47th streets, daily 8–8 (on Seventh Avenue)
☎ Times Square Information Center 212/869-1890
🚌 M6, M7, M27, M42, M104
🚇 1, 2, 3, 9, N, R
🚶 Free walking tour every Friday at noon from the Times Square Information Center
🍴 Broadway Joe's Steakhouse, 315 West 46th Street, tel 212/246-6513—steaks and seafood
🍴 Planet Hollywood, 1540 Broadway at 45th Street, tel 212/333-7827, serves burgers and other American favorites, but movie memorabilia and giant projection screens are the real stars
🛍️ Times Square Information Center

www.timessquarenyc.org
Get the latest news, events and tourist information, take a video tour or post a message.

SEEING TIMES SQUARE AND BROADWAY

Begin your visit at the Times Square Information Center, originally the attractive landmark Embassy Theater and now dominated by a branch of McDonald's. Even if you don't need information, take a look at the grand foyer. Over time, many of the old theaters have been renovated and now have landmark status. A special security force patrols the streets, and the area is as safe as any crowded urban neighborhood can be. If your visit to New York happens to coincide with New Year's Eve and you don't mind dense crowds, join the throngs in Times Square to see the glass ball drop at midnight to ring in the New Year. It's a great New York tradition.

HIGHLIGHTS

ED SULLIVAN THEATER
697–699 Broadway between 53rd and 54th streets
Built by Arthur Hammerstein as a memorial to his father, Oscar Hammerstein I, this theater was formerly called the Hammerstein Theater. The neo-Gothic vestibules, lobbies and auditorium are unique on Broadway. Used as a dance hall for many years, it made history when it became a television studio. "The Ed Sullivan Show," the longest-running TV show in history, was broadcast from here during the 1950s and 1960s. Today it is perhaps even more famous as the home of the "Late Show with David Letterman."

LYCEUM THEATRE
149 West 45th Street ☎ 212/239-6280
The oldest New York theater, saved from demolition in 1939, it is Broadway's most imposing structure with its magnificent Beaux Arts facade and powerful neo-Baroque columns. Inside are marble walls with murals by James Wall Finn. Many of Broadway's highly acclaimed comedies and dramas have been performed here, as well as classics by the National Actors Theatre. Such famous names as Ethel Barrymore, Bette Davis, Joseph Cotton, Melvyn Douglas, Alan Bates and Lauren Bacall have all performed at the Lyceum.

NEW VICTORY THEATER
209 West 42nd Street
www.newvictory.org
Built by Oscar Hammerstein I in 1899 and once known as Minsky's, the New Victory was restored and remodeled in 1995 and is the city's first full-time family-oriented performing arts center.

PARAMOUNT THEATRE BUILDING
1501 Broadway
The tallest building in Times Square when it was completed in 1927, the Paramount is crowned by a four-faced clock with a glass globe, a focal point of the area that is visible for miles when it's illuminated. The World Wrestling Entertainment's 2,000-seat theme restaurant, WWE New York, whose sign boasts the latest in fiber-optic technology, is in the old theater space; a 30ft (9m) video screen and 110 monitors

ensure that every diner can watch live broadcasts of shows like "Raw" and "Smackdown!", and appearances by WWE stars. Other entertainments vary from concerts to magic shows.

Transformed from a run-down, seedy area in the 1970s, Times Square is now respectable and much cleaner

BACKGROUND

Called Heere Straat (Main Street) by Dutch settlers, Broadway is New York's longest and oldest street. As the city's population grew, seedy bars, brothels and gambling dens opened on both sides. Even in the early 1800s, it bustled with pedestrians and

horse-drawn carriages; there were even traffic jams. In the 1860s a row of minstrel halls opened along Broadway, and by 1900 the area on and off Broadway around Union Square had become the city's theater district. In 1880, the advent of electricity began to turn Broadway between 14th and 34th streets into the Great White Way. In the 1890s, when Oscar Hammerstein built the Olympia Theater on Broadway between 44th and 45th streets, the city's theatrical entertainment moved to the area that is now Times Square; it was then known as Longacre Square and was renamed only in 1904, when the The New York Times moved into Times Tower on 42nd Street. In 1928, 14,900 electrical lights were added to the four sides of the Times Tower, creating the first moving electrical sign.

After the subway came to the Theater District, beginning in 1900, the crowds poured in. By the 1920s, movies had taken over many theaters. After this, the theaters started showing pornography and the crowd turned seedy. Sex joints drove out reputable business, and by the 1970s the district was crawling with hookers, pimps and other dubious characters.

During the 1990s, an aggressive clean-up operation—which included legislation against noise, gambling and prostitution, as well as new zoning laws—transformed the area. There's no question that the current state of the square and surrounding area has been an amazing show of effective planning, and a great triumph for the city.

Broadway is by far New York's longest street

TV SHOW TICKETS GUIDE

Tickets for live tapings of TV shows are free but usually hard to obtain because of the high demand, especially the immensely popular "Late Show with David Letterman." If you are seriously addicted to a show and you know six months in advance that you'll be in New York, send a postcard with your name, address, telephone number, the number of tickets you want, and your preferred dates.

Many studios hand out stand-by tickets on the day of taping, but you have to get up early and stand in line. In the dead of winter, you stand a better chance, as snow and cold winds put some people off. For more information call NYCVB at 212/484-1222. You can also phone or check show websites for information on ticket availability, waiting lists and stand-by tickets. When you attend a show, take photo ID, as it may be required.

"Late Show with David Letterman"
Send a postcard to Late Show Tickets, Ed Sullivan Theater, 1697 Broadway, New York, NY 10019, or register at **www.**cbs.com/latenight/ lateshow or telephone 212/247-6497 for stand-by tickets on the day of taping at 11am sharp. You must be 18 or over to attend.

"Total Request Live"
You can sometimes get tickets for the 3.30 MTV taping by telephoning TRL Ticket Reservation Hotline on 212/398-8549. If that doesn't work, turn up by 2pm (earlier if the day's guest is a major celebrity) outside the 1515 Broadway studio between 44th and 45th streets. A producer often roams around asking trivia questions about musicians and hands out tickets to those who answer correctly. You have to be between 18 and 24 to attend.

"Good Morning, America"
Visit **www.**abcnews.go.com/sections/GMA or telephone 212/580-5176 and you may be lucky and get to join Diane Sawyer and Charlie Gibson in their street-facing studio on Broadway at 44th Street. The show runs Monday to Friday from 7 to 9am.

"Montel"
Tickets to join the audience to see the Emmy award-winning talk show host Montel Williams can be obtained by visiting **www.**montel show.com and by emailing the form there, or by calling 212/989-8101. Three shows a day are taped on Wednesdays and Thursdays.

TIPS

● Broadway extends from Lower Manhattan to beyond Manhattan's northern tip, but Broadway as most visitors understand it refers to the area north–south between West 53rd and West 40th streets and east–west from Sixth to Eighth avenues. Most theaters are not on Broadway but on side streets.

● The TKTS booth (Broadway at 47th Street, tel 212/768-1818, www.tdf.org, Mon–Sat 3–8, Sun 11–7 for 8pm performances; 10–2 for Wed and Sat matinées; only cash or traveler's checks) sells day-of-show tickets for on and off-Broadway performances at 20–50 percent off face value. By 6pm the line is short.

● Times Square Information Center has a Metropolitan Transit Authority desk for transit maps and MetroCards; a Broadway Ticket Center sells full-price tickets; an HSBC Bank Center with ATMs and currency-exchange machines; computers with free internet access; free brochures and leaflets—some with discount vouchers.

The stratospheric Seagram Building, a fine skyscraper

Lucky commuters get to ride the Staten Island Ferry every day

An attractive promenade flanks the Hudson River Park in TriBeCa

SEAGRAM BUILDING

🔲 59 F17 • 375 Park Avenue 10022
☎ 212/572-7000 🕑 Mon–Fri 9–5 🚻

Erected in 1958 with interiors by Philip Johnson, this is New York City's only Mies van der Rohe building and one of the finest International-style skyscrapers in the world. The decision to set it toward the back of the granite-paved plaza was daring at the time, especially given real-estate values, but it ignited a taste for pedestrian plazas that lingers in Manhattan to this day.

The building is also notable as the site of the esteemed Four Seasons restaurant, famed venue for power lunches, and of the bustling Brasserie restaurant.

SOHO

See pages 132–133.

SOUTH STREET SEAPORT

See pages 134–135.

STATEN ISLAND FERRY

🔲 344 F27 • Whitehall Terminal, 1 Whitehall Street 10004 ☎ 718/815-2628 🕑 Daily 6am–10pm (Staten Island to Manhattan) or 6.30am–11pm (Manhattan to Staten Island), every 20–30 min on weekdays, less frequently on weekends and off-peak 🚢 Free, $3 for cars on certain ferries 🚌 M1, M6, M9, M15 🚇 1, 4, 5, 9, N, R www.ci.nyc.ny.us/html/dot

These commuter craft, which shuttle Staten Islanders to and from jobs in Manhattan, are—for tourists—a free, hour-long, round-trip excursion in the harbor—past the Statue of Liberty (▷ 136–137), Ellis Island (▷ 90–93) and Governors Island, with the Verrazano Narrows Bridge in the distance. In good weather, try for one of the old orange and green boats. The white boats are newer and have no outside deck. To get the best view, sit on the right side.

Avoid rush hours, and disembark at Staten Island. On your right as you get off, look for the boat-loading sign, which directs you to the next loading dock.

STATUE OF LIBERTY

See pages 136–137.

STUDIO MUSEUM IN HARLEM

🔲 Off map 59 E12 • 144 West 125th Street between Lenox and 7th Avenue 10027 ☎ 212/864-4500 🕑 Wed–Fri, Sun noon–6, Sat 10–6 🚢 Adult $7, child $3, under 12 free 🚌 M2, M7, M60, M100 🚇 2, 3 🔲 📧 🚻 www.studiomuseuminharlem.org

Specializing in 19th- and 20th-century African-American art, and 20th-century African and Caribbean art and artifacts, this small museum has a lot to offer. Rotating exhibitions, a full calendar of events, and the annual exhibition from their Artists-in-Residence program make this a museum well worth a visit. Exhibitions have included *Challenge of the Modern: African-American Artists 1925–1945*, which examined the modernist concepts adopted by black artists in the US and the Caribbean; and *Harlem Postcards 2003*. The small sculpture garden is charming. The gift shop offers a good selection of books, postcards and other items.

THEODORE ROOSEVELT BIRTHPLACE

🔲 60 E20 • 28 East 20th Street 10003 ☎ 212/260-1616 🕑 Guided tour only (30 min) Tue–Sat 9–5 🚢 Adult $3, under 17 free 🚌 M1, M6, M23 🚇 6, N, R www.nps.gov/thrb

Theodore (Teddy) Roosevelt, the great outdoorsman and 26th president of the United States, was born in New York in 1858 and spent his first 14 years in a fashionable brownstone just off Broadway. The house was demolished just before his death in 1919, but the lot where the house stood was acquired in 1923 by the Women's Roosevelt Memorial Association, which commissioned a female architect to reconstruct it as it had been in Roosevelt's youth. Rooms are furnished with objects preserved from the original house. The "lion's room" is filled with hunting and outdoor memorabilia. Roosevelt was sickly as a child, and a small gym that was intended to build up his health adjoins the nursery. There is also an exhibition about his eventful life.

TIMES SQUARE AND BROADWAY

See pages 138–140.

TRIBECA

🔲 61 E24 • Between Hudson River and Broadway, Chambers and Canal streets 🚌 M20 🚇 1, 2, 3, 9, A, C, E

TriBeCa (pronounced *try-beck-a*), the *Tri*angle *Be*low *Ca*nal Street, is where artists went in the late 1970s after sky-rocketing prices made SoHo (▷ 132–133) unaffordable to all but the rich. They converted cast-iron warehouses into loft apartments, and now, predictably, a wealthy group has moved in along with antiques shops, design shops and some very fine restaurants. Actor Robert De Niro brought the Tribeca Film Center to the area in 1989. There are some notable buildings, especially 2 White Street, dating from 1809; the Fleming Smith warehouse at 451 Washington Street, home of long-established Capsouto Frères bistro; and the Corinthian-columned, cast-iron 47 Worth Street. The area was greatly damaged on 9/11, but returned to full swing remarkably quickly.

Trinity Church

A historic church tucked among Lower Manhattan's skyscrapers, and the final resting place of a handful of great Americans.

Many famous names are buried in the churchyard

Figures from the Bible mark the entrance to the church

Gothic romance authors have used the church as a setting

RATINGS	
Historic interest	●●●○
Photo stops	●●●○
Specialist shopping	●●●○
Walkability	●●●●●

BASICS

✚ 61 E26 • Broadway at Wall Street 10006
☎ 212/602-0800
🕐 Daily 7–6
🚌 M1, M6
Ⓜ 4, 5, N, R
📷 Free guided tours daily 2pm
www.trinitywallstreet.org

As you walk up Broadway, north of Bowling Green, you come to Trinity Church. Now dwarfed by the surrounding skyscrapers, Richard Upjohn's 1846 rose-pink sandstone masterpiece, with beautiful stained-glass windows and an eight-sided, 280ft (85m) spire, was once the tallest building in New York. The church bell was presented to the church in 1704 by the Bishop of London. As you enter, notice the biblical scenes on the bronze doors, designed by Richard Morris Hunt and donated in memory of John Jacob Astor III. Look for the white marble altar, the wooden vault and the screen of the Chapel of All Saints. To the left, at the back of the church, is a small museum (Mon–Fri 9–11.45, 1–3.45, Sat 10–3.45, Sun 1–3.45) selling postcards, pamphlets outlining the church's history, books and videos, and gifts. The 30-minute guided tours of the church start from this museum. Classical music concerts take place in the church every Thursday from 1 to 2pm. Men must remove their hats as a sign of respect, even in the dead of winter, or will be reminded to do so by one of the church's wardens.

THE FIRST CHURCH

In 1697, by royal charter, the Anglican parish of Trinity became one of the largest landholders in Manhattan, and the first church was put up the next year, only to burn in the great fire of 1776, when the British army occupied New York. You will find the original royal charter for the church on display in the museum. During the struggle for independence, Trinity Church was a Loyalist bastion, but when the revolution ended, so did the Loyalists' hold on the city. A second building on the same spot was structurally flawed and was torn down in 1839. British architect Richard Upjohn, together with James Renwick, Jr., were commissioned to build the third Trinity Church. In the process, Upjohn made his reputation and went on to design many more churches around the country.

Before you leave the church, stroll around the small churchyard, a green oasis that's now estimated to be worth several million dollars for its prime location. Here are the graves of steamboat inventor Robert Fulton, statesman Alexander Hamilton, killed in a duel with Aaron Burr, and Francis Lewis, a signatory to the Declaration of Independence. The large cross in the churchyard is dedicated to Caroline Webster Schermerhorn Astor, the queen of 1800s high society.

Looking down Wall Street toward the Gothic Revival Trinity Church, with its imposing spire (right)

The opulence of Trump Tower is now the stuff of legend

A symbol of peace and unity— the United Nations headquarters

Washington Heights is dedicated to an American Revolution battle

THE SIGHTS

TRUMP TOWER

➕ 59 E17 • 725 Fifth Avenue 10022
☎ 212/832-2000 🚌 M1, M2, M3, M4
🚇 E, N, R, V 📶 🏻

Not to be confused with the older Trump Building, originally the Manhattan Company Building, or with other Trump structures about town, this one rose in the 1980s as a glass monument to the affluent lifestyle. Upper floors contain 263 plush apartments. (Trump himself was one of the first to move in.) Below them, the interior is a six-story atrium with escalators, waterfalls and glittering boutiques surrounded by pink marble, mirrors and shrubbery. It's ridiculously ostentatious but still quite the sight.

UKRAINIAN MUSEUM

➕ 61 F22 • 222 East Sixth Street between 2nd and 3rd Avenues 10003
☎ 212/228-0110 🕐 Wed–Sun 1–5
🚌 M101, M102, M103 🚇 6 📶 🏻
www.brama.com/ukrainian_museum

Ukrainian immigrants came to America in the 19th century and many stayed in New York and lived in the tenements on the Lower East Side, not far from this museum. Committed to preserving the cultural heritage of Ukrainians, this museum displays folk art items, including traditional costumes, decorative brass and silver jewelry, decorated Easter eggs, ceramics and woven and embroidered ritual cloths used as talismans at births, weddings, funerals and seasonal rituals. It also curates shows of works by important Ukrainian artists.

UNION SQUARE

See page 145.

UNITED NATIONS HEADQUARTERS

➕ 59 G18 • United Nations Plaza 10017
☎ 212/963-8687 🕐 Daily 9.30–4.45; closed Sat, Sun in Jan and Feb 🎫 Adult

$11.50, child (5–14) $6.50, under 5 not admitted 🚌 M15, M27, M42 🚇 4, 5, 6, 7 🎫 Tours every half-hour Mon–Fri 9.30–4.45, Sat and Sun 10–4.30
📶 📶 🏻
www.un.org

At the end of World War II John D. Rockefeller, Jr. donated $8.5 million to purchase this site for the United Nations complex. The 544ft (166m) Secretariat building that dominates the site opened in 1950. Alongside are the General Assembly building, the Conference building (fronting the river) and the Dag Hammarskjöld Library. Fittingly, architects from many countries contributed to the designs. A 45-minute guided tour covers the General Assembly Hall and Security Council Chamber. You can see donated exhibits such as stained glass by Marc Chagall, a replica Sputnik, and, in the park, sculptures by Barbara Hepworth and Henry Moore. Visit the landscaped grounds, with beautiful views. Arrive early at peak times.

UPPER WEST SIDE

➕ 58 C13 • Between 59th and 125th streets, west of Central Park 🚌 M7, M10, M11, M104 🚇 1, 2, 3, 9, A, B, C, D
📶 📶 🏻

The Upper West Side is a lively residential area with numerous historic districts, sumptuous landmark buildings, affordable hotels and excellent restaurants, and an affluent crowd that includes many actors, actresses, directors and musicians. The popular American Museum of Natural History (▷ 68–72) is here, as are the city's premier performing arts complex, the Lincoln Center (▷ 112–113), and the Cathedral Church of St. John the Divine (▷ 67). While you stroll, note the San Remo Apartment Building at 145–146

Central Park West, and the Trump International Hotel/Tower on Columbus Circle.

WASHINGTON HEIGHTS

➕ Page 7 • 155th Street to Dyckman Street 🚌 M4 🚇 1, 9, A, C 📶 📶 🏻

At the northern tip of Manhattan, this neighborhood of Latinos, Dominicanos, Greeks and Armenians does not attract many visitors. Yet there are some excellent restaurants and interesting attractions, including the medieval collections at the Cloisters (▷ 86) in Fort Tryon Park, which has spectacular views of the Hudson River. Washington Heights was the site of one of the earliest battles of the American Revolution, fought on November 16, 1776; Washington's troops lost to the British, who named the fort after the colonial governor, Sir William Tryon. John D. Rockefeller acquired the Cloisters property in 1917 and the museum opened in 1938.

WOOLWORTH BUILDING

➕ 61 E25 • 233 Broadway 10007
🚌 M1, M6, M15 🚇 2, 3, 4, 5, 6, N, R

Multimillionaire F. W. Woolworth, the department store mogul, hired fashionable architect Cass Gilbert to build the tallest building in the world in 1913. At 792ft (242m), this terracotta-faced, neo-Gothic masterpiece held the record until the Chrysler Building was completed in 1929 (▷ 85). In the 1980s much of the terracotta cladding was replaced. Inside, the lobby is a marvel of Skyros marble, with murals of *Labor and Commerce* and plaster depictions of some of the builders, including Gilbert, with a model of the building and Woolworth himself counting his cash.

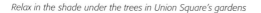

Relax in the shade under the trees in Union Square's gardens

UNION SQUARE

A focal point of the off-Broadway theater scene, with great restaurants, excellent art galleries and interesting museums.

On a sunny day, the park is a pleasant place to people-watch and relax. There are also sculptures of Washington (1856) and Lincoln (1866), both by Henry Kirke Brown, and Lafayette by Statue of Liberty sculptor Frédéric-Auguste Bartholdi. Nearby are the Center for Jewish History at 15 West 16th Street; the eclectic Forbes Magazine Galleries at 62 Fifth Avenue at 12th Street (▷ 99); and Theodore Roosevelt's reconstructed birthplace at 28 East 20th Street.

At last count there were some 100 restaurants in the Union Square area, including some of the city's top tables. In September, at a Union Square Park fundraiser called Harvest, you can sample signature dishes of top neighborhood chefs. Also in September, the free outdoor Manhattan Short Film Festival screens 14 of the world's best short films and gives new film-makers a chance to compete for prizes.

A VARIED HISTORY

Run down and threatening in the 1970s, Union Square is thriving and proud today. Every Monday, Wednesday, Friday and Saturday, a green market—one of the best farmers' markets in the United States—draws New Yorkers from all over the city and inspires local chefs. The bright idea of Barry Benepe (director of the green market)—who saw it as a way to simultaneously help Hudson Valley farmers and improve the neighborhood—it encouraged other communities to set up similar markets.

Union Square went residential in the 1840s, and America's greatest concentration of theaters, nightclubs, restaurants, hotels and luxury shopping followed. Union Square Park was laid out for the wealthy residents. In the 1800s, Ladies' Mile—Broadway and Sixth Avenue between 15th and 24th streets—was the height of fashionable shopping, until the turn of the 20th century when wealth moved uptown and the area deteriorated. In the late 1800s, Union Square was the center for demonstrations and political protests. In the early 1930s the editorial offices of The New Masses and the offices of the Communist Party's Yiddish-language paper moved here. A renovation of the square in 1936 discouraged further demonstrations.

The best chefs in town swear by the freshness and quality of produce at the farmers' market

RATINGS			
Historic interest	●	●	●
Photo stops	●	●	●
Specialist shopping	●	●	●	●
Value for money	●	●	●	●

BASICS

✚ 60 E21 • From East 12th Street to East 20th Street, between Third and Fifth avenues

🚌 M2, M3, M6, M7

🚇 4, 5, 6, L, N, Q, R

🎫 Free walking tour Sat 2pm, meet at the Lincoln statue near the Pavilion Building in Union Square Park

🍴 Old Town Bar & Restaurant, 45 East 18th Street between Broadway and Park Avenue, tel 212/529-6732

www.unionsquarenyc.org

Wall Street

The heart of New York's financial center and the historic site of George Washington's inauguration.

Shopping center underneath Wall Street

Playing chess in the street is a popular pastime today

The Stock Exchange, on the corner of Wall and Broad streets

This symbol of wealth is in fact a narrow 18th-century lane running from Broadway to South Street. The New York Stock Exchange (closed to the public since 9/11) stands on the corner of Broad Street and Wall Street. At the west end of the street on Broadway, framed between towering office buildings, is the Gothic Revival Trinity Church (▷ 142–143)—an impressive sight, and a great photo opportunity, with the many U.S. flags waving from their perches on the buildings along the street. Stop in front of Federal Hall National Monument (▷ 97); a statue of George Washington marks the spot where the first president took the oath of office. The two skyscrapers at Nos. 40 and 55 Wall Street rise up 930ft (282.5m) and 951ft (290m) respectively. This is an area steeped in history, evidenced by the many historical plaques, cornerstones, markers and notices. Take a look at the Morgan Bank headquarters at No. 60. Its bold arcade vies for attention as one of the tallest skyscrapers in the Financial District. Visit the white marble lobby.

Wall Street was named for the northern wall erected in 1653 to defend New Amsterdam from Native Americans. North of this wall were the *bouwerijs* (farms). After the English defeated the Dutch, and New Amsterdam was renamed New York, the wall started to crumble and in 1699 it was torn down. The bastion stones from the Dutch wall were carted off and used in the foundation of City Hall (▷ 77).

THE FIRST TRANSACTION
In 1792, 22 brokers and merchants stood in front of a buttonwood tree on Wall Street and made their first trading agreement. They were actively trading government securities, seeking to establish fixed commissions on transactions and favoring brokers who were signatories. This "Buttonwood Agreement," as it was called, eventually gave birth to the New York Stock Exchange. Their open-air trading activities moved indoors, probably to taverns, until premises on William Street were acquired in the 1860s.

The telegraphic ticker, new in 1867, has been replaced by today's latest market information display technology. The adrenaline rushes as hundreds of brokers on the trading floor, the size of a football field, trade billions of shares in about 3,000 companies. Sadly, this frenetic trading cannot be viewed live, because it is closed to visitors. Call 212/656-3000 for further information.

RATINGS	
Historic interest	●●●●●
Photo stops	●●●●
Specialist shopping	●●
Walkability	●●●●●

BASICS

✚ 61 F26 • Financial District

🚌 M1, M6, M15, M22

🚇 2, 3, 4, 5

📷 Free 90-min Wall Street walking tour every Thu, Sat noon; meet on the steps of the U.S. Customs House at 1 Bowling Green

🍴 John Street Bar & Grill, 17 John Street, tel 212/349-3278, daily 11.30–11

🍽 Mangia, 40 Wall Street, tel 212/425-4040, Mon–Fri 7–10

www.downtownny.com
Up-to-date information on Lower Manhattan's buses, subways, attractions, shops, hotels and transportation

TIP
● As the Financial District is deserted on weekends, visit on a weekday when this little street becomes a superhighway for stockbrokers in dark suits.

Wall Street is most famous internationally for the devastating Wall Street Crash in 1929

Whitney Museum
of American Art

●

More than 11,000 works by 1,700 prominent 20th- and 21st-century American artists, including Georgia O'Keeffe, Jasper Johns, Edward Hopper, Mark Rothko and Jackson Pollock. Provocative works by innovative and often controversial American independent film-makers, video artists, multimedia artists and photographers.

Taking a break at the museum

SEEING THE WHITNEY MUSEUM OF AMERICAN ART

Before entering the museum on Madison Avenue, take a few minutes to look at the striking granite, modernist building by Marcel Breuer and Hamilton Smith. In a neighborhood of traditional brownstone, limestone and brick row houses, this Brutalist architecture attracts attention, and when it was completed in 1966, many people thought it too heavy and dreary. Today, it is generally esteemed as daring and innovative as it rises in a series of inverted stairs above a sunken sculpture garden. As you enter, the ticket desk is to your left. At the ticket desk and checkout counter there are free Whitney calendars with the current exhibition schedule and leaflets about the current and upcoming temporary exhibitions. The free audiotours can be picked up at the end of the checkout counter.

Start your visit with the permanent collection, either on the second floor, De Kooning to Today, or on the fifth floor, Hopper to Mid-Century. New exhibitions are also staged (in the past these have featured individual artists and themed shows).

Works by contemporary artists are displayed to good effect in the museum galleries

HIGHLIGHTS

FIFTH FLOOR: HOPPER TO MID-CENTURY

The Leonard and Evelyn Lauder Galleries, which make up part of this floor, contain more than 200 works from the first half of the 20th century. As you leave the elevator on this floor, you will see the Early 20th-Century Urban Realism Gallery, with several paintings by Robert Henri, including a lovely portrait dating from 1916 of the museum's founder, Gertrude Vanderbilt Whitney, donated by her granddaughter, Flora. If you have the free audioguide, listen to Mrs. Whitney's granddaughter's description of her. The portrait depicts a woman of leisure, which surprises the granddaughter who remembers her as an energetic woman always on the go. On the opposite wall is a fine painting by William J. Glackens, *Hammerstein's Roof Garden* (c1901), which depicts wealthy New Yorkers at the beginning of the 20th century enjoying watching tightrope walkers, acrobats and jugglers on a hot summer's evening at Hammerstein's on the corner of Seventh Avenue and 42nd Street.

The Machine Age and Geometric Abstraction Gallery houses a collection of paintings of American factories and skyscrapers in a style called Precisionism. The artists' creations are a response to the explosion of industry in the early 20th century.

In the Early American Modernism Gallery are several paintings by Georgia O'Keeffe, including several of her dazzling flower paintings and *Summer Days* (1936), one of her many cow-skull paintings. You will also find her gorgeous *Music Pink and Blue II* (1919) and *Black and White* (1930).

The superb collection in the Edward Hopper Gallery displays such favorites as *7am* (1948), and his earlier *Small Town Station* (1918–20) and *Italian Quarter From Gloucester* (1912), as well as his particularly haunting painting, *Early Sunday Morning* (1930).

RATINGS	
Good for kids	● ● ●
Historic interest	● ●
Specialist shopping	● ● ● ●
Value for money	● ● ● ● ●

TIPS

● **Come Fridays from 6pm to 9pm. Admission is pay-what-you-wish and there are live musical performances.**

● **For a good cross section of the latest in American art and to see works by unknown but promising artists, visit when the Whitney Biennial is on (even-numbered years).**

● **There's a branch of the museum in the Altria Building at 120 Park Avenue (Mon–Wed, Fri 11–6, Thu 11–7.30; free).**

GALLERY GUIDE

Floors 1, 3, 4: Temporary exhibits

Floor 2: De Kooning To Today: Mildred and Herbert Lee Galleries include works by Jackson Pollock, Jasper Johns, Claes Oldenburg, Robert Rauschenberg, Roy Lichtenstein, Frank Stella, Robert Smithson, Alexander Calder and Paul Pfeiffer. Also temporary exhibits. Marisol's *Women and Dog* (1964) sculpture is four

Notice the curtains and blinds in the windows above the storefronts in this picture. By making each window different, some with yellow blinds and others with white curtains, he gives a sense that people live in each of these dwellings, and that something different is going on inside each one. Hold up your hands to block from your view the barber's pole and the fire hydrant, and notice how they give focus and balance to the painting.

The Realism in the 1930s Gallery has fine works by Thomas Hart Benton. *Poker Night* (1948) was a commissioned work based on the Broadway performance of "A Streetcar Named Desire."

In the Early Abstract Expressionism Gallery is a sculpture by Louise Bourgeois called *Quarantania* (1953). The artist produced this work when she was feeling very homesick for her native France while she studied in the United States. Her longing for her loved ones comes

The entrance lobby is a riot of modern lighting

The fourth-floor gallery was used for temporary exhibitions during the 2000 Whitney Biennial

sculptures of the artist. The one with the green skirt and pink blouse has her photo stuck to the head.

Floor 5: Hopper to Mid-Century: Leonard and Evelyn Lauder Galleries include works by William Glackens and Robert Henri; Machine Age and Geometric Abstraction Gallery has works in the Precisionist style; Early American Modernism Gallery includes Georgia O'Keeffe; Edward Hopper Gallery; Realism in 1930s Gallery displays Thomas Hart Benton, John Stuart Curry and Joe Jones; Early Abstract Expressionism Gallery includes Louise Bourgeois. Also temporary exhibits. *The Lord is My Shepherd* (1926), by Thomas Hart Benton, is a painting of a husband and wife who were the artist's deaf-mute neighbors on Martha's Vineyard.

out in this sculpture. The Surrealism in America Gallery contains Man Ray's *La Fortune* (1938), a statement about man's attempt to win at games.

SECOND FLOOR: DE KOONING TO TODAY
Roy Lichtenstein, *Little Big Painting*

In the Pop Gallery, *Little Big Painting* (1965) is a celebration of mass media and popular culture. The red, white and yellow with harsh black lines resemble an image of an abstract painting. With no trace of the artist's hand, no visible brushstroke, and the dot screen in the

Hail, Bright Aurora, *by an unknown artist*

background, Lichtenstein (1923–97) evokes mechanical printing, the culture of mass reproduction.

Alexander Calder, *Circus*

Calder's (1898–1976) fascination with the circus and his training as a mechanical engineer inspired him to create *Circus* (1926–31) and to breathe life into the tiny wire tightrope walkers, acrobats, weight-lifters and dancers in this mixed-media, miniature reproduction of an actual circus. The sculpture is accompanied by a continuous screening of a film of the affable ringmaster, Calder, in his studio with his wife, winding up the gramophone, as they performed for the Paris avant-garde in the 1920s.

Other Highlights

The Mildred and Herbert Lee Galleries, occupying almost all of this floor, display works by American artists after 1945. In the Abstract Expressionism Gallery, Jackson Pollock's *Number 27* (1950) is one of the many pieces he created by placing the canvas on the floor and drizzling paint on it in a very controlled and deliberate manner. The Life Is Art Gallery contains Jasper Johns's *Three Flags* (1958), which he viewed as a deconstruction of this potent symbol of America.

BACKGROUND

Gertrude Vanderbilt Whitney (1877–1942), the daughter of Cornelius Vanderbilt (1843–1899), studied sculpture at the Art Students League of New York and went on to become one of the country's most generous patrons of the arts. In 1914, she launched the Whitney Studio Club, at 8 West 8th Street in the West Village, next to her MacDougal Alley studio, to exhibit works of young, avant-garde American artists. She was particularly fond of revolutionary artists such as John Sloan, Everett Shin and George Luks, realist painters Edward Hopper and Thomas Hart Benton, and early modernist painters such as Max Weber and Stuart Davis.

In 1929, after years of collecting, Whitney offered her personal collection to the Metropolitan Museum of Art. When the Met refused it, she established the Whitney Museum of American Art in 1931 with 700 objects, many from her personal collection. Thus the museum became one of the few museums anywhere in the world to be founded by an artist. The Whitney moved to its present building in 1966.

THE SIGHTS

Railroad Crossing, *by Edward Hopper*

Enjoying the last of the evening sunshine from the Brighton Beach Boardwalk in Brooklyn

The elegant Palm House in Brooklyn Botanic Garden

Farther Afield

BROOKLYN

BRIGHTON BEACH

✚ Page 7 • Southern tip of Brooklyn
🚉 B1, B68 🅀 Q 🍴 📷 🏛
www.brightonbeachbid.com

The influx of Russian immigrants to this area on Brooklyn's Atlantic-pounded shore has earned it the nickname Little Odessa by the Sea. You'll appreciate why as you stroll along the ocean's-edge boardwalk and Brighton Beach Avenue. The dozens of supermarkets and delicatessens are stocked with caviar, knishes, vodka, sausages and foods you just don't see back home unless home is Russia. The nightlife recalls Las Vegas, with its scantily-clad dancers crowned with elaborate plumage.

BROOKLYN BOTANIC GARDEN

✚ Page 7 • 900 Washington Avenue, Brooklyn 11225 ☎ 718/623-7200
🕐 Apr–end Sep Tue–Fri 8–6, Sat–Sun 10–6; rest of year Tue–Fri 8–4.30, Sat–Sun 10–4.30 🎟 Adult $5, under 16 free. Free to all Tue and Sat 10–noon
🚉 B41, B43, B47, B48, B71 🅀 Q to Prospect Park, 2, 3 to Eastern Parkway ◀ Guided tours weekends 1pm 📷 🏛 🏛
www.bbg.org

These 52 acres (21ha), planted with more than 13,000 varieties from around the world, are a place for a quiet stroll when you've had enough of Manhattan. There are water-lily ponds, stately old trees and flowering shrubs, a local plantlife section and a conifer collection. The Cranford Rose Garden shelters more than 1,000 varieties of

rose. The stunning Cherry Esplanade draws large crowds in May for the blooming season and the Japanese hill-and-pond garden is one of the best of its type in the country. The Palm House, designed by McKim, Mead & White in 1914, and the contemporary greenhouses added in 1987, offer additional lovely spaces. You can see everything in two or three hours.

BROOKLYN HISTORICAL SOCIETY

✚ 345 H26 • 128 Pierrepont Street, Brooklyn 11201 ☎ 718/222-4111
🕐 Wed–Sat 10–5, Sun noon–5
🎟 Adult $6, members and under 12 free 🚉 2, 3, M, N ◀ Guided tours available 🏛
www.brooklynhistory.org

The Brooklyn Historical Society is a museum, library and educational center dedicated to preserving and exploring Brooklyn's heritage. It occupies a landmark Queen Anne-style building (1881) designed by

An early employee time recorder at the Brooklyn Historical Society

George B. Post, who embellished the interior with Minton tile floors, elaborately carved black ash, and stained glass by Charles Booth. Post applied bridge engineering techniques to create an open and dramatic two-story space in the center of the building. The museum has a collection of 9,000-plus objects relating to local history. They are used in shows such as Brooklyn Works, which traced the history of working people from early farming days through the industrial era (when Brooklyn was the fourth-largest city in the US) to today. The shows are accessible and include fascinating oral history. Prints and Dodger memorabilia are strong suits of the collection too. The society also offers walking tours of Brooklyn neighborhoods and a boat tour of the working waterfront (prices vary). The library (open by appointment) has a premier collection too, including a first edition of Walt Whitman's *Leaves of Grass*.

CONEY ISLAND

✚ Page 7 • Southern tip of Brooklyn 11224 🚉 B36, B74 🅀 F, Q, W
🍴 📷 🏛 🏛

Known as Sodom by the Sea in the 1880s, this Atlantic-washed corner of Brooklyn was also called Playground of the World. Coney Island lost its historic Thunderbolt roller coaster and Kensington Hotel in 2000, and before that Steeplechase Park was closed in 1964. In spite of losing some of its famous landmarks, Coney Island has a vibrant spirit of rebirth. The New York Aquarium, opened in 1957, is still going strong, Astroland

(Continued on page 154)

The Peaceable Kingdom *(1840–45), by Edward Hicks*

BROOKLYN MUSEUM

The second-largest art museum in New York City, and one of the largest in the country, attracts half a million visitors every year.

The Brooklyn Museum is housed in a grand Beaux Arts building designed by McKim, Mead & White in 1897, with an addition by Polshek Partners completed in spring 2004. The new plaza has two water features.

THE COLLECTIONS

The museum prides itself on its fine collection of Egyptian, Classical and Ancient Middle Eastern Art. It holds the third-largest collection of Ancient Egyptian artifacts dating from predynastic times to the Roman conquest. The renovated Morris A. and Meyer Schapiro Wing contains objects from 1350 BC, in the reign of Akhenaten and his wife Nefertiti, through to the time of Cleopatra. Jewelry, reliefs of major deities, decorated sarcophagi, coffins and a 2,600-year-old mummy are on display.

The Arts of Africa, the Pacific and the Americas galleries have astonishing collections. An ivory gong from the Edo people of Benin, works from Polynesia and Indonesia, and important textiles from the Andes are just some of the fascinating items. The Arts of Asia collection has objects from China, India, Iran, Korea, Japan, Tibet, Thailand and Turkey.

The collection of decorative arts, costumes and textiles features a 17th-century Dutch farmhouse and a 20th-century art deco library. The costumes of 19th-century America and Europe are a glimpse at finery we can hardly imagine today.

Paintings, sculptures, prints, drawings and photographs include works by Gilbert Stuart, Thomas Cole, George Caleb Bingham, Winslow Homer, Auguste Rodin, Edgar Degas, Camille Pissarro, Edward Steichen and Paul Strand, to name just a few.

EVENTS

First Saturdays of the month are enormously popular. A free program of art and entertainment, with food and drinks supplied, attracts thousands. The entertainment starts with spoken-word artists and members of the Brooklyn Philharmonic in Shakespeare Live from 6.30 to 9. The program of Hands-on-Art from 6.30 to 8.30 allows you to create your own Egyptian-inspired necklaces.

A sculpture in the grounds

RATINGS

Historic interest	● ● ●
Photo stops	● ● ●
Walkability	● ● ● ● ●
Value for money	● ● ● ●

BASICS

Page 7 • 200 Eastern Parkway, Brooklyn 11238-6052

718/638-5000

Wed–Fri 10–5, Sat–Sun 11–6, first Sat of the month (except Sep) 11–11

Adult $8, under 12 free; 1st Sat each month free 5–11

B41, B69, B71

2, 3

Free audiotour of permanent collection

Museum Café Wed–Fri 10–4, Sat, Sun and holidays 10.30–4.30

BMA Shop 10.30–5.30, until 11pm on First Saturdays

www.brooklynmuseum.org
Floorplan, information on permanent and temporary collections, events, schedule for First Saturdays, online shopping.

Fun on the Ferris wheel at
Coney Island in Brooklyn

Henry Ward Beecher at the
Plymouth Church of the Pilgrims

The Kennedy arch at the
entrance to Prospect Park

(Continued from page 152)

Park still has its Cyclone roller
coaster, and the Mermaid Parade
is on the summer solstice.

Nathan Handwerker opened
his hot-dog emporium here in
1916, and his famous hot dogs
are now sold all over New York.
Keyspan Park is the $39-million
home of the Brooklyn Cyclones
baseball team, behind Parachute
Jump on the Boardwalk.

NEW YORK TRANSIT MUSEUM

Page 7 • Boerum Place and
Schermerhorn Street, Brooklyn 11201
☎ 718/694-1600 ◷ Tue–Fri 10–4,
Sat–Sun noon–5 ◉ Adult $5, child
(under 17) $3 ◉ 2, 3, 4, 5 ⊞ Annex
Gallery and Store at Grand Central, tel
212/878-0106 ⑪
www.mta.info/museum

The New York Transit Museum
occupies a decommissioned
subway station in downtown
Brooklyn. The permanent
and temporary exhibitions

Have a go at the exhibits at the
New York Transit Museum

explore the history of buses
and trolleys in New York City.
Highlights are the vintage subway
and trolley cars.

PLYMOUTH CHURCH OF THE PILGRIMS

☩ 345 H26 • 75 Hicks Street, Brooklyn
11201 ☎ 718/624-4743 ◉ Phone for
prices ◉ Guided tour only (1hr 30 min)
Sun 11–2, advance reservation required
◉ 4, A, N, M
www.plymouthchurch.org

The Plymouth Church of the
Pilgrims, built in 1849, was the
first Congregational Church in
Brooklyn and a focal point of
the anti-slavery movement at
the time. Abraham Lincoln
worshiped here twice in 1860,
and many eminent writers
have spoken here. Elegant
and beautiful stained-glass
windows by Tiffany adorn this
otherwise modest church, and
in the courtyard next to it is a
superb bronze statue of Henry
Ward Beecher (1813–87) with
slaves, sculpted by Gutzon
Borglum (famous for his work
on Mount Rushmore).

Beecher, the most famous
preacher in America, preached
from this pulpit for 40 years,
often speaking out against slavery.

PROSPECT PARK

☩ Page 7 • Flatbush Avenue at Grand
Army Plaza. Information: Prospect Park
Alliance, 95 Prospect Park West, Brooklyn
11215 ☎ Information: 718/965-8999;
Lefferts Homestead Historic House
Museum: 718/789-2822 ◷ Daily
5am–1am. Museum: Apr–Oct Thu–Sun
12–5 ◉ Free ◉ B16, B41, B43, B48,
B69 ◉ 2, 3, F, Q ⊡ ⊡ ⊞ ⑪
www.prospectpark.org

Designed by Frederick Law
Olmsted and Calvert Vaux,
the designers of Central Park
(▷ 78–83), this 526-acre
(213ha) park is a pleasant
place to spend a day. At the

main entrance at Grand Army
Plaza are a triumphal arch and
a monument to President
John F. Kennedy.

In Leffert's Homestead is a
museum for children (tel 718/
965-6505; Apr–end Nov Fri–Sun
1–4). A zoo, skating rink, boathouse and pond, playgrounds,
and a lovely 1912 carousel
(Apr–end Oct; 50 cents) are very
popular with children, too.

The northeast corner has a
rose garden, Japanese gardens, a
sculpture garden and the
Brooklyn Museum (▷ 153).
Entertainment events throughout
the year draw large crowds.

The Audubon Center provides
maps and guides for self-guiding
tours, as well as free Discover
Nature self-guiding tours (tel
718/287-3400; Sat–Sun 3–4).

WATERFRONT MUSEUM

☩ Page 7 • 699 Columbia Street,
Marine Terminal, Brooklyn 11231
☎ 718/624-4719 ◉ Free ◉ 77
◉ F, G
www.waterfrontmuseum.org

An unusual museum in the last
surviving railroad barge, the
Waterfront stages a summer
music series on Friday nights in
July. The barge was designated
by the U.N. in 1998 as the
Regional Craft of the International
Year of the Oceans. It's worth a
visit to enjoy an unusual evening
of live music, from blues to swing
and country.

Day visitors learn about New
York Harbor, barge history and
how this particular barge was
rescued.

QUEENS

NEW YORK HALL OF SCIENCE

☩ Page 7 • 111th Street, Flushing
Meadows–Corona Park, Queens 11368
☎ 718/ 699-0005 ◷ Sep–end Jun

THE SIGHTS

Education through fun at the Hall of Science Playground

Staten Island's Conference House retraces American history

The Waterfront Museum is in the last old railroad barge

Mon–Thu 9.30–2, Fri 9.30–5, Sat–Sun 10–6; Jul–end Aug Mon 9.30–2, Tue–Fri 9.30–5, Sat–Sun 10.30–6 ♿ Adult $11, child (2–17) $8. Sep–end Jun Thu 2–5 free. Science Playground (age 6 and up, with adult supervision, Mar and Dec, weather permitting) $3, $2 if in groups 🚌 Q23, Q48 🚇 7 to 111th Street Queens 🎧 Audio tours $2 ▢ ▨ 🚻 www.nyscience.org

In this hands-on, interactive museum of science and technology, with more than 225 exhibits, trained Explainers answer questions about topics ranging from color or sound and light to microbiology and quantum physics. You can surf the net in the Technology Gallery, discover the wonders of science by conducting your own experiments in the Biochemistry Discovery Lab, or peer at the World of Microbes and the Realm of the Atom.

The Science Playground outside has more than 30,000sq ft (2,790sq m) of giant slides, windmills, waterplay features, kinetic sculptures and a 3-D spider web, where children can have fun.

QUEENS MUSEUM OF ART

➕ Page 7 • New York City Building, Flushing Meadows–Corona Park, Queens 11368 ☎ 718/592-9700 🕐 Jul–end Aug Wed, Thu, Sat–Sun 12–6, Fri 12–8; Sep–end Jun Wed–Fri 10–5, Sat–Sun 12–5 💲 Suggested donation: adult $5, child (under 5) free 🚌 Q48, Q88 🚇 7 to Willets Point/Shea Stadium www.queensmuseum.org

A $15-million renovation in 1994 by Rafael Viñoly expanded this museum for ambitious exhibitions of contemporary art.

The permanent collection includes beautiful glassware from the Tiffany Studio, which was in Queens from 1893 to 1938, and the Panorama of New York City, an 18,000sq ft (1,674sq m)

minutely detailed scale model of New York City, with every building in place. The largest architectural scale model, it was created for the 1964–65 World's Fair, and it is regularly updated to reflect the changes in New York buildings. The museum's Art Moderne building was erected to house the 1939 World's Fair and was used again during the 1964–65 Fair, for which the adjacent Unisphere was created. It is the largest globe in the world, built by U.S. Steel. From

The Unisphere outside the Queens Museum of Art

1946 to 1952 the museum building was home to the United Nations General Assembly.

STATEN ISLAND

ALICE AUSTEN HOUSE

➕ Page 6 • 2 Hylan Boulevard, Staten Island 10305 ☎ 718/816-4506 🕐 Mar–end Dec Thu–Sun noon–5 ♿ Adult $2, child free 🚌 S51 to Hylan Boulevard ▨ 🚻 www.aliceausten.8m.com

This unique museum is the restored Victorian house and garden of Alice Austen (1866–1952), one of America's early female documentary photographers. A visit here is fascinating for the quality of Austen's photographs, but also for the idea it gives of what middle-class life was like at the turn of the 20th century.

The house was declared a city landmark in 1971.

The photographs give you a glimpse into the world of a well-traveled young woman, who taught herself to operate the camera, develop heavy glass plates and make prints. Alice took her equipment with her everywhere when she traveled, despite it weighing as much as 50 pounds (23kg), and photographed the world around her, including New York street scenes, using costuming and satire to create the desired effect.

Exhibitions and events take place throughout most of the year and often feature works by other local artists. Take the Staten Island Ferry from Manhattan, then catch the S51 bus to Hylan Boulevard.

CONFERENCE HOUSE

➕ Page 346 • 7455 Hylan Boulevard, Staten Island 10307 ☎ 718/984-0415 🕐 Apr–end Dec Fri–Sun 1–4 💲 $3 🚌 S59 to Craig Avenue www.theconferencehouse.org

Originally called the Billop Manor House, Conference House was built around 1680. On September 11, 1776, Benjamin Franklin, John Adams and Edward Rutledge (a South Carolina governor and signatory to the Declaration of Independence) came here for a meeting with Admiral Lord Howe, Commander of Her Majesty's Atlantic Squadron. Howe hoped to persuade the colonists to give up their fight for independence and to return to the Mother Country, but the meeting lasted no more than three hours. The three visitors made it clear that they were not interested in his offer to return to the fold. The two-and-a-half-story house has beautifully furnished period rooms and offers a look at life in colonial America. Special events take place throughout the year.

The Garibaldi Meucci Museum is dedicated to two Italians

Restoration is widespread at Historic Richmond Town

There are plenty of beautiful buildings at Snug Harbor

THE SIGHTS

GARIBALDI MEUCCI MUSEUM

✚ Page 6 • 420 Tompkins Avenue 10305 ☎ 718/442-1608 🕐 Tue–Sun 1–5 📱 Telephone for prices 🚌 S52, S78 www.garibaldimeuccimuseum.org

The Italian national hero, and one of the founders of unified Italy, Giuseppe Garibaldi (1807–82) spent two years in this 1840s house after fleeing the conquering republicans in Italy. It was the home of one Antonio Meucci (1808–89), who in fact was the inventor of the telephone. He invented a prototype several years before Alexander Graham Bell got into the picture, but, as he failed to patent his idea, he never got the credit.

After Garibaldi died in 1884, a committee decided to commemorate his stay in Staten Island and a plaque was placed on the house. After Meucci's death, the house was given to the Italian community to preserve as a memorial to Garibaldi.

Today the house is owned and operated by The Order of Sons of Italy in America and displays artifacts about the lives of these two men. From the Staten Island Ferry, take either bus S78 or S52.

HISTORIC RICHMOND TOWN

✚ Page 6 • 441 Clarke Avenue, Staten Island 10306 ☎ 718/351-1611 🕐 Jan–end Jun and Sep–end Dec Wed–Sun 1–5; Jul–end Aug Wed–Fri 10–5, Sat–Sun 1–5 📱 Adult $5, child (5–17) $3.50, under 5 free 🚌 S74 🛒 🍴 🚻 www.historicrichmondtown.org

About 27 historic buildings are spread out over 100 acres (40ha) at this museum complex. It stretches across three centuries of daily life and culture on Staten Island, from its earliest days as a rural crossroad to its incorporation into Greater New York. The quaint atmosphere and helpful staff make the whole experience a very pleasurable day out. Special events take place throughout the year, including summer fairs, concerts and costumed re-enactments.

JACQUES MARCHAIS MUSEUM OF TIBETAN ART

✚ Page 6 • 338 Lighthouse Avenue, Staten Island 10306 ☎ 718/987-3500 🕐 Apr–Nov Wed–Sun 1–5; by appointment only, Dec–Mar 📱 Adult $5, child (under 13) $2 🚌 S74 to Lighthouse Avenue 🚻 🚻 www.tibetanmuseum.org

This lovely museum is one of New York's best-kept secrets. The Dalai Lama, when he visited in 1991, attested to the likeness of the stone cottage on Lighthouse Hill to a Tibetan mountain temple, with its terraced sculpture gardens and an attractive fish pond. The museum exhibits Tibetan, Nepalese and Mongolian art from the 17th to the 19th centuries. The Nepalese metalwork, encrusted with jewels, and the metal figures of deities and lamas, are exquisite. Informative explanations help you understand the significance of the jewelry, dance masks, ritual objects, incense burners, paintings and many other items from the world's Buddhist cultures. Special exhibitions and activities enhance a visit.

SNUG HARBOR CULTURAL CENTER

✚ Page 6 • 1000 Richmond Terrace, Staten Island 10301 ☎ 718/448-2500 🕐 Grounds daily dawn–dusk. Gallery Museum: Tue–Sun 10–5 📱 Gallery adult $3, child (under 12) $2. Grounds: free 🚌 S40 🛒 📱 🚻 🚻 www.snug-harbor.org

Snug Harbor, a National Historic Landmark District, spreads out over 83 acres (34ha). Its 26 buildings, a fine collection of Greek Revival, Beaux Arts, Italianate and Victorian architecture, housed "decrepit and worn-out" old sailors during the 1880s. By the 1960s, the buildings had fallen into disrepair. After a vast restoration project, however, they are now a focal point of Staten Island cultural life, with art exhibitions in the Newhouse Galleries (Wed–Sun) and other activities. Be sure to see the Main Hall (Tue–Sun), the oldest building, and its lavish ceiling mural, towering skylight dome and gilded weathervane.

Preparing flax at one of the Historic Richmond Town restoration projects

Seals bask in the sun in their landscaped habitat at the Bronx Zoo

THE BRONX

BRONX ZOO

The largest metropolitan wildlife park in the country, with more than 4,500 animals representing 55 species housed on 265 acres (107ha).

Plan to spend a whole day at this wonderful and hugely popular zoo, which has no fewer than three names—Bronx Zoo (unofficial), New York Zoological Park and International Wildlife Conservation Park. The animals, including endangered and threatened species, are well cared for and their surroundings are as near as possible to their habitats.

HIGHLIGHTS

One of the most impressive areas is the Wild Asia Complex, where you can see Indonesian tigers and Asian elephants, but only from the Bengali Express monorail. Jungle World's indoor re-creation of an Asian forest will envelop you, and it's home to leopards, lizards, tree kangaroos and white-cheeked gibbons, among other exotic wildlife from jungles around the world. In the Himalayan Highlands there are extremely rare snow leopards as well as red pandas.

The Congo Gorilla Forest is a 6.5-acre (9ha) re-creation of an African rainforest; among the treetop lookouts, wooded pathways and lush greenery are 400 animals, including western lowland gorillas, who can be entertaining. You'll also see okapi and red river hogs.

In the Butterfly Zone the size of some of the butterflies might surprise you, not to mention the enormous variety and beauty of these complicated insects.

The World of Darkness, as you might imagine, is devoted to the lives of nocturnal creatures, such as fruit-eating bats.

The Children's Zoo (Apr–end Oct) has wonderful activities—kids learn to see like an owl and hear like a fox—and a petting zoo.

The Bengali Express monorail (May–end Oct) is a 25-minute narrated ride above the roaming Siberian tigers, Indian rhinoceroses, Asian elephants, and other animals of the Indian subcontinent. It's a good way to see a lot without wearing yourself out. Other rides include the Skyfari aerial tram, camel rides and the Zoo Shuttle (Apr–end Oct).

In summer it can get very crowded, and if it is a very warm day the animals retreat from open sunny positions and it can be hard to see some of them.

RATINGS

Good for kids	●●●●●
Photo stops	●●●●●
Specialist shopping	●●●○○
Value for money	●●●●○

BASICS

✚ Page 7 • Bronx River Parkway and Fordham Road, Bronx 10460

☎ 718/367-1010

🕐 Apr–Oct Mon–Fri 10–5, Sat–Sun 10–5.30; rest of year daily 10–4.30

💵 Tue–Thu adult $11, child (2–12) $8, under 2 free; Wed suggested donation. Congo Gorilla Forest and camel rides $3; Children's Zoo, Skyfari, Zoo Shuttle, Butterfly Zone, Bengali Express $2 each. Pay-One-Price ticket that includes admission and all rides: adult $21, child $18

🚌 Bx11, tel 718/652-8400 for details

🚇 2 or 5 to Pelham Parkway or East Tremont Avenue

🎧 Tours by Friends of the Zoo, tel 718/220-5141

🍴 📷 ♿ 👥

www.bronxzoo.com

TIPS

● From Madison Avenue you can take the Liberty Lines Bx11 express bus directly to the zoo.

● Eat early or late or bring a picnic and drinks. Lines for the food stands can be long and slow on a busy, hot afternoon.

The New York Yankees have won 26 World Series, more than any other American baseball team

YANKEE STADIUM

Cheer the New York Yankees in their home stadium.

RATINGS	
Good for kids	●●●●
Photo stops	●●●
Specialist shopping	●●●●
Value for money	●●●●●

BASICS

✚ Page 7 • 161st Street and River Avenue, Bronx 10451
☎ 718/293-6000
🕐 Baseball season Apr–Oct
🎫 Tickets for games $12–$95, tel Ticketmaster 212/307-1212 or visit www.yankees.com
🚌 Bx6, Bx13
🚇 4, D
📷 One-hour behind-the-scenes tour, tel 718/579-4531, visit the website or buy tickets from one of the five Clubhouse Shops in Manhattan on the day of the tour. Adult $14, child $7
🍴 Sidewalk Café on the Plaza next to Gates 4 and 6; snacks and drinks throughout the stadium
🎁 Gift shops are on the Field Level sections 24, 25. Yankee Clubhouse stores have five Manhattan locations. Get the location details and opening hours from the website
🚻
www.yankees.com

Yankee Stadium, America's first triple-decker stadium, has been home of the New York Yankees since April 18, 1923. The most famous player of them all, Babe Ruth, hit a three-run homer on that inaugural day in front of 74,200 fans and the Yankees were victorious (4–1). After that, the stadium quickly became known as The House That Ruth Built. The stadium got electric lighting in 1946 and the first electronic message board in 1959. After CBS became its new owner in 1967, the Yankees spent two seasons at Shea Stadium while their own stadium was renovated. Upon their return, the Yankees went on to host the World Series.

The stadium is used for other events, including football, soccer, religious conventions, political assemblies and concerts.

At Monument Park, on Field Level Section 36, you can see a special walk honoring players whose uniform numbers have been retired. Old Timers' Day, usually held in July, brings back the grand old players for a bow before their cheering fans.

SEEING A GAME

There are seven main entrances, so make a mental note of where you enter to avoid confusion when you leave. Make sure that you have no reason to leave once you are inside, because you cannot re-enter the stadium using the same ticket. Arrive an hour and a half before the game Mondays to Fridays, two hours ahead on weekends to watch the batting practice. It can take some time to get through the entrance, so allow plenty of time to see the beginning of the game.

To get a behind-the-scenes tour, which starts at the Press Gate, go to the Advance Ticket window or any of the Clubhouse stores on the day of the tour and you can find out more about Yankee history, get a good look at the field, the dugout area, the press box, the Clubhouse and Monument Park.

Alcohol is sold up until the seventh inning of each game, but drunkenness is not tolerated; you can ask to sit in an alcohol-free section when you buy your tickets. Other rules ban bottles, cans, coolers or containers, large bags and briefcases, noisemakers, laser pens, beachballs, firearms and knives; and there's no smoking.

This chapter gives information on things to do in New York other than sightseeing.

Shops and performance venues are located on the maps at the beginning of each section.

What to Do

Hue-Man
Bookstore

West 95th Street
West 94th Street
West 93rd Street

UPPER WEST
West 92nd Street
SIDE
West 91st Street

Centra
Park
Reservo

13

West 90th Street
West 89th Street
West 88th Street
West 87th Street
West 86th Street

86th
Street

CENTRAL
PARK

86th
Stree

West 85th Street
West 84th Street

West 83rd Street

West 82nd Street

81st Street
Museum of
Nat Hist

Centra

14

West 81st Street
West 80th Street

Zabar's

American Museum
of Natural History

Belvedere
Lake

West 79th Street

79th
Street

West 78th Street

West 77th Street

**Kenneth
Cole**

West 76th Street

New-York
Historical
Society

79th street Transver

Centra

The
Lake

Hudson River

West 75th Street

San Remo
Apartments

West 74th Street

Ansonia
Building

West 73rd Street

West 72nd Street

72nd
Street

**Applause Theatre
and Cinema Books**

West 71st Street

The Dakota

72nd
Street

Strawberry
Fields

Olms

15

West
69th
Street

West
68th
Street

West 70th Street

West 69th Street

West 68th Street

West 67th Street

The
Sheep
Meadow

Freedom
Place

66th Street
Lincoln Center

West 66th Street

Juilliard School

West 65th Street

Tavern on
the Green

65th Street

West 64th Street

West 64th Street

16

West 63rd Street

West 62nd
Street

Lincoln
Center

West 63rd Street

West 62nd Street

West 61st Street

Museum of
Biblical Art

West 61st Street

Central
Park

West 60th Street

West 59th
Street

West 59th Street

**Time Warner
Center**

West 58th Street

59th Street
Columbut
Circle

COLUMBUS
CIRCLE

Central

Pa

WEST 57TH STREET

57th
Street

Carnegie
Hall

West 56th Street

**The Mysterio
Booksh**

West 55th Street

West 54th Street

West 53rd Street

7th
Avenue

17

West 52nd Street

West 51st Street

West 50th Street

50th
Street

59th
Street

49th
Street

West 49th Street

West 48th Street

B

Intrepid
Sea, Air and Space
Museum

West 46th
Street

C

West 47th Street

West 46th Street

West 45th Street

BROADWAY

D

De Witt
Clinton Park

Mill Rock Park

East 95th Street   East 95th Street
East 94th Street   East 94th Street
East 93rd Street
Kitchen Arts and Letters
East 92nd Street   East 92nd Street
Jewish Museum
East 91st Street   East 91st Street
Cooper-Hewitt National Design Museum
East 90th Street   East 90th Street
National Academy of Design
Guggenheim Museum   East 89th Street
East 88th Street   East 88th Street
Gracie Mansion
East 87th Street   East 87th Street
Carl Schurz Park
86th Street   East 86th Street
Neue Galerie   East 85th Street   East 85th Street
East 84th Street   East 84th Street
East 83rd Street   East 83rd Street
The Metropolitan Museum of Art
East 82nd Street   East 82nd Street
East 81st Street   East 81st Street
East 80th Street   East 80th Street
East 79th Street   East 79th Street
East 78th Street   East 78th Street
East 77th Street   East 77th Street
77th Street
East 76th Street   East 76th Street
Whitney Museum of American Art   East 75th Street   East 75th Street
East 74th Street   East 74th Street
Conservatory Water
East 73rd Street   East 73rd Street
John Jay Park
East 72nd Street   East 72nd Street
East 71st Street
Ralph Lauren
Frick Collection   Penhaligon's   East 70th Street   East 70th Street
Asia Society and Museum
East 69th Street   East 69th Street
Dolce & Gabbana
Donna Karan   68th Street Hunter College   East 68th Street
East 67th Street   East 67th Street
Nicole Miller
East 66th Street   East 66th Street
Giorgio Armani   Jean-Paul Gaultier   East 65th Street   East 65th Street
East 64th Street   East 64th Street
Shanghai Tang   Jimmy Choo
Floris   East 63rd Street   East 63rd Street
Lexington Avenue
FIFTH AVENUE   East 62nd Street   East 62nd Street
Sherry-Lehmann
East 61st Street   East 61st St
Calvin Klein   DKNY
Borrelli   Barneys   East 60th Street   East 60th Street
Argosy Books
Tod's   Bloomingdale's
FAO Schwarz   Crate & Barrel   East 59th Street   East 59th Street
Rizzoli   Bergdorf Goodman   Chanel   Border's Books, Music and Café   Hammacher Schlemmer
East 58th Street   East 58th Street
Coach   East 57th Street
WEST 57TH STREET   EAST 57TH STREET
Fendi   Tiffany   Dahesh Museum of Art
West 56th Street   Trump Tower   East 56th Street   West 56th Street
Manolo Blahnik   Henri Bendel   Suarez Handbags
Takashimaya   West 55th Street   East 55th Street
Gucci   Lacoste   East 54th Street
Museum of Modern Art   West 54th Street
Thomas Pink   East 53rd Street
Museum of Arts and Design   Museum of Television and Radio   Seagram Building
West 52nd Street   East 52nd Street
Jimmy Choo   Cartier
West 51st Street   St. Patrick's Cathedral   Municipal Art Society   East 51st Street
Radio City Music Hall   51st Street
West 50th Street   East 50th Street
GE Building   Saks Fifth Avenue
Rockefeller Center   Cole Haan   East 49th Street   East 49th Street
Caswell-Massey
West 48th Street   Morrell & Company   East 48th Street   East 48th Street
West 47th Street   East 47th Street   East 47th Street
DIAMOND DISTRICT
MIDTOWN MANHATTAN   East 46th Street   East 46th Street
West 45th Street   Paul Stuart   East 45th Street

Franklin Delano Roosevelt Drive
ROOSEVELT ISLAND
Roosevelt Island Main Street
Mount Vernon Hotel Museum and Garden
HIGHWAY 25   QUEENSBORO BRIDGE
Main Street
West Road   East Road
Sutton Place
Mitchell Pl
United Nations Headquarters

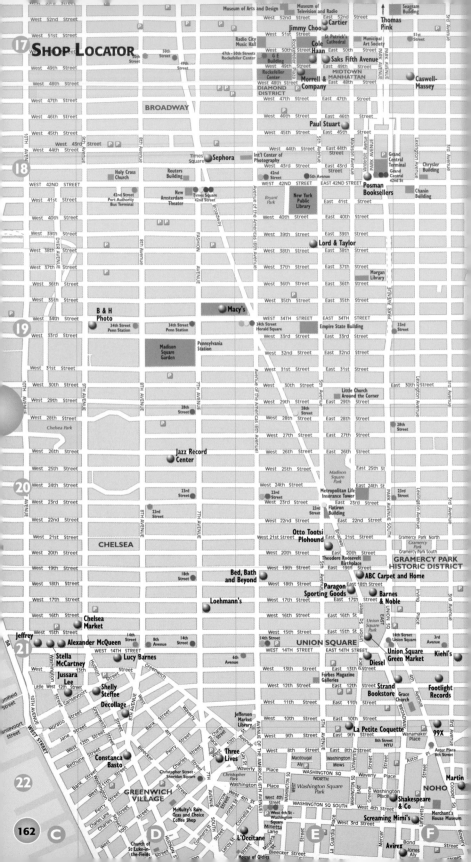

SHOP LOCATOR

Museum of Arts and Design
Museum of Television and Radio
Seagram Building

West 52nd Street
Thomas Pink
West 52nd Street

Jimmy Choo
Cartier
West 51st Street
51st Street

Cole Haan
St Patrick's Cathedral
Municipal Art Society
West 51st Street

Radio City Music Hall
47th–50th Streets Rockefeller Center
G E Building
West 50th Street

50th Street
49th Street

Saks Fifth Avenue
West 49th Street
MIDTOWN MANHATTAN

Rockefeller Center
Morrell & Company
West 48th Street
DIAMOND DISTRICT
West 47th Street

Caswell-Massey
West 47th Street

BROADWAY
West 46th Street

Paul Stuart
West 45th Street

West 44th Street
Grand Central Terminal
Chrysler Building

Times Square
Sephora
West 43rd Street
Int'l Center of Photography
East 43rd Street
Grand Central 42nd St

42nd Street
5th Avenue

Holy Cross Church
Reuters Building
EAST 42ND STREET
Posman Booksellers
Chanin Building

42nd Street Port Authority Bus Terminal
New Amsterdam Theater
Times Square 42nd Street
West 41st Street
Bryant Park
New York Public Library
East 41st Street

West 40th Street
West 40th Street
East 40th Street

West 39th Street
Lord & Taylor
East 39th Street

West 38th Street
West 38th Street
East 38th Street

West 37th Street
East 37th Street
Morgan Library

West 36th Street
East 36th Street

B & H Photo
West 35th Street
East 35th Street
Macy's

34th Street Penn Station
34th Street Penn Station
34th Street Herald Square
WEST 34th STREET
EAST 34th STREET
33rd Street

West 33rd Street
Empire State Building
East 33rd Street

Madison Square Garden
Pennsylvania Station
West 32nd Street
East 32nd Street

West 31st Street
East 31st Street

Chelsea Park
West 30th Street
Little Church Around the Corner
East 29th Street

West 29th Street
28th Street

West 28th Street
28th Street
East 28th Street
28th Street

West 26th Street
East 26th Street

Jazz Record Center
West 25th Street
East 25th St

Madison Square Park
West 24th Street
East 24th Street

23rd Street
West 23rd Street
Metropolitan Life Insurance Tower
23rd Street

CHELSEA
23rd Street
West 22nd Street
Flatiron Building
East 22nd Street

West 21st Street
Otto Tootsi Plohound
East 21st Street
Gramercy Park North

West 20th Street
Theodore Roosevelt Birthplace
East 20th Street
Gramercy Park South

Bed, Bath and Beyond
18th Street
West 19th Street
ABC Carpet and Home
East 19th St
GRAMERCY PARK HISTORIC DISTRICT

Paragon Sporting Goods
West 18th Street
East 18th Street
Barnes & Noble

Loehmann's
West 17th Street
East 17th Street

Chelsea Market
West 16th Street
East 16th St
Union Square Park

West 15th Street
East 15th St
UNION SQUARE
Union Square

Jeffrey
Alexander McQueen
14th Street
8th Street
14th Street
14th Street Union Square
3rd Avenue

Stella McCartney
Lucy Barnes
WEST 14th STREET
EAST 14th STREET
Union Square Green Market
Kiehl's

Jussara Lee
13th Street
West 13th Street
East 13th Street
Diesel

Shelly Steffee
Decollage
West 12th Street
Forbes Magazine Galleries
West 11th Street
Strand Bookstore
Grace Church
Footlight Records

Jefferson Market Library
West 10th Street
East 9th Street
La Petite Coquette
99X

Constanca Basto
Three Lives
GREENWICH VILLAGE
Christopher Street–Sheridan Square
Washington Square Park
8th Street NYU
Martin
NOHO

McNulty's Rare Teas and Choice Coffee Shop
WASHINGTON SQ SOUTH
West 4th St–Washington Square
Shakespeare & Co
Merchant's House Museum

162
Church of St-Luke-in-the-Fields
L'Occitane
Screaming Mimi's
West 3rd Street
Avirex
House of Oldies

C
D
E
F

SHOPPING

They say that you can buy anything you want in New York City, and it's true. New York's shopping ranges from large opulent department stores to tiny one-room boutiques. Many visitors come to New York just to shop, especially pre-Christmas, uptown at the flagship designer stores that line Madison and Fifth avenues, or downtown at the cutting-edge designers in SoHo and NoLita. More moderately priced wares can be found at stores around Herald Square and 34th Street, or in the branches of national chains scattered around Manhattan. There aren't any malls of note. Many stores open seven days a week (with late-night hours usually on Thursday). European visitors should note that American sizes differ from British and European sizes (▷ 315). Note too that the sales tax (added at the cash register) is 8.375 percent. Credit cards are accepted virtually everywhere.

Objets d'art and other decorative items from Greene Street, SoHo

116th Street and Lenox Avenue, textiles, jewelry, bowls made from gourds, wooden stools and other artifacts from Africa are for sale. The Annex Antique Fair and Flea Market in the parking lots at Sixth Avenue and 26th Street (tel 212/243-5343) is very popular. Get there early for the best pickings (it opens at 5am). The Sunday Columbus Avenue market (between 76th and 77th streets) is also fun. In summer, expect small neighborhood street fairs at which people sell all kinds of bric-à-brac, clothing, CDs, food and books. Green

Vintage clothing for both sexes at Screaming Mimi's

Top-quality produce, packaged and fresh, from Dean & DeLuca

SALES
The largest sales take place in January and July, and also around legal holidays—Presidents' Day, Memorial Day and Labor Day, for example.

To keep abreast of current and forthcoming sales check the relevant sections of *New York* magazine and *Time Out* or go online to www.dailycandy.com or www.nysale.com. Some of the best deals are found at sample sales, usually held in the spring and fall. Designers and manufacturers hold such sales to make space for their new design samples. Shopping fiends find

out about them by subscribing to S & B Report (tel 877/579-0222) or going online at www.lazarshopping.com. Online subscription is $75 a year. They are also listed at www.nysale.com. For visitors the best way to locate these sales is to go to a favorite designer or store and ask if they hold them. Or try walking around the Garment District, where people often give out flyers announcing them. Bring cash and note you may not be able to try items on. No refunds either.

MARKETS
Unlike European cities, New York has few outstanding markets, although one or two are worth visiting. At the African Market at

markets have become very popular. The most storied is at Union Square (▷ 178), but there are smaller ones around town in Abingdon Square in the West Village or Tompkins Square in the East Village, for example.

Savvy New Yorkers also shop the thrift stores and consignment shops. Some of the best are: Housing Works, 143 West 17th Street (tel 212/366-0820) and 306 Columbus Avenue (tel 212/579-7566), Encore, 1132 Madison Avenue (tel 212/879-2850) at 84th Street, and the Salvation Army, 112 4th Avenue (tel 212/673-2741).

SoHo

HOW TO GET THERE

🚇 4, 5, 6, or N, Q, R, W
🚌 M1, M5, M6

SoHo has some of the hippest loft-style stores in the city. Concentrate on Mercer, Greene, Wooster, Prince and Spring streets, between West Broadway and Broadway. Many stores are open seven days a week, and the area can be crowded with non-residents on weekends.

Emerge from the subway at Broadway and Prince Street and you'll find three destination stores. **Dean & DeLuca**, on the southeast corner, is a landmark of New York for lovers of top-quality food. Displays are gorgeous, a café serves delicious pastries, and top-of-the-line cooking equipment is also for sale.

Check out Eres for the ultimate in swimwear and lingerie

Across the street on the north-west corner, the **Prada** store was designed by Dutch architect Rem Koolhaas; rows of mannikins wear the latest must-have designs from this fashion powerhouse.

On the southwest corner, **Victoria's Secret** sells romantic lingerie and swimwear. Farther down Broadway, **The Puma Store**, at No. 521, sells oodles of walking and running shoes. At No. 504 check out **Bloomingdales Downtown** and also **Pearl River Mart** at No. 477. Nearby, on Broadway, between Houston and Canal

streets, branches of Seattle-based **Eddie Bauer** sell casual wear, and the rapidly expanding Spanish chain **Zara International**, among other brand-name stores, sells fashion.

West along Prince Street look for more names. **Phat Farm** (No. 129) has stylish hip-hop wear.

On Mercer, look for **Marc Jacobs** at No. 163, the hottest fashion name of the moment, and **APC** at No. 131, south of Prince Street, which sells well-designed Parisian-style basics. **Kate Spade**, the famous bag designer, has a store at Mercer and Broome streets. At the corner of Mercer and Grand streets are the precise fashions of **Yohji Yamamoto**.

On Greene Street **Helmut Lang** sells his iconic jeans and other avant-garde fashions at No. 80 and **Kirna Zabete**, at No. 96, shows fashions of the best of the current crop of international designers. If you appreciate kitchen and tableware, drop in at **Broadway Panhandler**, at 477 Broome Street between Greene and Wooster streets, which sells top brands at discount prices, another landmark of a good cook's New York.

Turn off Prince Street and head south down Wooster, and you'll find **BCBG by Max Azria** selling individual women's fashions at No. 120, and **Eres** selling beautiful swimwear and lingerie at No. 98.

WHERE TO EAT

Cupping Room Café, 359 West Broadway between Broome and Grand streets (tel 212/925-2898), is a fixture of SoHo, is casual and offers a menu of soups, burgers, salads and egg dishes.

Prada's store on Broadway is worth a visit just to see the design of the interior

At **Hampton Chutney**, 68 Prince Street between Crosby and Lafayette streets (tel 212/226-9996), tuck into southern Indian specialties—dosas, pancakes made with lentil flour, filled with both Indian and Western ingredients. You can get sandwiches on black, sourdough and other breads, too (▷ 278). **Fanelli's**, 94 Prince Street at Mercer (tel 212/226-9412), is reminiscent of the days when SoHo was a hang-out of artists. A good option for a burger or a plate of pasta, it also serves draft beer.

NoLita

WHAT TO DO

HOW TO GET THERE

🚇 4, 5, 6

🚌 M1, M6, M21

NoLita stands for *No*rth of *Li*ttle *Ita*ly. **It is a warren of streets anchored by St. Patrick's Old Cathedral on Mulberry Street (between Prince and Houston streets), which was New York's original Roman Catholic cathedral. Dedicated in 1815, it was designed by Joseph Mangin, co-architect of City Hall. After a disastrous fire in 1866, the cathedral that stands on Fifth Avenue and 50th Street replaced it as the seat of the archdiocese.**

The original congregation was largely Gaelic-speaking, poor Irish immigrants, and in those days the St. Patrick's Day parade terminated at the cathedral. At the turn of the 20th century, Italians

Map showing NoLita area with Bleecker Street, Broadway-Lafayette Street, East Houston Street, Mott Street, Mulberry Street, Elizabeth Street, Bowery, 2nd Avenue, Stanton Street, Chrystie Street, Jersey St, Prince Street, Little Singer Museum, St Patrick's Old Cathedral, Spring Street, Crosby Street, Broadway, Lafayette St, Kenmare Street, Broome Street, and stores: Me & Ro, Kelly Christy, Sigerson Morrison, Zero, Gas, Resurrection Vintage, Tracy Feith. LITTLE ITALY. F22, F23

Pick up some unique accessories in NoLita's boutiques

formed the majority; today most of the congregation is Spanish-speaking.

Several members of the famous restaurant family, the Swiss Delmonico's, are buried in the crypt.

Pierre Toussaint, a Haitian slave who came to America in 1787, was buried in the cemetery. He attained his freedom, subsequently worked as a hairdresser and donated most of his wealth to various charities— orphanages, seminaries and hospitals.

The area developed as a shopping district when SoHo rents became too expensive for new designers and artists. Here, along Mulberry, Mott and Elizabeth streets between Kenmare and Houston streets are numerous small storefronts selling the latest fashions and accessories. From the Spring Street Station, walk east on Spring Street to Mulberry Street.

On Mulberry **Tracy Feith**, at No. 209, is famous for his ready-to-go party outfits. No. 257 used to be the Ravenite Social Club, a favorite John Gotti hang-out. Today, of course, it's a boutique.

Mott Street, between Prince and Spring streets, shelters **Resurrection Vintage**, one of the city's finest vintage clothing stores, plus **Zero** at No. 225, where Maria Cornejo crafts her own avant-garde line, and **Gas** at No. 238, which displays this French designer's jewelry, made with brilliant colored semi-precious stones. **Sigerson Morrison**, around the corner on Prince Street, sells some ultra-fashionable shoes at No. 28—they're almost as good as Manolos but at a fraction of the price. There are also more eye-catching boutiques on Mott Street between Prince and Houston streets.

Elizabeth Street is NoLita's main drag and has a couple of outstanding stores. **Kelly Christy** at No 235 is one of the city's new young milliners and makes hats in every fabric and style, while **Me & Ro** at No. 239 are a duo who make some fun, inspired jewelry, often with Eastern motifs.

Stores in NoLita tend to be one-of-a-kind rather than chains

WHERE TO EAT

Tiny **Bread**, at 20 Spring Street between Elizabeth and Mott streets (tel 212/334-1015), prepares soups, salads and Italian-inspired dishes. French-inspired **Café Gitane**, 242 Mott Street at Prince Street (tel 212/334-9552), serves good coffee plus salads, sandwiches and more substantial plates, such as couscous. Drop in to **Café Habana**, 17 Prince Street at Elizabeth Street (tel 212/625-2001), for some spicy tacos or a hefty Cuban sandwich.

You'll find designer jewelry aplenty in boutiques such as Me & Ro on Elizabeth Street

Fifth Avenue

HOW TO GET THERE
🚇 A, C, E or N, Q, R, W
🚌 M1, M2, M3, M4, M5

After Madison Avenue, Fifth Avenue is the city's other famous shopping street, at least from 48th to 59th streets. Leave the subway stop at Fifth Avenue and 59th Street around the corner from the Plaza Hotel and stroll down Fifth Avenue.

Across the street looms the old General Motors Building. At the northeast corner of 58th Street **FAO Schwarz** is the city's legendary toy store. Farther down the Avenue are several of the city's great stores—**Bergdorf Goodman** at No. 754, **Henri Bendel** at No. 714, between 55th and 56th streets, and Japanese-owned **Takashimaya**, between 54th and 55th streets, with exquisite merchandise in

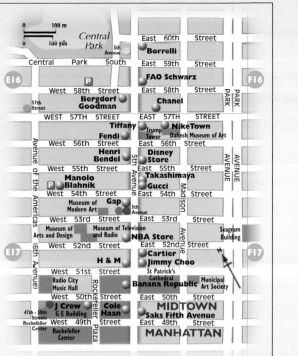

Go to Gap at No. 680 for practical, good-quality casuals

Jimmy Choo shoe

Well-cut, casual clothes for men and women at Banana Republic

exquisite settings. Duck off Fifth Avenue east along 57th Street to the French classic, **Chanel**, and high-tech **NikeTown**, home of the swoosh.

As you progress down the Avenue, top-end designer show-cases alternate with branches of national chains, making for sharp contrasts. At No. 720 **Fendi** sells its flamboyant, super-expensive accessories, while across the street a block farther south at No. 711, the **Disney Store** peddles character merchandise. **Gucci**, the premier Italian designer at No. 685, stands across from **Gap**, and a few blocks south at No. 666 is the **NBA Store**, which

stocks everything a basketball fan ever yearned for. **Tiffany** and **Cartier** are the two heavyweight jewelers on the Avenue, the first at No. 727, near 57th Street, and the second at No. 653 at 52nd Street. There are others, too—Bulgari, Van Cleef & Arpels, Harry Winston, and Wempe. **Jimmy Choo** displays his fantastic footwear at No. 645, at 51st Street. (**Manolo Blahnik** is just a few blocks away on 54th Street between Fifth and Sixth avenues.) At No. 640 **H&M** rolls out the designer knock-offs for the young shoppers, while at No. 626 **Banana Republic** concentrates its efforts on a more mature, more conservative audience. **Cole Haan** sells soft leather shoes and accessories at No. 620. At No. 626 **Saks Fifth Avenue** culls the best of the world's designers, including many you know and the most promising newcomers.

In Rockefeller Plaza (between 49th and 50th streets), look for **J. Crew**, which caters to the college crowd, recent graduates and wannabes.

WHERE TO EAT

Wander the subterranean hallways under the G. E. Building where you will find numerous restaurants and cafés. **Au Bon Pain**, 1211 Avenue of the Americas (tel 212/840-5093), is a reliable standby for soups, sandwiches and pastries. Stylish **Morrells Café**, 1 Rockefeller Plaza (tel 212/262-7700), has a wide selection of wines to accompany its light fare.

Madison Avenue

HOW TO GET THERE

🚇 A, C, E
🚌 M1, M2, M3, M4, M5

Madison Avenue sells the crème de la crème of international fashion. From 53rd Street and the Fifth Avenue subway station, walk east to Madison Avenue and turn left (north) for a leisurely stroll.

At the northwest corner of 53rd, **Thomas Pink** sells beautifully cut shirts in rainbow hues. Across the street, **Talbots** at No. 525 sells comfortable, reasonably priced fashions to well-heeled women. Farther up the avenue at No. 543, **Lacoste** has complete wardrobes for cruising, golf and tennis. At No. 595 **Coach** sells attractive well-made bags and accessories. **Ann Taylor** caters to the young professional

Bag from Coach

woman at No. 645, while the huge **Crate & Barrel** at No. 650 sells smart tableware, furniture and other items for the home. Italian shoemaker **Tod's** at No. 650 sells some of the most comfortable walking shoes ever made. Quintessential American designer **Calvin Klein**, who has lent his name to every conceivable wardrobe and houseware item, displays his talent at No. 654 at 60th Street. Designer Donna Karan has her **DKNY** store across the street at No. 655. **Barneys** is famous for its windows and for its highly selective range of all that's cutting edge in international design. Between 62nd and

72nd streets, famous names tumble one after the other— **Floris** at No. 703 with its alluring fragrances, **Shanghai Tang** displaying Asian-inspired fashions at No. 714, **Jean-Paul Gaultier** and **Giorgio Armani** (at 759 and 760 at 65th Street).

Farther up the Avenue are **Donna Karan** at No. 819, **Dolce & Gabbana** at No. 816, **Penhaligon's** at No. 870 and **Ralph Lauren**, in a spectacularly renovated 19th-century town house at No. 867 at 71st Street—this store is worth seeing just for the architecture. Equally dramatic stores are those of Donna Karan, and Jean-Paul Gaultier.

WHERE TO EAT

Brasserie, 100 East 53rd Street between Park and Lexington avenues (tel 212/751-4840), is a frenzied, streamlined, ultramodern space, where you can linger over lunch or grab a bite at the bar. The broad menu offers crepes, burgers, salads and bistro classics, as well as baguettes for a lighter snack (▷ 273). Food is served from early morning to late at night. **Pret à Manger**, 400 Park Avenue at 54th Street (tel 212/207-3725), is a branch of the British chain. It delivers freshly made sandwiches and wraps filled with appealing ingredients.

Shopping Directory

From large department stores and opulent designer stores to one-room boutiques, from diamonds to deckchairs and art supplies to zippers, you'll find it all in New York. Manhattan, though lacking the usual American city's bounty of malls, is itself like one huge open-air mall.

• ▷ 160–163 for shop locator maps
• ▷ 182–183 for chain stores chart
• ▷ 315 for clothing sizes

BOOKS

APPLAUSE THEATRE AND CINEMA BOOKS
Map 160 C15
211 West 71st Street between Broadway and West End Avenue
Tel 212/496-7511
www.applausebooks.com
Books about Broadway, plays and playwrights, dance and film fill the shelves.
🕐 Mon–Sat 11–7 🚇 72nd Street (1, 2, 3, 9) 🚌 M5, M7, M104

ARGOSY BOOKS
Map 161 F16
116 East 59th Street between Park and Lexington avenues
Tel 212/753-4455
www.argosybooks.com
This store, which has been operating since 1925, is one of the few remaining bookstores in the city for out-of-print and rare books. On its seven floors, it has an extensive stock of books, with particular strength in Americana, contemporary first editions, and the history of science and medicine. It also sells prints, autographs, and antique maps.
🕐 Sep–end Apr Mon–Fri 10–6, Sat 10–5; rest of year Mon–Fri 10–6
🚇 59th Street (4, 5, 6)
🚌 M1, M2, M3, M4, M98, M101, M102, M103

BARNES & NOBLE
Map 162 E21
Union Square North at 17th Street between Broadway and Park Avenue South
Tel 212/253-0810
www.bn.com
Although not the original of this megachain with

branches all over the country, it is large and comfortable enough to be considered the flagship store. The rise of this chain from a small store near New York University into this behemoth is certainly quite a story. Like most branches, this store has a

Browsing for a good read in one of the city's bookstores

café and comfortable chairs for reading, and sells music, software and magazines as well as books. The main college bookstore is at Fifth Avenue and 18th Street.
🕐 Daily 10–10 🚇 14th Street/Union Square (4, 5, 6, L, N, Q, R, W) 🚌 M1, M2, M3, M6, M7

BORDER'S BOOKS, MUSIC AND CAFÉ
Map 161 F16
461 Park Avenue at 57th Street (northeast corner)
Tel 212/980-6785
www.borders.com
The 'other' chain. It has a slightly more esoteric stock

and more personal feel than its competitor Barnes & Noble.
🕐 Mon–Fri 9am–10pm, Sat 10–8, Sun 11–8 🚇 59th Street (4, 5, 6), 59th Street (N, R, W) 🚌 M1, M2, M3, M4

HUE-MAN BOOKSTORE
Off map 160 D12
2319 Frederick Douglass Boulevard between 124th and 125th streets
Tel 212/665-7400
www.huemanbookstore.com
This bookstore stocks a large collection of classic and contemporary African-American fiction and non-fiction and holds author readings.
🕐 Mon–Sat 10–8, Sun 11–7 🚇 125th Street (A, B, C, D) 🚌 M10

KITCHEN ARTS AND LETTERS
Map 161 F13
1435 Lexington Avenue between 93rd and 94th streets
Tel 212/876-5550
You can find all of the classic cookery writers here—Julia Child, James Beard and M. F. K. Fisher—plus a host of others organized by category. Wonderful for rare and historic culinary volumes, too.
🕐 Mon 1–6, Tue–Fri 10–6.30, Sat 11–6 🚇 96th Street (6) 🚌 M98, M101, M102, M103

THE MYSTERIOUS BOOKSHOP
Map 160 D17
129 West 56th Street between Sixth and Seventh avenues
Tel 212/765-0900
www.mysteriousbookshop.com
An essential stop for the compulsive mystery reader as well as the collector of first editions and rare volumes. Sherlock Holmes, Raymond Chandler, P. D. James and Patricia Highsmith are all here. Recommendations from owner Otto Penzler and staff are sure-fire winners.
🕐 Mon–Sat 11–7 🚇 57th Street (N, Q, R, W), 57th Street (F) 🚌 M5, M6, M7

POSMAN BOOKSELLERS

Map 162 E18

9 Grand Central Terminal (Vanderbilt Avenue and 42nd Street)

Tel 212/983-1111

www.posmanbooks.com

A general bookstore which offers a good selection of journals and sharp insightful staff recommendations.

🅖 Mon–Fri 8am–9pm, Sat 10–7, Sun 11–6 🚇 42nd Street (4, 5, 6) 🚌 M1, M2, M3, M4, M42

RIZZOLI

Map 161 E16

31 West 57th Street between Fifth and Sixth avenues (north side)

Tel 212/759-2424

www.rizzoliusa.com

This gorgeous store has an excellent stock of art, design, and fashion books.

🅖 Mon–Fri 10–7.30, Sat 10.30–7, Sun 11–7 🚇 Fifth Avenue 59th Street (N, R, W), 57th Street (F) 🚌 M1, M2, M3, M4, M5, M6, M7, M57

ST. MARK'S BOOKSHOP

Map 163 F22

31 Third Avenue between St Mark's Place and 9th Street on east side

Tel 212/260-7853

www.stmarksbookshop.com

The original counterculture bookstore of the same name thrived on St. Mark's Place in the 1980s and 90s. It offers political and alternative titles plus a good general stock.

🅖 Mon–Sat 10am–midnight, Sun 11am–midnight 🚇 Astor Place (4, 5, 6) 🚌 M101, M102, M103

SHAKESPEARE & CO

Map 163 E22

716 Broadway between West 4th Street and Washington Place

Tel 212/529-1330

www.shakeandco.com

One of the city's few surviving small independent book chains. As the name suggests, it leans to literary and small press titles.

🅖 Mon–Sat 10am–11pm, Sun 10–7 🚇 Astor Place (4, 5, 6), 8th Street (N, R, W), West 4th Street (A, C, E, F, S, V) 🚌 M1, M5, M6

STRAND BOOKSTORE

Map 162 F21

828 Broadway at 12th Street

Tel 212/473-1452

www.strandbooks.com

New Yorkers come to this extraordinary bookstore to pore over the stacks and tables of publishers' review copies, sold at half price. Although you can browse, it's best to come with a title in mind, and ask the staff where to find it. The management claims to shelve 18 miles (29km) of books.

🅖 Mon–Sat 9.30am–10.30pm, Sun 11–10.30 🚇 14th Street/Union Square (L, N, Q, R, W, 4, 5, 6) 🚌 M1, M5, M6

You can track down a bargain at Strand Bookstore

THREE LIVES

Map 162 D22

154 West 10th Street at Waverly Place (southwest corner)

Tel 212/741-2069

www.threelives.com

The proprietor of this store provides super customer service and stocks an amazing variety of titles given the size of the place. A real neighborhood store, and one of the last personal bookstores in the city.

🅖 Wed–Sat 11–8.30, Sun 12–7, Mon–Tue 12–8 🚇 Christopher Street (1, 9), West 4th Street (A, C, E, F, V, S) 🚌 M5, M6, M8, M20

CLOTHING: BASICS AND SPORTSWEAR

APC

Map 163 E23

131 Mercer Street between Prince and Spring streets

Tel 212/966-9685

Atelier Production and Creation doesn't immediately suggest what you'll find here—good-looking, well-constructed Parisian-style basics. You can buy entire outfits, including cotton T's, turtlenecks, sweatshirts, dress shirts, leather jackets and very stylish jeans.

🅖 Mon–Sat 11–7, Sun 12–6 🚇 Prince Street (N, R, W) 🚌 M1, M6

BCBG BY MAX AZRIA

Map 163 E23

#1B, 120 Wooster Street between Prince and Spring streets

Tel 212/625-2723

www.bcbg.com

Bon Chic, Bon Genre brings you great style and fine quality from designer Max Azria. The women's fashions are stylish and sexy, suitable for day or night. Eye-catching accessories too, all at fair prices. Also at 770 Madison Avenue.

🅖 Mon–Sat 11–7, Sun 12–6 🚇 Prince Street (N, R, W) 🚌 M1, M6

BORRELLI

Map 161 E16

16 East 60th Street between Madison and Fifth avenues

Tel 212/644-9610

The ultimate Italian tailor favored by many a male film star offers exquisite shirts as well as a full line of beautiful suits, coats and sweaters, both custom-made and off the rack.

🅖 Mon–Sat 10–6, Sun 12–6 🚇 Fifth Avenue/59th Street (N, R, W) 🚌 M1, M2, M3, M4, M30

DKNY

Map 161 E16

655 Madison Avenue between East 60th and 61st streets

Tel 212/223-5569

www.dkny.com

Donna Karan delivers what New York women want—

comfortable clothes that coordinate easily. Black used to be her favorite color, but the current inventory offers plenty of colorful blouses, dresses, miniskirts, combat jackets and accessories. This striking glass-wrapped boutique opened in 1998. Also at 420 West Broadway and Spring Street.
🕐 Mon–Sat 10–8, Sun 11–7 🚇 Fifth Avenue/59th Street (N, R, W) 🚌 M1, M2, M3, M4, M30

EMPORIO ARMANI
Map 163 E23
410 West Broadway at Spring Street
Tel 646/613-8099
www.emporioarmani.com
At this flagship of Giorgio Armani's less expensive line, you get the same great design at a fraction of the price.
🕐 Mon–Sat 11–7, Sun 12–6 🚇 Spring Street (C, E), Prince Street (N, R, W) 🚌 M1, M6

HOTEL VENUS
Map 163 E23
382 West Broadway between Spring and Broome streets
Tel 212/966-4066
www.patriciafield.com
Patricia Field's latest and largest shop sells camp fashions made of rubber, PVC, leather, spandex, plastic and feathers. Styles range from bustiers and garter belts to micro minis. Not for the faint of heart, accessories, wigs and cosmetics are equally outrageous.
🕐 Daily 11–8 🚇 Spring Street (C, E), Prince Street (N, R, W) 🚌 M1, M6

JEFFREY
Map 162 C21
449 West 14th Street between Ninth and Tenth avenues
Tel 212/206-1272
It took courage for former Barneys shoe buyer Jeffrey Kalinsky to open this giant industrial-chic boutique in the blighted Meatpacking District before it became so very hip. Naturally, the shoe department is stellar, chock full of Manolos and other designer names. You will also find fashions by such

leaders as Fendi, Jil Sander, Celine, Prada, Gucci and Dolce & Gabbana. Service is gracious.
🕐 Mon–Fri 10–8 (Thu until 9), Sat 10–7, Sun 12.30–6 🚇 14th Street (A, C, E) Eighth Avenue (L) 🚌 M11, M14

LACOSTE
Map 161 E17
543 Madison Avenue between East 54th and 55th streets
Tel 212/750-8115
www.lacoste.com
The alligator has been around since French tennis champion René Lacoste, nicknamed "alligator," sold his first polo shirt in 1933. Today, Christophe Lemaire is re-energizing the company, adding fragrance,

Coordinate in style at DKNY on Madison Avenue

home fabrics, eyewear, underwear and footwear to the selection of golf, tennis and yachting sportswear.
🕐 Mon–Sat 10–7 (Thu until 8), Sun 12–5 🚇 Fifth Avenue/53rd Street (E, V), 51st Street/Lexington (6) 🚌 M1, M2, M3, M4

PAUL STUART
Map 162 E18
Madison Avenue at East 45th Street
Tel 212/682-0320
www.paulstuart.com
This pricey haberdashery, which opened in 1938, feels like something from Savile Row. It sells fine-quality suits, Italian dress shirts, Irish argyles and other good-looking

traditional fashions for men. Women will find similar—silk cashmere turtlenecks, pinstripe pantsuits and leather jackets.
🕐 Mon–Wed, Fri 8.30–6, Thu 8–7, Sat 9–6, Sun 12–5 🚇 42nd Street (B, D, F, V), 42nd Street/Grand Central (4, 5, 6, 7, S) 🚌 M1, M2, M3, M4, M5

PHAT FARM
Map 163 E23
129 Prince Street between West Broadway and Wooster streets
Tel 212/533-7428
www.phatfarm.com
A newer name on the hip-hop fashion scene, this line includes urban safari shirts and pants, scribble stitch jeans and jackets, plus hoodies, carpenter shorts and leather bomber jackets. Many bear the company logo.
🕐 Mon–Sat 11–7, Sun 12–6 🚇 Prince Street (N, R, W) 🚌 M1, M6

THE PUMA STORE
Map 163 E23
521 Broadway between Spring and Broome streets
Tel 212/334-7861
www.puma.com
Puma has made a dramatic return to the fashion scene, with shoes in olive and beige, as well as hot colors like canary yellow and lime green.
🕐 Mon–Sat 10–8, Sun 11–7 🚇 Prince Street (N, R, W)

SHANGHAI TANG
Map 161 E16
714 Madison Avenue between East 63rd and 64th streets
Tel 212/888-0111
www.shanghaitang.com
Asian cut and styling inform the youthful fashions at this store. Piping, clasps, and Chinese frog closures detail the women's jackets and blouses fashioned from pagoda prints. Kung fu and Fuji jackets with mandarin collars and knot buttons are favorites for men. Great fabric bags and home accessories too.
🕐 Mon–Sat 10–6, Sun 12–6 🚇 59th Street (4, 5, 6), Lexington Avenue/53rd Street (F) 🚌 M1, M2, M3, M4

STEVEN ALAN
Map 163 E24

103 Franklin Street between West
Broadway and Church Street
Tel 212/343-0692

Radical fashions for daring
fashionistas. The store stocks
the very latest international
designers such as Vanessa
Bruno, Alice Roi and Kateyone
Adeli.

🕐 Daily 11.30–7 🚇 Franklin Street
(1, 9) 🚌 M1, M6

THOMAS PINK
Map 161 E17

520 Madison Avenue between East
53rd and 54th streets
Tel 212/838-1928
www.thomaspink.co.uk

This British store sells formal,
business and casual shirts for
men and women in strikingly
beautiful colors and patterns,
as well as cufflinks—pretty
ones for her and elegant ones
for him.

🕐 Mon–Fri 10–7 (Thu until 8), Sat
10–6, Sun 12–6 🚇 Fifth Avenue/53rd
Street (E, V), 51st Street (6) 🚌 M1, M2,
M3, M4

CLOTHING: DESIGNER

ALEXANDER MCQUEEN
Map 162 C21

417 West 14th Street, between Ninth
Avenue and Washington Street
Tel 212/645-1797
www.alexandermcqueen.com

The British fashion shock jock,
who made his name at
Givenchy and is now designing
at Gucci, began his career on
Savile Row and at theatrical
costumer Angels and Bermans.
His shows are famous for their
theatricality and so are his
fashions, which are fantastical
but beautifully executed with
whimsical details.

🕐 Mon–Sat 11–7, Sun 12.30–6
🚇 14th Street (A, C, E), Eighth Avenue
(L) 🚌 M11, M14

CALVIN KLEIN
Map 161 E16

654 Madison Avenue at East 60th Street
Tel 212/292-9000

The beloved Bronx-born
American designer who

re-made the American fashion
industry in the 1970s has
expanded beyond refined
sportswear into shoes,
accessories and home
furnishings. He knows how
to cut and he knows how to
advertise. The boutique is a
paragon of minimalism by
British architect John Pawson,
worth seeing in its own
right.

🕐 Mon–Sat 10–6 (Thu until 7), Sun
12–6 🚇 Lexington Avenue/59th Street
(N, R, W, 4, 5, 6) 🚌 M1, M2, M3, M4

CHANEL
Map 161 E16

15 East 57th Street between Madison
and Fifth avenues

*Mix with stars of stage and
screen at Dolce & Gabbana*

Tel 212/355-5050
www.chanel.com

Coco Chanel created the little
black dress and added slacks
to a woman's wardrobe. Now
Karl Lagerfeld designs the
styles that will last forever and
the accessories (including the
quilted purse), shoes and
scents to go with them.
Two other stores on Madison
Avenue sell accessories and
jewelry only.

🕐 Mon–Sat 10–6.30 (Thu until 7, Sat
until 6) 🚇 Lexington Avenue/59th
Street (N, R, W, 4, 5, 6) 🚌 M1, M2, M3,
M4, M57

DOLCE & GABBANA
Map 161 E15

825 Madison Avenue between East
68th and 69th streets
Tel 212/249-4100
www.dolcegabbana.it

Domenico Dolce and Stefano
Gabbana have dressed
virtually every Hollywood and
Broadway star in fashions that
exude heat (distressed torn
pants and shirts, lots of corset
lacing). This spacious and
beautiful store is their flagship.

🕐 Mon–Fri 10–6 (Thu until 7), Sun
12–5 🚇 68th Street (6) 🚌 M1, M2,
M3, M4

DONNA KARAN
Map 161 E15

819 Madison Avenue between East 68th
and 69th streets
Tel 866/240-4700
www.donnakaran.com

In the elegant and dramatic
flagship of this very popular
American designer, the floating
staircase is worthy of Fred
Astaire and Ginger Rogers.

🕐 Mon–Sat 10–6 (Thu until 7)
🚇 68th Street (6) 🚌 M1, M2, M3, M4

EILEEN FISHER
Map 163 E23

395 West Broadway between Spring
and Broome streets
Tel 212/431-4567
www.eileenfisher.com

New Yorkers love the
comfortable easy-to-wear
clothes designed by Ms Fisher
—clothes that are versatile
enough to take a woman
through the day with minimal
changes. This is the flagship
store featuring her entire line.
Camisoles, tanks, skirts and
pants are all made of such
natural fabrics as cotton, linen,
and silk. March and August
sales are a big draw. Other
stores are on Madison Avenue
(at 53rd and 79th Streets) and
Fifth Avenue (at 22nd).

🕐 Mon–Thu 11–7, Fri–Sat 11–8, Sun
12–6
🚇 Spring Street (C, E)
🚌 M1, M6

GIORGIO ARMANI

Map 161 E16
760 Madison Avenue at 65th Street
Tel 212/988 9191
www.giorgioarmani.com
The ultimate designer for men and women makes suits in understated fabrics with superb detailing.
Mon–Sat 10–6 (Thu until 7) 68th Street (6) M1, M2, M3, M4

GUCCI

Map 161 E17
685 Fifth Avenue at East 54th Street
Tel 212/826-2600
840 Madison Avenue between 69th and 70th streets
Tel 212/717-2619
www.gucci.com
Tom Ford left Gucci in 2004 and now Frida Giannini has been elevated to creative director of womenswear and John Ray at menswear. Shop here for ultra-glamorous fashion.
Mon–Wed 10–6.30, Thu–Sat 10–7, Sun 12–6 Fifth Avenue/53rd Street (E, V), 68th Street (6) M1, M2, M3, M4

HELMUT LANG

Map 163 E23
80 Greene Street between Spring and Broome streets
Tel 212/925-7214
www.helmutlang.com
Austrian Helmut Lang crafts clothes that are lean, spare and beautifully cut, whether it's a gorgeous cashmere coat with a sheepskin lining, biker- and surfer-style garments, or skintight leggings in an electric hue. His entire line is sold here, including the iconic jeans.
Mon–Sat 11–7, Sun 12–6 Prince Street (N, R, W) M1, M6

ISSEY MIYAKE

Map 163 E24
119 Hudson Street at North Moore Street
Tel 212/226-0100
www.isseymiyake.com
This TriBeCa store, designed by Frank Gehry and his protégé Gordon Kipping, stocks all of Miyake's lines including the A-POC ("a piece of cloth"), each item created from a seamless cloth. A Gehry metallic sculpture defines the loft space.
Mon–Sat 11–7, Sun 12–6 Franklin Street (1, 9) M20

JEAN-PAUL GAULTIER

Map 161 E16
759 Madison Avenue between East 65th and 66th streets
Tel 212 249-0235
www.jeanpaulgaultier.com
The first US store designed by Philippe Starck is luxurious indeed, with its taffeta-covered walls and clothing racks with crystal fixtures. The fashions are exciting, dramatic,

Superbly designed suits at Giorgio Armani

beautifully draped and always au courant.
Mon–Sat 10–6 (Thu and Sat from 11), Sun 12–6 68th Street (6) M1, M2, M3, M4

MARC JACOBS

Map 163 E23
163 Mercer Street between Houston and Prince streets
Tel 212/343-1490
www.marcjacobs.com
Marc Jacobs is one of the city's hottest designers, turning out luxurious, updated vintage designs in soft, feminine colors. He also has two stores on Bleecker Street, one selling strictly accessories (retro flats plus), the other his highly successful, less expensive Marc by Marc Jacobs line, which includes his must-have cargo pants.
Mon–Sat 11–7, Sun 12–6 Prince Street (N, R, W) M1, M6

NICOLE MILLER

Map 161 E16
780 Madison Avenue between 66th and 67th streets
Tel 212/288-9779
www.nicolemiller.com
Nicole Miller's innovative, sexy and very wearable fashions attract a number of celebrity clients. She makes cowl-neck halter tops, distressed jersey tunics, bags and shoes, and simple evening gowns.
Mon–Fri 10–7, Sat 10–6, Sun 12–5 68th Street (6) M2, M3, M4

PRADA

Map 163 F23
575 Broadway at Prince Street
Tel 212/334-8888
www.prada.com
Dutch architect Rem Koolhaas designed this $40-million must-see store. The scooped-out ground floor functions as a performance space. Even the dressing rooms are very high-tech, and of the designer's five stores in Manhattan, this is the one to see.
Mon–Sat 11–7, Sun 12–6 Prince Street (N, R, W) M1, M6

RALPH LAUREN

Map 161 E15
867 Madison Avenue between East 71st and 72nd streets
Tel 212/606-2100
www.polo.com
Bronx native Ralph Lauren sells his distinguished cowboy and English country heritage looks in the Rhinelander Mansion, one of a handful of such turn-of-the-20th-century houses in Manhattan, renovated to gleaming splendor from its amazing hand-carved staircase to its Baccarat chandeliers and 19th-century oil paintings.
Mon–Wed 10–7, Thu 10–8, Fri–Sat 10–6, Sun 12–6 68th Street (6) M1, M2, M3, M4

STELLA McCARTNEY
Map 162 C21
429 West 14th Street between Ninth and Tenth avenues
Tel 212/255-1556
www.stellamccartney.com
Since graduating from London's Central St. Martin's College of Art and Design in 1995, Stella McCartney began her rise to stardom at Chloe and continues in partnership with Gucci. In this store, which opened in 2002, fitting rooms are lined with marquetry or hand-printed fabric. Her full line of well-tailored but nicely draped fashions is for sale.
Ⓞ Mon–Sat 11–7, Sun 12–6 Ⓣ 14th Street (A, C, E), Eighth Avenue (L) 🚍 M11, M14

YOHJI YAMAMOTO
Map 163 E23
103 Grand Street at Mercer Street
Tel 212/966-9066
www.YohjiYamamoto.co.jp
Impeccable design and draping informs the fashions, often black and white, of this serene designer. The store itself is an aesthetic gem.
Ⓞ Mon–Sat 11–7, Sun 12–6 Ⓣ Canal Street (A, C, E, J, M, N, Q, R, W, Z, 6) 🚍 M1, M6

CLOTHING: TRENDY BOUTIQUES

ALIFE RIVINGTON CLUB (SHOES)
Map 163 G23
158 Rivington Street between Clinton and Suffolk streets
Tel 212/375-8128
The unmarked steel door opens onto a space paneled in cherry wood, where sneakers are treated as high fashion, and you can find limited-edition American, European and Japanese lines in fantastic colors.
Ⓞ Daily 12–6.30 Ⓣ Delancey/Essex (F, J, M, Z) 🚍 M9

FORWARD
Map 163 G23
72 Orchard Street between Broome and Grand streets
Tel 646-264-3233
www.forwardnyc.com
This fashion incubator, supported by the neighborhood business association, regularly selects six emerging designers to create the merchandise and run the store. The stock changes constantly, so you might find dresses, jewelry, handbags, hats or lingerie.
Ⓞ Daily 12–7 Ⓣ Delancey/Essex (F, J, M, Z) 🚍 M9, M15

Kirna Zabete stocks a range of avant-garde designs

JUSSARA LEE
Map 162 C21
11 Little West 12th Street between Washington Street and Ninth Avenue
Tel 212/242-4128
www.caipirinha.com/jussara
This Korean-Brazilian designer's clothes have an edge but are eminently wearable. Coats, dresses, tops, pants, skirts and bathing suits are elegantly displayed here and at her flagship store.
Ⓞ Mon–Sat 11–7, Sun 12–7 Ⓣ 14th Street (A, C, E) 🚍 M11, M14

KIRNA ZABETE
Map 163 E23
96 Greene Street between Prince and Spring streets
Tel 212/941-9656
www.kirnazabete.com
Beth Buccini and Sarah Hailes assemble their choice of the avant-garde designers at this pretty store. You might find mohair and lace cardigans, sweatshirts by Matthew Williamson, Cacharel T's, frayed and patchwork pieces by Jessica Ogden, plus such other hard-to-find designers as Clements Ribeiro and Hussein Chalayan. Accessories, too.
Ⓞ Mon–Sat 11–7, Sun 12–6 Ⓣ Prince Street (N, R, W) 🚍 M1, M6

LUCY BARNES
Map 162 D21
320 West 14th Street between Eighth and Ninth avenues
Tel 212/255-9148
Edinburgh-born Lucy Barnes has been collecting vintage materials for years and uses them beautifully either whole or in part to make her nostalgic, feminine clothes. The designs and colors are stunning and often feature gorgeous embroidery, beading and patchwork. Prices are excellent considering the quality of the materials and the beauty of the designs.
Ⓞ Daily 11.30–7.30 Ⓣ 14th Street (A, C, E) 🚍 M11

MARTIN
Map 163 F22
206 East 6th Street between Second and Third avenues
Tel 212/358-0011
Greek togas seem to have inspired designer Anne Johnston's clothes, whether soft T's or hip street wear.
Ⓞ Tue–Sun 1–7 Ⓣ Astor Place (6) 🚍 M15, M103

MARY ADAMS THE DRESS
Map 163 G23
138 Ludlow Street between Rivington and Stanton streets
Tel 212-473-0237
www.maryadamsthedress.com
Neighborhood pioneer Mary Adams, who moved in during the early 1980s, sells beautifully light evening dresses in pastel hues.
🕐 Wed–Sat 1–6, Sun 1–5
🚇 Delancey/Essex (F, J, M, Z)
🚌 M9, M15

SHELLY STEFFEE
Map 162 D21
34 Gansevoort Street between Hudson Street and Ninth Avenue
Tel 917-408-0408
The sign outside reads Design Studio and that's how the clothes are displayed, in a museum-like fashion. The designs are sexy and fun. Capri pants have drawstrings at waist and calf; safari-style shirts are made from sheer material; and then there are more tailored separates.
🕐 Tue–Sat 12–9, Sun 12–6
🚇 14th Street (A, C, E) 🚌 M11, M14

37=1
Map 163 F23
37 Crosby Street between Grand and Broome streets
Tel 212-226-0067
Jean Yu makes dresses, lingerie and separates of the richest of silks. The garter belts are to die for. Prices are up there.
🕐 Tue–Sun 1–6 🚇 Canal Street (N, R)
🚌 M1, M6

TRACY FEITH
Map 163 F23
209 Mulberry Street between Spring and Kenmare streets
Tel 212/334-3097
Surf dude-turned-designer Tracy Feith dresses women in striking, playful, ready-to-party outfits. There's a gypsy glamour or ready-for-vacation air to all the clothes.
🕐 Mon–Sat 11–7, Sun 12–6 🚇 Spring Street (6), Broadway-Lafayette (F, S, V)
🚌 M1, M21

ZERO
Map 163 F23
225 Mott Street between Prince and Spring streets
Tel 212-925-3849
In this store you'll see capes, jackets and coats with an avant-garde look that Maria Cornejo sews in the back.
🕐 Mon–Fri 12.30–7.30, Sat–Sun 12.30–6.30 🚇 Prince Street (N, R)
🚌 M1, M6

| CLOTHING: VINTAGE |
DECOLLAGE
Map 162 D21
23 Eighth Avenue between West 12th and Jane streets
Tel 212-352-3338
It's worth a visit just to look

Designer clothes from yesteryear at Resurrection Vintage

at the new and vintage clothing on display in this wonderful fashion-as-art venue in a town house.
🕐 Mon–Fri 10–5, Sat 12–6 (spring–fall only) 🚇 14th Street (A, C, E)
🚌 M20

FOLEY & CORINNA
Map 163 G23
108 Stanton Street between Ludlow and Essex streets
Tel 212-529-2338
www.foleyandcorinna.com
Fashionistas and celebrities flock here to see the famous silk and vintage lace butterfly blouses, mohair and cashmere knit coats and other romantic hippie-chic fashions

created by Dana Foley, who began her career at a city flea market. Partner Anna Corinna selects the vintage clothing and accessories.
🕐 Sun–Thu 12–7, Fri–Sat 12–8
🚇 Delancey/Essex (F, J, M, Z)
🚌 M15, M21

99X
Map 163 F21
84 East 10th Street between Third and Fourth avenues
Tel 212-460-8599
www.99xny.com
Most of the 60s to 80s fashions here come from the UK. Customers can pick up mod and rocker outfits, as well as punk stuff and even some slender Teddy Boy ties and pork-pie hats.
🕐 Mon–Sat 12–8, Sun 12–7 🚇 Astor Place (6) 🚌 M1, M8, M103

RESURRECTION VINTAGE
Map 163 F23
217 Mott Street between Spring and Prince streets
Tel 212-625-1374
www.resurrectionvintage.com
This store has great vintage designer clothes—Pucci slips, pieces by Miyake and Vivienne Westwood, and 80s skateboard clothes from Alva, Thrasher and other brands. The owners also offer their own line of skirts and tops.
🕐 Mon–Sat 11–7, Sun 12–7
🚇 Broadway-Lafayette (F, S, V) 🚌 M1, M21, M103

SCREAMING MIMI'S
Map 163 F22
382 Lafayette Street between Great Jones and West 4th streets
Tel 212/677-6464
www.screamingmimis.com
The stock at this old-timer ranges from 1940s to 1980s. It's well displayed and in good condition. Cool and hip still, even though *Sex and the City* made it famous beyond a select circle of cognoscenti.
🕐 Mon–Sat 12–8, Sun 1–7
🚇 Broadway-Lafayette (F, S, V)
🚌 M1, M103

DEPARTMENT AND SPECIALTY STORES

BARNEYS
Map 161 E16
660 Madison Avenue between East 60th and 61st streets
Tel 212/826-8900, warehouse 212/450-8400
www.barneys.com

Barneys stocks only what's newest and hippest, so you'll find designers whose names everyone knows, as well as those known only to cognoscenti of the fashion scene—say, Proenza Schouler, Behnaz Sarafpour and Tess Giberson. The windows always make a statement, and people flock to the sales at the warehouse on 17th Street, between Seventh and Eighth avenues, where prices are slashed.

🕐 Mon–Fri 10–8, Sat 10–7, Sun 11–6 🚇 Fifth Avenue/59th Street (N, R, W), 59th Street (4, 5, 6) 🚌 M30

BERGDORF GOODMAN
Map 161 E16
754 Fifth Avenue between 57th and 58th streets
Tel 212/753-7300

Some shoppers actually dress up to visit this luxurious store, which showcases classics and new talent. The store is beautifully laid out, the shoe department marvelous and the designer boutiques extraordinary. You'll find great accessories throughout. The men's store is just across the street.

🕐 Mon–Sat 10–7 (Thu until 8), Sun 12–6 🚇 Fifth Avenue/59th Street (N, R, W) 🚌 M5, M30, M57

BLOOMINGDALE'S
Map 161 F16
Lexington Avenue at East 59th Street
Tel 212/705-2000
www.bloomingdales.com

Bloomingdale's, opened in 1879, is one of the most venerable names in Manhattan yet keeps up with every trend. It's an icon among its fans, and tourists and locals alike buy logo items emblazoned with

the store's name or sobriquet, "Bloomie's." On weekends locals come to schmooze.

🕐 Mon–Fri 10–8.30, Sat 10–7, Sun 11–7 🚇 59th Street/Lexington (4, 5, 6) 🚌 M98, M101, M102, M103

HENRI BENDEL
Map 161 E17
714 Fifth Avenue at 56th Street
Tel 212/247-1100
www.henribendel.com

Henri Bendel is synonymous with sophistication and elegance. The inventory and the clientele are similar to Bergdorf's, but the displays reveal the store's élan. If you want to see works by the hottest new designers, check

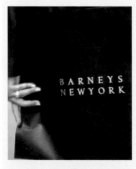

Head to Barneys for the hippest designs

out the New Creators boutique, which features such names as Michael Soheil, Peter Som, Alice Roi, Zac Posen and Behnaz Sarafpour.

🕐 Mon–Sat 10–8, Sun 12–7 🚇 Fifth Avenue/59th Street (N, R, W), Fifth Avenue/53rd Street (E, V) 🚌 M5, M30, M57

LORD & TAYLOR
Map 162 E18
424 Fifth Avenue between 38th and 39th streets
Tel 212/391-3344.
www.maycompany.com

This classic, established in 1826, targets traditional middle-aged shoppers, from Greenwich matrons to young working

women. The Christmas windows are a must-see.

🕐 Mon–Tue 10–8.30, Wed 9–8.30, Thu–Fri 10–8.30, Sat 10–7, Sun 11–7 🚇 42nd Street (B, D, F, V) 🚌 M2, M3, M5

MACY'S
Map 162 D19
Herald Square at 34th Street and Broadway
Tel 212/695-4400
www.macys.com

Macy's calls itself the "world's largest department store." The Cellar stocks housewares and culinary delights, and clothing, generally mainstream, comes from a range of well-known names. The store has good seasonal sales, and is famous for sponsoring both the Thanksgiving Day parade and the July 4th fireworks.

🕐 Mon–Sat 10–9, Sun 11–8 🚇 34th Street/Herald Square (B, D, F, N, Q, R, V, W) 🚌 M6, M7, M34

SAKS FIFTH AVENUE
Map 162 E17
611 Fifth Avenue between 49th and 50th streets
Tel 212/753-4000
www.saksfifthavenue.com

Comfortable Saks offers a very fine selection of clothing by an excellent range of established to up-and-coming designers for men and women.

🕐 Mon–Fri 10–7 (Thu until 8), Sat 10–7, Sun 12–6 🚇 Fifth Avenue/53rd Street (E, V), 47th–50th streets/Rockefeller Center (B, D, F, V) 🚌 M1, M2, M3, M4, M50

TAKASHIMAYA
Map 161 E17
693 Fifth Avenue between 54th and 55th streets
Tel 212/350-0100

Step in to this beautiful branch of Japan's largest department store even if you're not a shopper. The flower shop on the first floor is a lovely retreat from Fifth Avenue. Look for gold-leaf cups, black lacquer saucers and silk pillows.

🕐 Mon–Sat 10–7, Sun 12–5 🚇 Fifth Avenue/53rd Street (E, V) 🚌 M1, M2, M3, M4, M5

WHAT TO DO

DISCOUNT OUTLETS

New York magazine's "Sales and Bargains" feature highlights current sample and stock sales. Online, www.nysale.com and www.dailycandy.com keep up to date with what's on.

CENTURY 21

Map 163 E25
22 Cortlandt Street between Broadway and Church Street
Tel 212/227-9092
www.c21stores.com
Customers do their trying on in the aisles at this resource for discounted designer fashions. Look for Prada, Armani and Jil Sander among other designers at 40 to 75 percent off or more.
Mon–Fri 7.45am–8pm (Thu until 8.30), Sat 10–8, Sun 11–7 Cortlandt Street (E) M1, M6

INA

Map 163 E23
101 Thompson Street between Spring and Prince streets
Tel 212/941-4757
www.inanyc.com
The designer resale stock, discounted by 30 to 50 percent, changes daily, as models and the fashion set turn in their cast-offs. Look for Diane Von Furstenberg and Anna Sui. There's usually a fantastic array of Manolos, Pradas and Sigerson Morrisons, too.
Sun–Thu 12–7, Fri–Sat 12–8 Spring Street (C, E), Prince Street (N, R, W) M5, M6, M21

LOEHMANN'S

Map 162 D21
101 Seventh Avenue at 16th Street
Tel 212/352-0856
www.loehmanns.com
This place has been a name on the discount shopping scene ever since Frieda Mueller Loehmann began selling well-priced skirts and blouses out of her Brooklyn home in 1920. This flagship store has five floors of fashions to pick over. Discounts range from 30 to 65 percent.
Mon–Sat 9–9, Sun 11–7 14th Street (1, 2, 3, 9) M14, M20

FOOD AND WINE

CHELSEA MARKET

Map 162 D21
75 Ninth Avenue between 15th and 16th streets
Tel 212/243-6005
When you stroll through the first floor of this building, you can put together an entire meal including table decorations. You'll find bakers, fishmongers, florists, wine merchants, and such stores as Buon Italia, which sells

Dean & Deluca is a magnet for New York's gourmets

superb cheeses, sausages, sauces, oils and other products from Italy. A good place to while away a rainy hour.
Hours vary from store to store 14th Street (A, C, E) M11, M14

DEAN & DELUCA

Map 163 F23
560 Broadway at Prince Street
Tel 212/226-6800
www.deandeluca.com
A wonderful place to browse. Absolutely everything here is top quality—pastries, cheeses, meats, fishes, chocolates and packaged products, plus the baskets of hand-picked fruits and vegetables. There's also a coffee bar. There are five other branches in Manhattan.
Mon–Sat 9–8, Sun 9–7 Prince Street (N, R, W) M1, M5, M6

JACQUES TORRES CHOCOLATE

Map 163 D23
350 Hudson Street at King Street
Tel 212/414-2462
www.mrchocolate.com
Former Le Cirque dessert chef Jacques Torres is still the best chocolate maker in the city. The gems at his factory/shop and cocoa bar are sublime. The chocolates contain no preservatives, colorings or additives, and he makes his own peanut butter, marzipan, walnut, praline and pistachio pastes. The pithiviers are heavenly.
Mon–Sat 9–7 $50 per pound ($110 per kilo) Houston Street (1, 9)

KAM MAN FOODS

Map 163 F24
200 Canal Street at Mott Street
Tel 212/571-0330
This large Chinese food hall overflows with exotic products, from live fish and edible birds' nests to ginseng priced at hundreds of dollars. It also sells inexpensive Asian cookware.
Daily 9–9 Canal Street (J, M, Z) M1, M103

MORRELL & COMPANY

Map 162 E17
1 Rockefeller Plaza
Tel 212/688-9370
www.morrellwine.com
Morrell, in business since 1947, is the other great wine shop in Manhattan after Sherry-Lehmann (▷ 178). It has its own wine bar and café next door.
Mon–Fri 9–7, Sat 10–7 47th–50th streets/Rockefeller Center (B, D, F, V) M1, M2, M3, M4, M50

WHAT TO DO

SHERRY-LEHMANN

Map 161 E16
679 Madison Avenue at 61st Street
Tel 212/838-7500
www.sherry-lehmann.com
Even if you don't buy, this is a shop to browse. In business since 1934, it has a $10 million inventory of wines from every corner of the world, an attractive old-fashioned interior, and a friendly, knowledgeable staff. Besides the premier cru Bordeaux and Burgundies, you'll find ice wines from Canada, Swiss and Lebanese varieties, and selections of sake, port and Madeira. Prices are good, too. Stop by for the Wednesday tasting from 3 to 6.
Mon–Sat 9–7 Fifth Avenue/59 Street (N, R, W), 59th Street/Lexington Avenue 4, 5, 6) M1, M2, M3, M4, M30

UNION SQUARE GREEN MARKET

Map 162 E21
Union Square
Drop by this busy market to get a sense of the agricultural scene outside the city and to participate in a city happening.
Mon, Wed, Fri, Sat from 8am 14th Street/Union Square (L, N, Q, R, W, 4, 5, 6) M2, M3, M5, M7

ZABAR'S

Map 160 C14
2245 Broadway between West 80th and 81st streets
Tel 212/787-2000
www.zabars.com
The countermen who wield the knives at this culinary landmark are legendary for their skills and their attitude. Look for exquisite smoked salmon and other smoked fish, terrific cheeses, and, upstairs, cookware and tableware at great prices.
Mon–Fri 8–7.30, Sat 8–8, Sun 9–6 79th Street (1, 9) M104

CASWELL-MASSEY

Map 161 F17
518 Lexington Avenue at East 48th Street
Tel 212/755-2254
www.caswell-massey.com
This apothecary, founded in 1752, provided perfume to George Washington and Dolly Madison and continues to produce a range of delicious floral scents such as freesia, lilac, rose, geranium and lily of the valley. You can find rosewater and glycerin soap, sandalwood massage oil and appealing gift sets.
Mon–Fri 8–7, Sat 10–6, Sun 12–5 51st Street (6) M98, M101, M102, M103

Sherry-Lehmann offers a discerning selection of drinks

FLORIS

Map 161 E16
703 Madison Avenue between East 62nd and 63rd streets
Tel 212/935-9100
www.florislondon.com
Floris has been refining the art of making fragrance since 1730, when it opened on London's Jermyn Street. It's said that the elegant 19th-century English gentleman Beau Brummell (and more recently James Bond) loved No. 89, named for the store's London address. Today there are scents for men, women and the home (grapefruit, rosemary and seasonal spice); men's shaving and

grooming accessories are also available.
Mon–Sat 10–6 (Thu until 7) 5th Avenue/59th Street (N, R, W), 59th Street (4, 5, 6) M1, M2, M3, M4

KIEHL'S

Map 163 F21
109 Third Avenue between East 13th and 14th streets
Tel 212/677-3171
www.kiehls.com
Founded in 1851 and owned by L'Oréal since 2000, Kiehl's has been selling homeopathic remedies and natural cosmetics and treatment products since its inception. Natural herb-based moisturizers, cleansers, shampoos, eye creams, masques, facial scrubs, talc, lipsticks and toners line the shelves.
Mon–Sat 10–7, Sun 12–6 14th Street/Union Square (L, N, Q, R, W, 4, 5, 6), Third Avenue (L) M101, M102, M103

L'OCCITANE

Map 162 E22
247 Bleecker Street between Sixth and Seventh avenues
Tel 212/367-8428
www.loccitane.com
The great range of beauty and body products sold here incorporates almond, honey, apricot, bergamot and other natural ingredients. The most irresistible product has to be shea butter hand cream, made from the shea, fruit of a tree that grows in Burkina Faso.
Mon–Fri 11–8, Sat 10–8, Sun 11–7 West 4th Street (A, C, E, F, S, V), Christopher Street (1, 9) M1, M5, M6

PENHALIGON'S

Map 161 E15
870 Madison Avenue between 70th and 71st streets
Tel 212/249-1771
www.penhaligons.com
Classic British style reigns at this wood-paneled emporium, the American outpost of the famous British perfumer, established in 1841. The

seductive scents are handmade and have almost a cult following.

🕐 Mon–Sat 10–6, Sun 12–5 🚇 68th Street (6) 🚌 M1, M2, M3, M4

SEPHORA

Map 162 D18
1500 Broadway between 43rd and 44th streets
Tel 212/944-6789
www.sephora.com

If you have ever been intimidated, or overwhelmed by the typical make-up counter, then you'll appreciate Sephora. This European chain, which arrived in 1998, has an efficient self-service orientation and sells more than 200 brands of beauty products, from Adrienne Vittadini to Philosophy. There's a scent-testing bar, and treatments are arranged by skin type.

🕐 Daily 10am–midnight 🚇 Times Square (N, Q, R, W, 1, 2, 3, 9) 🚌 M6, M7, M10, M20

HOME FURNISHINGS

ABC CARPET AND HOME

Map 162 E21
888 Broadway between 19th and 20th streets
Tel 212/473-3000
www.abchome.com

Fabrics, furnishings and interior design artifacts from around the world are artfully displayed on 10 floors. Provençal armoires, Kashmiri silks, gorgeously dressed beds and Venetian chandeliers keep company with rugs from India, Nepal, Pakistan and China.

🕐 Mon–Fri 10–8, Sat 10–7, Sun 11–6.30 🚇 23rd Street (N, R, W) 🚌 M6, M7

BROADWAY PANHANDLER

Map 163 E23
477 Broome Street between Greene and Wooster streets
Tel 212/966 3434
www.broadwaypanhandler.com

Originally selling to professional kitchens, Broadway Panhandler now offers the very best cookware, tools, appliances and gadgets to domestic cooks at decent

prices. There are hundreds of different types of pots, pans and skillets available—about 10,000 items in all. Special weekend demonstrations bring in the likes of Jean-Georges Vongerichten, Eric Ripert and Jacques Pépin.

🕐 Mon–Fri 10.30–7, Sat 11–7, Sun 11–6 🚇 Prince Street (N, R, W) 🚌 M1, M6

KATE'S PAPERIE

Map 163 E23
561 Broadway between Prince and Spring streets
Tel 212/941-9816
www.katespaperie.com

Expensive but beautiful gifts can be found at this elegant store. Gorgeous stationery,

Professional cookware at Broadway Panhandler

handsome journals and date books, photo frames, alluring wrapping papers and ribbons, writing tools, and all kinds of ingenious paper items are attractively displayed.

🕐 Mon–Sat 10–8, Sun 10–7 🚇 Prince St (N, R) 🚌 M1, M6

PEARL RIVER

Map 163 E23
477 Broadway between Broome and Grand streets
Tel 212/431-4770
www.pearlriver.com

New Yorkers who have moved out of town often return here to browse the bargains—Asian-style robes, embroidered silk slippers, good-looking

ceramics, Asian cuisine ingredients, paper lanterns, and many other appealing objects.

🕐 Daily 10–7 🚇 Canal Street (N, R) 🚌 M1, M6

MUSIC

FOOTLIGHT RECORDS

Map 162 F21
113 East 12th Street between Third and Fourth avenues
Tel 212/533-1572
www.footlight.com

You need hours to browse all of the categories at this music-lover's store—from Big Band to Rock and Spoken Word. There's even an Old and Cool section, which includes Dame Edna doing *Peter and the Wolf*.

🕐 Mon–Fri 11–7, Sat 10–6, Sun 12–5 🚇 14th Street/Union Square (L, N, Q, R, W, 4, 5, 6) 🚌 M1, M2, M103

J & R MUSIC AND COMPUTER WORLD

Map 163 E25
1-34 Park Row (one block south of City Hall)
Tel 212/238-9000
www.jandr.com

This store, opened in 1971, stocks every conceivable brand of audio, video, computer, camera and cell phone, plus software and household appliances. Prices are excellent, and the staff are knowledgeable and helpful. The Music Store has separate stores for jazz, classical and pop.

🕐 Mon–Sat 9–7.30, Sun 10.30–6.30 🚇 Park Place (2, 3), City Hall (N, R, W), Brooklyn Bridge/City Hall (4, 5, 6) 🚌 M9, M15

JAZZ RECORD CENTER

Map 162 D20
236 West 26th Street between Seventh and Eighth avenues (8th floor, room 804)
Tel 212/675-4480
www.jazzrecordcenter.com

This store stocks all the great jazz names and all the jazz labels, plus books, videos and ephemera. It specializes in rare and out-of-print recordings.

🕐 Mon–Sat 10–6 🚇 28th Street (1, 9) 🚌 M20

SHOES AND ACCESSORIES

CARTIER
Map 161 E17
653 Fifth Avenue between 51st and
52nd streets
Tel 212/753-0111
www.cartier.com
Cartier opened in Paris in 1847
and has been famous for
beautiful design ever since,
creating such signature pieces
as the three-band ring and the
Portico Mystery Clock. Richard
Burton went to Cartier for the
diamond for Elizabeth Taylor.
Today, it sells beautiful
jewelry and watches, plus
leather goods and other
luxuries.
🕐 Mon–Fri 10–6, Sat 10–5.30, Sun
12–6 🚇 Fifth Avenue/53rd Street (E, V)
🚌 M1, M2, M3, M4, M50

COACH
Map 161 E16
595 Madison Avenue between East
57th and 58th streets
Tel 212/754-0041
www.coach.com
This successful leather
purveyor has a line of classics
as well as seasonal collections.
There are seven other
branches in the city.
🕐 Mon–Sat 10–8, Sun 11–6 🚇 Fifth
Avenue/59th Street (N, R, W), 59th
Street (4, 5, 6) 🚌 M1, M2, M3, M4,
M57

COLE HAAN
Map 161 E17
620 Fifth Avenue at 50th Street
Tel 212/765-9747
www.colehaan.com
Nike now owns this maker of
traditional, good-quality shoes
and is jazzing it up with new
ideas, colors and styles.
🕐 Mon–Sat 10–7 (Thu until 8), Sun
12–6 🚇 47th–50th streets/Rockefeller
Center (B, D, F, V) 🚌 M1, M2, M3, M4

CONSTANCA BASTO
Map 162 D22
573 Hudson Street between Bank and
11th streets
Tel 212/645-3233
www.constancabasto.com
This Brazilian shoe designer
has a striking orange candy-
stripe boutique studded with
gorgeous stilettos decorated
with jewels, plus other
beguiling footwear.
🕐 Tue–Sat 11–7, Sun 12–6 🚇 14th
Street (A, C, E) 🚌 M20

DOYLE AND DOYLE
Map 163 G22
189 Orchard Street between Houston
and Stanton streets
Tel 212/677-9991
Doyle and Doyle offers
some very alluring, historic
estate jewelry in prime
condition.
🕐 Tue–Sun 1–7 (Thu until 8)
🚇 Lower East Side/Second Avenue
(F, V) 🚌 M9, M15

*Accessorize to your heart's
content at Eye Candy*

ERES
Map 163 E23
98 Wooster Street between Spring and
Prince streets
Tel 212/431-7300
www.eresparis.com
In 1968 Eres opened in Paris
on place de la Madeleine,
selling the ultimate
swimwear—bikinis, suits and
other one-pieces. Today it
issues a cruise collection in
November and a summer
collection in January. Equally
beautiful and flattering lingerie
is offered as well now.
🕐 Mon–Sat 11–7, Sun 12–6 🚇 Prince
Street (N, R) 🚌 M1, M6

EUGENIA KIM
Map 163 G22
203 East 4th Street between Avenues A
and B
Tel 212/673-9787
www.eugeniakim.com
Former *Allure* editor Kim fell
into her career when she
fashioned a hand-feathered
cloche for herself, went
shopping, and attracted
attention from shop owners.
Her hats—many with a retro
look—are dashing, flamboyant,
beautifully crafted, and
expensive, made of straw and
cotton in cowboy, fedora, caps
and other shapes, and
trimmed with feathers, leather
and ribbons. On the wild side.
🕐 Mon–Sat 11–8, Sun 1–7 🚇 Astor
Place (6) 🚌 M9, M14

EYE CANDY
Map 163 F22
329 Lafayette Street between Bleecker
and Houston streets
Tel 212/343-4275
www.eyecandystore.com
The bags, costume jewelry and
sunglasses here are the stuff of
whimsical dreams.
🕐 Daily 12–8 🚇 Broadway-Lafayette
(F, V, S) 🚌 M1, M5, M6, M21

FENDI
Map 161 E17
720 Fifth Avenue between 56th and
57th streets
Tel 212/767-0100
www.fendi.it
The flashy Fendi label conveys
the message of money and
glitz, and women wear Fendi
for that reason. This flagship
store sells the full line:
handbags, shoes, accessories
and furs.
🕐 Mon–Sat 10–6.30, Sun 12–6
🚇 Fifth Avenue/53rd Street (E, V)
🚌 M1, M2, M3, M4, M57

GAS
Map 163 F23
238 Mott Street between Prince and
Spring streets
Tel 212/334-7290
This outpost of the St. Tropez
and Paris jeweler has lovely
inspirational handmade

jewelry made with semi-precious stones.
🕐 Mon–Sat 11–7, Sun 12–7
🚇 Broadway-Lafayette (F, S, V)
🚌 M1, M103

JIMMY CHOO
Map 161 E16
716 Madison Avenue, between 63rd and 64th streets (west side)
Tel 212/759-7078
645 Fifth Avenue between 51st and 52nd streets
Tel 212/593-0800
www.jimmychoo.com
Velvet-quilted sofas and satin-covered chairs set the tone at this flagship store selling the exquisite shoes and purses by this legendary Malaysian designer, who cobbled for Princess Diana. His line offers a variety of styles from pony boots and evening slides to kitten heels, stilettos and sandals made in all kinds of materials and fabrics, which are decorated with beads, crystals or embroidery, or just beautifully colored.
🕐 Mon–Sat 10–6 (Thu until 7), Sun 12–5 🚇 59th Street (4, 5, 6) or 68th Street (6) 🚌 M1, M2, M3, M4

KATE SPADE
Map 163 E23
454 Broome Street at Mercer Street
Tel 212/274-1991
www.katespade.com
The former *Mademoiselle* accessories editor, Kate started out in 1993, making handbags that emphasized utility, color and fabric. She opened her first store in 1996, and now sells a full line of exquisite nylon, leather and fabric bags, plus wallets, luggage, stationery, eyeglasses, fragrance and beauty products.
🕐 Mon–Sat 11–7, Sun 12–6 🚇 Prince Street (N, R, W) 🚌 M1, M6

KELLY CHRISTY
Map 163 F23
235 Elizabeth Street between Houston and Prince streets
Tel 212/965-0686
www.kellychristyhats.com
Kelly Christy makes eye-catching hats for men and women in all kinds of fabrics and in every conceivable style, from fedora to beret. Every hat is named to reflect a mood or character—recent examples are 'Miss Marple' and 'Let's skate'. Prices vary according to style and fabric and start at about $200.
🕐 Mon 12–5, Tue–Sat 12–7, Sun 12–6
🚇 Broadway-Lafayette (F, S, V)
🚌 M21, M103

Jimmy Choo offers a range of exquisite footwear

KENNETH COLE
Map 160 D14
353 Columbus Avenue between West 76th and 77th streets
Tel 212/873-2061
www.kennethcole.com
Good, clean styling and quality for the money have made Kenneth Cole a major fashion player. He started with urban shoes, but has expanded to include such fashionable footwear as satin pumps with ankle straps, plus sportswear, handbags, fragrance and other accessories.
🕐 Mon–Thu 10–7, Fri–Sat 10–8, Sun 11–7 🚇 79th Street (1, 9) 🚌 M7, M11

LA PETITE COQUETTE
Map 163 F22
51 University Place between 9th and 10th streets
Tel 212/473-2478
This may well be the best lingerie store in the city. In a boudoir setting, it sells swimwear and sexy top-of-the-line, multi-hued lingerie (camisoles, corsets, garter belts and other scanties).
🕐 Mon–Sat 11–7 (Thu until 8), Sun 12–6 🚇 8th Street (N, R, W) 🚌 M1, M3, M6

LE SPORTSAC
Map 163 E23
176 Spring Street between West Broadway and Thompson Street
Tel 212/625-2626
www.lesportsac.com
Fold-in-a-pouch bags made of rip-stop parachute nylon made this name famous after they were introduced in 1974. Today the brand continues to deliver practical, affordable totes, messenger bags and backpacks, now in fun prints and patterns including batik. A couture line features such materials as sheared mink and fox.
🕐 Mon–Sat 11–7, Sun 12–6 🚇 Spring Street (C, E) 🚌 M6

MANOLO BLAHNIK
Map 161 E17
31 West 54th Street between Fifth and Sixth avenues
Tel 212/582-3007
The sexy, strappy sandals, plain stiletto pumps, slingbacks and mules are beloved of the fashion and celebrity crowd, who pay $450 and up for these most glamorous accessories. They're fashioned from pony skin and other elegant materials in a brilliant palette.
🕐 Mon–Fri 10.30–6, Sat 10.30–5.30, closed Sun 🚇 Fifth Avenue/53rd Street (E, V) 🚌 M5, M6, M7

WHAT TO DO

ME & RO

Map 163 F23
239 Elizabeth Street between Houston and Prince streets
Tel 917-237-9215
www.meandrojewelry.com
The collection of Michelle Quan and Robin Renzi uses precious and semi-precious stones in stackable rings, bangles, necklaces and other pieces with a lotus petal motif or Sanskrit and Tibetan calligraphy.
🕐 Mon–Sat 11–7, Sun 12–6
🚇 Broadway-Lafayette (F, S, V)
🚌 M21, M103

MODELL'S

Map 163 E24
55 Chambers Street
Tel 212/732-8484
www.modells.com
Savvy New Yorkers come here to get the best deal on their running and athletic shoes (Adidas, New Balance, Reebok). The chain also stocks sports attire and gear, from treadmills and trampolines to baseball and yoga gear. Sports fans appreciate the prices on NFL, NBA and MLB souvenir stuff.
🕐 Mon–Fri 8.30–7.30, Sat 10–6, Sun 11–5 🚇 Chambers Street (E), City Hall (R), Park Place (1, 2, 3) 🚌 M1, M6

OTTO TOOTSI PLOHOUND

Map 162 E20
137 Fifth Avenue between 20th and 21st streets
Tel 212/460-8650
Otto Tootsi Plohound offers a selection of very cool and stylish shoes both from their own line and from other European and American designers.
🕐 Mon–Fri 11.30–7.30, Sat 11–8, Sun 12–7 🚇 23rd Street (N, R, W) 🚌 M2, M3, M5

CHAIN STORES

This chart tells you what to expect in many of the chain stores on New York's main shopping streets. Call the head office to find your nearest branch or check the website.

NAME	Clothing	Fashion accessories	Souvenirs	Books and music	Outdoor sport	Shoes	Pharmacy and toiletries	Stationery	Food	Household and electrical goods	HEAD OFFICE CONTACT NUMBER
Abercrombie & Fitch	✔	✔			✔	✔					614/283-6500 or 888-856-4480
Ann Taylor	✔	✔				✔					212/541-3300 or 800-342-5266
Anthropologie	✔	✔					✔			✔	800-309-2500
Banana Republic	✔	✔				✔					888-277-8953
Bed Bath and Beyond										✔	800-462-3966
Benetton	✔	✔				✔					800-535-4491
Bodyshop			✔				✔				800-263-9746
Brooks Brothers	✔	✔				✔		✔			800-274-1815
Club Monaco	✔	✔									212/886-2660
Crabtree & Evelyn			✔				✔		✔		860/928-2761 or 800-272-2873
Crate & Barrel										✔	847-272-2888 or 800-967-6696
Diesel	✔			✔							212/755-9200
Disney Store	✔		✔	✔							800-328-0368
Eddie Bauer	✔	✔			✔	✔					800-426-8020
Eileen Fisher	✔										800-345-3362
Gap	✔	✔				✔					800-333-7899
H & M	✔	✔									212/564-9922
J. Crew	✔	✔				✔					800-562-0258 or 800-932-0043
NBA Store	✔	✔	✔								877-622-0206
Old Navy	✔	✔				✔					800-653-6289
Pier 1 Imports										✔	817/252-8000 or 800-245-4595
Talbot's	✔	✔				✔					781/749-7600 or 800-992-9010
Toys "R" Us				✔					✔		800-869-7787
Urban Outfitters	✔	✔				✔					215/564-2313 or 800-282-2200
Victoria's Secret	✔	✔				✔	✔				800-411-5116
Virgin Megastore				✔							877-484-7446
Williams-Sonoma									✔	✔	877-812-6235 or 800-541-2233

SIGERSON MORRISON

Map 163 F23
28 Prince Street between Mott and
Elizabeth streets
Tel 212/219-3893
www.sigersonmorrison.com
The shoes from this exciting
designer are not as pricey as
Manolos but are stunning
nonetheless. Colors range
across the spectrum from red
to lavender, and materials
include pony skin, suede, satin
and metallic leather. Styles
range from slingback stilettos
to flats and boots.
🕐 Mon–Sat 11–7, Sun 12–6
🚇 Broadway-Lafayette (F, S, V), Prince
Street (N, R, W) 🚌 M21, M103

SUAREZ HANDBAGS

Map 161 E17
450 Park Avenue at East 56th Street
Tel 212/753-3758
Here, copies of designer
handbags are on offer for a
fraction of the price.
🕐 Mon–Sat 10–6, Sun 11–5 🚇 59th
Street (4, 5, 6) 🚌 M1, M2, M3, M4

TIFFANY

Map 161 E17
Fifth Avenue at 57th Street
Tel 212/755-8000
www.tiffany.com
Tiffany is famous for its superb
silver and crystal and its
beautiful design. Although
some items are astronomically
priced, it also displays more
moderately priced luxury
gifts—embossed note cards
($40 for 15) and singular silver
pieces. All are packaged in
the signature duck-egg blue
box tied with red or white
ribbon, which was introduced
when the store opened in
1837.
🕐 Mon–Fri 10–7, Sat 10–6, Sun 12–5
🚇 Fifth Avenue/59th Street (N, R, W),
57th Street (F) 🚌 M1, M2, M3, M4

TOD'S

Map 161 F16
650 Madison Avenue between East
59th and 60th streets
Tel 212/644-5945
www.tods.com

This Italian designer makes
ultra-comfortable shoes, plus
boots with equestrian styling.
They are relatively expensive,
but long-lasting.
🕐 Mon–Sat 10–6 (Thu until 7), Sun
12–5 🚇 59th Street/Fifth Avenue (N, R,
W) 🚌 M1, M2, M3, M4

SUPERSTORES

AVIREX

Map 163 F22
652 Broadway between Bleecker and
Bond streets
Tel 212/925-5456
www.avirex.com
Lusting for the bomber jacket
worn by Tom Cruise in *Top
Gun*? Head for Avirex, official
supplier of the U.S. Air Force's
A-2 leather flight jacket. It sells
unisex military fashions, biker
gear and varsity styles.
🕐 Mon–Sat 11–7, Sun 12–5
🚇 Broadway-Lafayette (F, S, V) 🚌 M1,
M5, M6

WHAT TO DO

LINE OF GOODS	WEB SITE
Stylish casual clothing for the American outdoors lifestyle	www.abercrombie.com
Elegant and casual women's fashion	www.anntaylor.com
Ethnically inspired clothing and eclectic housewares	www.anthropologie.com
Stylish fashion separates for men and women	www.bananarepublic.com
Everything and anything to go in the home	www.bedbathandbeyond.com
Contemporary fashions with Italian flair	www.benetton.com
Cosmetics and bath products made of natural ingredients	www.thebodyshop.com
Conservative and classic tailored fashions for men and women	www.brooksbrothers.com
Canadian chain selling chic basics and affordable high-fashion items	www.clubmonaco.com
Venerable British chain selling toiletries and British-oriented products like teas and jams	www.crabtree-evelyn.com
High-quality products for the home with a distinct West Coast style	www.crateandbarrel.com
Latest trends for kids from hip-hop style to surfer	www.diesel.com
Disney paraphernalia including clothes and furniture	www.disneystore.com
Casual stylish fashions with an outdoor orientation	www.eddiebauer.com
Casual, comfortable clothes for women	www.eileenfisher.com
The ubiquitous reasonably priced, casual clothing store	www.Gap.com
Low-cost versions of trendy youth-oriented fashion	www.hm.com
Casual preppy and collegiate fashions and affordable accessories	www.jcrew.com
Souvenir jerseys, posters, mugs and more for basketball fans	http://store.nba.com
Moderately priced high-street fashions for adults and children	www.oldnavy.com
Affordable, stylish home decor—from tableware to bed linens	www.pier1.com
Fine-quality, practical and affordable ladies' wear	www.talbots.com
Every toy imaginable plus a 60-foot (18m) Ferris wheel	www.toysrus.com
Practical casuals for the collegiate crowd	www.urbn.com
Sexy lingerie, sleepwear and swimwear are the staples at this famous chain	www.victoriassecret.com
Classical, pop and jazz CDs, including plenty of imports	www.virginmega.com
Upscale kitchen equipment, condiments and specialty ingredients	www.williams-sonoma.com

B & H PHOTO
Map 162 D19
420 Ninth Avenue between West 33rd and 34th streets
Tel 212/444-5000
www.bhphotovideo.com
Even if you're not in the market for a new camera, you might want to make a detour to this vast store to pick up inexpensive film in bulk. You'll also find every conceivable brand and type of camera, plus darkroom equipment and other accessories. Don't expect service—come knowing what you want to buy.
🕐 Mon–Thu 9–7, Fri 9–1, Sun 10–5 🚇 34th Street/Penn Station (A, C, E) 🚌 M11

BED, BATH AND BEYOND
Map 162 E21
620 Sixth Avenue between West 18th and 19th streets
Tel 212/255-3550
www.bedbathandbeyond.com
It can be overwhelming to shop at this huge store, which sells absolutely everything for the bedroom, bathroom, kitchen and dining room, plus storage and cleaning accessories, lamps and window treatments.
🕐 Daily 8am–9pm 🚇 18th Street (1, 9) 🚌 M5, M6, M7

CRATE AND BARREL
Map 161 E16
650 Madison Avenue at East 59th Street
Tel 212/308-0011
www.crateandbarrel.com
This chain sells affordable, good-looking designs for your home. The focus is on tableware (from linens to glasses). It also sells attractive outdoor dining stuff.
🕐 Mon–Fri 10–8, Sat 10–7, Sun 12–6 🚇 59th Street/Fifth Avenue (N, R, W) 🚌 M1, M2, M3, M4, M5

DIESEL
Map 162 E21
1 Union Square West at University Place
Tel 646-336 8552
www.diesel.com
This Italian clothes house always keeps one step ahead of the latest trends, whether it's hip-hop or surfer. Diesel jeans are de rigueur and so, too, are the shoes and bags. Also at 770 Lexington Avenue.
🕐 Mon–Sat 11–9, Sun 11–8 🚇 14th Street/Union Square (L, N, Q, R, W, 4, 5, 6) 🚌 M2, M3, M5, M14

FAO SCHWARZ
Map 161 E16
767 Fifth Avenue between 58th and 59th streets
Tel 212/644-9400
www.fao.com
This famous store has been in Manhattan since 1876. It stocks everything: action figures, stuffed toys, books, games, dolls, science and

FAO Schwarz featured in the Tom Hanks movie Big

nature toys, and electronics, plus furniture and fashions.
🕐 Mon–Sat 10–7, Sun 11–6 🚇 59th Street/Fifth Avenue (N, R, W) 🚌 M1, M2, M3, M4

HAMMACHER SCHLEMMER
Map 161 F16
147 East 57th Street between Lexington and Third avenues
Tel 212/421-9000
www.hammacher.com
Ingenuity meets the future. At this longtime innovator, which started as a hardware store on the Bowery in 1848, you will find such items as the upside-down tomato garden and the Roomba, a robotic cleaning device that navigates whole rooms removing dust from carpet and floor.
🕐 Mon–Sat 10–6 🚇 59th Street (4, 5, 6) 🚌 M57, M98, M101, M102, M103

PARAGON SPORTING GOODS
Map 162 E21
867 Broadway at 18th Street
Tel 212/255 8036
www.paragonsports.com
New Yorkers have been coming to this multilevel store for years to buy clothes and equipment for every conceivable type of sport or pastime. It stocks camping and hiking gear, binoculars for bird-watching, golfing gear, skis, snow and surfboards, tennis racquets and a terrific selection of brand clothing.
🕐 Mon–Sat 10–8, Sun 11–7 🚇 14th Street/Union Square (L, N, Q, R, W, 4, 5, 6) 🚌 M6, M7

PEARL PAINT
Map 163 E24
308 Canal Street between Mercer Street and Broadway
Tel 212/431-7932
www.pearlpaint.com
You won't find a better place for fine arts supplies at discounted prices than this multilevel store. The selection of oils, acrylics and other mediums, brushes, easels, markers, pens, pastels, sketchbooks, photo frames, drafting and sculpting tools is superb.
🕐 Mon–Fri 9–7, Sat 10–6.30, Sun 10–6 🚇 Canal Street (N, R) 🚌 M1, M6

TIME WARNER CENTER
Map 160 D16
10 Columbus Circle
Tel 212/823-6000
This, the first luxury shopping mall in Manhattan, will be familiar to suburbanites. Here under one roof are such big-name stores as Coach, Cole Haan, Davidoff, Godiva, L'Occitane, Hugo Boss, Thomas Pink, and Williams-Sonoma.
🕐 Mon–Sat 10–9, Sun 12–6 🚇 59th Street/Columbus Circle (A, C, B, D, 1, 9) 🚌 M7, M10

ENTERTAINMENT

The city's performance scene reflects the diversity of the metropolis. Theater patrons will find an array of options. There are 39 or so Broadway theaters, plus 450 non-profit theaters operating in the city.

CINEMA

The city is a veritable cinema paradiso. Numerous art houses operate, frequently showcasing individual directors or focusing on particular themes or eras. First-run movies are shown all over town in grand movieplexes.

CLASSICAL MUSIC, DANCE AND OPERA

Musical riches abound, led by the Metropolitan and City Operas and Carnegie Hall and

There is plenty of classical music on offer

the New York Philharmonic. All kinds of smaller groups and orchestras, plus independent opera companies, play at diverse venues—museums, music schools and churches. The New York City Ballet and American Ballet Theatre lead the traditional dance scene, while Merce Cunningham, Mark Morris, Alvin Ailey, Paul Taylor and Martha Graham are the leading modern dance companies.

COMEDY, POETRY AND THE SPOKEN WORD

The spoken word can be heard throughout the city, as the

intellectuals and literary lights meet, greet and sign at bookstores, lecture at the 92nd Street Y, or deliver their poetry at poetry fests and St. Mark's-in-the-Bowery. And don't forget stand-up comedy, a unique American cultural contribution, celebrated in New York City clubs, which gave birth to such brilliant comedians as Jerry Seinfeld, Jay Leno, Woody Allen, Rosie O'Donnell and Joan Rivers.

CONTEMPORARY LIVE MUSIC

Cabaret is flourishing in alluring rooms at the Carlyle and the Algonquin hotels. Musically, uptown tends to be more traditional; downtown leans to the avant-garde. Indie rock clubs abound on the Lower East Side and in the East Village. Cool jazz and other exotica can be heard at the Knitting Factory and Tonic. Jazz continues to thrive as it has always in New York. The leading venue is still the Village Vanguard, now under the watchful eye of Lorraine Gordon, but it has been joined by the $140 million Jazz at Lincoln Center in the Time Warner building on Columbus Circle. World music programming is featured all over town at Town Hall, Zankel Hall at Carnegie, and Symphony Space.

THEATER

The Great White Way attracts the most visitors with its brightly lit marquees and gilded theaters named after such luminaries as Ethel Barrymore, David Belasco and Eugene O'Neill. The Public Theater and BAM are the shining lights of Off-Broadway. The first, founded by Joe Papp, also delivers free summer

Shakespeare in the Park, while BAM is famous for its New Wave Festival. Off-Broadway has nurtured many playwrights too, such as Wally Shawn, Lanford Wilson and Tony Kushner, and several Broadway hits have emerged from here, notably *Rent*, *Avenue Q*, *A Chorus Line* and the *Heidi Chronicles*. Off-Off-Broadway stages quirky experimental showcases in tiny theaters with less than 100 seats, but it has nurtured such players as Eric Bogosian and Laurie Anderson.

PRACTICALITIES

Most box offices open from

Jazz has always flourished in New York

Monday to Saturday, 10am to 8pm, and Sunday from 11am to 6.30pm. Tickets can be purchased here without paying a fee. Standing Room Only tickets, when available, go on sale on the day of the performance.

Tickets can also be purchased through Telecharge (tel 212/239-6200) and Ticketmaster (tel 212/307-7171).

Best performance listings are found in *Time Out*, *New York* magazine, the *Village Voice* and the Friday edition of *The New York Times*. A good website is www.timeoutny.com.

ENTERTAINMENT LOCATOR

B

C

D

West 95th Street
Symphony Space,
Leonard Nimoy Thalia
Manhattan School of Music,
Miller Theatre,
Cotton Club,
Smoke
Cathedral Church of
St John the Divine
West 94th Street
Showman's Jazz Club,
Aaron Davis Hall,
Apollo Theater,
Classical Theater of Harlem
West 93rd Street
West 92nd Street
UPPER WEST
West 91st Street
SIDE

Central
Park
Reservoir

13

West 90th Street
West 89th Street
West 88th Street
West 87th Street
86th
Street
West 86th Street
86th
Street
CENTRAL
West 85th Street
West 84th Street
PARK
West 83rd Street
West 82nd Street
81st Street
Museum of
Nat Hist.
Centra

14

West 81st Street
West 80th Street
American Museum
of Natural History
Shakespeare in the Park
(Delacorte Theater)
Belveder
Lake
79th
Street
West 79th Street
West 78th Street
79th street Transvers
Stand-Up
New York
West 77th Street
New-York
Historical Society
West 76th Street
The
Lake
West 75th Street
Beacon
Theatre
West 74th Street
San Remo
Apartments
Ansonia
Building
West 73rd Street
West 72nd Street
The Dakota

Hudson River
Riverside Park
Riverside Drive
HIGHWAY 9A
West End Avenue
BROADWAY
Amsterdam Avenue
Columbus Avenue
Central Park West
West
Drive

72nd
Street
72nd
Street
Strawberry
Fields
West 71st Street
West 70th Street
Olmstr
West 69th Street
Freedom
Place
West 68th Street
West 69th
Street
West
68th
Street
Riverside Boulevard
Merkin
Concert Hall
West 67th Street
Makor
The
Sheep
Meadow

15

Juilliard School
64th Street
Lincoln Center
West 66th Street
Alice
Tully Hall
Tavern on
the Green
Bruno Walter
Auditorium
West 65th Street
Film Society of Lincoln Center
(Walter Reade Theater)
65th Street
Vivian Beaumont Theater
West 64th Street
Lincoln Center for
the Performing Arts
New York Society
for Ethical Culture
Mitzi Newhouse Theater
West 63rd Street
Lincoln
Center
Avery Fisher
Hall
Lincoln Plaza Cinemas
West 62nd
Street
New York State Theater
Museum of
Biblical Arts
Metropolitan
Opera House
West 61st Street
West 61st Street
Central
Park

16

West 60th Street
West 59th
Street
West End Avenue
12th Av
West 59th Street
Jazz at
Lincoln Center
59th Street
Columbus
Circle
COLUMBUS
CIRCLE
Central
Par
West 58th Street
57th
Street
West 57th STREET
HIGHWAY 9A

Carnegie
Hall
City
Center
WPP Theatre Four
(Women's Project Theatre)
West 56th Street
12th AVENUE
13th AVENUE
De Witt
Clinton Park
Alvin Ailey American
Dance Theater
Manhattan
Theatre
Club
West 55th Street
11th AVENUE
10th AVENUE
9th AVENUE
8th AVENUE
BROADWAY
7th AVENUE
West 54th Street
Studio 54
Chicago City
Limits
West 53rd Street
Broadway
Virginia
Roseland
Ballroom
Irish Arts
Center
West 52nd Street
Neil Simon
Iridium
Gershwin
Cadillac
Winter Garde
West 51st Street
Circle in the Square
Caroline's
Comedy
Club
West 50th Street
50th Street
Ambassador Theatre
49th Street
Eugene O'Neill
Walter Kerr
West 49th Street
Longacre
BROADWAY
Brooks Atkinson
Biltmore
Theatre
Barrymore
Theatre
Palac
West 48th Street
12th
Don't Tell Mama
West 47th Street
Richard Rogers
Lyceum
Imperial
Music Box
Marquis
West 46th Street
Danny's Skylight Room

17

West 52nd Street
West 51st Street
West 50th Street
West 48th Street
West 47th Street
West 46th Street
West 45th Street

186

B
Intrepid
Sea, Air and Space
Museum
West 46th
Street
9A
C
D

E

F

G

13

14

15

16

17

↑ Lenox Lounge, Schomburg Center for Research in Black Culture

East 95th Street

East 95th Street

Mill Rock Park

East 94th Street

Jewish Museum

East 93rd Street

East 93rd Street

East 92nd Street

92nd Street Y (Kauffman Concert Hall)

East 91st Street

East 91st Street

Cooper-Hewitt National Design Museum

National Academy of Design

East 90th Street

East 90th Street

Guggenheim Museum

East 89th Street

East 89th Street

East 88th Street

East 88th Street

Gracie Mansion

East 87th Street

East 87th Street

Carl Schurz Park

86th Street

East 86th Street

East 86th Street

Neue Galerie

East 85th Street

East 85th Street

Grace Rainey Rogers Auditorium (The Metropolitan Museum of Art)

East 84th Street

East 84th Street

East 83rd Street

East 83rd Street

East 82nd Street

East 82nd Street

East 81st Street

East 81st Street

ark

East 80th Street

East 80th Street

ad

East 79th Street

East 79th Street

PARK AVENUE

5th AVENUE

Lexington Avenue

3rd Avenue

2nd Avenue

1st Avenue

York Avenue

FRANKLIN DELANO ROOSEVELT DRIVE

East 78th Street

East 78th Street

77th Street

East 77th Street

East 77th Street

John Jay Park

Bemelmans Bar & Café Carlyle

East 76th Street

East 76th Street

East 75th Street

East 75th Street

Whitney Museum of American Art

East 74th Street

East 74th Street

Conservatory Water

East 73rd Street

East 73rd Street

East 72nd Street

East 72nd Street

ive

East 71st Street

East 71st Street

Asia Society

Frick Collection

Asia Society and Museum

East 70th Street

East 70th Street

Madison Avenue

East 69th Street

East 69th Street

East 68th Street

68th Street Hunter College

East 68th Street

Park Drive

North

East 67th Street

East 67th Street

East 66th Street

East 66th Street

Kosciuszko Foundation

East 65th Street

East 65th Street

East 64th Street

East 64th Street

Transverse Road

East 63rd Street

Lexington Avenue

PARK AVENUE

East 63rd Street

FIFTH AVENUE

East 62nd Street

East 62nd Street

Mount Vernon Hotel Museum and Garden

Dangerfield's

ROOSEVELT ISLAND

Roosevelt Island Main Street

Main Street

East 61st Street

Feinstein's at the Regency

East 61st St

Lexington Avenue

3rd Avenue

2nd Avenue

1st Avenue

York Avenue

West Road

East Road

Café Pierre

East 60th Street

5th Avenue

Florence Gould Hall

Chicago City Limits

East 60th Street

American Museum of the Moving Image

Highway 25

QUEENSBORO BRIDGE

Main Street

East 59th Street

59th Street

East

The Pond

South

West 58th Street

East 58th Street

East

57th Street

Paris Theatre

WEST 57TH STREET

EAST 57TH STREET

Trump Tower

West 56th Street

Dahesh Museum of Art

East 56th Street

West 56th Street

Avenue of the Americas (6th Avenue)

West 55th Street

Central Synagogue

West 55th Street

Museum of Modern Art

West 54th Street

York Theatre St Peter's Church

5th Avenue

West 54th Street

Lexington Avenue

Museum of Arts and Design

Museum of Television and Radio

West 53rd Street

East 53rd Street

Seagram Building

Rockefeller Center

West 52nd Street

YWCA Cine Club

East 52nd Street

Radio City Music Hall

Donnell Media Center New York Public Library

West 51st Street

51st Street

East 51st Street

St Patrick's Cathedral

Municipal Art Society

West 50th Street

East 50th Street

Mitchell Pl

47th - 50th Streets Rockefeller Center

GE Building

Rockefeller Center

West 49th Street

West 49th Street

East 49th Street

Cort

West 48th Street

5th Avenue

West 48th Street

East 48th Street

DIAMOND DISTRICT

West 47th Street

MIDTOWN MANHATTAN

East 47th Street

Japan Society

Lunt-Fontanne

West 46th Street

E

West 46th Street

East 46th Street

F

United Nations Headquarters

G

West 45th Street

West 45th Street

East 45th Street

Cinemas

Major cinema chains—AMC Empire, Cineplex Odeon, Loews and United Artists—have many theaters in the city showing first-run films. Those listed here screen more individual and varied fare. Most open around noon and operate continuously until late. You can get tickets in advance (for a surcharge) via websites such as fandango.com and movietickets.com. In the fall, the New York Film Festival is held at the Lincoln Center and other locations throughout the city. Spring is the time for the TriBeCa Film Festival.

AMERICAN MUSEUM OF THE MOVING IMAGE
Off map 187 G16
35th Avenue at 36th Street, Astoria, Queens
Tel 718/784-0077
www.movingimage.us
This museum in Queens, built on the site of the Astoria Studio, a former Paramount movie-production facility, hosts director festivals and retrospectives. Occasionally screenwriters answer questions at Friday and Saturday screenings. Take a look at how films are made in the core exhibition "Behind the Screen."
⚡ $10 🚇 Steinway Street (34th Avenue) (G, R, V), Broadway (N, W)

ANGELIKA FILM CENTER
Map 189 E22
Mercer and Houston streets
Tel 212/995-2000
www.angelikafilmcenter.com
This multiplex shows foreign films with subtitles, plus films by such artists as Atom Egoyan and other independent moviemakers. Pick up a latte at the café before or after the show.
⚡ $10.50 🚇 Broadway-Lafayette (F, S, V), Bleecker Street (6) 🚌 M1, M5, M6, M21

ANTHOLOGY FILM ARCHIVES
Map 189 F22
32 Second Avenue at East 2nd Street
Tel 212/505-5181
www.anthologyfilmarchives.org
Shows new film-makers along with old and rare vintage pieces and occasional tributes to particular directors.
⚡ $7–$8 🚇 Astor Place (6), Lower East Side/Second Avenue (F, V) 🚌 M15, M21

BAM ROSE CINEMAS
Off map 189 G25
30 Lafayette Street, Brooklyn
Tel 718/636-4100
www.bam.org
Screens at this house at the Brooklyn Academy of Music show contemporary first-run

Cinema Village is one of the city's independent cinemas

films, and tributes to American and foreign cinema, often with discussions with the directors.
⚡ $10 🚇 Nevins Street (2, 3), Dekalb Avenue (B, D, Q, N, R)

CINEMA VILLAGE
Map 189 E21
22 East 12th Street between University Place and Fifth Avenue
Tel 212/924-3363
www.cinemavillage.com
Renovated in 2000, this independent cinema, housed in a former fire station, now has three screens. Documentaries and old movies are the staples.
⚡ $9 🚇 14th Street/Union Square (L, N, Q, R, W, 4, 5, 6) 🚌 M1, M2, M14, M101, M103

FILM FORUM
Map 189 E23
209 West Houston Street between Sixth Avenue and Varick Street (Seventh Avenue)
Tel 212/727-8110 or 212/727-8112
www.filmforum.com
The leading cinema for independent films, it also shows domestic and foreign documentaries, as well as revivals.
⚡ $10 🚇 Houston Street (1, 9) 🚌 M5, M6, M20, M21

FILM SOCIETY OF LINCOLN CENTER
Map 186 C16
Walter Reade Theater, 165 West 65th Street
Tel 212/875-5600
www.filmline.com
This society hosts many different festivals—the New York Jewish Festival, Spanish Cinema Now, and Women in Film, for example.
⚡ $10 🚇 66th Street (1, 9) 🚌 M5, M7, M66, M104

IFC CENTER
Map 188 E22
323 Sixth Avenue (on the west side of Sixth Avenue at West 3rd Street)
Tel 212/924-7771
www.ifccenter.com
The Independent Film Channel renovated this old movie theater, creating the ultimate space for independent film entertainment. It has three cinemas with comfortable luxury seating and high-def digital and 35mm projection. A short is shown before each feature and there are no commercials. The restaurant is also an appealing feature.
🕐 Daily show times vary (starting at noon, with late 11pm Sun–Thu)
⚡ $10.75 🚇 West 4th Street (A, B, C, D, E, F, V) 🚌 M5, M6

LANDMARK SUNSHINE CINEMA

Map 189 F23

145 East Houston Street between First and Second avenues

Tel 212/358-7709 or 212/777-FILM (tickets)

www.landmarktheaters.com

This five-screener offers a medley of movies, from challenging documentaries such as *Bowling for Columbine,* foreign films and oldies, to first-run movies. Seating is raked and more comfortable than at other movie houses with similar programming.

$10.50 Second Avenue (F, V) M15, M21

LINCOLN PLAZA CINEMAS

Map 186 D16

1886 Broadway at 63rd Street

Tel 212/757-2280

www.lincolnplazacinema.com

A six-screener showing a select group of critically successful first-run movies and foreign films. For example, Gurinder Chadha's *Bend it Like Beckham* and Almodóvar's *Talk to Her* both played here.

$10.25 66th Street (1, 9) M5, M7, M66, M104

MAKOR

Map 186 D15

35 West 67th Street

Tel 212/601-1000

www.92Y.org

This club, part of a Jewish community center, hosts different programs, including mainly documentaries and oldies.

$9 66th Street (1, 9) M5, M7, M10, M66, M104

MOMA FILM

Map 187 E17

11 West 53rd Street

Tel 212/708-9480

www.moma.org

MoMA offers an ambitious film program of documentaries, historic retrospectives and director tributes.

$10 Rockefeller Center (B, D, F, V), 53rd Street/Fifth Avenue (E) M1, M2, M3, M4, M5, M6, M7

NEW YORK PUBLIC LIBRARY

Map 187 E17

Donnell Media Center, 20 West 53rd Street between Fifth and Sixth avenues

Tel 212/621-0609

Foreign films, shorts and documentaries, plus tributes to directors.

Free 53rd Street/Fifth Avenue (E, V) M1, M2, M3, M4, M5, M6, M7

PARIS THEATRE

Map 187 E16

4 West 58th Street between Fifth and Sixth avenues

Tel 212/688-3800

The films that play here are mostly foreign.

$10.50 Fifth Avenue/59th Street (N, R, W) M1, M2, M3, M4, M57

Catch a film from northern Europe at Scandinavia House

QUAD CINEMA

Map 188 E21

34 West 13th Street between Fifth and Sixth avenues

Tel 212/255-8800 or 212/255-2243

www.quadcinema.com

This four-screen art house shows foreign and independent films and works by new directors.

$9.50 14th Street (F, V), 14th Street/Union Square (L, N, Q, R, W, 4, 5, 6) M2, M3, M5, M6

SCANDINAVIA HOUSE

Map 188 E19

Victor Borge Hall, 58 Park Avenue between East 37th and 38th streets

Tel 212/779-3587

www.scandinaviahouse.org

Scandinavia House shows films by directors and actors from Denmark, Finland, Iceland, Norway and Sweden.

$8 42nd Street/Grand Central (4, 5, 6) M1

SYMPHONY SPACE LEONARD NIMOY THALIA

Off map at 186 C12

Broadway at 95th Street

Tel 212/864-5400

www.symphonyspace.org

Brilliant gems, like Fritz Lang's *Metropolis* and David Lynch's *Blue Velvet,* plus more recent independent films are shown here. There are also tributes to particular directors—Kurosawa, for example—and frequent double features.

$10 96th Street (1, 2, 3, 9) M96, M104

TWO BOOTS PIONEER THEATER

Map 189 G22

155 East 3rd Street at Avenue A

Tel 212/591-0434

www.twoboots.com

Opened in 2000 by the Two Boots pizza chain after they moved their East Village outlet to larger premises, this 100-seat house shows documentaries like *Bloody Sunday* and other foreign films, often followed by discussion sessions with the director.

$9 Lower East Side/Second Avenue (F, V) M14, M21

WHAT TO DO

Classical Music, Dance and Opera

CLASSICAL MUSIC

ALICE TULLY HALL
Map 186 C16
144 West 66th Street at Broadway
Tel 212/875-5050 or 212/721-6500
www.lincolncenter.org
This 1,096-seat hall is used
for chamber music, vocal
recitals, jazz and other musical
events. The Chamber Music
Society (tel 212/875-5788)
resides here.
🎫 $27.50–$52 🚇 66th Street (1, 9)
🚌 M5, M7, M66, M104

AVERY FISHER HALL
Map 186 C16
Lincoln Center, 111 Amsterdam Avenue
between West 64th and 65th streets
Tel 212/875-5030 or 212/721-6500
www.lincolncenter.org or
www.newyorkphilharmonic.com
Home to the New York
Philharmonic, this hall seats
2,700. Many other groups
perform here, including the
American Symphony Orchestra,
under Leon Botstein, and the
summer Mostly Mozart Festival.
During its season, the
Philharmonic opens its morning
rehearsals to the public (usually
on Thursdays at 9.45 for $15).
🎫 $25–$98 🚇 66th Street (1, 9)
🚌 M5, M7, M66, M104

BARGEMUSIC
Map 189 G25
Fulton Ferry Landing next to the
Brooklyn Bridge
Tel 718/624-2083
www.bargemusic.org
Anchored under Brooklyn
Bridge, this old coffee barge-
turned-125-seat concert hall is
the brainchild of violinist Olga
Bloom. A beguiling experience.
🎫 $25–$40 🚇 High Street (A), Clark
Street/Brooklyn Heights (2, 3)

BRUNO WALTER
AUDITORIUM
Map 186 C16
The New York Public Library for the
Performing Arts, 111 Amsterdam Avenue
between West 64th and 65th streets
Tel 212/870-1630, 212/642-0142
(programs)

Lectures, seminars, concerts
and films are the regular fare
at this 212-seat hall. The
library is a superb performing
arts archive.
🎤 Free 🚇 66th Street (1, 9) 🚌 M5,
M7, M66, M104

CARNEGIE HALL
Map 186 D17
Seventh Avenue at West 57th Street
Tel 212/247-7800
www.carnegiehall.com
"Practice, practice, practice" is
the answer to the old chestnut
of a question, "How do you
get to Carnegie Hall?" Many
well-practiced conductors and

*Carnegie Hall has an illustrious
past*

artists have played in this
famous hall, which was built
with Carnegie money in 1891,
from Tchaikovsky and Mahler
to the Beatles and the
Rolling Stones. Programming
includes the great orchestras
of the world, top-class
instrumentalists, the New York
Pops under Skitch Henderson,
and performers of jazz, folk,
pop and comedy. A small free
museum on the second floor
(tel 212/903-9629) displays
associated memorabilia.
🎥 Museum: daily 11–4.30; tours (tel
212/903-9765) Mon–Fri 11.30, 2 and 3
🎫 $10–$102 🚇 57th Street (N, Q, R,
W) 🚌 M6, M7, M57

CATHEDRAL CHURCH OF
ST. JOHN THE DIVINE
Off map 186 C12
1047 Amsterdam Avenue at 112th Street
Tel 212/316-7540
www.stjohndivine.org
Stop by to admire the still-
incomplete edifice, begun in
1892, and you may hear one of
the sanctuary's five organs. The
musical repertoire during arts
events ranges from choirs
singing Bach cantatas or
chanting Tibetan monks to
music made famous by Duke
Ellington and Judy Collins.
🎫 Varies 🚇 Cathedral Parkway/110th
Street (1, 9) 🚌 M4, M11

CENTRAL SYNAGOGUE
Map 187 F17
123 East 55th Street at Lexington Avenue
Tel 212/415-5500
www.92Y.org
Concerts at the synagogue
often feature well-known or
overlooked Jewish composers.
🎫 Varies 🚇 51st Street (6) 🚌 M98,
M101, M102, M103

COOPER UNION
Map 189 F22
41 Cooper Square at 7th Street
Tel 212/353-4140
www.cooperunion.edu
Diverse array of musical
performers and groups.
🎥 Varies 🎫 Varies 🚇 8th Street
(N, R, W), Astor Place (6) 🚌 M1

FLORENCE GOULD HALL
Map 187 E16
55 East 59th Street between Park and
Madison avenues
Tel 212/355-6160
www.fiaf.org
Chamber groups, opera
singers, pop and jazz artists,
dance companies, and actors
reading all entertain in
this 400-seat auditorium
associated with the
Alliance Française.
🎫 $30–$35 🚇 Fifth Avenue/59th
Street (N, R, W) 🚌 M1, M2, M3, M4,
M5, M57

FRICK COLLECTION

Map 187 E15
1 East 70th Street
Tel 212/288-0700
www.frick.org
The recitals in this exquisite
museum are a must.
 Varies 🚇 68th Street (6) 🚌 M1,
M2, M3, M4, M72

GRACE RAINEY ROGERS AUDITORIUM

Map 187 E14
The Metropolitan Museum of Art, Fifth
Avenue at 82nd Street
Tel 212/535-7710 or 212/570-3949
www.metmuseum.org
Small musical groups and
individuals entertain in this
mid-size 700-seat auditorium.
And the Met always has
chamber music in the Great
Hall Balcony on Friday and
Saturday evenings.
$35–$55 🚇 77th Street (6) 🚌 M1,
M2, M3, M4, M79

JUILLIARD SCHOOL

Map 186 C16
144 West 66th Street at Broadway
Tel 212/769-7406 or 212/721-6500
www.juilliard.edu
This world-famous performing
arts school is especially well
known for music. The young
artists who train here can be
seen in stimulating programs
in two auditoriums. Juilliard
also incorporates the School
for American Ballet, which is
the training ground for the
New York City Ballet. Dance
aficionados run to secure
tickets for the school's annual
workshop production in early
summer (tel 212/769-6600).
Most are free except for opera
programs and dance workshops
🚇 66th Street (1, 9)
🚌 M5, M7, M66, M104

KOSCIUSZKO FOUNDATION

Map 187 E16
15 East 65th Street
Tel 212/734-2130
www.kosciuszko.org
Programs featuring Polish
composers or artists.
Varies 🚇 68th Street (6) 🚌 M1,
M2, M3, M4

MANHATTAN SCHOOL OF MUSIC

Off map 186 C12
Broadway at 122nd Street
Tel 212/749-2802 or 917/493-4428
www.msmnyc.edu
This institution with a world-
class reputation has a large
concert hall and several
smaller venues. The
programming is diverse—
orchestras, chamber
ensembles—and ticket prices
reasonable.
Varies 🚇 125th Street (1, 9)
🚌 M4, M104

MERKIN CONCERT HALL

Map 186 C15
129 West 67th Street

The Frick Collection is a beautiful setting for music

Tel 212/501-3330
www.ekcc.org
National and international
chamber groups perform here.
You might find traditional
classical, new music or even a
group from Japan playing the
25-string koto.
$15–$45 🚇 66th Street (1, 9)
🚌 M5, M7, M104

MILLER THEATRE

Off map 186 C12
Columbia University, Broadway at 116th
Street
Tel 212/854-7799
www.millertheatre.com
Many cutting-edge classical
groups and composers are
presented here: John Zorn,
Julia Wolfe and John King,
for example.
Varies 🚇 116th Street (1, 9)
🚌 M104

NEW YORK PHILHARMONIC

Map 186 C16
Avery Fisher Hall, Broadway at 65th
Street
Tel 212/875-5656
www.newyorkphilharmonic.org
Established in 1842, this is the
oldest orchestra in the US.
Currently under the baton of
Lorin Maazel, the orchestra
performs more than 200
concerts annually. Dvorak's
New World Symphony was
premiered here in 1893.
$25–$108 🚇 66th Street (1, 9)
🚌 M5, M7, M66, M104

NEW YORK SOCIETY FOR ETHICAL CULTURE

Map 186 D16
2 West 64th Street at Central Park West
Tel 212/874-5210 or 866/468-7619
www.nysec.org
All kinds of cultural events are
held here, with lectures and
discussions often preceding
them.
🚇 66th Street (1, 9) 🚌 M10

92ND STREET Y

Map 187 F13
Kauffman Concert Hall, 1395 Lexington
Avenue at 92nd Street
Tel 212/415-5500, 212/427-6000 or
212/996-1100
www.92Y.org
The 92nd Street Y offers some
of the city's most varied
programming. It hosts music
recitals (Guarneri and Tokyo
string quartets, Janos Starker),
jazz, pop and folk, poetry and
literature readings (Thomas
Keneally, V. S. Naipaul), and
lectures on every conceivable
subject by contemporary
cultural leaders. A Jewish
cultural organization, it
celebrated its 130th
anniversary in 2004.
Varies 🚇 96th Street (6) 🚌 M96,
M98, M101, M102, M103

WEILL RECITAL HALL

Map 186 D17
881 Seventh Avenue
Tel 212/247-7800
www.carnegiehall.org
Small groups perform in this 250-seat hall in the Carnegie Hall complex (▷ 192). Well known for its Distinctive Debuts Series.
💵 $20–$92 🚇 57th Street (N, Q, R, W) 🚌 M6, M7, M57

ZANKEL HALL

Map 186 D17
881 Seventh Avenue
Tel 212/247-7800
www.carnegiehall.org
This 644-seat space in the Carnegie Hall complex (▷ 192) offers everything from early music and popular song to Afro-Cuban and other world music.
💵 $35–$90 🚇 57th Street (N, Q, R, W) 🚌 M6, M7, M57

DANCE AND OPERA

ALVIN AILEY AMERICAN DANCE THEATER

Map 186 D17
405 West 55th Street at Ninth Avenue
Tel 212/767-0590
www.alvinailey.org
In 2005 this exciting black modern dance company opened a brand-new permanent home with a 285-seat theater and 12 studios. Even if you don't go to a performance, stop by to see them working out in the first-floor studios.
💵 $25–$110 🚇 Columbus Circle (1, 9, A, B, C, D), 57th Street/7th Avenue (N, R, Q, W) 🚌 M11

AMATO OPERA THEATRE

Map 189 F22
319 Bowery at 2nd Street
Tel 212/228-8200
www.amato.org
The company has been putting on tiny productions of five or six operas annually since 1948. Mignon Dunn and Jon Frederic West performed here early in their careers. Seats 107.
💵 $25–$30 🚇 Bleecker Street (6), Lower East Side/Second Avenue (F, V) 🚌 M21, M103

AMERICAN BALLET THEATER

890 Broadway at 19th Street
Tel 212/477-3030
www.abt.org
This company performs regularly at City Center (see below) and at the Metropolitan Opera House (▷ 195) in the spring.

CITY CENTER

Map 186 D17
131 West 55th Street between Sixth and Seventh avenues
Tel 212/247-0430 or 212/581-1212
www.citycenter.org
The exotic Moorish-style building dating from 1922–24 is especially famous for dance productions. The Dance

The American Ballet Theatre performs a wide range of work

Theater of Harlem, Alvin Ailey American Dance Theater, Paul Taylor Dance Company, American Ballet Theatre and the San Francisco Ballet have all performed here. The Gilbert and Sullivan Players are also residents. Originally a Shriner's temple, the building was converted by Mayor Fiorello LaGuardia into a "people's theater" in 1943.
💵 $10–$65 🚇 57th Street (N, Q, R, W) 🚌 M5, M6, M7, M57

DANCE THEATER WORKSHOP

Map 188 D20
219 West 19th Street at Seventh Avenue
Tel 212/924-0077
www.dtw.org
In 1965 Jeff Duncan, Art Bauman and Jack Moore founded this choreographers' collective, and it still promises innovative performances here and at other city venues. Many famous dancers have begun careers here—Bill T. Jones, Mark Morris, Ann Carlson, Eiko and Koma—plus such theatrical talents as Bill Irwin, Whoopi Goldberg and Paul Zaloom.
💵 Varies 🚇 18th Street (1, 9) 🚌 M14, M20

DANCE THEATER OF HARLEM

Off map at 186 C13
Everett Center for the Performing Arts
466 West 152nd Street between Amsterdam and St. Nicholas avenues
Tel 212/690-2800
www.dancetheatreofharlem.com
This exciting company presents a series at the New York State Theater and also has open house every second Sunday of each month. Their appearance at the August street festival is also fun. The repertory ranges from classical to contemporary works.
🎫 July at New York State Theater
💵 Varies 🚇 155th Street (C) 🚌 M18, M100, M101

JOYCE SOHO

Map 189 E23
155 Mercer Street between Houston and Prince streets
Tel 212/431-9233 or 212/334-7479
www.joyce.org
This theater offers cutting-edge dance, often with an alternative perspective. Rehearsals are open to the public.
💵 $8–$20 🚇 Prince Street (N, R, W) 🚌 M1, M6, M21

THE JOYCE THEATER
Map 188 D21
175 Eighth Avenue southwest corner of 19th Street
Tel 212/691-9740 or 212/242-0800
www.joyce.org
The city's premier dance venue hosts top international and domestic dance companies and showcases such important dance series as Altogether Different. Expect to see the Eliot Feld Ballet, Pilobolus Dance Theater and many others.
Varies 23rd Street (C, E) M20, M23

THE JUDSON MEMORIAL CHURCH
Map 189 E22
55 Washington Square South
Tel 212/777-0033 or 212/477-0351
www.judson.org
For many decades this Baptist Church has nurtured avant-garde artists. It's most famous for the late Judson Poets Theater but it still hosts experimental dance series. Movement Research performs a regular series here.
Varies West 4th Street (A, C, E, F, S, V) M5, M6, M8

THE KITCHEN
Map 188 C21
512 West 19th Street between Tenth and Eleventh avenues
Tel 212/255-5793
www.thekitchen.org
At this fixture of the downtown scene established in 1971, the careers of such artists as Philip Glass, Laurie Anderson, Eric Bogosian, Robert Mapplethorpe and Cindy Sherman were nurtured. It's still going strong.
$5–$15 23rd Street (C, E) M11, M23

LINCOLN CENTER FOR THE PERFORMING ARTS
Map 186 C16
Columbus Avenue between 62nd and 66th streets
Tel 212/875-5000
www.lincolncenter.org
This huge complex is home to the Metropolitan Opera House, the New York State Theater, Avery Fisher Hall, the Vivian Beaumont and Mitzi E. Newhouse theaters, the New York Public Library of the Performing Arts, the Walter Reade movie theater and the Juilliard School. In summer there is dancing under the stars on the plaza as well as the Lincoln Center Festival,

The Metropolitan Opera House is a glamorous venue

a free event which presents hundreds of performing artists and companies of all kinds. For tours of the first three halls mentioned above call 212/875-5350 for reservations.
Varies 66th Street (1, 9) M7, M11, M66, M104

MERCE CUNNINGHAM STUDIO
Map 188 D22
55 Bethune Street at Washington Street (11th floor)
Tel 212/255-8240
www.merce.org
The Studio Performance Series for Emerging Choreographers uses this large studio space from September to July.

It seats 99. Cunningham, now in his 80s, still teaches here.
$15 14th Street (A, C, E), 14th Street (1, 2, 3, 9) M8, M11, M20

METROPOLITAN OPERA HOUSE
Map 186 C16
30 Lincoln Center Plaza between 63rd and 64th streets
Tel 212/362-6000
www.metopera.org
The Metropolitan Opera, which had its first season in 1883–84, moved to this building on the western side of Lincoln Center Plaza in 1966. Although modern, it is glamorous with its Chagall paintings, plush crimson carpeting, chandeliers and gold leaf. The back of each of the theater's 3,800-seats has a screen that shows subtitles during performances. Most productions are spectacular, with the best international stars. Season-ticket holders snap up most of the best seats (and the best-priced seats) but individual tickets are usually available. Beginning in May the American Ballet Theatre performs a traditional repertory plus more modern pieces by such choreographers as James Kudelka and Twyla Tharp.
$26–$215, standing room $15–$20 66th Street (1, 9) M5, M7, M11, M66, M104

NEW YORK GRAND OPERA
154 West 57th Street, Suite 125
Tel 212/245-8837
www.newyorkgrandopera.org
Founded in 1973, this company performs fully staged operas with full orchestra at Carnegie Hall and also gives free performances in Central Park. It is still directed by its founder, Vincent La Silva.
$20–$60 (Summer in Central Park free)

NEW YORK STATE THEATER

Map 186 C16
20 Lincoln Center Plaza at 63rd Street
Tel 212/870-5570
www.nycballet.com
www.nycopera.com
This 2,792-seat auditorium is home to the New York City Opera and the New York City Ballet. The New York City Opera is famous for its emphasis on the ensemble rather than soloists, and many prefer its stimulating productions over those of the Met. The New York City Ballet began in 1933, and is still going strong under artistic director Peter Martins. The company performs for 23 weeks in the State Theater and then moves upstate to Saratoga.

🎭 City Opera $32–$110 (standing room only $12), NY Ballet $30–78 🚇 66th Street (1, 9) 🚌 M5, M7, M11, M66, M104

STREB ACTION INVENTION LAB

Off map 189 G23 (Brooklyn)
51 North First Street between Wythe and Kent, Williamsburg, Brooklyn
Tel 718-384-6491
www.billburg.com
Harry Houdini and Evel Knievel inspire Elizabeth Streb's daring energetic stunt-like "Popaction" dancing in which she crashes through glass and leaps from ledges. She performs at this 200-seat theater and supper club and also in Grand Central and at the Joyce Theater and the Kitchen.

🎭 Varies 🚇 Bedford Avenue (L)

Comedy, Poetry and the Spoken Word

WHAT TO DO

BARNES & NOBLE

Map 188 E21
33 East 17th Street at Union Square and other locations
Tel 212/253-0810
www.bn.com
Barnes & Noble bookstores regularly sponsor readings, discussions and signings with numerous authors; the biggest names are most likely to appear at the Union Square branch.

🎭 Free 🚇 14th Street/Union Square (L, N, Q, R, W, 4, 5, 6) 🚌 M1, M2, M3, M6, M7, M14

BOWERY POETRY CLUB

Map 189 F22
308 Bowery between Bleecker and East 1st streets
Tel 212/614-0505 or 212/206-1515
www.bowerypoetry.com
All kinds of poets and performance artists play here. You might find *Communications from a Cockroach* and similar offbeat shows.

🎭 $5–$15 🚇 Bleecker Street (6) Broadway/Lafayette (F, S, V) 🚌 M21, M103

CAROLINE'S COMEDY CLUB

Map 186 D17
1626 Broadway between 49th and 50th streets
Tel 212/757-4100
www.carolines.com
First opened by Caroline Hirsch as a cabaret in Chelsea

Try Chicago City Limits for improvised comedy

in 1981, the club gained a name throughout the 1980s and 1990s for its comedy bookings. Now in its glitzy Times Square venue, it presents live entertainment 365 nights a year. Jerry Seinfeld and Rosie O'Donnell did their early stand-up here.

🕐 Mon–Wed 7.30, 9.30, Thu, Sun 8, 10, Fri–Sat 8, 10.30, 12.30am 🎭 $15–$40, plus 2-drink minimum 🚇 50th Street (1, 9) 🚌 M10, M20, M50

CHICAGO CITY LIMITS

Map 186 D17
318 West 53rd Street at Eighth Avenue
Tel 212/888-5233
www.chicagocitylimits.com
This comedy revue company relocated to New York from Chicago in 1979. The resident troupe puts on two-hour improv shows. Don't sit in the front row if you're worried about being heckled. Soft drinks served.

🕐 Wed–Sun 🎭 $10–$20 (plus 2-drink minimum) 🚇 50th Street (C, E) 🚌 M11

COMEDY CELLAR

Map 188 E22
117 MacDougal Street between West 3rd and Bleecker streets
Tel 212/254-3480
www.comedycellar.com
A cave-like venue that features nationally known comedians—Seinfeld, Stewart, Williams et al.

🕐 Sun–Thu 9, Fri 10.45, 12.30, Sat 7.30, 9.15, 11, 12.45am 🎭 $10–$15, plus 2-drink minimum 🚇 West 4th Street (A, C, E, F, S, V) 🚌 M5, M6

DANGERFIELD'S

Map 187 F16
1118 First Avenue between East 61st and 62nd streets
Tel 212/593-1650
www.dangerfields.com
Rodney Dangerfield is no longer a regular presence, but this classic seedy club, established in 1969, has hosted many a legend, from Jay Leno and Jim Carrey to Jackie Mason, Tim Allen and Andrew Dice Clay.

⏰ Sun–Thu 9, Fri 8.30, 10.30, Sat. 8, 10.30, 12.30am 💵 $12.50–$20, no minimum 🚇 59th Street (4, 5, 6) 🚌 M15, M57

DONNELL MEDIA CENTER
Map 187 E17
New York Public Library, 20 West 53rd Street between Fifth and Sixth avenues
Tel 212/621-0609
www.nypl.org
Cultural events and readings.
💵 Free 🚇 53rd Street/Fifth Avenue (E, V) 🚌 M1, M2, M3, M4, M5, M6, M7

THE DUPLEX
Map 188 D22
61 Christopher Street at Seventh Avenue South
Tel 212/255-5438
www.theduplex.com
A launching pad for Woody Allen, Joan Rivers and Rodney Dangerfield. The tradition continues in the upstairs cabaret room. Piano bar downstairs.
💵 Cover varies, plus 2-drink minimum 🚇 Christopher Street/ Sheridan Square (1, 9) 🚌 M8, M20

GOTHAM COMEDY CLUB
Map 188 E20
34 West 22nd Street between Fifth and Sixth avenues
Tel 212/367-9000
www.gothamcomedyclub.com
Old and new hands on the comedy scene play this upscale, elegant club in the Flatiron District, which opened in 1996.
💵 Varies 🚇 23rd Street (F, V) 🚌 M2, M3, M5, M6, M7, M23

HOUSING WORKS USED BOOK CAFÉ
Map 189 F23
126 Crosby Street at Jersey Street
Tel 212/334-3324
www.housingworks.org
This bookstore with a gallery has become a major literary hub, attracting hipsters to readings, parties and events. Every third Friday of the month, there's an acoustic music concert. All monies support the homeless with HIV and AIDS.

⏰ Mon–Fri 10–9, Sat 12–9, Sun 12–7 (readings/events vary) 💵 Free–$20 🚇 Prince Street (N, R), Broadway-Lafayette (F, S, V), Bleecker Street (6) 🚌 M1

NEW SCHOOL
Map 188 E21
Tishman Hall, 66 West 12th Street between Fifth and Sixth avenues
Tel 212/229-5488
www.nsu.newschool.edu
This prestigious university stages concerts, lectures and other performances including a new poetry series. *Inside the Actor's Studio*, which airs on Bravo, is one of the school's most popular events, but no single tickets are available.

Enjoying a good book at Poets House

🚇 14th Street (F, V) 🚌 M5, M6, M7, M14

NEW YORK PUBLIC LIBRARY
Map 188 E18
Fifth Avenue between 41st and 42nd streets
Tel 212/930-0855
www.nypl.org
In addition to exhibitions, the library also sponsors lectures by leading writers and critics. They are usually held in the Celeste Bartos Forum.
💵 Varies 🚇 42nd Street (B, D, F, V), Grand Central (4, 5, 6) 🚌 M1, M2, M3, M4, M42

92ND STREET Y
Map 187 F13
1395 Lexington Avenue at 92nd Street
Tel 212/415-5500
www.92Y.org
This major cultural force in the city has four performance spaces, programming everything from lectures given by heavy hitters like Bill Gates and Bill Clinton to readings sponsored in the Unterberg Poetry Center.
💵 $16–$50 🚇 96th Street (6) 🚌 M96, M98, M101, M102, M103

NUYORICAN POETS CAFÉ
Map 189 G22
236 East 3rd Street between Avenues B and C
Tel 212/505-8183
www.nuyorican.org
Originally a platform for Puerto Rican poets and artists, the café is still famous for its Wednesday and Friday night poetry slams. Expect to see theater, screenplay readings and even Latin jazz. Take a cab.
⏰ Tue–Sat 7–12, Sun 4–12 💵 Varies 🚇 Lower East Side/Second Avenue (F, V) 🚌 M9, M21

PEOPLE'S IMPROV THEATER
Map 188 E19/20
154 West 29th Street between Sixth and Seventh avenues
Tel 212/563-7488
www.thepit-nyc.com
Improvisation here comes with caustic social commentary and audience participation.
💵 Varies 🚇 28th Street (1, 9) 🚌 M5, M6, M7, M20

THE POETRY PROJECT
Map 189 F21
St. Mark's Church-in-the-Bowery
131 East 10th Street at Second Avenue
Tel 212/674-0910
www.poetryproject.com
This legendary outpost in the East Village, which hosted W. H. Auden, Allen Ginsberg and many others, has readings on Mondays and Wednesdays, among other events.
💵 Varies 🚇 Astor Place (6), First Avenue (L) 🚌 M8, M15

WHAT TO DO

POETS HOUSE
Map 189 F23
72 Spring Street between Crosby and Lafayette streets
Tel 212/431-7920
This 45,000-volume poetry library sponsors a fall and spring lecture series.
🖐 Free–$7 🚇 Spring Street (6), Spring Street (C, E) 🚌 M1

QUEENS COLLEGE
Music Building
Tel 718/997-4646
www.qc.edu/readings
The college offers a fall and spring series of readings by international poets and writers. No credit cards.
🕐 Tue at 7 🖐 $10–$15 🚇 Main Street (7) and bus Q 25/34 (best to call for directions)

STAND-UP NEW YORK
Map 186 C14
236 West 78th Street at Broadway
Tel 212/595-0850
www.standupny.com
Audiences here can be hard, but comics at this typical comedy club may emerge as the stars of tomorrow.
🖐 Cover varies, 2-drink minimum
🚇 79th Street (1, 9) 🚌 M79, M104

UPRIGHT CITIZENS BRIGADE THEATRE
Map 188 D20
307 West 26th Street between Eighth and Ninth avenues
Tel 212/366-9176
www.ucbtheatre.com
The city's hippest and most affordable comedy club. Expect manic, original and inventive improv-style sketches at the 150-seat theater.
🕐 Daily (show times vary) 🖐 $5–$20
🚇 23rd Street (C, E)

Contemporary Live Music

BLUES, COUNTRY, FOLK, REGGAE AND WORLD

ASIA SOCIETY
Map 187 F15
725 Park Avenue at East 70th Street
Tel 212/288-6400
www.asiasociety.org
The downstairs auditorium showcases arts and culture—dance, film, lectures and music—from Asia. Ravi Shankar made his American debut at the Asia Society.
🖐 Varies 🚇 68th Street (6) 🚌 M1, M2, M3, M4, M72

B. B. KING BLUES CLUB AND GRILL
Map 188 D18
237 West 42nd Street
Tel 212/997-4144
www.bbkingblues.com
Little Richard and Roberta Flack, among others, have all entertained at this large bi-level club. On Sunday the Harlem Gospel Choir shakes up the Sunday brunch from 12.30 to 2.30. Dance floor.
🖐 $10–$90 🚇 42nd Street/Times Square (N, Q, R, S, W, 1, 2, 3, 7, 9) 🚌 M10, M20, M42, M104

BITTER END
Map 189 E22
147 Bleecker Street at Thompson Street
Tel 212/673-7030
www.bitterend.com

You'll find the craic at the Irish Arts Center

The cradle of the antiwar folk music scene in the 1960s, the Bitter End is much more rock-oriented today. Performances every night.
🖐 $5–$15 🚇 West 4th Street (A, C, E, F, V, S) 🚌 M5, M6, M21

IRISH ARTS CENTER
Map 186 C17
553 West 51st Street between Tenth and Eleventh avenues
Tel 212/757-3318
www.irishartscenter.org
Comedy and music with a Celtic-Gaelic flavor are performed here the first Sunday of the month.
🖐 Varies 🚇 50th Street (C, E) 🚌 M11, M50

JAPAN SOCIETY
Map 187 F18
333 East 47th Street between First and Second avenues
Tel 212/832-1155
www.japansociety.org
Traditional and contemporary Japanese music concerts and cultural events are held in the 278-seat Lila Acheson Wallace Auditorium.
🖐 Varies 🚇 51st Street (6) 🚌 M15, M27, M50

LION'S DEN
Map 189 E22
214 Sullivan Street between Bleecker and West 3rd streets
Tel 212/477-2782
www.cegmusic.com
Folk and rock artists are the staples here.
🕐 Nightly (show times vary) 🖐 $8–$30
🚇 West 4th Street (A, C, E, F, S, V), Bleecker Street (6) 🚌 M5, M6, M21

PADDY REILLY'S MUSIC BAR
Off map 188 F19
519 Second Avenue at 29th Street
Tel 212/686-1210
www.paddyreillys.com
The Celtic house band, the Prodigals, plays Friday nights. Saturday is open mike night, and visitors make an attempt to play the bodhrán and the uillean pipes.
🕐 Daily 11am–4am 🖐 $5–$15
🚇 28th Street (6) 🚌 M15

WHAT TO DO

RODEO BAR
Map 188 F20
375 Third Avenue at East 27th Street
Tel 212/683-6500
www.rodeobar.com
This Southern-style roadhouse serves up Tex-Mex food and margaritas, along with such musicians as singer-songwriter Cindy Bullens and Tex-Mex rockabilly artist Rosie Flores.
Daily 11.30am–2am (music Mon–Sat 10–4, Sun 10–2) Free
28th Street (6) M101, M102, M103

TERRA BLUES
Map 189 E22
149 Bleecker Street between LaGuardia Place and Thompson Street
Tel 212/777-7776
www.terrablues.com
At this second-floor club, acoustic acts such as Honey Boy Edwards and Louisiana Red warm up the crowd. The bar has a good selection of bourbons.
$5–$15, plus 2-drink minimum West 4th Street (A, C, E, F, S, V) M5, M6

TOWN HALL
Map 188 D18
123 West 43rd Street between Sixth Avenue and Broadway
Tel 212/840-2824
www the-townhall-nyc.org
This 1,500-seat theater, founded in 1921 by the suffragist League for Political Education, offers eclectic programming with Broadway songs, cabaret, opera, pop performances and world music as well as lectures and readings. McKim, Mead and White designed the Georgian-style building.
$25–$85 42nd Street/Times Square (N, Q, R, S, W, 1, 2, 3, 7, 9), 42nd Street (B, D, F, V) M5, M6, M7, M42

VILLAGE UNDERGROUND
Map 189 E22
130 West 3rd Street between Sixth Avenue and MacDougal Street
Tel 212/777-7745
www.thevillageunderground.com
A subterranean club with a good line-up of artists ranging from salsa bands to blues artists. Sunday is open mike night.
Varies West 4th Street (A, C, E, F, S, V) M5, M6

WORLD MUSIC INSTITUTE
49 West 27th Street, Suite 930
Tel 212/545-7536
www.worldmusicinstitute.org
This organization sponsors world music concerts and

The Town Hall offers a wide range of performances

series at venues around town (Symphony Space, Cooper Union, Town Hall).

JAZZ AND CABARET
ARTHUR'S TAVERN
Map 188 D22
57 Grove Street between Seventh Avenue South and Bleecker Street
Tel 212/675-6879
This funky down-home bar has jazz most nights—usually traditional Dixieland.
Free Christopher Street/Sheridan Square (1, 9) M8, M20

BEMELMANS BAR
Map 187 E14
Carlyle Hotel, 35 East 76th Street
Tel 212/744-1600
www.rosewoodhotels.com
The murals and the sophistication of the scene make this a classic New York experience.
Daily 11am–2am (entertainment from 5.30 usually) $20–$25 at table, $10 at bar; no minimum 77th Street (6) M1, M2, M3, M4

BIRDLAND
Map 188 D18
315 West 44th Street between Eighth and Ninth avenues
Tel 212/581-3080
www.birdlandjazz.com
Perhaps the most elegant and comfortable jazz club in town. Charlie Parker inspired the original Birdland, which opened in 1949, and he was its first headliner. Expect to hear everyone from Roy Haynes and Lee Konitz to Diana Krall and Nicholas Payton.
Shows daily at 9pm and 11pm $20–$70, plus $20 minimum 42nd Street (A, C, E) M10, M11, M20, M42

BLUE NOTE
Map 188 E22
131 West Third Street at Sixth Avenue
Tel 212/475-8592
www.bluenotejazz.com
Tiny and ultra-expensive, the Blue Note is always jammed with fans grooving to the sounds of contemporary leaders in jazz, blues, Latin and R & B. It also sponsors a Latin Jazz Festival.
Daily at 9pm and 11.30pm $20–$65 at tables, $40–45 at bar, plus $5 minimum West 4th Street (A, C, E, F, S, V) M5, M6

WHAT TO DO

CAFÉ CARLYLE

Map 187 E14
35 East 76th Street at Madison Avenue
Tel 212/744-1600
Bobby Short has been playing here since 1968, sashaying from Cole Porter to Bessie Smith with ease and entertaining café society in high style. On Monday night, Woody Allen occasionally shows up with his clarinet and the Eddy Davis New Orleans Jazz Band.
Sets: Tue–Sat 8.45pm and 10.45pm $95, no minimum 77th Street (6) M1, M2, M3, M4

CAFÉ PIERRE

Map 187 E16
Fifth Avenue at 61st Street
Tel 212/838-8000
www.fourseasons.com
Kathleen Landis and Nancy Winston play and sing jazz and cabaret standards, along with customer requests.
Tue–Sat 8.30pm–12.30am, Sun–Mon 8.30pm–midnight Free, $25 minimum 59th Street/Fifth Avenue (N, R, W) M1, M2, M3, M4

CAJUN

Map 188 D21
129 Eighth Avenue between West 16th and 17th streets
Tel 212/691-6174
www.jazzatthecajun
One of the few places with traditional jazz bands every night.
Wed, Sun noon, Mon–Sat at 8pm, Sun 7.30pm Free 14th Street (A, C, E) M20

CORNELIA STREET CAFÉ

Map 188 D22
29 Cornelia Street between Bleecker and West 3rd streets
Tel 212/989-9319
www.corneliastreetcafe.com
This subterranean space hosts everything from structured free jazz and cabaret to poetry and performance art.
Free–$15 West 4th Street (A, C, E, F, S, V) M5, M6, M21

COTTON CLUB

Off map 186 C12
656 West 125th Street between Broadway and Riverside Drive
Tel 212/663-7980
www.cottonclub-newyork.com
Although its heyday was from 1923 to 1935 (then on 142nd Street), this famous Harlem landmark still has blues, jazz and gospel acts that seem straight out of the 1920s. Monday night is swing night.
Mon, Thu–Fri 8– 2, Sat–Sun noon–2am $15–$35 125th Street (1, 9) M104, Bx 15

DANNY'S SKYLIGHT ROOM

Map 186 D18
346 West 46th Street between Eighth

The Cotton Club is a New York institution

and Ninth avenues
Tel 212/265-8133
www.dannysgrandseapalace.com
Such cabaret artists as singer-pianist Blossom Dearie entertain in this elegant room.
None–$25, plus $15 or 2-drink minimum; dinner- show packages available 42nd Street (A, C, E) M11, M20

DETOUR

Map 189 F21
349 East 13th Street between First and Second Avenues
Tel 212/533-6212
www.jazzatdetour.com
This tiny casual no-cover jazz bar is the place to hear young emerging musicians and

singers playing traditional and experimental jazz.
Sun–Thu 4–2 (music 9–12.30), Fri–Sat 4–4 (music 10–1.30) 2-drink minimum 14th Street/Union Square (L, N, Q, R, W, 4, 5, 6), First Avenue (L) M14, M15

DON'T TELL MAMA

Map 186 D18
343 West 46th Street between Eighth and Ninth avenues
Tel 212/757-0788
Diverse singers and cabaret artists perform at this venue.
None–$40, plus 2-drink minimum 42nd Street (A, C, E) M11, M20

FEINSTEIN'S AT THE REGENCY

Map 187 E16
Regency Hotel, 540 Park Avenue at East 61st Street
Tel 212/339-4095 or 307-4100
www.loewshotels.com
It's lush, elegant and exclusive. Michael Feinstein plays on occasion. Dinner is available.
Shows Tue–Sat, usually at 8 $50–$75, plus $40 minimum Lexington/63rd Street (F), 59th Street (4, 5, 6), 59th Street (N, R, W) M1, M2, M3, M4, M57

IRIDIUM

Map 186 D17
1650 Broadway at 51st Street
Tel 212/582-2121
www.iridiumjazzclub.com
Guitar legend Les Paul plays every Monday night at this chic good-looking club. Top R&B and jazz names appear, plus there are Cuban jazz nights twice a month. On Sunday there's a jazz brunch buffet from 11 to 3, with shows at 12.30 and 2.30.
Sun–Thu 5–midnight (sets at 8 and 10), Fri–Sat 7pm–2am (sets at 8, 10 and 11.30) $25–$95 ($5 minimum at bar, $10 at table) 49th Street (N, R, W), 50th Street (1, 9) M6, M7, M50

JAZZ GALLERY

Map 189 F23
290 Hudson Street between Dominick and Spring streets
Tel 212/242-1063
www.jazzgallery.org
Opened in 1995, this exhibition and performance

space is used for jazz-oriented and jazz-influenced art, literature, drama and music.
🅒 Thu–Sat (sets at 9 and 10.30pm) 💲 $12–$65 🚇 Spring Street (C, E), Houston Street (1, 9) 🚌 M20, M21

JAZZ AT LINCOLN CENTER
Map 186 D16
Time Warner Center at Broadway and 60th Street
Tel 212/258-9800 or 212/721-6500
www.jazzatlincolncenter.org
Top-drawer jazz artists give performances in the 1230 seat Rose Theater, the 300- to 600-seat Allen Room (whose 50-foot-high (15m) glass wall overlooks Columbus Circle) and the more intimate Dizzy's Club Coca Cola, commemorating Dizzy Gillespie.
🅒 Varies 💲 Varies $30–$150; club has cover and minimum 🚇 59th Street (1, 9) 🚌 M5, M104

JAZZ STANDARD
Map 188 F20
116 East 27th Street between Park Avenue South and Lexington Avenue
Tel 212/576-2232
www.jazzstandard.com
The Union Square Café's Danny Myers established this popular downstairs venue with food from his ground-floor restaurant Blue Smoke. It's a sleek, comfortable place for music and a meal.
🅒 Daily 6.30–3 (show times vary) 💲 $15–$30 🚇 28th Street (6) 🚌 M1, M101, M102, M103

JOE'S PUB
Map 189 F22
Public Theater, 425 Lafayette Street between Astor Place and East 4th Street
Tel 212/539-8770 or 212/539 8778
www.joespub.com
A favorite cabaret club of many New Yorkers, named after Public Theater founder Joe Papp. It's comfortable the way a club should be, with couches and tables. DJs spin during Late Night at Joe's.
🅒 Daily 6–4 (shows usually at 8.30pm) 💲 $10–$40, plus 2-drink minimum 🚇 Astor Place (6) 🚌 M1, M8

KAVEHAZ
Map 188 E20
37 West 26th Street between Sixth Avenue and Broadway
Tel 212/343-0612
www.kavehaz.com
The name means coffeehouse in Hungarian, and this long narrow gallery café has plenty of atmosphere. It serves light snacks along with the cultural fare—usually two or three jazz bands per night and a monthly art exhibit.
🅒 Sun–Thu 5–12, Fri–Sat 5–2 (show times vary) 💲 Free 🚇 23rd Street (F, V) 🚌 M2, M3, M5, M6, M7

Jazz aficionados are spoilt for choice

LENOX LOUNGE
Off map 187 E12
288 Lenox Avenue between 124th and 125th streets
Tel 212/427-0253
www.lenoxlounge.com
This long-time Harlem hang-out for musicians has jazz every night except Tuesday.
🅒 Wed–Mon (8pm and 10pm) 💲 $20 on Fri and Sat 🚇 125th Street (2, 3) 🚌 M7, M102

OAK ROOM
Map 188 E18
Algonquin Hotel, 59 West 44th Street between Fifth and Sixth avenues
Tel 212/840-6800
www.algonquinhotel.com
By nurturing such artists as

Steve Ross, Michael Feinstein, Harry Connick, Jr. and Diana Krall, this room led a revival of cabaret. Dinner is available before the first show.
🅒 Tue–Thu 9pm, Fri–Sat 9pm and 11.30pm 💲 $50, plus 2-drink minimum, dinner packages 🚇 42nd Street (B, D, F, V) 🚌 M1, M2, M3, M4, M5, M6, M7

ST. PETER'S CHURCH
Map 187 F17
Citicorp Center, 619 Lexington Avenue at 54th Street
Tel 212/935-2200
www.saintpeters.org
The regularly held jazz vespers at this Lutheran church at Citicorp Center are well known among New Yorkers and musicians, along with the Wednesday jazz at noon.
💲 Varies 🚇 53rd Street/Lexington Avenue (E, V) 🚌 M57, M98, M101, M102, M103

SCHOMBURG CENTER FOR RESEARCH IN BLACK CULTURE
Off map 187 E12
515 Malcolm X Boulevard at 135th Street
Tel 212/491-2200
www.nypl.org
This African-American cultural archive sponsors an annual Women's Jazz Festival and a performance of Langston Hughes' *Nativity* in December.
💲 Varies 🚇 135th Street (B, C) 🚌 M7

SHOWMAN'S JAZZ CLUB
Off map 186 D12
375 West 125th Street between St. Nicholas and Morningside avenues
Tel 212/864-8941
In the 1940s and 50s, musicians often dropped in here after hours to jam or just hang out. Today musicians still frequent the place and you might find Grady Tate, George Benson or Ed Bradley whiling away the hours.
🅒 Tue–Thu 8.30pm–12.30am, Fri–Sat 10.30pm–3.30am 💲 Free, 2-drink minimum 🚇 125th Street (A, B, C, D) 🚌 M3

SMALL'S

Map 188 C22

183 West 10th Street between West 4th Street and Seventh Avenue South

Tel 212/929-7565

This just may be the least expensive, quality jazz club in the city. It's named appropriately; the downstairs space is narrow and spare. The focus is on the music, and there are no distractions such as a bar or food. The musicians jam into the wee hours, with many dropping in from other clubs after hours. Several big names got their break here, notably Zaid Nasser, Grant Stewart, Jason Lindner and Ari Roland.

🕐 Daily 10pm–8am 💵 Cover $10
🚇 14th Street (1, 2, 3, 9) 🚌 M20

SMOKE

Off map 186 C12

2751 Broadway between 105th and 106th Streets

Tel 212/864-6662

www.smokejazz.com

Intimate and comfortable with its plush couches, red velvet barstools and heavy drapes, this club was opened in 1999. It has headlined many great jazz artists including organist Dr. Lonnie Smith and trombonist Slide Hampton, but it is also a good place to see local artists.

🕐 Daily 9pm, 11pm, 12.30am
💵 Mon–Thu free, but $15 minimum, weekends cover varies $20–$25
🚇 103 Street (1, 9) 🚌 M104

SWEET RHYTHM

Map 188 D22

88 Seventh Avenue South between Grove and Bleecker streets

Tel 212/255-3626

The late Gil Evans played here when the place was called Sweet Basil. It's a casual spot where mainstream jazz artists play along with such singers as Carla Cook.

💵 $12–$25, plus $10 minimum
🚇 Christopher Street/Sheridan Square (1, 9), West 4th Street (A, C, E, F, S, V)
🚌 M8, M20

TISHMAN AUDITORIUM

Map 188 E21

New School, 66 West 12th Street between Fifth and Sixth avenues

Tel 212 229-5488

www.newschool.edu

The New School's Afro-Cuban Jazz Orchestra under Bobby Sanabria plays here.

💵 Varies 🚇 14th Street (F, V) 🚌 M2, M3, M5, M6

TONIC

Map 189 G23

107 Norfolk Street near Delancey Street

Tel 212/358-7051

www.tonicnyc.com

Very eclectic. This Lower East Side club has fast become a landmark for avant-garde

Jazz addicts can track down an after-hours jam

experimental music. Home for John Zorn's Masada, it has already completed many Live at Tonic recordings.

💵 $8–$15 🚇 Delancey Street (F, J, M, Z) 🚌 M9, M14

VILLAGE VANGUARD

Map 188 D21

178 Seventh Avenue at West 11th Street

Tel 212/255-4037

www.villagevanguard.com

Founded by Max Gordon in 1935, it's still the premier jazz club in the city, presided over by Lorraine Gordon since her husband died in 1989. The Vanguard is intimate, has terrific acoustics and features top-flight artists. All the great

names have played here— Coleman Hawkins, Lester Young and Thelonious Monk in the 40s, John Coltrane in the 60s, Keith Jarrett in the 70s, and Miles Davis and Bill Evans across the decades. Nowadays evenings often morph into a vibrant jam session. On Mondays, the Vanguard Jazz Orchestra, established by Thad Jones and Mel Lewis, plays.

🕐 Daily from 8pm (sets Sun–Thu 9 and 11, Fri–Sat 9, 11 and 12.30)
💵 Cover varies, plus $10 minimum
🚇 14th Street (1, 2, 3, 9) 🚌 M14, M20

ZINC BAR

Map 189 E22

90 West Houston Street between LaGuardia Place and Thompson Street

Tel 212/477-8337

Music-lovers and musicians come to this casual, tiny bar to hear newcomers as well as such famous names as George Benson and Max Roach. There's usually Brazilian music on Saturdays and Sundays.

🕐 Daily 6pm–3.30am (show times vary) 💵 Cover varies 🚇 West 4th Street (A, C, E, F, S, V), Houston Street (1, 9), Bleecker Street (6) 🚌 M5, M6, M21

ROCK AND POP

AARON DAVIS HALL

Off map 186 D12

City College of New York, West 135th Street and Convent Avenue

Tel 212/650-7100

www.aarondavishall.org

Harlem's principal center for the performing arts presents established and emerging artists of color in music, dance, theater and multimedia performances. Ashford & Simpson, Craig Harris and Jose Mangual Junior Band are a few who have performed here.

💵 Varies 🚇 137th Street/Broadway (1, 9) 🚌 M4, M5

WHAT TO DO

APOLLO THEATER
Off map 186 D12
253 West 125th Street between Frederick
Douglass Boulevard and St. Nicholas
Avenue
Tel 212/531-5305 or 212/307-7171 (tickets)
www.apollotheater.com
Originally a vaudeville theater, the Apollo has been a venue for black entertainers since 1934. Everyone from Duke Ellington and Billie Holiday to Aretha Franklin and Stevie Wonder have performed here. The Wednesday Amateur Night Competition is famous, drawing crowds who register their approval or disapproval with gusto. Today the entertainment ranges from musicians and singers to the Royal Shakespeare Company's adaptation of Salman Rushdie's novel *Midnight's Children*.
🎟 Varies 🚇 125th Street (A, B, C, D), Lenox (1, 2, 3) 🚌 M104

ARLENE GROCERY
Map 189 G23
95 Stanton Street between Ludlow and Orchard streets
Tel 212/358-1633
www.arlene-grocery.com
This former bodega is one of the best rock clubs in the city. The bar is pleasant, and the back room casually comfortable. It's the place to hear up-and-comers.
🕐 Daily 6pm–4am 🎟 Varies 🚇 Lower East Side/Second Avenue (F, V) 🚌 M15, M21

BEACON THEATRE
Map 186 C15
2124 Broadway at 74th Street
Tel 212/496-7070 or 212/307-7171
Many different artists perform here, from the Caribbean calypso artist The Mighty Sparrow to rock/pop groups.
🎟 $33–$90 🚇 72nd Street (1, 2, 3, 9) 🚌 M72, M104

BOWERY BALLROOM
Map 189 F23
6 Delancey Street between Bowery and Chrystie streets
Tel 212/533-2111
www.boweryballroom.com
When Patti Smith came out of retirement, it was to this rollicking tri-level venue in a 1929 Beaux Arts building that she returned. The club opened in 1997 and has comfortable lounges, good sound systems, a large stage and excellent sight lines. Beth Orton, Soul Asylum, Chris Robinson, David Byrne and Counting Crows are just a few of the bands that have played here.

Many legendary artists have performed at the Apollo Theater

🎟 $13–$35 🚇 Delancey/Essex (F, J, M, Z) 🚌 M103

CBGB DOWNSTAIRS LOUNGE
Map 189 F22
315 Bowery at Bleecker Street
Tel 212/982-4052
www.cbgb.com
Ever since it opened in 1973, this dark, funky place has been the home of underground rock (despite the fact that the name stands for "country bluegrass blues"). Here New Yorkers grooved to the Ramones, Patti Smith and all of the most important punk and post-punk bands from Blondie to Television and the Talking Heads. Sunday night, there's jazz in the downstairs lounge.
🎟 $7–$10 🚇 Bleecker Street (6) 🚌 M21, M103

COOPER UNION GREAT HALL
Map 189 F22
Seventh Street at Third Avenue
Tel 212/353-4195 or 212/279-4200
www.cooper.edu/ce
Everything from fado (Portuguese folk music) and contemporary classical music to Afro-Brazilian drum groups and samba bands can be heard in this hall at a private tuition-free college for the Advancement of Science and Art. Abraham Lincoln spoke here in 1860.
🎟 Free–$25 🚇 Astor Place (6), 8th Street (N, R, W) 🚌 M8, M101, M102, M103

KNITTING FACTORY
Map 189 E24
74 Leonard Street between Broadway and Church Street
Tel 212/219-3006 or 212/219-3055
www.knittingfactory.com
Innovative owner Michael Dorf opened this club in TriBeCa in 1987 to headline local and international bands playing experimental music— free jazz, rock and even klezmer (a mix of eastern European Jewish music with other styles). Its dedicated musical audience comes to three performance spaces: the Main Space, the smaller Old Office and Alterknit Theater, which hosts a weekly poetry open mike, and the Tapas Bar. The bar has plenty of beers on tap and free shows at midnight. The club also sponsors festivals and operates a record label.
🎟 $10–$30 🚇 Franklin Street (1, 9) 🚌 M1, M6

MADISON SQUARE GARDEN
Map 188 D19
4 Penn Plaza
Tel 212/465-6741
Located on top of Penn Station, this arena hosts sports events, concerts and other entertainment. Bob Dylan, Madonna, Michael Jackson, the Rolling Stones, Elton John and many other big star tours stop here.
🚇 34th Street/Penn Station (A, C, E, 1, 2, 3, 9) 🚌 M10, M16, M20, M34

MAKOR
Map 186 D15
35 West 67th Street at Columbus Avenue
Tel 212/601-1000
www.92Y.org
This venue, associated with a Jewish community center, offers an eclectic mix of musical entertainment ranging from rap to blues and gypsy to klezmer. It's strong on world music and brings in such performers as Nigerian Kofo the Wonderman and Maria del Mar Bonet from Mallorca.
💷 $15–$30 🚇 66th Street (1, 9) 🚌 M5, M7, M66, M104

MERCURY LOUNGE
Map 189 G22
217 East Houston Street between First Avenue and Avenue A
Tel 212/260-4700
www.mercuryloungenyc.com
This is a regular stop on the downtown music scene. Bands—both local and international—perform back to back in one raucous room. You might find Holly Go Lightly, who sang with punk Brit Billy Childish, doing garage rock, for example. The adjacent lounge is slightly more serene.
🕐 Daily 8pm–3am 💷 $8–$20 🚇 Lower East Side/Second Avenue (F, V) 🚌 M14, M21

ROSELAND BALLROOM
Map 186 D17
239 West 52nd Street between Broadway and Eighth Avenue
Tel 212/247-0200
www.roselandballroom.com
The original opened at 51st Street in 1919, but moved here in 1956. Once a legendary ballroom featuring the bands of Fletcher Henderson and Tommy Dorsey, today it hosts rock concerts and oldies dances (60s, 70s, 80s).
💷 $25–$27.50 🚇 50th Street (1, 9), 50th Street (C, E) 🚌 M6, M7, M10, M20, M50

Latin American rhythms at Sounds of Brazil (SOB's)

SOB'S
Map 189 D23
204 Varick Street at Houston Street
Tel 212/243-4940
www.sobs.com
Since 1982 this club (Sounds of Brazil) has been at the forefront of Afro-Latino music. The featured band might play hip-hop and rap or driving Latin salsa. Friday nights include a free Latin dance class.
💷 $10–$20, plus $20 minimum 🚇 Houston Street (1, 9) 🚌 M20, M21

SOUTHPAW
Off map 189 G25
125 Fifth Avenue between Sterling and St. John's Place, Park Slope, Brooklyn
Tel 718/230-0236
This club designed for rock shows has great acoustics, a good-size stage and a terrific sound system.
💷 Varies 🚇 Fourth Avenue (F, M, R, W)

SYMPHONY SPACE
Off map at 186 C12
2537 Broadway at 95th Street
Tel 212/864-5400 or 212/864-1414
www.symphonyspace.org
Since 1978 this alternative space occupying a renovated movie theater has been offering eclectic programming in two theaters, the Peter Jay Sharp Theatre and the Leonard Nimoy Thalia. It's known for its free shows, Wall to Wall 12-hour marathons celebrating particular artists (Joni Mitchell, for example); for its Face the Music and Dance, which pairs musicians with choreographers; and for its Selected Shorts, an evening of major actors reading short stories. Companies that perform regularly include the New Amsterdam Symphony Orchestra, the Gilbert and Sullivan Players and the Manhattan Chamber Orchestra. Many world music artists, including guitarist Djelimady Tounkara from Mali and Indian tabla player Zakir Hussain, also perform here under the auspices of the World Music Institute.
💷 $18–$50 🚇 96th Street (1, 2, 3, 9) 🚌 M96, M104

Theater

No fee applies when you buy your tickets at the box office; most open Monday to Saturday from 10am to 8pm and Sunday from 11am to 6.30pm. Standing Room Only tickets, which are sometimes available, go on sale when the box office opens on the day of the performance. Note the curtain times for each new production.

BROADWAY THEATERS

On Broadway, ticket prices range from $25 to $105 for major Broadway musicals and from $50 to $90 for dramas and comedies.

AL HIRSCHFELD
Map 188 D18
302 West 45th Street between Eighth and Ninth avenues
Tel 212/239-6200
Recently given the name of a theatrical caricaturist, this Moorish-style theater was built in 1924 and has lavish interiors. Avoid the side seats.
🕐 Tue–Sat 8, matinees Wed, Sat–Sun 2 🚇 42nd Street/Eighth Avenue (A, C, E) 🚌 M6, M7, M10, M11, M42, M104

AMBASSADOR THEATRE
Map 188 D17
219 West 49th Street between Broadway and Eighth Avenue
Tel 212/239-6200
Opened in 1921, this 1,125-seat auditorium is wider than it is deep, so viewing is good but with a mezzanine overhang.
🕐 Thu–Sat 8, Sun 7, Mon 8, Tue 7, matinees Sat–Sun 2 🚇 50th Street/Seventh Avenue (1, 9), 49th Street (N, R) 🚌 M6, M7, M10, M27, M50, M104

AMERICAN AIRLINES
Map 188 D18
227 West 42nd Street between Seventh and Eighth avenues
Tel 212/719-1300
www.roundabouttheatre.org
This restored 1918 theater with 750 seats is now the home of the Roundabout Theatre Company, founded in 1965 to perform the classics and new plays at affordable prices.
🕐 Tue–Sat 8, matinees Wed, Sat–Sun 2 🚇 42nd Street/Times Square (N, Q, R, S, W, 1, 2, 3, 7, 9) 🚌 M6, M7, M10, M42, M104

BARRYMORE THEATRE
Map 188 D18
243 West 47th Street between Seventh and Eighth avenues
Tel 212/239-6200
Ethel Barrymore starred in *The Kingdom of God* to open this theater in 1928. Fred Astaire gave his last stage

The American Airlines theater has been impressively renovated

performance here in *The Gay Divorcée* in the 1930s.
🕐 Tue–Sat 8, matinees Wed, Sat–Sun 2 🚇 50th Street (C, E), 50th Street (1, 9), 49th Street (N, R, W) 🚌 M10, M20, M104

BELASCO
Map 188 E18
11 West 44th Street between Broadway and Sixth Avenue
Tel 212/239-6200
Named after the bishop of Broadway David Belasco, this gem of a theater with 1,018 seats has some gorgeous Tiffany lamps and lovely murals by Everett Shinn. Avoid the side orchestra if you can.

🕐 Tue–Sat 8, matinees Wed, Sat 2, Sun 3 🚇 42nd Street/Times Square (N, R, S, W, 1, 2, 3, 7, 9), 42nd Street/Sixth Avenue (B, D, F) 🚌 M5, M6, M7, M10, M42, M104

BILTMORE THEATRE
Map 186 D18
261 West 47th Street between Broadway and Eighth Avenue
Tel 212/239-6200
This landmark theater (now with 650 seats) opened in 1925 and hosted such winners as *Hair* and Neil Simon's *Barefoot in the Park*. Recently it became the Broadway home of the Manhattan Theatre Club.
🕐 Tue–Sat 8, Sun 7, Sat, Sun 2 🚇 50th Street (C, E), 50th Street (1, 9) 🚌 M10, M20

BOOTH
Map 188 D18
222 West 45th Street between Broadway and Eighth Avenue
Tel 212/239-6200
Numerous hits have played at this Italianate 781-seat theater dating to 1913 and named after actor Edwin Booth.
🕐 Mon, Wed, Fri–Sat 8, Tue 7, matinees Wed and Sat 2, Sun 3 🚇 42nd Street/ Times Square (N, R, S, W, 1, 2, 3, 7, 9) 🚌 M6, M7, M10, M42, M104

BROADHURST
Map 188 D18
235 West 44th Street between Broadway and Eighth Avenue
Tel 212/639-6200
Named after Anglo-American playwright George Broadhurst, this theater was built by the Shuberts and has welcomed star-studded casts since opening in 1918. Seats 1,186.
🕐 Tue–Sat 8, matinees Wed, Sat 2, Sun 3 🚇 42nd Street/ Times Square (N, R, S, W, 1, 2, 3, 7, 9) 🚌 M6, M7, M10, M42, M104

BROADWAY

Map 186 D17
1681 Broadway between 52nd and 53rd streets
Tel 212/239-6200
This 1,752-seat theater was built as a movie house in 1924. Avoid the back of the house if you can.
🕐 Tue–Sat 8, matinees Wed, Sat 2, Sun 3 🚇 50th Street/Eighth Avenue (C, E), 50th Street/Seventh Avenue (1, 9) 🚌 M6, M7, M10, M27, M50, M104

BROOKS ATKINSON

Map 186 D18
256 West 47th Street between Broadway and Eighth Avenue
Tel 212/307-4100
www.nederlander.org
Built in 1926, this ornate theater is named for longtime *New York Times* theater critic Brooks Atkinson. With 1,086 seats, you may feel you're too far from the stage if you sit in the rear mezzanine.
🕐 Tue–Sat 8, matinees Wed, Sat 2, Sun 3 🚇 50th Street/Eighth Avenue (C, E), 50th Street/Seventh Avenue (1, 9) 🚌 M10, M27, M50, M104

CADILLAC WINTER GARDEN

Map 186 D17
1634 Broadway between 50th and 51st streets
Tel 212/563-5544
The building dates to 1885 when it served as an auction hall and stable. The Shuberts made it into a theater in 1910. Al Jolson first appeared here in blackface. Seats 1,482.
🕐 Wed–Sat 8, matinees Wed, Sat 2, Sun 3 🚇 50th Street/Eighth Avenue (C, E), 50th Street/Seventh Avenue (1, 9), 49th Street (N, R, W) 🚌 M6, M7, M10, M27, M50, M104

CIRCLE IN THE SQUARE (UPTOWN)

Map 188 D17
1633 Broadway at 50th Street
Tel 212/239-6200
Opened in 1972, this theater is in the same building as the Gershwin theater. All 681 seats have good sight lines.
🕐 Tue–Sat 8, matinees Wed, Sat 2, Sun 3 🚇 50th Street/ Eighth Avenue

(C, E), 50th Street/Seventh Avenue (1, 9) 🚌 M6, M7, M10, M27, M50, M104

CORT

Map 188 E17
138 West 48th Street between Sixth and Seventh avenues
Tel 212/239-6200
Named for producer John Cort, this 1,084-seat theater was modeled on the Petit Trianon and built in 1912. All seats have good sight lines.
🕐 Tue–Sat 8, matinees Wed, Sat 2, Sun 3 🚇 47th–50th streets/Rockefeller Center (B, D, F, V) 🚌 M6, M7, M10, M27, M50, M104

EUGENE O'NEILL

Map 186 D17

The Hilton Theater puts on major musical productions

230 West 49th Street between Broadway and Eighth Avenue
Tel 212/239-6200
Opened in 1926, the O'Neill was named for the great playwright in 1959.
🕐 Tue 7, Wed–Sat 8, matinees Wed, Sat 2, Sun 3 🚇 50th Street/Eighth Avenue (C, E), 50th Street/Seventh Avenue (1, 9) 🚌 M6, M7, M10, M27, M50, M104

GERSHWIN

Map 186 D17
222 West 51st Street between Broadway and Eighth Avenue
Tel 212/307-4100
www.nederlander.org
Owned by the Broadway producers the Nederlanders,

the Gershwin opened in 1972. The auditorium is on the second floor. It was renamed in 1983 after George and Ira.
🕐 Tue 7, Wed–Sat 8, matinees Wed, Sat 2, Sun 3 🚇 50th Street/Eighth Avenue (C, E), 50th Street/Seventh Avenue (1, 9) 🚌 M6, M7, M10, M27, M50, M104

HELEN HAYES

Map 188 D18
240 West 44th Street between Seventh and Eighth avenues
Tel 212/944-9450 or 212/239-6200
This small Colonial Revival-style theater was built in 1912 to house productions of new and experimental theater.
🕐 Tue–Sat 8, matinees Wed, Sat 2, Sun 3 🚇 42nd Street/Times Square (N, Q, R, S, W, 1, 2, 3, 7, 9), 42nd Street/Eighth Avenue (A, C, E) 🚌 M6, M7, M10, M42, M104

HILTON THEATER

Map 188 D18
213 West 42nd Street between Seventh and Eighth avenues
Tel 212/556-4750 or 212/307-4100
The Lyric (1903) and the Apollo (1920) were renovated and combined to create this 1,839-seat house ideal for spectacular musicals. Most seats have good sight lines.
🕐 Tue–Sat 8, matinees Wed, Sat 2, Sun 3 🚇 42nd Street/Times Square (N, Q, R, S, W, 1, 2, 3, 7, 9), 42nd Street/Eighth Avenue (A, C, E) 🚌 M6, M7, M10, M42, M104

IMPERIAL

Map 188 D18
249 West 45th Street between Broadway and Eighth Avenue
Tel 212/239-6200
Gypsy, Fiddler on the Roof and *Les Misérables* played at this 1923 theater. Seats 1,421.
🕐 Mon–Sat 8, matinees Wed, Sat 2 🚇 42nd Street/Times Square (N, Q, R, S, W, 1, 2, 3, 7, 9), 42nd Street/Eighth Avenue (A, C, E) 🚌 M6, M7, M10, M42, M104

JOHN GOLDEN THEATRE

Map 188 D18
252 West 45th Street between

Broadway and Eighth Avenue
Tel 212/239-6200

A small theater, named for producer John Golden and opened in 1927.

⊙ Tue–Sat 8, matinees Sat, Sun 2 🚇 42nd Street/Times Square (N, Q, R, S, W, 1, 2, 3, 7, 9), 42nd Street/Eighth Avenue (A, C, E) 🚌 M6, M7, M10, M42, M104

LONGACRE

Map 188 D17
220 West 48th Street between Broadway and Eighth Avenue
Tel 212/239-6200

Named for Longacre Square, as today's Times Square was known before the *New York Times* moved into the area, this 1,095-seat theater opened in 1913. Orchestra seats have the best sight lines.

⊙ Tue–Fri 8, Sat 5 and 9, Sun 3 and 7 🚇 50th Street/Seventh Avenue (1, 9), 49th Street (N, R), 47th–50th streets/Rockefeller Center (B, D, F, Q) 🚌 M6, M10, M27, M42, M50, M104

LUNT-FONTANNE

Map 188 D18
205 West 46th Street between Broadway and Eighth Avenue
Tel 212/575-9200 or 212/307-4747
www.nederlander.org

Designed by Carrère and Hastings in 1910, the theater was gutted in 1958. It seats 1,475 and was the New York home of *The Sound of Music*.

⊙ Tue–Wed 7, Thu–Sat 8, Sun 6.30, matinees Wed 2, Sat 2, Sun 1 🚇 42nd Street/Times Square (N, Q, R, S, W, 1, 2, 3, 7, 9), 50th Street/Seventh Avenue (1, 9), 50th Street/Eighth Avenue (C, E) 🚌 M6, M10, M27, M42, M50, M104

LYCEUM

Map 188 D18
149 West 45th Street between Broadway and Sixth Avenue
Tel 212/239-6200

Built in 1903 in Beaux Arts style, it's the oldest theater still in use on Broadway.

⊙ Tue–Sat 8, matinees Wed, Sat 2, Sun 3 🚇 49th Street (N, R), 47th–50th streets/Rockefeller Center (B, D, F) 🚌 M5, M6, M7, M10, M42, M104

MAJESTIC

Map 188 D18
245 West 44th Street between Broadway and Eighth Avenue
Tel 212/239-6200

This theater seating 1,607, which opened in 1927, has hosted hits from *Carousel* to *Phantom of the Opera*.

⊙ Mon–Sat 8, matinees Wed, Sat 2 🚇 42nd Street/Times Square (N, Q, R, S, W, 1, 2, 3, 7, 9), 42nd Street/Eighth Avenue (A, C, E) 🚌 M6, M7, M10, M42, M104

MARQUIS

Map 188 D18
1535 Broadway between 45th and 46th streets
Tel 212/382-0100 or 212/307-4100

The Music Box has a long history

www.nederlander.org
One of the newest large theaters on Broadway, with extra comforts, including well-raked seating. Seats 1,595.

⊙ Tue 7, Wed–Sat 8, matinees Wed, Sat 2, Sun 3 🚇 42nd Street/Times Square (N, Q, R, S, W, 1, 2, 3, 7, 9) 🚌 M6, M7, M10, M27, M42, M50, M104

MINSKOFF

Map 188 D18
200 West 45th Street between Seventh and Eighth avenues
Tel 212/ 307-4100
www.nederlander.org

This Nederlander theater, which was built in 1973, is rather impersonal. An escalator

takes you to the fourth-floor orchestra.

⊙ Tue 7, Wed–Sat 8, matinees Wed, Sat 2, Sun 3 🚇 42nd Street/Times Square (N, Q, R, S, W, 1, 2, 3, 7, 9) 🚌 M6, M7, M10, M42, M104

MUSIC BOX

Map 188 D18
239 West 45th Street between Broadway and Eighth Avenue
Tel 212/239-6200

Note the plaque, just inside the lobby, commemorating Irving Berlin, who built this theater in 1921 with producer Sam Harris to house his Music Box Revues.

⊙ Tue–Sat 8, matinees Sat 2, Sun 3 🚇 42nd Street/Times Square (N, Q, R, S, W, 1, 2, 3, 7, 9), 42nd Street/Eighth Avenue (A, C, E) 🚌 M6, M7, M10, M42, M104

NEDERLANDER

Map 188 D18
208 West 41st Street between Seventh and Eighth avenues
Tel 212/921-8000 or 212/307-4100
www.nederlander.org

When *Rent* moved from the East Village, it came to this theatre, and *Who's Afraid of Virginia Woolf?* opened here. Seats 1,189. Avoid side seats.

⊙ Mon–Tue, Thu–Sat 8, matinees Sat, Sun 2 🚇 42nd Street/Times Square (N, Q, R, S, W, 1, 2, 3, 7, 9) 🚌 M6, M7, M10, M27, M42, M50, M104

NEIL SIMON

Map 186 D17
250 West 52nd Street between Broadway and Eighth Avenue
Tel 212/757-8646 or 212/307-4100
www.nederlander.org

This ornate theater, opened in 1927, has been home to many musicals, including *Porgy and Bess, Funny Face* and *Hairspray*. Named for the playwright. Seats 1,334.

⊙ Tue 7, Wed–Sat 8, matinees Wed, Sat 2, Sun 3 🚇 50th Street/Eighth Avenue (C, E), 50th Street/Seventh Avenue (1, 9) 🚌 M6, M7, M10, M27, M50, M104

WHAT TO DO

NEW AMSTERDAM
Map 188 D18
214 West 42nd Street between Seventh
and Eighth avenues
Tel 212/282-2900 or 212/307-4747 or
212/282-2907 for tours
www.disneyonbroadway.com
Florence Ziegfeld
commissioned this Art
Nouveau beauty in 1903.
In 1997 the Walt Disney
Company restored the place
with its murals, stucco, tiles
and woodwork, and installed
The Lion King. Avoid side
seats.
Wed–Sat 8, Sun 6.30, matinees
Wed, Sat 2, Sun 1. Tours Mon 9.30–5.30,
Tue, Thu–Sat 9.30–11.30 Tours: adult
$12, children (under 12) $5 42nd
Street/Times Square (N, Q, R, S, W, 1, 2,
3, 7, 9), 42nd Street/Eighth Avenue (A,
C, E) M6, M7, M10, M42, M104

PALACE
Map 188 D18
1564 Broadway between 46th and 47th
streets
Tel 212/730-8200 or 212/307-4747
www.nederlander.org
The Palace opened as a
vaudeville house in 1913,
and such legends as Bob
Hope, Sophie Tucker, Jimmy
Durante and the Marx
Brothers all entertained here.
The Nederlanders restored it
in 1965.
Tue–Sat 8, matinees Wed, Sat 2, Sun
3 50th Street (1, 9), 49th Street (N, R)
M7, M10, M27, M50, M104

PLYMOUTH
Map 188 D18
236 West 45th Street between
Broadway and Eighth Avenue
Tel 212/239-6200
Drama and comedy from Noel
Coward's *Present Laughter* to
the Royal Shakespeare
Company's *Nicholas Nickleby*
have played at this 1918
theater. Seats 1,078.
Wed–Sat 8, Mon 8, Tue 7, matinees
Wed, Sat 2, Sun 3 42nd
Street/Times Square (N, Q, R, S, W, 1, 2,
3, 7, 9), 42nd Street/Eighth Avenue (A,
C, E) M6, M7, M10, M42, M104

RICHARD ROGERS
Map 188 D18
226 West 46th Street between
Broadway and Eighth Avenue
Tel 212/221-1211
Guys and Dolls and other hits
have entertained audiences at
this Renaissance Revival
theater, built in 1924. Named
for the composer, it seats
1,400.
Tue–Sat 8, matinees Wed, Sat 2,
Sun 3 42nd Street/Times Square
(N, Q, R, S, W, 1, 2, 3, 7, 9), 42nd Street/
Eighth Avenue (A, C, E), 50th Street
(1, 9) M10, M27, M50, M104

ROYALE
Map 188 D18
242 West 45th Street between

*The New Amsterdam is an Art
Nouveau gem*

Broadway and Eighth Avenue
Tel 212/239-6200
Laurence Olivier starred in *The
Entertainer* on this stage.
Opened in 1927, the Royale is
a perfect mid-size theater.
Tue–Sat 8, matinees Wed 2, Sun 3
42nd Street/Times Square (N, Q, R,
S, W, 1, 2, 3, 7, 9), 42nd Street/Eighth
Avenue (A, C, E) M6, M7, M10,
M42, M104

ST. JAMES
Map 188 D18
246 West 44th Street between Seventh
and Eighth avenues
Tel 212/239-5800
*Oklahoma!, The King and I,
Hello Dolly* and *The Producers*
have all played in this Beaux

Arts theater, dating to 1927.
Its mezzanine hangs over the
orchestra.
Tue 7, Wed–Sat 8, matinees Wed,
Sat 2, Sun 3 42nd Street/Times
Square (N, Q, R, S, W, 1, 2, 3, 7, 9),
42nd Street/Eighth Avenue (A, C, E)
M6, M7, M10, M42, M104

SHUBERT
Map 188 D18
225 West 44th Street between Seventh
and Eighth avenues
Tel 212/239-6200
This theater, opened in 1913,
is the cornerstone of the
Shubert family's empire.
Mon–Tue, Thu–Sat 8, Sun 7,
matinees Sat, Sun 2 42nd
Street/Times Square (N, Q, R, S, W, 1, 2,
3, 7, 9), 42nd Street/Eighth Avenue
(A, C, E) M6, M7, M10, M42, M104

STUDIO 54
Map 186 D17
254 West 54th Street between
Broadway and Eighth Avenue
Tel 212/239-6200
This former discotheque is
now a 920-seat theater.
Cabaret has played here.
Tue–Sat 8, Sun 7, matinees Sat, Sun
2 Seventh Avenue (B, D, E), 57th
Street (N, R, Q) M6, M7, M27, M50,
M57

VIRGINIA
Map 186 D17
245 West 52nd Street between
Broadway and Eighth Avenue
Tel 212/239-6200
The Theater Guild
commissioned this striking
theater with its Tuscan-style
facade, and it opened in 1925.
Tue–Sat 8, matinees Wed, Sat 2, Sun
3 50th Street (1, 9), 50th Street (C, E)
M6, M7, M10, M27, M50, M104

VIVIAN BEAUMONT THEATER
Map 186 C16
150 West 65th Street
Tel 212/239-6200
This is categorized as a
Broadway theater despite its
address. Its deep-thrust stage
allows for innovative directing.
Tue–Sat 8, matinees Wed, Sat 2,
Sun 3 66th Street (1, 9) M5, M7,
M66, M104

WHAT TO DO

WALTER KERR
Map 186 D17
219 West 48th Street between
Broadway and Eighth Avenue
Tel 212/239-6200
Named after the famous *New
York Times* critic, this is an
ideal house for serious drama
and classic comedy. Seats 947.
🎭 Tue–Sat 8, matinees Wed, Sat 2,
Sun 3 🚇 50th Street/Eighth Avenue
(C, E), 50th Street/Seventh Avenue
(1, 9) 🚌 M7, M10, M27, M50, M104

OFF-BROADWAY THEATERS
Off-Broadway theaters have
500 seats or fewer, and are
usually either in the East or
West villages or along
42nd Street between Eighth
and Eleventh avenues. Here
you'll see showcases,
experimental plays, musicals in
development and innovative
revivals. Several Broadway hits
have emerged from these
venues. Ticket prices range
from $25 to $65.

ACTOR'S PLAYHOUSE
Map 188 D22
100 Seventh Avenue South between
Bleecker and West Fourth streets
Tel 212/463-0060 or 212/239-6200
This small downstairs venue,
which has been around for
40 years, presents musical
revues, often with a gay
theme.
🎭 Mon, Wed–Fri 8, Sat 7, 10, Sun 7,
matinees Sun 3 🚇 Christopher
Street/Sheridan Square (1, 9) 🚌 M20

BOWERIE LANE
Map 189 F22
330 Bowery at Bond Street
Tel 212/677-0060
www.jeancocteaurep.org
The Jean Cocteau Repertory
Company (1971) presents five
to seven masterworks from
Euripides to Samuel Beckett
between August and June at
this beautiful old bank
building. Seats 140.
🚇 Broadway-Lafayette (F, V, S)
🚌 M21, M103

BROOKLYN ACADEMY OF
MUSIC (BAM)
Off map 189 G25
30 Lafayette Avenue
Tel 718/636-4100 or 212/307-4100
www.bam.org
New York's premier
progressive cultural complex is
in Brooklyn. It incorporates
several performance spaces—
the Howard Gilman Opera
House, seating 2,100; the
1,000-seat Harvey Lichtenstein
Theater; a café; and a four-
screen film complex. Every fall,
BAM stages the Next Wave
Festival of experimental opera,
music, theater, dance and film.
🚇 DeKalb Avenue (B, D, N, Q, R)
🚌 M51

*Bowerie Lane specializes in
repertory productions*

CHERRY LANE
Map 188 D22
38 Commerce Street between Hudson
and Bedford streets
Tel 212/989-2020
www.cherrylanetheater.com
In 1924 Edna St. Vincent Millay
and others turned a
warehouse into a theater.
Today the Cherry Lane
Alternative continues the
theater's tradition of producing
emerging playwrights.
🎭 Tue–Fri 8, Sat 5, 9, Sun 3
🚇 Christopher Street/Sheridan Square
(1, 9) 🚌 M20, M21

DARYL ROTH THEATER
Map 188 F21
101 East 15th Street at Union Square
Tel 212/375-1110 or 212/239-6200
Pulitzer Prize-winning Daryl
Roth owns this theater in an
old bank building. The space is
inherently dramatic.
🚇 14th Street/Union Square (L, N, Q,
R, W, 4, 5, 6) 🚌 M1, M2, M3, M6, M7,
M14

MANHATTAN ENSEMBLE
THEATRE
Map 189 E23
55 Mercer Street between Broome and
Grand streets
Tel 212/925-1900
www.met.com
Home to the Manhattan
Ensemble, founded by David
Fishelson, this theater presents
new plays that are often by
well-known playwrights.
🚇 Canal Street (J, M, N, Q), Spring
Street (C, E) 🚌 M1, M6

MANHATTAN THEATRE CLUB
261 West 47th Steet
Tel 212/581-1212 (tickets) or 212/399-
3000 (info)
www.manhattantheatreclub.com
Founded in 1970 to perform
new plays, this company is
based at the Biltmore (▷ 205).
🚇 57th Street (N, Q, R, W), 57th Street
(F) 🚌 M5, M6, M7

MINETTA LANE
Map 188 E22
18 Minetta Lane
Tel 212/420-8000
This charming Greenwich
Village theater is a major off-
Broadway player.
🚇 West 4th Street (A, C, E, F, S, V)
🚌 M5, M6, M8

MITZI NEWHOUSE THEATER
Map 186 C16
150 West 65th Street
Tel 212 239-6277 or 212/239-6200
www.lct.org
Spalding Gray performed
Swimming to Cambodia (1996)
at this Lincoln Center theater.
Its 299 seats are steeply raked.
🎭 Tue–Sat 8, matinees Wed, Sat 2,
Sun 3 🚇 66th Street (1, 9) 🚌 M5, M7,
M66, M104

WHAT TO DO

THE NEGRO ENSEMBLE COMPANY
Map 188 D18
303 West 42nd Street at Eighth Avenue
Tel 212/582-5860
www.negroensemblecompany.org
Founded in 1967, this group holds workshops for actors and playwrights.
🚇 42nd Street (A, C, E) 🚌 M10, M20, M42

NEW YORK THEATRE WORKSHOP
Map 189 F22
79 East 4th Street between Second Avenue and Bowery
Tel 212/780-9037 or 212/239-6200
www.nytw.org
A significant player on the Manhattan theater scene. *Rent* began life here, and the workshop staged Caryl Churchill's *A Number.* Seats 150.
🕐 Tue–Sat 8, matinees Sat, Sun 3
🚇 Broadway-Lafayette (F, S, V), Bleecker Street (6) 🚌 M1, M21

THE ONTOLOGICAL HYSTERIC THEATER AT ST. MARKS
Map 189 F21
131 East 10th Street between Second and Third avenues
Tel 212/420-1916 or 212/533-4650
www.ontological.com
An important home for the avant-garde. Richard Foreman presented his 35th-anniversary production here in 2003.
🚇 Astor Place (6), Eighth Street (N, R, W) 🚌 M8, M15

PLAYWRIGHTS HORIZONS THEATER
Map 188 C18
416 West 42nd Street between Ninth and Tenth avenues
Tel 212/564-1235
www.playwrightshorizons.org
This company is dedicated to the production of new American plays and musicals. The main stage seats 198 and the studio 96.
🚇 42nd Street (A, C, E) 🚌 M11, M42

PUBLIC THEATER
Map 189 F22
425 Lafayette Street between Astor Place and East Fourth Street
Tel 212/539-8500 or 212/239-6200
www.publictheater.org
In 1967 producer Joe Papp got the city to lease him the old Astor Library and converted it into five theater spaces.
🕐 Tue–Sat 8, Sun 7, matinees Sat, Sun 2 🚇 8th Street (N, R, W), Astor Place (6) 🚌 M1, M8

RADIO CITY MUSIC HALL
Map 187 E17
1260 Sixth Avenue at 50th Street
Tel 212/247-4777
www.radiocity.com

Radio City was saved from demolition in 1979

This theater with plenty of art deco paraphernalia was spectacularly refurbished in 1999 to the tune of $70 million. It has seats for 5,882 in the orchestra and on three mezzanines.
🕐 One-hour tours daily 11–3
🎫 Tours: adult $17, child (under 12) $10 🚇 47th-50th streets/Rockefeller Center (B, D, F, V) 🚌 M5, M6, M7

SECOND STAGE THEATER
Map 188 D18
307 West 43rd Street between Eighth and Ninth avenues
Tel 212/787-8302
www.secondstagetheater.com
Dutch architect Rem Koolhaas helped revamp the old bank

building that is home to this company. Seats 299.
🕐 Tue, Thu, Sat 8, Wed, Sun 7, matinees Wed, Sat 2, Sun 3 🚇 79th Street (1, 9) 🚌 M79, M104

SHAKESPEARE IN THE PARK
Map 186 D14
Delacorte Theater, 81st Street (West Side), 79th Street (East Side)
Tel 212/539-8500
www.publictheater.org
The Public Theater sponsors this summer festival in Central Park at the Delacorte Theater. Line up for free tickets from noon onwards.
🕐 Summer only Tue–Sun 🚇 79th Street (1, 9) 🚌 M1, M2, M3, M4, M79, M104

THEATER FOR THE NEW CITY
Map 189 F21
155 First Avenue between 9th and 10th streets
Tel 212/254-1109
www.theaterforthenewcity.org
Thought-provoking, often politically inspired dramas are the repertory of this community-oriented company, founded in 1970.
🕐 Thu–Sat 8, matinees Sun 3
🚇 Astor Place (6) 🚌 M8, M15

VINEYARD THEATRE
Map 188 F21
108 East 15th Street between Union Square and Irving Place
Tel 212/353-3366, 212/353-0303 or 212/239-6200
www.vineyardtheatre.org
Located in a residential tower, this off-Broadway theater has staged Pulitzer Prize-winning plays before they went to Broadway. Seats 120.
🕐 Tue–Sat 8, matinees Sun 3 🚇 14th Street/Union Square (L, N, Q, R, W, 4, 5, 6) 🚌 M14, M101, M102, M103

WPP THEATRE FOUR
Map 186 C17
424 West 55th Street
Tel 212/765-1706, tickets 212/757-3900
www.womensproject.org
Founded in 1978 by Julia Miles, the Women's Project Theatre is the nation's

pre-eminent women's theater company. Seats 199.

🕐 Tue–Sat 8, Sun 7.30, matinees Sat 2, Sun 3 🚇 59th Street (A, B, C, D, 1, 9) 🚌 M11, M57

YORK (THEATRE AT ST. PETER'S)
Map 187 F17
619 Lexington Avenue at 54th Street
Tel 212/935-5824
The material presented at the modern performing space in this church at Citicorp Center is often experimental and challenging. Seats 147.

🕐 Fri–Sat 8, Sun 7.30, matinees Sat, Sun 2.30 🚇 51st Street (6), Fifth Avenue/53rd Street (E, V) 🚌 M98, M101, M102, M103

OFF-OFF-BROADWAY

These small theaters seat 100 or under, offer contemporary works or innovative productions of traditional works, and often feature actors who don't belong to Actors Equity, the professional union. Performances range from the mundane to the inspiring, and ticket prices from $10 to $55.

BLEECKER STREET THEATRE
Map 189 F22
45 Bleecker Street between Bowery and Lafayette Street
Tel 212/253-9983 or 212/307-4100
www.45bleecker.com
Home of the Culture Project, which produces eclectic works by contemporary playwrights. Stadium-style seating for 45.

🕐 Tue–Fri 8, Sat 4, 8, Sun 4 🚇 Bleecker Street (6), Broadway/Lafayette (F, S, V) 🚌 M1, M21, M103

CENTER STAGE/NY
Map 188 E20
48 West 21st Street between Fifth and Sixth avenues, fourth floor
Tel 212/929-2228
www.labtheater.org
Thirteen actors founded the Labyrinth Repertory Company in 1992 to enable members to write, direct and act. Now it has 60 international

members, who produce annual productions here.

🎭 Varies 🚇 23rd Street (N, R, W), 23rd Street (F, V) 🚌 M2, M3, M5, M6, M7

CLASSICAL THEATER OF HARLEM
Off map 186 D12
Harlem School of the Arts Theater, 645 St. Nicholas Avenue near 141st Street
Tel 212/564-9983, tickets 212/868-4444
This company, founded in 1988, has been recognized outside Harlem only recently. It has garnered acclaim for recent productions of Genet's *The Blacks* and Euripides' *The Trojan Women*.

🚇 145th Street (A, B, C)

Shakespeare in the Park is a popular summer festival

FLEA THEATER
Map 189 E24
41 White Street between Broadway and Church Street
Tel 212/226-2407
www.theflea.org
Home to the Bat Theater Company, which presents works by playwrights who are breaking new boundaries—either society's or their own.

🚇 Canal Street (A, C, E) 🚌 M1, M6

LA MAMA EXPERIMENTAL THEATER CLUB
Map 189 F22
74A East 4th Street between Second Avenue and Bowery
Tel 212/475-7710
www.lamama.org

One of the most famous off-off-Broadway theaters was founded in 1961 by Ellen Stewart to nurture new playwrights. It has three theaters: the Annex, the First Floor and the Club, a cabaret space.

🕐 Thu–Sun 🚇 Astor Place (6) 🚌 M8, M15

THE MINT SPACE
Map 188 D18
311 West 43rd Street between Eighth and Ninth avenues
Tel 212/315-9434 or 212/279-4200
www.minttheater.org
Home of the Mint Theater, one of the most recognized companies off-off-Broadway. It performs stimulating plays, which may be drawn from foreign traditions. Seats 74.

🚇 42nd Street (A, C, E) 🚌 M11, M20, M42

PERFORMING GARAGE
Map 189 E23
33 Wooster Street at Grand Street
Tel 212/966-9796 or 212/966-3651
www.thewoostergroup.org
Home to the Wooster Group, an Obie-winning troupe founded in 1975 by Jim Clayburgh, Willem Dafoe, Spalding Gray and others. The group produces and develops experimental entertainment and theater.

🚇 Canal Street (A, C, E) 🚌 M6

THEATRE AT ST. CLEMENTS
Map 188 C18
423 West 46th Street between Ninth and Tenth avenues
Tel 212/246-7277 or 212/279-4200
Playwrights such as David Mamet and Terrance McNally have premiered works here, and many famous actors appeared here early in their careers. The plays often focus on contemporary spiritual, moral and ethical issues. The space is in an Episcopalian church and seats 151.

🕐 Wed–Fri 7.30pm, Sat 8pm, matinees Sat 2, Sun 3 🚇 42nd Street (A, C, E) 🚌 M11, M42

WHAT TO DO

NIGHTLIFE

New Yorkers take their nightlife very seriously. You can always find a "scene" somewhere in the city that never sleeps, with the party shifting from bar to dance club and back, and then to the Meatpacking District at dawn.

Some New York City clubs have a great deal of attitude. At the hottest dance clubs, there's a competition to get in, and people dress à la mode to ensure that they get past the velvet rope and the bouncer at the door. And there's always a VIP room and an A-list for guests (although you can often get on the list by calling in advance or going to www.sheckys.com or www.promony.com). So tough has it become to gain entry to the most fashionable clubs, that even a $1,000 bribe will not work. Hence PartyBuddys, tel 1/877-93-2839, www.partybuddys.com, which promises to shepherd visitors on a nightlife tour for a fee, starting at $350 per person. Still, there are plenty of more casual clubs available, especially the gay spots (see *Next*, *HX*, *Metro Source* and *Go* for listings), which are often a lot more fun.

There are bars to suit every taste. Great saloons with antique bars often have a lot of history attached. Cedar Tavern, for example, was associated with the Abstract Expressionists in the 1950s and P. J. Clarke's with many Damon Runyon types. In swank hotel bars such as the St. Regis's King Cole or the Carlyle's Bemelman's you can lounge in luxury. Rooftop bars are spectacular trysting places. Specialty bars serve up every liquor (beer, wine, champagne, vodka and sake). You'll find an extensive gay scene catering to different crowds and ages, concentrated mainly in Chelsea and Greenwich Village. Many lounges now have DJs spinning music, but they don't allow dancing because they usually lack a cabaret license.

The city's nightlife hot spots are Harlem, Chelsea, the East and West villages, and the Lower East Side. There's also plenty of action across the East River in Williamsburg, which now draws its own crowd from Manhattan. Drinking age is 21 (always carry a picture ID). British visitors should note that whiskey is rye, not Scotch.

New York has bars and clubs to suit every taste

DJs are in action at many lounges

The Bar and Lounge Scene

In addition to the outstanding hotel bars listed below, you might want to drop in at the following: The Villard at the New York Palace Hotel (24 East 51st Street, tel 212/303-7757); Thom's Bar at 60 Thompson Hotel (60 Thompson Street, tel 212/219-2000); The Whiskey, W Times Square (1567 Broadway at 47th Street, tel 212/930-7444); Underbar at W Hotel Union Square (201 Park Avenue South, tel 212/358-1560); the Monkey Bar at the Hotel Elysee (▷ 300), and the Rise Bar at the Ritz Carlton (Battery Park, tel 917/790-2525).

There is no cover for the bars listed here. Note, too, that there is a strict no-smoking law in the city, instituted in 2003. Only bars that derive 10 percent of their revenue from cigars can opt out of the law and allow smoking.

ANGEL'S SHARE
8 Stuyvesant Street (2nd floor) between 9th Street and Third Avenue
Tel 212/777-5415
Tucked away upstairs in a Japanese restaurant, this tiny bar is named for the alcohol that evaporates while whiskey is aging. The lychee daiquiri is well worth trying.
🕐 Daily 6pm–2.30am 🚇 Astor Place (6)

AUBETTE
119 East 27th Street between Park Avenue South and Lexington Avenue
Tel 212/686-5500
A fireplace makes this lounge a warm winter retreat. There are 12 wines by the glass, well-shaken cocktails and an

appealing fellow crowd.
 Mon–Fri 5–4, Sat–Sun 7pm–4am
 28th Street (6)

THE AUCTION HOUSE
300 East 89th Street between First and Second avenues
Tel 212/427-4458
Sotheby's meets New Orleans bordello at this wood-paneled, split-level lounge. Patrons sip cocktails on velvet sofas beneath gilt-framed portraits.
 Daily 7.30–4  86th Street (4, 5, 6)

B BAR
40 East 4th Street at Bowery
Tel 212/475-2220
B Bar has cooled as a hot spot, but its Tuesday night extravaganza, Beige, still draws gay society and other beauties. Large outdoor summer patio.
 Sun–Thu 10.30am–midnight, Fri–Sat 11.30am–3.30am  Broadway/ Lafayette (F, S, V), Bleecker Street (6)

BARAZA
133 Avenue C between East 8th and 9th streets
Tel 212/539-0811
No wonder this place is crowded: Just look at the prices and taste the sunshine in the mojitos and caipirhinas, and listen to the merengue, salsa and Afro-Cuban rhythms.
 Daily 7.30–4  Astor Place (6), First Avenue (L)

BARRAMUNDI
67 Clinton Street between Rivington and Stanton streets
Tel 212/529-6900
Manhattanites enjoy the odd woodsy Adirondack accents. The martinis and caipirhinas taste fine, and the crowd is friendly.
 Daily 6–4  Delancey/Essex (F, J, M, Z)

BED NY
530 West 27th Street between Tenth and Eleventh streets
Tel 212/594-4109
www.bedny.com
One of the latest of a crop of rooftop bars, this one has an exceptional draw—14 beds

with canvas sheets for lounging out Roman-style on summer nights and enjoying a vista of the sparkling cityscape, including the Empire State. Beds are also part of the scene in the 6th floor loft-like lounge-restaurant. Sunday afternoons there's a regular rooftop party; DJs entertain at other times too.
 Tue–Sat 7pm–4am, Sun 2pm–1am
 23rd Street (C, E)

BEMELMAN'S BAR
Carlyle Hotel, 35 East 76th Street between Park and Madison avenues
Tel 212/744-1600
Named for the illustrator of the beloved Madeleine books,

Champagne in a luxurious setting at the Bubble Lounge

Ludwig Bemelmans, this intimate bar attracts the city's most upscale tipplers with first-class cocktails and perfect piano music from Tony De Sare or the Chris Gillespie Trio most evenings (9.30–1.30).
 Daily noon–2am  Fri–Sat $20–$25 ($10 at bar)  77th Street (6)

THE BUBBLE LOUNGE
228 West Broadway between Franklin and White streets
Tel 212/431-3433
www.bubblelounge.com
This 1930s-style lounge celebrates champagne by serving more than 24 types by the glass and 350 by the bottle, amid luxurious red

sofas, marble tables and chandeliers.
 Mon–Thu 5–2, Fri–Sat 6–4
 Franklin Street (1, 9)

CAMPBELL APARTMENT
15 Vanderbilt Avenue in Grand Central Station (southwest corner)
Tel 212/953-0409
It's worth seeking out this quintessential New York bar. Originally designed as an office for wealthy businessman John W. Campbell, it's dark and richly decorated in a Renaissance style. Today it caters to suburbanites en route to their homes in Connecticut and Westchester County.
 Mon–Fri 3pm–1am, Sun 3–11pm
 42nd Street/Grand Central (4, 5, 6, S)

D.B.A.
41 First Avenue between East 2nd and 3rd streets
Tel 212/475-5097
Serious drinkers appreciate the massive selection of single malts (100) and beers (20 on tap) at this old-fashioned friendly bar. The backyard garden is great in summer.
 Daily 1pm–4am  Lower East Side/Second Avenue (F, V)

DECIBEL
240 East 9th Street between Second and Third avenues
Tel 212/979-2733
Subterranean, funky and cramped, this Japanese bar has a huge selection of sake. Take a booth and experiment.
 Mon–Sat 8–2, Sun 8–1  Astor Place (6)

DIVINE BAR
244 East 51st Street between Second and Third avenues
Tel 212/319-9463
A young professional singles crowd turns this long tapas bar into late-night Madrid. Flights of the 60 wines are available along with 40 different beers.
 Wed–Fri 5–1.30, Sat 7–2.30, Mon 5–12, Tue 5–12.30  51st Street (6), Lexington/53rd Street (E, V)

DOUBLE HAPPINESS

173 Mott Street between Broome and Grand streets
Tel 212/941-1282
This aptly named bar delivers on its promise, with well-made drinks, vibrant music and a beautiful young crowd.
🕐 Sun–Thu 6–2, Fri–Sat 6–4 🚇 Bowery (J, M, Z)

ELAINE'S

1703 Second Avenue between East 88th and 89th streets
Tel 212/534-8103
The writers, actors, politicians and socialites who gather here have their own tables, but everyone is welcome. Look for Liz Smith, Barbara Walters, Norman Mailer, Gay Talese, Woody Allen and many others.
🕐 Daily 6–2 🚇 86th Street (4, 5, 6)

ENOTECA I TRULLI

122 East 27th Street between Park Avenue South and Lexington Avenue
Tel 212/481-7372
This light and airy wine bar offers some 50 wines by the glass at the marble bar. Accompany them with some first-class cured meats, cheeses and olives from I Trulli next door.
🕐 Mon–Thu 12–10.30, Fri 12–11, Sat 5–11 🚇 28th Street (6)

EUGENE

27 West 24th Street between Fifth and Sixth avenues
Tel 212/462-0999
The razzle-dazzle of this club-lounge—fluted columns, red-velvet club chairs, a glassed-in dining room—appeals to an international jet-set crowd.
🕐 Thu, Fri 11pm–4am, Sat 10pm–4am 🚇 23rd Street (F, N, R, V)

FEZ UNDER TIME CAFÉ

380 Lafayette Street between Great Jones and East 4th streets
Tel 212/533-7000 or 212/533-2680 for events calendar
This casbah-style bar is plush and comfortable with pillow-studded sofas, under Moroccan-style hanging lamps, and whirling fans. The bar has

a good selection of cognacs and single malts.
🕐 Sun–Thu 6–2, Fri–Sat 6–4 🚇 Broadway-Lafayette (F, S, V), Bleecker Street (6)

FLUTE

205 West 54th Street between Seventh Avenue and Broadway
Tel 212/265-5169
Perfect, if pricey, for an after-theater celebration, this gilt-and-mirror subterranean bar serves 20 champagnes by the glass. Snag one of the private curtained alcoves.
🕐 Mon–Fri 5–4, Sat 7–4, Sun 7–2 🚇 Seventh Avenue (B, D, E)

Tempting drinks are on offer at Happy Ending

GLASS

287 Tenth Avenue between West 26th and 27th streets
Tel 212/904-1580
This sleek modernist space is fun and futuristic—worthy of the arty neighborhood. Check out the two-way mirrors in the bathrooms, and other visual tricks.
🕐 Thu–Sat 5–4, Tue–Wed 5–2 🚇 28th Street (1, 9)

GRACE

114 Franklin Street between West Broadway and Church Street
Tel 212/343-4200
Wall Streeters and politicos cozy up to the long mahogany bar for apple martinis and

tangerine margaritas in this lofty elegant space.
🕐 Daily 11.30am–4am 🚇 Franklin Street (1, 9)

HAPPY ENDING

302 Broome Street between Eldridge and Forsythe streets
Tel 212/334-9676
This duplex lounge still reveals traces of its former life as a massage parlor, from the bellybutton-level showerheads to the tiled sauna alcoves and the circular booths (which used to be tubs). Innovative drinks.
🕐 Tue–Wed 6–2, Thu 6–3, Fri–Sat 6–4 🚇 Delancey/Essex (F, J, M, Z)

HUDSON BARS

Hudson Hotel, 356 West 58th Street between Eighth and Ninth avenues
Tel 212/554-6000
The two bars are central to this hipster hotel. In the Hudson, a long ornate table serves as the bar. Late at night, the backlit floor becomes a dance floor. In the Library, there are leather chairs, ottomans and a fireplace.
🕐 Hudson Sun–Wed 4–1.30, Thu–Sat 4–3; Library Sun–Wed noon–1am, Thu–Sat noon–2.30am 🚇 59th Street/Columbus Circle (A, B, C, D, 1, 9)

IL POSTO ACCANTO

192 East 2nd Street between Avenues A and B
Tel 212/228-3562
A casual, friendly wine bar. Order appetizers to go with one of the 30 wines by the glass (all Italian).
🕐 Tue–Sun 6–2 🚇 Lower East Side/Second Avenue (F, V)

KING COLE BAR

St. Regis Hotel, 2 East 55th Street between Fifth and Madison avenues
Tel 212/753-4500
Named for the 1906 Maxfield Parrish mural *Old King Cole*, this bar claims to have invented the Bloody Mary (originally the Red Snapper). Excellent stock of cognacs, grappas and single malts.

Mon–Thu 11.30am–1am, Fri–Sat 11.30am–2am, Sun noon–midnight 🚇 Fifth Avenue/53rd Street (E, V)

KUSH
191 Chrystie Street between Stanton and Rivington streets
Tel 212/677-7328
www.kushlounge.com
Exotic Moroccan-inspired décor sets the stage for the hip crowd smoking hookahs and sipping drinks at this seductive lounge, with its private alcoves and sunken hookah lounge. Global music spins on the turntable most nights.
🕐 Tue–Wed 5pm–2am, Thu–Fri 5pm–4am, Sat 7pm–4am
🚇 Lower East Side/2nd Avenue (F, V), Bowery (J, M, Z)

LEVEL V
675 Hudson Street at 14th Street
Tel 212/699-2410
This basement lounge at Vento is the latest hotspot in the meatpacking district. Black leather couches, glass tables and dramatic lighting set the scene for a chic and coiffed young crowd. VIPS are ushered into the private vaulted brick stalls. Best to make a reservation.
🕐 Thu–Sat 8pm–4am, Tue–Wed 8pm–2am 🚇 14th Street (A, C, E), Eighth Avenue (L)

LIGHT
129 East 54th Street between Lexington and Park avenues
Tel 212/583-1333
Singles gather around the bar at this atmospheric red-velvet party spot. It is far from light.
🕐 Mon–Thu 5–2, Fri 5–4, Sat 9–4
🚇 Lexington Avenue/53rd Street (E, V), 51st Street (6)

LOT 61
550 West 21st Street between Tenth and Eleventh avenues
Tel 212/243-6555
This still-trendy lounge occupies a garage that once housed trucks. Sliding panels divide the space into sitting areas, which are a pastiche of

funky 1940s, fake zebra and posh Polynesian. Damien Hirst contributed some of the art.
🕐 Fri–Sun 10–4 🚇 23rd Street (C, E)

LUNA PARK
Union Square Park between Broadway and 17th Street
Tel 212/475-8464
The quintessential Manhattan summer scene, this open-air bar/restaurant occupies the northern end of Union Square Park. Decent Mediterranean fare, too.
🕐 May–Sep Mon–Fri noon–midnight, Sat noon–1am, Sun noon–11 🚇 14th Street/Union Square (L, N, Q, R, W, 4, 5, 6)

Enjoy a cocktail in one of New York's many bars

MARIE'S CRISIS
59 Grove Street
Tel 212/243-9323
A mixed crowd of gays and straights gather around the upright piano and sing along to Broadway show tunes at this downstairs bar.
🕐 Daily 4–4 🚇 Christopher Street/Sheridan Square (1, 9)

MARION'S CONTINENTAL
354 Bowery between East 4th and Great Jones streets
Tel 212/475-7621
A steady clientele gathers for reasonably priced martinis and theme nights. On Monday, for example, the Pontani Sisters cavort around as if they were

in the Ziegfeld Follies.
🕐 Daily 5.30–2
🚇 Broadway/Lafayette (F, S, V), Bleecker Street (6)

MARKT
40 West 14th Street at Ninth Avenue
Tel 212/727-3314
In summer, the outdoor tables are always occupied at this Belgian-style bar. Belgian brews are on tap, to wash down mussels and shellfish.
🕐 Mon–Fri 11.30–4.30, 5.30–midnight, Sat–Sun 10–4.30, 5.30–1 🚇 14th Street (A, C, E)

MERC BAR
151 Mercer Street between Houston and Prince streets
Tel 212/966-2727
The ultra-hip have moved on, but this bar still has comfortable seating, seductive lighting and groovy music. The front banquettes are great for people-watching in summer.
🕐 Mon–Wed 5–1.15, Thu–Sat 5–3.30, Sun 6–1.15 🚇 Broadway/Lafayette (F, S, V), Bleecker Street (6)

METROPOLITAN MUSEUM ROOF GARDEN
Metropolitan Museum of Art, 1000 Fifth Avenue at 82nd Street
Tel 212/879-5500
Classy all the way. What better accompaniment to a drink than a view of the sun setting over Central Park? The balcony bar is chic with its chamber music and jazz groups.
🕐 Roof Garden Tue–Thu, Sun 9.30–5.15, Fri–Sat 9.30–8; Balcony Bar Fri–Sat 5–8 🚇 86th Street (4, 5, 6), 77th Street (6)

MORGANS BAR
Morgans Hotel, 237 Madison Avenue between East 37th and 38th streets
Tel 212/726-7600
This basement hideaway draws more than its fair share of celebrities. Sink into the leather chairs and enjoy the candlelight and well-made cocktails. Go after 10 to catch the place at its best.
🕐 Mon–Fri 5–2, Sat 6–3.15, Sun 6–midnight 🚇 33rd Street (6)

WHAT TO DO

N

33 Crosby Street between Broome and Grand streets
Tel 212/219-8856
This tiny narrow bar serves sangria with tasty tapas. Good selection of sherry and Spanish wine.
🕐 Sun–Thu 5–2, Fri–Sat 5–4 🚇 Spring Street (6)

THE PARK

118 Tenth Avenue between West 17th and 18th streets
Tel 212/352-3313
This gargantuan complex with an attractive outdoor courtyard is famous for having hosted J Lo's birthday bash.
🕐 Mon–Thu 4–1, Fri–Sun 4–4 🚇 14th Street (A, C, E), Eighth Avenue (L)

PEN TOP BAR

Peninsula Hotel, 700 Fifth Avenue at 55th Street
Tel 212/903-3097
Who can resist an invitation to a well-dressed outdoor rooftop bar in the middle of Manhattan? You'll pay dearly for the privilege, but that's what makes memories.
🕐 Mon–Thu 5–midnight, Fri–Sat 5–1 🚇 Fifth Avenue/53rd Street (E, V), 51st Street (6)

PRAVDA

281 Lafayette Street between Houston and Prince streets
Tel 212/226-4944
Caviar and other Russian snacks accompany the vodka at this classy lounge, which is more dacha than imperial palace. Sixty-five vodkas are available, many infused with bizarre ingredients like ginger, mango and horseradish.
🕐 Wed–Thu 5–2, Fri–Sat 5–3, Sun 6–1, Mon–Tue 5–1 🚇 Broadway/Lafayette (F, S, V), Bleecker Street (6)

PUNCH AND JUDY

26 Clinton Street between Houston and Stanton streets
Tel 212/982-1116
Theater-style seating sets the scene up front at this sleek and comfortable wine bar, where you can sink back into red velvet couches and sample 32 wines by the glass.
🕐 Daily 6–2 🚇 Delancey/Essex (F, J, M, Z)

RAINBOW GRILL BAR

30 Rockefeller Plaza at 49th Street between Fifth and Sixth avenues
Tel 212/632-5000
www.rainbowroomny.com
You can spend a fortune dining and dancing at the Rainbow Room—or head to this bar and dream among the starlit towers of Midtown over some cocktails. Jackets required.
🕐 Sun–Thu 5–midnight, Fri–Sat 5–1, dining and dancing selected Fri–Sat 🚇 47th–50th Streets (B, D, F, V)

You can lounge in luxury in the city's finest bars

ROYALTON VODKA BAR

Royalton Hotel, 44 West 44th Street between Fifth and Sixth avenues
Tel 212/869-4400
Tucked away off the lobby of the ultra-hip Royalton, this cocoon-like bar is perfect for pre- or post-theater drinks.
🕐 Mon–Thu 5–12.45, Fri–Sat 5–1.45 🚇 42nd Street (B, D, F, V)

RUBYFRUIT

531 Hudson Street between Charles and West 10th streets
Tel 212/929-3343
www.rubyfruitnyc.com
Couches and antique chairs are clustered around the fireplace in the upstairs bar, which attracts an over-35 crowd and the occasional celebrity lesbian. There is a convivial restaurant downstairs.
🕐 Mon–Thu 3–2, Fri–Sat 3pm–4am, Sun 11.30am–2am 🚇 Christopher Street (1, 9)

RUSSIAN VODKA ROOM

265 West 52nd Street between Broadway and Eighth Avenue
Tel 212/307-5835
A huge selection of flavored vodkas, apple-cinnamon and horseradish, for example, are poured into martinis or drunk straight, the preference of the Russians who gather at this old-fashioned basement bar. Inexpensive menu.
🕐 Tue–Thu 4–2, Fri–Sat 4–3, Sun–Mon 4–1 🚇 50th Street (C, E)

ST. ANDREW'S

120 West 44th Street between Broadway and Sixth Avenue
Tel 212/840-8413
Scotch-lovers crowd the front bar at this traditional pub-style restaurant. Here they can select their favorites from about 175 or so single malts. Go early or late if you want to avoid the crush.
🕐 Tue–Sat 11.30am–4am, Sun–Mon noon–2am 🚇 42nd Street (B, D, F, V)

SAKAGURA

211 East 43rd Street between Second and Third avenues
Tel 212/953-7253
In the basement of a high-rise building, this bar could have been lifted from Japan. Shelves are lined with 200 different types of sake, and you can order flights of four selections.
🕐 Mon–Thu noon–2.30, 6–midnight, Fri noon–2.30, 6–1, Sat 6–2, Sun 6–11 🚇 42nd Street/Grand Central (4, 5, 6)

SERENA BAR AND LOUNGE

Hotel Chelsea, 222 West 23rd Street between Seventh and Eighth avenues
Tel 212/255-4646
Society and fashion doyenne Serena Bass established this cellar hot spot opulent with

lounges outfitted in velvet, suede, marble and mirrors, and a mover-and-shaker crowd. On Wednesday nights DJs celebrate downtown culture.

 Tue–Fri 6–4, Sat 7–4 🚇 23rd Street (1, 9)

SLIPPER ROOM
167 Orchard Street at Stanton Street
Tel 212/253-7246
The name captures the mood of this lounge, where aspiring cabaret artists entertain.

 Wed–Sat 8–4, Tue 8–2 🚇 Lower East Side/Second Avenue (F, V)

SOHO 323
323 West Broadway
Tel 212/334-2232
South Beach is the obvious influence on this two-story lounge. Decorous palm fronds (some stenciled, others for real) grace the space, while patrons lounge on sofas or wicker ottomans sipping 'Twos and Threes', a combination of champagne, Chambord and litchi puree. The upstairs venue has a cabana-style bar and minimal décor.

 Mon–Sat 5pm–4am
🚇 Canal Street (C, E)

STARLIGHT
167 Avenue A between 10th and 11th streets
Tel 212/475-2172
Starlight offers more than drinking. In the back, artists of all sorts take the small stage. It could be drag, comedy, improvisation, poetry or whatever.

 Sun–Thu 6–3, Fri–Sat 6–4 🚇 Astor Place (6), First Avenue (L)

STONEWALL
53 Christopher Street between Seventh Avenue South and Waverly Place
Tel 212/463-0950
www.stonewall-place.com
It's nondescript, but this place has acquired near-mythic status for the gay movement. Here in 1969 some transvestites, using their stilettos, took a stand against

the police.

 Daily 4–4 🚇 Christopher Street/Sheridan Square (1, 9)

SUGARCANE
245 Park Avenue South between 19th and 20th streets
Tel 212 475-9377
The gimmick at this Latino lounge is the "Cocktail Tree," a $50 sampler holding the drinks menu. The DJ spins Brazilian-Caribbean sounds for the sophisticates engaged in conversation at the sleek bar or on the banquettes around the room.

 Tue–Sat 4.30pm–2am, Sun–Mon 4.30pm–midnight 🚇 23rd Street (6), 23rd Street (N, R, W)

A night on the town, New York style

SWIFT HIBERNIAN LOUNGE
34 East 4th Street between Bowery and Lafayette Street
Tel 212/227-9438
Numerous brews are on tap at this slice of Dublin in Manhattan named for satirist Jonathan Swift. Locals and Irish expats are the main patrons.

 Daily noon–4am 🚇 Broadway/Lafayette (F, S, V), Bleecker Street (6)

TAO
42 East 58th Street between Madison and Park avenues
Tel 212/888-2288
A large golden Buddha presides over this loft space, which is so crowded with

good-looking singles after work that it made it into an episode of *Sex and the City*.

 Wed–Fri 11.30am–1am, Sat 5–1, Sun 5–midnight, Mon–Tue 11.30am–midnight, 🚇 Fifth Avenue/59th Street (N, R, W), 59th Street (4, 5, 6)

TEMPLE BAR
332 Lafayette Street between Houston and Bleecker streets
Tel 212/925-4242
This ultra-expensive bar attracts models and their moneyed coterie. A beautiful scene.

 Mon–Wed 5–1, Thu–Sat 5–2 🚇 Broadway/Lafayette (F, S, V), Bleecker Street (6)

TOP OF THE TOWER
Beekman Tower, 3 Mitchell Place on First Avenue at 49th Street
Tel 212/980-4796
This 26th-floor eyrie is neither overhyped nor overpriced—a miracle considering how romantic the place is and how bewitching the views are.

 Sun–Thu 5–1, Fri–Sat 5–2 🚇 51st Street (6), 53rd Street/Lexington (E, V)

TOWNHOUSE
236 East 58th Street at Second Avenue
Tel 212/754-4649
www.townhouseny.com
Upscale professionals gather around the piano at this club-bar.

 Sun–Wed 4–3, Thu–Sat 4–4 🚇 59th Street (4, 5, 6)

XUNTA
174 First Avenue between East 10th and 11th streets
Tel 212/614-0620
On Thursdays flamenco and rippling guitar music provide an atmospheric setting for sangria and tapas at this lively bar. Good selection of sherry, too.

 Sun–Thu 5–midnight, Fri–Sat 5–2 🚇 14 Street (L), Lower East Side/Second Avenue (F, V)

Traditional Old New York

CEDAR TAVERN
82 University Place between 11th and 12th streets
Tel 212/741-9754
In the 50s, the Cedar Tavern (then at No. 24) was the HQ of artists Jackson Pollock and Willem de Kooning. Today's crowd is likely to be NYU students. In summer, head to the glass-enclosed roof garden.
Mon–Sat 9am–3.30am, Sun noon–3am 14th Street/Union Square (L, N, Q, R, W, 4, 5, 6)

CHUMLEY'S
86 Bedford Street between Barrow and Grove streets
Tel 212/675-4449
Originally opened in 1922 as a speakeasy, the bar attracted writers (note their book jackets on the walls), who have been replaced by locals and students.
Mon–Thu 5–midnight, Fri 5–1, Sat noon–1am, Sun noon–midnight
Christopher Street/Sheridan Square (1, 9)

EAR INN
326 Spring Street between Greenwich and Washington streets
Tel 212/226-9060
This 1817 bar near the Hudson River used to cater to sailors and stevedores and now attracts writers and artists.
Daily noon–4am Spring Street (C, E), Canal Street (1, 9)

FANELLI CAFE
94 Prince Street at Mercer Street
Tel 212/226-9412
Step through the etched-glass doors and you could be in London. A few artists still gather here, and you can get pub food in the back room.
Mon–Thu 10am–2am, Fri 10am–4am, Sat 10am–4am, Sun 11am–12.30am Prince Street (N, R)

JOE ALLEN
326 West 46th Street between Eighth and Ninth avenues
Tel 212/581-6464
It's really a restaurant, but the bar is ideal for a pre- or post-theater drink. American menu.
Sun, Wed, Sat 11.30am–11.45pm, Mon–Tue. Thu–Fri noon–11.45
42nd Street (A, C, E)

LANDMARK TAVERN
626 Eleventh Avenue at the southeast corner of 46th Street
Tel 212/247-2562
The Landmark Tavern is worthy of its name, since it

Enjoy a drink in a literary setting at Chumley's

opened in 1868. The mahogany bar, antique mirrors and tile floor provide a historic patina. The traditional pub fare is good.
Daily 11.30am–3am (kitchen closes at 11pm) 42nd Street (A, C, E), 50th Street (C, E)

McSORLEY'S OLD ALE HOUSE
15 East 7th Street between Second and Third avenues
Tel 212/473-9148
McSorley's, established in 1854, became infamous for refusing to admit women until 1970. The walls are plastered with old newspaper clippings. Students are the main patrons.

Mon–Sat noon–1am, Sun 1–1
Astor Place (6), 8th Street (N, R)

OLD TOWN BAR
45 East 18th Street between Broadway and Park Avenue
Tel 212/529-6732
At this authentic hang-out, dating from 1892, look for the private booths. Tiled floors, a long mirrored bar, pressed-tin ceiling and original gas lamps complete the look. No jukebox, conversation reigns.
Mon–Wed 11.30am–12.30am, Thu–Fri 11.30am–1am, Sat noon–1am, Sun 1–11.30 14th Street/Union Square (L, N, Q, R, W, 4, 5, 6)

P.J. CLARKE'S
915 Third Avenue at 55th Street
Tel 212/317-1616
A tiny building overshadowed by skyscrapers, the bar played a major role in Billy Wilder's 1945 film *The Lost Weekend*. A 2003 renovation preserved its old New York feel.
Daily 11.30am–4am 59th Street (4, 5, 6)

PETE'S TAVERN
129 East 18th Street at Irving Place
Tel 212/473-7676
The writer O'Henry supposedly wrote *The Gift of the Magi* in a beer-stained booth here. In summer, snag a sidewalk table if you can.
Mon–Sat 11am–2.30am, Sun noon–2.30am 14th Street/Union Square (L, N, Q, R, W, 4, 5, 6)

WHITE HORSE TAVERN
567 Hudson Street at 11th Street
Tel 212/989-3956
Dylan Thomas, Brendan Behan and Jack Kerouac all slaked their thirst here. In summer, the benches and picnic tables make perfect perches for Village people-watching.
Sun–Thu 11am–2am, Fri–Sat 11am–4am Christopher Street/ Sheridan Square (1, 9), 14th Street (A, C, E)

WHAT TO DO

Clubs

New York has loads of attitude, and it is on display at its worst at the entrances to dance clubs. At a few places, the henchmen at the door are rude and obnoxious. At many clubs, as the week gets closer to the weekend the door policies get stricter. In some places, the action doesn't warm up until after midnight.

APT
419 West 13th Street between Ninth Avenue and Washington Street
Tel 212/414-4245
www.aptwebsite.com
You must be on the A-list to snag one of the sofas in the upstairs apartment-style lounge (with a big bed as well as coffee tables). The sleek basement lounge is more accessible, but you still need to look good at this designer nightlife spot.
🕐 Sun–Wed 6–2, Thu–Sat 6–4 (downstairs Sun–Wed 10–2, Thu–Sat 10–4)
💷 $0–$20 🚇 14th Street (A, C, E), Eighth Avenue (L)

BAKTUN
418 West 14th Street between Ninth Avenue and Washington Street
Tel 212/206-1590
www.baktun.com
A plain but vibrant club, especially at the weekly Saturday drum 'n bass party, when club kids trance in to the double-sided video screens. Live instrumental and electronic music, plus special events (kodo drummers from Japan) are featured other nights.
🕐 Mon, Wed–Sat 9–4 💷 Varies
🚇 14th Street (A, C, E)

CHINA CLUB
268 West 47th Street between Broadway and Eighth Avenue
Tel 212/398-3800
www.chinaclubnyc.com
This glitzy spot has been pulsating and attracting celebrities for 25 years. Today, sports figures and music heavies still head to its VIP lounge especially on Monday nights. Other nights are dedicated to house, salsa, merengue and R & B.
🕐 Mon–Sat 10–4 (doors open sometimes at 6 for after-work events)
💷 $15–$20 🚇 49th Street (N, R, W), 50th Street (1, 9)

CIELO
18 Little West 12th Street between Ninth Avenue and Washington Street
Tel 212/645-5700
Tough to get into unless you're beautiful or famous since it only accommodates

New York's hottest clubs have a lot of attitude

300 standing. It's comfortable, with a small sunken dance floor (which throbs at 2am) and plenty of intimate nooks. Latin-flecked house and tribal and hot guest DJs attract the crowds.
🕐 Mon–Wed 10–4, Thu–Sat 11–4, Sun 6–midnight 💷 $5–$20 🚇 14th Street (A, C, E)

CLUB SHELTER
20 West 39th Street between Fifth and Sixth avenues
Tel 212/719-4479
Upstairs the ultimate garage party has been playing for more than a decade. Downstairs is LoverGirlNYC, a major lesbian event.

🕐 Sat 11pm–noon 💷 $10–$25
🚇 42nd Street (B, D, F, V), Fifth Avenue (7)

COPACABANA
560 West 34th Street at Eleventh Avenue
Tel 212/239-2672
www.copacabanany.com
Serious dancers come to this flashy Latin club to dance to live bands playing salsa, merengue and other Latin rhythms. Tuesday includes free buffet from 6 to 8. No T's for men, and no jeans or sneakers.
🕐 Tue 6–2.30, Fri–Sat 10–5
💷 $10–$25 🚇 34th Street (A, C, E)

CORAL ROOM
512 West 29th Street between Tenth and Eleventh avenues
Tel 212/244-1965
Hokey, but fun and easy to get into. It's famous for the large aquarium behind the bar. On Sundays, Chelsea's gay clubbers pile in. Other nights, you never know whom you'll find—suits, slicks or suburban types.
🕐 Wed–Mon 10.30–4 💷 $20
🚇 23rd Street (C, E)

CROBAR
530 West 28th Street between Tenth and Eleventh avenues
Tel 212/629-9000
www.crobar.com
Crobar has to be the largest club anywhere. It's so vast that it attracts a party crowd of every sort, shape and variety—punk, rock, gay, straight, suburban—which gets high on the chaotic crush. Music is similarly multi.
🕐 Fri–Sat 10–5 💷 $20–$30 🚇 23rd Street (C, E)

DISCOTHEQUE

17 West 19th Street between Fifth and Sixth avenues
Tel 212/352-9999
www.discothequenyc.com
Soul, retro R & B and disco draw models and their banker escorts to this glitzy, hard-to-get-into club. The DJ line-up is always top drawer. Occasionally, there's a male revue for women and other entertainment.
Thu–Sun 10–4 $10–$25 23rd Street (N, R, W), 18th Street (1, 9)

EL FLAMINGO

547 West 21st Street between Tenth and Eleventh avenues
Tel 212/243-2121
www.elflamingo.com or www.donkeyshow.com
This club/lounge is home to a hilarious musical revue called the *Donkey Show*. Afterwards, the show patrons can join a disco diva party dancing with the scantily clad cast members.
Fri 9, Sat 7.30, 10 $40–$45 including show and dancing
23rd Street (C, E)

EXIT 2

610 West 56th Street between Eleventh and Twelfth avenues
Tel 212/582-8282
www.exit2nightclub.com
The wildest night at this huge dance warehouse is the Saturday night reggae party. The awesome space can accommodate 4,000. Thursday night is hip-hop and Friday is Latin.
Thu 11–4, Fri 11–4, Sat 10–4 $20–$30 59th Street/Columbus Circle (A, B, C, D, 1, 9)

GO

73 Eighth Avenue between West 13th and 14th streets
Tel 212/463-0000
Dramatic lighting intensified by the all-white walls and an eye-candy crowd makes this a current favorite. The sounds mix hip-hop, R & B and house. Usual hassle to secure entry.

Tue–Sat 10–4 $20 14th Street (A, C, E)

LOTUS

409 West 14th Street between Ninth and Tenth avenues
Tel 212/243-4420
www.lotusnewyork.com
European jet-setters flock to this chic supper club with attitude, attracted by the international DJs and the luxe balcony lounge and basement dance club. It's tough to get past the fu dogs at the door. Make a dinner reservation and bring the platinum.
Dinner Tue–Sat 7–11; club Tue–Sat 11–4 $20 14th Street (A, C, E)

New York's clubs offer an eclectic range of music

MARQUEE

289 Tenth Avenue between 26th and 27th streets
Tel 646/473-0202
www.marqueeny.com
Currently this club has a lot of buzz and attracts a celebrity crowd who appreciate its plush comforts, French elegance (glittering contemporary chandeliers, velvet banquettes), cabaret room and good sightlines for watching the scene. Monday night's Charm School University is an uproarious parody; Baby Tuesday caters to the fashion industry. The crowd is mainly straight, but there's a smattering of

fashion-conscious gays too. Hip hop, house, funk and soul are the main musical themes.
Tue–Sat 10pm–4am Cover $5–$20 23rd Street (C, E)

PIANOS

158 Ludlow Street between Stanton and Rivington streets
Tel 212/505-3733
www.pianosnyc.com
Don't expect piano entertainment at this bi-level bar, because the name is a relic of a previous occupant. People show up for the alternative music on Friday and Monday. Sunday it's stand-up comedy.
Daily 5–4 $5–$10 DeLancey/Essex Street (F, J, M, Z)

SPIRIT

530 West 27th Street between Tenth and Eleventh avenues
Tel 212/268-9477
www.Spiritny.com
A current haunt for many New York City celebrities from the fashion and music worlds, this club aims to provide a holistic experience by providing a dance area, a spiritual wellness facility providing massage and chakra adjustment, and a restaurant serving organic vegetarian cuisine. The New Age club attracts a diverse group of people to see the musical and dance troupes and hear the DJs spin Sufi trance, soul and R & B.
Fri–Sun (doors open at 11pm) Cover $20–$30 23rd Street (C,E)

SWING 46

349 West 46th Street between Eighth and Ninth avenues
Tel 212/262-9554
www.swing46.com
At this 1940s-style jazz club, you can lindy and jitterbug to top-notch live bands. Friday and Saturday is always swing. The management provides lessons to neophytes.
Daily 5–1 or 2 $10–$12 42nd Street (A, C, E)

SPORTS AND ACTIVITIES

New York City is a major sports destination, whether you fancy watching a game of baseball, football, basketball, ice hockey or tennis. If you want to take part in something yourself, try jogging in Central Park or working out at one of the many gyms.

Local and regional rivalries drive the professional sports scene. In baseball it's the Yankees (Bronx) versus the Mets (Queens). In addition, whenever the Yankees play the Red Sox, it's a grudge game because Boston has never forgiven New York for stealing Babe Ruth. The biggest sports are football (Giants and Jets) and basketball (Knicks and New Jersey Nets). Ice hockey has fanatical fans too, supporting the Rangers,

Islanders and New Jersey Devils, making for internecine rivalries between Manhattan, Long Island and New Jersey. Most seats are sold in advance by subscription to corporations and individuals. Tickets are available without fee at the box office, there's an extra fee for phone and online orders. Agencies like TicketMaster (tel 212/307-7171 or www.ticketmaster.com) usually charge a fee of from $4 to $8 per ticket. Tickets to any of these sports are tough to get and/or expensive, but you can always take a seat in one of the many raucous sports bars around town and see the action there, or at the large ESPN Zone in Times Square.

The major sports seasons are: baseball April–end October; basketball November–end April; soccer March–end October; football and ice hockey September–end April.

Despite the American women's global success in soccer, women's professional sports struggle for audience

support, although such teams as basketball's Liberty have loyal fans.

New Yorkers also enjoy a variety of exercise and activities. They go to the gym, walk, run, cycle, skate, rollerblade and play tennis, softball and street basketball. Equestrians can ride in Central Park. They have also rediscovered the waterfront and now enjoy kayaking and sailing from several downtown piers. The more sedentary count bowling and pool as sports.

Basketball is one of the city's biggest sports

Many New Yorkers exercise in Central Park

BASEBALL

BROOKLYN CYCLONES

Keyspan Park, 1904 Surf Avenue between 17th and 19th streets, Coney Island
Tel 718/449-8497 or 718/507-TIXX
www.brooklyncyclones.com
This minor-league club has the fans cheering, because going to the game here is the way baseball used to be. Sitting in the bleachers at this waterfront stadium is just the ticket, especially for old Dodgers fans.
💵 $5–$12 (single tickets available mid-Apr) 🚇 Stillwell Avenue/Coney Island

(W) 🚌 B36, B64, B74 (Stillwell/Surf Avenue)

NEW YORK METS

Shea Stadium , Roosevelt Avenue at 126th Street, Flushing, Queens
Tel 718/507-8499
www.mets.com
When the Brooklyn Dodgers left New York in 1957, the Mets in effect replaced them. Even though they haven't won a championship since 1986 and often finish at the bottom of their league, they continue to draw fans. You can usually get tickets unless they're

playing the Yankees or the Boston Red Sox. Shea Stadium, right underneath the landing path to LaGuardia airport, is noisy.
💵 $8–$60 🚇 Willets Pt/Shea Stadium (7) 🚢 On Sat–Sun only: New York Waterway (tel 800/533-3779) operates from the South Street Seaport, East 34th Street or East 90th Street for $18 round-trip. Reservations recommended.

NEW YORK YANKEES

Yankee Stadium, East 161st Street and River Avenue, the Bronx
Tel 212/307-1212 for tickets, 718/579-4531 for tours
www.yankees.com
Since the Yankees began playing in 1903 as the New York Highlanders, they've racked up 26 World Championships. Tickets are tough to get for certain games (opening day, games against the Mets, the play-offs, the series) but not for other games. Even if you don't go to a game, take the one-hour tour to see the dugout, clubhouse and scoreboard operations of a stadium associated with several baseball legends.
$8–$90 ⬛ 161st Street/Yankee Stadium (C, D, 4) ⬛ New York Waterway (tel 800/533-3779) operates from the South Street Seaport, East 34th Street or East 90th Street for $18 round-trip. Reservations recommended.

STATEN ISLAND YANKEES

Richmond County Bank Ballpark at St.George
Tel 718/720-9265 or 718/720-9200
www.siyankees.com
This minor-league team plays in a stadium overlooking the harbor. It's fun to take the trip on the Staten Island Ferry.
$9–$11 ⬛ South Ferry (1, 9) to Staten Island Ferry ⬛ Staten Island Ferry

WHAT TO DO

BASKETBALL

NEW JERSEY NETS
Continental Airlines Arena, East Rutherford, N.J.
Tel 201/935-3900 or 1800-7NJNETS
www.nba.com or
www.meadowlands.com
This Atlantic Division basketball team has been on a winning streak thanks to All-star point guard Jason Kidd, Vince Carter and Richard Jefferson.
$15–$120 ⬛ NJ Transit bus from 42nd Street/Port Authority Bus Terminal at Eighth Avenue

NEW YORK KNICKS

Madison Square Garden, 2 Pennsylvania Plaza, Seventh Avenue between West 31st and 33rd streets
Tel 212/465-5867 or 212/465-6741 (Madison Square Garden), 212/307-7171 for tickets
www.nyknicks.com or www.thegarden.com
The Knicks are the city's hottest ticket. This team and the Boston Celtics are the only charter members of the NBA left. Walt Frazier, Bill Bradley and Willis Reed made them golden in the 1970s, and Patrick Ewing helped them to the play-offs in 1994 and 1999. Since Ewing left, they have struggled. Today Allan Houston is the guy to

Visit Larry and Jeff's to explore the city on two wheels

watch. The Knicks City Dancers are pure Americana. Spike Lee is just one of the celebrity fans in attendance. For tours, call 212/465-5802.
$10–$100 ⬛ 34th Street/Penn Station (A, C, E, 1, 2, 3, 9) ⬛ M20, M34

NEW YORK LIBERTY

Madison Square Garden, 2 Pennsylvania Plaza, Seventh Avenue between West 31st and 33rd streets
Tel 212/564-9622
www.nyliberty.com
This team, launched in the summer of 1997, has become a star in the Women's National Basketball Association (WNBA) and has played in many WNBA finals. Look for Tari Phillips to

wow the crowds and get mascot Maddie waving and whooping.
$10–$69.50 ⬛ 34th Street/Penn Station (A, C, E, 1, 2, 3, 9) ⬛ M20, M34

BICYCLING

LARRY & JEFF'S
1690 Second Avenue between East 87th and 88th streets
Tel 212-722-2201
This store rents road and mountain bikes and is conveniently close to Central Park.
⬛ Daily 10–7 (until 8 during daylight savings) ⬛ $30 day (3 1/2hrs or more) ⬛ 86th Street (4, 5, 6) ⬛ M15, M86

BIRDWATCHING

CHARLES A. DANA DISCOVERY CENTER
Central Park, 110th Street between Fifth and Lenox avenues
Tel 212/860-1370
www.centralparknyc.org or www.nyc.gov/parks
Exhibits relate to the natural life in the park, and the center sponsors related activities in the park. For ranger-led activities call 1-866-NYCHAWK.
⬛ Daily 10–5 ⬛ Free ⬛ Central Park North (2, 3) ⬛ M4

NEW YORK CITY AUDUBON SOCIETY

Tel 212/691-7483
www.nycas.org
The New York City Audubon Society allows visitors to join its birdwatching walks in Central Park for a fee of $5.

BOWLING

BOWLMOR LANES
110 University Place between 12th and 13th streets
Tel 212/255-8188
www.bowlmor.com
This funky bowling alley has 42 lanes with automatic scoring. At Monday's Night Strike (10pm–3am), DJs spin music as you bowl.
⬛ Sun, Tue–Wed 11am–1am, Thu 11am–2am, Fri–Sat, Mon 11am–4am ⬛ $8.45–$8.95 per game (shoe rental $5) ⬛ 14th Street/Union Square (L, N, Q, R, W, 4, 5, 6) ⬛ M3

LEISURE TIME

625 Eighth Avenue at West 42nd Street
(2nd floor)
Tel 212/268-6909
www.leisuretimebowl.com
Cocktails are prominently
advertised at the entrance to
this 30-lane alley in the Port
Authority Bus Terminal. Sports
bar and video arcade.
🕐 Sun–Thu 10am–midnight, Fri–Sat
10am–3am 💲 $6–$8 per game (shoe
rental $5) 🚇 42nd Street (A, C, E)
🚌 M20, M42

CRICKET

VAN CORTLANDT PARK

Van Cortlandt Park, Park South and
Bailey Avenue
The Caribbean communities
brought cricket to the city and
this is the best place to find a
cricket game in progress.
🕐 Dawn–dusk in summer 💲 Free
🚇 242nd Street (1, 9)

FOOTBALL

NEW YORK GIANTS

Giants Stadium, The Meadowlands,
East Rutherford, N.J.
Tel 201/935-8111 or 201/935-8222 for
tickets www.giants.com or
www.meadowlands.com
Also known as the Big Blue
Wrecking Crew, its fans are
maniacally loyal and tickets are
impossible to get. The team
won their first NFL title in
1927; their golden years were
in the late 1950s and 1960s
when Frank Gifford, Roosevelt
Brown and Sam Huff were in
the line-up. The team made it
to the Super Bowl in 2003.
💲 Single tickets unavailable 🚌 NJ
Transit bus from 42nd Street/Port
Authority Bus Terminal at Eighth Avenue

NEW YORK JETS

Giants Stadium, The Meadowlands,
East Rutherford, N.J.
Tel 516/560-8100 or 516/560-8200
www.newyorkjets.com or
www.meadowlands.com
This American Football League
team has been playing since
1960, but only gained
credibility after they drafted
Joe Namath in 1965 and won
the Super Bowl in 1969.

They moved to Giants Stadium
in 1984. Tickets are hard to
come by—you have to wait
15 years for season tickets.
💲 Season ticket only 🚌 NJ Transit bus
from 42nd Street/Port Authority Bus
Terminal Eighth Avenue

GOLF

VAN CORTLANDT GOLF COURSE

Tel 718/543-4595
www.americangolf.com
The oldest public golf course
in the US is not exactly grade
A, but it will do. Eighteen
holes, 6,122 yards, with
clubhouse and snack bar.
🕐 Dawn–dusk 💲 $37–$43 for
non-residents 🚇 242nd Street (1, 9)

New Yorkers are fanatical about football

HORSE RACING

AQUEDUCT

108th Street and Rockaway Boulevard,
Ozone Park, Queens
Tel 718/641-4700
www.nyra.com
This racetrack, which opened
in 1894, is only 30 minutes by
train from Times Square.
🕐 Mid-Oct to early May Wed–Sun
1pm post time 💲 $1–$4 🚇 Aqueduct
Racetrack (A)

BELMONT PARK

2150 Hempstead Turnpike and
Plainfield Avenue , Elmont, Queens
Tel 516/488-6000
www.nyra.com
This beautiful 430-acre
(174 ha) racecourse is the

largest in North America. In
June, it hosts the Belmont
Stakes, the third leg of the
Triple Crown.
🕐 May–end Jul, Sep–end Oct
Wed–Sun, 1pm post time 💲 $2–$5
🚂 Long Island Railroad's *Pony Express*
from Penn Station

THE MEADOWLANDS

East Rutherford, New Jersey
Tel 201/935-8500
www.meadowlands.com
Trotters run from January
through August and
thoroughbreds from
September through
December at this track.
🕐 Wed–Sat, 7.30pm post time
💲 Free–$2 🚌 Transit bus from 42nd
Street/Port Authority bus terminal at
Eighth Avenue

YONKERS RACEWAY

Yonkers, New York
Tel 914/968-4200
www.yonkersraceway.com
One of the premier harness
racing tracks in the nation is
in the city, just north of the
Bronx. The track celebrated
its centennial in 1999. The
most illustrious race run here
is the Night of Champions,
with a $1.2 million purse.
🕐 Wed–Sun, 7.40pm post time
💲 $2.25–$4.25 🚇 Woodlawn (4) and
Beeline 20 bus

HORSEBACK RIDING

CLAREMONT RIDING ACADEMY

175 West 89th Street between
Columbus and Amsterdam avenues
Tel 212/724-5100
Here, only experienced riders
who can ride at all paces and
post to the trot English-style
can rent horses to ride in
Central Park.
🕐 Daily 7am–sunset 💲 $50 per hr
(lessons $60 for 30 min) 🚇 86th Street
(B, C) 86th Street (1, 9)

ICE HOCKEY

NEW JERSEY DEVILS
Continental Airlines Arena, East Rutherford, N.J.
Tel 201/935-3900, 201-507-8900 or 1-800-NJDEVILS
www.newjerseydevils.com or www.meadowlands.com
The Devils, who have won the Stanley Cup only twice, are currently the premier hockey team in the metro region, thanks largely to brilliant goalie Martin Brodeur and longtime players like Scott Niedermayer. Tickets are easily available.
 $20–$90 🚌 NJ Transit bus from 42nd Street/Port Authority Bus Terminal at Eighth Avenue

NEW YORK ISLANDERS
Nassau Coliseum, Long Island
Tel 516/794-4100
www.newyorkislanders.com
Tickets to contests of this Long Island team are easier to come by than tickets to Rangers games, even though the Islanders won four straight Stanley Cups between 1980 and 1983. The two teams have an edgy rivalry even more cutting after the Islanders' place in the 2003 play-offs.
🖐 $19–$120 ($40–$265 during play-offs) 🚆 LIRR to Hempstead then bus, or Westbury and cab

NEW YORK RANGERS
Madison Square Garden, 2 Pennsylvania Plaza, Seventh Avenue between West 31st and 33rd streets
Tel 212/465-4459, 212/307-7171 for tickets, 212/465-6225 for guest relations, 212/465-5802 for tours and 212/465-6741 for the Garden
www.newyorkrangers.com or www.thegarden.com
The Rangers may have the highest payroll in the National Hockey League, but they haven't made the play-offs for several seasons. They won their last Stanley Cup in 1993–94. Yet tickets are virtually impossible to get. The institutionalized violence on the ice rarely extends into the stands, but it's wise not to cheer the other team.
🖐 $27–$150 🚇 34th Street/Penn Station (A, C, E, 1, 2, 3, 9) 🚌 M20, M34

JOGGING

CENTRAL PARK RESERVOIR
This 1.6-mile (2.6km) gravel path is the favorite track for Upper West Siders and Upper East Siders.
🖐 Free 🚇 86th Street (4, 5, 6), 86th Street (B, C) 🚌 M1, M2, M3, M4, M10, M86

KAYAKING

DOWNTOWN BOATHOUSE
Pier 26, 241 West Broadway at North Moore Street
Tel 646/613-0375
www.downtownboathouse.org

Central Park is a great place for joggers

This organization offers free kayaking trips and instruction on the Hudson River from Pier 26 and Pier 64.
🕐 Mid-May to mid-Oct 🖐 Free 🚇 Franklin Street (1, 9) 🚌 M20

MANHATTAN KAYAK COMPANY
Pier 63 at West 23rd Street
Tel 212/924-1788
www.manhattankayak.com
This company offers instruction and over 30 local tours for beginners, intermediates and advanced paddlers. Longer tours go to the Verrazano Bridge and farther.
🕐 Mid-Apr to end Oct 🖐 Short tours $50–65, long tours $75–$250 🚇 23rd Street (C, E) 🚌 M11, M23

NEW YORK KAYAK COMPANY
Pier 40 at Houston Street
Tel 212/924-1327
www.nykayak.com
This company offers classes and guided tours, which last two or three hours.
🕐 Tours early May to mid-Oct 🖐 Classes: $40 per hr; tours: $80–$120 🚇 Houston Street (1, 9) 🚌 M21

POOL

PRESSURE
110 University Place between 12th and 13th streets
Tel 212/255-8188
www.pressurenyc.com
This bubble on the roof of Bowlmor Lanes is the ultimate pool hall/multimedia lounge. It has 21 tables, plus a huge bar/lounge with seven 42-inch plasma screens.
🕐 Fri–Sat 9pm–3am, Thu 7pm–3am 🖐 Thu $23 per hr, Fri–Sat $26 per hr 🚇 14th Street/Union Square (L, N, Q, R, W, 4, 5, 6) 🚌 M2, M3, M14

SLATE
54 West 21st Street between Fifth and Sixth avenues
Tel 212/989-0096
www.slate-ny.com
This is one of the city's best billiard-pool halls, with 31 tables.
🕐 Thu–Sat 11am–4am, Sun–Wed 11am–3am 🖐 $7–$17 per hr 🚇 23rd Street (N, R, W), 23rd Street (F, V) 🚌 M2, M3, M5, M6, M7

ROWING

LOEB BOATHOUSE
Central Park near East 72nd Street
Tel 212-517-2233
www.thecentralparkboathouse.com
Weather permitting, you can rent bicycles and rowboats for use on the lake year round.
🕐 Daily 10am–dusk 🖐 Bicycles $9–$21 per hr, rowboats $10 per hr 🚇 68th Street (6), 72nd Street (B, C) 🚌 M1, M2, M3, M4, M10

RUNNING

NEW YORK MARATHON
New York Road Runners Club, 9 East 89th Street at Fifth Avenue
Tel 212/860-4455
www.nyrrc.org

Thirty thousand athletes compete in this marathon, watched by 2.5 million spectators. The finish line is in Central Park.

🕐 First Sun in Nov

SKATING

BLADES BOARD & SKATE
120 West 72nd Street at Columbus Street
Tel 212/787-3911
www.blades.com
This is the most convenient of these stores to Central Park, where you can rent in-line skates. There's also a branch at Chelsea Piers.

🕐 Mon–Sat 11–8, Sun 11–7
💷 Rentals $21.65 for 24 hr 🚇 72nd Street (1, 2, 3, 9) 🚌 M7, M11, M72

EMPIRE SKATE CLUB
Tel 212/774-1774
www.empirestate.org
The club sponsors group skates, skating events and tours. Year-round skates include the Sunday morning roll from Columbus Circle at 11am and the Tuesday night skate from Blades at 120 West 72nd Street at 8pm.

💷 Club membership $25 (you don't have to be a member to join group skates)

ROCKEFELLER CENTER ICE RINK
1 Rockefeller Center Plaza, Fifth Avenue between 49th and 50th streets
Tel 212/332-7654
www.restaurantassociates.com
It's dreamlike to glide on this legendary rink under the golden statue of Prometheus. Live DJ Thursday 7–11pm.

🕐 Oct–late Apr Mon–Thu 9am–10.30pm, Fri–Sat 8.30am–midnight, Sun 8.30am–10pm
💷 Mon–Wed $9, Thu–Sun adult $13, child (under 12) $7/8, skate rental $7 🚇 47th–50th streets/Rockefeller Center (B, D, F, V) 🚌 M1, M2, M3, M4, M50

WOLLMAN RINK
Central Park at 62nd Street
Tel 212/439-6900
www.wollmanskatingrink.com

You can skate against the backdrop of the Manhattan skyline at this romantic outdoor rink—or, in summer, roller skate or blade.

🕐 Mon–Tue 10–2.30, Wed–Thu 10–10, Fri–Sat 10am–11pm, Sun 10–9 💷 Adult $8.50–$11, skate rental $4.75 🚇 59th Street/Fifth Avenue (N, R, W) 🚌 M5

SOCCER

METROSTARS
Giants Stadium, Continental Airlines Arena
Tel 1-888-4METROTIX
www.metrostars.com
Despite the triumph of the women's soccer team in the World Cup, soccer has failed to capture the

The city offers a wide range of skating options

imagination of the American public. The MetroStars' dismal performance hasn't helped. Coach Bob Bradley looks to a better future with newcomers Jeff Agoos and Gilberto Flores.

💷 $20–$75 🚌 NJ Transit bus from 42nd Street/Port Authority Bus Terminal at Eighth Avenue

SPORTS CENTER

CHELSEA PIERS
Piers 59–62 between 17th and 23rd streets
Tel 212/336-6000 or 212/336-6400 for golf, 212/336-6500 for field house, 212/336-6100 for Skyrink
www.chelseapiers.com
This is the city's ultimate sports facility, where many sports are

catered to. There's also a four-tiered golf driving range, basketball and sand volleyball courts, and a huge gym.

🕐 Daily 6am–midnight 💷 Day pass $50, golf $20 minimum for 80 balls after 5pm (118 balls before 5pm), ice-skating adult $10 🚇 23rd Street (C, E) 🚌 M23

TENNIS

DEPARTMENT OF PARKS AND RECREATION
830 Fifth Avenue at 64th Street
Tel 212/360-8111 or 212/408-0243 for pool information
www.centralparknyc.org
The best tennis courts are: Central Park and 93rd Street (tel 212/280-0205), 30 hard courts; Riverside Drive and 96th Street (tel 212/496-2006), eight clay courts; Riverside Drive and 119th Street (tel 212/496-2006), eight hard courts.

🕐 Tennis courts: early Apr–late Nov; office: Mon–Fri 9–4, Sat 9–12 💷 Tennis $7 pass for one hour of play obtainable at office above or at Central Park courts 🚇 Fifth Avenue/59th Street (N, R, W) 🚌 M1, M2, M3, M4

U.S. OPEN TENNIS CHAMPIONSHIP
USTA National Tennis Center, Flushing Meadows–Corona Park, Queens
Tel 718/760-6200 or 516/354-2590
www.usopen.org or www.usta.com
This two-week tournament is one of four in tennis' Grand Slam. Tickets to any session admit you to major matches played in Arthur Ashe stadium, and also to other courts. You can see more tennis if you buy daytime tickets, since many of the outer courts are not used at night. Tickets go on sale at the end of April; most are sold via subscription and what remain are usually in the stratosphere—but that's less an issue for day sessions, when most of the action is on the outer courts.

🕐 Late Aug–end Sep 💷 $56–$104 🚇 Willets Pt/Shea Stadium (7) 🚆 LIRR to Shea Stadium

HEALTH AND BEAUTY

Almost every neighborhood in New York has a selection of health clubs with fitness equipment, classes and assorted frills—sometimes a pool. Massages, nutrition consultations and personal trainers may be available by appointment. Most offer day passes for visitors for a price (anywhere from $20 to $50). It's best to go at off-peak hours—between 12 and 2 and from 5 till 8 the clubs may be so crowded you have to sign up to use the machines.

The city has always had yoga studios and fancy hair salons, but it has seen an enormous growth of day spas and other pampering facilities. Some are world-class, like La Prairie in the Ritz; others cater to New Age constituencies, while still others hustle passers-by for a quick back massage. The Brazilian nail salons are considered extra-special.

HEALTH CLUBS

ASPHALT GREEN
555 East 90th Street between York and East End avenues
Tel 212/369-8890
www.asphaltgreen.org

Swimming is just one of the fitness options at Asphalt Green

This 5.5-acre (2.25ha) sports complex has Manhattan's only Olympic-size pool. It also has indoor and outdoor running tracks, fields for team sports, a large rooftop terrace with views of the East River, and a multi-level fitness center with 50-plus exercise classes.
🕐 Mon–Fri 5.30am–10pm, Sat–Sun 8–8 💧 Day pass $25 🚇 96th Street (6) 🚌 M15, M31, M86

BALLY TOTAL FITNESS
335 Madison Avenue at 43rd Street
Tel 212/983-5320
www.ballyfitness.com
This national chain has eight

facilities in Manhattan. The Madison Avenue club has an 80ft (24m) swimming pool plus cardio equipment, weights, and aerobics classes (kick-boxing, Pilates, step, yoga, spinning and kwando).
🕐 Mon–Fri 5.30am–10pm, Sat–Sun 9–6 💧 Day pass $25 🚇 42nd Street (4, 5, 6) 🚌 M1, M2, M3, M4, M42

CHELSEA PIERS
Piers 59–62 at 23rd Street and the Hudson River
Tel 212/336-6000
www.chelseapiers.com
The city's ultimate sports complex, built on four Hudson River piers, has facilities for 21 sports. In summer, the beach, sundecks, large pool and kayaking layout are inviting. There's a climbing wall as well as 200-meter and quarter-mile tracks, an ice rink, and rows of cardiovascular, circuit and strength-training equipment. There are courts for basketball, indoor sand volleyball and touch football, plus a boxing ring, golf driving range and batting cages. Some 125 classes a week offer everything from aerobics to yoga. Other facilities include a sports medicine clinic, café and spa.
🕐 Mon–Fri 6am–11pm, Sat–Sun 8am–9pm 💧 Day pass $50 🚇 23rd Street (C, E) 🚌 M23

CRUNCH FITNESS
54 East 13th Street between Broadway and University Place
Tel 212/475-2018
www.crunch.com
Crunch, which has 12 locations in the city, is

The Greenhouse Spa is one of the city's finest

the very popular premier brand of Bally Fitness. Each place has whimsy and pop style. The instructors are first rate, and the studio is known for its innovative classes, from street stomp to cycle karaoke.
🕐 Mon–Fri 6am–10pm, Sat–Sun 8–8 💧 Day pass $24 🚇 14th Street/Union Square (L, N, Q, R, W, 4, 5, 6) 🚌 M1, M2, M3, M5

EQUINOX FITNESS CLUB

521 Fifth Avenue at 44th Street
Tel 212 972-8000
www.equinoxfitness.com
All 17 Equinox clubs in
Manhattan are sleek
and sophisticated and
almost invariably offer
spinning, Pilates, yoga,
cardio-boxing and cardio
machines.
Mon–Thu 5.30am–10pm, Fri
5.30am–9pm Day pass $35
42nd Street/Grand Central (4, 5, 6)
M1, M2, M3, M4, M5

NEW YORK HEALTH AND RACQUET CLUB

24 East 13th Street between Fifth
Avenue and University Place
Tel 212/924-4600
www.HRCBEST.com
The nine Manhattan branches
of this chain offer sports,
equipment and classes
from tai chi and karate to
aqua-cise. Each branch has
a pool, and the one at 57th
and Lexington comes
complete with a full spa.
Members have access to a
beach and tennis club in
New Rochelle, as well as a
yacht docked at 23rd Street.
Mon–Fri 6am–11pm, Sat–Sun
7am–8pm Day pass $50 14th
Street/Union Square (L, N, Q, R, W, 4, 5,
6) M1, M2, M3, M5

NEW YORK SPORT CLUBS

128 Eighth Avenue at 16th Street
Tel 212/627-0065
www.nysc.com
This chain has close to
100 locations around town,
mostly aerobic studios
with cardio-fitness machines
and free weights, plus a
full program of exercise
classes—cardio-kick-boxing,
step, abs, Pilates and yoga.
Massage treatments are
usually available, too.
Mon–Thu 6am–11pm, Fri
6am–10pm, Sat–Sun 8am–9pm
Day pass $25 18th Street (1, 9)
M20

SPORTS CLUB/LA

330 East 61st Street between First and
Second avenues
Tel 212/355-5100
45 Rockefeller Plaza
Tel 212/218-8600
www.TheSportsClubLA.com
The spectacular 61st Street
location of this urban country
club occupies 150,000 square
feet (13,500sq m) and offers
50 fitness classes, five squash
courts, two basketball courts,
a climbing wall, weights, and a
cardio deck with more than
200 machines. There's even
rooftop tennis and golf.
Mon–Fri 5am–11pm, Sat–Sun 7am–
9pm Day pass $35 with member
only 59th Street (4, 5, 6) M15

*Stretch your muscles while
enjoying great views at Clay*

SPAS AND TREATMENT CENTERS

AVON SALON AND SPA

725 Fifth Avenue between 56th and
57th streets, sixth floor
Tel 212/755-2866
www.avonsalonandspa.com
Many clients come here
for eyebrow shaping by
the self-styled Queen of the
Arch, Eliza Petrescu. There's
also a hair salon, plus facials,
massage, waxing and
body treatments.
Mon 8–6, Tue–Fri 7.30am–8pm, Sat
8.30–6, Sun 11–6 Facial $100–$180,
massage $100–$140 59th
Street/Fifth Avenue (N, R, W) M1,
M2, M3, M4, M57

CLAY

25 West 14th Street between Fifth and
Sixth avenues
Tel 212/206-9200
www.insideclay.com
Sleek, serene and minimal,
Clay combines bodywork
therapies with exercise
(weights, cardio-boxing,
yoga). The fireside lounge
and rooftop deck are bonuses.
Mon–Thu 8am–9.30pm, Fri 8–8,
Sat–Sun 9.30–8 Massage $110–$185
14th Street/Union Square (L, N, Q,
R, W, 4, 5, 6) M2, M3, M5, M14

CORNELIA DAY RESORT

663 Fifth Avenue between 52nd and
53rd streets
Tel 212/871-3050
www.cornelia.com
New York's weather and urban
ambience does not lend itself
to outdoor pampering à la
California. That may be
changing with the rooftop
massages available here and
the underwater shiatsu
massage offered in the watsu
pool. It also offers a full range
of spa services—facials, algae
wraps and massages.
Mon–Fri 9–9, Sat 9–7, Sun 11–6
Facial $175, massage from $150
5th Avenue/53rd Street (E, V)
M1, M2, M3, M4

THE GREENHOUSE SPA

127 East 57th Street between Park and
Lexington avenues
Tel 212/644-4449
www.greenhousespa.com
This premier spa uses
Elemis skin and body care
products. Bask in relaxing
treatments such as coconut
rub and milk ritual wrap,
and lime and ginger salt
glow. Massage and
hydro-massage are available.
Mon–Fri 9–8, Sat 9–6, Sun 10–6
Facial $75–$135, massage
$65–$160 59th Street/Lexington
Avenue (N, R, W), 59th Street (4, 5, 6)

INSPARATIONS AT THE 92ND STREET Y

139 Lexington Avenue at 92nd Street
Tel 212/415-5795
www.insparations.com

People on the run appreciate the mini-facial ($45) and hot-rock massages that are available.

🕐 Tue–Fri 9–9, Sat 12–8, Sun 10–7, Mon 11–7 💆 Facial $90–$130, massage $75–$130 🚇 86th Street (4, 5, 6) 🚌 M98, M101, M102, M103

J. SISTERS

35 West 57th Street between Fifth and Sixth avenues
Tel 212/750-2485
www.jsisters.com

In 1987, seven Brazilian sisters opened a nail salon to deliver "serious" Brazilian-style manicures and pedicures. They have now branched out to provide superb bikini waxing, facials and massage.

🕐 Tue, Fri–Sat 8–5.30, Wed–Thu 8–7.30 💆 Manicure $45–$55, pedicure $65–$75, facial $60–$90 🚇 57th Street (F), 59th Street/Fifth Avenue (N, R, W) 🚌 M1, M2, M3, M4, M5, M6, M7, M57

JENIETTE

58 East 13th Street between University Place and Broadway
Tel 212/529-1616
www.jeniette.com

Since 1979 this East Village salon has been providing good manicures, pedicures facials and massage at much lower prices than uptown. It uses Dinur products.

🕐 Mon–Wed, Fri–Sat 10–7, Thu 10–8, Sun 11–6 💆 Manicure $10–$18, facial $60, massage $75–$120 🚇 14th Street/Union Square (L, N, Q, R, W, 4, 5, 6) 🚌 M1, M5, M6, M14

LE PETIT SPA

140 East 34th Street between Lexington and Third avenues
Tel 212/685-0773
www.lepetitspanyc.com

This small salon offers a full array of treatments. Fit in a mini facial or body polish when you're in a rush.

🕐 Daily 10–8 💆 Facial $100, massage $75–$95 🚇 33rd Street (6) 🚌 M98, M101, M102, M103, M34

OASIS DAY SPA

108 East 16th Street near Union Square, 2nd floor
Tel 212/254-7722
www.nydayspa.com

Candlelight and soft music add to the charms of this popular spa, offering 15 massage treatments.

🕐 Mon–Fri 10am–10.15pm, Sat–Sun 9am–9.15pm 💆 Facial $95–$200, massage $85–$160 🚇 14th Street/Union Square (L, N, Q, R, W, 4, 5, 6) 🚌 M1, M2, M3

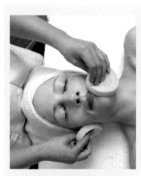

Feel the stress ebb away at Oasis Day Spa

PAUL LABRECQUE SALON AND SPA

171 East 65th Street between Lexington and Third avenues
Tel 212/595-0099
www.paullabrecque.com

London-trained Labrecque has coiffed the rich and famous for decades. The ultimate facial at this attractive salon provides five levels of hydration. It also offers sensual body treatments and massage treatments (Thai, Reiki, rolfing, phyto-essence and acupuncture).

🕐 Mon–Fri 8am–9pm, Sat 9–8, Sun 10–8 💆 Facial $110–$160, massage $105–$160 🚇 68th Street (6) 🚌 M98, M101, M102, M103

RESCUE BEAUTY LOUNGE

34 Gansevoort Street between Hudson and Greenwich streets, second floor
Tel 212/206-6409
www.rescuebeauty.com

Rescue takes a medical approach to pampering, maintaining hospital standards of cleanliness. This is the place to get the ultimate manicure or pedicure.

🕐 Tue–Fri 11–8, Sat–Sun 10–6 💆 Manicure $23–$50, pedicure $45–$100, facial $85–$160, massage $120 🚇 14th Street (A, C, E), Eighth Avenue (L) 🚌 M11, M20

SOHO SANCTUARY

119 Mercer Street near Prince Street
Tel 212/334-5550
www.sohosanctuary.com

This spa and yoga studio achieved a reputation when Julia Roberts made frequent visits. It offers facials, body wraps and massage.

🕐 Tue–Fri 10–9, Sat 10–6, Sun 12–6, Mon 3–9 💆 Facial $110–$170, massage $110–$175 🚇 Prince Street (N, R, W) 🚌 M1, M6

SPAS IN HOTELS

Many hotels in the city have spas and fitness centers. Below are two of the best.

AFFINIA SPA AND WELLNESS CENTER

Benjamin Hotel, 125 East 50th Street between Lexington and Third avenues, third floor
Tel 212/715-2517
www.affiniaspa.com

Treatments available include aromatherapy massage, reflexology and hydrotherapy.

LA PRAIRIE SPA

Ritz Carlton, 50 Central Park South at Sixth Avenue
Tel 212/521-6135
www.ritzcarlton.com/new_york_central_park/spa

Treatments include detoxification, shiatsu massage and exfoliation.

CHILDREN'S NEW YORK

With its towering buildings, vibrant streets, sights and sounds, New York is wonderful for kids. Even a ride on the subway is exciting. A few of the family-friendly institutions are listed below. Also check the Sports and Activities section and the Shopping section (especially Niketown and the Disney Store). In addition, many seasonal events appeal to kids—performances of the Big Apple Circus and the *Nutcracker* at Christmas as well as the Radio City Christmas Spectacular; the Ringling Brothers' circus in spring; and the parades and fairs that take place throughout the year. As you research your visit, it's worth calling concert halls and museums in advance to find out what special events will be on while you're in town; reserve ahead for those that interest you.

FILM, TV, THEATER AND MUSIC

BACKSTAGE AT LINCOLN CENTER
Tel 212/769-7020
These one-hour tours, run by

Theater tailor-made for children at the New Victory

the Opera Guild, take you backstage to the shops where the sets and costumes are made and to rehearsal rooms and storage areas.
🕐 Oct–Jun (weekdays 3.30, Sun 10.30). Advance reservations needed ✋ Adult $10, child (6 and up) $5 (under 6 not admitted) 🚇 66th Street (1, 9) 🚌 M5, M7, M104

LITTLE ORCHESTRA SOCIETY
Avery Fisher Hall, Lincoln Center, Broadway and West 65th Street
Tel 212/971-9500
www.littleorchestra.org
This company organizes two family concert series: Happy Concerts (children aged 6 to

12) and the Lollipops (tots aged 3 to 5).
✋ $10–$35 🚇 66th Street (1, 9) 🚌 M5, M7, M104

LOEWS IMAX THEATER
1998 Broadway and 68th Street
Tel 212/336 5020
For some kids, the 3-D IMAX experience is too intense; those who tolerate it are usually enthralled. The screen is eight stories high. Programming changes roughly every two months.
✋ Adult $12, child $9 🚇 66th Street (1, 9) 🚌 M5, M7, M104

NBC STUDIO TOUR
30 Rockefeller Plaza, 49th Street between Fifth and Sixth avenues
Tel 212/664-3700
www.shopnbc.com
Hour-long tours of the NBC network's studios begin with a short video of Katie Couric and Matt Lauer tracing the story of NBC from its origins in radio to the present. Visitors peek into studios and also see how shows are produced. The tour ends in a theater with a demonstration of HD TV.
🕐 Mon–Sat 8.30–5.30, Sun 9.30–4.30 ✋ Adult $17.95, child (6–16) $15.50 (under 6 not admitted) 🚇 47th–50th streets/Rockefeller Center (B, D, F, V) 🚌 M1, M2, M3, M4, M5, M6, M7

NEW VICTORY THEATER
209 West 42nd Street between Broadway and Eighth Avenue
Tel 212/239-6200
www.newvictory.org

The city's first theater designed for family programming is an intimate space and a must. All types of theater take place here. Every show is age rated from 4 to 12-plus, but shows here suit all ages.
✋ $10–$30 🚇 42nd Street/Times Square (N, Q, R, S, W, 1, 2, 3, 7, 9) 🚌 M6, M7

PAPER BAG PLAYERS
Sylvia and Danny Kaye Playhouse Hunter College, East 68th Street between Park and Lexington avenues
Tel 212/772-4448
The members of this beloved troupe make their costumes and sets out of cardboard

Liberty Helicopters offer a view with a difference

and paper bags and perform original offbeat plays and revues.
🕐 Jan–Mar Sat 2, Sun 1 and 3 ✋ $20–$25 🚇 68th Street (6) 🚌 M1, M2, M3, M4, M98, M101, M102, M103

TADA THEATER AND DANCE ALLIANCE
15 West 28th Street at Sixth Avenue
Tel 212/252-1619
www.tadatheater.com
Young professionals aged 8 to 17 put on entertaining shows and revues at this theater company-and-school.
✋ Adult $18, child $8 🚇 23rd Street (F, V) 🚌 M5, M6, M7

THEATREWORKS USA
Auditorium, Equitable Tower, 787 Seventh Avenue between West 51st and 52nd streets
Tel 212/627-7373
www.theatreworksusa.org
This group puts on plays and musicals for children based on such favorites as *The Lion, the Witch and the Wardrobe* and *Charlotte's Web.*
Sep–Apr Sat–Sun 12 or 2 (call ahead) $25 50th Street (1, 9), 49th Street (N, R, W) M6, M7

THE "TODAY SHOW"
NBC Studios, Rockefeller Plaza
Kids may enjoy crowding against the barriers for a chance to be seen on nationwide TV. Just show up at dawn at the corner of 49th Street and Rockefeller Plaza.
Mon–Fri 7–10 Free
47th–50th streets/Rockefeller Center (B, D, F, V) M1, M2, M3, M4

YOUNG PEOPLE'S CONCERTS
Lincoln Center
Tel 212/875-5656 or 212/721-6500
www.newyorkphilharmonic.org or www.lincolncenter.org
Sponsored by the New York Philharmonic, these concerts introduce kids to great artists and great music. Children can attend demonstrations and workshops given by members of the orchestra. There's also a program for teens.
Four Saturdays during the year $6–$25 66th Street (1, 9) M5, M7, M104

MUSEUMS AND ATTRACTIONS

AMERICAN MUSEUM OF THE MOVING IMAGE
35th Avenue at 36th Street, Astoria, Queens
Tel 718/784-0077
www.movingimage.us
The permanent exhibit traces the process of making, producing and distributing movies and TV programs. Children enjoy the interactive exhibits and making their own short animations.
Wed–Thu noon–5, Fri 12–8,
Sat–Sun 11.30 6 Adult $10, child (5–18) $5, under 5 free Broadway (N), Steinway Street (R, G) Q66, Q101 or Queens Artlink

AMERICAN MUSEUM OF NATURAL HISTORY
▷ 68–72

BROOKLYN MUSEUM OF ART
▷ 153

CHILDREN'S MUSEUM OF MANHATTAN
212 West 83rd Street between Broadway and Amsterdam Avenue
Tel 212/721-1223
www.cmom.org
The Children's Museum of Manhattan was designed to

Educational fun at the Children's Museum of Manhattan

be a first museum experience for kids from 10 months to 10 years old. It has plenty of sensory exhibits, plus a regular schedule of sing-alongs and other wonderful programs.
Sep–late Jun Wed–Sun 10–5; late Jun–end Aug Tue–Sun 10–5 Adult $8, child (under 1) free 86th Street (1, 9), 81st Street (B, C) M7, M11, M79, M104

CHILDREN'S MUSEUM OF THE ARTS
182 Lafayette Street between Broome and Grand streets
Tel 212/274-0986
Children aged from 1 to 11 are welcome at this
playground-cum-museum, which offers all kinds of hands-on art projects.
Wed–Sun noon–5 $6, child (under 1) free Spring Street (6), Prince Street (N, R) M1

CONEY ISLAND
▷ 152

ELLIS ISLAND
▷ 90–93

EMPIRE STATE BUILDING
▷ 94–96

FORBES MAGAZINE GALLERIES
▷ 99

GUGGENHEIM MUSEUM
▷ 110–111

INTREPID SEA, AIR AND SPACE MUSEUM
▷ 101

MADAME TUSSAUD'S
234 West 42nd Street between Eighth and Seventh avenues
Tel 800/246-8872
www.madame-tussauds.com
The New York version of this famous London waxworks museum opened in 2000. It has the usual collection of lifelike figures (here, geared to a New York audience, you'll see such luminaries as Joan Rivers, Woody Allen and Michael Jordan).
Sun–Thu 10–8, Fri–Sat 10–10 Adult $28, child (4–12) $22, under 4 free 42nd Street (A, C, E), 42nd Street/Times Square (N, Q, R, S, W, 1, 2, 3, 7, 9) M5, M6, M7, M42

METROPOLITAN MUSEUM OF ART
▷ 114–119

MUSEUM OF THE CITY OF NEW YORK
▷ 123

MUSEUM OF COMIC AND CARTOON ART
594 Broadway (4th floor) between Houston and Prince
Tel 212/254-3511
www.moccany.org

Adults seeking to relive their childhoods and older kids who love their super heroes enjoy coming here. The museum aims to promote the art of telling stories through pictures. Exhibits are dedicated to the works of such seminal figures as Harvey Kurtzman, founder of *MAD* magazine, or are theme-oriented like the recent Toon Town exhibit, which explored the love affair that cartoonists have had with New York City.

🕐 Fri–Mon 12–5 💷 $3, under 12 free 🚇 Broadway-Lafayette (B, D, F, V, 6), Prince Street (N, R, W) 🚌 M1, M6

MUSEUM OF MODERN ART
▷ 125

MUSEUM OF TELEVISION AND RADIO
▷ 124

NEW YORK HALL OF SCIENCE
47-01 111th Street at 48th Avenue, Flushing Meadows–Corona Park, Queens
Tel 718/699-0005
www.nyscience.org
This museum was one of the first hands-on science museums in the US. The entire basement is filled with interactive exhibits. Permanent exhibits demonstrate biology, chemistry and physics, and special shows explore such topics as Optical Illusions. There's also a large outdoor science playground.

🕐 Mon–Thu 9.30–2, Fri 9.30–5, Sat–Sun 10–6 💷 Adult $11, child (5–17) $8 (free Fri 2–5, Sun 10–11) 🚇 111th Street (7) 🚌 Q23, Q48

NEW YORK TRANSIT MUSEUM
Boerum Place and Schermerhorn Street, Brooklyn
Tel 718/694-1600
www.mta.nyc.ny.us/mta/museum
Vintage subway cars and other interactive exhibits tell the story of the subway.

🕐 Tue–Fri 10–4, Sat–Sun noon–5 💷 Adult $5, child (3–17) $3, under 3 free 🚇 Borough Hall (2, 3, 4, 5), Hoyt Street (A, C, G), Jay Street (F)

SONY WONDER TECHNOLOGY LAB
Sony Plaza, East 56th Street between Madison and Fifth avenues
Tel 212/833-8100
www.sonywondertechlab.com
Interactive exhibits on four floors here demonstrate the latest in communications, robotics, medical technology and entertainment. It's not as much of a hard sell as you might expect. Reservations are needed and can be made two weeks in advance.

🕐 Tue–Sat 10–5, Sun noon–5 💷 Free 🚇 Fifth Avenue/53rd Street (E, V), Fifth Avenue/59th Street (N, R, W) 🚌 M1, M2, M3, M4

The New York Transit Museum is perfect for would-be drivers

SOUTH STREET SEAPORT MUSEUM AND MARKETPLACE
▷ 134–135

STATUE OF LIBERTY
▷ 136–137

TIMES SQUARE
▷ 138–140

PARKS AND GARDENS
BROOKLYN BOTANIC GARDEN
▷ 152

CENTRAL PARK
▷ 78–83

NEW YORK BOTANICAL GARDEN
Kazimiroff (Southern) Boulevard at 200th Street, Bronx
Tel 718/817-8700
www.nybg.org
This lovely retreat with 250 acres (101ha) has two special areas for kids—the 8-acre (3-ha) Adventure Garden, and the Family Garden. The conservatory is beautiful and so are the many specialty gardens.

🕐 Apr–Oct Tue–Sun 10–6; Nov–Mar 10–5 💷 Adult $13, child (2–12) $5 (less for grounds only) 🚇 Bedford Park Boulevard (B, D, 4) then walk, or take Bx 26 bus 🚌 Bx 19, Bx 26 🚉 Botanical Garden Station (Metro North)

WAVE HILL
675 West 249th Street at Independence Avenue, Bronx
Tel 718-549-3200
www.wavehill.org
The setting of this park in the toney Riverdale section of the Bronx is spectacular. So are the beautiful gardens and greenhouses. On weekends, there's often a Family Art Project scheduled.

🕐 Tue–Sun 9–5.30 (Oct 15–Apr 14 until 4.30) 💷 Adult $4, child $2, under 6 free (free Tue and mornings on Sat) 🚇 231st Street (1, 9), then Bx 7 or Bx 10 🚌 Bx 7, Bx 10 🚉 Riverdale (Metro North, tel 212/532-4900)

TOY STORE
FAO SCHWARZ
767 Fifth Avenue between 58th and 59th streets
Tel 212/644-9400
www.fao.com
This is the toy store to end all toy stores. It's a fantasyland for kids and adults alike, with departments dedicated to everything from antique and classic toys to magic sets.

🕐 Mon–Sat 10–7, Sun 11–6 🚇 Fifth Avenue/59th Street (N, R, W) 🚌 M1, M2, M3, M4

TRIPS AND TOURS

CIRCLE LINE CRUISES

Pier 83, West 42nd Street and Hudson River
Tel 212/563-3200
www.circleline.com

Circling around Manhattan in a boat is the best way to grasp the contours of the island and the extraordinary city piled high upon it. Depending on the attention span of your kids, you can opt for the shorter two-hour afternoon trip or the longer three-hour version. The narration can be great or mediocre, but the fresh air, the passing river craft and the sights along the way make it fun. The same company also runs day-long tours up the Hudson River.

Call for departure times and schedules. Operates Thu–Mon only in winter
Adult $28, child (under 12) $15 ($23/12 respectively for 2-hr cruise)
42nd Street (A, C, E) then M42
M42, M50

LIBERTY HELICOPTERS

West 30th Street and Twelfth Avenue
Tel 212/967-6464
www.libertyhelicopters.com

Helicopters take off from the heliport on 5-, 10- or 15-minute tours hovering above the city and the Hudson River. If you can afford it, why not?
$63 (5 min), $108 (10 min), $169 (15 min) 34th Street (A, C, E)
M11, M34

MADISON SQUARE GARDEN

4 Penn Plaza, Seventh Avenue between West 31st and 34th streets
Tel 212/465-5800

One-hour tours go to the locker rooms, the luxury boxes and the sports bar and restaurant of this vast 20,000-seat arena, home to the Knicks and Liberty basketball teams and to the Rangers hockey team. Or just see a game or special event. The Westminster Dog Show and the Westminster Cat Show are sure-fire hits.

Daily 10–3 Adult $17, child (2–12) $12, under 2 free 34th Street (A, C, E), 34th Street/Penn Station (1, 2, 3, 9) M10, M20, M34

ROOSEVELT ISLAND TRAM

Second Avenue at 60th Street
Tel 212/832-4555
www.rioc.com

Kids who have never ridden a cable-car at a ski resort will get a kick out of this aerial tramway trip across the East River and back.

Sun–Thu 6am–2am, Fri–Sat 6am–3.30am $2
59th Street (4, 5, 6) M15, M57

STATEN ISLAND FERRY

Whitehall Terminal, 1 Whitehall Street
Tel 718/727-2508 or 718/815-2628

The view from the decks of the harbor, the Statue of Liberty and the Lower Manhattan skyline is stunning—and free.

Spectacular views from the Staten Island ferry

Daily Free South Ferry (1, 9), Whitehall Street (N, R, W)
M1, M6, M15

YANKEE STADIUM
▷ 158

WILDLIFE ATTRACTIONS

BRONX ZOO
▷ 157

CENTRAL PARK WILDLIFE CENTER

Fifth Avenue and 64th Street
Tel 212/439-6500
www.wcs.org

A perfectly sized zoo for kids, this Manhattan classic is populated by youngsters' favorites—sea lions, polar bears, monkeys, pandas, penguins and tropical birds. The Tisch Children's Zoo is great for little ones, with fish, birds and llamas, and pigs and other domestic animals.

Daily 10–5 (Sat, Sun and holidays until 5.30) Adult $6, child (3–12) $1, under 3 free Fifth Avenue (N, R), 68th Street (6) M1, M2, M3, M4

NEW YORK AQUARIUM

Surf Avenue and West 8th Street, Coney Island, Brooklyn
Tel 718-265-3400
www.nyaquarium.com

There are daily dolphin and sea lion shows in summer at this small park, which also houses penguins, walruses, Beluga whales, sharks and seals—300 species in all. Most exhibits are outside. In the Discovery Center kids can pick up starfish, crabs and other small sea creatures.

Memorial Day–Labor Day, Mon–Fri 10–6, Sat–Sun 10–7; Apr–Memorial Day and Labor Day–Oct 31 Mon–Fri 10–5, Sat–Sun 10–5.30; Nov–Mar daily 10–4.30 Adult $11, child (2–12) $7, under 2 free Stillwell Avenue (D), 8th Street (F, Q) From Manhattan, call 718/330-1234

CONCERTS FOR KIDS

The following venues offer musical and performing arts series or single performances for families at various times of year:
Brooklyn Center for the Performing Arts at Brooklyn College (tel 718-951-4500, www. brooklyncenter.com); Carnegie Hall, Seventh Avenue and 57th Street (tel 212/247-7800, www.carnegiehall.org); Metropolitan Opera, Lincoln Center (tel 212/769-7008, www.lincolncenter.org); Jazz at Lincoln Center (tel 212/258-9800, www.jalc.org); Chamber Music Society, Lincoln Center (tel 212/875-5788, www. chambermusicsociety.org).

FESTIVALS AND EVENTS

Note that the Convention & Visitors Bureáu often has information about these events. Call 212/484-1222 or check www.nycvisit.com. Other useful websites are www.nyc.com and www.nyctourist.com.

FEBRUARY

CHINESE NEW YEAR
Depends on the lunar calendar
Firecrackers blast and dragon and lion dancers sashay through the streets of Chinatown.
☎ 212/484-1222
www.chinatown-online.com

NEW YORK ARMORY ANTIQUES SHOW
Second weekend
The city's most prestigious antiques fair in the Seventh Regiment Armory.

Independence Day sees a spectacular firework display

☎ 212/472-1180 (during show only); 212/484-1222

WESTMINSTER KENNEL DOG SHOW
Second weekend
More than 2,500 canines strut their stuff at Madison Square Garden.
☎ 800/455-3647
www.westminsterkennelclub.org

MARCH

ST PATRICK'S DAY PARADE
March 17
Bagpipers and bands, politicians and New York's finest march down Fifth Avenue from 86th to 44th streets celebrating the patron saint of Ireland.
☎ 212/484-1222
www.saintpatricksdayparade.com

MARCH–APRIL

EASTER PARADE
Depending on when Easter falls
People with a bent for fashion stroll down Fifth Avenue between 49th and 57th streets showing off their often wacky and wonderful hats.

APRIL

NEW YORK INTERNATIONAL AUTO SHOW
10 days inc. last two weekends in April
Heaven for car enthusiasts.
Jacob Javits Convention Center
☎ 800/282-3336
www.autoshowny.com,
www.javitscenter.com

MACY'S FLOWER SHOW
Last two weeks
More than 30,000 varieties of flower are arrayed in the store in celebration of spring.
☎ 212/494-4495

CHERRY BLOSSOM FESTIVAL
Late April, depending on when trees flower
A range of traditional Japanese activities and performances take place against a backdrop of gorgeous pink cherry blossoms in the Brooklyn Botanic Garden.
☎ 718/623-7200
www.bbg.org

MAY

NINTH AVENUE INTERNATIONAL FOOD FESTIVAL
Second or third weekend
Between 37th and 57th streets, Ninth Avenue is lined with stands selling food of all kinds.

Musical entertainment, too.
☎ 212/484-1222
www.9th-ave.com

FLEET WEEK
Third week
The tall ships and aircraft carriers sail in a majestic parade into New York Harbor and up the Hudson River. The festival includes military demonstrations, tugs of war and cooking fests, and culminates in a Memorial Day celebration. The best part is the posses of sailors roaming New York City streets in their crisp white uniforms.
☎ 212/245-0072
www.fleetweek.com

Macy's Flower Show is a riot of color

WASHINGTON SQUARE
Outdoor Art Exhibit Memorial Day weekend
The streets around Washington Square are lined with artists, photographers and craftspeople selling their work.
☎ 212/982-6255
www.nycgv.com

JUNE

BELMONT STAKES
First weekend in June
The last leg of the Triple Crown is run at Belmont on Long Island.
☎ 516/488-6000
www.nyracing.com

PUERTO RICAN DAY PARADE
Second weekend in June
The city is awash with Puerto Rican flags.
☎ 212/484-1222

LESBIAN AND GAY PRIDE PARADE
Last Sunday in June
The flamboyant parade from 52nd Street to Greenwich Village, via Fifth Avenue, is the culmination of a week of gay-oriented celebrations.
☎ 212/807-7433
www.nycpride.org

JULY

INDEPENDENCE DAY HARBOR FESTIVAL AND FIREWORKS
July 4
New York City celebrates the nation's birth with a festival in Lower Manhattan and some spectacular fireworks launched from barges in the East River.
☎ 212/484-1222

AUGUST

HARLEM WEEK
Most of August
A host of Harlem events—film, jazz and food festivals among them—celebrate the culture and heritage of African-Americans and Hispanics.
☎ 212/862-8477 or 212/484-1222
www.harlemdiscover.com

SEPTEMBER

WEST INDIAN PARADE AND CARNIVAL
Labor Day
Thousands flock to Brooklyn to see the dancers and bands sashaying along to reggae, soca and calypso. Caribbean food adds to the festivities.
☎ 212/484-1222

WIGSTOCK
Labor Day
An informal East Village gathering of transvestites has become a major event. Venues change, but the biggest party is usually at the 13th Street pier on the west side of Manhattan.
www.wigstock.nu www.gaycenter.org

FEAST OF SAN GENNARO
Eleven days including the first and second weekend
The patron saint of Naples is paraded down Mulberry Street at this fiesta, with all kinds of Italian food and street entertainment.
☎ 212/484-1222
www.sangennaro.org

NEW YORK FILM FESTIVAL
17 days in late September or early October
The Film Society of Lincoln Center organizes this major film festival. The hub is the Walter Reade Theatre.
☎ 212/875-5600
www.filmlinc.com

Harlem Week runs throughout August

OCTOBER

BLESSING OF THE ANIMALS
First Sunday
At churches throughout the city, animals are blessed on St. Francis Day. The biggest event takes place at the Cathedral of St. John the Divine. People bring their pets.
☎ 212/316-7540
www.stjohndivine.org

HALLOWEEN PARADE
What started as an impromptu procession of drag queens in Greenwich Village has become a huge event with big-name sponsors. The costumes are amazing, but line up early to get a glimpse.
☎ 212/484-1222
www.halloween-nyc.com

NOVEMBER

NEW YORK CITY MARATHON
First weekend
Thousands of runners thunder across the Queensborough Bridge into Manhattan and race for the finish in Central Park.
☎ 212/423-2249
www.nyrrc.org

MACY'S THANKSGIVING DAY PARADE
Last Thursday
Families line the route from 77th Street and Central Park West to Herald Square to see the immense helium balloons.
☎ 212/484-1222

DECEMBER

LIGHTING OF THE CHRISTMAS TREE
Usually the first week in December
It's a media event, usually starring popular singers. Stake out your place early—or avoid the area altogether because crowds make it impossible to get through.
Rockefeller Center
☎ 212/332-6868
www.rockefellercenter.com

RADIO CITY SPECTACULAR
Through December 30
Busloads of revelers come to the city to see the Rockettes kick up a storm in their stylish chorus line for this seasonal show, which always includes a Parade of the Wooden Soldiers.
☎ 212/247-4777
www.radiocity.com

NEW YEAR'S EVE CELEBRATION
December 31
Times Square fills with thousands of partyers who show up to watch the ball drop announcing the official start of the next year.

New York is best explored on foot and this section describes 10 walks that take in the most interesting parts of the city. The locations of the walks are marked on the map on the inside front cover of the book.

These pages also give suggestions for excursions outside the city center.

Out and About

42ND STREET TO THE UN HEADQUARTERS

This walk along 42nd Street is architecturally fascinating, taking you past some of the finest buildings in the city, including nine designated landmarks. It's a great stroll for families. Times Square is exciting, surprising and lots of fun, with its flashing billboards, electronic news and stock tickers, and theater marquees and posters. The walk ends at the United Nations complex in a quiet, peaceful spot alongside the East River.

THE WALK

Distance: 1.5 miles (2.4km)

Allow: 2 hours

Start at 42nd Street/Port Authority subway

End at United Nations Building, 46th Street and First Avenue

HOW TO GET THERE

Subway: A

Bus: M15, M27, M42, M50

Leave the 42nd Street/Port Authority subway station and turn right, then proceed to the corner of West 42nd Street and Eighth Avenue.

1 Times Square and 42nd Street are famous today for their theaters, giant neon advertisements and megastores. Look back toward Ninth Avenue and you will catch a glimpse of an older side of the area: Holy Cross Church, one of its oldest buildings, dates from 1887.

Face east toward Seventh Avenue and you'll see the gleaming spire of the Chrysler Building in the distance. Walk east toward it, passing the AMC 25-screen multiplex, formerly the Empire Theater, on your right. Next door is Madame Tussaud's and next to that the Candler Building.

2 The Candler Building was named for a salesman for the Coca-Cola Company, which built this white terracotta tower in 1914. Two doors farther east is the New Amsterdam Theater, lavishly restored by the Walt Disney Company with an outstanding art nouveau foyer.

To see the building directly opposite, the New Victory Theater, you will need to cross this very busy street. So continue east to the traffic lights and use the crosswalk. The New Victory Theater, once known as Minsky's, was built in 1899 by Oscar Hammerstein I.

Restoration in 1995 has retained the beautiful old-fashioned interior. Continue east along West 42nd Street on this side of the street. Two doors east of the New Victory is the Reuters Building, and just east of that, Times Square (▷ 138–140), the triangle created by 42nd Street, Seventh Avenue and Broadway.

3 The 25-story tower at No. 1 Times Square became the home of the *New York Times* on December 31, 1904; the inaugural fireworks display was almost outshone by the illuminated globe lowered from the roof to herald the New Year. Almost 100 years later, the globe is still lowered every New Year's Eve, and for many New Yorkers and visitors Times Square is still the place to celebrate the holiday. The tower now functions as an office block.

On the southeast corner of West 42nd Street and Broadway, on the right, is the former Knickerbocker Hotel, commissioned by Colonel John Jacob Astor. The songwriter George M. Cohan lived here for a time. Now condominiums, there is talk of returning it to its original use.

Continue east along 42nd Street, crossing Broadway and Sixth Avenue (now officially known as Avenue of the Americas).

4 The flashy glass building leaning away from traffic on the north side of 42nd Street, 41 West 42nd Street, is the W. R. Grace Building, built in 1974 by architects Skidmore, Owings and Merrill.

Cross to the south side of the street and Bryant Park. Bryant Park sits on top of the subterranean stacks of the New York Public Library. During the World's Fair of 1853, the first to be held on United States soil, the

park was the site of the Crystal Palace. To reach the library, continue east along 42nd Street to Fifth Avenue. The library rises ahead of you on the southwest corner of 42nd Street and Fifth Avenue.

5 The majestic Beaux Arts New York Public Library (▷ 127) is guarded by two stone lions, Patience and Fortitude, who sit at the base of an imposing front stairway. Inside the building, the marble entrance area on the ground floor and the usually packed second-floor Main Reading Room are well worth a look.

Return to 42nd Street and continue along east, crossing Madison Avenue. On your left at Park Avenue is Grand Central Terminal. Cross the street and plunge in.

6 Inside Grand Central Terminal (▷ 102–104), the ceiling in the Main Concourse, decorated with the constellations of the zodiac, and the Dining Concourse downstairs, are a treat.

Back on 42nd Street, continue east to Lexington Avenue and the Chanin Building (on the southwest corner). Named for the brothers who developed the Times Square Theater District, the building has an art deco bas-relief on the facade, the work of Edward Trumbull. Continue to the northwest corner for the Chrysler Building.

7 The Chrysler Building (▷ 85) is one of the world's great 20th-century buildings—completed in 1929. Around the 30th floor a brick frieze depicts hubcaps and there are 9ft (3m)-high pineapples and giant stainless-steel radiator caps. The art deco foyer is made of African marble and chrome.

OUT AND ABOUT

Neon signs in Times Square

The magnificent Chrysler Building (above); flags from all over the world fly outside the United Nations Building (above right)

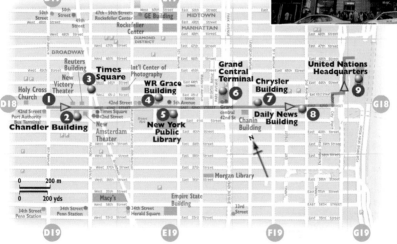

OUT AND ABOUT

Continue to 220 East 42nd Street and you'll come to the Daily News Building.

❽ The Daily News Building (▷ 87) was until 1995 the home of America's first tabloid newspaper.

Cross Second Avenue and continue on 42nd Street until you come to an area with steps on both sides of the street. These lead to the charming Tudor City apartments. From the top of the steps there's a splendid view of the United Nations Building, the East River and, beyond it, the borough of Queens. Turn left onto Tudor City Place, then right onto 43rd Street. Here, steps

lead down to Ralph Bunche Park. Cross United Nations Plaza (as First Avenue is called here) and turn left.

❾ At the United Nations Headquarters (▷ 144), view the General Assembly lobby (foyer) and stroll through the gardens. The entrance to the complex is on 46th Street. John D. Rockefeller, Jr. donated the $8.5 million needed for the site.

WHEN TO GO

Crowds will not be out in full force if you begin your walk on a weekday morning before 10. If you wish to visit the United Nations Building at the end of

the walk, arrive early—the last tour begins at 4.45pm.

WHERE TO EAT

The Dining Concourse at Grand Central Terminal, 42nd Street at Park Avenue (tel 212/340-2210), is just the place to refuel; for variety at affordable prices, it can't be beaten. The Oyster Bar & Restaurant (tel 212/490-6650), on the same level, offers excellent seafood, but at higher prices.

PLACES TO VISIT

Madame Tussaud's Wax Museum

✉ 234 West 42nd Street

☎ 212/512-9600

🕐 Sun–Thu 10–8, Fri–Sat 10–10

💲 Adults $28, child (4–12) $22

NORTHEAST CORNER OF CENTRAL PARK TO GRANT'S TOMB

This northeast corner of Central Park boasts beautiful gardens, commissioned by parks commissioner Robert Moses in 1936. You will also find a pretty pond, meandering paths, woods and picturesque waterfalls. Just outside the park is the largest church in the United States, the Cathedral Church of St. John the Divine. Nearby is Grant's Tomb, where the great Civil War general Ulysses S. Grant lies in rest.

THE WALK

Distance:	2 miles (3.2km)
Allow:	2 hours
Start at	Fifth Avenue and 105th Street
End at	122nd Street and Riverside Drive

HOW TO GET THERE

Bus: M4 to Madison Avenue and 104th Street; walk one block west to Fifth Avenue

Leave Madison Avenue by turning left onto East 105th Street, and walk one block west to the entrance gate of the Conservatory Garden, across the street from El Museo del Barrio (▷ 87) on Fifth Avenue.

❶ The Conservatory Garden— actually a complex of gardens — is at its best in July and August. As you enter, go straight toward the Classical fountain in the area known as the Italian Garden. Walk to your left to tour the maze-like English Garden. To the right of the Italian Garden is the lovely French Garden, with the charming Untermeyer Fountain (also called "Three Dancing Maidens"). Go past this fountain and walk through the gate toward the pond on your right, whose Dutch name, Harlem Meer, means "little sea."

Skirt around the pond, keeping to the right, with the pond on your left.

❷ The Charles A. Dana Discovery Center, halfway around the pond, displays natural history exhibits in a Victorian-style building.

Continue around the pond and keep to the right of the Lasker Pool and ice-skating rink. Take the path up some steps, then down a few steps, then to the right and walk under the Huddlestone Arch. Still keeping right, with a pretty little waterfall on your left, walk about 300 yards (273m), and you'll come to a very small rustic wooden bridge on your left. Cross the bridge, keeping to the right and you'll come to the Glenspan Arch. There's a small waterfall beyond the arch and a small pool is just beyond that. Ahead of you, a couple of paths lead to Central Park West, which you can see. The path to the right takes you out to 103rd Street and Central Park West.

On Central Park West, leave the park, turn right and follow the busy street, past Strangers Gate on the right, to Frederick Douglass Circle. Cross Central Park West at

110th Street and continue left around the circle until you come to the traffic lights. Cross 110th Street and immediately turn left. You are now in Harlem. Continue west on 110th Street for two blocks to Amsterdam Avenue, passing the entrance to Morningside Park. Turn right and walk north to 111th Street and the Cathedral Church of St. John the Divine.

❸ The enormous Cathedral Church of St. John the Divine (▷ 67) is well worth exploring. The Peace Fountain in the Children's Sculpture Garden depicts a bronze Michael the Archangel slaying the devil.

Leaving the cathedral, cross to the west side of Amsterdam Avenue and follow 112th Street west one block to Broadway. Tom's Restaurant, familiar to fans of the TV show "Seinfeld," is on the right. If you are tired and do not want to continue, catch a bus on the west side of Broadway or take the M4 to Midtown East or the M104 to Midtown West. To continue the walk, go north up Broadway to 122nd Street, passing Columbia University (▷ 77), New York City's oldest institution of higher learning, on your right. Turn left onto 122nd Street and walk two blocks west, passing the Manhattan School of Music on your left, to Riverside Drive. Riverside Church is on your left.

❹ From its 392ft (119m) tower, Riverside Church (▷ 126) offers a magnificent view across the Hudson River.

❺ Nearby is the General Grant National Memorial (▷ 99), where Grant and his wife, Julia,

The "Three Dancing Maidens" Fountain in the French Garden, part of the Conservatory Garden

OUT AND ABOUT

Cathedral of St. John the Divine (top); Columbia University is one of the most prestigious in the US (above)

rest side by side in two black sarcophagi. The Gaudí-style mosaic benches and tables surrounding the tombs are a good spot for a picnic.

From here you can walk back to Broadway and get the M4 or M104 bus downtown.

WHEN TO GO

Do this walk when the weather is pleasant and you want to have a quiet stroll away from crowds. Although the park is generally safe by day and is patrolled, this is not a walk to do alone. Pack a picnic to enjoy along the way.

WHERE TO EAT

Tom's Restaurant, 2880 Broadway at 112th Street (tel 212/864-6137).

PLACES TO VISIT

General Grant National Memorial
✉ Riverside Drive at West 122nd Street
☎ 212/666-1640
🕓 Daily 9–5

Riverside Church
✉ 490 Riverside Drive
☎ 212/870-6700
🕓 Gift shop: Tue–Thu, Sat 10.30–5, Wed 10.30–7, Sun 9.45–10.45, noon–4

The tranquil waterfall at Glenspan Arch (above right); the facade of Ulysses S. Grant's majestic tomb

OUT AND ABOUT

GREENWICH VILLAGE: IFC CENTER TO WASHINGTON SQUARE

Some of the country's finest literature and most radical ideas have developed in the area covered by this stroll. From the revolutionary Thomas Paine, who decried taxation without representation in colonial times, to the Stonewall rioters, whose protests sparked the gay liberation movement beginning in 1969, Village people have long been at the forefront of liberalism in America.

THE WALK

Distance: 1.9 miles (3km)

Allow: 2 hours

Start/End at West 4th Street/ Washington Square subway station

HOW TO GET THERE

Subway: A, C, E, F trains

Bus: M5, M6

Leave the subway on Avenue of the Americas (6th Avenue), cross the avenue at West 4th Street and position yourself in front of the IFC Center. Turn to your left (as you face the theater) and head along the avenue to Carmine Street. Turn right.

1 Along Carmine Street you pass first the Unoppressive, Non-Imperialist Bargain Books store on the left and then the House of Oldies Rare Records (on the right), both worth a browse.

Continue to Seventh Avenue South, cross it, and turn right. At St. Luke's Place (also called Leroy Street), go left. On your left you will pass J. J. Walker Park, once a graveyard, which locals claim is the resting place of the lost son of Louis XVI and Marie Antoinette. The brick and brownstone houses along this street date from the 1850s. Theodore Dreiser wrote *An American Tragedy* while he was living at No. 16. At Hudson Street, turn right, and walk two blocks to Barrow Street where you turn left.

2 On Barrow Street, take a look at the pretty garden behind the Church of St. Luke-in-the-Fields, built in 1822. The gate is on your right just before you reach Greenwich Street.

Backtrack along Barrow Street to Hudson Street, and stop for a snack or light lunch at the popular Belgian café, Petite

Abeille. Go across Hudson Street to 81 Barrow Street, where a plaque gives some architectural history of the area. Continue heading east on Barrow, then turn right onto Commerce Street. To the right at the bend in Commerce Street is the Cherry Lane Theater.

3 Cherry Lane Theater, an Off-Broadway venue, was founded in 1924 by the Pulitzer Prize-winning poet Edna St. Vincent Millay. Samuel Beckett's *Waiting for Godot* and *Endgame* both premiered here, as have plays by Edward Albee, David Mamet and many others.

Continue east on Commerce Street for one block and then turn right on Bedford Street. Notice the first two houses on your right.

4 The Isaacs-Hendricks House, 77 Bedford Street, is the oldest in the West Village. The narrowest house in the city is at No. 75, which was home to Edna St. Vincent Millay in 1923–24. The actor Cary Grant also lived here when he was young.

Return along Bedford Street, past Chumley's, a famous speakeasy, which put in an appearance in Warren Beatty's *Reds* and Woody Allen's *Sweet and Lowdown*. John Steinbeck, Eugene O'Neill, e e cummings and F. Scott Fitzgerald are among past patrons whose book jackets hang on the walls. It's great for drinks or dinner. When you reach Grove Street, turn left.

5 The pretty, leafy Grove Court, 10–12 Grove Street, was once dubbed "Ale Alley" because of the original Irish tenants' fondness for a brew.

Return to the corner of Grove and Bedford streets. The oldest

wooden house in the Village stands at 17 Grove Street. Continue one block roughly north on Bedford Street to Christopher Street, and turn right.

6 The long-established McNulty's Rare Teas and Choice Coffee Shop is at 109 Christopher Street, and from its looks it hasn't changed much since it opened in 1895. Go in and enjoy the aroma.

Continue east on Christopher Street and cross Seventh Avenue South.

7 Tiny Christopher Park, which was part of a tobacco farm from 1633 to 1638, is to your right. Stop for a rest on the bench next to George Segal's sculpture *Gay Liberation*, then look behind you at the Stonewall Bar and Club, where gay resistance to police arrests provoked the Stonewall Riot in 1969, the start of the gay rights movement. There's a modest plaque on the building. Christopher Street is also called Stonewall Place from the park up to Greenwich Avenue.

Walk along the Stonewall side of Christopher Street to Greenwich Avenue, and turn left. Go north one block, turn right onto West 10th Street and you'll come to Patchin Place; No. 4 was famously the home of e e cummings. Continue on West 10th Street one block east.

8 The ornate landmark Jefferson Market Library, at 425 Sixth Avenue, is a former courthouse built in 1877. The tower originally served as a fire-watching lookout.

Continue on West 10th Street, crossing Avenue of the Americas, until you come to Fifth Avenue.

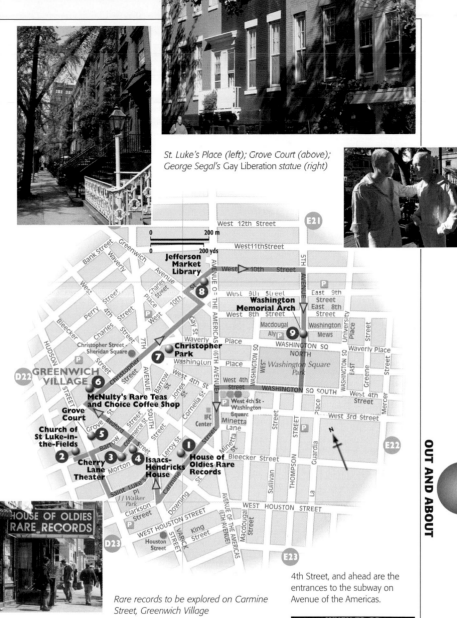

St. Luke's Place (left); Grove Court (above); George Segal's Gay Liberation statue (right)

Rare records to be explored on Carmine Street, Greenwich Village

Turn right and walk four blocks south on Fifth, through Washington Memorial Arch.

9 The original wooden arch was erected in 1889, in honor of George Washington 100 years after his inauguration. The marble Stanford White arch you see now was erected in 1895. The residential Washington Mews, on the east side of Fifth Avenue just north of the arch, were originally built as carriage houses for the wealthy residents of the fine town houses on Washington Square Park south of the arch. In the mews, John Dos Passos lived at No. 14A and Sherwood Anderson at No. 54. Washington Square Park, the focus of Greenwich Village, was once a potter's field and was the site of public executions until the 1800s.

Walk straight through the park to Washington Square South and turn right. This becomes West 4th Street, and ahead are the entrances to the subway on Avenue of the Americas.

WHEN TO GO

If you want to visit shops along the way, it is best to do this walk between 10 and 5 Monday to Saturday.

WHERE TO EAT

Petite Abeille, 466 Hudson Street (tel 212/741-6479, open 24 hours).
Chumley's, 86 Bedford Street (tel 212/675-4449).

SOHO'S PUCK BUILDING TO THE SOHO GRAND HOTEL

If you enjoy gallery-hopping or architecture, put this walk at the top of your list. SoHo, *South of Houston* (pronounced *how-stun*), a landmark district famous for the prefabricated cast-iron facades of its buildings, is full of galleries where some of the city's most interesting contemporary artists show their work.

THE WALK

Distance: 2 miles (3.2km)
Allow: 1.5 to 2 hours
Start at Broadway/Lafayette subway station
End at Canal Street subway station

HOW TO GET THERE

Subway: F and downtown 6
Bus: M6

Leave the Broadway/Lafayette Street subway and turn right (south) on Lafayette.

1 The restored Puck Building is at 295 Lafayette Street. Don't miss the statue of Puck, decorated with gold leaf, above the door. Here the satirical magazine *Puck* was published, in German (1876–96) and in English (1877–1918). A plaque on the Houston Street side of the building relates its history. With its deliciously complex red brickwork, the building was instantly revered as a prime example of New York commercial design.

Continue south along Lafayette, and turn right on Prince Street, then left on Broadway.

2 The Little Singer Building at 561 Broadway was designed by Ernest Flagg. It was very avant-garde in 1904 with its curled steel, recessed glass and textured terracotta. It suggested the next great architectural step: replacing cast-iron floor supports with steel—the basis of the modern skyscraper.

Walk two blocks south to the corner of Broadway and Broome. Look across Broadway to the northeast corner of Broome and Broadway.

3 The Haughwout Building, dating from 1857, is SoHo's oldest cast-iron beauty. Cast-iron facades were ornate,

stylish, cheap, easy to assemble and recyclable. The Haughwout Building architect based the facade on a window arch from a Venice library, repeating it 92 times. The first Otis elevator was installed here, inaugurating an era of ever-higher buildings.
Turn right onto Broome Street and right again onto Mercer Street. Go north on Mercer.

4 Stop for drinks at Bar 89, two doors down—and make sure you check out the now-you-see-through-them-now-you-don't doors on the toilet facilities on the mezzanine.

Continue to Prince Street and turn left (west), then go left again onto Greene Street, where there are more cast-iron buildings.

5 Many of these structures started out as warehouses. By 1962, a lot of them had been abandoned, and there were plans to raze the neighborhood in order to accommodate a highway, but the area was saved from demolition when residents protested. Rents were low here at the time so many artists, attracted to the huge, light-filled spaces, set up their homes and studios here;

by the 1970s, artists had almost completely taken over. Landmark designation for the neighborhood came in 1973. As you walk south on Greene Street, watch for Nos. 72–76, known as the King of Greene Street, with cast-iron Corinthian columns, and Nos. 28–30, the Queen of Greene Street, with a Second Empire roof.

Return along Greene to Grand Street and turn right. Walk one block west to Wooster Street and turn right. On the corner of Broome and Wooster streets, a shop called Vintage New York has more than 200 wines for you to sample, all from New York State.

6 On Wooster Street, the Tony Shafrazi Gallery is worth a visit at No. 119. Keith Haring and Julian Schnabel have exhibited here. At No. 120, the well-established Howard Greenberg Gallery is devoted to 20th-century photography. At No. 141, the innovative New York Earth Room exhibits great mounds of earth.

When you reach West Houston Street, turn left and walk one block west to West Broadway, where you turn left again and walk south all the way down to Canal Street.

7 Just north of Canal Street is the SoHo Grand Hotel. Have a look at the postmodern industrial interiors, then join the hip crowds at the bar.

Continue south on West Broadway, and turn right at Canal Street. You'll see the Canal Street station for A, C and E subway lines two blocks along and, two blocks beyond that, the 1 and 2 train stations.

The gold Puck statue outside the building of the same name

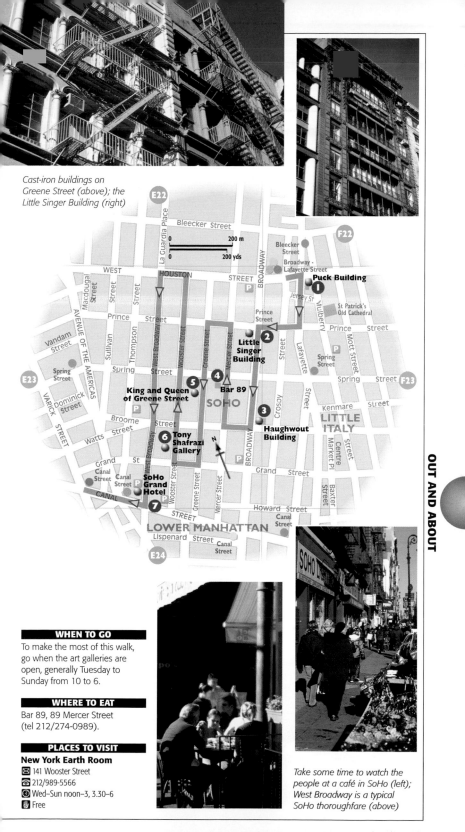

Cast-iron buildings on Greene Street (above); the Little Singer Building (right)

WHEN TO GO
To make the most of this walk, go when the art galleries are open, generally Tuesday to Sunday from 10 to 6.

WHERE TO EAT
Bar 89, 89 Mercer Street (tel 212/274-0989).

PLACES TO VISIT
New York Earth Room
✉ 141 Wooster Street
☎ 212/989-5566
🕐 Wed–Sun noon–3, 3.30–6
🎟 Free

Take some time to watch the people at a café in SoHo (left); West Broadway is a typical SoHo thoroughfare (above)

BOWLING GREEN TO SCHERMERHORN ROW

New York city began here in the 17th century, so if you are interested in the city's history, this is the walk for you. From Bowling Green to South Street Seaport, this area encompasses some of the city's greatest treasures.

THE WALK

Distance:	2.5 miles (4km)
Allow:	2 to 2.5 hours
Start at	Bowling Green subway station
End at	Fulton Street subway station (A, 2, 3)

HOW TO GET THERE

Subway:	4, 5
Bus:	M6

Leave Bowling Green station, and you'll see Battery Park ahead of you. Taking the path to the right, walk toward Castle Clinton.

1 Castle Clinton (tel 212/344-7220, Mon–Sun 8.30–5) was the immigrant clearing center before Ellis Island. You'll pass a temporary memorial to the victims of the World Trade Center, *The Sphere*, a sculpture which once stood between the towers as a symbol of world peace and is now a symbol of hope. In 1850, P. T. Barnum brought Europe's greatest soprano, Jenny Lind, to Castle Clinton, securing international stardom for both "the Swedish nightingale" and for himself as her promoter. Inside the gate to your right, a small museum displays dioramas depicting the castle's various uses from fort and entertainment center to ticket office for boat trips to the Statue of Liberty (▷ 136–137) and Ellis Island Immigration Museum (▷ 90–93).

Leave through the gate straight ahead and walk to your right, keeping to the path as it veers left past Slip 6.

2 In the water, just beyond Slip 6, is the site of the *American Merchant Mariners Memorial*, a sculpture of a sinking ship by Marisol, dedicated to all merchant mariners

who have served the United States from the Revolutionary War to the present day.

Turn back and walk east past the ferries to Slip 3. Walk up the steps to your left.

3 Albino Manca's sculpture of a bronze eagle with a funeral wreath, the *East Coast Memorial*, honors the memory of all the people who died in American waters during World War II.

Take the path west back toward Castle Clinton and turn right at the east gate. Walk past the Hope Garden to the point where Battery Place, Broadway and State Street meet. This small park is Bowling Green, where a statue of King George III was torn down by fervent nationalists in 1776.

4 The imposing neoclassical US Custom House on the right houses the National Museum of the American Indian. The rotunda inside the Great Hall is well worth viewing.

Pass Bowling Green and walk north on Broadway, passing Arturo DiModica's bronze *Charging Bull* on your right outside the Museum of American Financial History. Continue past this symbol of stockmarket prosperity to Trinity Church, on your left.

5 Trinity Church is historic (▷ 142–143). Many famous people are buried in the churchyard, including statesman Alexander Hamilton, steamboat inventor

Robert Fulton and Captain James Lawrence, whose last words ("Don't give up the ship") are now legendary.

As you leave the churchyard, cross to the east side of Broadway and continue east on famous Wall Street, straight ahead.

6 Wall Street (▷ 146–147) is where you will find the New York Stock Exchange, now closed to the public, halfway down the street on your right. No. 40 is the Trump Building.

Walk east on Wall Street to William Street and go left, then left again onto Pine Street.

7 On Pine Street, steps lead up to the Chase Manhattan Plaza, where sculptor Jean Dubuffet's *Group of Trees* takes center stage. Below the plaza is Isamu Noguchi's sunken sculpture garden.

Return to William Street by descending the steps to the right of the *Group of Trees*. Turn left to view the four abstract metal sculptures in Louise Nevelson Plaza. Across the street from the largest sculpture is the Federal Reserve Bank, designed to look like a Florentine palazzo. Just past the bank is Maiden Lane. Here turn left onto Maiden Lane, then right onto Nassau Street, and then right again onto John Street. At No. 44 is the United Methodist Church, with a fine Palladian front window. Continue east on John Street for five blocks, then left onto Water Street.

8 The South Street Seaport Historic District (▷ 134–135) is full of boutiques and restaurants, more shopping mall than historic, but the atmosphere is festive and it's fun to be on the water; you have fine views of the East River, Brooklyn Bridge

The Sphere, a memorial to the World Trade Center tragedy, temporarily in Battery Park

OUT AND ABOUT

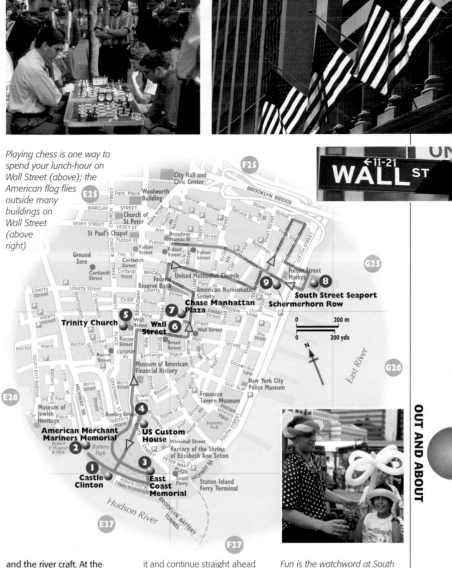

Playing chess is one way to spend your lunch-hour on Wall Street (above); the American flag flies outside many buildings on Wall Street (above right)

and the river craft. At the northern end of Water Street is Manhattan's oldest saloon, the Bridge Café, dating from 1847, where you can have a drink and a meal.

Turn right (east) onto Dover Street, then right again onto Front Street. When you get to Beekman Street, turn left to the city's fish market, Fulton Street Market. Go across South Street and walk to the end of Pier 17, and go up the steps for a spectacular view of Brooklyn Bridge (▷ 74–75). Then head toward South Street, cross over

it and continue straight ahead along Fulton Street.

❾ Schermerhorn Row, the Federal-style buildings along this street, were built as warehouses or counting houses in the early 1800s and named for the developer.

Continue west on Fulton Street to William Street and the subway station.

WHEN TO GO
To fully appreciate the bustle of Wall Street it is best to do this walk on weekdays.

Fun is the watchword at South Street Seaport

WHERE TO EAT
Bridge Café, 279 Water Street (tel 212/227-3344), or any of the eateries at South Street Seaport.

PLACES TO VISIT
National Museum of the American Indian
- 1 Bowling Green
- 212/668-6624
- Mon–Wed, Fri–Sun 10–5, Thu 10–8
- Free

OUT AND ABOUT

CITY HALL PARK TO WASHINGTON SQUARE PARK

Starting out from City Hall Park, you'll walk past the famous Woolworth Building, the world's tallest building until 1930 when the Chrysler Building spired even higher. Beyond lies Ground Zero, the site of the World Trade Center. You'll continue to SoHo and what remains of once-bustling Little Italy.

THE WALK

Distance: 3 miles (4.8km)
Allow: 2 to 2.5 hours
Start at Park Place subway station
End at West 4th Street/Washington Square

HOW TO GET THERE

Subway: 2, 3
Bus: M6

When you leave Park Place subway station, City Hall and its park are on your left at the northern end of City Hall Park.

❶ The principal designer of City Hall (▷ 77) was a Frenchman, Joseph François Mangin, who also worked on the place de la Concorde in Paris. This mini-palace is where the mayor and city council have their offices. A wrought-iron fence keeps the rest of us out. In the park in front of City Hall is a statue of Nathan Hale, a spy for Washington's army, hanged by the English in 1776. Just before his execution he uttered his famous last words of regret that he had "but one life to lose for my country." The same area was the site of the 1863 Draft Riots (▷ 33). Behind City Hall facing

Chambers Street is the old Tweed Courthouse, now the Department of Education. In 1872, when Boss Tweed (▷ 33) ran the city and milked taxpayers of millions of dollars, the estimated cost of constructing the courthouse was $250,000. But by the time Tweed paid off friends and lined his own pockets to the tune of some $10 million, the tab was $14 million. Tweed died penniless in jail in 1878. Across Broadway is Cass Gilbert's Woolworth Building (▷ 144), between Park Place and Barclay Street, a skyscraper with lavish Gothic ornamentation and an amazingly rich lobby.

Continue south down Broadway.

❷ St. Paul's Chapel, on Broadway between Fulton and Vesey streets, is Manhattan's only remaining pre-Revolution building. George Washington worshiped here during the two years that New York was the nation's capital, and inside you can see his pew.

Turn right on Fulton Street and continue west.

❸ Along the fence protecting the site of the World Trade Center (now known as Ground Zero, ▷ 108) at the end of Fulton Street, on Church Street, photos, flags, candles, flowers, teddy bears and other memorials to the victims of the tragedy can still be seen. Alongside the memorial, people sell T-shirts, photographs and hats to anyone willing to buy such reminders of the 9/11 disaster. Reconstruction on this site is already underway. If you wish to have a closer look,

The glistening Woolworth Building was built in 1913

cross Church Street to the viewing wall.

Turn right on Church Street.

❹ At the corner of Church and Barclay streets is the Church of St. Peter, founded in 1785, and New York's oldest Catholic parish church.

Turn right on Park Place and you'll see City Hall Park ahead. Walk east through the park to get a good view of Brooklyn Bridge. Take Park Row to Centre Street and walk north to the US Courthouse.

❺ The US Courthouse, designed by architect Cass Gilbert, is on the corner of Centre Street and Foley Square.

A little farther north are the criminal courts. As you approach Canal Street, the proximity to Chinatown becomes obvious: Open-fronted shops sell everything from Chinese lanterns to refrigerator magnets and made-in-China trinkets. When you reach the corner of Centre Street and Canal Street, turn right. Walk two blocks east, then turn left on Mulberry Street and walk north.

❻ You are now in the heart of Little Italy (▷ 109), with a handful of Italian restaurants and cafés. Two blocks north, at 195 Grand Street, is Ferrara, founded in 1892, with strong coffee and sweet pastries.

Continue north on Mulberry Street to Prince Street, and turn left.

❼ On the southeast corner of Prince Street and Broadway is Dean & DeLuca, a temple to food and cuisine offering beautiful displays of the finest pastries, meats, fishes and produce, plus good coffee at

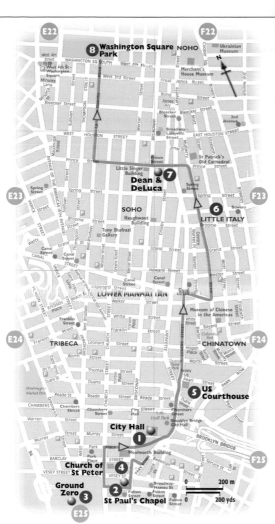

City Hall was completed in 1802 in the Federal style (above)

Chinatown canopies and Ground Zero memories (above)

the front counter. Cross Broadway and continue along Prince Street and turn right on West Broadway toward Houston Street.

As you cross Houston Street, West Broadway becomes LaGuardia Place.

8 Three blocks north is Washington Square Park. Once a hanging ground and a burial site for more than 10,000 unidentified paupers, this space became a public park in 1828.

After a rest in the park, you can catch a downtown train from West 4th Street/Washington Square back to Chambers Street near City Hall.

WHEN TO GO

The area around City Hall Park is at its liveliest on weekdays.

WHERE TO EAT

Ferrara, 195 Grand Street, between Mulberry and Mott streets (tel 212/226-6150).

Ferrara's, an Italian institution on Grand Street, where you can get great pastries and coffee (right)

MACY'S TO ROCKEFELLER CENTER

Some of New York's most striking sights are along this route—the Empire State Building, the Diamond District and Rockefeller Plaza, where you may be tempted to stop in at the NBC Experience Store to pick up a "Will & Grace," "Friends" or "Law & Order" T-shirt.

THE WALK

Distance: 3 miles (4.8km)
Allow: 2.5 hours
Start at 34th Street/Penn Station subway station
End at 34th Street/Herald Square

HOW TO GET THERE

Subway: 1, 2, 3, 9
Bus: M10

Leave the 34th Street/Penn Station subway so you come out onto West 34th Street at Seventh Avenue (also known as Fashion Avenue).

❶ You are standing in front of Macy's, arguably New York's most famous department store. Encompassing two entire city blocks, this store is so big you could spend days here.

Head east on West 34th Street. Continue to Broadway, cross it and turn left onto Sixth Avenue (Avenue of the Americas), keeping to the right as you go through the intersection. Six blocks north on Sixth, past lots of shops and banks, is Bryant Park on your right, where you can rest or get a coffee in the park. Continue north past the park. At the corner of 43rd Street is the International Center of Photography (▷ 101).

❷ The Diamond District is concentrated on 47th Street between Fifth and Sixth avenues. Notice the diamond-motif street lights illuminating the corners. Millions of dollars worth of gems are traded daily in the businesses here.

Continue north on Sixth Avenue.

❸ At 49th Street you'll see the 70-story G. E. Building towers to the right at 30 Rockefeller Plaza. This building is the headquarters of General Electric and NBC (National Broadcasting Corporation) and is part of the Rockefeller Center (▷ 128–130), a city landmark. The ground floor of the building is worth visiting; note José Maria Sert's sepia murals depicting the progress of man. At the Rainbow Room Restaurant on the 65th floor of the G. E. Building there are spectacular views of the city.

Continue on Avenue of the Americas (Sixth Avenue) to 50th Street.

❹ Stop to admire the land-mark art deco Radio City Music Hall (▷ 129), another city landmark and important element of the Rockefeller Center. Most famous for its Rockettes Christmas spectacu-lar, it also hosts other music shows throughout the year. This was the world's largest indoor theater when it opened in 1932. Hour-long guided tours are worth the time and the money. The block-long entry, with its 24-carat-gold ceiling and two-ton glass chandeliers, is spectacular. Just past Radio City, at 1290

Avenue of the Americas, is the AXA Financial Center. Stop in to view the foyer's magnificent multi-panel murals by Thomas Hart Benton depicting the nation's economic and social life on the eve of the Depression.

Back on Avenue of the Americas, go north a block to 52nd Street and turn right. The CBS Building, constructed in a dark granite in 1965, is on the corner of Avenue of the Americas and 52nd Street, a part of which is also known as Swing Street because of the many jazz clubs that flourished along here after the repeal of Prohibition.

❺ At 25 West 52nd Street is the Museum of Television and Radio (▷ 124). Next door at No. 21 is the 21 Club, a still-fashionable Prohibition-era hang-out, now a fine restaurant. Note the jockeys above the door.

At the corner of 52nd Street and Fifth Avenue, turn right and walk south a block.

❻ At St. Patrick's Cathedral (▷ 131), the largest Catholic cathedral in America, the flying buttresses and 330ft (100m) twin towers vie for your attention.

Turn left on 51st Street, and walk east past the cathedral toward Madison Avenue. Cross Madison Avenue.

❼ On the southeast corner of 51st and Madison is the New York Palace Hotel, which rises out of the Villard Houses, twin brownstone mansions built in 1884 by the Bavarian-born journalist, financier and railroad tycoon Henry Villard.

Continue walking east on 51st as far as Park Avenue. Turn left and walk one block north.

Macy's is the one everyone thinks of when they think stores

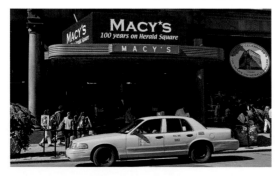

OUT AND ABOUT

8 The bronze-glass tower at 375 Park Avenue is the Seagram Building (▷ 141), a lively place in summer and a delight at Christmas with a tree and lights. Diagonally across the avenue is Lever House, built in 1952 with an avant-garde metal- and glass-curtain wall that reflects everything around.

Go left on East 53rd Street, walk west to Sixth Avenue and turn left again. Walk four blocks south.

9 The Rockefeller Center is a great place to shop, stop for a snack or just wander around.

From here you can take the subway to Herald Square.

WHEN TO GO
Avoid this walk on Sunday if you want to shop and visit St. Patrick's Cathedral. Monday to Saturday from 10 to 6 is best.

WHERE TO EAT
Rainbow Room in the Rockefeller Center (212/632-5000) or Rockefeller Center Café, 20 West 50th Street (212/332-7620)

PLACES TO VISIT
Museum of Television and Radio
✉ 25 West 52nd Street
☎ 212/621-6800
⏰ Tue–Sun noon–6, Thu until 8

Radio City Music Hall
✉ 1260 Sixth Avenue
☎ 212/247-4777
⏰ Daily 11–3
🎫 Hour-long behind the scenes tours every 30 min

Bryant Park is a pleasant green space to stop for a snack in summer (left)

Radio City Music Hall (top); St. Patrick's Cathedral (above)

OUT AND ABOUT

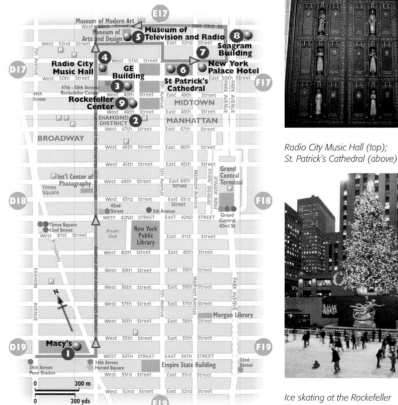

Ice skating at the Rockefeller Center at Christmas

CENTRAL PARK WEST HISTORIC DISTRICT

This walk begins with a quick look at the Dakota Building, where former Beatle John Lennon was shot in 1980, then stops at his memorial across the street in Central Park. In the 1960s, with private contributions of about $165 million, Upper West Side tenements were razed and Lincoln Center was built in their stead, a very pleasant complex of pedestrian open spaces, theaters, concert halls, cinemas and museums. Many actors, actresses and movie directors work and live in the neighborhood—it's fun to see if you can spot any.

THE WALK

Distance: 1.5 miles (2.4km)
Allow: 1.5 to 2 hours
Start/End at 72nd Street subway station

HOW TO GET THERE

Subway: B, C
Bus: M10

Leave the 72nd Street subway at the corner of 72nd Street and Central Park West.

❶ The Dakota (▷ 87) is on the northwest corner of Central Park West and 72nd Street. Look at the front of the building on 72nd Street, where John Lennon was shot. His wife, Yoko Ono, still lives in the building.

Walk east across Central Park West and follow the path straight ahead to Strawberry Fields.

❷ Here there is a memorial to Lennon, a black-and-white mosaic called *Imagine*.

Go back to Central Park West, turn left, and walk south. Note the residential streets lined with 19th-century brownstones to your right. Turn left into the park at West 67th Street.

❸ Here, at Tavern on the Green, celebrities show up for gala events and film premieres and tourists come (and pay the price) to enjoy the seating on the leafy patio in summer. The Sheep Meadow, straight ahead, is a 15-acre (6ha) expanse created as part of the Olmsted and Vaux design for Central Park; at the time it reminded many city-dwellers of the rural landscapes they had left behind when they emigrated to the United States.

Return to Central Park West and go south for two blocks. Turn right on 65th Street to Columbus Avenue. Cross Broadway and Columbus Avenue. On the west of Broadway is the Lincoln Center.

❹ The Lincoln Center (▷ 112–113) includes Alice Tully Hall (on the northwest corner of 65th Street) and Avery Fisher Hall (on the southwest corner). Much of the movie *West Side Story* was shot in the tenements that once stood on this spot. Walk south from Avery Fisher about 300 yards (274m) to the Lincoln Center central plaza, with its fountain. On the south side of the plaza is the home of the New York City Ballet, the New York State Theater; rising over the plaza on the west is the Metropolitan Opera House with Austrian chandeliers and Marc Chagall murals visible through the glass facade. To the south of the Met is a pleasant open area where open-air concerts are held in summer and the Big Apple Circus holds forth over the year-end holidays. The pond sculpture, Henry Moore's *Reclining Figure*, and the Vivian Beaumont Theater lie to the north.

Go up the steps to the Juilliard School to the north, turn right then left down the steps to Broadway. Cross 66th Street, then cross Broadway to your right. Walk east on 66th to Columbus Avenue and turn left. On the right stands the contemporary ABC Building at No. 147 Columbus. Continue along Columbus to West 70th Street and turn left.

❺ At 135 West 70th, near the corner of 70th and Broadway is the Pythian Temple, now a condominium; designed by Thomas W. Lamb, and built in 1926, it was dedicated to Pythianism, the cult of the oracle at Delphi, and Assyrian sages still guard the entrance. Bill Haley and the Comets recorded "Rock Around the Clock" here in 1954. Across the street, at 154 West 70th Street, is Café Mozart, with extravagant cakes and pastries.

Continue west to Amsterdam Avenue then turn right. As you approach West 72nd Street, you'll see one of the few remaining old subway buildings from the early 1900s on your left and a pleasingly harmonious new structure, an expansion of the venerable subway station, across 72nd on the north side of the street. Cross West 72nd Street.

❻ The magnificent Beaux Arts Ansonia Building rises at 2109 Broadway between West 73rd and West 74th streets. Caruso, Stravinsky and Toscanini all lived at the Ansonia, and the sound-proofing between apartments and floors continues to attract distinguished musicians, singers and conductors.

Turn right on West 73rd Street; 18 row houses, between Nos. 248 and 272, are the earliest houses in the neighborhood, dating from 1885. Turn left on Central Park West.

❼ Designed in 1930 by architect Emery Roth, the towers of the San Remo Apartments at 145–146 Central Park West grace the skyline. Residents have included Paul Simon and Dustin Hoffman.

Continue north on Central Park West to 77th Street.

❽ The New-York Historical Society (▷ 126) is on the corner of 77th and Central Park West. The fascinating collections and unusual variety of gifts in the shop make this worth a stop.

Cross West 77th Street.

OUT AND ABOUT

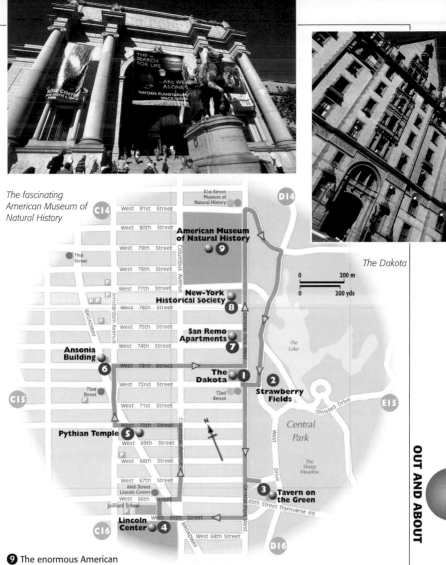

The fascinating American Museum of Natural History

The Dakota

81st Street Museum of Natural History

West 81st Street

West 80th Street

West 79th Street

American Museum of Natural History 9

West 78th Street

West 77th Street

New-York Historical Society 8

West 76th Street

West 75th Street

San Remo Apartments 7

West 74th Street

Ansonia Building 6

West 73rd Street

The Dakota 1

West 72nd Street

2 **Strawberry Fields**

72nd Street

The Lake

Olmsted Drive

Central Park

The Sheep Meadow

Pythian Temple 5

West 70th Street

West 69th Street

West 68th Street

West 67th Street

Lincoln Center

West 66th Street

Juilliard School

3 **Tavern on the Green**

65th Street Transverse Rd

Lincoln Center 4

West 65th Street

West 64th Street

C14

D14

C15

E15

C16

D16

0   200 m
0   200 yds

N

Columbus Avenue

Amsterdam Avenue

BROADWAY

Central Park West

West Drive

9 The enormous American Museum of Natural History (▷ 68–72) is on your left. Go to the main entrance to admire the bronze statue of President Theodore Roosevelt seated upon a horse, then step inside to look at William Mackay's beautiful murals depicting events from Roosevelt's life in the Roosevelt Memorial Hall.

After leaving the museum, walk up Central Park West, and at the 81st Street traffic lights take the entrance to the park straight ahead of you. As soon as you enter, take the path immediately to your right and walk south along this path to West 72nd Street and back to the 72nd Street subway station.

WHEN TO GO
This walk is very pleasant on Sunday afternoons. Most shops and restaurants are open then.

WHERE TO EAT
Café Mozart, 154 West 70th Street (tel 212/595-9797).

PLACES TO VISIT
American Museum of Natural History
✉ Central Park West at 79th Street
☎ 212/769-5100
🕐 Daily 10–5.45, Fri until 8.45

New-York Historical Society
✉ 2 West 77th Street
☎ 212/873-3400
🕐 Tue–Sun 10–6

Sheep grazed in The Sheep Meadow until 1934

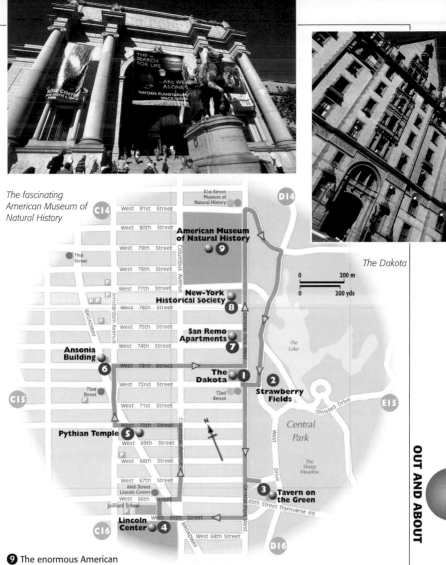

OUT AND ABOUT

FORT TRYON PARK

Go to Fort Tryon Park for fresh air, a walk in the woods, spectacular views of the Hudson River from Manhattan's highest natural point, gardens and a medieval-style monastery.

THE WALK

Distance: 1.5 miles (2.4km)
Allow: 1.5 to 2 hours
Start/End at Margaret Corbin Circle at 190th Street subway station

HOW TO GET THERE

Subway: A to 190th Street
Bus: M4

Leave the M4 bus at 190th Street rather than taking it to the Cloisters, the last stop. If you arrive by the A train, get off at 190th Street and take the elevator to street level and turn to your right as you come out of the station.

1 One of the earliest battles of the American Revolutionary War was fought in Fort Tryon Park on November 16, 1776. General George Washington's troops were outnumbered 4,000 to 600 and lost to the British, who named the fort after the colonial governor, Sir William Tryon. Although the area around the park is known as Washington Heights, the British name for the fort was never changed.

John D. Rockefeller acquired the property in 1917 and in 1938 established the Cloisters, a branch of the Metropolitan Museum of Art, to house a large collection of medieval art. Frederick Law Olmsted, Jr., designed the gardens using more than 250 species of plant. Olmsted's stone walls, arches, terraces and stairs recall medieval Europe, making these 62 acres (25ha) a special spot.

Margaret Corbin Circle is named after a brave American woman who took over her husband's cannon after he was fatally wounded in the Fort Tryon battle, and who is the only woman buried at West Point. To your left, on the west side of the circle, stands a small stone building that was the gatehouse for the Billings estate. Cornelius K. G. Billings was a wealthy horseman from Chicago who spent more than $2 million building his Tryon Hill mansion between 1901 and 1905.

Make your way through the huge stone gateway ahead and onto the Promenade. Turn immediately to your left onto this walkway.

2 The 3-acre (1.2ha) Heather Garden here enjoys a breathtaking view across the Hudson River to New Jersey's Palisades and the George Washington Bridge. With its many heathers, brooms, perennials and shrubs, this garden is one of the largest heather gardens on the east coast. By May, 5,000 bulbs are in full bloom, with more than 30 varieties of daffodils and tulips, and 1,000 lilies are in flower from June to September.

From the Heather Garden, return to the Promenade and follow it for about 300 yards (273m) to Linden Terrace.

3 In 1909, Billings erected a stela in Linden Terrace as a memorial to the Continental Army's defense of the site. Linden trees shade the pretty spot, and there are benches, parapets and splendid river views. At the northeast corner of the terrace, steps lead up to a flagpole. Standing here, you are on the highest natural point in Manhattan.

Return down the steps you have just come up to the Promenade, which veers to the left and down some stone steps. At the bottom of the steps continue along the path to your right.

4 You can see the Cloisters (▷ 86) straight ahead to the north. Stroll northward with the river on your left and, if you wish to have a quick look inside the museum, cross the road at the crosswalk (pedestrian crossing) on your right and continue along the path straight ahead. The entrance on your left leads to the gift shop, which sells Tiffany-like glass, art books, educational children's toys, videos and CDs to a background soundtrack of medieval music.

Continue north on the path you left to visit the Cloisters and stroll through the very pleasant woods and lawns. If you stay on the path closest to the road (Margaret Corbin Drive) that runs through the park, you'll come to the New Leaf Café.

5 The stunning location, trendy food and affordable prices of the New Leaf Café, an enterprise of actress Bette Midler's New York Restoration Project, make it a very pleasant rest stop. Proceeds support ongoing work in the park.

The path leads back to the park's main entrance at Margaret Corbin Circle.

WHEN TO GO

It is best not to go on Mondays when the Cloisters and the restaurant are closed. Even if you do not spend time viewing the exhibits, a quick look at the Cloisters is well worthwhile.

WHERE TO EAT

New Leaf Café, Fort Tryon Park (tel 212/568-5323; closed Mon).

PLACES TO VISIT

The Cloisters
✉ Fort Tryon Park ☎ 212/923-3700
🕐 Mar–Oct Tue–Sun 9.30–5.15; rest of year Tue–Sun 9.30–4.45 💲 $15 adult, child (under 12) free

Margaret Corbin Circle, at the entrance to the park, is the start and finish of the walk (below); a blue jay in the park (below right)

OUT AND ABOUT

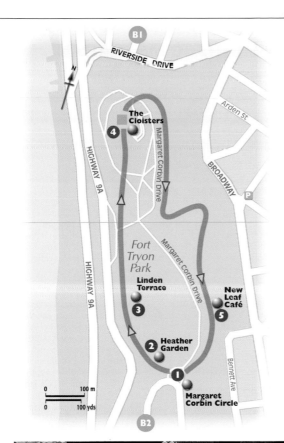

The impressive Cloisters (above); a walled walk around the park (below)

One of the many beautiful walkways that make up the Cloisters, which houses medieval European art (below)

BROOKLYN HEIGHTS TO MANHATTAN

If Brooklyn were not part of New York City, it would be America's sixth-largest city. Historic Brooklyn Heights, with its many landmark churches, fine brownstones and leafy streets, remains one of the city's most distinguished residential areas. The walk across Brooklyn Bridge provides stunning views of Lower Manhattan.

THE WALK

Distance: 2.5 miles (4km)

Allow: 2 to 2.5 hours (allow time to enjoy the view of Manhattan from Brooklyn Bridge)

Start at High Street/Brooklyn Bridge subway station

End at Brooklyn Bridge/City Hall subway station

HOW TO GET THERE

Subway: A, C

Leave the High Street/Brooklyn Bridge subway station. As you come out of the station, you see Cadman Plaza Park, with its tall trees, paths and benches. On the right side of the park is Cadman Plaza West. Walk south on this street the length of the park.

❶ Stop for a moment at the large stone monument on your left, dedicated to the Brooklyn men and women who fought during World War II. With its trees and benches, this park is a pleasant place to sit.

Continue on Cadman Plaza West, crossing Tillary Street. Pass the Korean War Veterans Plaza on your left and continue to the Federal Building and the Romanesque Revival US Post Office and Courthouse. Cross Johnson Street.

❷ The enormous building on the left is the Supreme Court of New York. Pause to admire the statue of Christopher Columbus in front of the building and the bronze bust of Senator Robert F. Kennedy, the assassinated brother of President John F. Kennedy.

❸ Straight ahead is an elaborate fountain and behind it is the

Greek Revival Brooklyn Borough Hall, built in 1848.

Just past Borough Hall is Joralemon Street. Walk west on Joralemon a block and a half to Sidney Place, on your left. Look down this little street to the big red church, St. Charles Borromeo Roman Catholic Church, built in 1849. Three blocks farther west on Joralemon, turn right on Hicks Street. Walk one block north.

❹ Grace Church, at 254 Hicks Street, is one of many New York City churches designed by Richard Upjohn; it dates from 1849. Visit the charming entrance court off Hicks Street and cool off in the shade of the enormous elm tree.

Continue a block north on Hicks to Remsen Street, and turn right. Go one block east and cross Henry Street.

❺ On your left is Richard Upjohn's Cathedral of Our Lady of Lebanon, the first round-arched, Early Romanesque Revival ecclesiastical building in the United States. Notice the medallions on the entrance doors. Originally the dining room doors on the French luxury liner *Normandie*, they were bought at an auction in 1945.

Continue another block east on Remsen, and turn left on Clinton Street. Walking north, as you cross Montague Street, look at St. Ann and the Holy Trinity Episcopal Church, a major work of James Renwick, Jr., on your left; it is one of the most important Victorian Gothic churches in the

The statue of Bobby Kennedy outside the Supreme Court of New York

SENATOR
ROBERT
FRANCIS
KENNEDY

NOVEMBER 20, 1925
JUNE 6, 1968

United States. At the end of Clinton Street, turn left on Cadman Plaza West, left again on Clark Street and then right on Henry Street. Walk two blocks to Orange Street and turn left.

❻ The Plymouth Church of the Pilgrims, built in 1849 on Orange Street between Henry and Hicks streets, was the center of anti-slavery sentiment during antebellum days. Abolitionist minister Henry Ward Beecher preached against slavery here. Abraham Lincoln worshiped here twice, and the building was a key part of the Underground Railroad, which helped get escaped slaves to freedom in the north. Beautiful stained-glass windows adorn this otherwise modest church, and in the courtyard next to it stands a bronze statue of Henry Ward Beecher by Gutzon Borglum, who sculpted the famous presidents' heads at Mount Rushmore.

Return to Henry Street and turn left. There are many cafés, restaurants and delis along here. At the traffic lights, turn right on Middagh Street and, at Cadman Plaza West, take the path ahead across the park. On your left is a plaque with information about the peregrine falcons that often roost here. At the fork in the path, keep left and you'll come to Washington Street. Turn left, and just before you come to the traffic lights at Prospect Street, go up the steps on your left.

❼ You now leave Brooklyn Heights across Brooklyn Bridge (▷ 74–75), on the wide wooden pedestrian walkway. In 1883 Brooklyn Bridge became the world's longest suspension bridge, spanning the East River and connecting Brooklyn to Manhattan. This spectacular bridge, with its web of steel cables, remains as much a marvel today as it did when it was first built.

OUT AND ABOUT

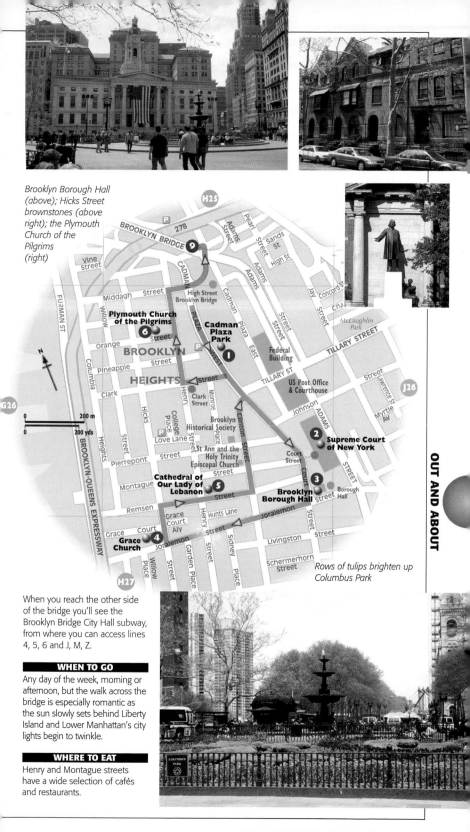

Brooklyn Borough Hall (above); Hicks Street brownstones (above right); the Plymouth Church of the Pilgrims (right)

Rows of tulips brighten up Columbus Park

When you reach the other side of the bridge you'll see the Brooklyn Bridge City Hall subway, from where you can access lines 4, 5, 6 and J, M, Z.

WHEN TO GO

Any day of the week, morning or afternoon, but the walk across the bridge is especially romantic as the sun slowly sets behind Liberty Island and Lower Manhattan's city lights begin to twinkle.

WHERE TO EAT

Henry and Montague streets have a wide selection of cafés and restaurants.

HUDSON RIVER VALLEY

The Hudson River flows 315 miles (508km) from the Adirondack Mountains to New York and out into the Atlantic. The splendor of this valley can be seen in the paintings by the Hudson River School artists of the 19th century, and still today the area is lovely, especially in the fall, when the colorful foliage brightens the shoreline.

BASICS

Historic Hudson Valley
☎ 914/631-8200
www.hudsonvalley.org

National Trust for Historic Preservation
☎ 914/631-4481

National Park Service
☎ 845/229-9115

HOW TO GET THERE

By train: Most of the valley north of New York City is easily visited by train. From Grand Central Terminal, take the Metro-North Hudson Line to the closest station; local taxis meet trains at most stations, or you can book one through Rivertowns Taxi (tel 914/478-2222).

By car: Follow the West Side Highway to the Henry Hudson Parkway and then the Saw Mill River Parkway (all one road, really, but with three different names). It's best to get specific directions from the Saw Mill by phoning each sight.

By river: The New York Waterway offers day-long excursions up the Hudson River, leaving from Pier 78 on Manhattan's west side (tel 1800/533-3779, www.newyorkwaterway.com).

HUDSON RIVER MUSEUM

The Hudson River Museum (tel 914/963-4550; May–end Sep Wed–Sun noon–5, Fri noon–8) is built around a historic house and a modern addition. Collections encompass art and history, and there's a planetarium. At the Museum Café, you can have a light lunch with splendid views of the Hudson River and the Palisades in New Jersey. Take Metro-North to Yonkers, then grab a cab (about $5).

SUNNYSIDE TO LYNDHURST

Sunnyside, a National Historic Landmark, was the home of Washington Irving, who wrote *The Legend of Sleepy Hollow* and was America's first internationally known author. The cottage (tel 914/631-8200; Apr–end Dec Wed–Mon 10–4; Mar Sat–Sun 10–4) was built in the 18th century and enlarged by Irving in 1835. Guided tours of the house and grounds are available up to one hour before closing time. There is a visitor center, museum shop and seasonal café. From Grand Central Terminal, catch a train to Tarrytown, where taxis will be waiting.

Lyndhurst, a spectacular Gothic Revival-style mansion (tel 914/631-4481; mid-Apr to end Oct Tue–Sun 10–5; rest of year Sat–Sun 10–4), was the home of railroad tycoon Jay Gould. The surrounding lawns have amazing Hudson River views. You can call a cab to take you to Sunnyside, or walk on the footpath.

PHILLIPSBURG MANOR AND KYKUIT

Phillipsburg Manor, on Route 9 in Sleepy Hollow, is a restored colonial farm once owned by the powerful Phillips family (Apr–end Dec Wed–Mon 10–4). Guided tours are available and houses and outbuildings like the barn and working grist mill are staffed by interpreters in period costume who explain early Hudson River Valley life.

Kykuit is a National Trust Historic Site that was home to four generations of the wealthy Rockefeller family. The sumptuous mansion is filled with priceless antiques and works of art, and sculptures fill the beautifully landscaped gardens. Guided tours (mid-Apr to end Nov Wed–Mon 10–3) begin at Phillipsburg Manor; tickets go on sale at 9am and are issued on a first-come, first-served basis (children under 10 are not admitted).

VAN CORTLANDT MANOR

This 18th-century Hudson Valley mansion belonged to the Van Cortlandt family for more than 260 years. Pierre Van Cortlandt was the first lieutenant-governor of New York State. The house has many original furnishings, and the kitchen is a tour highlight with its original hearth and beehive oven (Apr–end Oct Wed–Mon 10–5; Nov–end Dec Wed–Mon 10–4; Mar Sat–Sun 10–4).

WEST POINT, FRANKLIN D. ROOSEVELT NATIONAL HISTORIC SITE TO VANDERBILT MANSION

Farther upstate, there are several other landmarks on the eastern banks of the Hudson, most notably West Point Military Academy. Nearby is Cold Spring,

A long wooden footbridge leads to Phillipsburg Manor

OUT AND ABOUT

a charming riverfront town known for its antiques shops and garrison, home to another 19th-century mansion Boscobel (tel 845/265-3638). Next stop would be Beacon, a riverfront town that is being revived with the help of such institutions as DIA Arts. Farther north are two sites associated with the Roosevelts. The best way to visit is by car.

Your first stop is the United States Military Academy at **West Point** (tel 914/938-2638). America's most respected academy has turned out some great generals, presidents and astronauts. The museum displays guns, uniforms, medals and flags from various conflicts, and the grounds are beautiful in their own right.

Franklin D. Roosevelt National Historic Site (tel 845/229-8114; daily 9–5) was the Depression-era president's birthplace. The house, library and museum have a large collection of family memorabilia. Franklin and his formidable wife, Eleanor, are buried in the rose garden; a white marble monument marks their graves.

From this point a shuttle bus will take you to the **Eleanor Roosevelt National Historic Site** (daily 9–5) in the grounds of the Roosevelt estate.

Vanderbilt Mansion (tel 845/229-7770; daily 9–4, visit by guided tour only), 2 miles

The Monument to the American Soldier in the US Military Academy at West Point (above); Sunnyside, where Irving got his inspiration to write The Legend of Sleepy Hollow *(right)*

(1km) north of the Roosevelt Historic Site, is a lavish Beaux Arts mansion that was designed by architects McKim, Mead and White for the grandson of railroad magnate Cornelius Vanderbilt. Inside you will see all the splendors money can buy, from Renaissance to rococo furniture and works of art. The gardens are exquisite, and there are several walking trails that skirt the river.

WHERE TO EAT

In Tarrytown there are three good places to find something to eat: Equus Restaurant, The Castle (tel 914/631-3646); Main Street Café, 24 Main Street (tel 914/524-9770); and Striped Bass, 236 Main Street (tel 914/366-4455).

Fall foliage surrounds the Victory Monument in the US Military Academy at West Point

LONG ISLAND

Long Island is 125 miles (202km) long and between 12 and 23 miles (19 and 37km) wide. It lies east of New York City and is washed by the Atlantic Ocean on the south and Long Island Sound on the north. The rocky northern shoreline, scalloped with beaches, coves and bluffs, and sometimes called the Gold Coast, has attracted the affluent since the late 19th century. The Hamptons, at the east of the island, on the Atlantic shore, has become the playground of wealthy families, who have built fine summer houses and mansions. The delightful Atlantic-pounded beaches along the southern shore offer an escape from city heat in summer. The western part of the island, which consists of the Manhattan boroughs of Brooklyn and Queens, is densely populated, but the farther east you go, the more rural it becomes. Here are historic homes, fishing ports, historic whaling towns, museums and state parks.

BASICS

ℹ️ NYC & Company
☎ 212/484-1222
🕐 Mon–Fri 8.30–6, Sat–Sun 9–5
www.nyc.visit.com

HOW TO GET THERE

By train: Go to Pennsylvania Station on 7th Avenue between 31st and 33rd streets. From here catch a Long Island Railroad train to the town nearest the place of interest.

By car: From New York, travel from Manhattan east on the Long Island Expressway (I-495). Buses and trains are often a better way to get to Long Island, but you usually need a car to get around the various sights, so it's best to take your own wheels.

OLD WESTBURY GARDENS AND SAGAMORE HILL HISTORIC SITE

Old Westbury Gardens

(tel 516/333-0048) was the home of financier John S. Phipps (1874–1958), his wife Margarita and their four children. The Charles II-style manor house is furnished with English antiques and decorative arts. The surrounding 160 acres (64ha), with 88 breathtaking acres (36ha) of formal gardens, walkways, architectural follies and woodlands, are dotted with ponds and lakes. The gardens are between the Long Island Expressway and Jericho Turnpike (Route 25). By car, take Exit 39 (Glen Cove Road) off the I-495. Follow the service road east for 1 mile (1.5km), turn right on Old Westbury Road and continue for half a mile.

Sagamore Hill National Historic Site is northeast of Old Westbury, the home of President Theodore Roosevelt from 1885 until his death in 1919. The house is furnished as it was when he lived here (tel 516/922-4788; Memorial Day–Labor Day daily 10–4; rest of year Wed–Sun). Tours last half an hour and are offered on a first-come, first-served basis. They are limited in size, so arrive early if possible (by noon in summer they are often sold out). To get there by car, take Exit 41N (Oyster Bay) off I-495 onto Route 106 North. Travel for 4 miles (6km) to Route 25A, where you will turn right and travel 2.5 miles (4km) to the third traffic light. At the bottom of a long hill, turn left onto Cove Road and continue for

Sagamore Hill House (left); the Atlantic Ocean washes onto Robert Moses State Park on Fire Island (below), south of Long Island

The Vanderbilt Museum at Centerport was built in 1910 by William K. Vanderbilt

1.5 miles (2.5km). Turn right onto Cove Neck Road for 1.5 miles (2.5km).

WALT WHITMAN BIRTHPLACE TO OLD BETHPAGE VILLAGE

Walt Whitman (1819–92) was one of America's finest poets and essayists. At his birthplace (tel 631/427-5240; Jun 15–Labor Day daily 11–4; rest of year Wed–Fri 1–4, Sat–Sun 11–4), south of Sagamore Hill, you will see Whitman memorabilia, including photographs and excerpts from his writings and letters. To get there from I-495, take Exit 49N onto Route 110 North. Turn left onto Walt Whitman Road in Huntington Station. As the site is very popular with school groups, you may want to phone ahead.

Old Bethpage Village (tel 516/572-8400; Mar–end Oct Wed–Sun 10–5; rest of year Wed–Fri 10–4, Sat–Sun 10–5) is 100 acres (40ha) of vintage shops, farms, a one-room school-house, a church, gardens and homes filled with antiques, staffed by costumed interpreters explaining what life was like on Long Island in the 19th century. Special events are lively and fun.

The Theodore Roosevelt Sanctuary at Sagamore Hill

New York offers more tours than any city in the world. There are walking tours, bicycle tours, harbor tours, art and theater tours, behind-the-scenes tours, bus tours, limo tours, train tours, multilingual tours and special-interest tours such as ethnic, food and shopping tours. Some major bookstores have shelves of books about New York, many of them with self-guiding tours themed around everything from nature to literary history. The list of tour operators below is a small sample of what's available.

Details; www.nycvisit.com (click on Visitors, Things To Do and Tours)

BICYCLE TOURS

CENTRAL PARK BICYCLE TOURS
2 Columbus Circle/Broadway at 59th Street
Tel 212/541-8759
www.centralparkbiketour.com
Rent a bicycle and ride around Central Park with a knowledgeable guide for two hours. Tours daily at 10am, 1pm and 4pm
Adult $35, child (under 16) $20. Rental only: $20 for 2 hours, $25 for 3 hours, $35 all day

BUS TOURS

ON LOCATION TOURS
Tel 212/209-3370
www.screentours.com
Coaches depart from different locations. Reservations are recommended. Manhattan TV Tour is a 3-hour tour to 60 locations; "Sex and the City" Tour is a 4-hour tour; the "Sopranos" Tour is also 4 hours.
Manhattan TV tour: adult $32, child 6–9 $17, under 6 free. "Sex and the City" tour: $37. "Sopranos" tour: $42

HELICOPTER TOURS

Helicopters leave from the Downtown Manhattan Heliport at Pier 6 and South Street and from the VIP Heliport at West 30th Street.

LIBERTY HELICOPTER TOURS
Tel 212/967-6464
www.libertyhelicopters.com
Fly over Manhattan's skyscrapers, New York Harbor and the five boroughs.
$63, 5–7 min; $169, 15–17 min

RIVER TOURS

CIRCLE LINE
Tel 212/563-3200
www.circleline.com
Cruises from the Circle Line (Pier 83 at West 42nd Street/12th Avenue or Pier 16, South Street Seaport at Fulton Street and East River) are worth every penny. Take the 3-hour Full Island cruise, the 1-hour Semi-Circle cruise, 1-hour Seaport Liberty cruise, or a combination of packages. Combos are more expensive. Cruises with live music (adults only) operate from May to September. In spring and fall remember that it's at least 10 degrees colder on the water—and more when you consider wind chill in a moving boat.
Adult $18–28, child under 12 $10–15. Cruises $30–45

WALKING TOURS

Here are a few that are highly recommended. Call ahead for up-to-date schedules.

BIG APPLE GREETER
Tel 212/669-8159
www.bigapplegreeter.org
A free public service. The guides—volunteer New Yorkers—are matched with visitors according to language and interests. Give at least a week's advance notice (longer during peak season).

BIG ONION WALKING TOURS
Tel 212/439-1090
www.bigonion.com
Two-hour tours. Guides have degrees in American history. No reservations necessary.
Adult $15, child $10

GRAND CENTRAL PARTNERSHIP
Tel 212/883-2420
www.grandcentralpartnership.org
Free tours of Grand Central Terminal every Friday lunchtime at 12.30. Just show up outside Grand Central Terminal at Philip Morris at 42nd Street and Park Avenue.

THEMED WALKING TOURS

HERITAGE TRAILS
Tel 212/269-1500 exn 209
Fifty landmarks on four different trails in Lower Manhattan. Free maps are available at the Federal Hall National Memorial Information Desk.

MUNICIPAL ARTS SOCIETY
Tel 212/439-1049
www.mas.org
Architectural tours of Grand Central Terminal and other sites, including Ground Zero, Madison Avenue, Rockefeller Center and Martin Luther King Boulevard in Harlem. Guides are professional architects, historians, educators and writers.
Adult $12–15

NEW YORK GALLERY TOURS
Tel 212/946-1548
www.nygallerytours.com
Ten modern art galleries in two hours in Chelsea, SoHo and other locations.
Adult $15

OUT AND ABOUT

Little Italy : Ray's Pizza
Prince St

Eating and Staying

EATING OUT IN NEW YORK

You can dine around the world in New York City and you can spend a pittance or a fortune or somewhere in between. The choice is yours. Some New Yorkers dine out every night, others save the top-class choices for special occasions. Dining trends change from season to season. The biggest news is the "food mall of the stars" at the Time Warner Center and an obsession with super-expensive sushi.

RESERVATIONS, DRESS CODES AND OTHER NOTES

In general, it's wise to make a reservation for dinner, especially on weekends. Indeed, top-class restaurants require reservations and will ask you to provide a telephone number for confirmation. If you want a table at Jean-Georges, Le Bernardin, Alain Ducasse or similar, call well in advance. Sometimes, at these "famous" restaurants, it can be tough to get through even to the reservationists. Just keep trying. If you're on your own and want to eat on the run, you may be able to eat at the bar in one of these fancy restaurants. Note that some restaurants do not take reservations for parties under six people. In Midtown, luncheon reservations are also essential.

The United States is a more casual culture than most and strict dress codes have disappeared. Nonetheless few places still do require a jacket and tie at dinner so remember to ask when making a reservation. In general, casual smart is the way to go.

Smoking is not allowed in public spaces period. The majority of restaurants have full bars; some sell beer and wine only, and a few have no liquor but will allow you to bring your own. At premier restaurants, there will be a substantial corkage fee if you bring your own wine.

Vegetarians will find a welcome. Many of the top-class dining rooms offer vegetarian menus, and even fast-food joints are offering more healthful options on their menus these days.

Breakfast may be served all day at coffee shops and diners. Otherwise, the normal breakfast hours are from 7 to 11am. Lunch usually runs from 11.30am to 2 or 2.30pm and dinner from 5pm to 10 or 11pm, depending on the day of the week. Most top-class restaurants close for lunch on Saturday and Sunday. Many restaurants offer brunch on Sunday or both Saturday and Sunday.

TAXES, TIPPING AND OTHER FINANCIAL CONSIDERATIONS

A sales tax of 8.65 percent will be added to your dining bill. Americans tip more generously than most other nationalities. The minimum (with good service) is 15 percent; many people double the tax for a 17.3 percent tip. Many restaurants offer prix fixe menus, which often provide good value. In January and late June, a special promotion offers a three-course menu for $20.12 (luncheon) or $35 (dinner) at numerous restaurants; this promotion is often extended so it's always worth checking if it's available.

DESSERT AND COFFEE

Greenwich Village has been famous for its coffeehouses since the 1950s. Of the few that remain Caffe Reggio (119 MacDougal Street, tel 212/475-9557) is one of the best, a genuine Italian coffeehouse where you can idle away an afternoon over a few espressos. Le Gamin (183 Ninth Avenue at 21st Street, tel 212/243-8864) is a similar French version. Palacinka (28 Grand Street, tel 212/625-0362) is a small, busy café attracting an artsy SoHo crowd for the restaurant's namesake Eastern European crepes bathed in chocolate, or fresh fruit sauces. The Paris-inspired Payard Patisserie & Bistro (1032 Lexington Avenue, tel 212/717-5252) displays the creations of former Restaurant Daniel pastry chef, François Payard. The pastry case displays all kinds of gems plus handmade chocolates; sorbets are also available. Crowds make their way to the tiny storefront Magnolia Café (401 Bleecker Street, tel 212/462-2572) to taste the cupcakes iced with thick ultrasweet buttercream. In the East Village, Veniero's (342 East 11th Street, tel 212/674-7070) has been making and selling delicious Italian pastries for aeons.

EATING

The United States of America is a nation of immigrants. Traditional American food has evolved out of the traditions of the immigrant populations—German, Jewish, Italian, Scandinavian, Latino, Asian—plus Native American and African-American. Each group has contributed its ingredients and techniques to the current food scene. The Germans brought sauerkraut, sausages and pumpernickel; the Hungarians goulash and stuffed cabbage; the Cubans black bean soup and Cuban

cuisines, most notably Southern, Cajun, Southwestern and Tex-Mex.

DRINKS

The New York bar scene is extremely varied. Bars range from cheap dives charging a few dollars for a drink to luxury lounges charging anywhere from $10 for a cocktail. Despite the campaign against drinking and driving, most bars offer happy hours when they charge half price for drinks or offer two for the price of one.

sandwiches; the Irish corned beef and cabbage; the Japanese sushi and teriyaki; the Jews chopped liver pastrami and knishes; the Greeks kebabs; the Lebanese baba ganoush and falafel; the Mexicans salsa, tacos and refried beans; the Moroccans couscous; the Russians blinis and caviar; the Spanish tapas, chorizo and paella; the Swedes gravlax; and the Welsh leek and potato pie. Many of these dishes (or American modifications) have become common fare on all-American menus at standard American restaurants and even at lowly diners. The United States also boasts some distinctive regional

Note that American bartenders expect to be tipped (at least 10 percent). As far as drinks go, international beers and microbrews are readily available; cocktails are in vogue and every day brings a new concoction to light. Food is always available. It ranges from burgers and wings to more sophisticated fare. Most bars open from mid-morning to anywhere from 1am to 4am. Note that the drinking age is 21; expect to be "carded" (to show a photo ID), so carry an identification with photo. Buy wine and liquor at a liquor store; supermarkets sell beer only.

SOME NEW YORK DINING INSTITUTIONS

New York does have some unique dining institutions. The most famous is the deli. Among delis, the most traditional is the Jewish deli, which sells a variety of smoked fishes and meats, plus such items as bagels, pastrami and corned beef sandwiches, chopped liver, pickles and knishes. The word deli is also used for small neighborhood grocery stores, often operated by Korean merchants. They sell coffee, bagels, sandwiches, salads and other grocery items.

The coffeeshop/diner is another traditional dining haven. It will have counters and stools as well as table service. Here people secure endless cups of coffee, and breakfast, lunch or dinner selections taken from a vast (usually laminated) menu. The city has plenty of fast-food outlets too (McDonald's, etc). Look for street vendors too. They sell everything from hot salty pretzels to soups, hot dogs and ethnic snacks. The other dining establishment that is endemic to New York is the pizza parlor. The most visible coffee vendor is Starbucks, which seems to be on every corner, but there are plenty of independent cafés, especially in the West and East villages.

Hot dogs from a Manhattan street vendor

EATING

LATE NIGHT/24-HOUR

Despite New York's reputation as a 24/7 town, it's not that easy to find food in the wee hours. Among tried-and-true late-night oases, the hip but strangely unpretentious Blue Ribbon (97 Sullivan Street, tel 212/274-0404) draws clubbers and workers, including many chefs for sesame-glazed catfish, tofu ravioli, paella, and oysters on the half shell. It's open from 4pm to 4am daily.

The Coffee Shop (29 Union Square West, tel 212/243-7969), which looks like what you'd expect, is like nothing you'd find in Peoria with its Brazilian ownership and varied fare.

At Empire Diner (210 Tenth Avenue, tel 212/243-2736), you'll pay for the stylish chrome-and-black art deco setting as well as for the classic egg dishes, sandwiches and meat loaf. It's open around the clock except on Monday. In the Meatpacking District, Florent (69 Gansevoort Street, tel 212/989-5779) serves bistro-style food to night owls, clubbers and meat-market workers—onion soup, blood sausage, steak frites and the usual breakfast favorites.

Singles can almost always eat at the bar in Manhattan. If the place is full, or if you want to eat on the run, just ask.

AMERICAN MENU READER

The famous Oyster Bar in Grand Central Terminal

Bagel
An unsweetened dense eggless bread cooked in water and then baked. It's shaped with a hole in the middle.

Boston baked beans
Navy beans flavored with molasses and salt pork

Chicken-fried steak
Batter-dipped steak

Chowder
Thick soup traditionally made with clams or corn

Cobbler
Fruit pie topped with a biscuit-style crust

Egg cream
A thick drink made with chocolate syrup, milk and seltzer

Eggplant
Aubergine

Eggs over easy
Fried eggs that have been turned over so they are cooked through

Eggs sunnyside up
Fried eggs that have not been turned over

French toast
Bread coated with beaten eggs and sautéed. Served with maple syrup.

Grits
Corn kernels with the bran and germ removed

Hero
An extra-large long roll

Key lime pie
Made with special lime variety from Florida

London broil
A particular cut of flank steak

Lox
Cured salmon

Meat loaf
Ground beef, turkey and pork combined with breadcrumbs and egg and baked

New York cheesecake
Jewish-style dense and creamy cake, which may be plain or topped with fruit

On the rocks
With ice

Pot roast
Braised beef

Pretzel
An elongated biscuit, which is shaped and twisted into a knot. It's sprinkled with coarse salt and sold warm from carts on the street.

Salisbury steak
A beef patty

Scotch
Scottish whiskey

Stack of pancakes
Three or four thick batter cakes served with maple syrup

Sub
Short for submarine; another name for an extra-large long roll

Straight up
No ice

Waldorf salad
Apples, celery and walnuts in mayonnaise; first created at the Waldorf Astoria

Whiskey
American rye

EATING

RESTAURANTS BY CUISINE

The restaurants listed alphabetically on pages 270 to 290 are grouped here by cuisine.

American contemporary
Annisa
Aureole
Blue Hill
Blue Ribbon Bakery
Cafe Gray
Craft and Craftbar
Cru
Eleven Madison Park
Etats-Unis
Gotham Bar & Grill
Gramercy Tavern
The Harrison
Ouest
Per Se
Prune
Red Cat
River Café
Sarabeth's
Tasting Room
Tavern on the Green
Town
Union Square Café
Veritas
WD-50

American regional
Mesa Grill

American traditional
'21' Club

Asian
Biltmore Room
Spice Market

Barbecue
Blue Smoke
Virgil's Real Barbecue

Burgers
Corner Bistro

Caribbean
Maroons
Negril Village

Chinese
Dim Sum Go Go
Shun Lee Palace
66

Continental
Four Seasons

Deli
Barney Greengrass
Katz's Deli
Second Avenue Deli

Eclectic
Spotted Pig

French
Aix
Alain Ducasse
Artisanal
Balthazar
Bouley
Brasserie
Café Boulud
Chanterelle
Daniel
DB Bistro Moderne
Fleur de Sel
Jean-Georges
JoJo
Le Zinc
Montrachet
Odeon
Pastis

Greek
Estiatorio Milos
Molyvos
Periyali

Indian
Banjara
Devi
Hampton Chutney
Mirchi
Tabla
Tamarind

Italian
Babbo
Bar Pitti
Bread
Cesca
Felidia
Fiamma Osteria
Gonzo
I Coppi
L'Impero
Lupa
Peasant

Japanese
Bond Street
Jewel Bako
Masa
Nobu
Sugiyama
Sushi Yasuda
Taka
Tomoe Sushi

Korean
Do Hwa
Woo Lae Oak

Latin American
Calle Ocho
Pio Pio

Malaysian
Nyonga

Mexican
Dos Caminos
Hell's Kitchen
La Palapa
Maya
Mi Cocina
Pamano
Rosa Mexicano
Zarela

Moroccan/Middle Eastern
Chez Es Saada
Moustache

Noodle shops
Big Wong
Honmura An

Pizza
John's Pizzeria Pizza
Otto Enoteca Pizzeria

Russian
Uncle Vanya Café

Scandinavian
Aquavit
Good World Bar and Grill

Seafood
Aquagrill
Blue Fin
Esca
Grand Central Oyster Bar
Le Bernardin
Mermaid Inn
Oceana
Pearl Oyster Bar

Soul
Amy Ruth's
Londel's

Spanish
Bolo
Casa Mono
Pintxos
Pipa

Steak
Mark Joseph Steakhouse
Peter Luger Steakhouse
Strip House

Thai
Holy Basil
Pam Real Thai
Kittichai
Vong

Vegetarian
Angelica Kitchen

Vietnamese
Le Colonial
Nam

HOTELS WITH EXCEPTIONAL DINING ROOMS

Four Seasons
Hotel Wales
Le Parker Meridien
Mandarin Oriental
Mark
Mercer Hotel
New York Palace
Ritz-Carlton (Central Park South)
Royalton
Sherry Netherland
Surrey
Trump International Hotel
W-NY

Restaurant Locator

West 95th Street
West 94th Street
West 93rd Street
West 92nd Street
UPPER WEST SIDE
West 91st Street
West 90th Street
West 89th Street
West 88th Street
Aix
West 87th Street
Barney Greengrass
West 86th Street
86th Street
West 85th Street
West 84th Street
West 83rd Street
Ouest
West 82nd Street
Calle Ocho
West 81st Street
81st Street Museum of Nat Hist
West 80th Street
American Museum of Natural History
West 79th Street
79th Street
West 78th Street
Ruby Foo's
West 77th Street
New-York Historical Society
West 76th Street
Cesca
West 74th Street
Ansonia Building
West 73rd Street
San Remo Apartments
West 72nd Street
The Dakota
72nd Street
72nd Street
West 71st Street
West 70th Street
Strawberry Fields
West 69th Street
Freedom Place
West 68th Street
Riverside Boulevard
West 67th Street
West 66th Street
Lincoln Center
Juilliard School
West 65th Street
Tavern on the Green
West 64th Street
Picholine
West 63rd Street
Lincoln Center
Rosa Mexicano
Museum of Biblical Art
West 62nd Street
Jean-Georges (Trump International Hotel Tower)
West 61st Street
West 60th Street
Cafe Gray, Masa, Per Se
59th Street Columbus Circle
West 59th Street
COLUMBUS CIRCLE
Alain Ducasse (Essex House)
West 58th Street
57th Street
Carnegie Hall
WEST 57TH STREET
West 56th Street
Sugiyama
Molyvos
West 55th Street
Uncle Vanya Café
Estiatorio Milos
West 54th Street
West 53rd Street
De Witt Clinton Park
West 52nd Street
West 51st Street
Le Bernardin
West 50th Street
50th Street
50th Street
49th Street
West 49th Street
West 48th Street
Pam Real Thai
Blue Fin (W Times Square Hotel)
West 47th Street
Hell's Kitchen
BROADWAY
West 46th Street
Intrepid Sea, Air and Space Museum
West 45th Street

Amy Ruth's, Londel's

CENTRAL PARK

Central Park Reservoir

Central [Park]

Belvedere Lake

79th street Transverse

The Lake

The Sheep Meadow

Hudson River

Riverside Park

Riverside Drive

West End Avenue

HIGHWAY 9A

B C D

13 14 15 16 17

266

East 95th Street East 95th Street
East 94th Street East 94th Street
East 93rd Street East 93rd Street
Jewish Museum **Sarabeth's**
East 92nd Street East 92nd Street
East 91st Street East 91st Street
Cooper-Hewitt National Design Museum East 90th Street **Pio Pio**
National Academy of Design East 90th Street
Guggenheim Museum East 89th Street
East 88th Street East 88th Street Gracie Mansion
East 87th Street East 87th Street Carl Schurz Park
86th Street East 86th Street East 86th Street
Neue Galerie East 85th Street East 85th Street
East 84th Street East 84th Street
The Metropolitan Museum of Art East 83rd Street East 83rd Street
East 82nd Street East 82nd Street
East 81st Street East 81st Street
Etats-Unis East 80th Street East 80th Street
East 79th Street East 79th Street John Jay Park
East 78th Street East 78th Street
East 77th Street East 77th Street
77th Street
Café Boulud East 76th Street East 76th Street
Whitney Museum of American Art East 75th Street
East 74th Street East 74th Street
Conservatory Water East 73rd Street East 73rd Street
East 72nd Street East 72nd Street
East 71st Street East 71st Street
Frick Collection Asia Society and Museum East 70th Street
East 69th Street East 69th Street
68th Street Hunter College East 68th Street
East 67th Street East 67th Street
East 66th Street East 66th Street
Daniel **JoJo** East 65th Street **Maya**
FIFTH AVENUE East 64th Street
Lexington Avenue East 63rd Street
East 62nd Street East 62nd Street
Aureole East 61st Street Mount Vernon Hotel Museum and Garden
East 60th Street East 60th Street
5th Avenue HIGHWAY 25
59th Street **Felidia** QUEENSBORO BRIDGE Main Street
East 58th Street **Dawat**
WEST 57th STREET EAST 57TH STREET **Le Colonial** West 57th Street
Town (Chambers Hotel) Trump Tower Dahesh Museum of Art **Shun Lee Palace**
West 56th Street West 56th Street
Aquavit West 55th Street West 55th Street
Oceana **Vong**
Museum of Modern Art West 54th Street West 54th Street
Lexington Avenue
West 53rd Street **Brasserie**
Museum of Arts and Design Museum of Television and Radio Seagram Building **Four Seasons**
"21" Club West 52nd Street East 52nd Street
Radio City Music Hall St Patrick's Cathedral Municipal Art Society **Zarela**
West 50th Street 51st Street
G E Building **Pampano**
Rockefeller Center Rockefeller Plaza East 49th Street
West 48th Street West 48th Street
DIAMOND DISTRICT **Diwan**
West 47th Street MIDTOWN MANHATTAN East 47th Street
West 46th Street East 46th Street
West 45th Street West 45th Street

Lexington Avenue Park Avenue 3rd Avenue 2nd Avenue 1st Avenue York Avenue Madison Avenue 5th Avenue Avenue of the Americas (6th Avenue)

FRANKLIN DELANO ROOSEVELT DRIVE

Mill Rock Park
ROOSEVELT ISLAND
Roosevelt Island Main Street
River
West Road East Road
Transverse Road Park Drive North The Pond

E F G 13 14 15 16 17

17

Museum of Arts and Design
Museum of Television and Radio
Seagram Building
Brasserie
Four Seasons
"21" Club

West 52nd Street
West 51st Street
Le Bernardin
West 50th Street
Radio City Music Hall
St. Patrick's Cathedral
Municipal Art Society
47th–50th Streets Rockefeller Center
G E Building
West 49th Street
Pam Real Thai
Rockefeller Center
West 48th Street
MIDTOWN MANHATTAN
Blue Fin
(W Times Square Hotel)
DIAMOND DISTRICT
Diwan
West 47th Street
West 46th Street
Hell's Kitchen
BROADWAY
West 45th Street

18

Int'l Center of Photography
DB Bistro Moderne
West 44th Street
East 44th Street
Grand Central Terminal
Times Square
Virgil's Real Barbecue
West 43rd Street
East 43rd Street
Grand Central 42nd St
Esca
Holy Cross Church
Reuters Building
WEST 42ND STREET
EAST 42ND STREET
Grand Central Oyster Bar
Chanin Building
L'Impero

42nd Street Port Authority Bus Terminal
New Amsterdam Theater
Times Square 42nd Street
West 41st Street
Bryant Park
New York Public Library
East 41st Street
DYER AVENUE
West 40th Street
East 40th Street
FASHION AVENUE
West 39th Street
East 39th Street
West 38th Street
East 38th Street
West 37th Street
East 37th Street
Morgan Library
West 36th Street
East 36th Street
West 35th Street
East 35th Street
Macy's
34th Street Herald Square
Empire State Building

19

34th Street Penn Station
34th Street Penn Station
34TH STREET
EAST 34TH STREET
33rd Street
Madison Square Garden
Pennsylvania Station
West 32nd Street
East 32nd Street
Artisanal
West 31st Street
East 31st Street
West 30th Street
50th Street
East 30th Street
Little Church Around the Corner
West 29th Street
28th Street
East 29th Street
28th Street
West 28th Street
East 28th Street
Chelsea Park
West 27th Street
East 27th Street
Blue Smoke
West 26th Street
East 26th Street
Dos Caminos
West 25th Street
East 25th Street
Madison Square Park
Biltmore Room
West 24th Street
23rd Street
Eleven
Tabla
Madison Park
East 24th Street
Metropolitan Life Insurance Tower

20

Red Cat
West 23rd Street
23rd Street
West 22nd Street
East 23rd Street
23rd Street
Bolo
Tamarind
CHELSEA
Flatiron Building
West 21st Street
Periyali
Fleur de Sel
Veritas
Theodore Roosevelt Birthplace
Gramercy Park North
Gramercy Park
Gramercy Park South
West 20th Street
Gramercy Tavern
West 19th Street
Craft and Craftbar
GRAMERCY PARK HISTORIC DISTRICT
18th Street
Pipa
East 18th Street
West 18th Street
Devi
Casa Mono
West 17th Street
East 17th Street
Union Square Café
West 16th Street
Maroons
Mesa Grill
West 15th Street
Union Square Park

21

Spice Market
14th Street
8th Avenue
14th Street
WEST 14TH STREET
UNION SQUARE
EAST 14TH STREET
14th Street Union Square
3rd Avenue
West 13th Street
6th Avenue
Pastis
Forbes Magazine Galleries
East 13th Street
Mi Cocina
Corner Bistro
Gonzo
Strip House
Grace Church
Gotham Bar & Grill
West 11th Street
Jefferson Market Library
West 10th Street
Cru
West 9th Street
Otto Enoteca Pizzeria
8th Street NYU
Astor Place 8th Street
Spotted Pig
Blue Hill
Babbo
WASHINGTON SQ NORTH
Wanamaker Place

22

GREENWICH VILLAGE
Taka
Annisa
Washington Square Park
WASHINGTON SQUARE SOUTH
NOHO
McNulty's Rare Teas and Choice Coffee Shop
Negril Village
Merchant's House Museum
John's Pizzeria Pizza
Church of St. Luke-in-the-Fields
Mirchi
Pearl Oyster Bar
West 3rd Street
Bond Street
Dok Suni
House of Oldies

C D E F

RESTAURANT LOCATOR

The prices given are for a two-course lunch (L) for one person and a three-course à la carte dinner (D) for one person. The wine price is the starting price for a bottle of wine.

AIX
Map 266 C13
2398 Broadway at 88th Street
Tel 212/874-7400
www.aixnyc.com
Didier Virot has brought robust Provençal cuisine to the Upper West Side at this tri-level restaurant. He adds his twists to such dishes as pistou, which is enhanced with lemon cream, or foie gras sautéed with almonds, marinated in Calvados and vanilla and served in cinnamon reduction. Desserts are innovative (apple-rosemary brioche with honey Calvados sauce, anyone?).
Ⓒ Sun–Thu 5.30–10.30, Fri–Sat 5.30–11
Ⓓ D $60, Wine $32
Ⓠ 86th Street (1, 9)
Ⓜ M104

ALAIN DUCASSE
Map 266 D16
Essex House, 155 West 58th Street between Sixth and Seventh avenues
Tel 212/265-7300
www.alain-ducasse.com
When three-Michelin-star

chef Alain Ducasse opened this opulent restaurant, he was criticized for affectation, but now he draws acclaim from even the toughest critics. The crimson salon is luxe, and so is the service. Start with champagne and finish with the candy cart (caramels, nougat, macaroons). The dishes that will appear in between are sublime: sea bass with leek, potato and black truffle, fresh crab seasoned with citrus fruit and black

pepper with a delicate velouté of sweetcorn. The 1,400 international wine selections tilt toward France.
Ⓒ Mon–Sat 6.30–9
Ⓓ D $150–$175, Wine $56
Ⓠ 57th Street (F, N, Q, R, W)
Ⓜ M6, M7

AMY RUTH'S
Off map 266 D12
113 West 116th Street between Malcolm X Boulevard and Adam Clayton Powell Jr. Blvd
Tel 212/280-8779
It's named for the owner's grandmother, who taught her Southern-style cooking. Most items on the menu are named for someone, such as the Reverend Al Sharpton (chicken and waffles). At dinner, look for lusty Southern fried chicken, oxtail stew and fried or baked catfish. No alcohol.
Ⓒ Mon–Thu 7.30am–11pm, Fri–Sun 24hrs
Ⓓ L $17, D $22
Ⓠ 116th Street (2, 3, B, C)
Ⓜ M3, M7, M116

ANGELICA KITCHEN
Map 269 F21
300 East 12th Street between First and Second avenues
Tel 212/228-2909
This plain, 60s-like spot proves that vegetarian cuisine does not have to be bland. Go for the hearty

soups, excellent chili or tasty noodle dishes and sandwiches. No alcohol. No credit cards.
Ⓒ Daily 11.30–10.30
Ⓓ L $15, D $20
Ⓠ 14th Street/Union Square (4, 5, 6, L, N, Q, R, W)
Ⓜ M14, M15

ANNISA
Map 268 D22
13 Barrow Street between Bleecker and West 4th streets
Tel 212/741-6699
www.annisarestaurant.com
At this minimalist restaurant Chef Anita Lo cooks coherent fusion cuisine. For appetizers, oysters might arrive with three root vegetables, while roasted kabocha squash and maiiake mushrooms could be combined with bitter chocolate. Smoked lamb hominy is enriched with chili and lime. No credit cards.
Ⓒ Mon–Sat 5.30–10, Sun 5.30–9.30
Ⓓ D $55, Wine $27
Ⓠ West 4th Street (A, C, E, F), Christopher Street/Sheridan Square (1, 9)
Ⓜ M20, M21

AQUAGRILL
Map 269 E23
210 Spring Street at Sixth Avenue
Tel 212/274-0505
Every day brings a fresh selection of seafood—cod, halibut, grouper, monkfish, tuna—which can be prepared to your specifications,

roasted, poached or grilled, or served in such dishes as sea bass with smoked pepper and crispy bacon in thyme vinaigrette. Star of the show is the oyster bar, which offers about 24 varieties. Prices are fair.
Ⓒ Tue–Thu noon–3, 6–10.45, Fri noon–3, 6–11.45, Sat noon–3.30, 6–11.45, Sun noon–3.30, 6–10.30
Ⓓ L $30, D $45, Wine $29
Ⓠ Spring Street (C, E)
Ⓜ M6

EATING

AQUAVIT
Map 267 E17
65 East 55th Street between Madison and Park avenues
Tel 212/307-7311
www.aquavit.org
In a sleek modern space, Chef Marcus Samuelsson creates contemporary interpretations of Swedish–Scandinavian cuisine: Oysters come with a mango-curry sorbet; mushroom broth is poured over delicately smoked arctic char. There's a wide selection of aquavits, plus 250 wines (15 by the glass). Jackets are required in the dining room, but the front café is more casual and offers more traditional Scandinavian fare.
🕐 Daily noon–2.30, 5.30–10.30
🍴 L $35, D $75, Wine $45
🚇 Fifth Avenue (E, V)
🚌 M1, M2, M3, M4, M5, M6, M7

ARTISANAL
Map 268 E19
2 Park Avenue at 32nd Street
Tel 212/725-8585
This gem is all about cheese, and the quality of the 250 varieties in the walk-in cheese vault is astonishing, ranging from cabecou de Rocamadour to callu de cabreddu. Savor them straight or in a fondue. Not to worry if you don't eat cheese: Escargots, moules and main dishes such as crisp skate wing with blood orange Grenobloise and steak frites complete the menu. Some 170 wines are available by the glass.
🕐 Mon–Thu noon–11, Fri–Sat noon–midnight, Sun noon–10
🍴 L $34, D $46, Wine $28
🚇 33rd Street (6)
🚌 M1

AUREOLE
Map 267 E16
34 East 61st Street between Madison and Park avenues
Tel 212/319-1660
www.aureolerestaurant.com
Aureole's chef/owner Charlie Palmer is one of the most highly regarded talents on the American culinary scene. This elegant Upper East Side town-house with a grand staircase and towers of wine, liquor and flowers, is made for special occasions. Palmer uses ultra-fresh ingredients in such signature dishes as slow-

BABBO
Map 268 E22
110 Waverly Place between MacDougal Street and Sixth Avenue
Tel 212/777-0303
www.babbonyc.com
With his ponytail and orange clogs, Mario Batali has a lust for life that's infectious and an originality that is breathtaking. At Babbo, his flagship restaurant, the welcome is warm and the food some of the freshest and lustiest anywhere. Try the handmade beef cheek ravioli or the prosciutto with spicy fig jam. The deep all-Italian wine list is a revelation.
🕐 Mon–Sat 5.30–11, Sun 5–11
🍴 D $60, Wine $25
🚇 West 4th Street (A, C, E, F, S, V)
🚌 M5, M6

poached Maine lobster with heirloom tomatoes, which is served with lemon-verbena-infused consommé, and seared Hudson Valley foie gras.

The wine list features 600 selections, 25 by the glass. In summer, sit in the courtyard.
🕐 Mon–Fri noon–2.30, Mon–Thu 5.30–11, Fri–Sat 5–11
🍴 L $46, D prix fixe $79 3-course, $89 6-course, Wine $40
🚇 59th Street (4, 5, 6), 59th Street/Fifth Avenue (N, R, W)
🚌 M1, M2, M3, M4

BALTHAZAR
Map 269 F23
80 Spring Street between Broadway and Lafayette Street
Tel 212/965-1414
www.balthazarny.com
Keith McNally has cloned a classic Paris brasserie with smoky gilded mirrors, tile floor, red-leather banquettes and a vast 27ft (8m) bar. Bistro fare includes the seafood platter piled high with oysters, clams, shrimp and scallops; chicken

paprika; and skate in brown butter. The place is crowded and vibrant and loaded with celebrity cachet. Bread and pastries come from the adjacent bakery. The 300-selection wine list is totally French.
🕐 Mon–Thu 7.30–11.30, noon–5, 5.45–1.30, Fri 7.30–11.30, noon–5, 5.45–2.30, Sat 7.30–3.30, 5.45–2.30, Sun 7.30–3.30, 5.30–12.30
🍴 L $30, D $40, Wine $26
🚇 Prince Street (N, R), Spring Street (6)
🚌 M1, M5

BANJARA
Map 269 F22
97 First Avenue at 6th Street
Tel 212/477-5956
Sixth Avenue is lined with Indian restaurants, but Banjara is the best of the lot. Northern Indian cuisine is the specialty. The tandoori dishes are particularly good with their fine smoky flavor. Also appealing are the pasanda lamb, cooked in a yogurt-based curry sauce, and the palak ghost—lamb cooked in a purée of spinach, tomatoes, ginger and cumin seeds.
🕐 Daily 12–12
🍴 L $20, D $30, Wine $19
🚇 Astor Place (6)
🚌 M8, M15

BAR PITTI
Map 269 E22
268 Sixth Avenue between Bleecker and Houston streets
Tel 212/982-3300
Actors, writers, fashion designers and Village residents gather at this European-style boîte. In summer, the sidewalk dining affords great people-watching and the chance to observe comings and goings next door at celebrity hot spot Da Silvano. Your best bet is to select one of the reliable meat, fish or pasta chalkboard specials. Otherwise, choose one of the typical pastas, perhaps spaghetti with clam sauce. No credit cards.
🕐 Daily noon–midnight
🍴 L $25, D $35, Wine $30
🚇 West 4th (A, C, F, S, V), Houston Street (1, 9)
🚌 M5, M6

EATING

BARNEY GREENGRASS

Map 266 C13
541 Amsterdam Avenue between West
86th and 87th streets
Tel 212/724-4707
www.barneygreengrass.com

An Upper West Side tradition
since 1929, Barney Greengrass
is frantic on weekends, when
locals come to feast on
huge platters of smoked
fish—whitefish, sable, sturgeon
and lox—or sandwiches made
with similar contents, plus
fresh caviar, chopped herring
salad, cheese blintzes,
borscht and other such
specialties. During the week,
it's less frenzied. Credit
cards are taken on bills of $25
or more only.
🕐 Tue–Fri 8.30–4, Sat–Sun 8.30–5
🍴 L $15, D $20
🚇 86th Street (1, 9)
🚌 M7, M86, M104

BIG WONG

Map 269 F24
67 Mott Street between Bayard and
Canal streets
Tel 212/964-0540
At this Manhattan restaurant
you're guaranteed a cheap,
tasty meal. Don't expect any
decor, tablecloth or efficient
service. You're here for
noodles (with duck, chicken,
shrimp), congee and other
standard Cantonese dishes.
No credit cards.
🕐 Daily 7.30am–10pm
🍴 L $15, D $20
🚇 Canal Street (J, M, N, Q, R, W, Z, 6)
🚌 M1

BILTMORE ROOM

Map 268 D20
290 Eighth Avenue between 24th and
25th streets
Tel 212/807-0111
www.thebiltmoreroom.com
The traditional grand decor of
marble, mirror and chandelier
belies the inspiration for the
cuisine which is Asian and
occasionally world. The most

eye-catching intro dish is
the giant prawns in sarong,
a composition of prawns,
beets in honey ginger
vinaigrette, avocado tomato
salad and mango mint
salsa. Go for the Indian
spiced salmon or the Algerian
rack of lamb.
🕐 Mon–Thu 5.30–10.30, Fri–Sat
5.30–11, Sun 5.30–10
🍴 L $55, D $55, Wine $40
🚇 23rd Street (C, E)
🚌 M20

BLUE FIN

Map 268 D18
W Times Square Hotel
1567 Broadway at 47th Street
Tel 212/918-1400
www.Brguestrestaurants.com
The vast, theatrical Blue Fin
made a culinary and design
splash when it opened in
2002. It offers the freshest
fish, prepared simply in such
dishes as salmon in a warm
bacon sherry vinaigrette,
or poached halibut in
ancho-chili-and-vegetable
broth. Sushi is available on
the first floor of the two-story
space, which has a dramatic
floating staircase that looks
out over a school of black
fish suspended from the
ceiling against an undulating
ocean-like white wall. There
are 600 wines on the list,
30 by the glass.
🕐 Daily 7–11, 11.30–4, Sun–Mon
5–midnight, Tue–Thu 5–12.30, Fri–Sat
5–1
🍴 L $30, D $45, Wine $32
🚇 49th Street (N, R, W), 50th Street
(1, 9)
🚌 M10, M20, M27, M104

BLUE HILL

Map 268 E22
75 Washington Place, between
MacDougal and Sixth Avenue
Tel 212/539-1776
www.bluehillnyc.com
Candlelight and extravagant
bouquets set the inviting
tone of this below-ground
dining room. It's named for
a farm in Massachusetts
where the chef finds his
seasonal, locally grown
ingredients. Expect corn shoots
in June, squash and apples
in fall. The menu offers six
appetizers and seven entrées—
say, fall mushrooms braised
and steamed with fingerling
potato tart, followed by
roasted trout with a pistou

of vegetables with puréed
basil, or poached duck
with a stew of organic carrots
with toasted spices. Desserts
are enticing.
🕐 Mon–Sat 5.30–11, Sun 5.30–10
🍴 D $55, Wine $35
🚇 W 4th Street (A, C, E, F, S, V)
🚌 M5, M6

BLUE RIBBON BAKERY

Map 269 D22
33 Downing Street at Bedford Street
Tel 212/337-0404
Refreshing sandwiches made
with house-baked breads and

tasty small plates draw
crowds at lunch, while such
dinner entrées as New
Orleans barbecue shrimp
and filet mignon with tomato,
onion and watercress
salad and potato cake
draw night-time customers.
There are so many small
plates—mushroom ravioli,
sweet sopressata, smoked
red trout—you could eat
for two months without
repetition. Cheese lovers
appreciate the choice of goat,
cow and sheep cheeses.
Extensive wine list.
🕐 Tue–Thu noon–midnight, Fri
noon–2am, Sat 11.30am–2am, Sun
11.30am–midnight
🍴 L $22, D $45, Wine $28
🚇 Houston Street (1, 9)
🚌 M20

BLUE SMOKE

Map 268 F20
116 East 27th Street between Park
Avenue South and Lexington Avenue
Tel 212/447-7733
www.bluesmoke.com
The secret of barbecue is
slow cooking and well-
blended spices. Danny Meyer
studied it for three years and
traveled 62,000 miles before
opening this rustic red-hot
restaurant. Barbecue addicts
drool over the rib sampler.
Eight beers are on tap, while
the 50-selection wine list

pairs well with the food. A good jazz room downstairs shares the interesting upstairs menu.

🕘 Wed–Fri 11am–1am, Sat noon–1am, Sun noon–11, Mon–Tue 11.30–11

🍴 L $25, D $36, Wine $27

Ⓢ 23rd Street (6)

🚌 M1, M101, M102, M103

BOLO

Map 268 E20

23 East 22nd Street between Broadway and Park Avenue

Tel 212/228-2200

www.bolorestaurant.com

The contemporary Spanish cuisine shines here against an understated decor. Chef Bobby Flay knows how to successfully assemble contrasting and complementary flavors— anchovies in sour orange, clams in saffron and tomato among the tapas, and rioja- glazed tuna or pork tenderloin with caramelized date sauce among the more substantial dishes. Good selection of wines (13 by the glass) and spectacular array of sherries.

🕘 Mon–Fri noon–2.30, Sun–Thu 5.30–10, Fri–Sat 5.30–11

🍴 L $30, D$50, Wine $24

Ⓢ 23rd Street (N, R, W, 6)

🚌 M1, M2, M3, M6, M7

BOND STREET

Map 269 F22

6 Bond Street between Broadway and Lafayette Street

Tel 212/777-2500

The buzz has lessened at this sleek Japanese spot in a SoHo brownstone, but the glistening sushi and sashimi are as beautiful as ever. Among the appetizers, expect seared duck with shitake and truffle glaze, or monkfish filet with spicy-and-sour salsa. Desserts are innovative Japanese. Traditional tatami rooms are upstairs; downstairs there's a fashionable lounge serving exotic saketinis.

🕘 Mon–Sat 6pm–midnight, Sun 6–11

🍴 D $45, omakase $60–$100, Wine $35

Ⓢ Broadway/Lafayette (F, S, V)

🚌 M1, M5, M6

BOULEY

Map 269 E24

120 West Broadway at Duane Street

Tel 212/964-2525

www.bouley.net

David Bouley made his name

in 1987 when he opened the original Bouley. This gem is his encore. The dining rooms are gorgeous: One is in Venetian stucco with a fireplace; the other has crimson vaulted ceilings and glazed walls hung with Impressionist paintings. The exquisitely prepared cuisine makes occasional Asian references, as in the chilled lobster with Serrano ham, mango and artichoke, in a Thai curry dressing. Don't miss the Valrhona chocolate soufflé.

🕘 Daily 11.30–3, 5.30–11.30

🍴 L $55, D $75, Wine $45

Ⓢ Chambers Street (A, C, E, 1, 2, 3, 9)

🚌 M6, M20

BRASSERIE

Map 267 F17

100 East 53rd Street between Park and Lexington avenues

Tel 212/751-4840

www.restaurantassociates.com

From its theatrical entrance ramp to its buzzing bar, Brasserie is one very cool room and so very New York. The French-Mediterranean menu is satisfying, ranging as it does from salad Niçoise and burgers (with oyster mushrooms, bacon and roasted onions) to duck cassoulet and rice-crusted black sea bass in lemongrass and lime broth. Great sushi and a raw bar, too.

🕘 Mon–Fri 7am–1am, Sat 11am–1am, Sun 11–10

🍴 L $35, D $50, Wine $29

Ⓢ 53rd Street/Lexington Avenue (E, V), 51st Street (6)

🚌 M1, M2, M3, M4, M98, M101, M102, M103

BREAD

Map 269 F23

20 Spring Street between Elizabeth and Mott streets

Tel 212/334-1015

This small casual café makes delicious panini, soups, salads and daily plates. Try the gazpacho in summer

and the prosciutto di Parma with truffle oil, bruschetta, spicy shrimp salad, and delicious bread and tomato soup in winter. There is a choice of wines with 12 wines sold by the glass.

🕘 Daily 11–11

🍴 L $15, D $25

Ⓢ Spring Street (6), Bowery (J, M, Z), Grand Street (S)

🚌 M1

CAFÉ BOULUD

Map 267 E15

20 East 76th Street between Fifth and Madison avenues

Tel 212/772-2600

www.danielnyc.com

Many diners consider this casually smart 1930s-style Parisian neighborhood restaurant their favorite Daniel Boulud restaurant. Three Daniel muses inspire the menu—classics, seasons and ethnic cuisines. You will find a pot au feu and a good bouillabaisse; and entrées inspired by Tuscany, Morocco, Vietnam, Spain and the Caribbean. The 450 wine selections are categorized by varietal.

🕘 Tue–Sat noon–2.30, 5.45–11, Sun–Mon 5.45–11

🍴 L $40, D $60, Wine $25

Ⓢ 77th Street (6)

🚌 M1, M2, M3, M4, M79

CAFE GRAY

Map 266 D16

10 Columbus Circle 3rd floor

Tel 212/823-6338

Despite the views of Central Park, the room is not worthy of the cuisine prepared by Swiss-born Gray Kunz, formerly of Lespinasse. He is a consummate artist able to draw on techniques from around the world to create such dishes as lamb chops on carrots melding orange, lemon, cumin and cayenne or branzino in a verbena flavored bouillon.

🕘 Mon–Sat 11.30–2.15, Mon–Tue 5.30–10, Wed–Sat 5.30–11

🍴 L $40, D $60, Wine $40

Ⓢ 59th Street/Columbus Circle (A, B, C, D, 1, 9)

🚌 M5, M7, M10, M20, M104

EATING

CALLE OCHO

Map 266 D14
446 Columbus Avenue between West
81st and 82nd streets
Tel 212/873 5025
www.calleochonyc.com

Calle Ocho has brought a
limited menu of very good
Latin cuisine to the Upper West
Side. Start with one of the
refreshing ceviches (say,
lobster with lemon, lime and
jalapeño) or appetizers like
arepa with spicy braised short
ribs. Fish and meat dishes are
tasty, both the coffee-glazed
tuna or the basil chimichurri
chicken with roasted almond
sauce.
🕐 Mon–Thu 6–11, Fri 6–midnight, Sat
5–midnight, Sun 11.30–3, 5–10
🍴 D $45, Wine $22
🚇 81st Street (B, C)
🚌 M7, M11, M79

CASA MONO

Map 268 F21
52 Irving Place at 17th Street
Tel 212/253-2773
Mario Batali has turned to
Spain for inspiration at this
small tapas bar reminiscent
of those found in Barcelona
and Madrid. It's crowded and
noisy and the dishes invite
experimentation. There might
be bacalao croquettes with
orange flavored aioli, cockles
with scrambled eggs and
Serrano ham, or oxtails with
piquillo peppers along with
more substantial dishes and
great artisanal cheeses.
Affordable wine and sherry
selection.
🕐 Daily 11.30–2.30, 5.30–midnight
🍴 L $25, D $36, Wine $20
🚇 14th Street/Union Square L, N, Q, R,
W
🚌 M1, M2, M3, M6, M7, M101, M102,
M103

CESCA

Map 266 C15
164 West 75th Street (at Amsterdam
Avenue)
Tel 212/787 6709
www.cescanyc.com
Popular casual Italian trattoria
turning out some very fine
cuisine. Settle into a velvet-
covered booth and order the
veal meatballs in broth or the
roasted oysters under a spicy
tomato zabaglione and crisp
pancetta. It's tasty, relaxing
and eminently affordable.
🕐 Tue–Fri 11.30–2, Tue–Thu 5–11,
Fri–Sat 5–11.30, Sun 5–10
🍴 L $20, D $45, Wine $23
🚇 72nd Street (1, 2, 3, 9)
🚌 M7, M11, M104

CHANTERELLE

Map 269 E24
2 Harrison Street at Hudson Street
Tel 212/966-6960
www.chanterllenyc.com
The presentation of the superb
food is simply exquisite at
this ultra-spacious classic.
The menu changes monthly,
but the cuisine is always full-
flavored. Conclude with one
of the luscious desserts—
molten vanilla cake with spring
strawberries, for example.
🕐 Tue–Sat noon–2.30, 5.30–11, Mon
5.30–11
🍴 L $35, 3-course prix fixe $43, D
3-course prix fixe $95, tasting $115,
Wine $30
🚇 Franklin Street (1, 9)
🚌 M20

CHEZ ES SAADA

Map 269 F22
42 East 1st Street between First and
Second avenues
Tel 212/777-5617
The exotic neo-Moroccan
experience that begins at an
unmarked door leading into a
casbah-style bar continues at
the rose-petal-strewn stairway
leading down to a grotto-like
dining room. The tagines and
couscous are completely au
courant, as are such house
specialties as pan-seared
salmon with lentils, onions,
and slow-roasted tomatoes.
The traditional mezze—katafi-
wrapped prawns with harissa
yogurt—make a wonderful
meal in themselves.
🕐 Mon–Thu 6–midnight, Fri–Sat
6pm–1am
🍴 D $36, Wine $30
🚇 Lower East Side/Second Avenue (F, V)
🚌 M15, M21

CORNER BISTRO

Map 268 D21
331 West 4th Street between Jane Street
and Eighth Avenue
Tel 212/242-9502
The distressed graffiti-covered
tables and booths at this plain
West Village bar remain the
best place in town to grab

burgers. Made with 8oz (225g)
hunks of ground chuck, they
come plain or topped with
bacon or blue cheese. Other
sandwiches and decent chili
are also available. Good jukebox and beer. No credit cards.
🕐 Mon–Sat 11.30am–4am, Sun
noon–4am
🍴 L $10, D $15
🚇 14th Street (A, C, E)
🚌 M14, M20

CRAFT AND CRAFTBAR

Map 268 E20
43 East 19th Street between Broadway
and Park Avenue South
Tel 212/780-0880
When Tom Colicchio conceived
Craft he wanted diners to
create their own dishes from
a menu that was essentially not
any more than a list of
ingredients. This is still the
focus, but the chef now
supplies more direction with
superb results. Most dishes are
roasted (striped bass, quail) or
braised (red snapper, short
ribs). Desserts can be perfect
fresh fruits, intense sorbets or
decadent confections like the
toffee steamed pudding. The
cheeses are stunning. The
leather, copper and steel, and
plain wood furnishings and
fittings recall the Arts & Crafts
movement. Casual Craftbar
takes a similar focus-on-the-
ingredients approach to
sandwiches, fried oysters
and braised dishes.
🕐 Mon–Fri noon–2, Sun–Thu 5.30–10,
Fri–Sat 5.30–11
🍴 L $50, D $60, Wine $28
🚇 23rd Street (N, R, W), 23rd
Street (6)
🚌 M1, M2, M3, M6, M7

EATING

DB BISTRO MODERNE

Map 268 E18
55 West 44th Street between Fifth and Sixth avenues
Tel 212/391-2400
www.danielnyc.com
This most casual and contemporary of Boulud's restaurants, with its carved wood furniture, beaded curtains and fabric-wrapped ceiling panels, is a great Theater District choice. It's famous for its $27 sirloin burger—a fistful of ground sirloin wrapped around red wine-braised short ribs with truffle and foie gras, served with tomato confit and fresh horseradish. Other delights include: roast salmon with honeyed eggplant (aubergine) and stuffed zucchini (courgette) flowers; Muscovy duck breast with blood orange jus. Extensive wine list.
🕐 Mon–Sat noon–2.30, 5.45–11, Sun 5–10
🍴 L $45, D $60, Wine $25
🚇 42nd Street/Grand Central (S, 4, 5, 6, 7), 42nd Street (B, D, F, V)
🚌 M1, M2, M3, M4, M42

CRU

Map 268 E22
24 Fifth Avenue at Ninth Street
Tel 212/529-1700
www.cru-nyc.com
The 3,000-selection wine list (50 by the glass) is a gift to wine lovers to be accompanied by some carefully prepared contemporary European cuisine in elegant surroundings. Start with crudo or appetizers, which will supply such delights as fluke with mango and caviar or tuna with caper espresso and olives praline. Entrees are equally exciting, even revelatory—just try the silky poussin baked in buttermilk and finished with orange paprika carrots and chanterelles and parsley root.
🕐 Mon–Sat 5.30–11 (closed Mon in Aug)
🍴 D $62, Wine $35
🚇 8th Street (N, R, W)
🚌 M2, M3, M5, M8

DANIEL

Map 267 E16
60 East 65th Street at Park Avenue
Tel 212/288-0033
www.danielnyc.com
Lyons-born chef Daniel Boulud opened this restaurant in 1993. It has all the romance of

an Italian Renaissance palazzo, and dining here is a joyous experience. Signature dishes include the creamy oyster velouté with lemongrass and caviar, roast squab stuffed with foie gras and black truffle, and chocolate fondant with nougatine. Warm madeleines, home-made chocolates and petits fours conclude the meal. The predominantly French wine list offers more than 1,600 selections. Jacket and tie required.
🕐 Mon–Thu 5.45–11, Fri–Sat 5.30–11
🍴 D 3-course prix fixe $92, tasting menus $103–$168, Wine $30
🚇 63rd Street/Lexington (F), 68th Street (6)
🚌 M1, M2, M3, M4, M66

DAWAT

Map 267 F16
210 East 58th Street between Second and Third avenues
Tel 212/355-7555
www.restaurant.com/dawat
Cookbook author Madhur Jaffrey consults on the menu at this comfortable Indian, aptly named "invitation to feast." The spices are skillfully blended to subtle effect in such dishes as shrimp in coconut sauce flavored with

curry leaves and smoked tamarind; chicken tikka; and baby goat in cardamom sauce. Appealing rice and vegetarian specialties.
🕐 Mon–Sat noon–3, 5–11, Sun 5–11
🍴 L $60, D $65, Wine $23
🚇 59th Street/Lexington Avenue (6)
🚌 M15, M57, M98, M101, M102, M103

DEVI

Map 268 E21
8 East 18th Street between Fifth Avenue and Broadway
Tel 212/691-1300
Antique palace doors, etched colored glass lanterns, and raw silk will transport you to India in a minute. And so will the food, which draws inspiration from street food and from good regional cuisine. Goan shrimp are cooked with balchao, a vinegar based sauce; fishes are baked in banana leaf to retain their flavor; Manchurian cauliflower is a fiery mixture of tomato sauce with scallions and chilies. All are redolent with cilantro (coriander), mint, tamarind and coconut.
🕐 Mon–Sat noon–2.30, Mon–Thu 5.30–10.30, Fri–Sat 5.30–11, Sun 5–10
🍴 L $20–$25 prix fixe, D $40, 7-course tasting menu $95, vegetarian $55, Wine $30
🚇 14th Street/Union Square (L, N, Q, R, W, 4, 5, 6)
🚌 M2, M3, M5, M6, M7

DIM SUM GO GO

Map 269 F24
5 East Broadway between Catherine and Oliver streets
Tel 212/732-0797
At this small, modernist restaurant you can find the latest in Chinese cuisine: updated dim sum, presented in bamboo steamers or on pupu platters. Expect jicama and lotus root dumplings, crabmeat stuffed in green spinach dough, wood mushrooms and carrot dumplings. Pork buns and shrimp dumplings are the kitchen's nod to tradition.
🕐 Daily 10am–10.30pm
🍴 L $16, D $20
🚇 East Broadway (F), Canal Street (J, M, N, R, Q, W, Z, 6)
🚌 M9, M15, M22

EATING

DIWAN

Map 267 F16
148 East 48th Street between Lexington
and Third avenues
Tel 212/607 5426

This uptown Indian trendsetter
serves more than traditional
dishes like vindaloos, chicken
murgh and tandoori. You can
also expect butter chicken,
apricot Cornish hens, lamb in
almond sauce, and sea bass
with fenugreek sauce.
🕐 Sun–Thu 11.30–2.30, 5–10.30,
Fri–Sat 11.30–2.30, 5–11
🍴 L $15, D $40, Wine $20
🚇 51st Street (6)
🚌 M50, M98, M101, M102, M103

DO HWA

Map 269 D22
55 Carmine Street between Bedford
Street and Seventh Avenue South
Tel 212/414-1224
At Do Hwa (formerly Dok Suni)
you'll experience a Korean
barbecue and learn how to roll
ingredients into a lettuce leaf.
Start with a traditional soup
such as sea kelp with beef.
Follow with pork ribs in spicy
chili pepper, garlic and ginger
sauce, or with bulgogi,
thin grilled slices of rib eye
marinated in soy and garlic
and rolled in lettuce with
rice and miso. Also at 119 First
Avenue (tel 212/477-9506).
No credit cards.
🕐 Mon–Fri 12–3, Tue–Sat 5–midnight,
Sun–Mon 5–11
🍴 L $15, D $32, Wine $27
🚇 West 4th Street (A, C, E, F, S, V)
🚌 M5, M6, M20, M21

DOS CAMINOS

Map 268 E20
373 Park Avenue South between 26th
and 27th streets
Tel 212/294-1000
www.brguestrestaurants.com
This is as far from an enchilada
hut as you can get. The space is
celebratory, the bar stocks 150
tequilas, and the fare covers all
the bases—guacamole made
tableside; shrimp, scallop and
tuna ceviche; chicken mole; and
and pan-roasted snapper
with pineapple-passion fruit
sauce. Desserts run to ice
creams and sorbets such
as guava-mango sorbet.
🕐 Mon–Fri noon–4, Sat–Sun 11.30–4,
Sun–Tue 5–10, Wed–Thu 5–11, Fri–Sat
5–midnight
🍴 L $25, D $40, Wine $26
🚇 28th Street (6)
🚌 M1

ELEVEN MADISON PARK

Map 268 E20
11 Madison Avenue at 24th Street
Tel 212/889-0905
This dramatic dining space,
once the brokers' hall of the
Metropolitan Life insurance
company, is worthy of the
cuisine created by Kerry
Heffernan. The fish dishes

are fragrant and moist
(seared Arctic char in black
truffle vinaigrette), and meat
dishes robust (grilled hanger
steak in shallot sauce).
Appetizers include seared
foie gras in a sauternes
coulis. The international
wine list leans to the French,
and there are 36 options by
the glass.
🕐 Mon–Fri 11.30–2, Sat noon–2,
Mon–Thu 5.30–10.30, Fri–Sat 5.30–11,
Sun 5.30–10
🍴 L $45, D $60, Wine $32
🚇 23rd Street (6)
🚌 M1, M2, M3

ESCA

Map 268 D18
402 West 43rd Street at Ninth Avenue
Tel 212/564-7272
Esca, another star in Mario
Batali's firmament, prepares
fish Southern Italian style.
The menu changes daily, but
you might find Mediterranean
sea bass in sea salt or
Amalfi-style fritto misto,

with crispy scrod, skate,
calamari, steamers, oysters
and shrimp. Appetizers run
to crispy Neapolitan-style

eel and juicy morsels from
a serious raw bar.
🕐 Mon–Sat noon–2.30, Mon 5–10.30,
Tue–Sat 5–11.30, Sun 4.30–10.30
🍴 L $35, D $50, Wine $28
🚇 42nd Street (A, C, E)
🚌 M11

ESTIATORIO MILOS

Map 266 D17
125 West 55th Street between Sixth and
Seventh avenues
Tel 212/245-7400
www.milos.ca
Some 19 selections of fish
are priced by the pound and
range from pompano and
monkfish to tuna and
swordfish. Your choice will
be filleted at the table.
Appetizers lean to the briny,
like calamari stuffed with
three types of cheese and
fresh mint. Honey, nuts
and yogurt come to the fore
in the traditional sweets.
🕐 Mon–Sat noon–3, 5.30–11,
Sun 5–11
🍴 L 3-course prix fixe $35, D $67,
Wine $35
🚇 57th Street (F), 57th Street (N,Q,
R, W)
🚌 M10, M20

ETATS-UNIS

Map 267 F14
242 East 81st Street between Second
and Third avenues
Tel 212/517-8826
French though the motif
maybe, this is still an
American neighborhood
restaurant. The bistro-style
menu changes daily. Look
for veal in Riesling with shitake
and oyster mushrooms, and
a charcoal-grilled swordfish
in sweet red pepper purée.
Desserts are delicious and
there is a good selection
of cheeses.
🕐 Daily 6–11
🍴 D $50, Wine $20
🚇 77th Street (6)
🚌 M15, M79, M98, M101, M102, M103

FELIDIA

Map 267 F16
243 East 58th Street between Second
and Third avenues
Tel 212/758-1479
www.lidiasitaly.com
Owner Lidia Bastianich is a
tireless promoter of Italian
cuisine. Felidia is one of the
city's top Italian restaurants—
expensive but worth it.
The Istrian wedding pillows,
stuffed with rum, raisins

EATING

FOUR SEASONS

Map 267 F17
99 East 52nd Street between Park and
Lexington avenues
Tel 212/754-9494
www.fourseasonsrestaurant.com
Titans and moguls have regular tables at this modernist power restaurant designed by Philip Johnson and Mies van der Rohe. When it opened in 1959, it helped launch the city's food revolution. The square bar at the center of the rosewood-paneled Grill Room is a great cocktail spot. The pièce de résistance is the Pool Room, with a large fountain as centerpiece. Chef Christian Albin's signature dish is roast duck, which is carved table-side. The soufflés are justly famous. First-rate wine list.
🕐 Mon–Fri noon–2, 5–9.30, Sat 5–11
🍴 L $70, D $100, Wine $77
🚇 51st Street (6), Fifth Avenue/53rd Street (E, V)
🚌 M50, M98, M101, M102, M103

and three cheeses, are a signature dish, but chef Fortunato Nicotra has added many regional dishes,

such as roasted goose ravioli. The wine list concentrates on great Italian selections.
🕐 Mon–Thu noon–2.30, 5–11, Fri noon–2, 5–11.30, Sat 5–11.30
🍴 L $40, 3-course prix fixe $29.50, D $55, Wine $35
🚇 59th Street (4, 5, 6)
🚌 M15, M57, M98, M101, M102, M103

FIAMMA OSTERIA

Map 269 E23
206 Spring Street between Sixth Avenue and Sullivan Street
Tel 212/653-0100
www.brgnestrestaurants.com
An Italian bistro with attitude, this bi-level restaurant is as much about Hollywood styling as it is about food. Red wine braised octopus and corona beans with olives and peppers, stracci with rabbit Bolognese and other exceptional pastas, plus veal chops perfumed with sage and served with caramelized sweet and sour cipollini onions are some of the beguiling dishes.
🕐 Mon–Fri noon–2.30, Sun–Thu 5.30–11, Fri–Sat 5.30–midnight
🍴 L $36, D $60, Wine $32
🚇 Spring Street (C, E)
🚌 M6

FLEUR DE SEL

Map 268 E20
5 East 20th Street between Broadway and Fifth Avenue
Tel 212/460-9100
www.fleurdeselnyc.com
It may look unassuming but the food is not at this French gem. Many dishes have surprising elements.

Imagine venison in a beet licorice sauce, sea bass with Malbec wine sauce or rack of lamb with horseradish crème and rosemary jus. Desserts are equally thrilling.
🕐 Daily noon–2, Mon–Thu 6–10.30, Fri–Sat 5.30–10.30, Sun 5.30–9
🍴 L prix fixe $30, D prix fixe $52, 6-course $82, Wine $37
🚇 23rd Street (N, R, W)
🚌 M2, M3, M5, M6, M7

GONZO

Map 268 D21
140 West 13th Street between Sixth and Seventh avenues
Tel 212/645-4606
Gonzo may be moderately priced, but the rustic food is very good, made with ultra-fresh ingredients and served to a hip lively crowd in a comfortable setting. Start your meal with a plate of sliced meats and cheeses or cicchetti, such as beet and Gorgonzola salad, or chickpea and sun-dried tomato spread. The pastas and pizzas are inventive. Among entrées, the Venetian calf's liver is superb.
🕐 Daily 5.30–midnight
🍴 D $40, Wine $28
🚇 14th Street
🚌 M5, M6, M20

GOOD WORLD BAR AND GRILL

Map 269 G24
3 Orchard Street between Canal and Division streets
Tel 212/925-9975
Distinctive Swedish cuisine is served in this lively, refreshing dining room. Here, several kinds of herring are offered, along with gravlax, Swedish meatballs and game in season. A Swedish interpreted burger comes with capers and beets.
🕐 Daily noon–4am
🍴 L $30, D $35, Wine $28
🚇 East Broadway (F), Grand Street (S)
🚌 M15

GOTHAM BAR & GRILL

Map 268 E21
12 East 12th Street between Fifth Avenue and University Place
Tel 212/620-4020
www.gothambarandgrill.com
Unique among Manhattan celebrity chefs, Alfred Portale has not yet created his own mini-chain. This may be why his fresh-tasting dramatically presented contemporary cuisine continues to excite even after more than 20 years. Rack of lamb is Portale's signature dish, but you can't go wrong with the truffle crusted halibut with verjus sauce or the Snake River Farms pork with caramelized cipollini onions. The warm apple and mango tartes tatin and the warm Gotham chocolate cake are sublime. Extra-special tea selections.
🕐 Mon–Fri noon–2.15, Mon–Thu 5.30–10, Fri 5.30–11, Sat 5–11, Sun 5–10
🍴 L $35, D $70, Wine $40
🚇 14th Street/Union Square (L, N, Q, R, W, 4, 5, 6)
🚌 M2, M3, M5

EATING

GRAMERCY TAVERN
Map 268 E20
42 East 20th Street between Broadway and Park Avenue South
Tel 212/477-0777
www.gramercytavern.com

Danny Meyer's stellar restaurant, under chef Tom Colicchio, still shines. Both the main dining room (a warren of several cozy rooms) and the more casual tavern in the front are striking and comfortable. The truly warm hospitality and the seamless service make this one of the city's top tables. You can't go wrong on this menu, which offers a seared foie gras paired with a rhubarb tart, arugula and sherry vinegar, and a roasted monkfish wrapped with pancetta. Twenty-five wines from the superb list are available by the glass. Desserts are equally as delightful as the main dishes.
Dining room: Mon–Fri noon–2, Mon–Thu 5.30–10, Fri–Sat 5.30–11; Tavern: Sun–Thu noon–11, Fri–Sat noon–midnight
L $35, 3-course prix fixe $36, D 3-course prix fixe $76, tasting menu $95; Tavern L $35, D $40, Wine $20
23rd Street (N, R, W)
M1, M2, M3, M6, M7

GRAND CENTRAL OYSTER BAR
Map 268 E18
Grand Central Terminal, 42nd Street and Park Avenue
Tel 212/490-6650
www.oysterbarny.com
You don't have to love oysters to love this legendary room in the lower level of Grand Central. Since it opened in 1913 the Guastavino-tiled space has starred in many a movie. Today, it's jammed at lunch and busy in the early evening with people

sampling the 20–30 fresh fish choices, or slurping down oysters in a dozen varieties, all flown in daily. The chowders and chowderlike panroasts are famous.
Mon–Fri 11.30–9.30, Sat noon–9.30
L $35, D $45, Wine $25
42nd Street/Grand Central (4, 5, 6)
M1, M2, M3

HAMPTON CHUTNEY
Map 269 F23
68 Prince Street between Crosby and Lafayette streets
Tel 212/226-9996
South Indian dosas and uttapas are the specialties of this counter-style eatery. The classic dosa is filled with spiced potato here, but many Western-inspired variations are offered, from avocado, tomato, arugula and jack cheese, to tuna with cilantro-chutney dressing. Good sandwiches on black, sourdough and other breads, too. Chai and lassi are the choice drinks.
Daily 11–9
$12
Prince Street (N, R), Broadway/Lafayette (F, S, V), Spring Street (6)
M1, M6

THE HARRISON
Map 269 E24
355 Greenwich Street at Harrison Street
Tel 212/274-9310
www.theharrison.com
With its tufted leather banquettes and weathered wood paneling, this friendly, inviting restaurant is the kind of neighborhood spot where people drop in regularly. The food is brimming with flavor; the skillet calf's liver comes with bacon, onion and potato strudel in a rich sherry sauce; while sautéed skate is redolent of treviso, pancetta and preserved lemon. The spicy French fries are superb.

Mon–Thu 5.30–11, Fri–Sat 5.30–11.30, Sun 5–10
D $45, Wine $25
Franklin Street (1, 9)
M20

HELL'S KITCHEN
Map 268 D18
679 Ninth Avenue between West 46th and 47th streets
Tel 212/977-1588
Here, a contemporary interpretation of Mexican cuisine uses prime American ingredients. Start with calamari in smoked chipotle broth, or chayote and portobello mushroom roll with chipotle pepper sauce. The strong exotic drinks from the bar match the interesting and robust flavors.
Tue–Fri 11.30–3, Sun–Tue 5–11, Wed–Sat 5–midnight
L $20, D $37, Wine $24
42nd Street (A, C, E)
M11

HOLY BASIL
Map 269 F22
149 Second Avenue between East 9th and 10th streets
Tel 212/460-5557 or 212/645-8965
www.holybasilrestaurant.com
This is one of the city's best Thai restaurants. Here, the

kitchen balances the flavors of sweet and salt associated with the cuisine. The stars are the fish dishes, such as the whole crisp fish, which you can order in red chili sauce or a delicious tamarind sauce. Wine selections pair well with the food.
Mon–Thu 5–11.30, Fri 5–midnight, Sat 3–midnight, Sun 3–11.30
D $30, Wine $23
Astor Place (6)
M15

HONMURA AN
Map 269 E23
170 Mercer Street between Houston and Prince streets
Tel 212/334-5253

EATING

When restaurant critic Ruth Reichl chose this as one of the first restaurants she would review after arriving at the *New York Times*, she shocked the city's culinary establishment. This noodle house continues to ladle out the food she praised—hot and cold udon and soba with toppings and dipping sauces (nori, mushrooms, salmon caviar and wild greens). The tasting plates are superb (slices of duck marinated in red wine and sweet soba or blanched asparagus with sesame seed dressing).

◷ Wed–Sat noon–2.30, Tue–Thu 6–10, Fri–Sat 6–10.30, Sun 6–9.30

🍴 L $22, D $40, Wine $44

Ⓜ Broadway/Lafayette (F, S, V), Prince Street (N, R), Bleecker Street (6)

🚌 M1, M6

I COPPI

Map 269 G22
432 East 9th Street between First Avenue and Avenue A
Tel 212/254-2263
www.icoppinyc.com

This restaurant is like a piece of Tuscany in Manhattan. Wood tables and rush-seated chairs create a rustic charm accompanied by music from the opera and floral bouquets. Tuna carpaccio is paper-thin and spiked with green peppercorn sauce; sliced pears with Gorgonzola and stracchino cheese make for a perfect salad. Among the secondi, there might be grilled wild boar, or wild striped bass with caper and black olives. The wine list leans to Italy.

◷ Mon–Thu 5–11, Fri 5–11.30, Sat 11.30–3, 5–10, Sun 11.30–4, 5–10.30

🍴 D $50, Wine $22

Ⓜ Astor Place (6)

🚌 M8, M14, M15

L'IMPERO

Off map 268 F18
45 Tudor City Place (access from East 41st Street)
Tel 212/599-5045
www.limpero.com

Tucked away in Tudor City, L'Impero is a lovely hideaway. The dining rooms are comfortable and seductively lit, the service gracious, and the food extremely good and even affordable. Taste the roasted lobster with chickpeas, the extraordinary

JEAN-GEORGES

Map 266 D16
Trump International Hotel Tower
1 Central Park West between 60th and 61st streets
Tel 212/299-3900
www.jean-georges.com

Jean-Georges Vongerichten is the toast of the town. Thoroughly French, he has developed a signature cuisine that is intensely flavored and highly textured, based on vegetable and fruit essences, oils, vinaigrettes and broths. Stellar examples are the peekytoe crab and English pea fondue with rhubarb gelée and shiso purée, and the veal tenderloin with fricasee of mushrooms, fava beans, and Meyer lemon with liquid Parmesan. It's hard to snag a table here, so consider dining in the less formal Nougatine at the same address. There's a 700-plus-strong wine list. Terrace dining in summer.

◷ Mon–Fri 12–2.30, 5.30–11, Sat 5.30–11, closed Sun

🍴 L $45, 3-course $20 (in Nougatine), 2-course $24; D $60, 4-course prix fixe $95, 7-course prix fixe $125, Wine $22

Ⓜ 59th Street/Columbus Circle (A, C, B, D, 1, 9)

🚌 M7, M10, M20

pastas (farfalle with sweetbreads, bitter greens, chanterelles and shallots or the duck and foie gras agnolotti), and delicious secondi like the roast capretto. The wine list is excellent and fairly priced.

◷ Mon–Thu noon–2.30, 5.30–10.30, Fri noon–2.30, 5–11.30, Sat 5–11.30

🍴 L $36, D $50, tasting menu $95, Wine $26

Ⓜ 42nd Street/Grand Central (4, 5, 6)

🚌 M15, M27, M42, M50

JEWEL BAKO

Map 269 F22
239 East 5th Street between Second and Third avenues
Tel 212/979-1012

This tiny restaurant is the domain of sushi artist Kazuo Yoshida. Sushi cognoscenti either experience nirvana or complain because they want it done their way. Tables and golden bamboo chairs are set under a bamboo-lined barrel-vaulted ceiling. Diners are presented with slices of sea bass, pike, eel, mackerel and octopus, sprinkled variously with sea salt, yuzu pepper, sesame or grated daikon, or smeared with wasabi paste.

◷ Mon–Sat 6.30–10.30

🍴 D $50, omakase $50, tasting menu $85, Wine $36

Ⓜ Astor Place (6)

🚌 M8, M15, M103

JOHN'S PIZZERIA PIZZA

Map 268 D22
278 Bleecker Street between Sixth and Seventh avenues
Tel 212/243-1680

The pizza served at this John's Pizzeria is frequently touted as the best in the city, and it is extraordinarily good indeed. Note that this

is not a pizza parlor; slices are not available. Instead, take a booth and order a whole pie loaded with toppings—more than 50 are available. No credit cards.

◷ Mon–Sat 11.30–11.30, Sun noon–11.30

🍴 L $20, D $30, Wine $18

Ⓜ West 4th Street (A, C, E, F, S, V), Christopher Street/Sheridan Square (1, 9)

🚌 M5, M20

EATING

JOJO

Map 267 F16

160 East 64th Street between Lexington and Third avenues

Tel 212/223 5050

www.jean-georges.com

Jean-Georges was 29 in 1986, when he opened the bistro that made him a name in New York. The town house dining rooms remain sumptuous and glowing, with their plum banquettes, sconces and flattering illumination. The signature appetizer is still shrimp dusted in orange powder. Desserts are also exceptional—just try the molten chocolate cake.

 Daily noon–2.30, 5.30–10

 L $45, D $60, Wine $36

 63rd Street/Lexington (F)

 M66, M98, M101, M102, M103

KATZ'S DELI

Map 269 G22

205 East Houston Street between Ludlow and Orchard streets

Tel 212/254-2246

www.homedelivery.com

The site of the hilarious climactic scene in *When Harry Met Sally* is the last remaining deli in what was

once a thriving Jewish neighborhood. Opened in 1888, it upholds deli traditions: nondescript surroundings and immense knishes and pastrami sandwiches. Credit cards accepted on bills of $20 and more only.

 Sun–Tue 8am–10pm, Wed–Thu 8am–11pm, Fri–Sat 8am–3am

 L $15, D $20

 Lower East Side/Second Avenue (F, V)

 M14, M15, M21

KITTICHAI

Map 269 E23

60 Thompson Street between Broome and Spring streets

Tel 212/219-2000

www.kittichairestaurant.com

Lush drapes and a reflecting pool set the dramatic tone at this sizzling downtown boîte. Named for the chef, who knows how to produce great flavors using kaffir lime, lemongrass, Thai basil, chili coriander and coconut with the requisite balance between sweet, sour, salty and spicy. The Thai riffs include a loin of lamb with Thai basil pesto, and sea bass in caramelized red curry.

 Daily noon–3, Sun–Thu 6–11, Fri–Sat 6–midnight

 L $30, D $40, Wine $35

 Spring Street (C, E)

 M1, M6

LA PALAPA

Map 269 F22

77 St. Mark's Place between First and Second avenues

Tel 212/777-2537

www.lapalapa.com

At this dark and sultry Mexican, cookbook author Diana Kennedy is the inspiration for much of

the cooking, which reveals the complex flavors of epazote, cactus pads, avocado leaves and numerous chilies. The balance is always right, whether in the shrimp with red mole sauce, or the baked cod with guajillo, garlic and achiote barbecue sauce. Meat dishes are also well spiced. Then there are the extras—pinto beans with smoked bacon and chayotes in spicy cream.

 Mon–Fri noon–midnight, Sat–Sun 11am–midnight

 L $25, D $35, Wine $26

 Astor Place (6)

 M8, M15

LE BERNARDIN

Map 266 D17

155 West 51st Street between Sixth and Seventh avenues

Tel 212/489-1515

www.le-bernardin.com

Le Bernardin, the best seafood restaurant in the city, may also be the best restaurant in the city. The teak-paneled room is spacious and comfortable, the service discreet and precise, and the food exquisite. Chef Eric Ripert's dishes are designed to show off the flavor and texture of the specific type of fish. Cod is served in a sage and garlic broth, halibut poached in lemongrass and coconut, and monkfish oven roasted and served with lemon-paprika sauce. Signature appetizers— tuna carpaccio; a scallop wrapped in a cabbage leaf with foie gras and truffles and steamed; and black bass ceviche topped with coriander, mint, jalapeños and tomatoes—are all gems. Desserts are equally inspirational.

 Mon–Fri noon–2.30, Mon–Thu 5.30–10.30, Fri–Sat 5.30–11

 L prix fixe $49, D 3-course prix fixe $92, Wine $45

 47th–50th streets/Rockefeller Center (B, D, F, V), 49th Street (N, R, W)

 M5, M6, M7

LE COLONIAL

Map 267 F16

149 East 57th Street between Lexington and Third avenues

Tel 212/752-0808

www.lecolonialnyc.com

The bamboo-and-fans French colonial ambience is a perfect backdrop for the southeast Asian cuisine at this striking spot. Start with chao tom (grilled shrimp wrapped around sugarcane with angel-hair noodles, lettuce, mint and peanut dipping sauce) or the delicious steamed ravioli with chicken and mushrooms. The steamed sea bass dishes are outstanding.

 Mon–Fri noon–2, Sun–Mon 5.30–10.30, Tue–Thu 5.30–11, Fri–Sat 5.30–11.30

 L $30, D $40, Wine $38

 59th Street (4, 5, 6), 59th Street/Lexington Avenue (N, R, W)

 M57, M98, M101, M102, M103

EATING

LE ZINC

Map 269 E24
139 Duane Street
Tel 212/513-0001
www.lezincnyc.com
Lace curtains, a zinc counter
and French posters may
make this bistro look French,
but the cuisine is international.
The Waltucks, who own this
place as well as Chanterelle,
keep everything top quality

but still affordable. Besides
bistro dishes like hanger
steak in red wine, terrines,
charcuterie and skate with
pine nuts and redcurrants,
you might find Asian-inspired
appetizers. Desserts are
courtesy of Chanterelle's
excellent pastry chef. Good
wine list.
🕐 Daily 8am–midnight
🍴 L $25, D $40, Wine $21
🚇 Chambers Street (A, C), Chambers
Street (1, 2, 3, 9)
🚌 M1, M6

LONDEL'S

Off map 266 D12
2620 Frederick Douglass Boulevard
between 139th and 140th streets
Tel 212/234-6114
www.londelsrestaurant.com
The South has given the
United States its most
distinctive cuisine, and this
restaurant serves some of the
best, from the Southern fried
chicken and barbecue back
ribs to the blackened catfish.
Order collard greens or
candied yams on the side,
and bread pudding with
rum sauce. You'll have
had a feast. Live music on
Friday and Saturday.
🕐 Tue–Sat 11.30–4, 5–midnight, Sun
11–5
🍴 L $18, D $30, Wine $25
🚇 145th Street (A, B, C, D)
🚌 M10

LUPA

Map 269 E22
170 Thompson Street between Bleecker
and Houston streets
Tel 212/982-5089
www.luparestaurant.com
Lupa, beloved Food Channel
host Mario Batali's moderately
priced restaurant, has the feel
of a casual Roman trattoria.
The cuisine starts with ultra-
fresh staples, many of which
are made on the premises,
notably the pasta, sausages
and cheeses featured as

appetizers. The simple, intense
main dishes range from a
classic saltimbocca to bucatini
all' amatriciana, made with
bacon, onions and cilantro.
Side dishes such as the braised
escarole and the cauliflower
with capers are worthy, too.
🕐 Mon–Fri noon–2.30, 5–11.30,
Sat–Sun noon–2.30, 4.45–11.30
🍴 L $27, D $35, Wine $21
🚇 West 4th Street (A, C, E, F, S, V)
🚌 M5, M6, M21

MARK JOSEPH STEAKHOUSE

Map 269 F25
261 Water Street at Peck Slip
Tel 212/277-0020
www.markjosephsteakhouse.com
Those who have had enough
of Peter Luger's sawdust-on-
the-floor style claim that this
sleek and more modern meat
specialist is the city's best
steakhouse. The porterhouse is
the choice cut. Add a salad
and an order of the addictive
hash-brown potatoes, finish
with the apple galette or a
slice of pecan pie.
🕐 Mon–Fri 11.30–10, Fri 11.30–11, Sat
5–11
🍴 L $30, D $60, Wine $30
🚇 Broadway-Nassau (A, C), Fulton
Street (J, M, Z, 2, 3, 4, 5)
🚌 M9, M15

MAROONS

Map 268 D21
244 West 16th Street between Seventh
and Eighth avenues
Tel 212/206-8640
www.maroons.citysearch.com
Southern and Jamaican
flavors are the draw at this
small, unassuming restaurant.
This is one place you can find
fried green tomatoes, luscious
fried chicken, fiery Jamaican
jerk chicken and other regional
delights.
🕐 Tue–Sun 11.30–3.30, daily
5.30–midnight
🍴 L $25, D $35, Wine $21
🚇 18th Street (1, 9), 14th Street (A, C, E)
🚌 M20

MASA

Map 266 D16
Time Warner Center
10 Columbus Circle 4th Floor
Tel 212/823-9800
www.masanyc.com
Currently the Holy Grail of
dining in Manhattan. Here,
sushi chef Mr Takayama (from
Tokyo via Los Angeles) holds
forth behind his hinoki counter
creating whatever he has
selected as the freshest and
best from around the world. It
seats only 26 (10 at the sushi
bar) and sushi lovers swear
that it is nirvana.
🕐 Tue–Fri noon–1.30, Mon–Sat 6–9.30
🍴 $350 prix fixe ($100 penalty for
cancellations within 48 hours of
reservation), Wine $35
🚇 59th Street/Columbus Circle (A, B,
C, D, 1, 9)
🚌 M5, M7, M10, M20, M104

MAYA

Map 267 F16
1191 First Avenue between East 64th
and 65th streets
Tel 212/585-1818
www.modernmexican.com
Sophisticated Mexican cuisine
is the draw here. The chile
relleno stuffed with seafood
and gouda cheese is a palate-
pleasing combination and the
guacamole, served in the stone
pestle in which it's made, is
among the best in the city.
The pork tenderloin marinated
with onion-orange salsa is
ultra tender and richly flavored.
A winner. No credit cards.
🕐 Tue–Thu 5–11, Fri–Sat 5–11.30,
Sun–Mon 5–10
🍴 D $42, Wine $28
🚇 Lexington Avenue/63rd Street (F),
68th Street (6)
🚌 M15

MERMAID INN

Map 269 F22

96 Second Avenue between 5th and 6th streets

Tel 212/671 5070

www.themermaidnyc.com

This is the closest that Manhattan can come to a seafood shack complete with ocean paraphernalia and navigational charts. The menu opens with a small selection of raw shellfish and follows with everything from chowder and spaghetti fra diavolo to zaruela brimming with lobster tail, cod and squid. No desserts are available, except what the house provides for free.

🕐 Mon–Sat 6–1

🍴 D $30, Wine $24

🚇 Astor Place (6), Eighth Street (N, R, W)

🚌 M15, M103

MESA GRILL

Map 268 E21

102 Fifth Avenue between 15th and 16th streets

Tel 212/807-7400

www.mesagrill.com

When Bobby Flay opened this restaurant in 1991, he

introduced New Yorkers to the spices of the Southwest, and the place continues to excite. The red walls recall Sedona rock, the shrimp and fresh corn with black pepper tamale is hot off the grill, and the cactus pear margaritas cool the heat. Follow the cornmeal-crusted oysters and mango habanero sauce with sixteen-spice chicken in cilantro-pumpkin seed sauce. Brunches are distinctive as well—it's not everywhere you'll find tequila-smoked-salmon quesadilla.

🕐 Mon–Fri noon–2.30, Sat 11.30–2.30, Sun 11.30–3, Sun–Fri 5.30–10.30, Sat 5–11

🍴 L $25, D $48, Wine $26

🚇 14th Street/Union Square (L, N, Q, R, W, 4, 5, 6)

🚌 M2, M3, M5, M14

MI COCINA

Map 268 D21

57 Jane Street at Hudson Street

Tel 212/627-8273

Mi Cocina was one of the city's first restaurants to offer authentic regional Mexican cuisine. Start with the shrimp

in spicy chile adobo or the corn tamale filled with guajillo chile sauce and Mexican white cheese. To follow, there are rich mole-coated chicken enchiladas or lighter dishes like the chicken marinated with lime, oregano and blue agave tequila. The brightly painted rooms decked with folk art strike just the right note, and the small garden courtyard is romantic on a summer evening.

🕐 Sat–Sun 11.30–2.30, Sun–Thu 4.30–10.30, Fri–Sat 4.30–11.30

🍴 D $40, Wine $25

🚇 14th Street (A, C, E)

🚌 M20

MIRCHI

Map 268 D22

29 Seventh Avenue South between Bedford and Morton streets

Tel 212/414-0931

www.mirchiny.com

This sleek neo-Indian offers fiery street food and regional dishes and a list of wines that pair well with it all. Among the *chats* (snacks), try the bhel poori, made with puffed rice, onion and tomato and served with tamarind and cilantro chutneys. Peppery Chettinad chicken comes from South India; Gujarat contributes chickpea cakes with chilies and cilantro; the herb-swathed fish is a Sind specialty. The tandoor turns out succulent meats and fish spiced variously with chili, coriander, ginger and garlic.

🕐 Mon–Fri noon–3, 5.30–midnight, Sat noon–1am, Sun noon–11

🍴 $33, Wine $20

🚇 Houston Street (1, 9)

🚌 M20, M21

MOLYVOS

Map 266 D17

871 Seventh Avenue between West 55th and 56th streets

Tel 212/582-7500

www.molyvos.com

This large space with a café, a bar and two dining rooms, brings Greece to Manhattan. The Greek dips and spreads are irresistible, including the garlicky roasted eggplant (aubergine) purée and the tzatziki, a blend of yogurt, cucumber, garlic, mint, dill and lemon. Also outstanding are the cold meze such as grilled baby octopus with olives, fennel, lemon and oregano, and fava beans mashed with olive oil. Marinated lamb shanks, whole grilled fish and

rabbit stew are traditional main courses. The 165-bottle wine list includes more than 50 Greek wines; 10 are available by the glass.

🕐 Mon–Sat noon–3, 5.30–11.30 (Sat until midnight), Sun noon–11

🍴 L $30, D $43, Wine $32

🚇 Seventh Avenue (B, D, E), 57th Street (N, R, Q, W)

🚌 M10, M20

MONTRACHET

Map 269 E24

239 West Broadway between Walker and White streets

Tel 212/219-2777

www.myriadrestaurantgroup.com

The focus is on the plate in this spare, minimal classic. Chef Chris Gesualdi expresses his distinctive style in such dishes as roasted salmon with Riesling and magret of duck with verjus and huckleberries. Appetizers range from lobster and corn soup to foie gras with oxtail and candied root vegetables. Chocolate and fruit are the core dessert ingredients.

🕐 Mon–Thu 5.30–9.45, Fri noon–2, 5.30–10.45, Sat 5.30–10.45

🍴 L $33, D 3-course prix fixe $35 and $46, D $56, Wine $28

Canal Street (A, C, E), Franklin Street
(1, 9)
 M6, M20

MOUSTACHE
Map 269 G21
265 East 10th Street between First
Avenue and Avenue A
Tel 212/228-2022
This unadorned restaurant
serves great, inexpensive
Middle Eastern cuisine.
A favorite specialty is the ouzi—
filo dough wrapped around
fragrantly spiced basmati rice,
chicken, carrots, sweet peas,
onions, raisins and almonds.
Pizzas come with eight differ-
ent toppings. No credit cards.
 Daily noon–midnight
 L $25, D $30, wine $18
 First Avenue (L), Astor Place (6)
 M8, M14, M15

NAM
Map 269 E24
110 Reade Street at West Broadway
Tel. 212 267 1777
Nam stands out for its style
and for its authentic and often
unique dishes. Particularly
alluring are the appetizers.
Banh xeo, for example, is a
crepe filled with mushrooms,
bean sprouts, coconut-flavored
rice, shrimp and chicken; ca
tim nuong—simple but
addictive—consists of grilled
Asian eggplant (aubergine)
with ginger, lime, garlic and a
little chili. Among the many
main dishes, the crisp red
snapper and the chicken with
chile lemongrass sauce are
excellent dinner choices.
 Mon–Fri noon–2, Sun–Thu 5.30–10,
Fri–Sat 5.30–11
 L $22, D $28, Wine $28
 Chambers Street (1, 9)
 M20

NEGRIL VILLAGE
Map 269 E22
70 West 3rd Street between La Guardia
Place and Thompson Street
Tel 212/477-2804
The neo-Caribbean dishes sit
wonderfully on the tongue at
this sultry restaurant. It's
hard to choose between the
succulent curried goat, and
such specialties as the ackee
and the saltfish. Tropical
desserts include key lime
cheesecake with mango coulis.
The downstairs rum lounge
pours 50 different rums.
 Mon–Fri noon–midnight,, Sat–Sun
noon–2am

NOBU
Map 269 E24
105 Hudson Street between Franklin
and North Moore streets
Tel 212/219-0500
www.myriadrestaurantgroup.com
Celebrities flock to Drew
Nieporent's TriBeCa hotspot
for the artistic sushi and
sashimi fashioned by chef
Nobu Matsuhisa. If you can
afford it, choose the omakase
menu, which will deliver the
chef's inspirations for the day.
Or choose from baby
abalone, live scallop or
sashimi drizzled with garlic
and ginger-flavored olive oil.
Masu sake is served in small
cedar cups with salted rims;
finish with green tea crème
caramel. Reservations are
hard to come by; the next
best thing is to drop in to
Next Door Nobu.
 Mon–Thu 5.45–midnight, Fri–Sat
5.45–1, Sun 5.45–11
 D $50, omakase $80–120,
Wine $40
 Franklin Street (1, 9)
 M20

 L $22, D $40, Wine $20
 West 4th Street (A, C, E, F, S, V)
 M5, M21

NYONYA
Map 269 F23
194 Grand Street between Mott and
Mulberry streets
Tel 212/334-3669
Malaysian cuisine draws on
many different Asian cooking
traditions—Chinese, Indian, Thai
and Malay. You can sample
some of the country's appealing, sometimes spicy dishes at
this plain favorite. You have a
wide choice of rice, noodle,
casserole and other dishes; start
with a roti (Indian pancake) or
the satays, and follow with a
fiery sambal or a curry made
with lemongrass, chili and
coconut milk. No credit cards.
 Daily 11am–11.30pm
 L $20, D $25
 Grand Street (S)
 M1

OCEANA
Map 267 E17
55 East 54th Street between Madison
and Park avenues
Tel 212/759-5941
www.oceanarestaurant.com
With its nautical interior,
Oceana is something like a

streamlined yacht, even
though it's in a handsome
town house. The French-Asian
cuisine is bold and often
surprising, as exemplified by,
for example, the loup de mer
accompanied by a tamarind
and wasabi sauce, and the
salmon roulade, which is
stoked up with smoked bacon
and peppered green apple and
served in a red wine and olive
sauce. The international wine
list offers 1,100 selections,
15 by the glass.
 Mon–Fri noon–2.30, Mon–Fri
5.30–10.30, Sat 5–10.30
 L 3-course prix fixe $48, D 3-course
prix fixe $72, Wine $30
 53rd Street/Fifth Avenue (E, V)
 M1, M2, M3, M4

ODEON
Map 269 E24
145 West Broadway between Thomas
and Duane streets
Tel 212/233-0507
www.theodeonrestaurant.com
In the early 1980s this
cafeteria-turned-hip-bistro was
the incubator of the downtown
scene. Odeon still has Venetian
blinds on the windows and

chrome stools at the bar, but
nowadays it caters to
neighborhood residents as well
as downtown celebrities, with
a typical bistro menu of onion
soup gratinée, moules and
steak frites. This is a great
late-night stop.
 Mon–Fri 11.45am–2am, Sat–Sun
11am–2am
 L $28, D $42, Wine $18
 Chambers Street (A, C, E),
Chambers Street (1, 2, 3, 9)
 M6, M20

EATING

OTTO ENOTECA PIZZERIA

Map 269 E22
1 Fifth Avenue at 8th Street
Tel 212/995-9559
www.ottopizzeria.com
Mario Batali continues to apply his genius to educating the average American palate to real Italian cuisine and wine. Here, the arena is pizza, which you can have with marinara, or—a better idea—in one of the combinations dreamed up by Mario, such as topped with porcini and taleggio or with tomato, fennel, bottarga (silver mullet roe), pecorino and mozzarella. The wine card is extraordinary, and the gelati are the best in the city, period.
Daily 11.30am–11.30pm
L $18, D $27, Wine $20
West 4th Street (A, C, E, F, S, V)
M2, M3, M5

OUEST

Map 266 C14
2315 Broadway between West 83rd and 84th streets
Tel 212/580-8700
www.ouestny.com
This lively, entertaining restaurant helped raise the Upper West Side's culinary reputation with Tom Valenti's fresh seasonal menu. Settle into one of the cherry-red booths and order the luscious short ribs, one of the braised or roasted meats such as the roast free-range chicken with garlic jus, or a fish dish such as seared tuna with white bean purée, black olive-lemon compote and red pepper coulis. The nightly specials attract crowds, especially on Monday, when the kitchen turns out the chef's signature braised lamb shanks. Desserts are Italian-inspired.
Tue–Thu 5–10.30, Fri–Sat 5–11.30, Sun 10–2, 5–10.30
D $50, Wine $26
86th Street (1, 9)
M 104

PAM REAL THAI

Map 266 C17
404 West 49th Street between Ninth and Tenth avenues
Tel 212/333-7500
www.pamrealthai.com
At this authentic Thai, none of the sweet, sour and salt dishes have been compromised to suit a more timid palate. The traditional favorites are all available: superb hot and milder curries, fiery salads made with green papaya, ground pork with lime dressing, noodle dishes and, best of all, duck with chili sauce and lime leaves. Bring your own bottle. No credit cards.
Daily 11.30–11
L $15, D $20
50th Street (C, E, 1, 9)
M11, M50

PAMPANO

Map 267 F17
209 East 49th Street between 2nd and 3rd avenues
Tel 212/751-4545
www.modernmexican.com
Placido Domingo loves to eat and so he helped open this restaurant where chef Richard Sandoval, who hails from Mexico City, via California, produces great contemporary Mexican using such exciting ingredients as huitlacoche, epazote, pomegranate, queso blanco and every conceivable kind of pepper. The chile rellenos are roasted not fried and stuffed with seafood and tart manchego. Start with any one of the great ceviches and continue with one of the terrific seafood dishes. Meat lovers are out of luck although the lamb in adobo orange sauce is tasty. The outdoor terrace is as close to the beach as you can get in midtown Manhattan.
Mon–Fri 11.30–2.30, Mon–Wed 5–10, Thu–Sat 5–10.30, Sun 5–9.30
L $30, D $51, Wine $32
51st Street (6)
M15, M27, M50, M101, M102, M103

PASTIS

Map 268 D21
9 Ninth Avenue at Little 12th Street
Tel 212/929-4844
www.balthazarny.com

PER SE

Map 266 D16
Time Warner Center, 10 Columbus Circle 4th Floor
Tel 212/823-9335
The room has urban chic and fine views, but diners come to taste the superlative cuisine of Thomas Keller, whom many consider America's finest chef. He has arrived from the Napa Valley and his famous French Laundry. The menu changes daily, but the diners can expect perfectly prepared dishes right down to the finest details. His "oysters and pearls" (oysters, tapioca and osetra caviar) and his "macaroni and cheese" (lobster mascarpone in a lobster broth topped with a wheel of crisp Parmesan) are legendary signature dishes. The wine list has 500 selections to pair with the exquisite food. It's hard to snag one of the 16 tables.
Fri–Sun 11.30–1.30, daily 5.30–10
5-course tasting menu $125, 9-course $150, Wine $40
59th Street/Columbus Circle (A, B, C, D, 1, 9)
M5, M7, M10, M20, M104

At Pastis, you could just as easily be on Paris' rue St Denis around the corner from Les Halles. Every detail rings true: the zinc bar, the smoky mirrors, the tiles and the French ads. Then there are the *plats* (dishes)—onion soup gratinée, croque monsieur, skate *au beurre noir*, steak and moules frites, and, at breakfast, wonderful brioche and egg dishes. Owner Keith McNally's heritage shows through in the fish and chips and the beans on toast. Wine is served in tumblers. Expect lines, and look out for celebrities in summer.
Mon–Fri 9–11.30, Sat–Sun 9–10 (continental breakfast), Mon–Fri noon–5, Sat–Sun 10–5 (brunch), daily 6–midnight (supper Sun–Wed until 1am, Thu until 2am and Fri–Sat until 3am)
L $30, D $35, Wine $18
14th Street (A, C, E)
M11, M14

PEARL OYSTER BAR

Map 268 E22
18 Cornelia Street
Tel 212/691-8211

The fiercely loyal patrons of this spot with a marble bar don't mind lining up for New England favorites such as oysters, creamy chowder and the fried oyster sandwiches doused in rémoulade sauce. The pièce de résistance is the delicious lobster roll encased in a toasted bun.

🕐 Mon–Fri noon–2.30, Mon–Sat 6–11
🍴 L $30, D $40, Wine $28
🚇 West 4th Street (A, C, E, F, S, V)
🚌 M5, M6, M20

PEASANT

Map 269 F23
194 Elizabeth Street between Prince and Spring streets
Tel 212/965-9511
www.peasantnyc.com

This cozy storefront has become a popular chef's hang-out. As the name suggests it produces bold rustic Italian cuisine from its wood-fired ovens. Wood-roasted sardines, roasted clams and really fine pizzas are carefully prepared. The grilled fishes are flavored with the best olive oil, lemon and herbs and cooked to perfection.

🕐 Tue–Sat 6–11, Sun 6–10
🍴 D 40, Wine $22
🚇 Bowery (J, M, Z), Spring Street (6)
🚌 M1, M6

PERIYALI

Map 268 E20
35 West 20th Street between Fifth and Sixth avenues
Tel 212/463-7890
www.periyali.com

This was the first authentic Greek restaurant to open in Manhattan, and it has remained a premier Greek destination. The ambience is warm and appealing (white plaster, dark wood beams and attractive displays of appetizers). Everything is carefully prepared, from the fragrant avgolemono soup to the grilled lamb chops with fresh rosemary.

🕐 Mon–Fri noon–3, Mon–Thu 5.30–10.30, Fri 5.30–11, Sat 5.30–11.30
🍴 L $30, D $40, Wine $32
🚇 23rd Street (N, R, W)
🚌 M2, M3, M5, M6, M7

PETER LUGER STEAKHOUSE

Off map 269 G25
178 Broadway between Bedford and Briggs streets, Williamsburg, Brooklyn
Tel 718/387-7400

Many people will tell you that this old-fashioned beer hall-style restaurant serves the city's best steak. The meat itself is carefully selected, aged on the premises and cooked to perfection. All the traditional cuts are available, but the most fun is the porterhouse, which is sliced tableside. Don't miss the creamed spinach and mashed potatoes. No credit cards.

🕐 Mon–Thu 11.45–10, Fri–Sat 11.45–11, Sun 12.45–10
🍴 L $40, D $60, Wine $27
🚇 Marcy Ave (J, M, Z)

PICHOLINE

Map 266 D16
35 West 64th Street between Central Park West and Broadway
Tel 212/724-8585

The Mediterranean cuisine at Picholine is superb. Among the entrees, the licorice-lacquered squab is exquisite, perfectly complemented by foie gras, glazed turnips and spiced rhubarb marmalade. The wild mushroom and duck risotto is a perennial favorite. It's easy to fill up with such delicious entrees and the main courses on offer—but be sure to save room for one more course. Picholine also has one of the city's most fabulous cheese trays.

🕐 Sat 11.45–2, Tue–Wed 5.15–11, Thu–Sat 5.15–11.45, Sun 5–9
🍴 L prix fixe $35, D 3-course prix fixe $72, Wine $31
🚇 66th Street (1, 9)
🚌 M10, M20

PINTXOS

Off map 269 D23
510 Greenwich Street between Canal and Spring streets
Tel 212/343-9923

Pintxos are Basque tapas, and this unassuming restaurant offers 18 of them—and they are your best bet here, even though the menu also offers eight or so meat and fish entrées. Look for spicy chorizo, Basque anchovies, stuffed mussels and white asparagus, which all go wonderfully well with the available wines.

🕐 Mon–Thu 11.30–10, Fri 11.30–11, Sat 4.30–11
🍴 L $25, D $30, Wine $22
🚇 Spring Street (C, E), Houston Street (1, 9)
🚌 M20

PIO PIO

Map 267 F13
1746 First Avenue between East 90th and 91st streets
Tel 212/426-5800

This is the Peruvian version of the Boston Chicken chain. Order a quarter, half or whole chicken, marinated in secret spices. Then add some ceviche tostones, red beans or yuca frita and a beer, and you've got yourself a tasty meal. Amex credit cards only.

🕐 Daily 11–11
🍴 $15
🚇 86th Street (4, 5, 6)
🚌 M15

PIPA

Map 268 E21
ABC Carpet and Home, 38 East 19th Street between Broadway and Park Avenue South
Tel 212/677-2233

Nuevo Latin king Douglas Rodriguez does Spanish at this lively restaurant, whose name means "great time." You can make a meal of the wonderful tapas—succulent fried oysters with banana-and-lentil salad, horseradish aioli and crispy bacon; shrimp with garlic oil and chilies; or sautéed chorizo. Or you can follow up with a rice, meat or fish dish, or perhaps a gorgeous paella. The white or red sangria are perfect accompaniments, or go for one of the rum drinks.

🕐 Mon–Thu noon–11, Fri noon–midnight, Sat 11am–midnight, Sun 11–10
🍴 L $20, D $40, Wine $32
🚇 4th Street/Union Square (L, N, Q, R, W, 4, 5, 6)
🚌 M1, M2, M3, M6, M7

PRUNE

Map 269 F22
54 East 1st Street between First and
Second avenues
Tel 212/677-6221
Everything is meticulously
prepared at this small,

idiosyncratic restaurant. Dinner
entrées might include roast
duck with green olives, or
whole grilled fish with fennel
oil and salt. Order one of the
carefully prepared vegetable
accompaniments. Choose,
perhaps, between the roast
beets or the bitter greens salad
with oil and lemon juice to
compliment the beautifully
presented dishes.
🄖 Sat–Sun 10–3.30, Mon–Thu 6–11,
Fri–Sat 6–midnight, Sun 5–10
🄙 D $47, Wine $24
🄡 Lower East Side/Second Avenue
(F, V)
🄜 M15, M21

RED CAT

Map 268 C20
227 Tenth Avenue between West 23rd
and 24th streets
Tel 212/242-1122
www.theredcat.com
A downtown art crowd packs
this vivacious, inviting bistro
a narrow crimson room
illuminated by large Moroccan
lanterns. The contemporary
kitchen puts plenty of flavor
into its creations–take, for
example, the crisp skate wing
in caper brown butter, or the
calves' liver au poivre. Tasty
Parmesan fries spiked with
mustard aioli are one of the
most popular side orders.
Desserts are eclectic but
equally delicious. The wine
list is carefully chosen, and
17 selections are available
by the glass.
🄖 Mon–Thu 5.30–11, Fri–Sat
5.30–midnight, Sun 5–10
🄙 D $40, Wine $20
🄡 23rd Street (C, E)
🄜 M11, M23

RIVER CAFÉ

Map 269 G25
1 Water Street at Old Fulton Street,
Brooklyn
Tel 718/522-5200
www.rivercafe.com
Opened in 1977, this old-timer
tucked on a barge under the
Brooklyn Bridge is still one
of the city's most romantic
restaurants, with magical views
of the river and downtown
Manhattan skyline. A dynasty
of great American chefs from
Larry Forgione to the current
Brad Steelman have made the
kitchen famous. Nowadays you
might start with the tuna
tartare with coconut sauce,
then go on to the rack of
lamb with lavender flower
glaze or the sautéed black
sea bass with turmeric
coconut sauce. The chocolate
Brooklyn Bridge remains a
signature dessert. There are
500 selections on the wine list.
🄖 Mon–Sat noon–3, 5.30–10, Fri–Sat
noon–3, 5.30–11, Sun 11.30–3, 5.30–10
🄙 L $40, D 3-course prix fixe $78,
Wine $19
🄡 High Street (A, C), York Street (F)

ROSA MEXICANO

Map 266 D16
61 Columbus Avenue at West 62nd
Street NE corner
Tel 212/977-7700
www.rosamexicano.com
A waterfall studded with
sculptures of Acapulco-style
divers, among other decorative
notes, sets a flashy scene at
this authentic Mexican. The
guacamole, which is made
at the table, is fragrant with
cilantro (coriander) and

oregano, and the menu offers
unusual regional dishes such
salmon al guajillo, beef short
ribs marinated in lime and beer
and *budin Azteca*, a flavorsome
tortilla pie.
🄖 Mon–Fri noon–3, Sat–Sun
11.30–2.30, Tue–Sat 5–11.30, Sun 4–10,
Mon 5–10.30

🄙 L $30, D $42, Wine $24
🄡 59th Street/Columbus Circle (A, B,
C, D, 1, 9)
🄜 M5, M7, M11, M104

RUBY FOO'S

Map 266 C14
2182 Broadway at 77th Street
Tel 212/724-6700
www.brguestrestaurants.com
This, the original Ruby Foo's,
made a big splash when it
opened in 1996 on the Upper
West Side with its dramatic
staircase and red lacquer walls.
The pan-Asian cuisine was the
other big draw then and now,
ranging from dim sum and
sushi to hot-and-sour shrimp
with water chestnuts and
coconut sticky rice, and seven-
flavored beef with ginger
mashed potatoes and chile-
lime salsa. Have fun.
🄖 Mon 11.30–11.30, Tue–Sat
11.30am–12.30pm, Sun 11.30–4.30,
5–11.30
🄙 L $30, D $40, Wine $23
🄡 79th Street (1,9)
🄜 M104

SARABETH'S

Map 267 E13
1295 Madison Avenue between East
92nd and 93rd streets
Tel 212/410-7335
Sarabeth Levine is most
famous for her luscious
baking and breakfasts, but
that does not mean that she
can't turn out equally wonderful lunch and dinner fare.
Try her short ribs in zinfandel
or her hazelnut-crusted sea
bass, and you'll be a fan.
At breakfast, don't miss the
cinnamon French toast or
the pumpkin waffles–and
plan on a light lunch
afterwards.
🄖 Mon–Sat 8am–10.30pm, Sun
8am–10pm (breakfast until 3.30)
🄙 L $20, D $40, Wine $25
🄡 96th Street (6)
🄜 M1, M2, M3, M4

SECOND AVENUE DELI

Map 269 F21
156 Second Avenue between East 9th
and 10th streets
Tel 212/677-0606
www.2ndavedeli.com
The names on the sidewalk
outside this deli recall the
days when the neighborhood
was the Yiddish Theater
District. The interior is
comfortable, the service
swift and good-natured.

Favorite dishes: chopped liver, chicken soup, hefty sandwiches filled with pastrami, corned beef and tongue and, as entrees, the goulash and boiled beef.

⏰ Sun–Thu 7am–midnight, Fri–Sat 7am–3am

💲 L $20, D $35

🚇 Astor Place (6), Third Avenue (L)

🚌 M8, M15

SHUN LEE PALACE

Map 267 F17

155 East 55th Street between Lexington and Third avenues

Tel 212/371-8844

It's still the best Chinese restaurant in the city, even though it's been around since 1972. It may be expensive, but the dining rooms are comfortable and elegant and the Shanghai, Szechuan and Cantonese cuisine is beautifully presented. Besides such traditional dishes as crispy sea bass Hunan style and lobster in black bean sauce, you will find such extraordinary specialties as Grand Marnier prawns and red cooked short ribs Hang Chow style. There's a branch near the Lincoln Center at 43 West 65th Street between Central Park West and Columbus Avenue (tel 212/595-8895)—a good bet for a leisurely meal or a pre-concert snack.

⏰ Mon–Sat noon–11.30, Sun noon–11

💲 L $40, 3-course prix fixe $20, D $50, Wine $40

🚇 Lexington Avenue/53rd Street (E, V), 51st Street (6)

🚌 M57, M98, M101, M102, M103

66

Map 269 E24

241 Church Street between Leonard and Worth streets

Tel 212/925-0202

This is not just another Chinese restaurant; it's Jean-Georges Vongerichten's elegant and energized interpretation of Chinese cuisine. Architect Richard Meier's design pairs frosted glass and steel mesh with Eames chairs and Saarinen tables. The chefs are definitely Chinese, deftly turning out jewel after jewel, the likes of which you won't find in Chinatown—crab with lotus-seed crust, Meyer lemon chicken. Other Chinese favorites get a new twist.

⏰ Daily noon–3, Mon–Thu 6–midnight, Fri–Sat 6pm–1am, Sun 5.30–10.30

💲 L $30, D $60, Wine $31

🚇 Franklin Street (1,9)

🚌 M6

SPICE MARKET

Map 268 D21

403 West 13th Street at Ninth Avenue

Tel 212/675-2322

www.jean-georges.com

Expect a sensual experience. Beguiling and theatrical are the only words to describe this Southeast Asian space swathed in teak lit by silk lanterns, and dotted with palm trees. It's Jean-Georges Vongrichten's stage for exciting spicy street food. Roll the spring rolls in lettuce with fresh mint and cilantro (coriander) and dip them in sweet lime and rice vinegar broth, sample the fiery pork vindaloo or the black pepper shrimp with pineapple.

⏰ Mon–Wed 6–midnight, Thu–Sat 6–1

💲 D $40, Wine $26

🚇 14th Street (A, C, E, L)

🚌 M 11

SPOTTED PIG

Map 268 D22

314 West 11th Street at Greenwich Street

Tel 212/620-0393

www.thespottedpig.com

It may have Mario Batali as part owner, but it is the chef April Bloomfeld who is drawing crowds at this small "gastro pub." She comes most recently from London's River Cafe and delivers some gutsy cuisine—veal kidneys, lamb with salsa verde, roast cod with parsley sauce and her beloved gnudi (gnocchi with sheep's milk ricotta and brown butter and sage). Note though that the menu changes constantly at this lively ongoing party.

⏰ Mon–Fri noon–5, Sat–Sun 11–5, daily 5.30–2

💲 D $40, Wine $24

🚇 Christopher Street (1, 9), 14th Street (A, C, E, L)

🚌 M11, M20

STRIP HOUSE

Map 269 E21

13 East 12th Street between Fifth Avenue and University Place

Tel 212/328-0000

www.theglaziergroup.com

Recalling a 19th-century bordello with its tufted leather

banquettes and swathe of velvet, this place serves up juicy succulent beef, notably the New York strip. Other cuts are available along with a couple of fish dishes, wild striped bass with artichokes, pancetta and basil sauce, for example.

⏰ Mon–Thu 5–11.30, Fri–Sat 5–midnight, Sun 5–11

💲 D $60, Wine $35

🚇 14th Street/Union Square (L, N, Q, R, W, 4, 5, 6)

🚌 M2, M3, M5

SUGIYAMA

Map 266 D17

251 West 55th Street between Broadway and Eighth Avenue

Tel 212/956-0670

www.sugiyama-nyc.com

Here, the seasons inform chef Nao Sugiyama's Kaiseki cuisine. You have a choice of four menus: 8-course, 10-course, 12-course and pre-theater. Each includes an appetizer, sashimi, soup, a sizzling dish on hot stone and dessert. The selection of sake by the glass and by the bottle is extensive.

⏰ Tue–Sat 5.30–11.45

💲 D $60 8-course, $80 10-course, $100 12-course, $45 pre-theater, Sake $48

🚇 59th Street/Columbus Circle (A, B, C, D, 1, 9)

EATING

SUSHI YASUDA

Off map 268 F18
204 East 43rd Street between Second and Third avenues
Tel 212/972-1001
www.sushiyasuda.com

Here owner Naomichi Yasuda displays his artistry, selecting the best fish, evaluating its texture, masterfully cutting it to release the best flavor, and

cooking and seasoning the rice to perfection. Then he crafts a meal for the individuals who sit down at his sushi bar, according to their tastes and experience, and to the size of their mouths. It's custom-made perfection, but naturally it comes at a high price. For a delightful meal request one of his eight tuna specialties or one of the eel pieces for which he is renowned.

🕐 Mon–Fri noon–2.15, 6–10.15, Sat 6–10.15, closed 2nd and 4th Sat of each month
🍽 L $80, D $100, Wine $18 (sake)
🚇 42nd Street/Grand Central (S, 4, 5, 6, 7)

TAKA

Map 268 D22
61 Grove Street between Bleecker and Seventh Avenue South
Tel 212/242-3699

Takako Yoneyama is a female sushi master, rare in a culture that has denied women such a role because their body temperature is one degree higher than a man's. At this atypical restaurant with Western-style paintings and

TABLA

Map 268 E20
11 Madison Avenue at 25th Street
Tel 212/009 0007

Danny Meyer's Tabla delivers a superb dining experience with its plush decor, gracious service and fragrant cuisine. In the sensual coral and jade jewel box of a room upstairs, the menu offers Bombay native Floyd Cardoz's dishes, which use the spices of South India—tamarind, kokum, clove, cinnamon and black pepper. Goan-spiced crab cake, rice-flaked black bass, and duck samosa, set off by shaved fennel, almonds and dried fruit chutney are just a few favorites. The sorbets are packed with flavor. The wine selections pair beautifully with the food (16 by the glass). On the ground floor, the informal and very affordable Bread Bar serves a selection of tandoori dishes and small plates of superb Indian breads.

🕐 Mon–Fri 12–2, 5.30–10.30, Sat 5.30–10.30, Sun 5.30–10
🍽 L $50, D $80, 3-course prix fixe $57, Wine $32
🚇 23rd Street (N, R, W), 23rd Street (6)
🚌 M2, M3

bentwood chairs, she wields her knives creatively and delivers a bento box containing sushi, sashimi, shumai and other small dishes that's a real bargain.

🕐 Tue–Sun 5–11
🍽 D $35
🚇 Christopher Street/Sheridan Square (1, 9)
🚌 M20

TAMARIND

Map 268 E20
41-43 East 22nd Street between Broadway and Park Avenue South
Tel 212/674-7400
www.tamarinde22.com

The dining room of this Indian restaurant is sleek, modern and comfortable (although noisy), the cuisine fresh and the wine list expansive. The flavor of the restaurant's namesake fruit infuses many of the wonderful dishes, such as the shrimp cooked in coconut sauce flavored with curry

leaves and smoked tamarind, but there are other flavors as well—the she-crab soup with sweet spices, ginger and saffron is another winner. The lamb vindaloo is authentically spiced, as are many of the vegetarian dishes. Some are refreshingly new—*bhindi do piazza*, which is okra flavored with brown onions and dried mango, for example. Even the desserts shine.

🕐 Daily 11.30–3, 5.30–11.30
🍽 L $25, D $40, Wine $30
🚇 23rd Street (N, R), 23rd Street (6)
🚌 M1, M2, M3, M6, M7

TASTING ROOM

Map 269 F22
72 East 1st Street between First and Second avenues
Tel 212/358-7831

This small restaurant offers just a dozen jewel-like tasting dishes. Based on seasonal vegetables, fish and meat, they range from chilled venison consommé to

seabass escabeche with red onion, saprasata and sherry vinaigrette. Every dish has a surprise element, like the candied fennel that comes with the brown butter-lemon tart. The 300 American wines, 10 by the glass, include some hard-to-find selections.

🕐 Tue–Sat 5.30–11.30
🍽 D $45, Wine $30
🚇 Lower East Side/Second Avenue (F, V)
🚌 M15

TAVERN ON THE GREEN

Map 266 D16
Central Park West at 67th Street
Tel 212/873-3200
www.tavernonthegreen.com

Visitors are drawn to this bauble of a restaurant at the edge of Central Park, shaded by stately trees outlined after dark by thousands of twinkling fairy lights. The view from the

EATING

Crystal Room and the summer dining terrace creates a certain magical, festive look. Against all odds, the Tavern delivers a memorable dining experience—despite its stature as a prime visitor destination, despite its size, and despite the breadth of its menu, which ranges from prime rib with Yorkshire pudding to sautéed rainbow trout in brown butter sauce. The wine list boasts 1,000 selections, a 1975 Chateau Petrus among them. From May to mid-October you can dance under the stars in the garden areas from 9pm.

🕐 Mon–Fri 11.30–3.30, Sat–Sun 10–3.30, Sun–Thu 5–10.30, Fri–Sat 5–11.30
🍽 L $40, prix fixe $32, D $60, prix fixe $45, pre-theater $36, Wine $32
🚇 66th Street (1, 9)
🚌 M10

TOMOE SUSHI
Map 269 E22
172 Thompson Street between Bleecker and Houston streets
Tel 212/777-9346
Around the corner from New York University, this plain sushi parlor does a brisk trade among students and other sushi aficionados, drawn by its reasonable prices. About 30 different sushi choices and 30 varieties of maki rolls are available, along with traditional hot dishes and noodles.

🕐 Mon 5–11, Wed–Sat 1–3, 5–11
🍽 L $25, D $30
🚇 West 4th Street (A, C, E, F, S, V)
🚌 M5, M6, M21

TOWN
Map 267 E17
Chambers Hotel
15 West 56th Street between Fifth and Sixth avenues
Tel 212/582-4445
www.townnyc.com
Strands of crystal beads suspended in the two-story loft space in this stylish

subterranean dining room swathed in suede and blond wood sparkle magically. Chef Geoffrey Zakarian's fusion cuisine sparkles, too. Start with the fragrant octopus fricassée in lemongrass broth, or the lobster bisque, zapped with ginger, coconut and wood sorrel. Zakarian poaches or roasts his fish to retain moisture, glazing swordfish with mushroom tapenade and serving with smoked tomato and marjoram coulis, for instance; the venison is simply slow-roasted to exquisite tenderness. Desserts are show-stoppers.

🕐 Daily 7am–10.30am, Mon–Fri noon–2, Mon–Thu 5.30–10.30, Fri–Sat 5.30–11, Sun 11–2, 5.30–9
🍽 L $45, 3-course prix fixe $36, D 4-course prix fixe $78, 5-course prix fixe $89, Wine $35
🚇 53rd Street/Fifth Avenue (E, V)
🚌 M1, M2, M3, M4, M57

'21' CLUB
Map 267 E17
21 West 52nd Street between Fifth and Sixth avenues
Tel 212/582-7200
www.21club.com
The hamburger makes headlines for its price ($29 and climbing), but this storied locale is about so much more than the sandwich. Two college students opened it as a speakeasy in Greenwich Village in 1920; it was frequented by Humphrey Bogart, F. Scott Fitzgerald and Joe Di Maggio after relocating to this town house in 1929. Old-fashioned and masculine, it purveys fist-size medallions of beef flambéed with cognac and Dijon, chicken hash and Dover sole, along with newer, lighter dishes like black sea bass in champagne sauce. The daily special ice creams, gussied up or plain, are the choice desserts, and the wine cellar is renowned. Jacket and tie required.

🕐 Mon–Fri noon–2.30, Mon–Sat 5.30–9
🍽 L $60, D $80, Wine $28
🚇 47th–50th streets (B, D, F, V)
🚌 M1, M2, M3, M4, M5, M6, M7

UNCLE VANYA CAFE
Map 266 D17
315 West 54th Street between Eighth and Ninth avenues
Tel 212/262-0542
Russian home cooking starts at this plain storefront restaurant: hearty borscht, beef dumplings with sour cream, stuffed cabbage rolls and beef Stroganoff with kasha. It's all good and filling and costs very little. Try one of the Georgian wines, if you dare.

🕐 Mon–Sat noon–11, Sun 2–10
🍽 L $20, D $25, Wine $25
🚇 50th Street (C, E)
🚌 M10, M11, M20

UNION SQUARE CAFÉ
Map 268 E21
21 East 16th Street between Fifth Avenue and Union Square West
Tel 212/243-4020
Union Square Café remains a darling of the downtown publishing industry because it delivers on every aspect of the dining experience from the comfortable but not-too-fussy setting to the warm but thoroughly professional service. Michael Romano's bold Tuscan cuisine is thoughtfully imaginative and always flavorful. The meats and fishes

are grilled to perfection and enhanced with just the right combination of ingredients. Try the grilled salmon with Meyer lemon citronette, or the organic chicken with mustard-cognac sauce. The signature warm banana tart with honey-vanilla ice cream and macadamia brittle is perfect. The 200-plus wine list is organized by varietal.

🕐 Mon–Sat noon–2.30, Mon–Thu 6–10.30, Fri–Sat 6–11.30, Sun 5.30–10
🍽 L $35, D $50, Wine $22
🚇 14th Street/Union Square (L, N, Q, R, W, 4, 5, 6)
🚌 M2, M3, M5, M7

VERITAS

Map 268 E20
43 East 20th Street between Broadway
and Park Avenue South
Tel 212/353-3700
www.veritas-nyc.com
With 2,700 selections, Veritas
has the most comprehensive
wine list in the city. And the
kitchen offers some gutsy
cuisine to go with the wines.
Expect pepper-crusted venison
with Armagnac or juniper,
or braised veal in Barolo
reduction. Even a dish like red
snapper brings a surprise—here
it arrives in Thai red curry nage.
Hot chocolate and doughnuts
is the signature dessert.
🕐 Mon–Sat 5.30–10, Sun 5–9.30
🍴 D 3-course prix fixe $72, Wine $15
🚇 23rd Street (N, R), 23rd Street (6)
🚌 M1, M2, M3, M6, M7

VIRGIL'S REAL BARBECUE

Map 268 D18
152 West 44th Street between Sixth
Avenue and Broadway
Tel 212/921-9494
www.virgilsbbq.com
The aroma of hickory wood
smoke alone is enough
to draw you into this vast
barbecue emporium.
Here, the huge platters
of Memphis-style barbecue

or fried chicken arrive with
grits or mashed potatoes
and biscuits and gravy.
Po'boys, also known as
hero sandwiches, round out
the southern-style menu.
🕐 Tue–Sat 11.30am–midnight, Mon
11.30–11, Sun 11.30–10
🍴 L $20, D $40, Wine $20
🚇 42nd Street/Times Square (N, Q, R,
S, W, 1, 2, 3, 7, 9), 42nd Street (B, D,
F, V)
🚌 M5, M6, M7

VONG

Map 267 F17
200 East 54th Street at Third Avenue
Tel 212/486-9592
When Jean-Georges launched
his French-Asian cuisine,
it was revolutionary. Today,
it's just plain beautiful, and
the explosive flavors still
dance on the tongue.
Vongerichten worked in
Thailand, Hong Kong and
Singapore in the 1980s,
and the flavors of lemongrass,
cilantro (coriander), ginger and
coconut milk changed his life.
🕐 Mon–Fri noon–2.30, 6–11, Sat 5–11,
Sun 5.30–9
🍴 L $50, 3-course prix fixe $20.12,
D $60, tasting menu $68, 3-course
pre-theater $38, Wine $32
🚇 53rd Street/Lexington Avenue (F,
V), 51st Street (6)
🚌 M98, M101, M102, M103

WD-50

Map 269 G23
50 Clinton Street between Stanton and
Rivington streets (east side of the street)
Tel 212/477-2900
www.wd-50.com
Wylie Dufresne made the
Lower East Side a dining
destination when he cooked
at 71 Clinton Street. Now he
has his own place, a sleek

postmodern dining room
where he mixes exciting
but harmonious flavor
combinations—octopus with
celery pesto, pineapple and
almonds, striped bass with
passion fruit. Desserts are
also creative.
🕐 Mon–Sat 6–11, Sun 6–10
🍴 D $55, Wine $34
🚇 Delancey (F), Essex (J, M, Z)
🚌 M9, M21

WOO LAE OAK

Map 269 E23
148 Mercer Street between Houston
and Prince streets
Tel 212/925-8200
www.woolaeoaksoho.com
Here, you'll find a stylized
American version of Korean
cuisine. Start with the hot
Dungeness crab wrapped in
spinach crepes, or tuna tartare
served over Korean pear.
Among the selections for the
on-the-table barbecue there
are 17 meats, fishes and
vegetables, including ostrich,
squid and tripe. Among other
dishes, short ribs are swathed
in sweet soy sauce, and then
come soups, casseroles
and rice dishes. Don't forget
the kimchi—the pickle dishes
that are a perennial presence
on the Korean table.
🕐 Sun–Thu noon–11, Fri–Sat
noon–11.30
🍴 L $15, prix fixe $20, D $45, prix fixe
$40 and $50, Wine $34
🚇 Broadway/Lafayette (F, S, V), Prince
Street (N, R), Bleecker Street (6)
🚌 M1, M5

ZARELA

Map 267 F17
953 Second Avenue between 50th and
51st streets
Tel 212/644-6740
www.zarela.com
Don't be fooled by the festive
ambience of this restaurant,
for it offers some of the most
authentic regional Mexican
cuisine in the city. Whether

or not you are looking for
northern fajitas and flautas, or
Oaxacan moles and coastal
Veracruz-style dishes, you will
find it here along with rare
seasonal specialties.
🕐 Mon–Fri noon–3, Mon–Thu 5–11,
Fri–Sat 5–11.30, Sun 5–10
🍴 L $23, prix fixe $25, D $35, prix fixe
$40, Wine $21
🚇 Lexington/53rd Street (E, V), 51st
Street (6)
🚌 M15

EATING

MAJOR RESTAURANT CHAINS

New York is a good place for eclectic and unusual eating, but there are also plenty of tried and tested chains, where you know exactly what you're getting and how much you'll have to pay.

	Price range ($–$$$)	Alcohol	Child menu	Takeout	Phone number	Website
RESTAURANTS						
Baluchi's	$$	Yes	No	Yes	212/594-5533	www.baluchis.com
Burritoville	$	No	Yes	Yes	212/563-9010	www.burritoville.com
California Pizza Kitchen	$$	Yes	Yes	Yes	310/342-5000	www.californiapizzakitchen.com
Lemongrass Grill	$$	Yes	No	Yes	718/399-7100	www.lemongrassgrill.com
Patsy's Pizzeria	$$	Yes	No	Yes	212/688-5916	www.patsyspizzeria.com
Pizza Hut	$	Some	Yes	Yes	972/338-7700	www.pizzahut.com
Pizzeria Uno	$$	Yes	Yes	Yes	617/323-9200	www.pizzeriauno.com
TGI Friday's	$$	Yes	Yes	Yes	972/662-5400	www.Fridays.com
Two Boots Pizzeria	$	Some	Yes	Yes	212/777-2668	www.twoboots.com
Xando Cosi	$	Yes	Yes	Yes	847/444-3200	www.xandocosi.com
Zen Palate	$$	No	No	Yes	212/614-9345	www.zenpalate.com

SANDWICHES AND FAST FOOD						
Au Bon Pain	$	No	No	Yes	617/423-2100	www.aubonpain.com
Burger King	$	No	Yes	Yes	305/378-3000	www.burgerking.com
Cosí Sandwich Bar	$	Yes	No	Yes	847/444-3200	www.getcosi.com
Kentucky Fried Chicken	$	No	Yes	Yes	800/225-5532	www.kfc.com
Le Pain Quotidien	$	No	No	Yes	212/625-9009	www.painquotidien.com
Little Pie Company	$	No	No	Yes	212/414-2324	www.littlepiecompany.com
McDonald's	$	No	Yes	Yes	800/244-6227	www.mcdonalds.com
Pret à Manger	$	No	No	Yes	646/728-0750	www.pretamanger.com
Subway	$	No	Yes	Yes	203/877-4281	www.subway.com
Wendy's	$	No	Yes	Yes	614/764-3100	www.wendys.com

EATING

COFFEE SHOPS						
Dean and DeLuca	$	No	No	Yes	877/826-9246	www.deananddeluca.com
Krispy Kreme Donuts	$	No	No	Yes	800/457-4779	www.krispykreme.com
Starbucks	$	No	No	Yes	800/782-7282	www.starbucks.com

STAYING IN NEW YORK

Traditionally the priciest hotels in New York have been relatively traditional, formal places. However the last two decades have seen a number of ultra-chic hotels open around the city, offering guests luxurious amenities in modern, stylish settings. The restaurants, lounges and bars in these places also attract trendy New Yorkers, as well as visitors to the city. There are plenty of hotel rooms, but it is hard to find a comfortable room under $150. If money is no object, reserve a room at the Carlyle or the Four Seasons.

Accommodation in New York ranges from cutting-edge luxury with impeccable service to less expensive options in local neighborhoods

STAYING

For less expensive options, check out the inexpensive chains—Red Roof, Super 8 and others. The city also has some bed-and-breakfasts, which charge less than the average hotel and provide good-value extras. Hostels are the least expensive lodging options (see the box on the opposite page).

It used to be that all the best hotels were in Midtown but that has changed dramatically. Now, there are first-class luxury hotels downtown in SoHo, Greenwich Village and the Financial District. Still, there are more bargains away from Midtown. New York City hotels range in size from vast 2,000-room monstrosities to smaller establishments with 250 rooms or less. If you stay at a large convention hotel, expect to find crowded lobbies, more lines and slower service. Most hotels have similar amenities. The average hotel room comes with air conditioning, private bathroom, cable TV, telephone, coffeemaker, hairdryer, iron and ironing board. The level of luxury and the quality and range of the service are the real distinctions between hotels. Top-class hotel rooms boast luxe fabrics and linens (Frette, Pratesi), high-tech electronics and telephony, and high staff-to-guest ratios, which guarantees prompt, courteous service. Space is at a premium in Manhattan, so expect rooms to be on the small side. Double-glazed windows, which are usually standard, help reduce noise. Most hotels have complimentary coffee/tea service, and newspapers either in the lobby or delivered to your room.

The Peninsula is a luxurious choice on Fifth Avenue

Today there is no such thing as a standard rack rate. Prices fluctuate with customer demand. To get the best rate on a hotel room, always call the hotel directly and ask for the best available rate and what special discounts are available. Alternatively, go online to such discount services as hotels.com, quickbook.com or hoteldiscounts.com to secure the best rates. Winter (Jan–end Feb) and summer (Jul–end Aug) are the least expensive seasons. Depending on the hotel, weekend rates may be higher or lower than midweek. Parking charges of $35 and up will add substantially to any bill. Note, too, that 13.625 percent will be added to your bill, plus $2 occupancy tax on a standard room and $4 on a one-bedroom suite.

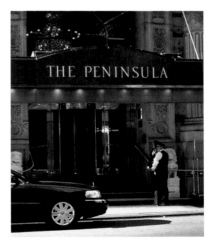

HOSTELS IN NEW YORK

BIG APPLE HOSTEL (Map 296 D18)
119 West 45th Street between Sixth and Seventh avenues,
10036, tel 212/302-2603, www.bigapplehostel.com

CHELSEA CENTER HOSTEL (Map 296 D19)
313 West 29th Street between Eighth and Ninth avenues,
10031, tel 212/643-0214, www.chelseacenterhostel.com

CHELSEA INTERNATIONAL HOSTEL
(Map 296 D20)
251 West 20th Street between Seventh and Eighth avenues,
10011, tel 212/647-0010, www.chelseahostel.com

HOSTELLING INTERNATIONAL
(Off map 294 C12)
891 Amsterdam Avenue at 104th Street, tel 212/932-2300,
www.hinewyork.org/home

WEST SIDE YMCA (Map 294 D16)
5 West 63rd Street between Central Park West and
Broadway, 10023, tel 212/875-4100, www.ymcanyc.org

WHITEHOUSE (Map 297 F22)
340 Bowery between 2nd and Great Jones streets, 10012,
tel 212/477-5623, www.whitehousehotelofny.com

HOTELS BY AREA

The hotels are listed alphabetically on pages 298–309. Here they are listed by area.

LOWER EAST SIDE
Off-SoHo Suites

GREENWICH VILLAGE/MEAT MARKET/CHELSEA
Abingdon Guest House
Chelsea
Chelsea Lodge
Hotel Gansevoort
Inn on 23rd Street
Maritime Hotel
Washington Square
Larchmont

SOHO/TRIBECA
Cosmopolitan Hotel-Tribeca
Mercer
SoHo Grand
Tribeca Grand

UNION SQUARE/FLATIRON DISTRICT/GRAMERCY PARK
Gershwin
Giraffe
Inn at Irving Place
Union Square Inn

MADISON SQUARE PARK/ MURRAY HILL
Avalon
Grand Union
Hotel Chandler
Marcel
Morgans

70 Park Avenue
Thirty Thirty
Wolcott

MIDTOWN WEST/THEATER DISTRICT
Algonquin
Americana Inn
Belvedere
Blakely
Broadway Inn
Bryant Park Hotel
Casablanca
Dream Hotel
Hudson
Le Parker Meridien
Mansfield
Moderne
Ritz Carlton
Royalton
Shoreham
Travel Inn
Warwick
Westpark
Wyndham

LINCOLN CENTER/UPPER WEST SIDE
Beacon
Excelsior
Lucerne
Mandarin Oriental
Newton
On the Avenue

Roger Williams
Trump International Hotel and Tower

MIDTOWN EAST
Beekman Tower
Benjamin
Edison
Elysee
Four Seasons
Habitat
Kimberly
Le Parker Meridien
Library
Metro
Millennium UN Plaza
New York Palace
Peninsula
St. Regis
Sherry-Netherland
Waldorf-Astoria Hotel And Towers
W-New York

UPPER EAST SIDE
Carlyle
Gracie Inn
Lowell
Lyden Gardens
Mark
Pickwick Arms
Pierre
Surrey
Wales

STAYING

Hotel Locator

West 95th Street

B   C   Newton   Hostelling International   D

West 94th Street

West 93rd Street

UPPER WEST

West 92nd Street

SIDE

West 91st Street

West 90th Street

West 89th Street

West 88th Street

BROADWAY   West 87th Street

West End Avenue   Amsterdam Avenue   Columbus Avenue

West 86th Street   86th Street

86th Street   CENTRAL

West 85th Street

West 84th Street

West 83rd Street

Central Park West   West

81st Street Museum of Nat Hist

West 82nd Street

Riverside Park   West 81st Street

Excelsior   Central

Central Park Reservoir

14   Hudson River   Riverside Drive   West End Avenue

West 80th Street

Lucerne   American Museum of Natural History

West 79th Street   79th Street

West 78th Street

On the Avenue   West 77th Street   New-York Historical Society

Belvedere Lake

West 76th Street

West 75th Street

BROADWAY

Beacon   West 74th Street   San Remo Apartments   The Lake

Ansonia Building   West 73rd Street

West 72nd Street   The Dakota

72nd Street   72nd Street   Strawberry Fields

West 71st Street   Central Park West   West

15   West 70th Street

Olmsted

West 69th Street   West 69th Street   The Sheep Meadow

Freedom Place   West 68th Street   Riverside Boulevard

West 67th Street

66th Street Lincoln Center   Tavern on the Green

West 66th Street   Central Park West

Juilliard School   65th Street

West 65th Street

West 64th Street   West 64th Street

16   Lincoln Center   West Side YMCA   Central Park

West 63rd Street   West 63rd Street

West End Avenue   West 62nd Street   Amsterdam Avenue   BROADWAY

HIGHWAY 9A   West 62nd Street   Museum of Biblical Art

West 61st Street   West 61st Street

West 60th Street   Trump International Hotel & Tower   59th Street Columbus Circle

West 59th Street   West 59th Street   Columbus Circle   Central Park

12th Av   Mandarin Oriental   COLUMBUS CIRCLE

West 58th Street

12th Avenue   Hudson   Westpark   57th Street

WEST 57TH STREET   Carnegie Hall

12TH AVENUE   West 56th Street   9th Avenue   10th Avenue   Le Parker Meridien Blakely

Moderne   8th Avenue   7th Avenue

West 55th Street   BROADWAY

11th Avenue   West 54th Street   Dream Hotel

West 53rd Street   7th Avenue

17   De Witt Clinton Park   West 52nd Street

West 51st Street

West 50th Street   50th Street

West 49th Street   50th Street   49th Street

West 48th Street   Belvedere

9A   West 47th Street   Edison   8th Street

294   Intrepid Sea, Air and Space Museum   BROADWAY

B   West 46th Street   C   10th Avenue   9th Avenue   D   Broadway Inn

West 45th Street   Big Apple Hostel

13

Mill Rock Park

East 95th Street   East 95th Street
East 94th Street   East 94th Street
East 93rd Street   East 93rd Street
Jewish Museum   **Wales**   East 92nd Street
East 92nd Street
East 91st Street   East 91st Street
Cooper-Hewitt National Design Museum   East 91st Street
National Academy of Design   East 90th Street   East 90th Street
Guggenheim Museum   East 89th Street   Gracie Mansion
East 88th Street   East 88th Street   Carl Schurz Park
East Drive   East 87th Street   East 87th Street
86th Street   East 86th Street   East 86th Street
Neue Galerie   East 85th Street   East 85th Street
East 84th Street   East 84th Street
The Metropolitan Museum of Art   East 83rd Street   East 83rd Street
East 82nd Street   East 82nd Street
East 81st Street   East 81st Street   **Gracie Inn**
Park   East 80th Street   East 80th Street
East 79th Street   East 79th Street
road   East 78th Street   East 78th Street
Mark   East 77th Street   77th Street   East 77th Street   John Jay Park
Carlyle   East 76th Street   East 76th Street
Surrey   East 75th Street   East 75th Street
Whitney Museum of American Art   East 74th Street   East 74th Street
Conservatory Water   East 73rd Street   East 73rd Street
East 72nd Street   East 72nd Street
Drive   East 71st Street   East 71st Street
Frick Collection   Asia Society and Museum   East 70th Street   East 70th Street
East 69th Street   East 69th Street
68th Street Hunter College   East 68th Street   East 68th Street
East 67th Street   East 67th Street
East 66th Street   East 66th Street
Lyden Gardens   East 65th Street   East 65th Street
FIFTH AVENUE   East 64th Street   East 64th Street
Lexington Avenue   East 63rd Street   East 63rd Street
Lowell   East 62nd Street   East 62nd Street   Mount Vernon Hotel Museum and Garden
The Pond   **Pierre**   East 61st Street   East 61st St
North   **Sherry-Netherland**   East 60th Street   East 60th Street   HIGHWAY 25
5th Avenue   **Ritz Carlton**   East 59th Street   59th Street   QUEENSBORO BRIDGE   Main Street
West 58th Street   East 58th Street   East 58th Street
Wyndham   **Four Seasons**   East 57th Street
Avenue of the Americas   WEST 57TH STREET   EAST 57TH STREET
Dahesh Museum of Art   **Habitat**
West 56th Street   Trump Tower   East 56th Street   West 56th Street
Shoreham   West 55th Street   East 55th Street   West 55th Street
Warwick   **Peninsula**   **St Regis**   East 54th Street
Museum of Modern Art   **Elysée**   East 53rd Street
Museum of Arts and Design   Museum of Television and Radio   West 52nd Street   Seagram Building   East 52nd Street
Radio City Music Hall   West 51st Street   **New York Palace**   **Benjamin**   **Pickwick Arms**   East 51st Street
47th–50th Streets Rockefeller Center   West 50th Street   St Patrick's Cathedral   Municipal Art Society   51st Street   **Kimberly**   **Beekman Tower**   Mitchell Pl   East 50th Street
G E Building   West 49th Street   **Waldorf-Astoria Hotel & Towers**   **W-New York**   East 49th Street
Rockefeller Center   West 48th Street   East 48th Street
West 47th Street   East 47th Street
DIAMOND DISTRICT   **MIDTOWN MANHATTAN**   East 47th Street   United Nations Headquarters
West 46th Street   East 46th Street
West 45th Street   East 45th Street   **Millennium UN Plaza**

FRANKLIN DELANO ROOSEVELT DRIVE

ROOSEVELT ISLAND

Roosevelt Island   Main Street

West Road   East Road   Sutton Place   York Avenue   1st Avenue   2nd Avenue   3rd Avenue   Lexington Avenue   Park Avenue   Madison Avenue   5th Avenue

HOTEL LOCATOR

Prices are for a double room for one night, excluding sales tax. All the hotels listed accept credit cards unless otherwise stated.

ABINGDON GUEST HOUSE
Map 296 D21
13 Eighth Avenue at West 12th Street, 10014
Tel 212/243-5384
www.abingdonguesthouse.com
Located in two historic three-story red-brick town houses above a coffee shop in Greenwich Village, the guest house is unmarked. The nine rooms are individually decorated and well furnished with antiques. Amenities include private bath (with hairdryer), cable TV and telephone. The patio garden is a bonus.
🛏 $179–$239
🛈 9
🚇 14th Street (A, C, E), Christopher Street/Sheridan Square (1, 9)
🚌 M20, M14

ALGONQUIN
Map 296 E18
59 West 44th Street between Fifth and Sixth avenues, 10036
Tel 212/840-6800
www.algonquinhotel.com
It's famous for being the place where in the 1920s Robert Benchley, Dorothy Parker and the rest of the Vanity Fair/New Yorker crowd gathered regularly for lunch at the Round Table. The rooms are moderate in size and furnished with reproductions of American antiques. The wood-paneled Oak Room is the city's best cabaret, and there's a fitness center.
🛏 $209–$499, suite from $309
🛈 150 rooms, 24 suites
🚇 42nd Street (B, D, F, V)
🚌 M5, M7, M42

AMERICANA INN
Map 296 E18
69 West 38th Street between Fifth and Sixth avenues, 10018
Tel 212/840-6700
www.newyorkhotel.com
Rooms here are bright, modern and comfortable, if plainly decorated. They are equipped with cable TV and telephone. All rooms share a bath, and each floor has a kitchenette.
🛏 $85–$95
🛈 53
🚇 42nd Street (B, D, F, V)
🚌 M5, M6, M7

AVALON
Map 296 E19
16 East 32nd Street at Madison Avenue, 10016
Tel 212/299-7000
www.theavalonny.com
This small hotel is near the Empire State Building and has

traditionally furnished rooms. Executive suites have fax, Bose radio and cordless phone. Complimentary breakfast and evening champagne are set out in the mahogany-paneled library off the lobby. The Avalon Bar and Grill serves contemporary American cuisine. Guests have access to a gym nearby.
🛏 $199–$380, suite from $315, including breakfast
🛈 70 rooms, 30 suites
🚇 33rd Street (6)
🚌 M1, M2, M3, M4, M34

BEACON
Map 294 C15
2130 Broadway between 74th and 75th streets, 10023
Tel 212/787-1100
www.beaconhotel.com
Less than 10 blocks from the Lincoln Center and close to Central Park, this 25-story hotel offers good value. Guests can save money using the kitchenette with stove, microwave and refrigerator. Amenities

include TV, telephone and hairdryer. Fitness center.
🛏 $165–$230, suite from $225
🛈 120 rooms, 110 suites
🚇 72nd Street (1, 2, 3, 9)
🚌 M7, M11, M104

BEEKMAN TOWER
Map 295 F17
3 Mitchell Place (East 49th Street and First Avenue), 10017
Tel 212/355-7300
www.affinia.com
This all-suite hotel, in a 1928 art deco building near

the UN, has accommodations that include bedroom, sitting room and fully equipped kitchen. The deluxe suites have such extras as VCRs and two-line phones. The bar/restaurant on the top floor is one of the most romantic aeries in the city. Fitness center on-premises.
🛏 $209–$440, 2-bedroom suite from $500
🛈 174 suites
🚇 51st Street (6)
🚌 M15

BELVEDERE
Map 294 D17
319 West 48th Street between Eighth and Ninth avenues, 10036
Tel 212/245-7000
www.newyorkhotel.com
The most expensive hotel in the Empire Hotel group, the Belvedere has handsome sizable rooms with kitchenettes fitted with microwave, refrigerator and coffeemaker. Executive rooms are also available. On premises, the Churrascaria Plataforma is a Brazilian steakhouse.
🛏 $150–$250
🛈 400 rooms and suites
🚇 50th Street (C, E)
🚌 M11, M20, M50

STAYING

BENJAMIN

Map 295 F17
125 East 50th Street at Lexington
Avenue, 10022
Tel 212/715-2500
www.affinia.com

Conveniently situated in
Midtown, this Manhattan
Suites hotel offers good-
looking rooms and excellent
facilities in a handsome 1927

building. The rooms are
furnished with mahogany
pieces. Guests can select from
a ten-type pillow menu. The
Affinsa Wellness Spa (▷ 228)
is a bonus. Seafood restaurant
and chop house.

$179–$489
209
51st Street (6)
M50, M98, M101, M102, M103

BLAKELY

Map 294 D17
136 West 55th Street between Sixth and
Seventh avenues, 10019
Tel 212/245-1800
www.blakelyny.com

The rooms are handsome
with a traditional English
flavor conveyed in foxhunt
prints and cherry furnishings.
Amenities include full

kitchenettes with microwave
and mini-fridge plus the
latest in tech—flat screen
TVs, DVD/CD players, cordless
phones and complimentary
WiFi. Comforts run to Frette
bathrobes and Penhaligon
toiletries. Restaurant-bar and
fitness center.

$225–$345, suite from $325
58 rooms, 55 suites
57th Street (N, Q, R, W), 57th
Street (F)
M5, M6, M7, M57

BROADWAY INN

Map 296 D18
264 West 46th Street between
Broadway and Eighth Avenue, 10036
Tel 212/997-9200
www.broadwayinn.com

In the Theater District, this
cozy small hotel could be
found in London or any
other European city. The
second-floor lobby welcomes
guests to a comfortable
hearth and book-lined
aerie. The rooms vary in size,
but it's one of the few places
in town where a solo traveler
can rent a single room—and
save money doing so.
They are basically decorated
and have such amenities
as cable TV, telephone
and hairdryer. Suites have
extras such as a refrigerator
and microwave. Quietest
rooms are in the back.
No elevator.

$159–$299, suite from $250,
including breakfast
30 rooms, 11 suites
42nd Street (A, C, E), 42nd
Street/Times Square (N, Q, R, S, W, 1, 2,
3, 7, 9)
M6, M7, M20, M27, M104

BRYANT PARK HOTEL

Map 296 E18
40 West 40th Street at Fifth Avenue
Tel 212/869-0100
www.bryantparkhotel.com

Occupying the American
Radiator Building, a
dramatic 24-story black
brick building designed by
Raymond M Hood in 1924,
this hotel is well located
for midtown sites and the
theater district, but far enough
away from the mall-like
atmosphere of Times
Square itself. The Italian-style
minimalist rooms have all
of the latest amenities—Bose
CD player, fax and dual-line
phone. Great cellar bar that
is worth the high tabs.
Fitness center, too.

$295–$420, suite from $395
113 rooms, 14 suites
42nd Street (B, D, F, V)
M1, M2, M3, M4, M5, M42

CARLYLE

Map 295 E14
35 East 76th Street between Madison
and Park avenues, 10021
Tel 212/744-1600
www.rosewoodhotels.com

This is a striking art deco
building. The rooms boast
large bathrooms and every
conceivable amenity. The
public areas are classics,
particularly Bemelman's
Bar with its charming
murals and the café
where Bobby Short plays.
Facilities include fitness
center and pool.

$350–$595, suite from $550
124 rooms, 56 suites
77th Street (4, 5)
M1, M2, M3, M4

CASABLANCA

Map 296 D18
147 West 43rd Street between Sixth and
Seventh avenues, 10036
Tel 212/869-1212
www.casablancahotel.com

Close to the Theater District,
the boutique-style Casablanca
is small and personal and

offers stylish, modern, well-
equipped rooms. The public
areas have a Moroccan feel
with tiles and rattan chairs.

$189–$349, suite from $315,
including breakfast and evening wine
and cheese (weekdays only)
40 rooms, 8 suites
42nd Street/Times Square (N, Q, R,
S, W, 1, 2, 3, 7, 9), 42nd Street (B, D, F, V)
M6, M7, M10, M20

STAYING

CHELSEA

Map 296 D20
222 West 23rd Street between Seventh
and Eighth avenues, 10011
Tel 212/243-3700
www.chelseahotel.com

Many artists and bohemians
have stayed or lived here since
it opened in 1884, including
Mark Twain and Dylan Thomas.
The rooms vary in size and
decor. Serena's, the bar
opened by Serena Bass,
attracts a Brit-pack crowd.
🖐 $175–$300, suite from $300
ℹ 375 rooms (250 permanent
residents)
🚇 23rd Street (C, E), 23rd Street (1, 9)
🚌 M20, M23

CHELSEA LODGE

Map 296 D20
318 West 20th Street between Eighth
and Ninth avenues, 10001
Tel 212/243-4499
www.chelsealodge.com
In very fashionable Chelsea,
this small hotel occupies

a handsome red-brick
town house, which has been
lovingly restored by the
owners. The rooms are
decorated in plain American
country style with patterned
wallpaper and eclectic
furnishings. Most have
hardwood floors and
small TVs, plus sink and
shower. Toilet is in the hall.
🖐 $110
ℹ 22
🚇 23rd Street (C, E)
🚌 M11, M20

COSMOPOLITAN
HOTEL–TRIBECA

Map 297 E24
95 West Broadway at Chambers Street,
10007
Tel 212/566-1900
www.cosmohotel.com

This hotel has a great
downtown location and
good-looking rooms. They're
all furnished with industrial-
style carpeting and
Scandinavian-style pieces,
but they have private bath,
TV and telephone.
🖐 $129–$139
ℹ 105
🚇 Chambers Street (1, 2, 3, 9),
Chambers Street (A, C)
🚌 M20

DREAM HOTEL

Map 294 D17
210 West 55th Street between
Broadway and Seventh Avenue
Tel 212/247-2000
www.dreamny.com
From the minute you enter
the lobby you know that this
hotel is all about design.
A crystal boat is suspended
from the ceiling and an
enormous aquarium
dominates the space. The
rooms are dramatically furnished with blue satin headboards and lit blue too.
Bathrooms are hip-minimalist.
The rooms have the latest tech
amenities—plasma TV, iPod
with Bose speakers. Lounges
are found in the lobby, on
the rooftop and underground.
Plus Deepak Chopra has
located an Ayurvedic center
here.
🖐 $215–$460, suite from $519
ℹ 204 rooms and 16 suites
🚇 7th Avenue (B, D, E), 57th
Street/7th Avenue (N, Q, R, W)
🚌 M10, M20

EDISON

Map 296 D18
228 West 47th Street between
Broadway and Eighth Avenue, 10036
Tel 212/840-5000.
www.edisonhotelnyc.com
Theater patrons appreciate
this art deco 1931 hotel in the
center of the Theater District.
The entrance lobby is some-
what bland but functional.
The rooms are moderately
priced and have cable TV
and telephone. Restaurant and
bar too.
🖐 $160–$190, suite from $220
ℹ 800 rooms and suites
🚇 50th Street (C, E), 50th Street (1, 9)
🚌 M6, M7, M20, M27, M104

ELYSÉE

Map 295 E17
60 East 54th Street, 10022
Tel 212/753-1066
www.elyseehotel.com

This little gem of a hotel, built
in 1926, has comfortable
rooms decorated with fine
French antique reproductions
and luxurious fabrics.
Bathrooms are marble and
brass. The Monkey Bar, named
for its murals, was once home
to such regulars as Tallulah
Bankhead. Guests have use of
a nearby sports club.
🖐 $245–$325, suite from $400,
including Continental breakfast and
wine and cheese (weekday evenings)
ℹ 86 rooms, 15 suites
🚇 53rd Street/Fifth Avenue (E, V),
51st Street (6)

EXCELSIOR

Map 294 D14
45 West 81st Street between Columbus
Avenue and Central Park West, 10024
Tel 212/362-9200
www.excelsiorhotelny.com
One of the few hotels on
the Upper West Side, near
the Natural History Museum,
the Excelsior offers spotless
modern rooms equipped
with cable TV, dual-line
phone with data port, and

such niceties as bathrobes. Small, decently equipped exercise room.

🛏 $169–$269, suite from $239
🏨 116 rooms, 80 suites
🚇 81st Street (B, C)
🚌 M7, M11, M10, M79

GERSHWIN
Map 296 E20
7 East 27th Street between Fifth and Madison avenues, 10016
Tel 212/545-8000
www.gershwinhotel.com
The Gershwin attracts young budget travelers, who stay in plain doubles or dormitory-style rooms with 10 beds. Rooms have cable TV and phone. On weekends, live bands play in the Gallery Lounge.

🛏 $107–$229, suite from $200, dorm for two $53, women only dorm $43, coed dorm $33
🏨 130 rooms, 6 suites
🚇 28th Street (N, R, W)
🚌 M2, M3

SPECIAL

FOUR SEASONS
Map 295 E16
57 East 57th Street between Madison and Park avenues, 10022
Tel 212/758-5700
www.fourseasons.com

The service at this hotel is legendary; staff are trained to cater to a guest's every whim. I. M. Pei designed the 53-story building, which opened in 1993. The rooms, averaging 600-sq feet (55sq m) are the largest in the city and include a dressing area. The suites have walk-in closets and balconies with grand city views. The large fitness center contains a full spa, and the restaurant and bar are both top-of-the-line.

🛏 $575–$775, suite from $1,250
🏨 305 rooms, 63 suites
🚇 59th Street (4, 5, 6)
🚌 M1, M2, M3, M4

GIRAFFE
Map 296 F20
365 Park Avenue South between 26th and 27th streets, 10016
Tel 212/685-7700
www.hotelgiraffe.com
A small boutique hotel in the Flatiron neighborhood evokes the 1920s and 1930s. Each floor has only seven rooms,

decorated in glamorous colors and materials. Many have balconies. On-premises restaurant, plus access to a nearby health club.

🛏 $329–$399, suite from $349, including breakfast and wine and cheese (weekday evenings)
🏨 52 rooms, 21 suites
🚇 23rd Street (6)
🚌 M1

GRACIE INN
Map 295 G14
502 East 81st Street between York and East End avenues, 10028
Tel 212/628-1700
www.gracieinn.com
Slightly off the beaten track, near the mayor's mansion, this inn attracts long-term guests to 12 apartments in a five-story building. Each has a kitchenette, plus TV and phone with data port. The penthouses have waterbeds, whirlpool tubs and sundecks. Wireless and DVD on request. Breakfast delivered to the room is a welcome indulgence.

🛏 Studio $139–$179, 1-bedroom suite from $189
🏨 12 rooms, 2 suites
🚇 77th St (6)
🚌 M15, M31, M79

GRAND UNION
Map 296 E19
34 East 32nd Street between Madison and Park avenues, 10016
Tel 212/683-5890
www.hotelgrandunion.com
This old-fashioned hotel in the trend-setting Flatiron neighborhood has clean basic rooms that are equipped

with small refrigerators and phones with data ports. Coffee shop.

🛏 $120–$180
🏨 95
🚇 33rd Street (6)
🚌 M1, M2, M3, M34

HABITAT
Map 295 F17
130 East 57th Street at Lexington, 10022
Tel 212/753-8841
www.habitatny.com
Little wonder that budget travelers love this place. It has a great location, and the contemporary rooms are clean, comfortable and attractively decorated. Some have shared bath. All have cable TV and telephone with data port.

🛏 Shared bath $75–$135, private bath $99–$230, suite from $240
🏨 250 rooms, 50 suites
🚇 59th Street (4, 5, 6)
🚌 M59, M98, M101, M102, M103

HOTEL CHANDLER
Map 296 E19
12 East 31st Street between Fifth and Madison avenues, 10016
Tel 212/889-6363
www.hotelchandler.com
This 14-floor boutique hotel in the Murray Hill neighborhood occupies a 1903 Beaux Arts building, which has been carefully renovated and decorated in retro style. Rooms are small but chic, with CD and DVD. The library room has a desktop PC and 40-inch flat screen TV, and the 12:31 bar attracts a hip after-work crowd. There is a fitness room with sauna.

🛏 $179–$355, suite from $425
🏨 120 rooms, 8 suites
🚇 33rd Street (6)
🚌 M2, M3, M5

HOTEL GANSEVOORT

Map 296 D21
18 Ninth Avenue at 13th Street
Tel 212/206-6700
www.hotelgansevoort.com

This meat-packing district hotel adopts South Beach style with such dramatic features as heated rooftop pool, kaleidoscopic illuminated glass columns that change color and mood, and a Japanese restaurant with a fetching outdoor courtyard bar-dining area. Rooms are decorated in minimalist style and hues (fabric headboards, stainless-steel sinks), and feature the latest amenities—plasma TVs and complimentary WiFi. Spa and fitness center occupy a lower level.

🏨 $365–$545, suite from $625
ℹ️ 167 rooms, 20 suites
Ⓜ 14th Street (A, C, E)
🚌 M11

HUDSON

Map 294 D16
356 West 58th Street between Eighth and Ninth avenues, 10019
Tel 212/554-6000
www.morganshotelgroup.com

The Hudson is Ian Schrager's and Philippe Starck's latest "hotel as on-going party". Guests arrive in the ivy-draped lobby via escalators encased in a chartreuse-green tube. Starck trademarks include oversized chairs and other objects like the 500-gallon watering can in the garden courtyard. The rooms are small and furnished with minimalist stainless-steel pieces, plus the latest technical amenities. The Library lounge has plenty of leather, a hearth and a dramatically lit antique billiard table. A long gilded table serves as a bar in the lounge, which converts into a dance club at night. Landscaped roof terrace a bonus.

🏨 $245–$360, suite from $330
ℹ️ 1000 rooms, 11 suites
Ⓜ 59th Street/Columbus Circle (A, B, C, D, 1, 9) 🚌 M1, M20, M57

INN AT IRVING PLACE

Map 296 F21
56 Irving Place between East 17th and 18th streets, 10003
Tel 212/533-4600
www.Innatirving.com

These two 1834 town houses have plenty of ersatz atmosphere. Rooms have fireplaces and four-poster beds dressed with Frette linens, plus antique reproductions. Amenities include two-line telephones with data port, VCRs and CD players. Guests sit on tufted chairs around the fireplaces in Lady Mendl's at afternoon tea. Lounge, too.

🏨 $325–$495, suite from $500, including breakfast
ℹ️ 5 rooms, 6 junior suites
Ⓜ 14th Street/Union Square (L, N, Q, R, W, 4, 5, 6) 🚌 M1, M2, M3, M14

INN ON 23RD STREET

Map 296 D20
131 West 23rd Street between Sixth and Seventh avenues, 10011
Tel 212/463-0330
www.innon23rd.com

If you prefer a bed-and-breakfast, then this inn in a 19th-century town house (with an elevator!) has much to offer. The Fisherman family has furnished it with family heirlooms and eclectic pieces. The rooms have such modern amenities as dual-line phone (local calls are free). Bathrooms are small. Guest amenities include an inviting second-floor library and an honor bar with liquor, wine and beer, plus a microwave.

🏨 $189–$269, suite from $329, including breakfast
ℹ️ 14
Ⓜ 23rd Street (F, V), 23rd Street (1, 9)
🚌 M5, M6, M7, M20, M23

KIMBERLY

Map 295 F17
145 East 50th Street between Third and Lexington avenues, 10022
Tel 212/755-0400
www.kimberlyhotel.com

This small personal hotel in Midtown has a European flavor. Originally built in 1985 as an apartment house, it has large rooms with fully equipped kitchens. Some rooms have balconies; they all have three dual-line phones

LE PARKER MERIDIEN

Map 294 D17
118 West 57th Street between Sixth and Seventh avenues, 10019
Tel 212/245-5000
www.parkermeridien.com

The rooms in this French hotel are furnished with sleek modernist pieces and contain the latest amenities—32-inch TV, ergonomic chairs, fax, DVD, CD player and free high-speed internet access. Hip bistro-style Seppi's serves Mediterranean fare, while Norma's luxury all-day breakfast is famous. Jack's Lounge produces exotic cocktails. There is an excellent 42nd-floor fitness center with a rooftop jogging track.

🏨 $255–$660, suite from $580
ℹ️ 600 rooms, 100 suites
Ⓜ 57th Street (N, Q, R, W)
🚌 M6, M7, M57

and fax/printer. Restaurant, bar and supper club round out the amenities. Guests have membership at the New York Health and Racquet Clubs.

🏨 $209–$385, suite from $229
ℹ️ 26 rooms, 158 suites
Ⓜ 51st Street (6)
🚌 M50, M98, M101, M102, M103

LARCHMONT

Map 297 E21
27 West 11th Street between Fifth and Sixth avenues, 10011
Tel 212/989-9333
www.larchmontHotel.com

LIBRARY

Map 296 E18

299 Madison Avenue at 41st Street, 10017

Tel 212/983-4500

www.libraryhotel.com

It's not just the design concept that book lovers appreciate at this boutique property, it's also the service. Each floor of the hotel is dedicated to a subject category from the Dewey Decimal system and each room has a collection of art and books related to a sub-category. The decor is modern and minimalist. Amenities include multi-line phones with high-speed internet access. Refreshments are served in the second-floor book-lined Reading Room. There's also an Italian restaurant and complimentary passes to a nearby fitness center.

💷 $325–$425, suite from $415, including breakfast and afternoon wine and cheese

🛈 52 rooms, 8 suites

🚇 Grand Central/42nd Street (S, 4, 5, 6, 7)

🚌 M1, M2, M3, M4, M42

This is a great buy on an extra-quiet side street in Greenwich Village. It has plenty of character and appeals to European travelers who don't mind shared bathrooms (bathrobe and slippers provided). The rooms are attractively decorated, ultra clean and well equipped with air conditioning, cable TV and telephone.

💷 $90–$135, including breakfast

🛈 58

🚇 14th Street (F, V), Sixth Avenue (L)

🚌 M2, M3, M5, M6

LOWELL

Map 295 E16

28 East 63rd Street between Madison and Park avenues, 10021

Tel 212/838-1400

www.lowellhotel.com

This little-known hotel, in an elegant 1920s town house, draws a regular clientele. The rooms are furnished with antiques and the suites are spectacular, with fireplaces and large garden terraces. There's 24-hour room service and concierge, and also two restaurants and fitness center.

💷 $375–$585, suite from $745

🛈 23 rooms, 47 suites

🚇 59th Street (4, 5)

🚌 M1, M2, M3, M4

LUCERNE

Map 294 C14

201 West 79th Street between Broadway and Amsterdam Avenue, 10024

Tel 212/875-1000

www.newyorkhotel.com

This hotel, in a 1903 landmark building, is a bargain. Rooms are spacious enough for queen or king beds, and have marble bathrooms. The suites have sitting areas as well as kitchenette with refrigerator and microwave. Facilities include a decent fitness center.

💷 $195–$330, suite from $225, including breakfast

🛈 190 rooms, 60 suites

🚇 79th Street (1, 9)

🚌 M7, M11, M79

LYDEN GARDENS

Map 295 F16

215 East 64th Street, between Second and Third avenues, 10021

Tel 212/320-3022

www.affinia.com

The suites at this well-located hotel have fully equipped kitchens, grocery shopping service and guest laundry. There's also a fitness center.

💷 $244–$420

🛈 131

🚇 68th Street (6)

🚌 M15, M72, M98, M101, M102, M103

MANSFIELD

Map 296 E18

12 West 44th Street between Fifth and Sixth avenues, 10036

Tel 212/944-6050

www.mansfieldhotel.com

Occupying a 1904 Beaux-Arts building with many original features, the hotel is convenient for the theater

MANDARIN ORIENTAL

Map 294 D16

80 Columbus Circle at West 60th Street, 10023

Tel 212/805-8800

www.mandarinoriental.com

This hotel soars majestically above Columbus Circle commanding views of Central Park, the Hudson River and the Manhattan skyline from floors 35 through 54 of the new Time Warner Center. Rooms are sumptuously furnished and designed. Bathrooms have deep tubs and glass wall showers plus flat panel TVs. Room service can be ordered from Asiate an Asian-inspired fine dining restaurant. MO Bar (on the 35th floor) has been attracting a lot of buzz. Facilities include a two-story spa, and a fitness center with 75-foot lap pool. The hotel has access to all of the facilities in the Time Warner Center.

💷 $499–$695, suite from $1,099

🛈 203 rooms, 48 suites

🚇 59th Street (A, B, C, D, 1, 9)

🚌 M5, M7, M10, M104

and Midtown shopping. The elegantly furnished rooms have sleigh beds with steel mesh headboards, metal and fabric armoires, plus VCRs. Nearby health club.

💷 $199–$439, suite from $300, including breakfast

🛈 100 rooms, 24 suites

🚇 42nd Street (B, D, F, V)

🚌 M1, M2, M3, M4, M5, M42

MARCEL

Map 296 F20

201 East 24th Street between Second and Third avenues, 10011

Tel 212/696-3800

www.nychotels.com

The rooms at this hotel are serene and minimal. Sheathed in blond wood and furnished in taupe, they have such modern clever design accents as high hats over the beds. They also have exceptional amenities for the price: dual-line phones with data ports and CD players, for instance. On-premises restaurant.

💷 $135–$249

🛈 100

🚇 23rd Street (6)

🚌 M15, M23, M101, M102, M103

MARITIME HOTEL

Map 296 D21

363 West 16th Street at Ninth Avenue
Tel 212/242-4300
www.themaritimehotel.com
In Chelsea and close to nightlife central, the Meatpacking District, this hotel was formerly the headquarters of the Maritime Union. In keeping with that history, the rooms are small and cabin-like with teak paneling and port-hole windows. Furnishings are modern and the rooms feature the latest technology—flat panel TVs and high-speed internet access. It has two attention-grabbing restaurants. Matsura is a dramatic basement supper-club style Japanese restaurant; there's also a Mediterranean café with a large outdoor terrace garden landscaped with magnolia trees and lily pond.

🛏 $245–$315
🛎 125
🚇 14th Street (A, C, E)
🚌 M11

MARK

Map 295 E14

25 East 77th Street between Fifth and Madison avenues, 10021
Tel 212/744-4300
www.mandarinoriental.com
In the center of the fashionable Upper East Side,

the Mark is the city's first boutique hotel. Small and elegant, it has a neoclassic Italian style. Piranesi prints accent the marble lobby. Rooms incorporate dressing areas, and bathrooms have large soaking tubs, heated towel racks and Molton Brown toiletries. Fax and VCR are standard. Facilities include restaurant-bar and a well-equipped fitness center.

🛏 $310–$620, suite from $450
🛎 119 rooms, 57 suites
🚇 77th Street (6)
🚌 M1, M2, M3, M4, M79

METRO

Map 296 E19

45 West 35th Street between Fifth and Sixth avenues, 10001
Tel 212/947-2500
www.hotelmetronyc.com
This has to be one of the best-value hotels in the city. It has a good Midtown location and plenty of art deco style. The rooms are nicely decorated with good-looking beds, nightstands and chairs and equipped with cable TV, and phone with data port. The marble bathrooms have hairdryers. Guests can relax in the library, which actually has books, or on the rooftop garden terrace. The sleek Metro Grill provides room service.

🛏 $170–$275, suite from $350, including breakfast
🛎 179 rooms and suites
🚇 34th Street (B, D, F, N, Q, R, V, W)
🚌 M2, M3, M5, M6, M7

MERCER

Map 297 E23

147 Mercer Street between Prince and Spring streets, 10012
Tel 212/966-6060
www.mercerhotel.com
The Hollywood crowd loves this East Coast version of Andre Balaz's Château Marmont. The SoHo location is ultra-hip, but the place is discreet, comfortable and tranquil. The loft-style rooms are spacious and minimalist. Christian Liaigre used neutral colors, glass, fabrics like linen, and rich woods from Africa. Extras include a mini-bar stocked by Dean and DeLuca and three telephones including a portable. If that's not enough, then the Mercer Kitchen under star chef Jean Georges Vongerichten is the clincher. Access to a nearby fitness center is provided.

🛏 $425–$650, suite from $1,200
🛎 68 rooms, 8 suites
🚇 Prince St (N, R, W)
🚌 M1, M6

MILLENNIUM UN PLAZA

Off map 295 G18

1 UN Plaza at 44th Street and First Avenue, 10017
Tel 212/758-1234
www.millenniumhotels.com
Across the street from the UN, this flashy hotel attracts

---

international diplomats and other wealthy visitors. Many of the rooms, which are located from the 28th floor and up, have splendid views of the skyline and the East River. They are well equipped with two-line phones with data port and printer/fax/copier. Traditional rooms feature mahogany and cherry furnishings, while more classicly furnished rooms with their blond woods look more contemporary. The fitness center has indoor pool and tennis court. The Ambassador Grill and lounge serves contemporary American cuisine.

🛏 $179–$429, add $100 for junior suite, $200 for one-bedroom suite
🛎 382 rooms, 45 suites
🚇 42nd Street/Grand Central (S, 4, 5, 6, 7)
🚌 M15, M27, M50

MODERNE

Map 294 D17

243 West 55th Street between Broadway and Eighth Avenue, 10019
Tel 212/397-6767
www.nychotels.com
This small retro-style hotel in a fine location near Carnegie Hall is reliable. The rooms are sleekly decorated (padded high back bed, built-in nightstands, op art) and equipped with the latest gadgetry—VCR, CD player and telephone with data port—plus hairdryer and an extra phone in the bathroom.

🛏 $139–$349, suite from $225
🛎 29 rooms, 5 suites
🚇 Seventh Avenue (B, D, E), 59th Street/Columbus Circle (A, B, C, D, 1, 9)
🚌 M10, M20, M104

MORGANS

Map 296 E19

237 Madison Avenue between East 37th and 38th streets, 10016
Tel 212/686-0300
www.morganshotelgroup.com
In 1984 Ian Schrager opened this hotel, his first in New York City. It's discreet (no nameplate visible) and more sedate than most. Minimalist furnishings decorate the rooms, which are ultra-comfortable with their club chairs, ottomans and window seats, and good looking, too, with suede headboards and

---

STAYING

bird's-eye maple cabinets. Bathrooms have whirlpool tubs and stainless-steel fixtures, granite floors and eye-catching black and white tile. The rooms also have the latest amenities. The dramatic cellar bar and the restaurant Asia de Cuba attract a fashion-conscious crowd. Residents have complimentary access to a nearby fitness club.

🏨 $235–$425, suite from $365
🛏 113 rooms, 28 suites
Ⓜ 33rd Street (6), 42nd Street/Grand Central (S, 4, 5, 6, 7)
🚌 M1, M2, M3, M4, M42, M34

NEW YORK PALACE

Map 295 E17
455 Madison Avenue between 50th and 51st streets, 10022
Tel 212/888-7000
www.newyorkpalace.com

Six landmark brownstones designed by McKim, Mead and White make up the core of this luxury hotel. Owner Sultan of Brunei has spent lavishly on the decor of the public areas and the guest rooms. Several gorgeous Louis Comfort Tiffany windows and alabaster sculptures by Saint-Gaudens grace the interiors. The accommodations are located in a 55-story tower. Business travelers appreciate the executive amenities: fax, three phones and spacious desk. The restaurant Istana offers an olive bar (30-plus), numerous sherries, and tapas at afternoon tea and contemporary American cuisine. Fitness center available.

🏨 $340–$595, suite from $1,000
🛏 821 rooms, 75 suites
Ⓜ 51st Street (6)
🚌 M1, M2, M3, M4, M50

NEWTON

Map 294 C13
2528 Broadway between 94th and 95th streets, 10025
Tel 212/678 6500
www.newyorkhotel.com

This reliable hotel caters to the workers in the entertainment industry who appreciate the value of the rooms here. They are equipped with cable TV and phone and prettily decorated in an old-fashioned way. Some share a bathroom.

🏨 $75–$180, suite from $150
🛏 98 rooms, 12 suites
Ⓜ 96th Street (1, 2, 3, 9)
🚌 M104

OFF-SOHO SUITES

Map 297 F23
11 Rivington Street between Chrystie and Bowery streets, 10002
Tel 212/979-9815
www.offsoho.com

It's pushing the envelope when the location is described as SoHo. It is, in fact, on the Lower East Side, the last of Manhattan's gentrified neighborhoods. Savvy travelers will appreciate the low prices of these suites, which have

bedroom living/dining area. Ideal for two couples traveling together, as each suite shares a kitchen and bath. They are well equipped with cable TV, telephone, modular jack, VCR and minibar. Fitness center available.

🏨 $89–$129, quads $119–$209
🛏 36 suites
Ⓜ Bowery (J, M, Z)
🚌 M103

ON THE AVENUE

Map 294 C14
222 West 77th Street between Broadway and Amsterdam Avenue, 10024
Tel 212/362-1100
www.stayinny.com

A few blocks from the Natural History Museum,

this small hotel built in 1922 is part of the Citylife Hotel Group, which has rescued and refurbished several historic buildings in Manhattan. The rooms, furnished in sleek modern style (duvets on beds, retro chairs), feature vibrant paintings by Alfonso Muñoz. Amenities include two phones. The three floors of penthouse suites have fine views.

🏨 $179–$349, suite from $400
🛏 250 rooms, 16 suites
Ⓜ 79th Street (1, 9)
🚌 M79, M104

PENINSULA

Map 295 E17
700 Fifth Avenue at 55th Street, 10019
Tel 212/956-2888
www.peninsula.com

This small hotel in a beautiful 23-story 1902 Beaux Arts building has a premier location, luxurious interiors and superb service. The rooms contain the latest amenities: fax, hands-free telephone, TV in the bathroom, dual-line phone with data

port, and bedside electronic control of all the electrical systems. The furnishings are luxurious and made even more so by the mood lighting. The Pen-Top Bar & Terrace is ideal for summertime trysts and Fives is an inviting bar/restaurant overlooking Fifth Avenue. Large outstanding fitness center, too, with an indoor pool, sundeck and spa.

🏨 $460–$760, suite from $760
🛏 185 rooms, 54 suites
Ⓜ 59 Street/Fifth Avenue (E, V)
🚌 M1, M2, M3, M4, M57

PICKWICK ARMS

Map 296 F17
230 East 51st Street, between Second
and Third avenues, 10022
Tel 212/355-0300
www.pickwickarms.com

One of the most reliable budget hotels in Manhattan, the Pickwick Arms attracts many international tour groups to its central and safe location. Single women in particular appreciate the last. The rooms are plain and comfortable with cable TV and telephone as standard amenities. Some single rooms have shared or corridor bathroom. The hotel has a restaurant, wine bar and a rooftop terrace.

🛏 Shared bath $79–$109, double $99–$199
🛈 350
🚇 51st Street (6)
🚌 M15, M50, M98, M101, M102, M103

PIERRE

Map 295 E16
2 East 61st Street at Fifth Avenue, 10021
Tel 212/940-8101
www.fourseasons.com

Overlooking Central Park, this 41-story hotel, built in 1930, is the quintessence of luxury,

service and refinement. Named after the son of Jacques Pierre, owner of the Hotel Anglais in Monte Carlo, it is currently under Four Seasons management and offers the same premier service. Both the rooms and the public areas are traditionally decorated with antiques. Trompe-l'oeil work decorates the Rotunda, where breakfast, afternoon tea and cocktails are served, and the marble, etched glass, silk and satin of the Café Pierre are extravagant. Even the fitness center is elegant.

🛏 $420–$645, suite from $750
🛈 149 rooms, 52 suites
🚇 59th Street/Fifth Avenue (N, R, W)
🚌 M1, M2, M3, M4

ROGER WILLIAMS

Map 296 E19
131 Madison Ave at 31st Street, 10016
Tel 212/448-7000
www.rogerwilliamshotel.com

In 1997 Unique Hotels Group renovated this fine old hotel (1928). They transformed the lobby, lining it with limestone and coating the fluted columns with zinc. In the good-size rooms they installed sleek contemporary maple furnishings, shoji window screens, and such amenities as VCRs, CD players, 27-inch TVs, and three phones. Bathrooms have hairdryers, Frette robes and Aveda toiletries. Cappuccino and espresso are available 24 hours. There's also a fitness studio.

🛏 $245–$385, suite from $500
🛈 183 rooms, 2 suites
🚇 33rd Street (6)
🚌 M1, M2, M3

ROYALTON

Map 296 E18
44 West 44th Street between Fifth and Sixth avenues, 10036
Tel 212/869-4400
www.morganshotelgroup.com

The first hotel conceived by Ian Schrager, the late Steve Rubell and Philippe Starck became an instant sensation and a magnet for the city's movers and shakers. Some even dubbed the lobby-restaurant 44 the Condé Nast cafeteria. The rooms are sleekly decorated in contemporary

minimalist style using trendy materials like slate, steel and glass. Bathrooms have oval tubs, and rooms come equipped with VCRs, fax and cassette players as standard. The Round Bar is a pleasant place for a drink. The fitness center is open 24 hours.

🛏 $245–$550, suite from $345
🛈 165 rooms, 3 suites
🚇 42nd Street (B, D, F, V)
🚌 M1, M2, M3, M4

RITZ CARLTON

Map 295 E16
50 Central Park South, 10019
Tel 212/308-9100
www.ritzcarlton.com

On the corner of Sixth Avenue and Central Park, this sparkling 33-story hotel has magnificent views. The lobby sets an opulent tone with its limestone walls, inlaid onyx floor and Samuel Halpert paintings. The rooms are luxuriously decorated in soft shades with brocade drapes and other plush fabrics. Room amenities include flat-screen TVs, DVDs and multi-line cordless phones. Park-view rooms have telescopes for birdwatching. Bathrooms have deep tubs with neck pillows, Frederic Fekkai toiletries and Frette candles. Pratesi linens and Bang and Olufsen stereo grace the suites. The Ritz Carlton is famous for its exceptional service, which here even extends to complimentary Burberry trench coats. The modern Restaurant Atelier offers innovative French cuisine. The Star Lounge specializes in elegant afternoon tea and classic cocktails. The full service La Prairie spa (▷ 228) is the first to open in the US. Fitness center, too. Note that Ritz Carlton also has another hotel overlooking the Statue of Liberty at Battery Park (tel 212/344-0800).

🛏 $525–$995, suite from $1,495
🛈 237 rooms, 40 suites
🚇 59th Street/Fifth Avenue (N, R, W), 57th Street (F)
🚌 M5, M6, M7

ST. REGIS

Map 295 E17
2 East 55th Street at Fifth Avenue,
10022
Tel 212/753-4500
www.stregis.com

Colonel John Jacob Astor IV conceived this beautiful 1904 Beaux Arts style hotel. The hallmarks of luxury, marble, gold leaf, tapestries and Louis XVI furniture are joined by the latest in technical wizardry. The service—each floor has 24-hour butler service—is also extraordinary. Suites have such extras as CD player/stereo, VCR, fax and a daily delivery of roses. The King Cole Bar is famous for the 1932 murals painted by Maxfield Parrish and for the creation of the first Bloody Mary in 1934 (originally called the "Red Snapper"). Tea in the Astor Court is one of the city's best. Carita of Paris spa and a fitness center.

🛏 $475–$795, suite from $1,200
🛏 222 rooms, 93 suites
Ⓜ Fifth Avenue/53rd Street (E, V)
🚌 M1, M2, M3, M4

70 PARK AVENUE

Map 296 E19
70 Park Avenue at 38th Street
Tel 212/973-2400
www.70parkavenuehotel.com
In the quiet Murray Hill neighborhood, Kimpton's first property in New York City has been designed in contemporary style, but with comfort in mind, even though the rooms are on the small side. Guests can select their own pillows and blankets. Deep soaking tubs invite repose in the bathrooms. Yoga mats and a 24-hour yoga channel are also available. Tech equipment runs to 42-inch flat panel TVs, DVD/CD

players and KioPhones that can be used for e-mail and web surfing. Pets are welcome. The Silverleaf Tavern offers contemporary American fare.

🛏 $225–$525, suite from $295
🛏 193 rooms, 14 suites
Ⓜ Grand Central/42nd Street (4, 5, 6, 7)
🚌 M1, M2, M3, M4, M42

SHERRY-NETHERLAND

Map 295 E16
781 Fifth Avenue between 59th and 60th streets, 10022
Tel 212/355-2800
www.sherrynetherland.com
The Sherry-Netherland is unique because it's a building cooperative, which means that the owners individually decorate their units, and that the number of guest rooms available fluctuates between 100 and 150. It's also one of the best situated and most opulent cooperatives. The building dates from 1927 and much of its luxury detailing was taken from a nearby Vanderbilt mansion that was being torn down. It has plenty of genuine European style—there are even elevator operators—so it's not surprising that Harry Cipriani chose to open a restaurant here. There is a bar and fitness center for guests, too.

🛏 $425–$600, suite from $650
🛏 150 rooms and suites
Ⓜ 59th Street/Fifth Avenue (N, R, W)
🚌 M1, M2, M3, M4

SHOREHAM

Map 295 E17
33 West 55th Street between Fifth and Sixth avenues, 10019
Tel 212/247-6700
www.shorehamhotel.com
This mid-size Midtown hotel, right behind the Museum of Modern Art, has been imaginatively updated and now boasts the latest looks and the most up-to-date technology and amenities in the rooms. Mesh headboards shimmer above the beds. The decor includes plenty of aluminum, plus entertainment musts such as VCRs and CD players. Choice rooms are in the back. Restaurant and bar available.

SOHO GRAND

Map 297 E23
310 West Broadway between Canal and Grand streets, 10013
Tel 212/965-3000
www.sohogrand.com
Since the CEO of Hartz pet food owns this stylish downtown hotel, it puts out a welcome mat for animals. It was a pioneer, too, when it opened in art-oriented SoHo. A cast-iron staircase studded with coke-bottle glass leads up to the vibrant lobby. Cool tones create the ambience in the rooms, but there are plenty of guest comforts—bathrobes, Frette linens and velvet drapes, plus VCR and CD player. Restaurant, two bars and fitness center.

🛏 $309–$599, suite $3,500
🛏 358 rooms, 2 suites
Ⓜ Canal Street (A, C, E)
🚌 M5

🛏 $199 $429, suite from $339, including Continental breakfast
🛏 143 rooms, 31 suites
Ⓜ 53rd Street/Fifth Avenue (E, V)
🚌 M1, M2, M3, M4, M5, M6, M7

SURREY

Map 295 E15
20 East 76th Street at Madison Avenue, 10021
Tel 212/288-3700
www.affinia.com
The Surrey's large suites with kitchenettes and dining area are attractively decorated and well equipped, with dual-line phones, VCRs, irons and ironing boards and bathrobes. Another reason to stay here? Eminent chef Daniel Boulud's Café Boulud is on the premises. Facilities include a fitness center.

🛏 $275–$545
🛏 250 suites
Ⓜ 77th St (6)
🚌 M1, M2, M3, M4, M79

STAYING

THIRTY THIRTY

Map 296 E19
30 East 30th Street between Madison
and Park avenues, 10016
Tel 212/689-1900
www.thirtythirty-nyc.com
On the edge of the burgeoning
Flatiron District in a
refurbished 1902 building,
this hotel is decent value. The
rooms sport the latest minimal
look, but they are small and
exhibit some European-style
solutions—TVs suspended on
the walls and very limited
furnishings. Still, they do
have such conveniences as
telephone with data port and
hairdryer. Superior rooms
have 27-inch TVs. Bathrooms
are tiled and have glass
shower doors.
🅦 $139–$279
ⓘ 243 rooms, 15 suites
Ⓢ 33rd Street (6)
Ⓜ M1, M101, M103

TRAVEL INN

Map 296 C18
515 West 42nd Street between Tenth
and Eleventh avenues, 10036
Tel 212/695-7171
www.newyorkhotel.com
The great benefits of this
Manhattan hotel are the outdoor pool and the free parking.
The rooms are decorated in
typical motel style. Coffeeshop
and fitness center.
🅦 $105–$210
ⓘ 160
Ⓢ 42nd Street (A, C, E)
Ⓜ M42, M11

TRIBECA GRAND

Map 297 E24
2 Avenue of the Americas at White
Street, 10013
Tel 212/519-6600
www.tribecagrand.com
With its luxurious 98-seat
private screening room, this
hotel, close to SoHo and the
Village, caters to the independent film crowd. The lobby
opens to a dramatic atrium
lounge/restaurant. The rooms
are modern and come with
such gadgets as wireless key-
boards, a bathroom TV with
waterproof remote, Bose
radio and fax/printer. Bliss
and Kiehl products in the
bathroom and the Dean &
DeLuca snacks are alluring
extras. The business center is
exceptionally well equipped,
and the workstations have
flat-panel screens. Hartz owns

the place, so pets are welcome. Fitness center.
🅦 $319–$609, suite from $1,299
ⓘ 365 rooms, 4 suites
Ⓢ Franklin Street (1, 9)
Ⓜ M6

TRUMP INTERNATIONAL HOTEL AND TOWER

Map 294 D16
1 Central Park West at Columbus Circle,
10023
Tel 212/299-1000
www.trumpintl.com
You have to admire Donald
Trump for taking one of the
worst buildings in the country,
recognizing its strengths, and
transforming it into such a
stylish hotel. The location is
superb, with breathtaking
views of Central Park and
easy access to the Lincoln
Center and Midtown. The
rooms, located between the
third and 17th floors, are
stylish, and each has fax, CD
player and VCR; suites have
whirlpool tubs and even
telescopes. The restaurant
Jean-Georges is another draw.
Excellent fitness center with
lap pool and spa.
🅦 $399–$650, suite from $565
ⓘ 38 rooms, 129 suites
Ⓢ 59th Street/Columbus Circle (A, B,
C, D, 1, 9)
Ⓜ M10, M20

UNION SQUARE INN

Map 297 F21
209 East 14th Street between Second
and Third avenues
Tel 212/614-0500
www.unionsquareinn.com
Even though most rooms are
small with wall pegs for closets
and only showers in the tiled
bathrooms, this place is
attractive and modern and
offers decent value. No
elevator. Coffeeshop.
🅦 $119–$159, including breakfast
ⓘ 43
Ⓢ 14th Street/Union Square (L, N, Q,
R, W, 4, 5, 6)
Ⓜ M14, M15, M101, M102, M103

W-NEW YORK

Map 295 F17
541 Lexington Avenue between East
49th and 50th streets, 10022
Tel 212/755-1200
www.whotels.com
W is the hip Starwood Hotels
chain. Here, as elsewhere in
the group, the lobby is a living
room space, where you can
relax on ottomans or play

board games. Natural
elements are always evident,
too: pots of grass, waterfalls,
polished chunks of tree trunk
as coffee tables and bouquets
of grasses and seedpods, for
example. Rooms are modern
and equipped with Web TV,
two-line phones, VCRs and CD
players. Good food and
beverage outlets polish the
image—Rande Gerber's
Whiskey Blue and Drew
Nieporent's Heartbeat
Restaurant. The spa and fitness
center is a standout.
🅦 $239–$550, suite from $1,000
ⓘ 647 rooms, 67 suites
Ⓢ 51st Street (6)
Ⓜ M50, M101, M102, M103

WALDORF-ASTORIA HOTEL AND TOWERS

Map 295 F17
301 Park Avenue between 49th and
50th streets, 10022
Tel 212/355-3000
www.waldorfastoria.com or
www.waldorf-towers.com
The Waldorf opened in 1931 to
rave reviews. The largest hotel
in the world at the time, it
remains monumental—some
would say overwhelming. The
Towers, which occupies the
28th to 42nd floors, have a
separate entrance and the
most luxurious rooms; this is
where residents and heads of
state stay when they come to
town. The clubby Bull and Bear
is popular for steaks, while

Peacock Alley is famous
for its afternoon tea.
Oscar's is a very chic
coffeeshop and Inagiku
is authentically Japanese.
Large fitness center; excellent
business center.
🅦 Waldorf $239–$629, suite from
$339; Waldorf Towers $399–$799, suite
from $599
ⓘ 1,049 rooms, 197 suites (Waldorf),
79 rooms, 101 suites (Towers)
Ⓢ 51st Street (6)
Ⓜ M1, M2, M3, M4, M50

STAYING

WALES

Map 295 E13
1295 Madison Avenue between 92nd and 93rd streets, 10128
Tel 212/876-6000
www.waleshotel.com

The Hotel Wales is a study in old-fashioned luxury in a nine-story building on the quiet Upper East Side near Museum Mile and Central Park. The rooms are traditional with plush chairs and half-poster beds, with VCRs and CD players; some have views of Central Park, just two blocks away. Sarabeth's Kitchen, with yummy breakfast pastries and teas, and the charming rooftop terrace are bonuses. Small fitness studio.

🛏 $219–$399, suite from $300, including breakfast
ℹ 46 rooms, 41 suites
Ⓜ 96th Street (6)
🚌 M1, M2, M3, M4, M96

WARWICK

Map 295 E17
65 West 54th Street at Sixth Avenue, 10019
Tel 212/247-2700
www.warwickhotels.com
William Randolph Hearst built this impressive hotel in 1927 as his East Coast hideaway

and guest facility. Many a Hollywood celebrity settled into residence here, including Cary Grant. The rooms are large with such old-fashioned and rare amenities as walk-in closets and extra-large marble bathrooms, plus modern ones such as fax machines and two dual-line phones. They are furnished in English style with Asian accents. Facilities include two restaurants, bar and well-equipped fitness center.

🛏 $220–$425, suite from $385
ℹ 359 rooms, 67 suites
Ⓜ 57th Street (F)
🚌 M5, M6, M7, M57

WASHINGTON SQUARE

Map 297 E22
103 Waverly Place between Fifth and Sixth avenues, 10011
Tel 212/777-9515
www.washingtonsquarehotel.com
On the northwest corner of Washington Square Park, this small hotel has a

casual bohemian air (in the 1960s Joan Baez and Bob Dylan were frequent visitors). The rooms are small, basic and unimaginative, but the price is right. They do have cable TV and telephone with data port. Facilities include an attractive restaurant-lounge (with occasional jazz) and exercise room.

🛏 $150–$210, including breakfast
ℹ 175
Ⓜ West 4th Street (A, C, E, F, S, V)
🚌 M5, M6, M8

WESTPARK

Map 294 D16
6 Columbus Circle (between Eighth and Ninth avenues), 10019
Tel 212/246-6440
www.westparkhotel.com
Conveniently situated near Carnegie Hall in an attractive historic building, this hotel's rooms are quite plain, but are equipped with all the necessary amenities: air conditioning, cable TV, dual-line telephone with data port, hairdryer. Some of the rooms have views of Central Park.

🛏 $139–$199, suite from $189
ℹ 87 rooms, 3 suites
Ⓜ 59th Street/Columbus Circle (A, B, C, D, 1, 9)
🚌 M10, M11, M20, M57

WOLCOTT

Map 296 E19
4 West 31st Street between Fifth Avenue and Broadway, 10001
Tel 212/268-2900
www.wolcott.com.
Close to the Empire State Building, this hotel has comfortable rooms decorated in a quaint, old-fashioned style (candy-stripe wallpaper, patterned bed cover, wing chair, swing arm lamps). The standard amenities you can expect in the rooms include cable TV, telephone with data port, hairdryer and air conditioning. There is a fitness room for guests use.

🛏 $109–$230 junior, suite add $20
ℹ 144 rooms, 23 suites
Ⓜ 28th Street (N, R, W), 34th Street/Herald Square (B, D, F, N, Q, R, V, W)
🚌 M2, M3, M5, M6, M7

SPECIAL

WYNDHAM

Map 295 E16
42 West 58th Street between Fifth and Sixth avenues, 10019
Tel 212/753-3500
www.hotelwyndham.com
Given its location and attributes, this place is great value. Although it has the name Wyndham, it is not part of that chain. It's a quirky place relying on its good word-of-mouth and a great Midtown location, just a block from Central Park and a short walk from both the Lincoln Center and the Theater District. The decor is old-fashioned, as is the service and the attitude, which is a pleasant bonus. Suites come with pantries, refrigerators and walk-in closets. All rooms have cable TV and telephone.

🛏 $179–$399, suite from $250
ℹ 100 rooms, 100 suites
Ⓜ 57th Street (F), 59th Street/Fifth Avenue (N, R, W)
🚌 M1, M2, M3, M4, M5, M6, M7

STAYING

MAJOR HOTEL CHAINS

Company	Description	Number of Hotels in Manhattan	Contact Number and Website
Best Western	Decent quality, budget accommodation	4	602/957-4200; www.bestwestern.com
Clarion Hotels	A Choice Hotels International brand. It's moderately priced and offers full amenities.	2	301/592-5000 www.clarionhotel.com
Comfort Inn	Strictly budget. Rooms-only; no extras (restaurants, for example). Owned by Choice Hotels International	4	301/592-5000; 800/228-5150 www.comfortinn.com
Courtyard Marriott	A moderately priced Marriott brand that appeals to business travelers.	3	301/380-3000 www.courtyard.com
Crowne Plaza	The second-tier full-service brand of Intercontinental	2	770/604-2000; 800/227-6963 www.crowneplaza.com
Days Inns/Hotels	Decent-quality budget accommodations	1	800/329-7466 www.daysinn.com
Doubletree Suites	Hilton's all-suite hotel	2	310/278-4321; www.doubletree.com
Embassy Suites	Another Hilton all-suite hotel; trademark is complimentary breakfast and evening hors d'oeuvres	1	800/362-2779 www.embassysuites.com
Four Points	Starwood's budget brand	1	800/640-8100; www.fourpoints.com
Hampton Inn	Hilton's moderately priced brand	4	800/426-7866; www.hamptoninn.com
Hilton	International full-service hotel chain	4	800/445-8667; www.hilton.com
Holiday Inn/ Holiday Inn Express	Consistent good-value accommodations. Express is the budget line. Owned by Intercontinental	4	770/604-2000 www.holiday-inn.com
Howard Johnson	Moderately priced accommodations	3	800/446-4656; www.hojo.com
Hyatt	International full-service hotel chain	2	312/750-1234; 800/233-1234; www.hyatt.com
La Quinta	Budget chain	1	866/725-1661; 800/642-4241 www.lq.com
Marriott Hotels	The premier brand of this international chain	3	301/380-3000; 800/228-9290 www.marriott.com
Quality Inn Hotels	Decent-quality hotels for business and leisure travelers. Owned by Choice Hotels	2	301/592-5000; 800/4choice www.qualityinn.com
Radisson	Full-service international chain	1	800/333-3333; www.radisson.com
Ramada Inns	Full-service moderately priced hotel chain. Ramada Limited brand lacks in-house dining	2	800/272-6232 www.ramada.com
Red Roof Inns	Modern, high-quality budget accommodations	1	800/567-7720 www.redroof.com
Renaissance	Marriott's moderately priced full-service brand	1	301/380-3000 www.renaissancehotels.com
Sheraton	Owned by Starwood, Sheraton offers good-quality modern full-amenity hotels	3	914/640-8100 www.sheraton.com
W Hotels	The hip brand owned by Starwood Hotels	5	914/640 8100; www.whotels.com
Westin	This Starwood's brand appeals to business travelers	2	914/640-8100 www.starwood.com

Planning

GEOGRAPHY

New York City is in the northeast United States. Four of the five boroughs that comprise New York City are islands. Manhattan, the most populous, is bordered on the east by the East River and on the west by the Hudson River. The narrow Harlem River separates it from the Bronx to the north, and Long Island Sound separates it from Long Island to the south. The city has a waterfront of 578 miles (930km). The Bronx is the only borough on the mainland and it is bounded by water to the south, east and west. The surrounding landscape is flat, although the highest point, at Todt Hill on Staten Island, is the highest point on the Atlantic coast south of Maine at 409ft (124m).

During the Ice Age, most of New York State was covered by glaciers, with southern Long Island and Staten Island being the exceptions. The movement of the glaciers produced nine distinct physiographic regions.

The four seasons are very distinct in this region, and New Yorkers endure, without too many complaints, the cold, damp winters and hot, humid summers.

DAYLIGHT HOURS

Be aware of the number of daylight hours you have when planning your days out in and around the city. There are some areas, away from central tourist areas, that are best avoided after dark.

Carl Schurz Park (above); cooling off at a fire hydrant (left)

TEMPERATURE

Below left are the average daily maximum and minimum temperatures for New York City. Precipitation in December, January, February and March can fall in the form of snow.

WINTER

The city's average annual snowfall is 29.2 inches (74cm), most of it falling in January and February. However, even after heavy snowfall, plows quickly remove the snow and disruptions are minimal. The strong winds, more pronounced as you approach the East or Hudson rivers, makes it feel colder than it really is.

SUMMER

In July and August, the hottest months, humidity can be as high as 90 percent, the sun can be fierce, and everyone feels lethargic and sticky. Avoid these months if you suffer from the heat. If you do decide to visit then, make sure to wear sunscreen during the day both in the city and at the beaches.

THE BEST TIME TO VISIT

The most pleasant time to visit, and therefore the most expensive, as it is peak season, is May to early June and September to mid-November.

From May to early June, the days are delightfully comfortable and the evenings cool; showers are always a possibility. From September to late October, days are still warm but evenings start getting cooler. The leaves change to gold and red in mid- to late October, which is very pretty but

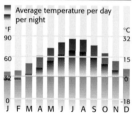

TEMPERATURE

■ Average temperature per day per night

■ Average no. of days above 65°F below 32°F

RAINFALL

Average rainfall

AVERAGE SUNRISE/SUNSET TIMES		
	SUNRISE	SUNSET
Jan	7.15	4.45
Feb	6.50	5.30
Mar	6.10	6.00
Apr	5.15	6.30
May	4.30	7.00
Jun	4.30	7.30
Jul	4.35	7.30
Aug	5.00	7.00
Sep	5.30	6.00
Oct	5.30	5.20
Nov	6.35	4.45
Dec	7.15	4.30

PLANNING

- Radio and television news end with a weather report and a short-range forecast (▷ 323).
- Visit www.weather.com, the Weather Channel's 10-day forecast.
- Visit www.cnn.com/weather for CNN's five-day forecast and satellite pictures.

not as spectacular as in New England, farther north. By November, days are much cooler and there is more rain and wind.

TIME ZONES

New York is on Eastern Standard Time, five hours behind GMT. Daylight Saving Time, four hours behind GMT, is from early April to late October. An easy way to remember this is: In April, the clocks "spring" ahead one hour, and in October they "fall" behind one hour.

TIME ZONES		
CITY	TIME DIFFERENCE	TIME AT NOON IN NEW YORK
Amsterdam	+6	6pm
Berlin	+6	6pm
Brussels	+6	6pm
Chicago	-1	11am
Dublin	+5	5pm
Johannesburg	+7	7pm
London	+5	5pm
Madrid	+6	6pm
Montreal	0	noon
Paris	+6	6pm
Perth, Australia	+13	1am
Rome	+6	6pm
San Francisco	-3	9am
Sydney, Australia	+15	3am
Tokyo	+14	2am

DOCUMENTATION FOR NON-US VISITORS

SECURITY

Since 9/11, security in the US has been stepped up. Restrictions are tight on what baggage you can check in and what you can carry on board, both for domestic and international flights (see www.tsa.gov for the latest information). Expect your belongings to be searched at airports, at museums and at the entryways of many office buildings. Prohibited items may be confiscated. If you are carrying bottled water, you may be asked to take a sip of it, as proof that it is not chemically suspicious. Co-operation will facilitate easy access. For the most up-to-date information on security in and around the city visit the city's official tourism office at www.nycvisit.com.

VISA AND PASSPORT REQUIREMENTS

Canadian citizens do not require a passport, but all other nationalities must have a machine-readable passport to enter the United States. Canadians may be asked for identification and proof of

citizenship before entering the country, such as a birth certificate or photo ID. Non-resident foreign visitors must show their machine-readable passport, their visa if required, and their round-trip ticket when entering the United States. Upon entry, expect to be fingerprinted and photographed.

For up-to-date information on visa requirements and how to obtain one, it is vital that you contact the American embassy in your home country months before your journey. Passport and visa requirements can change at short notice so always check before you travel.

CUSTOMS ALLOWANCES

Visitors arriving in New York from outside the country are required to fill in a Customs Declaration before landing in the United States, and they must declare everything except personal effects, which include either 200 cigarettes or 50 cigars or 2.2lbs (1kg) of smoking tobacco, providing you are 21 or older. You may also bring in 1 liter (33.8fl oz) of alcohol.

Visitors are not allowed to bring in any fruits, vegetables, plants, meat or meat products, firearms or ammunition.

If you have any questions,

CUSTOMS WEBSITES
Australia
1-300-363-263 or 61-2-6275-6666
www.customs.gov.au
Canada
800/461-9999 or 204/983-3500
or 506/636-5064
www.cra-arc.gc.ca
Ireland
353 1 647 4444
www.revenue.ie
New Zealand
(0800) 428-786 or 64-(09) 300-5399
www.customs.govt.nz
United Kingdom
0845 010 9000 or 44 20 8929 0152
www.hmce.gov.uk

telephone the Customs Information Line on 202/354-1000 or contact your nearest United States consulate or embassy before departing, or visit www. customs.ustreas.gov and click on "Traveler Information." If you are bringing more than $10,000 into the country, you must declare it on the customs form given to passengers during your inbound flight. You may bring in only $100 worth of gifts duty-free, however.

WHAT YOU CAN TAKE HOME

If you buy expensive items, you can often avoid paying New York City's 8.375 percent sales tax by having the items shipped back to your home. Ask when making the purchase, but before paying. Because rules vary for each country, contact the customs service in your country by telephone or check its website.

PLANNING

COUNTRY	ADDRESS	WEBSITE
Australia	Moonah Place, Yarralumla ACT 2600, tel 61 2 6214 5600	http://canberra.usembassy.gov/
Canada	490 Sussex Drive, Ottawa, ON K1N 1G8, tel 1 800 283-4356	www.usembassycanada.gov
France	2 avenue Gabriel, 75382 Paris, tel 33 1 43 12 22 22	http://france.usembassy.gov/
Germany	Neustädtische Kirchstr. 4-5, 10117 Berlin, Federal Republic of Germany tel 030 8305-0	http://berlin.usembassy.gov/
Ireland	42 Elgin Road, Ballsbridge, Dublin 4, tel 353 1 668 8777	http://dublin.usembassy.gov/
Italy	via Vittorio Veneto 119/A, 00187 Roma, tel 39 06 46741	http://www.usembassy.it/
New Zealand	29 Fitzherbert Terrace, Thorndon, Wellington, tel 644 462 6000	http://wellington.usembassy.gov/
Spain	Calle Serrano 75, 28006 Madrid, tel 91 587 2200	http://madrid.usembassy.gov/
South Africa	PO Box 9536, Pretoria 0001, 877 Pretorius St, Pretoria, tel 27 12 43 4000	http://pretoria.usembassy.gov/
UK	24 Grosvenor Square, London, W1A 1AE, tel 020 7499-9000	http://london.usembassy.gov/

TRAVEL INSURANCE

The US does not have reciprocal healthcare arrangements with other countries. Ensure you purchase full travel insurance in your country before departing. Check that it covers cancellations, lost luggage and medical expenses up to at least $1 million, including dental care. Medical costs in the US are high, so make sure you have good medical coverage. The cost of insurance depends on your age, health, type and length of your trip. One-year coverage is very economical if you are planning more than one trip per year. Family coverage is also good value if you are traveling with a spouse and children.

PRACTICALITIES

CLOTHING

Casual clothing is acceptable in restaurants, museums and attractions throughout New York City. In summer, men must wear a shirt to enter most restaurants, although only a handful of the city's restaurants require men to wear a jacket and tie. Of course, there is no shortage of stores where you can buy any clothing that you may have forgotten to bring with you. In public places, you will be expected to wear shoes (no bare feet), and men are expected to remove their hats in churches.

Comfortable walking shoes are a must. In winter, you will need a hat or earmuffs, scarf, gloves or mittens, boots, a sweater and a warm coat or jacket. If you want to go ice skating or sledding in Central Park, you can either bring your own gear or rent skates once you're there.

In spring, bring a sweater and a spring coat or jacket. In summer, prepare for hot, humid weather, and be sure to bring a sun hat or cap and sunglasses. In the fall, pack a sweater and a light jacket or coat as well as lighter clothes in case of warm weather. Rainwear and an umbrella, however, are a must all year round.

SHOPPING

Don't overpack. Shopping in New York is fun, and you can readily find anything you may need—umbrella vendors seem to materialize on almost every significant street corner when it rains (you can pick an umbrella up for just $5), and you can readily acquire sunglasses on the street on fine days.

Clothes, accessories, electronic equipment and many other items come in wider selections than in most of the rest of the United States and are cheaper than in many European countries.

For every shopper, bargain-hunting can be rewarding. Be aware, however, that the "Going out of business" sales advertised on posters at electronic equipment stores in the Theater District are bogus—these "sales" are a come-on to attract naïve customers. Before buying, get the model number of the product you want and check other retailers' prices online or you will almost certainly pay too much; if you're spending a significant sum of money, it's better to patronize a reputable specialist retailer. In vintage and second-hand shops it is always worthwhile to ask for a better price—sometimes you will get it.

Keep in mind that many stores close on public holidays; SoHo is fairly closed on Mondays and the Lower East Side is shuttered on Saturdays and very slow on Friday afternoons.

MEASUREMENTS

If you are more used to metric measurements than imperial, the conversion table below will be very useful.

CONVERSION CHART		
FROM	TO	MULTIPLY BY
Inches	Centimeters	2.54
Centimeters	Inches	0.3937
Feet	Meters	0.3048
Meters	Feet	3.2810
Yards	Meters	0.9144
Meters	Yards	1.0940
Miles	Kilometers	1.6090
Kilometers	Miles	0.6214
Acres	Hectares	0.4047
Hectares	Acres	2.4710
Gallons	Liters	4.5460
Liters	Gallons	0.2200
Ounces	Grams	28.35
Grams	Ounces	0.0353
Pounds	Grams	453.6
Grams	Pounds	0.0022
Pounds	Kilograms	0.4536
Kilograms	Pounds	2.205
Tons	Tonnes	1.0160
Tonnes	Tons	0.9842

PLANNING

CLOTHING SIZES

The chart below indicates how UK and European clothing and shoe sizes compare with those in the US

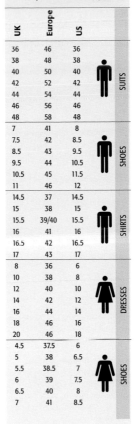

UK	Europe	US	
36	46	36	
38	48	38	SUITS
40	50	40	
42	52	42	
44	54	44	
46	56	46	
48	58	48	
7	41	8	
7.5	42	8.5	
8.5	43	9.5	SHOES
9.5	44	10.5	
10.5	45	11.5	
11	46	12	
14.5	37	14.5	
15	38	15	
15.5	39/40	15.5	SHIRTS
16	41	16	
16.5	42	16.5	
17	43	17	
8	36	6	
10	38	8	
12	40	10	DRESSES
14	42	12	
16	44	14	
18	46	16	
20	46	18	
4.5	37.5	6	
5	38	6.5	
5.5	38.5	7	SHOES
6	39	7.5	
6.5	40	8	
7	41	8.5	

VOLTAGE AND ADAPTERS

The power supply in the US is 110/120 volts AC (60 cycles). American plugs have two-prong flat pins, so you will need an adapter if you have plugs with two round pins, or three pins.

It is best to buy an adapter before departing or in the airport shop as they can be difficult to find in the US, although some department stores and pharmacies stock them. You will also need a voltage transformer for European appliances.

COMFORT AND ETIQUETTE
Public restrooms

Restrooms are normally labeled "Women" and "Men" or use a male/female symbol. You may notice that they are labeled in Spanish as well as English in airports, some restaurants and clubs. Public restrooms are found in visitor centers (▷ 324) and in Grand Central Terminal (▷ 102–104), but New Yorkers stop in hotels, large bookstores, department stores or cafés—theoretically restrooms in eating places are for patrons only, but in some restaurants it's an option. Restrooms in public buildings are wheelchair-accessible and may offer facilities for baby-changing. Restrooms in most parts of the city are clean and well supplied with soap, hand-dryers and paper. A few in Chinatown are substandard.

Traveling with children

New York is family-friendly for the most part, with special discounts for children, special prices for meals and plenty of attractions to keep them happy. Many hotels let kids stay for free and most museums do not charge for young children. Look for special things to do in the "Weekend" section of the Friday *New York Times*, *New York* magazine's "Cue" section and in *Time Out New York*. Special performances can sell out or fill up early, so expect to plan ahead. For baby-sitting services there's the Baby Sitters' Guild (tel 212/682-0227 or www.babysittersguild.com).

Laundry services

Most hotels either offer laundry services or will recommend one. Before you make your reservation, check what the hotel offers.

Smoking

In April 2003, when Mayor Bloomberg banned smoking in all public places, including restaurants, clubs, bars and anywhere an employee may be exposed to a patron's smoke, it was very controversial. Today it is widely accepted. People who want to smoke must go outside. There is no smoking on buses, subways or trains, but you may smoke in the privacy of your hotel room—providing it is a designated smoking room.

Dealing with beggars

It is your choice whether to give money to beggars. If you would prefer not to, simply keep on moving if a beggar approaches you on the street and asks for money. Don't make eye contact and don't engage in conversation. On the subway, you may come across beggars who deliver a monologue about their hard times and about how your donation will help their family. Again, if you prefer not to give, don't make eye contact, and shake your head "no" if you are approached personally.

On subways

If all seats are taken, move to the center of the subway car so you don't block the doors. If a senior citizen, an adult with a young child, a pregnant woman or person with a disability gets on and there are no available seats, offer yours. It's the civilized thing to do, and your fellow passengers —at least the civilized ones—will admire you for it.

GAY AND LESBIAN NEW YORK

The Stonewall Riot on Christopher Street in Greenwich Village is credited with starting the gay liberation movement in New York City in 1969. Today, gay and lesbian visitors will find New York an easy place to visit. The West Village, especially Christopher Street, is full of shops, restaurants and services with a gay orientation, as is Chelsea, on Eighth Avenue from 16th to 23rd streets.

Finding help

● The International Gay & Lesbian Travel Association (tel 800/448-8550 or 954/776-2626, www.iglta.org) is a specialist travel agency.
● Lesbian, Gay, Bisexual & Transgender Community Center (208 West 13th Street, between Seventh and Eighth avenues, tel 212/620-7310, www.gaycenert.org) is an excellent source of information on what's happening in the city and where to stay.
● Gay and Lesbian Switchboard of NY Project (tel 212/989-0999, www.glnh.org) offers peer counseling and information on events.

What's happening

For current gay and lesbian nightlife, pick up a copy of *Metro, Go, HX, New York Blade, Next* and *Village Voice*, all of them free publications. *Time Out New York*, available at all street news-stands and many other retail outlets, has an excellent section on what's on for gay and lesbian visitors.

PLANNING

PLACES OF WORSHIP

With its rich cultural mix, this city of immigrants offers a place to worship for every kind of belief. Listings in newspapers note the topic of the current week's theme. For the most extensive list of churches, temples, synagogues and mosques, look in the *Yellow Pages*.

PLACES OF WORSHIP	
Baptist	Abyssinian Baptist Church (132 Odell Clark Place at West 138th Street between Adam Clayton Powell Boulevard and Lenox Avenue, tel 212/862-7474).
Buddhist	New York Buddhist Church (Riverside Drive between 105th and 106th streets, tel 212/678-0305).
Greek Orthodox	St. Nicholas Greek Orthodox Church (155 Cedar Street, tel 212/227-0773).
Interfaith	Cathedral of St. John the Divine (1047 Amsterdam Avenue at 112th Street, tel 212/316-7540).
Jewish	Temple Emanu-El (1 East 65th Street at Fifth Avenue, tel 212/744-1400) is reform.
Muslim	Mosque of the Islamic Culture Center (Third Avenue at 96th Street, tel 212/722-5234).
Roman Catholic	St. Patrick's Cathedral (Fifth Avenue between 50th and 51st streets, tel 212/753-2261).

St. Patrick's Cathedral, with its two spires, is dwarfed by Midtown skyscrapers

MONEY

TAXES

In New York City an 8.375 percent sales tax is added at the cash register. You will pay this on most purchases, except on clothing under $110. The hotel tax is 13.25 percent, plus $2 per room per night. The parking garage tax is 18.25 percent.

TIPPING

You must tip people in the service sector because their livelihood depends on tips. Employers pay them a minimum wage, in most cases, and expect tips to make up the rest of their income. If you tip less than expected, you are sending a message that the service was less than satisfactory.

● **In restaurants**, tip waiters, waitresses and bartenders at least 15 percent of the bill—to figure it out quickly just double the 8.375 percent sales tax listed on the bill. Tip 20 percent in expensive restaurants, and always round up for good service. The head waiter in upscale restaurants expects 5 percent and the cloakroom attendant expects $1 when they give you back your coat.

● **In taxis**, tip the driver 20 percent, more if the journey is short.

● **In hotels**, tip the bellboy $1 or $2 for each suitcase he carries up to your room or down to the lobby. The chambermaid expects $2 for a few nights' stay. The hall porter expects $1 or $2 for getting you a taxi.

● **At the airport or train station**, tip the porter who transports your luggage $1 or $2 per bag.

FOR NON-US VISITORS
Changing money

If you are coming from outside the United States, change money before you leave home so that you can pay taxis, trains or buses on arrival. The commission at airport bureaux de change is higher than in most banks. Dollar bills of a higher denomination than $20 may not be accepted by taxi drivers, so it is best to always have small bills available. There are bureaux de change throughout Manhattan, but you get better service in banks and at the visitor center in Times Square (▷ 324). There are ATMs all

MONEY VOCABULARY	
$	dollar
¢	cent
a penny	1 cent
a nickel	5 cents
a dime	10 cents
a quarter	25 cents
a half dollar	50 cents
5 bucks	5 dollars

over the city. Expect to pay up to $3 per transaction if you are using a bank other than your own.

● **American Express Travel Services** has many offices in the city, including one on the mezzanine level at Macy's in Herald Square (tel 212/695-8075).

● **TravelEx** has a number of offices (tel 212/265-6063 or www.us.thomascook.com).

● **Chase Manhattan Bank** (tel 212/935-9935 or www.chase. com) has more than 400 branches with bureaux de change.

How to get money

Most people use credit cards to pay for hotels, restaurant meals and shopping. However, some restaurants and other establishments accept only cash. If you rent a car, a credit card will be essential. MasterCard, Visa and American Express are the cards most often accepted (but Amex occasionally is not accepted). Diner's Club and Carte Blanche are accepted by most restaurants and many hotels, but not all. Discover, enRoute, Eurocard and JCB are also often accepted, but not always.

Traveler's checks in US dollars, although less common than in the past, remain a safe way to carry money. Keep a copy of the serial numbers separate from the checks and record the ones you cash, so that any lost or stolen checks can be replaced quickly. Checks from American Express (tel 800/221-7282 or www.americanexpress.com) are the most widely accepted. Most restaurants and large stores will accept traveler's checks as payment but will ask to you to produce your passport. Most banks will cash them, but charge between 1 percent and 4 percent on the value for doing so. American Automobile Association members can avoid fees by purchasing checks from an AAA office.

Stolen credit cards or traveler's checks
If your credit card is stolen, report the theft to the bank so that charges can be blocked. Also notify the police. The bank's toll-free number is usually on the back of the credit card. It's a good idea to photocopy the front and

back sides of everything in your wallet, or at least write down the numbers you need to report the card lost, and carry this information separately.

Exchange rates
For the latest market conversion rates, visit www.oanda.com or www.x-rates.com.

MONEY-SAVING TIPS
● CityPass (tel 707/256-0490, www.citypass.com) is a book of tickets to six attractions and will

10 EVERYDAY ITEMS AND HOW MUCH THEY COST

Takeout sandwich	$6
Bottle of water	$2
Cup of tea or coffee	$1
Pint of beer	$6
Glass of wine	$10
Daily newspaper	25c–$1.25
Roll of camera film	$8
20 cigarettes	$7.75
An ice cream	$2.50
A gallon of fuel (petrol)	$?

save you hours of waiting in line at attractions, as well as 50 percent on admission to the American Museum of Natural History (▷ 68–72), Empire State Building (▷ 94–96), Guggenheim Museum (▷ 110–111), *Intrepid* Sea-Air-Space Museum (▷ 101) and MoMA (▷ 125), as well as on two-hour Circle Line harbor cruises (▷ 232). The CityPass costs $53 ($41 for ages 6–17) and can be purchased at any attraction. It is good for nine days once you begin using it.

BANKNOTES AND COINS

Local currency One US dollar is worth 100 cents. Paper bills come in denominations of $1, $5, $10, $20, $50 and $100. Bills are all the same size and color, so look carefully at the numbers on them before handing them over. Each type of coin is a different size, so they are easier to differentiate (coins and bills are not shown actual size).

1 cent
penny

5 cents
nickel

10 cents
dime

25 cents
quarter

50 cents

Dollar

Coin images courtesy United States Mint.

(Money-Saving Tips continued)

● **New York Pass** (250 West 49th Street, New York 10019, tel 877/714-1999, www.newyorkpass.com) an all-inclusive passport to New York City that gets you admission to and discounts at 65 attractions. The New York Pass can be purchased at Madame Tussaud's (234 West 42nd Street), the Empire State Building's Skyride (350 Fifth Avenue) or online. Passes cost $49 ($39 for children under 13) for one day, or you can buy them for two ($89/59), three ($109/84) or seven ($139/99) days.

● **"Pay-what-you-wish"** is the admission scheme adopted by some attractions; a suggested admission is posted, but you decide how much you actually pay. Some museums are free one day a week or for a couple of evening hours. To save on museum admission prices, visit during the hours given in the table above.

● **The Official NYC Guide** (810 Seventh Avenue, New York

MUSEUM ADMISSION		
	PAY-WHAT-YOU-WISH	**FREE**
American Folk Art Museum		Fri 5.30–7.30pm
Bronx Zoo	All day Wed	
Brooklyn Botanic Garden		Sat 10–noon, All day Tue
Brooklyn Museum of Art	1st Sat each month	After 5pm
Guggenheim Museum	Fri 6–8pm	
Jewish Museum	Thu 5–8pm	
MoMA	Fri 4–7.45pm	
Museum of Arts and Design	Thu 6–8pm	
New York Botanical Garden	All day Wed	Sat 10–noon
Whitney Museum of American Art	Fri 6–9pm	

10019, tel 800/NYC-VISIT or 212/397-8222, www.nycvisit. com) is published by NYC & Company, the city's official tourism marketing organization, and contains discount vouchers for hotels, stores, restaurants, cruises and museums. Buy the book online, or pick up a copy from one of the visitor centers.

The New York Pass can bring you substantial savings on many attractions

HEALTH

New York City has some of the best hospitals and doctors in the country, so if you should be in need of care, you have come to the right place. But make sure you have full insurance (▷ 314).

INOCULATIONS
If you are arriving in the United States from Canada or from a European Union member country, you will probably not need inoculations. However, check with your travel agent or with a US consulate or embassy (▷ 314). All visitors to the United States are advised to be fully immunized against tetanus and diptheria.

WHAT TO TAKE
If you will be in New York during the summer, make sure to have sunscreen, which you can easily purchase from any pharmacy upon arrival. You should bring any medication you require with you and, if it is prescription medicine, pack it in your in-flight baggage. Take copies of your prescription to be on the safe

A New York pharmacy

side. If the bag in which you are carrying medication gets lost or stolen, the copy of the prescription will make it easier to get a replacement.

If you require medication containing habit-forming drugs or narcotics, such as some cough medicines, diuretics, heart drugs, tranquilizers, sleeping pills, anti-depressants, stimulants, etc., make sure they are properly labeled and that you have a prescription or written statement from your doctor confirming that you are taking these under a

doctor's direction and that you require them while traveling.

If you suffer from heart problems, epilepsy or diabetes, it is a good idea to wear a Medic Alert Identification Tag so that the doctor can easily get access to your medical records through the 24-hour hotline in case of an emergency. You can get this tag by phoning 800/825-3785 or visit www.medicalert.org.

DRINKING WATER
The tap water in New York is safe to drink, as is water from public water fountains. However, bottled water is sold throughout the city in stores, restaurants and vending machines.

BUYING MEDICATIONS
The 24-hour pharmacies listed opposite are all located in convenient places.

Travelers from abroad may require a prescription in the United States to purchase certain medications, such as birth control pills, inhalers and codeine, that they can buy over the counter in their own country.

PLANNING

Pharmacies are generally open from 9am to 5pm and can be recognized by signs in the window—either a mortar and pestle or a caduceus (a staff with two entwined snakes and two wings at the top, which symbolize a physician).

FINDING A DOCTOR

If you need to find a doctor in New York, contact any one of the health services listed below. They are reputable healthcare providers accustomed to treating visitors.

DOCS at New York Healthcare (55 East 34th Street between Park and Madison avenues, tel 212/252-6001) is a walk-in medical center for non-emergency cases. New York University Downtown Hospital (tel 212/312-5000) offers referrals. N.Y. Hotel Urgent Medical Services (952 Fifth Avenue between 76th and 77th streets, tel 212/737-1212, www.travelmd.com) was set up by a New York City doctor to treat visitors. Whether you need a prescription, a medical examination or a dentist, a specialist will come to your hotel

HEALTHY FLYING

● Visitors from Europe, Australia or New Zealand may be concerned about the effect of a long-haul flight on their health. The most widely publicized concern is deep vein thrombosis (DVT). Misleadingly labeled "economy class syndrome," DVT is when a blood clot forms in the body's deep veins, particularly in the legs. The clot can move around the bloodstream and can be fatal.

● You are most at risk if you are elderly, pregnant, using the contraceptive pill, smoke or are overweight. If you think you are at increased risk of DVT, see your doctor before departing. Flying increases the likelihood of DVT because passengers are often seated in a cramped position for long periods of time and may become dehydrated.

● Other health hazards for flyers are airborne diseases and bugs spread by the air-conditioning system on board. These hazards are largely unavoidable but if you have a serious medical condition, seek advice from a doctor before flying.

To minimize risk:

Drink water (not alcohol)

Don't stay immobile for hours at a time

Stretch and exercise your legs periodically

Do wear elastic flight socks, which support veins and reduce the chances of a clot forming

EXERCISES

1 ANKLE ROTATIONS	2 CALF STRETCHES	3 KNEE LIFTS

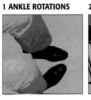

Lift feet off the floor. Draw a circle with the toes, moving one foot clockwise and the other counterclockwise

Start with heel on the floor and point foot upwards as high as you can. Then lift heels high keeping balls of feet on the floor

Lift leg with knee bent while contracting your thigh muscle. Then straighten leg pressing foot flat to the floor

room. He or she will produce appropriate identification. The hotel visit fee is $200 to $300, with higher rates at night and on weekends. You can also go to the office for a fee of $165—either drop in or phone for an appointment. Emergency rooms (ER rooms) in some hospitals have walk-in clinics where you can go for non-emergencies (and pay a slightly lower rate than in the emergency area), but you will probably have to wait for a long time. Or you can always ask the hotel staff to suggest a doctor.

IF YOU HAVE TO GO TO THE HOSPITAL

Before you go, phone your travel insurance company's emergency number to find out which hospitals accept your insurance. You will need to show your insurance card at the hospital

PHARMACIES OPEN 24 HOURS		
NAME	**ADDRESS**	**TELEPHONE**
Duane Reade	224 West 57th Street/Broadway	212/541-9708
Duane Reade	485 Lexington Avenue/47th Street	212/682-5338
Duane Reade	2025 Broadway/70th Street	212/579-9955
Rite Aid	146 East 86th Street/Lexington Avenue	212/876-0600

PLANNING

before any treatment will be given.

INSURANCE FOR NON-US VISITORS

Although you are not required to have health insurance in order to visit the United States, it would be extremely unwise not to. The US does not have reciprocal health agreements with other countries and the cost of healthcare is very high, whether you need a doctor's visit or dental care or have a medical emergency. An emergency room visit usually carries a minimum charge of $300, and that's before you begin receiving treatment. Make sure that you have a good insurance policy that covers all healthcare, including dental care (▷ 314).

OPTICIANS

Lenscrafters has several Midtown locations. Go to 45th Street and Fifth Avenue, tel 212/302-4882 www.lenscrafters.com

Cohen's Optical has numerous locations in Manhattan, including 2561 Broadway tel 212/666-2615 and 2 West 14th Street tel 212/989-3937 www.cohensfashionoptical.com

ALTERNATIVE MEDICINE

Alternative medical treatments are widely available in New York City.

American Academy of Medical Acupuncture
www.medicalacupuncture.org
Chiropractic Federation of New York
64 East 34th Street, tel 212/532-0185
North American Society of Homeopaths
www.homeopathy.org

Chinatown offers a wide selection of herbal and alternative treatments, including acupuncture. You will find, among others:

Grand Meridian Herbs, Acupuncture and Massage
209 Grand Street, New York 10013, tel 212/965-1503
Kamwo Herbs
211 Grand Street, New York 10013, tel 212/966-6370
Zon Foo Acupuncture and Medical
36 East Broadway, 2nd Floor, New York 10002, tel 212/925-2501

COMMUNICATIONS

TELEPHONE CHARGES
Public pay phones

Local calls cost 25 cents for the first three minutes. Even if you are making a local call, one that has the 212 or 646 area code, you must still dial 1, then the area code, before the seven-digit number. This includes calls from Manhattan to other boroughs, (area codes 718 and 347).

All calls that are not local are so-called long-distance calls, which cost more; for these, you again have to dial 1 followed by the area code and seven-digit number.

Paying by card

Prepaid calling cards, sold at many convenience stores and news-stands in denominations up to $50, are the easiest and probably the cheapest way to phone home.

TIP

Hotel-room phones may be convenient but they are costly, because most hotels impose a high surcharge on calls dialed from rooms. To avoid these surcharges, use a public pay phone. Many hotels have internet access in the lobby, so you can email, as long as you have a credit card.

Public pay phones throughout New York City take phonecards. Airport public telephones all accept MasterCard, Visa and American Express.

TELEPHONES AND NON-US VISITORS
Telephone numbers

Local and long-distance calls: dial 1 + area code + 7-digit number
Word telephone numbers: Some numbers are made easy to remember by using the letters on the dial rather than the numbers, for example, 1-800/WHITNEY. Find the letters on the dial to call these numbers.

Toll-free numbers

There is no charge for telephone

COUNTRY CODES FROM THE UNITED STATES

Dial 011 followed by the country code, the city code, then the telephone number

Australia	(011) 61
Belgium	(011) 32
France	(011) 33
Germany	(011) 49
Greece	(011) 30
Ireland	(011) 353
Italy	(011) 39
Netherlands	(011) 31
New Zealand	(011) 64
Spain	(011) 34
Sweden	(011) 46
United Kingdom	(011) 44

numbers with area codes 800, 888 and 877. The 911 emergency number is also free.

High-toll numbers

Telephone numbers with area codes 700 and 900 are chat lines, dating services or other specialized services that can charge anywhere between 95¢ and $15 per minute.

Cell phones and laptops

If your cell phone is not equipped to make calls from the US, you may as well leave it at home. If you plan to use a laptop while traveling, make sure that the battery is fully charged before you leave home. At airport

Public pay phones can be an economical way to keep in touch

security, you may be asked to take the laptop out of the case. Security officers may ask you if it is yours, if it is new and if anyone else has been using it. Make sure that you have an adapter for your laptop, and a converter for voltage if necessary, if it does not have a US two-prong, flat-pin plug and does not work on 110/120 volts. If you plan to use it a lot, bring an extra battery.

EMAIL

Go to www.mail2web.com and type in your email address and password to retrieve your email from any web browser. You can also open a free email account

Mail boxes are blue

via www.hotmail.com or www.mail.yahoo.com.

You can check your email from most hotel lobbies, at internet cafés or Kinko's copy shops (www.kinkos.com), which are found throughout the city.

Alternatively, use the free terminals at the Times Square Information Center at 1560 Broadway (▷ 324).

CYBER-CAFÉS

There are more and more of these around town (see below for two well-known cafés).

POST OFFICES

The main post office is on Eighth Avenue between 31st and 33rd streets (tel 800/275-8777). Throughout the city there are numerous branches, which are listed in the *Yellow Pages*. Most branches are open Monday to Friday 8, 9 or 10am to 6pm. A few open Saturday 9am to 4pm.

POSTAGE RATES
As of March 2005, a regular letter costs:
Within the US, minimum of 37 cents
Across the border to Canada, minimum of 60 cents
Overseas, minimum of 80 cents

CYBER CONNECTIONS	
Kinko's	**NY Computer Café**
60 West 40th Street	247 East 57th Street
Tel 212/921-1060	Tel 212/872-1704
www.kinkos.com	www.nycomputercafe.com
Daily 24 hours	Mon–Fri 8am–11pm, Sat 10am–11pm,
Also at many other locations	Sun 11–11

FINDING HELP

The crime rate in New York has plummeted over the past 10 years and it is now one of the safest large cities in the United States. However, it is big and crowded, and crimes do occur, so always be aware of your surroundings and people around you. If someone does try to steal your property, let them take it, then report the crime to the police.

PERSONAL SECURITY

● Do not keep all your money, credit cards and traveler's checks in the same place.
● Do not carry large sums of money with you. Use the

New York City policeman

hotel safe if you have brought valuables or have large amounts of cash.
● Do not walk alone at night in deserted areas, and do not go into parks after dark unless there is a concert and a large crowd is already there.
● If someone "falls" in front of you, be aware that this may be a ploy to distract you while an accomplice picks your pocket.
● Wear shoulder bags and cameras over one shoulder and across your front—in bandolier style. Do not let your handbag dangle from the back of your chair in restaurants; put it on your lap rather than risk making it an easy target.

OBEY THE LAWS

● Drinking laws are strictly enforced in New York. It is against the law to drive with an open container of alcohol in the car and also, of course, to drive while intoxicated.

• Smoking in all public places, such as restaurants, museums, on public transportation or in public offices, is illegal in New York (laws were passed in April 2003). You must smoke outside—as you will see many New Yorkers doing.

LEGAL AGE	
To purchase tobacco	18 years
To gamble or play the lottery	18 years
To purchase/consume alcohol	21 years
To rent a car	25 years

IF YOU ARE ARRESTED

• Remember that New York has been on high alert at different times since 9/11 and that even when these alerts are not in effect, there is a high police presence in the streets, at public places, in airports and at other metropolitan locations. Never joke about matters of security—it's a crime.
• Visitors from abroad need to be aware that the police can arrest you if you break the law, if they have a strong suspicion that

you have been involved in a crime, or if your behavior or activities make them suspect that you are involved in criminal activities.

If you are arrested, you have the right to remain silent, to make a telephone call, and you have the right to contact a lawyer. Anything you say can be used as evidence against you. Your best option is to contact your embassy or consulate (see below) and ask for their assistance.

CONSULATES FOR VISITORS FROM OVERSEAS	
Australia	212/351-6500
Canada	212/596-1700
Ireland	212/319-2555
New Zealand	212/832-4038
United Kingdom	212/745-0200

EMBASSIES FOR VISITORS FROM OVERSEAS			
COUNTRY	ADDRESS	TELEPHONE	WEBSITE
Australia	1601 Massachusetts Avenue, NW, Washington DC 20036	202/797-3000	www.austemb.org
Canada	501 Pennsylvania Avenue, NW, Washington DC 20001	202/682-1740	www.canadianembassy.org
Ireland	2234 Massachusetts Avenue, NW, Washington DC 20008	202/462-3939	www.irelandemb.org
New Zealand	37 Observatory Circle NW,, Washington DC 20008	202/328-4800	www.nzemb.org
United Kingdom	3100 Massachusetts Avenue, NW, Washington DC 20008	202/588-6500	www.britainusa.com

MEDIA

At the newspaper stands on many streets throughout the city, you can buy newspapers in English, Spanish and, at some, a few other languages, as well as a wide variety of magazines.

NEWSPAPERS

• *The New York Times* is the city's most widely read daily (www.nytimes.com), published seven days a week. The Sunday edition includes a magazine and special sections for sports, travel, real estate, etc.
• The *Daily News* is a tabloid published seven days a week and offers a large quantity of Sunday supplements.
• The *New York Post* is another tabloid published daily.
• The *Wall Street Journal* is the much-respected New York-based national financial newspaper.
• The *New York Observer* is the pink-hued weekly full of media and political gossip.

Taking the time out to sit and watch the world go by—and possibly to log on to the internet

MAGAZINES

• *The New Yorker* (www.new yorker.com) is a national literary and news magazine with New York listings and reviews; published every Monday.
• *New York Magazine* (www.newyorkmetro.com), published every Monday, is a good source of information on restaurants, theaters, movies, books, art, television and bargains around town.
• *The Village Voice* (www. villagevoice.com) is published weekly every Tuesday, with extensive listings of music, clubs, arts and entertainment.
• *Time Out* (www.timeoutny. com) is a very good comprehensive weekly magazine with plenty of listings on just about everything going on around town.

To buy newspapers from other countries, go to **Universal News & Magazines** (234 West 42nd Street between Seventh and

MAJOR RADIO STATIONS	
www.nyradioguide.com	
AM:	
Sports	620 (WSNR)
News and Talk	020 (WNYC feeds from NP Rand; the BBC World Service)
Multi-ethnic	930 (WPAT)
News	1130 (WBBR)
News around the clock	880 and 1010 (WINS)
FM:	
Classic and talk	93.9 (WYNC-FM)
Classical	96.3 (WQXR, the radio station of the New York Times)
Top 40	108.3 (also known as Z-100).

NATIONAL TV STATIONS
2 (CBS)
4 (NBC)
5 (Fox)
7 (ABC)
9 and 11 (independent)
13 (PBS)

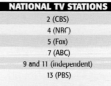

Eighth avenues, tel 212/221-1809) or **Hotaling News Agency** (624 West 52nd Street between Eleventh and Twelfth avenues, tel 212/974-9419).

Number 9 West 57th Street (right); billboard for one of New York's radio stations (below)

MAJOR TV STATIONS
On cable, NY1 is all about New York, and more than 50 stations on cable, available in most hotels, supply movies, weather updates and home shopping. If you're traveling with kids, ask whether the Disney Channel is available.

OPENING TIMES AND PUBLIC HOLIDAYS

New York never sleeps. The working week is Monday through Friday, 9am to 5pm, but some banks are open on Saturday mornings and many stores are open longer hours; most stores are open all weekend. Some pharmacies are open 24/7, as are some coffee shops and bureaux de change.

Always phone in advance if timing is critical or if you're making a detour to visit a particular place.

PUBLIC HOLIDAYS
On public holidays many museums, some restaurants and all public office buildings close. New Year's Day, Christmas and Thanksgiving are the biggest, most widely celebrated holidays, when most New York businesses grind to a halt. Airports and train stations are particularly busy in the period leading up to these holidays, when many New Yorkers travel out of town to be with family or friends. However,

it is also a time when the city is festive and celebrations are enjoyed by visitors as well as New Yorkers (for a list of parades ▷ 324). Much of the city closes down or slows during the Jewish High Holidays—Rosh Hashanah and Yom Kippur—in September and early October.

PUBLIC HOLIDAYS
January 1
New Year's Day
3rd Monday in January
Martin Luther King Day
3rd Monday in February
Presidents' Day
March/April
Easter (half day Good Friday)
Last Monday in May
Memorial Day
July 4
Independence Day
1st Monday in September
Labor Day
2nd Monday in October
Columbus Day
November 11
Veterans' Day
4th Thursday in November
Thanksgiving Day
December 25
Christmas Day

OPENING HOURS			
	OPEN	**CLOSED**	**COMMENTS**
Stores	Mon–Sat, 10–7		Many closed Sun Upper East
	Sun noon–6		Side, Sat Lower East Side
Banks	Mon–Fri 9.30–3.30	Sat–Sun	Some close at 3, some open
			Sat morning
Offices	Mon–Fri 9–5	Sat–Sun	
Museums	Tue–Sun		Some open Mon or close
			another day
Galleries	Tue–Sat 10–6	Mon	
Doctors	Mon–Fri 9–5	Sat–Sun	▷ 319
Pharmacies	Daily 9–7 or 9–9		Shorter hours and Sun
			closing in commercial
			neighborhoods, some 24hrs
Grocery stores	Daily 7am–9pm		As above
Restaurants	Daily (see listings)	Some close one	Many serve until 11pm or
		day a week	midnight, a few between 4pm
			and 5.30pm

EVENTS AND PARADES

Lively events worth planning a trip around take place throughout the year. If you are in New York during a parade, don't miss it. The two biggest are the St. Patrick's Day Parade and the Macy's Thanksgiving Day Parade, which is televised nationwide. The crowd scene is almost as entertaining as the parade. Check local listings for dates, times and parade routes, and plan to show up early for either of them to get a choice viewing spot.

TOURIST OFFICES

Major visitor centers, listed below, are well worth visiting on your first or second day. Many brochures offer discount vouchers, which will save you a few dollars at attractions or restaurants. In addition, most hotels offer a good selection of maps and free brochures.

Times Square Information Center

(1560 Broadway between 46th and 47th streets, tel 212/768-1560, www.timessquarenyc.org, daily 8–8)
This is New York's central tourist office and has free brochures, maps, helpful staff, a Broadway Ticket Center and a Metropolitan Transportation Authority that sells MetroCards (▷ 43), as well as providing ATMs, currency-exchange machines and free internet. It's worth visiting even if

New York's marathon goes from Staten Island to Central Park

EVENTS	
January or early February	
Chinese New Year in Chinatown	
April–October	
Baseball season	
May	
Ninth Avenue International Food Festival	
June	
Metropolitan Opera park concerts, Museum Mile celebration	
July	
Independence Day fireworks over the East River	
July–August	
Shakespeare in the Park	
August–September	
Lincoln Center Out-of-Doors Festival; Harlem Week	
September	
Feast of San Gennaro, in Little Italy	
September–October	
New York Film Festival	
Early November	
New York Marathon	
December	
Tree lighting at Rockefeller Center, New Year's Eve celebrations	

PARADES
January
Three Kings' Day
Martin Luther King Day Parade
March
St. Patrick's Day
Greek Independence Day Parade (parade of circus animals to Madison Square Garden)
March or April
Easter Parade, Fifth Avenue between 44th and 59th streets
June
Puerto Rican Day Parade
Lesbian and Gay Pride
October
Columbus Day Parade
Halloween Parade in Greenwich Village
November
Macy's Thanksgiving Day

you think you don't need to. Some of the free walking tours start from here.

NYCVB Visitor Information Center

(810 Seventh Avenue between 52nd and 53rd streets, tel 212/484-1222, Mon–Fri 8.30 to 6)
Smaller than the Times Square complex, this information center has free brochures and leaflets. The interactive terminal with touch-screen access to visitor information is extremely useful. Buy advance tickets to major attractions here and your CityPass (▷ 317), and pick up a copy of the *Official New York City Guide*.
The center provides an ATM (cashpoint), plus telephones that are directly connected to American Express offices.

Lower East Side Visitors Center

(261 Broome Street between Orchard and Allen streets, tel 888/825-8374 or 212/226-9010, www.lowereastsideny.com, daily 10–4)
Provides pamphlets covering local shopping, dining and nightlife entertainment.

PLANNING

BOOKS, MAPS, MOVIES AND TELEVISION

BOOKS
Non-fiction
The Historical Atlas of New York City: Eric Homberger, Henry Holt and Company, New York, 1998
A fascinating book on the history of New York, always a pleasure to read. Excellent graphics, maps and photographs.

New York City (A Short History): George J. Lankevich, New York University Press, New York, 2002
A fascinating look at New York's political and social history from the first settlers to the election of Mayor Michael Bloomberg.

New York: Songs of the City: Nancy Groce, Watson-Guptill Publications, New York, 1999
A delightful musical journey through New York's five boroughs, with anecdotes and facts about people in the music industry, lyrics of old tunes about New York, and beautifully reproduced music sheet covers and posters.

Fiction
Novelists and short-story writers have always been attracted to New York, and many American classics have been set here. For short stories pick up O. Henry's *The Voice of the City* (1908) or Damon Runyon's *Guys and Dolls* (1932). Novels such as F. Scott Fitzgerald's *The Beautiful and the Damned* (1922), John Dos Passos's *Manhattan Transfer* (1925), J. D. Salinger's *The Catcher in the Rye* (1951) and Truman Capote's *Breakfast at Tiffany's* (1958) are all popular reads. More recent novels include Tom Wolfe's *Bonfire of the Vanities* (1987) and *The New York Trilogy* (1988) by Paul Auster.

MAPS AND OTHER PUBLICATIONS
Fodor's *New York City 2004*
Fodor's shows you the way on and off the beaten path, with detailed reviews and expert inside track knowledge.

Fodor's *Gold Guide to New York City* Information on where to go, what to see and how to get there, written by New York City-based shopping experts,

The place for literary bargains

restaurant critics and other specialists. It includes detailed descriptions of hundreds of restaurant and hotel choices, information on sights, and listings of stores and sports opportunities. Useful web links and Smart Travel Tips help in planning.

AIA *Guide to New York City*: Norval White & Elliot Willensky, Three Rivers Press, New York, 2000
The American Institute of Architects' guide to parks and buildings in all five boroughs is a treasure of architectural knowledge and opinion. With structures arranged in geographical order, it's fun to have as you amble around town, but it's hefty.

Guide to New York City Landmarks: John Wiley & Sons, Inc. 1998
This guide to the city's landmarks and historic districts is ideal for walking tours.

MOVIES
New York has been the setting of great movies by some great directors. Why not watch a few of them before you visit?

42nd Street (1933), Hal Wallis
King Kong (1933), Merian C. Cooper
Guys and Dolls (1955), Samuel Goldwyn
Breakfast at Tiffany's (1961), M. Jurrow, R. Shepherd
West Side Story (1961), Robert Wise

Mean Streets (1973), Martin Scorsese
Taxi Driver (1976), Martin Scorsese
New York, New York (1977), Martin Scorsese
Saturday Night Fever (1977), John Badham
Manhattan (1979), Woody Allen
Broadway Danny Rose (1984), Woody Allen
The Cotton Club (1984), Francis Ford Coppola
Desperately Seeking Susan (1985), Susan Seidelman
Radio Days (1987), Woody Allen
When Harry Met Sally (1989), Rob Reiner
A Bronx Tale (1993), Robert De Niro
Pollock (2000), Ed Harris
Gangs of New York (2002), Martin Scorsese
The Hours (2002), Stephen Daldry

TELEVISION
High drama, farce and comedy are played out on the streets of New York daily, and on the screens in people's homes throughout the world when they tune into the following popular TV shows set in or about New York City. Many of them can also be seen on video or DVD.

Friends (now in rerun)
Law & Order
NYPD Blue (now in rerun)
Seinfeld (now in rerun)
Sex and the City (now in rerun)
Will & Grace

PLANNING

ACCOMMODATIONS
● All New York Hotels
www.allnewyorkhotels.net
Search for a hotel (including
discount hotels) by name or
criteria
● Hotel Conxions
www.hotelconxions.com
Finds great deals on city hotels
● New York hotels
www.new-york.hotels-nb.com
Assists with reservations at any of
the hotels they list
● Room Connection
www.RoomConnection.com
A central reservation service for
hotels in New York City
● YMCA Guest Rooms
www.ymcanyc.org Main YMCA
site with links to YMCAs around
Greater New York

BROADWAY AND
OFF-BROADWAY TICKETS
● Playbill's Online Theater
Club
www.playbillclub.com
A membership club that gives
discounts to top shows
● TeleCharge
www.telecharge.com
● Theater Direct International
www.broadway.com
● TheaterMania
www.theatermania.com
● Ticketmaster
www.ticketmaster.com

MONEY
● TravelEx Worldwide Money
www.travelex.com

NEW YORK CITY
INFORMATION
● Alliance for Downtown New
York
www.downtownny.com
Everything you need to know
about Downtown, including links
to a free bus service and an
interactive map
● The Bronx Tourism Council
www.ilovethebronx.com
● Brooklyn Tourism Council
www.brooklynX.org
● Citysearch
www.newyork.citysearch.com
Attractions, events, hotels, real
estate, restaurants and
shopping
● Customs information for
entering New York City
www.customs.ustreas.gov
● New York Convention &
Visitors Bureau
www.nycvisit.com

● New York Metro
www.nymetro.com
New York magazine and Metro
TV website
● New York Today
www.nytoday.com
The New York Times site, a guide
for New Yorkers and visitors on
what's on and what to do
● Times Square Business
Improvement District
www.timessquarebid.org
The official site for Times Square
and what's going on there

NEWS, REVIEWS AND
WHAT'S ON
● New York magazine
www.newyorkmag.com
● The New York Times
www.nytimes.com
● The New Yorker
www.newyorker.com
● New York Press
www.nypress.com
A free weekly newspaper
● Time Out New York
www.timeoutny.com
● Village Voice
www.villagevoice.com
A major culturally hip
publication

RADIO
New York City is the United
States's top radio outlet. The
radio dial is literally cacophonous,
and if you live in an area without
a similar level or choice, just
turning on the radio and flipping
the dial is an experience. A few
top stations are:
● WYNC-FM 93.9 (820-AM)
www.wnyc.org
● 1010 WINS-AM Radio
www.1010wins.com

Keeping in touch is easy

● WBGO-FM 88.3 Radio
www.wbgo.org
● WQXR-FM 96.3
www.wqxr.com
New York Times radio station,
with classical music
● WFAN-AM 660
www.wfan.com
Sports and news talk
● WOR-AM 710
www.wor710.com
Venerable NYC talk radio

TRANSPORTATION
● Airports
www.panynj.gov/airports
● Trains
www.amtrak.com
● Airtrain Newark
www.airtrainnewark.com
An on-airport service and shuttle
from Newark Liberty International
Airport Train Station to Newark
Liberty Airport
● American Automobile
Association
www.aaa.com
● Subways and buses
www.mta.info

GENERAL
● The Baby Sitters' Guild
www.babysittersguild.com
For child care at any time
● Smart Pages
www.smartpages.com
Telephone numbers in the U.S.
● Weather
www.weather.com or
www.cnn.com/weather
A comprehensive weather
service

PLANNING

GLOSSARY FOR NON-US VISITORS

You will see signs in Spanish throughout the city, especially in subways, and hear a wide variety of languages in various neighborhoods. But the New York vocabulary also has its idiosyncrasies, as you will see below.

arugula	rocket (salad)
automated teller machine (ATM)	cashpoint
Band-Aid/bandage	plaster
bill	banknote
car (on a train)	carriage
cart	trolley
check (restaurant)	bill
cilantro	coriander
cookie	biscuit
cot	camp bed
counterclockwise	anticlockwise
crib	cot
crosswalk	zebra crossing
day care	crèche
desk clerk	receptionist
dessert	pudding
diaper	nappy
directory assistance	directory enquiries
eggplant	aubergine
elevator	lift
emergency room (hospital)	casualty
faucet	tap
flashlight	torch
french fries	chips
gas	petrol
gas station	garage
hood (car)	bonnet
house trailer/RV	caravan
Jello™	jelly
jelly	jam
license plate	number plate
liquor store	off-licence
long-distance bus	coach
mail	post
main street	high street
one-way ticket	single ticket
pants	trousers
panty-hose	tights
parking lot	car park
pavement	road surface, usually referring to the street
pharmacy	chemist
phone booth	phone box
potato chips	crisps
private school	public school

public holiday	bank holiday
pull-off	lay-by
rent	hire
restrooms	toilets
round-trip ticket	return ticket
row houses	terrace
sidewalk	pavement
soccer	football
soda	fizzy soft drink
street musician	busker
stroller	pushchair/buggy
sweater	jumper, jersey
takeout	takeaway
taxi stand	taxi rank
two-lane highway	dual carriageway
traffic circle	roundabout
truck	lorry
trunk (car)	boot
underpass	subway
underpants (men's)	pants
undershirt	vest
vest	waistcoat
washcloth	face flannel
wharf/pier	quay
yard (residential)	garden
zucchini	courgette

balcony	gallery
brownstones	four- and five-story 19th-century row houses originally faced with cheap brown sandstone
checkroom	cloakroom
crosstown	an east–west direction across the city
downtown	a direction south of any point
first balcony	dress circle
jaywalking	crossing the street illegally, or not at the crosswalk
orchestra seats	stalls
upstate	the state of New York north of New York City
uptown	a direction north of any point

BUILDING FLOOR NUMBERING

The first floor in America is the ground floor to British visitors, the second floor is the first floor, and so on. This is worth watching out for when visiting museums, galleries and other public buildings.

PLANNING

NEW YORK NEIGHBORHOODS

New York is divided into the five boroughs of Manhattan, Brooklyn, the Bronx, Queens and Staten Island, each with their own distinct character.

MANHATTAN

Attractions, many of them world famous, line the streets of Manhattan, the area stretching from Battery Park at its tip to Harlem in the north, beyond Central Park.

Financial District

The oldest part of the city and the nexus of the securities industry anchored by the New York Stock Exchange and Wall Street. It's still primarily a business district, although residents have moved in over the last decade.

Battery Park City

A 92-acre (35ha) complex, built on landfill from the creation of the World Trade Center in 1974. It includes housing, commercial and retail space, plus a marina and the Museum of Jewish Heritage.

TriBeCa

It means *Triangle Below Canal* and is defined by Canal and Barclay streets and Broadway and the Hudson River. In 1980, the Odeon restaurant opened and pioneer residents followed, settling into the warehouses and manufacturing buildings. It now has the highest real-estate values in the city and plenty of celebrity cachet. Home to TriBeCa Film Studios, it's still a mixed-use neighborhood of gritty warehouse lofts, loft-style restaurants and low-end retail.

Civic Center

The focal point of City government, incorporating the courts, police and immigration. City Hall is at the center of the area. It's dwarfed by the nearby Municipal Building, designed by McKim, Mead and White.

Chinatown

In the 1840s, Chinatown was just eight blocks. Today it includes about 30 blocks, from Kenmare and Delancey streets to East Broadway and Worth Street, and from Broadway to Allen Street. Shop for fish, meat, vegetables and herbal remedies or dine in the many affordable restaurants.

Little Italy

Very little of this once vibrant community survives. Most of the Italians have moved to the suburbs and Chinese residents have replaced them. It consists largely of Mulberry Street, which is lined with tourist-oriented restaurants, plus one or two genuine delis.

NoLita

It stands for *North* of *Little Italy*. The narrow streets around St. Patrick's Cathedral, once the heart of the Italian community, are now lined with hip designer boutiques.

SoHo

In 1973 the 20 blocks between Houston, Canal, West Broadway and Broadway were designated a Historic District, protecting the best stock of cast-iron buildings in the city. Artists had already begun reclaiming the manufacturing and warehouse spaces and pioneering a loft lifestyle. Today the artists and most of the art galleries have moved on; the area is now an ultra-expensive, chic shopping mall crowded with non-residents on weekends.

Bowery

A long street connecting Chinatown to the East Village, it was once the city's Skid Row, lined with flophouses and numerous stores selling kitchen supplies and lighting fixtures. Today it is being gentrified.

Lower East Side

The traditional gateway for every wave of immigrants, from the Jewish and the Italians to the Puerto Ricans, this was the last Manhattan neighborhood to be updated. Today, young professionals and artists occupy the tenements and congregate at the clubs and bars along Orchard, Clinton and other streets. Remnants of the Puerto Rican community survive, and so does the bargain bazaar on Sunday along Orchard Street. The boundaries stretch from 14th Street to Fulton and Franklin and from the East River to Broadway, incorporating Chinatown, Little Italy and the East Village neighborhoods.

Greenwich Village/ West Village

This area stretches from 14th to Houston streets and from the Hudson River to Bowery and Fourth Avenue. Originally a poor neighborhood housing the workers and stevedores who worked the waterfront, it became a bohemia around 1900, attracting a mixture of artists, writers and anarchists. Today, it's a mixed neighborhood. The gay population has mostly moved to Chelsea, and now "successful" singles and families occupy the town houses and apartments. Small boutiques line the west end of Bleecker Street. The southern section around Bleecker Street and Sixth Avenue still has an Italian flavor.

Meatpacking District

Sandwiched between the West Village and Chelsea around 14th Street, this gritty neighborhood is being redeveloped. Restaurants, bars, clubs and stores are opening and hotels too.

NoHo

Between SoHo and Greenwich Village (from Houston to Eighth Streets and Mercer to Bowery/ Third Avenue), this youth-oriented neighborhood has plenty of fashionable shopping, bars and restaurants. The acronym stands for *North* of *Houston*.

East Village

This was originally an extension of the Lower East Side, settled by Jewish and Ukrainian/Polish communities. In the 1960s and 70s it became the center of the counter-culture. It has been rapidly redeveloped and is now filled with restaurants, bars and a young street scene.

Alphabet City

It refers to avenues A, B, C and D between Houston and 14th streets. In the 1970s, First Avenue marked the DMZ and the streets east of First were considered dangerous drug supermarkets. Gentrification

PLANNING

began in 1983 when Operation Pressure Point started cleaning up the drug trade, and buildings on Tompkins Square became co-ops. Today young professionals occupy the tenement apartments; there's a thriving dining and bar scene, including a substantial number of gay bars and clubs. The original Hispanic population has been dispersed.

Gramercy Park
This genteel and dignified neighborhood radiating from the eponymous gated garden square remains primarily residential. It stretches from 18th to 23rd streets and from Park Avenue South to Third Avenue.

Union Square/Flatiron District
This hot new neighborhood leading south from the Flatiron Building on 22nd Street and around Madison Square has plenty of bars, restaurants and clubs. The Green Market at Union Square is a must on Saturday. The former Ladies' Mile along Sixth Avenue between 15th and 24th streets is now occupied by large national chain stores. The boundaries go from 14th to 23rd streets and from Park to Sixth avenues.

Chelsea
Today Chelsea is the center of the gay community and the new focus for contemporary art anchored by DIA on 22nd Street and numerous warehouse/garage galleries along 24th Street. It has a lively club and restaurant scene. The boundaries stretch from 14th to 30th streets and from Sixth Avenue to the Hudson River.

Murray Hill
A quiet residential neighborhood between 34th and 40th streets between Madison and Third avenues. It is becoming increasingly commercial on the fringes. The Morgan Library and the Episcopalian church, where the Roosevelts worshiped, set the tone.

Midtown
The commercial heart of the city between 34th and 59th streets on the West Side and from 40th to 59th streets on the East Side. It includes major attractions, shops, restaurants, theaters, TV studios, Nasdaq and corporate offices.

Times Square/Theater District
The old peep shows, hookers and junkies have been displaced, and the area around 42nd Street and Broadway is now occupied by an array of major corporations and national chain stores—Condé Nast, Reuters, ESPN Zone, Toys R-Us and many others, who share the area with new hotels, clubs and theaters.

Clinton/Hell's Kitchen
Real-estate developers have rediscovered this neighborhood from 42nd to 59th streets between Eighth Avenue and the Hudson River. It was formerly known as Hell's Kitchen and was the site of slaughterhouses, freight yards and factories.

Upper East Side
It stretches from 59th to 96th streets from Fifth Avenue to the East River. The section from 59th to 78th streets between Fifth and Park avenues is often referred to as the Gold Coast, where those who can afford it live. Farther east it was not always elegant, but it became more so in 1956 when the Third Avenue El was demolished and Madison Avenue became an ultra-chic shopping street. Today it is filled with private clubs, consulates, art galleries, restaurants and fine residences. Museum Mile extends along Fifth Avenue from 81st Street north past the Metropolitan Museum of Art.

Yorkville
High-rise apartments line the streets of what was formerly the German section between Lexington and Third avenues on 86th Street.

Carnegie Hill
Between 86th and 96th streets between Fifth and Third avenues, this is primarily a low-key wealthy residential district, anchored by the Carnegie mansion (now the Cooper-Hewitt National Design Museum). The area is home to such prestigious private schools as Dalton, Spence and Horace Mann, plus the Guggenheim and the Jewish Museum.

East Harlem/Spanish Harlem
From 96th to 142nd streets, between Park Avenue and the East River, this area is still home to El Barrio, the community

established by the Puerto Ricans, who first arrived at the end of World War I and increased in numbers after World War II. Today it's a mixed neighborhood of Italians, African-Americans and Hispanics.

Lincoln Square
The square is the area around the Lincoln Center. Wealthy individuals, many of them successful performers, occupy the towers, and the area buzzes with bars, restaurants and stores. The ABC and CNN studios are a major presence.

Upper West Side
Broadway cuts right through this section that extends from 59th to 125th streets between the Hudson River and Central Park West. The blocks around 72nd Street were the center of an old German/East-European, primarily Jewish, liberal intellectual community. In the 1970s and 80s, Columbus and Amsterdam avenues were gentrified and the old single-room occupancy hotels returned to handsome residences. Today, it's often referred to as a Manhattan suburb, because of its family orientation, although it has become more fashionable recently, as new chic restaurants have opened. Central Park West is lined with expensive cooperatives overlooking Central Park. Notable attractions include the American Museum of Natural History .

Morningside Heights
Columbia University dominates this neighborhood, along with Barnard, Teachers College, the Cathedral of St. John the Divine and the Union Theological and Jewish Theological seminaries.

Harlem
Stretching from 110th Street to the Harlem River and from Fifth to St. Nicholas avenues, Harlem is the city's most famous black community. Originally a suburb for the wealthy, it was settled in the late 19th century by Jewish immigrants from Germany. When the subway arrived in the early 20th century, most of the black community moved in from midtown Manhattan and also from the southern states, and it became a mecca for black artists, writers and musicians. In the 1920s the Harlem Renaissance

brought whites and blacks together to the clubs, theaters and jazz joints. Later it became a blighted community, destroyed by the riots of the 1960s. Today it has been rediscovered by the middle classes and increasingly by whites in search of reasonably priced houses. The restaurants and churches attract visitors.

Washington Heights/Inwood
This is the last stop in Manhattan. It has been home to many different immigrant groups. Today, it's largely a Dominican community, although young professionals are moving in. It's also home to the Cloisters.

BROOKLYN
With the highest population of the five boroughs (2.5 million), Brooklyn is a healthy rival to Manhattan. It's full of world-class museums, spacious parks, landmark buildings and lively neighborhoods.

Greenpoint
This is an old Polish neighborhood where young professionals have moved because of its proximity to Manhattan.

Williamsburg
Primarily a Jewish and African-American neighborhood, recently it has been discovered by the young and hip. It's now reminiscent of 1950s Greenwich Village.

DUMBO
One developer alone has created this neighborhood (Down Under the Manhattan Bridge Overpass) by renting to artists and musicians. It's likely to become the next "hot" neighborhood à la SoHo.

Brooklyn Heights
This is a former premier residential neighborhood. The Promenade has magnificent views of the Manhattan skyline.

Cobble Hill
This is another affluent residential neighborhood where the streets are lined with elegant brownstones. Atlantic Avenue supports a major Middle Eastern community.

Prospect Park
The Brooklyn Botanic Gardens are in Prospect Park and the Brooklyn Museum of Art is adjacent to the gardens.

Carroll Gardens
Fine brownstones made this primarily Italian neighborhood an attractive residential area for those who could not afford to buy in Manhattan.

Fort Greene
After it was designated a historic district in 1978, professionals started buying the handsome brownstones. It's home to the Brooklyn Academy of Music.

Park Slope
Brooklyn's "alternative" village on the western edge of Prospect Park. The main commercial streets are 7th and 5th avenues.

Crown Heights
The city's largest West Indian community, plus a thriving Hasidic Jewish community.

Brighton Beach/Coney Island
Often called Little Odessa due to its Russian Jewish community, Brighton Beach has a boardwalk, clubs, restaurants and stores servicing the Russian community.

Next door, Coney Island was the city's great blue-collar playground from the late 1890s to the early 1930s. In the 1960s it became drug infested and dangerous. Today it is being revived. It's home to the New York Aquarium.

QUEENS
An international melting pot, Queens has the most diverse population of the five boroughs, and is also the largest. Named for Queen Catherine of Braganza, Charles II's wife, it is a good place to go to sample ethnic life and cuisine.

Astoria
The old Greek neighborhood has survived. Astoria was also a film-making area and some of the studios have been revived, including one that houses the American Museum of the Moving Image.

Long Island City
This is Queens' most industrialized area. The gritty waterfront area is being revamped.

Forest Hills
This wealthy, largely Jewish enclave, only a short commute from Manhattan, has handsome apartment houses, and good restaurants and social services.

Jackson Heights
This is a major South American and Indian enclave on 82nd Street.

Corona, Shea Stadium and Flushing Meadows Park
The stadium is the home of the Mets. The park has the National Tennis Center, the New York Hall of Science and the Queens Museum of Art. Corona is mainly a Dominican, Colombian and Mexican community.

Flushing Meadows
This is an area populated by Chinese, Koreans, Vietnamese, Malaysians and Japanese.

THE BRONX
The Bronx was once an expensive retreat for the wealthy. Development in the 1920s brought more well-heeled residents, then it got a reputation as a crime-laden area, and now has been turned into a much more tourist-friendly borough, with plenty of attractions and beautiful parks.

Fordham
The Bronx Zoo and the New York Botanical Garden are in this neighborhood. Arthur Avenue is a colorful Italian area.

Riverdale
The most desirable residential neighborhood in the borough and the location of Wave Hill, an 1843 estate once home to Mark Twain and Teddy Roosevelt and now a public garden and cultural center.

Van Cortlandt Park and Woodlawn Cemetery
Many famous people are buried at Woodlawn, including F. W. Woolworth, Irving Berlin and Duke Ellington. Van Cortlandt Park is a delightful space with forests and hills to explore.

City Island
New Yorkers come to this historic fishing community for fresh fish.

STATEN ISLAND
Staten Island is more than twice the size of Manhattan. Its residents are largely blue collar, still living a fairly autonomous, rural life away from busy Manhattan. Attractions include Alice Austen House, Snug Harbor Cultural Center and Historic Richmond Town.

MILL ROCK

UPPER WEST SIDE
332-333

Central Park

Carl Schurz Park

Franklin D Roosevelt Island

UPPER EAST SIDE
334-335

LONG ISLAND CITY

QUEENSBORO

Hudson River

QUEENS

THEATER DISTRICT
336-337

338-339

MIDTOWN

CONNECTICUT

NEW YORK

NEW
346-347

Newark

JERSEY

New York

New York's Outer Boroughs

CHELSEA

Madison Square Park

Gramercy Park

STUYVESANT TOWN

EAST VILLAGE ALPHABET CITY

340-341

Washington Square Park

342-343

East River Park

SOHO

LITTLE ITALY

LOWER EAST SIDE

WILLIAMSBURG BRIDGE

TRIBECA

City Hall Park

East River

MANHATTAN BRIDGE

FINANCIAL DISTRICT
344-345

BATTERY PARK CITY

Battery Park

BROOKLYN HEIGHTS

—————— Main road

—————— Other road

—————— Minor road/path

⊨===⊨ Railway

▬ Park

▬ Important building

● Featured place of interest

Subway station:
● 1, 2, 3, 9
● 4, 5, 6
● 7
● A, C, E
● B, D, F
● L
● M, J, Z
○ N, R, Q, W
● S (42 St Shuttle)
○ S (Grand St Shuttle)
● S (Franklin Av Shuttle)
● V (0530-2300 Mon-Fri)

▬ Railway station

🅿 Parking

332-345 0 —— 300 m / 0 —— 250 yds

346-347 0 —— 8 km / 0 —— 5 m

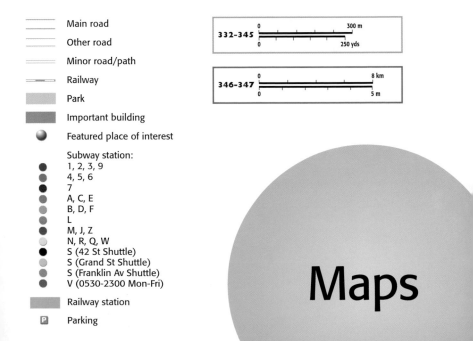

Maps

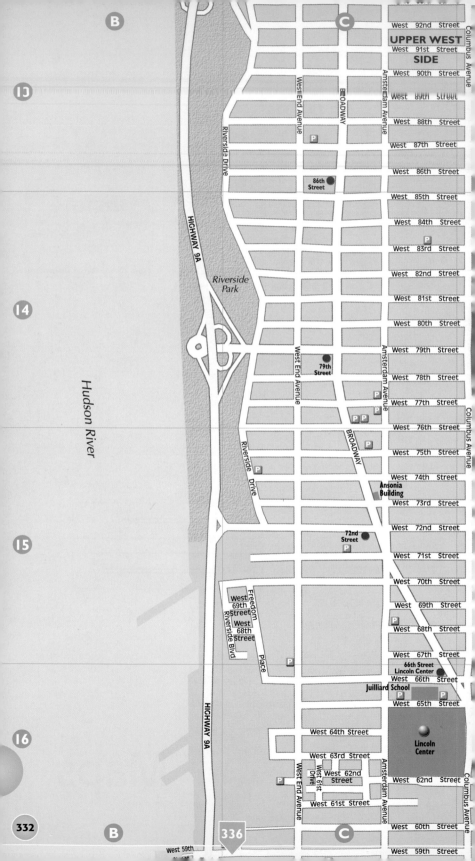

West 92nd Street

UPPER WEST
West 91st Street
SIDE

West 90th Street

West End Avenue

BROADWAY

Amsterdam Avenue

Columbus Avenue

West 89th Street

West 88th Street

West 87th Street

Riverside Drive

West 86th Street

86th Street

West 85th Street

West 84th Street

West 83rd Street

HIGHWAY 9A

West 82nd Street

West 81st Street

Riverside Park

West 80th Street

West 79th Street

West End Avenue

79th Street

West 78th Street

West 77th Street

West 76th Street

BROADWAY

West 75th Street

Riverside Drive

West 74th Street

Ansonia Building

West 73rd Street

West 72nd Street

72nd Street

West 71st Street

Hudson River

West 70th Street

West 69th Street

Freedom Place

Riverside Blvd

West 69th Street

West 68th Street

West 68th Street

West 67th Street

66th Street Lincoln Center

West 66th Street

Juilliard School

West 65th Street

West 64th Street

Lincoln Center

West 63rd Street

Amsterdam Avenue

Columbus Avenue

West End Avenue

West 61st Street

West 62nd Street

HIGHWAY 9A

West Drive 61st

West 62nd Street

West 61st Street

West 60th Street

West 59th Street

West 59th Street

J3

J4

J5

J6

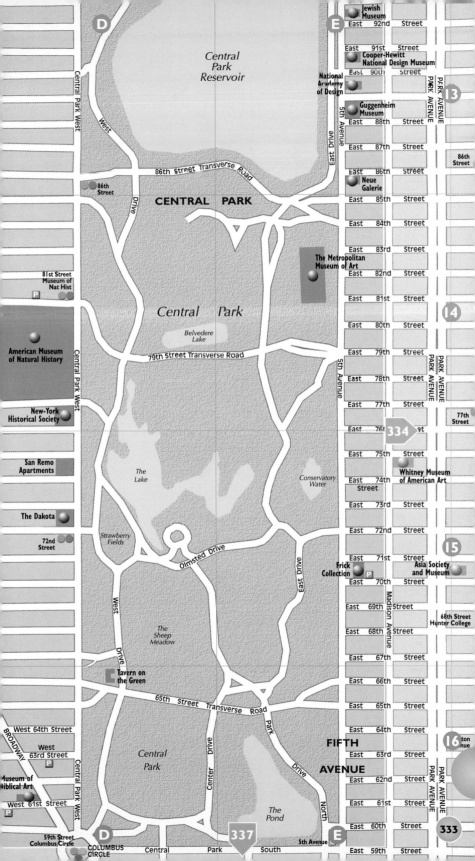

Central Park Reservoir

Central Park

CENTRAL PARK

Central Park

Belvedere Lake

The Lake

Strawberry Fields

The Sheep Meadow

Central Park

The Pond

D

Central Park West

West

Drive

86th Street Transverse Road

81st Street Museum of Nat Hist

American Museum of Natural History

New-York Historical Society

San Remo Apartments

The Dakota

72nd Street

Central Park West

79th Street Transverse Road

Olmsted Drive

West

Drive

Tavern on the Green

65th Street Transverse Road

West 64th Street

BROADWAY

West 63rd Street

Museum of Biblical Art

West 61st Street

59th Street Columbus Circle

COLUMBUS CIRCLE

Central

Center Drive

Park

Park Drive

South

North Drive

E

Jewish Museum

East 92nd Street

East 91st Street

Cooper-Hewitt National Design Museum

East 90th Street

National Academy of Design

Guggenheim Museum

East 88th Street

East 87th Street

East 86th Street

Neue Galerie

East 85th Street

East 84th Street

East 83rd Street

The Metropolitan Museum of Art

East 82nd Street

East 81st Street

East 80th Street

East 79th Street

East 78th Street

East 77th Street

East 76th Street

East 75th Street

Whitney Museum of American Art

East 74th Street

East 73rd Street

East 72nd Street

East 71st Street

Frick Collection

East 70th Street

Asia Society and Museum

East 69th Street

Madison Avenue

East 68th Street

68th Street Hunter College

East 67th Street

East 66th Street

East 65th Street

East 64th Street

FIFTH

East 63rd Street

AVENUE

East 62nd Street

East 61st Street

East 60th Street

5th Avenue

East 59th Street

5th Avenue

5th Avenue

PARK AVENUE

PARK AVENUE

PARK AVENUE

86th Street

77th Street

ton nue

PARK AVENUE

13

14

334

15

16

337

333

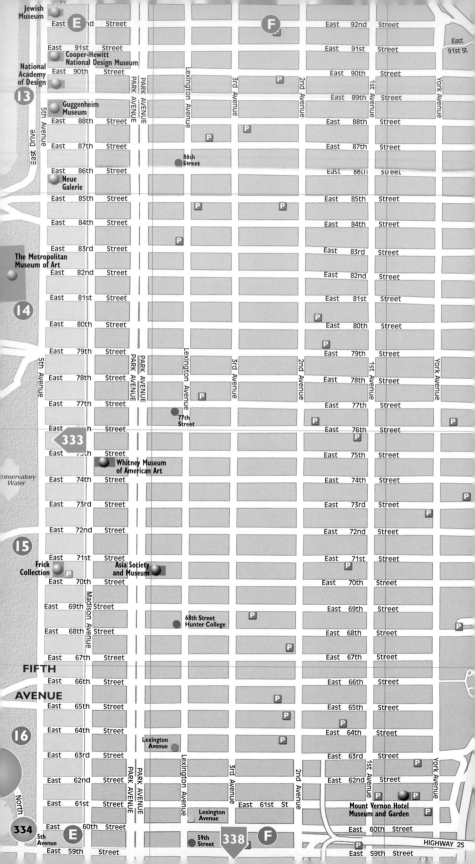

Jewish
Museum

East 92nd Street

East 91st Street

East 91st St

Cooper-Hewitt
National Design Museum

East 90th Street

National
Academy
of Design

East 90th Street

13

Guggenheim
Museum

East 88th Street

East 89th Street

East 88th Street

East 87th Street

East 87th Street

86th
Street

East 86th Street

East 86th Street

Neue
Galerie

East 85th Street

East 85th Street

East 84th Street

East 84th Street

East 83rd Street

East 83rd Street

The Metropolitan
Museum of Art

East 82nd Street

East 82nd Street

14

East 81st Street

East 81st Street

East 80th Street

East 80th Street

East 79th Street

East 79th Street

East 78th Street

East 78th Street

East 77th Street

East 77th Street

77th
Street

East 76th Street

East 76th Street

333

East 75th Street

East 75th Street

Whitney Museum
of American Art

East 74th Street

East 74th Street

Conservatory
Water

East 73rd Street

East 73rd Street

East 72nd Street

East 72nd Street

15

East 71st Street

East 71st Street

Frick
Collection

Asia Society
and Museum

East 70th Street

East 70th Street

East 69th Street

East 69th Street

68th Street
Hunter College

East 68th Street

East 68th Street

East 67th Street

East 67th Street

FIFTH

East 66th Street

East 66th Street

AVENUE

East 65th Street

East 65th Street

East 64th Street

East 64th Street

16

East 63rd Street

East 63rd Street

Lexington
Avenue

East 62nd Street

East 62nd Street

East 61st Street

East 61st St

Mount Vernon Hotel
Museum and Garden

Lexington
Avenue

East 60th Street

334

East 60th Street

5th
Avenue

E

59th
Street

338

F

HIGHWAY 25

East 59th Street

East 59th Street

5th Avenue

Park Avenue

Lexington Avenue

3rd Avenue

2nd Avenue

1st Avenue

York Avenue

Madison Avenue

North

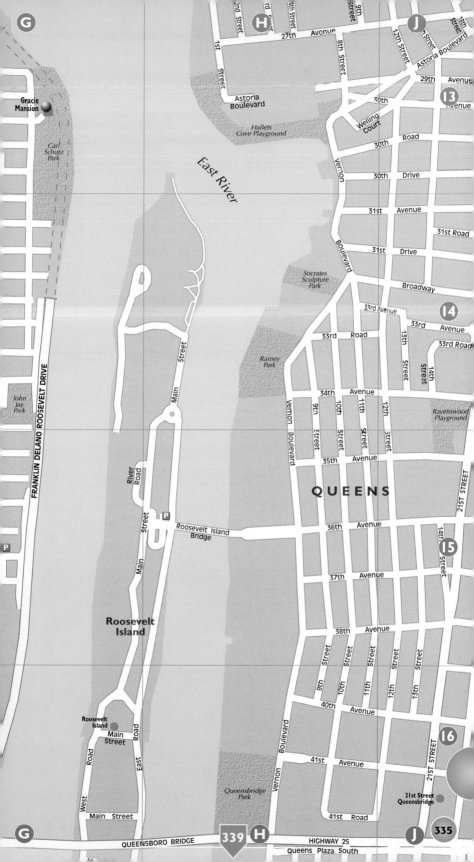

Gracie
Mansion

Carl
Schutz
Park

East River

FRANKLIN DELANO ROOSEVELT DRIVE

John Jay
Park

P

Main Street

River Road

P

Roosevelt Island
Bridge

**Roosevelt
Island**

Roosevelt
Island

Main
Street

West Road

East Road

Main Street

2nd Street

3rd Street

4th Street

9th Street

27th Avenue

1st Street

Astoria
Boulevard

Hallets
Cove Playground

8th Street

12th Street

h Street

18th Street

Astoria Boulevard

29th Avenue

Avenue

30th

Welling
Court

30th Road

Vernon

30th Drive

31st Avenue

31st Road

Boulevard

31st Drive

Socrates
Sculpture
Park

Broadway

33rd Avenue

33rd Avenue

33rd Road

13th Street

33rd Road

14th Street

Rainey
Park

Ravenswood
Playground

Vernon Boulevard

34th Avenue

9th Street

10th Street

11th Street

12th Street

35th Avenue

QUEENS

21st STREET

36th Avenue

14th Street

37th Avenue

38th Avenue

9th Street

10th Street

11th Street

12th Street

13th Street

40th Avenue

Vernon Boulevard

41st Avenue

21st STREET

21st Street
Queensbridge

Queensbridge
Park

41st Road

QUEENSBORO BRIDGE

HIGHWAY 25
Queens Plaza South

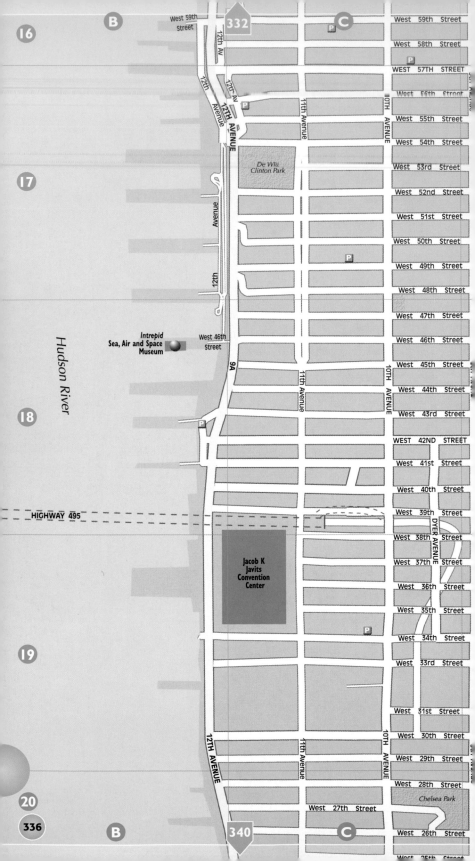

B

332

C

West 59th Street

12th Av

12th Avenue

12TH AVENUE

Avenue

12th

9A

11th Avenue

De Witt Clinton Park

10TH AVENUE

West 59th Street
West 58th Street
WEST 57TH STREET
West 56th Street
West 55th Street
West 54th Street
West 53rd Street
West 52nd Street
West 51st Street
West 50th Street
West 49th Street
West 48th Street
West 47th Street
West 46th Street
West 45th Street
West 44th Street
West 43rd Street
WEST 42ND STREET
West 41st Street
West 40th Street
West 39th Street
West 38th Street
West 37th Street
West 36th Street
West 35th Street
West 34th Street
West 33rd Street
West 31st Street
West 30th Street
West 29th Street
West 28th Street

Intrepid Sea, Air and Space Museum

West 46th Street

Hudson River

HIGHWAY 495

Jacob K Javits Convention Center

DYER AVENUE

12TH AVENUE

11th Avenue

10TH AVENUE

Chelsea Park

B

340

C

West 27th Street

West 26th Street

West 25th Street

P

P

P

P

P

P

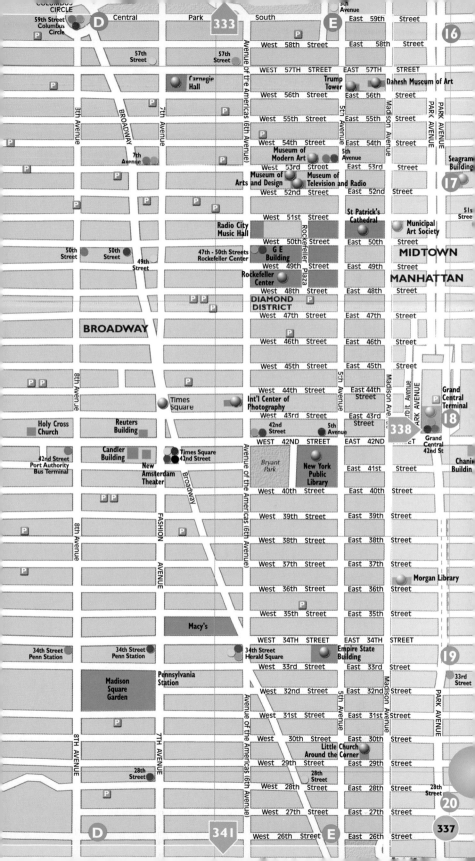

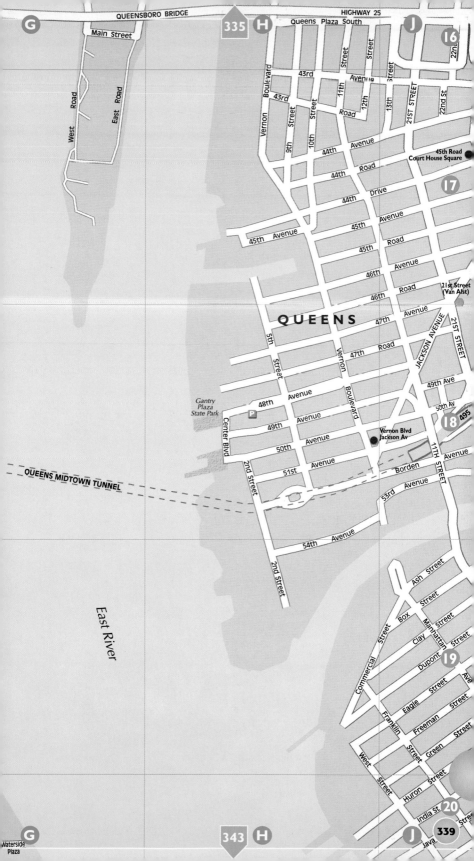

Queens Plaza South

Main Street

West Road

East Road

43rd Street

43rd Road

9th Street

10th Street

11th Street

12th Street

13th Street

Avenue

Street

Street

21ST STREET

22nd St

22nd

44th Avenue

44th Road

45th Road
Court House Square

17

44th Drive

45th Avenue

45th Avenue

45th Road

46th Avenue

46th Road

21st Street
(Van Alst)

QUEENS

47th Avenue

47th Road

5th Street

Vernon

47th Road

JACKSON AVENUE

21ST STREET

49th Ave

50th Av

18
495

Gantry Plaza State Park

48th Avenue

Center Blvd

49th Avenue

Boulevard

50th Avenue

Vernon Blvd
Jackson Av

51st Avenue

2nd Street

11TH STREET

Avenue

Borden

- - - QUEENS MIDTOWN TUNNEL - - -

53rd Avenue

54th Avenue

East River

Ash Street

Box Street

Manhattan Street

Clay Street

Commercial Street

Dupont Street

19

Eagle Street

Franklin Street

Freeman Street

Green Street

West Street

Huron Street

India St

20

Java

339

West 26th Street
West 25th Street
West 24th Street
West 23rd Street

10TH AVENUE

9TH AVENUE

West 22nd Street
West 21st Street

P

West 20th Street

11TH AVENUE

West 19th Street
West 18th Street
West 17th Street
West 16th Street

P

West 15th Street

9A

WEST 14TH STREET

West

Washington

13th

Little West 12th Street

Bloomfield
Street

10TH AVENUE

Gansevoort

Street

Gansevoort
Street

WEST STREET

Horatio

Street

Jane Street

West 12th

Bethune

Bank

Chelsea
Waterside Park

Hudson River

21

22

23

10

Waterside Pla

20

FRANKLIN DELANO ROOSEVELT DRIVE

Service Drive

Loop

Stuyvesant Oval

Avenue C Loop

Loop

Avenue C

East 16th Street

East 15th Street

East River

Service Drive

Avenue B

EAST 14TH STREET

East 13th Street

East 12th Street

Szold Place

East 11th Place

Avenue D

East 10th Street

21

East 9th Street

East 8th Street

East 7th Street

East 6th Street

Street

East 5th Street

East 5th Walk

East 4th Street

East 4th Walk

East

Avenue B

Avenue C

East 3rd Street

Avenue D

East 3rd Street

Louis Street

River

FRANKLIN DELANO ROOSEVELT DRIVE

22

EAST HOUSTON STREET

Attorney Avenue

Hamilton Fish Park

Columbia Street

Baruch Drive

Mangin Street

Baruch Place

Park

Franklin D Roosevelt Drive

Clinton Street

Attorney Street

Ridge Street

Pitt Street

Stanton Street

Rivington Street

Street

Suffolk Street

WILLIAMSBURG BRIDGE APPROACH

P

LOWER EAST SIDE

Broome

Ridge Street

Pitt Street

Willett Street

Columbia Street

Broome Street

Lewis Street

Suffolk St

Norfolk St.

Grand Street

23

Montgomery St

Henry Street

Madison Street

Jackson St

Cherry Street

Franklin D Roosevelt Drive

Seward Park

Corlears Hook

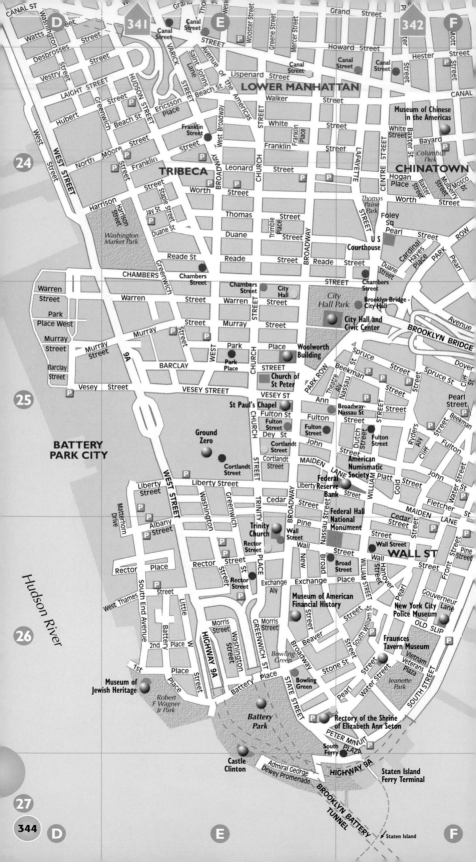

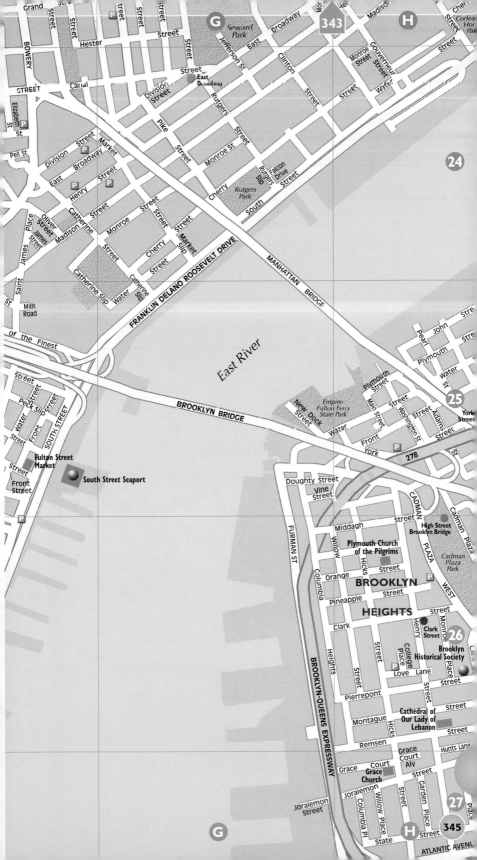

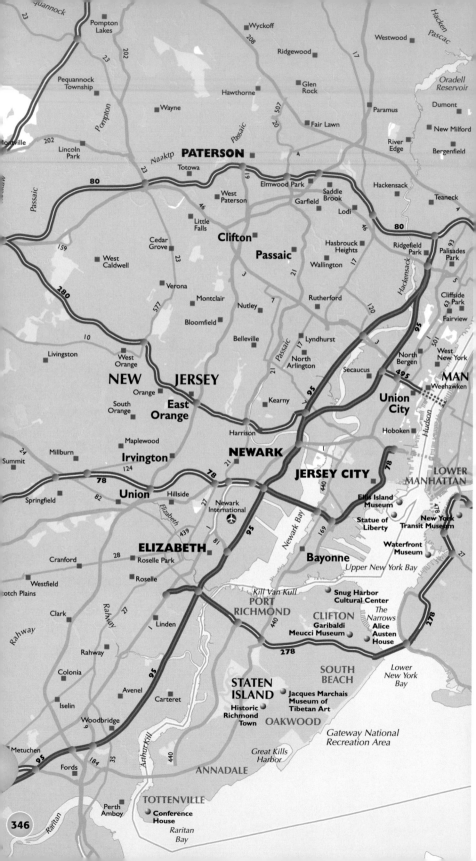

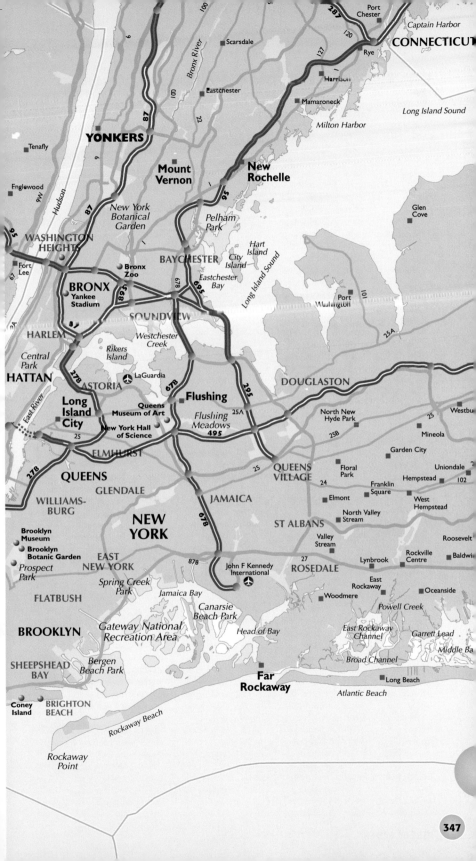

Port
Chester
Captain Harbor
CONNECTICUT

287

120

127

Scarsdale
Eastchester

Bronx River

Rye

Harrison
Long Island Sound

Mamaroneck

Milton Harbor

Tenafly

YONKERS

**Mount
Vernon**

**New
Rochelle**

95

87

Englewood

9W

Hudson

Glen
Cove

**New York
Botanical
Garden**

*Pelham
Park*

95

87

**WASHINGTON
HEIGHTS**

Fort
Lee

Bronx
Zoo

BAYCHESTER

*Hart
Island*

City
Island

Long Island Sound

67

895/95

BRONX

Yankee
Stadium

678

95

Eastchester
Bay

Port
Washington

101

25A

SOUNDVIEW

HARLEM

*Central
Park*

*Westchester
Creek*

*Rikers
Island*

87

HATTAN

278

ASTORIA

LaGuardia

678

295

DOUGLASTON

25A

East River

**Long
Island
City**

**Queens
Museum of Art**

Flushing

*Flushing
Meadows*

North New
Hyde Park

Westbu

25

25

**New York Hall
of Science**

495

258

Mineola

Garden City

ELMHURST

QUEENS

GLENDALE

278

25

25

JAMAICA

**QUEENS
VILLAGE**

Floral
Park

Franklin
Square

Uniondale

102

Hempstead

**NEW
YORK**

24

Elmont

West
Hempstead

**WILLIAMS-
BURG**

**Brooklyn
Museum**

**Brooklyn
Botanic Garden**

*Prospect
Park*

**EAST
NEW YORK**

678

North Valley
Stream

ST ALBANS

Valley
Stream

Roosevelt

878

John F Kennedy
International

27

Lynbrook

Rockville
Centre

Baldwi

ROSEDALE

FLATBUSH

*Spring Creek
Park*

Jamaica Bay

*Canarsie
Beach Park*

East
Rockaway

Woodmere

Oceanside

Powell Creek

BROOKLYN

**Gateway National
Recreation Area**

Head of Bay

East Rockaway
Channel

Garrett Lead

Middle Ba

**SHEEPSHEAD
BAY**

*Bergen
Beach Park*

Broad Channel

Long Beach

**Far
Rockaway**

Atlantic Beach

**Coney
Island**

**BRIGHTON
BEACH**

Rockaway Beach

*Rockaway
Point*

The following indexes list hotels, restaurants and cafés, stores, theaters and music and dance venues.

ACKNOWLEDGMENTS

Abbreviations for the credits are as follows:
AA = AA World Travel Library, t (top), b (bottom), c (center), l (left), r (right)

UNDERSTANDING NEW YORK

5 AA/C Sawyer; 8tl AA/C Sawyer; 8tr AA/S McBride; 8ctr AA/C Sawyer; 8cbr AA/R Elliott; 8br AA/P Kenward; 9tl Jean-Georges; 9cl Photodisc; 9bl AA/D Corrance; 9cr AA/T Souter; 9b AA/C Sawyer; 10tl AA/C Sawyer; 10cl AA/C Sawyer; 10bl AA/P Kenward; 10tr AA/D Corrance; 10cr AA/C Sawyer; 10br AA/C Sawyer.

LIVING NEW YORK

11 AA/P Kenward; 12/3bg AA/C Sawyer; 12tl AA/C Sawyer; 12/3t AA/C Sawyer; 12c AA/R Elliott; 12cr AA/C Sawyer; 12cl AA/P Kenward; 12bl AA/C Sawyer; 13tr AA/R Elliott; 13cl AA/C Sawyer; 13c AA/R Elliott; 13cr AA/R Elliott; 13br AA/C Sawyer; 14/5bg AA/C Sawyer; 14tl AA/S McBride; 14tc AA/C Sawyer; 14tr AA/S McBride; 14c AA/R Elliott; 14cl AA/C Sawyer; 14bl AA/C Sawyer; 14/5c AA/S McBride; 15tl AA/C Sawyer; 15cl AA/C Sawyer; 15tr AA/R Elliott; 15cr AA/C Sawyer; 16/7bg AA/C Sawyer; 16tl AA/D Corrance; 16tr AA/S McBride; 16c AA/E Rooney; 16cr AA/C Sawyer; 16br AA/D Corrance; 16/7c AA/C Sawyer; 17tl AA/C Sawyer; 17tr AA/C Sawyer; 17cl AA/C Sawyer; 17c AA/C Sawyer; 17cr AA/R Elliott; 18/9bg AA/C Sawyer; 18tl AA/C Sawyer; 18tc AA/C Sawyer; 18tr AA/C Sawyer; 18cl AA/D Corrance; 18cr AA/S McBride; 18cbl AA/R Elliott; 18bl AA/C Sawyer; 19tl AA/P Kenward; 19tr AA/C Sawyer; 19cl AA/C Sawyer; 19cr Getty Images; 20/1bg AA/C Sawyer; 20tl AA/C Sawyer; 20tr AA/C Sawyer; 20cl AA/C Sawyer; 20cr AA/D Corrance; 20cr AA/C Sawyer; 20bc AA/C Sawyer; 21tl The Kobal Collection; 21tc AA/C Sawyer; 21c AA/R Elliott; 21r AA/P Kenward; 22/3bg AA/C Sawyer; 22tl AA/C Sawyer; 24tr AA; 22cl Nova Development Corp; 22cr Getty Images; 22b AA/D Corrance; 22/3t Nova Development Corp; 23cl Getty Images; 23tc AA/C Sawyer; 23tr AA/C Sawyer; 23c Nova Development Corp; 24bg AA/C Sawyer; 24l Getty Images; 24tc Federal Reserve Board, Washington, D.C; 24tr AA/C Sawyer; 24cr AA/C Sawyer.

THE STORY OF NEW YORK

25 Illustrated London News; 26/7bg AA; 26cl Mary Evans Picture Library; 26cr Corbis; 26bl Corbis; 26/7b AA; 26/7c Mary Evans Picture Library; 27l Mary Evans Picture Library; 27c AA; 27br Mary Evans Picture Library; 28/9bg AA; 28cl Mary Evans Picture Library; 28cr Mary Evans Picture Library; 28bl AA/R Elliott; 28/9 Representation of the Terrible Fire of New York in 1776 (engraving) by French School th(18th century), Museum of the City of New York, USA/Bridgeman Art Library; 29cl AA; 29c Mary Evans Picture Library; 29bl AA; 29br Mary Evans Picture Library; 30/1bg New York Looking South from Union Square, pub. By John Bachman, 1849 (litho) by C Bachman (19th century), Museum of the City of New York, USA/Bridgeman Art Library; 30d View of the Ruins after the Great Fire in New York, Dec. 16th & 17th 1835, engraved by W I Bennett, pub, by L P Glover, by Bernardo Belottto Canaletto (1720-80), Museo di Goethe, Rome, Italy/Bridgeman Art Library; 30c Hulton Archives/Getty Images; 30cr Mary Evans Picture Library; 30/1 New York Looking South from Union Square, pub. by John Bachman, 1849 (Litho) by C Bachman (19th century), Museum of the City of New York, USA/Bridgeman Art Library; 31cl Hulton Archives/Getty Images; 31c Hulton Archives/Getty Images; 31bl AA/C Sawyer; 31br Hulton Archives/Getty Images; 32/3bg AA; 32c Illustrated London News; 32cr Mary Evans Picture Library; 32bl AA; 33d Illustrated London News; 33c AA; 33bl Hulton Archives/Getty Images; 33br AA/R Elliott; 34/5bg AA/C Sawyer; 34cl AA/C Sawyer; 34cr AA/C Sawyer; 34bl Hulton Archives/Getty Images; 34br Mary Evans Picture Library; 34/5 AA/C Sawyer; 34cl Mary Evans Picture Library; 35c Hulton Archives/Getty Images; 35bc AA/R Elliott; 35br AA/C Sawyer; 36/7bg AA/R Elliott; 36cl AA/P Kenward; 36cr Corbis; 36bl AA/R Elliott; 36/7 AA/R Elliott; 37cl Corbis; 37c Hulton Archives/Getty Images; 37cr Hulton Archives/Getty Images; 3br AA/C Sawyer; 38bg AA/C Sawyer; 38c Getty Images; 38cr AA/S McBride; 38bl AA/C Sawyer; 38br AA/C Sawyer.

ON THE MOVE

39 AA/C Sawyer; 40/1 Digital Vision; 42t Digital Vision; 42b NY Airport Service; 43t AA/S L Day; 43b AA/S L Day; 44/5 AA/S L Day; 44 AA/C Sawyer; 46/7 AA/S L Day; 46 AA/C Sawyer; 47c AA/R Elliott; 47b AA/S McBride; 48/9 AA/C Sawyer; 48tr AA/C Sawyer; 48br AA/C Sawyer; 49tl AA/C Sawyer; 50 AA/C Sawyer; 51t AA/D Corrance; 51cr AA/D Corrance; 51br AA/C Sawyer; 52/3 Digital Vision; 52 AA/E Rooney; 53t AA/C Sawyer; 53b AA/C Sawyer; 54/5 AA/C Sawyer; 54cr AA/C Sawyer; 54b AA/C Sawyer; 55 Printed by Permission Greyhound Lines, Inc; 56t AA/C Sawyer; 56c AA/N Sumner.

THE SIGHTS

57 AA/C Sawyer; 62l AA/R Elliott; 62r AA/C Sawyer; 63l AA/D Corrance; 63r AA/R Elliott; 64l AA/C Sawyer; 64r AA/C Sawyer; 65l AA/C Sawyer; 65r AA/D Corrance; 66l AA/C Sawyer; 66r AA/C Sawyer; 67tl Downtown Alliance; 67tr AA/C Sawyer; 67bl Asia Society & Museum/Frank Oudeman; 68 AA/C Sawyer; 69t American Museum of Natural History; 69cr AA/C Sawyer; 69c American Museum of Natural History; 69r D Finnin/American Museum of Natural History; 69b American Museum of Natural History; 70t AA/R Elliott; 70cl American Museum of Natural History; 70c American Museum of Natural History; 70cr American Museum of Natural History; 70bl American Museum of Natural History; 72 D Finnin/American Museum of Natural History; 73t AA/C Sawyer; 73cr AA/C Sawyer; 73br AA/C Sawyer; 74t AA/C Sawyer; 74cl AA/C Sawyer; 74cr AA/C Sawyer; 75 AA/D Corrance; 76t Don Perdue; 76cl Don Perdue; 77tl AA/C Sawyer; 77tc AA/C Sawyer; 77tr Dahesh Museum of Art; 78t AA/E Rooney; 78cl AA/C Sawyer; 78c AA/C Sawyer; 78cr AA/C Sawyer; 79t AA/S McBride; 79br AA/S McBride; 80tl AA/S McBride; 80tr AA/S McBride; 80c AA/S McBride; 80cr AA/S McBride; 82 AA/D Corrance; 83l AA/S McBride; 83c AA/C Sawyer; 83r AA/C Sawyer; 84t AA/C Sawyer; 84l AA/S McBride; 85t AA/C Sawyer; 85cr AA/C Sawyer; 85br AA/S McBride; 86t AA; 86l AA/C Sawyer; 87tl AA/C Sawyer; 87tc AA/D Corrance; 87tr AA/C Sawyer; 88t AA/C Sawyer; 88cl AA/C Sawyer; 88c AA/S McBride; 88cr AA/C Sawyer; 88bl AA/S McBride; 89 AA/C Sawyer; 90 AA/C Sawyer; 91 Corbis; 92t By courtesy of the Ellis Island Immigration Museum; 92cl By courtesy of the Ellis Island Immigration Museum; 92c Corbis; 92cr AA/R Elliott; 92bl AA/S McBride; 94 AA/C Sawyer; 95 AA/C Sawyer; 95cl AA/C Sawyer; 95cr AA/S McBride; 96 AA/C Sawyer; 97t AA P Kenward; 97r Federal Hall; 98t AA/C Sawyer; 98cl AA/C Sawyer; 98bl AA/C Sawyer; 99t AA/C Sawyer; 99tc AA/C Sawyer; 99tr AA/C Sawyer; 100t Frick Collection; 100cl Frick Collection; 101tl AA/C Sawyer; 101tc AA/C Sawyer; 101tr AA/R G Elliott; 102 AA/S McBride; 103t AA/S McBride; 103cl AA/S McBride; 103c AA/S McBride; 103cr AA/S McBride; 104tl AA/S McBride; 104tr AA/S McBride; 105t AA/S McBride; 105cl AA/C Sawyer; 105c AA/S McBride; 105cr AA/C Sawyer; 106 AA/S McBride; 107cl AA/C Sawyer; 107c AA/P Kenward; 107cr AA/S McBride; 107b AA/C Sawyer; 108t AA/C Sawyer; 108cl AA/C Sawyer; 109tl Jewish Museum; 109tc AA/C Sawyer; 109tr Lower East Side Tenement Museum; 110t AA/C Sawyer; 110cl AA/S McBride; 110c Flask, Glass and Fruit, 1877 by Paul Cezanne (1839-1906) Solomon R Guggenheim Museum, New York, USA/Bridgeman Art Library; 110cr AA/C Sawyer; 111t Robert Harding Picture Library; 111br Jeanne Hebuterne in a Yellow Jumper, 1918-19 (oil on canvas) by Amedeo Modigliani (1884-1920), Solomon R Guggenheim Museum, New York, USA/Bridgeman Art Library; 112t AA/P Kenward; 112cl AA/C Sawyer; 112c Lincoln Center/Steve J Sherman; 112cr AA/E Rooney; 113 AA/P Kenward; 114t AA/C Sawyer; 114cl AA/C Sawyer; 114c Lady at the Tea Table, 1885 (oil on canvas) by Mary Stevenson Cassatt (1844-1926), Metropolitan Museum of Art, New York, USA/Bridgeman Art Library; 114cr AA/R Elliott; 115 AA/R Elliott; 116 AA/D Corrance; 118 Corbis; 119t AA/D Corrance; 119cl AA; 119c The Dance Lesson, c 1879 (pastel) by Edgar Degas (1834-1917) Metropolitan Museum of Art, New York, USA/Bridgeman Art

Library; 119cr AA/C Sawyer; 120tl AA/R G Elliott; 120tc Mount Vernon Hotel Museum; 120tr Museum of American Financial History; 121t AA/R Elliott; 121cr AA/C Sawyer; 122t © Photo SCALA, Florence, The Pierpont Morgan Library, 2001; 122cl AA/C Sawyer; 123tl Museum of the Chinese in Americas; 123tr Museum of Arts and Design; 124tl AA/R Elliott; 124tc Maika, Neue Galerie, © Christian Schad Stiftung Aschaffenburg/VG Bild-Kunst, Bonn and DACS, London 2004; 124tr AA/R Elliott; 125t © Photo SCALA, Florence, Museum of Modern Art, 2003; 125cr Museum of Modern Art/©2005 Timothy Hursley; 126tl Courtesy of the NY City Police Museum; 126tc New York Historical Society; 126tr AA/C Sawyer; 127t AA/R Elliott; 127cr AA/E Rooney; 128t AA/S McBride; 128cl AA/S McBride; 128c AA/S McBride; 128cr AA/C Sawyer; 129 AA/C Sawyer; 130tl AA/C Sawyer; 130cl AA/C Sawyer; 130r AA/C Sawyer; 130bl AA/S McBride; 131tl AA/S McBride; 131tc AA/C Sawyer; 131tr AA/C Sawyer; 132t AA/S McBride; 132cl S McBride; 132c AA/C Sawyer; 132cr AA/C Sawyer; 132bl AA/C Sawyer; 133 AA/C Sawyer; 134t AA/C Sawyer; 134cl AA/S McBride; 134cr AA/C Sawyer; 134bl South Street Seaport; 135t AA/C Sawyer; 135b AA/C Sawyer; 136t AA/E Rooney; 136cl AA/C Sawyer; 136c AA/E Rooney; 136cr AA/P Kenward; 136bl AA/R Elliott; 137 AA/C Sawyer; 138 AA/C Sawyer; 139 AA/C Sawyer; 140tl AA/C Sawyer; 140cl AA/C Sawyer; 141tl AA/C Sawyer; 141tc AA/C Sawyer; 141tr AA/C Sawyer; 142t AA/C Sawyer; 142cl AA/P Kenward; 142c AA/C Sawyer; 142cr AA/C Sawyer; 143 AA/P Kenward; 144tl AA/C Sawyer; 144tc AA/C Sawyer; 144tr AA/C Sawyer; 145t AA; 145r AA/C Sawyer; 146 AA/C Sawyer; 147t AA/C Sawyer; 147cl AA/C Sawyer; 147c AA/C Sawyer; 147cr AA/C Sawyer; 148/9 AA/R Elliott, ©ADAGP, Paris and DACS, London 2004; 148c Whitney Museum of American Art View 2/Jeff Goldberg, Esto; 148bl AA/R Elliott; 150cl AA/P Kenward; 150cr Whitney Museum of American Art View 1/Jeff Goldberg, Esto; 150b Corbis; 151 Railroad Crossing, 1922-23 by Edward Hopper (1882-1967) Whitney Museum of American Art, New York, USA/Bridgeman Art Library; 152tl AA/R Elliott; 152tr AA/C Sawyer; 152b Brooklyn Historical Society; 153t The Peaceable Kingdom, c 1840-45) by Edward Hicks (1780-1849), Brooklyn Museum of Art, New York, USA/Bridgeman Art Library; 153cr AA/C Sawyer; 154tl AA/R Elliott; 154tc AA/C Sawyer; 154tr AA/C Sawyer; 154bl NY Transit Museum; 155tl NY Hall of Science; 155tc AA/C Sawyer; 155tr Waterfront Museum/Frank Zimmerman; 155c AA/R Elliott; 156tl Garibaldi Meucci Museum; 156tc AA/C Sawyer; 156tr AA/C Sawyer; 156bl Historic Richmond Town; 157t AA/R Elliott; 157cr Bronx Zoo; 158t Getty Images; 157l Photodisc.

WHAT TO DO

159 Photodisc; 164t AA/M Jourdan; 164cl Screaming Mimi's; 164c AA/C Sawyer; 165/5c AA/C Sawyer; 165cl AA/C Sawyer; 165cr AA/C Sawyer; 166cl AA/S McBride; 166cr AA/S McBride; 166b Me & Ro; 167cl AA/C Sawyer; 167c Jimmy Choo; 167cr AA/C Sawyer; 168 AA/C Sawyer; 169t AA/M Jourdan; 169c AA/K Paterson; 170t AA/M Jourdan; 170 AA/R G Elliott; 171t AA/M Jourdan; 171c AA/C Sawyer; 172t AA/M Jourdan; 172c AA/C Sawyer; 173t AA/M Jourdan; 173c AA/C Sawyer; 174t AA/M Jourdan; 174c Kirna Zabete; 175t AA/M Jourdan; 175c Mark Bulkin; 176t AA/M Jourdan; 176c AA/C Sawyer; 177t AA/M Jourdan; 177c AA/C Sawyer; 178t AA/M Jourdan; 178c AA/P Kenward; 179t AA/C Sawyer; 179c Broadway Panhandler; 180t AA/M Jourdan; 180c Eye Candy; 181t AA/M Jourdan; 181c Jimmy Choo; 182t AA/M Jourdan; 183t AA/M Jourdan; 184t AA/M Jourdan; 184c AA/C Sawyer; 185t Digital Vision; 185cl Digital Vision; 185c Digital Vision; 190t AA/C Sawyer; 190c AA/S Collier; 191t AA/C Sawyer; 191c Jonathan B Ragle; 192t Digital Vision; 192c AA/C Sawyer; 193t Digital Vision; 193c Frick Collection/John Bigelow Taylor; 194t Digital Vision; 194c AA/P Kenward; 195t Digital Vision; 195c AA/C Sawyer; 196t Brand X Pics; 196c Chicago City Limits; 197t Brand X Pics; 197c Michael Moran; 198t Brand X Pics; 198c AA/C Coe; 199c © Bob Colton/Black Star; 199t Brand X Pics; 200c AA/C Sawyer; 201t Digital Vision; 201c Digital Vision; 202t Digital Vision; 202c Digital Vision; 203t Digital Vision; 203c AA/C Sawyer; 204t Digital Vision; 204c Sob's; 205t AA/C Sawyer; 205c American Airlines Theatre; 206t AA/C Sawyer; 206cc AA/C Sawyer; 207t AA/C Sawyer; 207c AA/C Sawyer; 208t AA/C Sawyer; 208c AA/C Sawyer; 209t AA/C Sawyer; 209c Bowerie Lane; 210/1t AA/C Sawyer; 210c AA/P Kenward; 211c Carol Rosegg; 212t AA/T Souter; 212cl Brand X Pics; 212cr Brand X Pics; 213t AA/T Souter; 213c Bubble Lounge; 214t AA/T Souter; 214c Happy Ending; 215t AA/T Souter; 215c Photodisc; 216t AA/T Souter; 216c Photodisc; 217t AA/T Souter; 217c Photodisc; 218t Piano's; 218c AA/C Sawyer; 219t Piano's; 219c Brand X Pics; 220t Piano's; 220c Brand X Pics; 221t Photodisc; 221cl AA/P Kenward; 221cr AA/C Sawyer; 222t Photodisc; 222c AA/C Sawyer; 223t Photodisc; 223c Photodisc; 224t Photodisc; 224c AA/R G Elliott; 225t Photodisc; 225c AA/P Kenward; 226t Photodisc; 226cl Asphalt Green; 226cr Greenhouse Spa; 227t Photodisc; 227c Clay; 228t Photodisc; 228c Oasis Day Spa; 229t AA/R G Elliott; 229cl New Victory Theatre; 229cr Liberty Helicopters; 230t AA/R G Elliott; 230c Children's Museum of Manhattan; 231t AA/R G Elliott; 231c Steve Williams © 2003; 232t AA/R G Elliott; 232c AA/C Sawyer; 233t AA/S L Day; 233cl AA/S L Day; 233cr AA/P Kenward; 234t AA/S L Day.

OUT AND ABOUT

235 AA/P Kenward; 237tl AA/C Sawyer; 237tc AA/C Sawyer; 237tr AA/C Sawyer; 237cr AA/C Sawyer; 238 AA/N Lancaster; 239t AA/C Sawyer; 239cr AA/R Elliott; 239cb AA/N Lancaster; 239b AA/N Lancaster; 241tl AA/N Lancaster; 241tr AA/C Sawyer; 241cr AA/C Sawyer; 241bl AA/N Lancaster; 242 AA/C Sawyer; 243tl AA/C Sawyer; 243tr AA/C Sawyer; 243bc AA/C Sawyer; 243br AA/C Sawyer; 244 AA/C Sawyer; 245tl AA/C Sawyer; 245tr AA/C Sawyer; 245cr AA/C Sawyer; 245br AA/E Rooney; 246 AA/R Elliott; 247tr AA/C Sawyer; 247ctr AA/C Sawyer; 247cbr AA/C Sawyer; 247br AA/C Sawyer; 248 AA/C Sawyer; 249tr AA/C Sawyer; 249c AA/S McBride; 249cr AA/C Sawyer; 249b AA/C Sawyer; 251tl AA/C Sawyer; 251tr AA/C Sawyer; 251b AA/C Sawyer; 252/3 AA/N Lancaster; 253tr AA/P Kenward; 253ctr AA/C Sawyer; 253cb AA/C Sawyer; 253b AA/N Lancaster; 254 AA/N Lancaster; 255tl AA/N Lancaster; 255tr AA/N Lancaster; 255c AA/C Sawyer; 255b AA/N Lancaster; 256 AA/R Elliott; 257t AA/R Elliott; 257c AA/R Elliott; 257b AA/R Elliott; 258c AA/R Elliott; 258/9 AA/R Elliott; 259t AA/R Elliott; 259c AA/R Elliott; 260l AA/C Sawyer; 260c AA/C Sawyer; 260r AA/C Sawyer.

EATING AND STAYING

261 AA/C Sawyer; 262l AA/C Sawyer; 262cl AA/P Kenward; 262cr AA/C Sawyer; 262r AA/P Kenward; 263l AA/C Sawyer; 263c AA/C Sawyer; 263r AA/R Elliott; 263bl AA/R Elliott; 264l AA/C Sawyer; 264c AA/C Sawyer; 264r AA/D Corrance; 264cb AA/S McBride; 270c AA/S Collier; 270r S Collier; 272tl AA/S McBride; 272cr AA/S Collier; 276bc AA/S Collier; 277l AA/S Collier; 278tc AA/S McBride; 278r AA/S Collier; 279r AA/S McBride; 280l AA/S McBride; 281l AA/S Collier; 281c AA/S Collier; 282l AA/S Collier; 282tc AA/S Collier; 284bc AA/S Collier; 285l AA/S McBride; 287cr AA/S Collier; 288tl AA/S Collier; 288bl AA/S Collier; 288cr AA/S Collier; 289tl AA/S McBride; 289r AA/S Collier; 290cl AA/S Collier; 291t AA/S McBride; 291c AA/S McBride; 291b AA/N Lancaster; 292l AA/C Sawyer; 292cl AA/C Sawyer; 292cr AA/C Sawyer; 292r AA/C Sawyer; 292b AA/C Sawyer; 293l AA/C Sawyer; 293cl AA/C Sawyer; 293cr AA/C Sawyer; 293r AA/C Sawyer.

PLANNING

311 AA/C Sawyer; 312t AA/C Sawyer; 312c AA/E Rooney; 316 AA/C Sawyer; 318t Leisure Pass North America LLC; 318b AA/C Sawyer; 320 AA/C Sawyer; 321t AA/C Sawyer; 321b AA/C Sawyer; 322 AA/S Collier; 323tr AA/P Kenward; 323cr AA/R Elliott; 324 AA/E Rooney; 325 AA/R Elliott; 326 AA/S Collier.

Project editor
Betty Sheldrick

Interior design
David Austin, Glyn Barlow, Alan Gooch, Kate Harling, Bob Johnson,
Nick Otway, Carole Philp, Keith Russell

Additional design
Jo Tapper, Nautilus Design

Picture research
Carol Walker

Cover design
Tigist Getachew

Internal repro work
Susan Crowhurst, Ian Little, Michael Moody

Production
Lyn Kirby, Helen Sweeney

Mapping
Maps produced by the Cartography Department of AA Publishing

Main contributors
Coleen Degnan-Veness, Marilyn Wood

Copy editors
Sheila Hawkins, Sarah Hudson, Jo Perry

Updater
Marilyn Wood

Revision management
Cambridge Publishing Management Ltd

See It New York City
ISBN 1-4000-1658-4
ISBN-13: 978-1-4000-1658-7
Second edition

Published in the United States by Fodor's Travel Publications and simultaneously in Canada
by Random House of Canada Limited, Toronto.
Published in the United Kingdom by AA Publishing.

Color separation by Keenes
Printed and bound by Leo, China
10 9 8 7 6 5 4 3 2 1

Special sales: This book is available for special discounts for bulk purchases for sales promotions or
premiums. Special editions, including personalized covers, excerpts of existing books, and corporate
imprints, can be created in large quantities for special needs. For more information, write to Special
Markets/Premium Sales, 1745 Broadway, MD 6-2, New York, NY 10019 or e-mail
specialmarkets@randomhouse.com

A02359
Mapping in this title produced from New York data © Tele Atlas N. V. 2003
Relief map images supplied by Mountain High Maps ® Copyright © 1993 Digital Wisdom, Inc
Weather chart statistics supplied by Weatherbase © Copyright 2003 Canty and Associates, LLC

Important Note: Time inevitably brings changes, so always confirm prices, travel facts, and other
perishable information when it matters. Although Fodor's cannot accept responsibility for errors,
you can use this guide in the confidence that we have taken every care to ensure its accuracy.

Fodor's Key to the Guides

AMERICA'S **GUIDEBOOK LEADER** PUBLISHES GUIDES FOR **EVERY KIND OF TRAVELER**. CHECK OUT OUR MANY SERIES AND FIND YOUR **PERFECT MATCH**.

FODOR'S GOLD GUIDES
America's favorite travel-guide series offers the most detailed insider reviews of hotels, restaurants, and attractions in all price ranges, plus great background information, smart tips, and useful maps.

COMPASS AMERICAN GUIDES
Stunning guides from top local writers and photographers, with gorgeous photos, literary excerpts, and colorful anecdotes. A must-have for culture mavens, history buffs, and new residents.

FODOR'S CITYPACKS
Concise city coverage in a guide plus a foldout map. The right choice for urban travelers who want everything under one cover.

FODOR'S WHERE TO WEEKEND
A fresh take on weekending, this series identifies the best places to escape outside the city and details loads of rejuvenating activities as well as cool places to stay, great restaurants, and practical information.

FODOR'S AROUND THE CITY WITH KIDS
Up to 68 great ideas for family days, recommended by resident parents. Perfect for exploring in your own backyard or on the road.

FODOR'S TRAVEL HISTORIC AMERICA
For travelers who want to experience history firsthand, this series gives in-depth coverage of historic sights, plus nearby restaurants and hotels. Themes include the Thirteen Colonies, the Old West, and the Lewis and Clark Trail.

FODOR'S FLASHMAPS
Every resident's map guide, with 60 easy-to-follow maps of public transit, parks, museums, zip codes, and more.

FODOR'S LANGUAGES FOR TRAVELERS
Practice the local language before you hit the road. Available in phrase books, cassette sets, and CD sets.

THE COLLECTED TRAVELER
These collections of the best published essays and articles on various European destinations will give you a feel for the culture, cuisine, and way of life.

FODOR'S HOW TO GUIDES
Get tips from the pros on planning the perfect trip. Learn how to pack, fly hassle-free, plan a honeymoon or cruise, stay healthy on the road, and travel with your baby.

KAREN BROWN'S GUIDES
Engaging guides—many with easy-to-follow inn-to-inn itineraries—to the most charming inns and B&Bs in the U.S.A. and Europe.

OTHER GREAT TITLES FROM FODOR'S
Baseball Vacations, The Complete Guide to the National Parks, Family Vacations, Golf Digest's Places to Play, Great American Drives of the East, Great American Drives of the West, Great American Vacations, Healthy Escapes, National Parks of the West, Skiing USA.

At bookstores everywhere.   www.fodors.com/books

Dear Traveler

From buying a plane ticket to booking a room and seeing the sights, a trip goes much more smoothly when you have a good travel guide. Dozens of writers, editors, designers, and cartographers have worked hard to make the book you hold in your hands a good one. Was it everything you expected? Were our descriptions accurate? Were our recommendations on target? And did you find our tips and practical advice helpful? Your ideas and experiences matter to us. If we have missed or misstated something, we'd love to hear about it. Fill out our survey at www.fodors.com/books/feedback/, or e-mail us at seeit@fodors.com. Or you can snail mail to the See It Editor at Fodor's, 1745 Broadway, New York, New York 10019. We'll look forward to hearing from you.

Tim Jarrell
Publisher